T0137926

Communications
in Computer and Information Science 1655

More information about this series at https://link.springer.com/bookseries/7899

Constantine Stephanidis · Margherita Antona ·
Stavroula Ntoa · Gavriel Salvendy (Eds.)

HCI International 2022 – Late Breaking Posters

24th International Conference on Human-Computer Interaction
HCII 2022, Virtual Event, June 26 – July 1, 2022
Proceedings, Part II

Springer

Editors
Constantine Stephanidis
University of Crete and Foundation for
Research and Technology – Hellas (FORTH)
Heraklion, Crete, Greece

Margherita Antona
Foundation for Research and Technology
Hellas (FORTH)
Heraklion, Crete, Greece

Stavroula Ntoa
Foundation for Research and Technology
Hellas (FORTH)
Heraklion, Crete, Greece

Gavriel Salvendy
University of Central Florida
Orlando, FL, USA

ISSN 1865-0929   ISSN 1865-0937 (electronic)
Communications in Computer and Information Science
ISBN 978-3-031-19681-2   ISBN 978-3-031-19682-9 (eBook)
https://doi.org/10.1007/978-3-031-19682-9

This Springer imprint is published by the registered company Springer Nature Switzerland AG
The registered company address is: Gewerbestrasse 11, 6330 Cham, Switzerland

Foreword

Human-computer interaction (HCI) is acquiring an ever-increasing scientific and industrial importance, as well as having more impact on people's everyday life, as an ever-growing number of human activities are progressively moving from the physical to the digital world. This process, which has been ongoing for some time now, has been dramatically accelerated by the COVID-19 pandemic. The HCI International (HCII) conference series, held yearly, aims to respond to the compelling need to advance the exchange of knowledge and research and development efforts on the human aspects of design and use of computing systems.

The 24th International Conference on Human-Computer Interaction, HCI International 2022 (HCII 2022), was planned to be held at the Gothia Towers Hotel and Swedish Exhibition & Congress Centre, Göteborg, Sweden, during June 26 to July 1, 2022. Due to the COVID-19 pandemic and with everyone's health and safety in mind, HCII 2022 was organized and run as a virtual conference. It incorporated the 21 thematic areas and affiliated conferences listed on the following page.

A total of 5583 individuals from academia, research institutes, industry, and governmental agencies from 88 countries submitted contributions, and 1276 papers and 275 posters were included in the proceedings that were published just before the start of the conference. Additionally, 296 papers and 181 posters are included in the volumes of the proceedings published after the conference, as "Late Breaking Work". The contributions thoroughly cover the entire field of human-computer interaction, addressing major advances in knowledge and effective use of computers in a variety of application areas. These papers provide academics, researchers, engineers, scientists, practitioners, and students with state-of-the-art information on the most recent advances in HCI. The volumes constituting the full set of the HCII 2022 conference proceedings are listed in the following pages.

I would like to thank the Program Board Chairs and the members of the Program Boards of all thematic areas and affiliated conferences for their contribution and support towards the highest scientific quality and overall success of the HCI International 2022 conference; they have helped in so many ways, including session organization, paper reviewing (single-blind review process, with a minimum of two reviews per submission) and, more generally, acting as good-will ambassadors for the HCII conference.

This conference would not have been possible without the continuous and unwavering support and advice of Gavriel Salvendy, Founder, General Chair Emeritus, and Scientific Advisor. For his outstanding efforts, I would like to express my appreciation to Abbas Moallem, Communications Chair and Editor of HCI International News.

July 2022

Constantine Stephanidis

HCI International 2022 Thematic Areas and Affiliated Conferences

Thematic Areas

- HCI: Human-Computer Interaction
- HIMI: Human Interface and the Management of Information

Affiliated Conferences

- EPCE: 19th International Conference on Engineering Psychology and Cognitive Ergonomics
- AC: 16th International Conference on Augmented Cognition
- UAHCI: 16th International Conference on Universal Access in Human-Computer Interaction
- CCD: 14th International Conference on Cross-Cultural Design
- SCSM: 14th International Conference on Social Computing and Social Media
- VAMR: 14th International Conference on Virtual, Augmented and Mixed Reality
- DHM: 13th International Conference on Digital Human Modeling and Applications in Health, Safety, Ergonomics and Risk Management
- DUXU: 11th International Conference on Design, User Experience and Usability
- C&C: 10th International Conference on Culture and Computing
- DAPI: 10th International Conference on Distributed, Ambient and Pervasive Interactions
- HCIBGO: 9th International Conference on HCI in Business, Government and Organizations
- LCT: 9th International Conference on Learning and Collaboration Technologies
- ITAP: 8th International Conference on Human Aspects of IT for the Aged Population
- AIS: 4th International Conference on Adaptive Instructional Systems
- HCI-CPT: 4th International Conference on HCI for Cybersecurity, Privacy and Trust
- HCI-Games: 4th International Conference on HCI in Games
- MobiTAS: 4th International Conference on HCI in Mobility, Transport and Automotive Systems
- AI-HCI: 3rd International Conference on Artificial Intelligence in HCI
- MOBILE: 3rd International Conference on Design, Operation and Evaluation of Mobile Communications

Conference Proceedings – Full List of Volumes

http://2022.hci.international/proceedings

24th International Conference on Human-Computer Interaction (HCII 2022)

The full list with the Program Board Chairs and the members of the Program Boards of all thematic areas and affiliated conferences is available online at:

http://www.hci.international/board-members-2022.php

HCI International 2023

The 25th International Conference on Human-Computer Interaction, HCI International 2023, will be held jointly with the affiliated conferences at the AC Bella Sky Hotel and Bella Center, Copenhagen, Denmark, 23–28 July 2023. It will cover a broad spectrum of themes related to human-computer interaction, including theoretical issues, methods, tools, processes, and case studies in HCI design, as well as novel interaction techniques, interfaces, and applications. The proceedings will be published by Springer. More information will be available on the conference website: http://2023.hci.international/.

General Chair
Constantine Stephanidis
University of Crete and ICS-FORTH
Heraklion, Crete, Greece
Email: general_chair@hcii2023.org

http://2023.hci.international/

Contents – Part II

Interactive Technologies for Learning

Digital Transformation in Business, Government, and Organizations

Automated Driving and Urban Mobility

Robots, Agents, and Intelligent Environments

AI in HCI: Methods, Applications, and Studies

Studies on Social Computing

Virtual Services During Covid-19 Using Social Media of Minister of Public Health

Isnanda Rahmadani Bagastiwi[✉], Haryadi Arief Nuur Rasyid, and Fajar Junaedi

Department of Communication, Universitas Muhammadiyah Yogyakarta, Kasihan, Indonesia
Isnanda.bagas@gmail.com, haryadiariefnurrasyid@umy.ac.id

Abstract. This study aims to examine the role of social media in filtering the spread of COVID-19 information. Covid-19 information is crowdsourcing Information. Anxiety caused by social media information must be addressed through explicit government regulations on handling COVID-19. As a result, governments must understand the emotions and sentiments conveyed on social media. Based on this point of view, this study examines the role of the government in responding to health information from social media through the ministry of health. This study uses a qualitative exploration method with the NvivoPlus12 tool in processing Ministry of Health data in providing health education, covid-19 information, and policy responses to COVID-19. This analysis shows that the ministry of health functions based on the type of information presented through official accounts, first, as a means of socialization. Second, providing real-time information as a medium for public information. Third, the Ministry of Health cooperates with other ministries to encourage policies, especially the handling of COVID-19. This finding is in line with the United Nations 2020 research that virtual services can be realized by using social media to build services and convey Information; In addition, this function makes it easier to know the community's response so that policies and management of COVID-19 run smoothly.

Keywords: Services · Covid-19 · Social media · Information

1 Introduction

Covid-19, or coronavirus disease, is a viral outbreak currently being experienced in all parts of the world; this has a lot to do with the economic state of our society and our health care system. In the context of Covid-19, WHO has set communication standards to prevent misinformation and rumors, detect events, and respond to public complaints. Social media is beneficial, especially during crises and health emergencies. When people need information about the response of the community, government, or organization to crises and emergencies, social media becomes the right, fast, and real-time information platform [2].

Social media has an essential role in meeting information needs [3]. Today, social media is essential for sharing individual thoughts and opinions because of its easy access. It provides an opportunity for malicious users to post fake content intentionally created to influence people. To create controversy and play with public emotions. Spread of contaminated Information such as Rumors, Hoaxes, and Accidental Misinformation. The web has become an emergency that can have a hazardous impact on society and individuals [4]. Based on data from the Ministry of Communication and Information of the Republic of Indonesia shows that data on social media users in Indonesia continues to increase from 2018–to 2021, namely in 2018 by 130 million users, 2019 by 150 million users, 2020 by 170 million users, and in 2021 in the first semester by 180 million users [5].

Social media is widely considered the optimal location for finding and disseminating health information [6]. Usually, health information is distributed by public organizations, health organizations, and service organizations [7]. In this case, the Indonesian Ministry of Health has disseminated data related to COVID-19 on their official Twitter account with 488.5 thousand followers [8]. Social media can be a source of accurate and reliable information relevant to the public or other fellow health professionals to reduce the spread of misinformation about COVID-19; this can be achieved by providing accurate and reliable information based on recommendations provided by the relevant health authorities and professional associations to ensure the public understands the importance of the message and thereby minimizes the adverse consequences of a pandemic [9].

Based on the explanation above, this study aims to analyze the social media function of the Ministry of Health from the perspective of virtual services. We understand that social media has a varied role, but there are still limitations to research on virtual services using social media in recent studies. Therefore, this study further explores the function of social media as a virtual service tool by the Ministry of Health.

2   Overview of Literature

Social media as a communication tool builds relationships [10], and social media as a medium of innovation builds interactive communication [11]. As an innovative medium, social media helps the government communicate and coordinate with the community [12]. Social media offers various services, such as public complaints, services, and news reporting, and serve as a platform for creating online communication that connects the public with information [13]. Otherwise, there are various social media services for the public sector. Twitter is a social media platform used in disseminating information and has been known and used by government agencies, the private sector, and civil society [5]. The government can use Twitter to provide information [14]. The use of Hashtags can confirm that indirectly the use of these hashtags can be part of the dissemination of information [5]. Some local governments have used social media Twitter as a tool for virtual communication services between communities [14]. Twitter can also be used as a policy-making tool, and this is because Twitter is considered an elite medium in a crisis or emergency. As elite media, Twitter incorporates interactive communication with other users to obtain information from various sources [15].

The emergence of technological developments, namely the internet, has become a factor that cannot be separated in life [16]. Nowadays, people need fast access to information [17]. Obtaining information about surrounding matters is very important for survival, especially in the current state of the Covid-19 virus pandemic [18]. COVID-19 is a massive challenge at the global level [19]. In the first few months of 2020, information and news about COVID-19 quickly spread on social media and social networking sites [20]. With the rapid spread of information, it is also challenging to contain fake news during these uncertain conditions [17]. Sharing misinformation has implications beyond the dangers of the coronavirus itself [21]. Most of the world's people are uncertain and anxious about misinformation circulating [17].

3 Method

This study uses a qualitative approach called Q-DAS (Qualitative Data Analysis Software) with computer-assisted data analysis tools Nvivo software [22], data retrieval through the Indonesian Ministry of Health's Twitter account via NCapture from NVivo 12 Plus. Nvivo functions to translate data sets from Twitter and parse unstructured social media data [23]. The qualitative approach using Nvivo aims to describe the role of the Ministry of Health from the information conveyed through twitter.

4 Results and Discussions

As the number of COVID-19 worldwide increases, people also need quick access to information [17]. This study shows that the need for information is answered through the Twitter account of the Ministry of Health; according to Juditha [17], this step is an effort to prevent hoaxes. Through Twitter, the Ministry of Health provides relatively high content per month; see Fig. 1. Figure 1 shows that the intensity of information is relatively consistent; starting from June-March, in the middle period, the Ministry of Health provides various information.

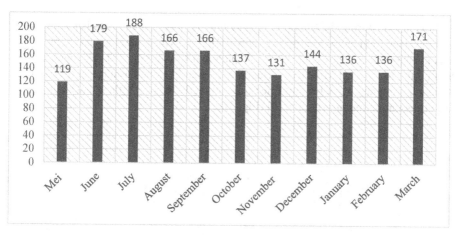

Fig. 1. Updating news about COVID-19

From the data above, the Ministry of Health's Twitter account for the last 11 months, namely from July 2021-March 2022, has tweeted the most in July 2021 with 188 tweets. The following month with the most tweets was not February 2022, with a tweet frequency of 187 tweets, and in June 2021, with a Tweets frequency of 179 tweets. Judging from the data above the Indonesian Ministry of Health's account, During this pandemic, there are many present tweets about COVID-19. With Frequency, The number of Tweets made was 1798 tweets. This shows that twitter has become a place of government in disseminating information [5].

Twitter incorporates interactive communication with other users to obtain information from various sources [15]; this is done on the Ministry of Health's Twitter by frequently mentioning it with other agencies, which function to spread Information about COVID-19 more widely. This also proves that many agencies use Twitter to disseminate information [14, 5]. To help spread Information about Covid-19 quickly, the Ministry of Health's account also includes mentions in every tweet, such as the following accounts:

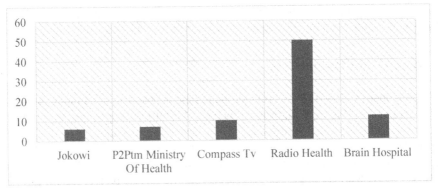

Fig. 2. Accounts that interact with The Ministry of Health of the Republic of

Information during the COVID-19 pandemic has physical characteristics identified with hashtags frequently used by accounts [24]. On Twitter, hashtags are popular and can indicate what content is uploaded. The picture below shows what hashtags are often used by the Indonesian Ministry of Health accounts; in using hashtags in the Ministry of Health accounts, it can be confirmed that indirectly the use of these hashtags can be part of disseminating information [5] (Fig. 3).

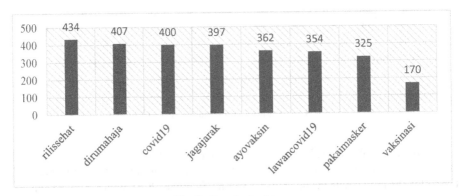

Fig. 3. Popular hashtags

Figure 2 From the results of the data above, the Indonesian Ministry of Health's account using hashtags about covid 19 is the most #at home with the use of 405 hashtags; after that there is the hashtag #covid19 with the use of 399 hashtags and the next is the hashtag #jagajarak with the usage of 395 hashtags, it can be seen that the Ministry of Health's account has given full attention to the issue of COVID-19. In this meeting, the government also used hashtags so that Information about COVID-19 is easy to find and obtain [25, 14]. In addition to hashtags, several words are often tweeted by the Ministry of Health's Twitter account, showing what information is most often spread by this Ministry of Health account. The following image shows the most frequently tweeted words by the account Fig. 4.

Fig. 4. Word frequency

Based on the data above, he has further analyzed using Word Cloud to find words often discussed on the Indonesian Ministry of health's Twitter account. It can be seen that the Ministry of health's Twitter account using Indonesian words and hashtags ranks the most frequently used, such as "covid" and "Vaksinissi". This proves that the Ministry of health's Twitter account uses many of these keywords when disseminating information in their tweets. With the frequency of the word about covid, people don't need to worry about the wrong information circulating [17].

5   Conclusion

Based on the explanation above, this study concludes that the Ministry of Health has maximized the Twitter account to become a virtual government service in the health sector very well seen from the intensity of the tweets carried out, especially the strategy from the Ministry of Health of the Republic of Indonesia which made the Ministry of health's Twitter account to spread Information about COVID-19 using The hashtag released Sehat is the official hashtag from the Ministry of Health, making it easier to find information. Indonesians who follow the @KemenkesRI account get complete data on various Information about COVID-19. With this, the Ministry of Health has succeeded in making Twitter a means of socialization, a means of Information, and an account trusted by the public.

References

1. Ehlers, L., Müskens, W.M., Jensen, L.G., Kjølby, M., Andersen, G.: National use of thrombolysis with Alteplase for acute Ischaemic stroke via telemedicine in Denmark. CNS Drugs **22**(1), 73–81 (2008). https://doi.org/10.2165/00023210-200822010-00006
2. Yoo, E., Rand, W., Eftekhar, M., Rabinovich, E.: Evaluating information diffusion speed and its determinants in social media networks during humanitarian crises. J. Oper. Manag. **45**, 123–133 (2016)
3. Kurnia, N.D., Johan, R.C., Rullyana, G.: Hubungan Pemanfaatan Media Sosial Instagram Dengan Kemampuan Literasi Media Di Upt Perpustakaan Itenas. Edulib **8**(1), 1 (2018). https://doi.org/10.17509/edulib.v8i1.10208
4. Varshney, D., Vishwakarma, D.K.: Hoax news-inspector: a real-time prediction of fake news using content resemblance over web search results for authenticating the credibility of news articles. J. Ambient. Intell. Humaniz. Comput. **12**(9), 8961–8974 (2020). https://doi.org/10.1007/s12652-020-02698-1
5. Azmi, N.A., Fathani, A.T., Sadayi, D.P., Fitriani, I., Adiyaksa, M.R.: Social Media Network Analysis (SNA): Identifikasi Komunikasi dan Penyebaran Informasi Melalui Media Sosial Twitter. J. Media Inform. Budidarma **5**(4), 1422–1430 (2021)
6. Park, H., Reber, B.H., Chon, M.-G.: Tweeting as health communication: health organizations' use of Twitter for health promotion and public engagement. J. Health Commun. **21**(2), 188–198 (2016)
7. Lachlan, K.A., Spence, P.R., Lin, X., Najarian, K., Del Greco, M.: Social media and crisis management: CERC, search strategies, and Twitter content. Comput. Hum. Behav. **54**, 647–652 (2016)
8. Ahram, T., Taiar, R. (eds.): IHIET 2021. LNNS, vol. 319. Springer, Cham (2022). https://doi.org/10.1007/978-3-030-85540-6
9. Erku, D.A., et al.: When fear and misinformation go viral: pharmacists' role in deterring medication misinformation during the 'infodemic' surrounding COVID-19. Res. Soc. Adm. Pharm. **17**(1), 1954–1963 (2021). https://doi.org/10.1016/j.sapharm.2020.04.032
10. Stromback, J., Kiousis, S.: Political Public Relations: Principles and Applications. Taylor & Francis (2011)
11. J. I. Criado, R. Sandoval-Almazan, and J. R. Gil-Garcia, "Government innovation through social media," *Government information quarterly*, vol. 30, no. 4. Elsevier, pp. 319–326, 2013
12. Getchell, M.C., Sellnow, T.L.: A network analysis of official Twitter accounts during the West Virginia water crisis. Comput. Hum. Behav. **54**, 597–606 (2016)
13. Chun, S.A., Luna-Reyes, L.F.: Social media in government. Gov. Inf. Q. **29**(4), 441–445 (2012)
14. Furqon, M., Hermansyah, D., Sari, S., Sukma, A., Akbar, Y., Rakhmawati, N.A.: Analisis sosial media pemerintah daerah di indonesia berdasarkan respons warganet. J. Sosioteknologi **17**(2), 2–4 (2018)
15. Zhang, C.B., Lin, Y.H.: Exploring interactive communication using social media. Serv. Ind. J. **35**(11–12), 670–693 (2015)
16. Fitriani, Y.: Analisis pemanfaatan berbagai media sosial sebagai sarana penyebaran informasi bagi masyarakat. Paradig. Komput. dan Inform. **19**(2), 148–152 (2017)
17. Juditha, C.: Perilaku Masyarakat Terkait Penyebaran Hoaks Covid-19 People Behavior Related To The Spread Of Covid-19's Hoax. J. Pekommas **5**(2), 105–116 (2020)
18. Widjaja, V., Widodo, N.M.: Pengaruh Teknologi Internet Terhadap Pengetahuan Masyarakat Jakarta Seputar Informasi Vaksinasi Covid-19. Temat. J. Teknol. Inf. Komun. **8**(1), 1–13 (2021)

19. Al-Dmour, H., Salman, A., Abuhashesh, M., Al-Dmour, R.: Influence of social media platforms on public health protection against the COVID-19 pandemic via the mediating effects of public health awareness and behavioral changes: integrated model. J. Med. Internet Res. **22**(8), e19996 (2020)
20. Ahmad, A.R., Murad, H.R.: The impact of social media on panic during the COVID-19 pandemic in Iraqi Kurdistan: online questionnaire study. J. Med. Internet Res. **22**(5), e19556 (2020)
21. Radwan, E., Radwan, A.: The spread of the pandemic of social media panic during the COVID-19 outbreak. Eur. J. Environ. Public Heal. **4**(2), em0044 (2020)
22. Isyanto, P., Sapitri, R.G., Sinaga, O.: Micro influencers marketing and brand image to purchase intention of cosmetic products Focallure. Syst. Rev. Pharm. **11**(1), 601–605 (2020)
23. Kaefer, F., Roper, J., Sinha, P.N.: A software-assisted qualitative content analysis of news articles: examples and reflections (2015)
24. Purnomo, E.P., et al.: How public transportation use social media platform during Covid-19: study on Jakarta public transportations' Twitter accounts? Webology **18**(1), 1–19 (2021). https://doi.org/10.14704/WEB/V18I1/WEB18001
25. Riyanto, S.J., Farida, N.: Social Network Analysis Komunikasi Kesehatan Pengguna Twitter Dengan Tagar# vaksinuntukkita Di Era Covid-19. AGUNA J. Ilmu Komun. **3**(1), 47–55 (2022)

Comparing Twitter Sentiment and United States COVID-19 Vaccination Rates

Aaron Cooper, Matteo Danforth, and April Edwards(✉)

United States Naval Academy, Annapolis, MD 21402, USA
aedwards@usna.edu

Abstract. As more people use social media as a source of news and information, it is important to understand its impact on individual health decisions. This article compares the sentiment expressed in COVID-19 related tweets with national rates for first dose vaccinations as recorded by the Centers for Disease Control and Prevention. To conduct the study, the text from over 570,000 COVID-related tweets from January 2021 to December 2021 was captured. The tweets were segregated by month and Google Cloud's Natural Language API was used determine the sentiment in each tweet, with each post labeled as having positive, negative, or neutral sentiment. Overall, there was greater prevalence of negative sentiment as compared with positive sentiment during the period of review, with 45% of tweets negative, 33% positive and 22% neutral. The number of positive and negative tweets was more balanced in the early months of 2021 (when the vaccine was first available) and became decidedly more negative in the later part of the year, as misinformation about the vaccines spread prolifically on social media. This comparison of the tweet sentiment to first-time vaccine doses in the US shows that misinformation about vaccines on social media appears to have had an impact on behavior. Vaccine adoption declined significantly in the latter half of 2021, even as vaccines and information from public health officials regarding their efficacy became more available to the general public. These findings are validated by subsequent analysis of word usage by month, with positive comments about vaccines and vaccination in January through May coinciding with high vaccination rates, and a negative conversational shift to variants, increased deaths and suspicion about vaccine safety and effectiveness later in the year during a stagnation period in vaccinations.

Keywords: COVID-19 · Social media analysis · Sentiment analysis

1 Introduction

Social media platforms have experienced unprecedented growth in daily active users (DAU) since the end of 2019, with one of the main contributing factors believed to be the COVID-19 pandemic and nationally mandated quarantine that went into effect in early 2020 [1]. Quarterly data of monetizable DAUs (mDAUs) worldwide show that the largest increases in mDAUs occurred between quarter four of 2019 and quarter one of 2020 (152 million users to 166 million) and between quarter one and two of 2020 (166

© The Author(s), under exclusive license to Springer Nature Switzerland AG 2022
C. Stephanidis et al. (Eds.): HCII 2022, CCIS 1655, pp. 10–17, 2022.
https://doi.org/10.1007/978-3-031-19682-9_2

million to 186 million) [2]. These quarterly increases resulted in 34 million new mDAUs on Twitter between October 2019 to June 2020, a time that also spanned the outbreak of the COVID-19 pandemic and national quarantine efforts. According to Tweet Binder, as of May 2020 there were over 628 million tweets using the hashtags using the phrase "COVID-19" [3].

The increased number of posts on social media platforms factors into the "infodemic" that has been occurring online regarding the COVID-19 pandemic. The World Health Organization defines an "infodemic" as too much data including false or misleading information in digital and physical environments during a disease outbreak [4], which has a variety of consequences. These consequences include risk-taking regarding health-related decisions and mistrust of credible health information. While the presence of misinformation on social media does not necessarily entail belief, more research is needed to determine the impact that misinformation regarding COVID-19 has had during the pandemic [5].

To address this topic, our research compares Twitter sentiment of COVID-19 related tweets from January 2021 to December 2021 with vaccination rates in the United States as recorded by the Centers for Disease Control and Prevention (CDC). After collecting over 500,000 tweets, we capture sentiment in the data both quantitively (using natural language processing to extract the sentiment from each tweet) and qualitatively (through an analysis of term frequency data). These analyses are then compared with vaccination rates to gain insight into the relationship between sentiment on social media with acceptance of vaccination during the COVID-19 pandemic.

2   Data

We used "Coronavirus Twitter Data: A collection of COVID-19 tweets with automated annotations" [6] to collect COVID-related tweets. This dataset contains tens of millions of records from February 2020 to present, with a separate download for each day. For the purposes of these experiments, we sampled data from the first day of each month of 2021. These dates were chosen because the existence of an effective vaccine was first announced in early November 2020 (days before the 2020 US Presidential Election), and the vaccines become widely available in early 2021. Each of the 12 downloads (one per month) contained approximately 1.3 million tweet ids. We sampled from among these, choosing 100,000 tweets from each month, and attempted to rehydrate the resulting tweets using Tweepy [7] and the Twitter API [8]. A large number of tweets were unavailable due to disabled user accounts, deleted tweets, or other factors. Ultimately, the full text of approximately 570,000 tweets were eventually recovered from Twitter, an average of 47,634 tweets per month.

3   Sentiment Analysis Using Natural Language Processing

3.1   Methodology

To quantitatively determine the sentiment of each tweet, we used Google Cloud's Natural Language API, a tool that "derives insight from unstructured text using Google machine learning" [9]. The API returns a *score* which indicates the overall emotion of a text and *magnitude* which indicates how much emotional content is present in the text [10]. The differentiation and use of both allows the user to determine the overall sentiment of a document while also giving insight into the prevalence of emotionally charged words. The *score* value has a range of $[1, -1]$ with a 1 representing emotionally positive and -1 emotionally negative. A sentiment score of 0 represents either a lack of emotional content or mixed emotional content. The *magnitude* value has a range of $[0, \infty]$ with 0 representing no emotional content detected and the value increasing as emotional content is detected.

To provide context to the numeric results, we also completed a qualitative term frequency analysis for each month using word clouds. To generate each word cloud, we combined the tweet text for each month. Stop words, html tags, and links were discarded. We also discarded terms that appeared in virtually every tweet, including: "COVID", "Coronavirus", "El Covid", and "La Covid." A word cloud was then generated with the top 100 frequently occurring terms (words or short phrases) from each month using the Python wordcloud library [11].

3.2 Results

An analysis of tweet sentiment by month appears in Fig. 1. Perhaps unsurprisingly, there was more negative content overall, with 45% of the tweets receiving a negative score from the Google API in comparison the 22% neutral and 33% positive. Notably the only months that showed a greater number of positive than negative tweets were February and July. Furthermore, sentiment became more decidedly negative in the latter half of 2021, as COVID variants emerged, and booster shots were needed to increase the effectiveness of vaccines.

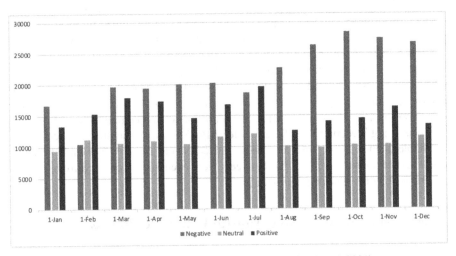

Fig. 1. Tweet sentiment by Month (Jan. 1 2021–Dec. 1 2021)

The most frequent word used on January 1, 2021 was "Wuhan;" "China" also appeared frequently. News articles from these dates refer to Chinese citizens ringing in the new year as 'ring out' a 'good riddance' to 2020, after an unarguably hard year for the city of Wuhan as the believed epicenter of the pandemic. Another term that was prominent in the word cloud was the name "Blancas", referring to an El Paso school teacher Zelene Blancas who passed away 28 December, 2020 after a nine week battle with COVID-19. Blancas would be one of many individuals who would receive notable recognition on social media during their battles with COVID-19.

The word cloud for February (see Fig. 2) reflects the optimism about the vaccine with phrases such as "vaccines," "committed," "strength," "one people," and "Relief Bill." The first highlights the spike in COVID-19 vaccine searches as revealed by a Google Trends search. Positive news around this time included a Department of Homeland Security statement regarding equal access for persons in the US seeking to receive a vaccine for COVID-19. "Relief Bill" refers to a two-hour Senate meeting that included a discussion of COVID-19 relief legislation for US citizens. On the other hand, a CBS 60 Minutes Special that drew more than 9 million viewers aired close to February 1st was far more negative. The 60 Minutes Special reported on China collecting American's DNA and health care data, and featured families who lost members after battles with COVID-19. Recall that February was the only month that showed substantially more positive sentiment than negative, indicating that the 60 Minutes Special did not overwhelm the positive sentiment at that time.

Fig. 2. 01 February word cloud

The July word cloud (Fig. 3) demonstrates the shortcomings of using automated tools without qualitative context analysis. "Death" is by far the most prominent term in the July word cloud, which also sees frequent mention of the Delta variant, and "long," which is a reference to ongoing health problems experienced by some individuals who contracted COVID. Furthermore, the frequency of the terms 'vaccine' and 'vaccination' are dropping out of the conversation. In late June and early July there was a 10% spike in US COVID-19 cases, and it was clear that the early optimism that vaccines would put the pandemic behind us was replaced with a new reality as a summer surge caused by the Delta variant began.

By September, the tide had fully turned, with negative sentiment growing substantially (Fig. 1). This change in attitude is fully reflected in the word cloud as well (Fig. 4), with terms like "fake" and "don need." The reference to Chloe Mrozak is in reference to a story about a woman who obtained a fake vaccination card to gain entrance to Hawaii. Ms. Mrozak was charged with falsifying documents and arrested. This was one of several stories around this time which showed public resistance to taking the COVID vaccines, with some people denying the existence of COVID entirely.

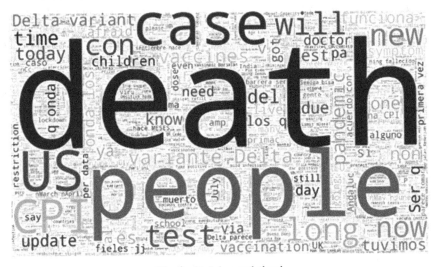

Fig. 3. 01 July word cloud

The word clouds (all of which are available at https://github.com/acoop2/Twitter_Analysis) show monthly fluctuation in the online discussion around COVID throughout 2021, with distinctive themes (represented by key terms) appearing from month to month. As the national conversation evolves, social media discussion follows the trends in an emotional and visceral way. Recall that almost 80% of tweets demonstrated emotionality (only 22% were neutral), as individuals reacted to each new piece of information.

Fig. 4. 01 September word cloud

4   Comparison of Social Media Sentiment and Vaccination Rates

To compare the social media conversation with its potential impact on vaccination rates in the United States, we collected data on first dose vaccinations from the Center for Disease Control (CDC) [12] and summarized the data by month (Fig. 5). The data show a large spike in March and April 2021 (Fig. 5 top). The numbers decline sharply by June and vaccine participation stays low for the remainder of 2021 despite the strong push

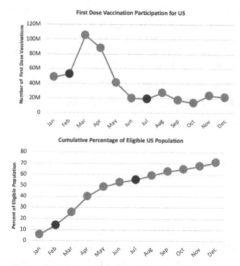

Fig. 5. Number (left) and cumulative percent (right) of first dose vaccinations in the United States from January to December 2021 (source: CDC)

via public health messaging that strongly encouraged people to get the vaccine. Figure 5 (bottom) shows the cumulative participation of eligible individuals, with a sharp rise from February through May; the increase was 9% in February, 12% in March, 14% in April, and 9% in May. Afterwards there is incremental improvement of only 2–3% per month from June through December.

The blue markers in Fig. 5 represent the months when there was a greater prevalence of positive vs. negative sentiment in the Twitter data. The comparison of sentiment with vaccination rates gives insight into the impact of social media on vaccination behavior. Referring to the word cloud from February (Fig. 2), we saw the prominence of positive terms such as "committed", "strength", and "vaccine" used frequently. Vaccinations surged in the subsequent months. However, even though there was a slightly larger number of positive than negative tweets in July, it appears as if the largely negative tone that was demonstrated in our qualitative analysis (Fig. 3) had an impact on vaccinations. As social media sentiment grows more strongly negative from August through December, first-dose vaccination participation remains low, and the small rate of growth may be due to additional populations becoming eligible to receive the vaccine [13]. See Table 1 for the vaccine milestone timeline.

The spikes in March and April 2021 coincide with the positive sentiment in Twitter data and the surge in vaccine participation. However, even as vaccines receive full FDA approval and people become eligible for vaccines at younger ages, there is no corresponding boost in first dose vaccinations (Table 1 and Fig. 5). It appears that negative public sentiment in social media analysis overrides positive news from official sources.

Table 1. Vaccine eligibility milestones

Date	Milestone
Dec 2020	Vaccines receive emergency use authorization from FDA First doses available to vulnerable populations and healthcare workers
March 2021	Eligibility expands to include teachers and other school staff
April 2021	Eligibility expands to all people ages 16 and older
May 2021	Eligibility expands to ages 12–15
August 2021	Full FDA approval received for Pfizer vaccine
October 2021	Eligibility expands to ages 5–11

5   Discussion

There is no clear answer as to why vaccination rates declined so sharply in the 2nd half of 2021 and why there is still a large percentage (over 23% as of May 2022) of Americans who have still not received a first dose [12]. A recent survey shows that a majority of those unvaccinated are concerned about long term side effects, don't trust the vaccine, or don't trust the government [14]. Research shows that misinformation plays a large role in vaccine hesitancy, resulting in confusion, distress, and mistrust [15, 16]. It is also clear that social media plays a role in the spread of misinformation due to the proliferation of negative messages to a broad audience [17, 18].

While the large number of negative tweets coincides with the stagnation in vaccination rates, this does not imply causation. Additional research is required to determine if social media content affects health decisions.

References

1. The Washington Post: Twitter sees record number of uses during pandemic, but advertising sales slow (2020). https://www.washingtonpost.com/business/economy/twitter-sees-record-number-of-users-during-pandemic-but-advertising-sales-slow/2020/04/30/747ef0fe-8ad8-11ea-9dfd-990f9dcc71fc_story.html. Accessed May 2022
2. Statista: Number of monetizable daily active Twitter users (mDAU) worldwide from 1st quarter 2017 to 1st quarter 2022 (2022). https://www.statista.com/statistics/970920/monetizable-daily-active-twitter-users-worldwide/. Accessed May 2022
3. Tweet Binder: How many tweets about Covid-19 and Coronavirus? (2020). https://www.tweetbinder.com/blog/COVID-19-coronavirus-twitter/. Accessed May 2022
4. World Health Organization: Infodemic (n.d.). https://www.who.int/health-topics/infodemic#tab=tab_1. Accessed May 2022
5. Bridgman, A.: The causes and consequences of COVID-19 misperceptions: understanding the role of news and social media. Harvard Kennedy School Misinformation Rev. 1(3) (2020)
6. Huang, X., Jamison, A., Broniatowski, D., Quinn, S., Dredze, M.: Coronavirus Twitter data: a collection of COVID-19 tweets with automated annotations. Zenodo (2020). https://doi.org/10.5281/zenodo.6513067
7. Roesslein, J.: Tweepy: Twitter for Python! (2020). https://github.com/tweepy/tweepy
8. Twitter Developer. https://developer.twitter.com/en. Accessed May 2022
9. Google Cloud: Natural language API demo (n.d.). https://cloud.google.com/natural-language#section-2. Accessed May 2022
10. Google Cloud: Natural language API basics (n.d.). https://cloud.google.com/natural-language/docs/basics#interpreting_sentiment_analysis_values. Accessed May 2022
11. Word Cloud GitHub. https://amueller.github.io/word_cloud/. Accessed May 2022
12. Centers for Disease Control and Prevention: COVID Data Tracker (n.d.). https://covid.cdc.gov/covid-data-tracker/vaccinations_vacc-total-admin-rate-total. Accessed May 2022
13. Department of Health and Human Services. (n.d.) COVID-19 Vaccines. https://www.hhs.gov/coronavirus/covid-19-vaccines/index.html. Accessed May 2022
14. Harman, T., et al.: Different conspiracy theories have different psychological and social determinants: Comparison of three theories about the origins of the COVID-19 virus in a representative sample of the UK population. Front. Polit. Sci. 3, 44 (2021)
15. Hughes, J., et al.: The impact of risk perceptions and beliefs in conspiracy theories on COVID-19 pandemic-related behaviours. PLoS ONE 17(2), e0263716 (2022)
16. Boyd, K.: Beyond politics: additional factors underlying skepticism of a COVID-19 vaccine. Hist. Philos. Life Sci. 43(12) (2021)
17. Wong, J., Yang J.: Comparative risk: dread and unknown characteristics of the COVID-19 pandemic versus COVID-19 vaccines. Risk Anal. (2021)
18. Lockyer, B., et al.: Understanding COVID-19 misinformation and vaccine hesitancy in context: findings from a qualitative study involving citizens in Bradford, UK. Health Expect. 24(4), 1158–1167 (2021)

Digital Content Management of Twitter for Climate Change Using Hashtag

Anisa Septia Firnanda[(⊠)], Fajar Junaedi, and Erwan Sudiwijaya

Department of Communication, University of Muhammadiyah Yogyakarta, Kasihan, Indonesia
firnanda145@gmail.com, {fajarjun,erwansudiwijaya}@umy.ac.id

Abstract. Environmental issues have become a big issue in the last few decades. Environmental damage, changes in natural resources caused by human activities. This study aims to identify the activity of spreading #Iniaksiku by using the *Social Network Analysis* (SNA) method on the Twitter social media network. This research method uses qualitative analysis with N'Vivo 12 plus analysis tool. Based on the analysis of information content provided by @earthhourjogja by the community with social media activities through twitter earthhourjogja about concern for climate change. The results of this study are to educate and invite the public to take care of the environment such as reducing plastic waste, saving on electricity, protecting the earth, protecting the earth, and protecting the environment, clean garbage in rivers and seas using the hashtag #iniaksiku. According to the frequency of words that often appear in the hashtag #iniaksiku in the @earthourjogja account, 122 tweets appear. The hashtag #iniaksiku also ranks first at the top and is often on the @earthhourjogja twitter account timeline. The results of data analysis which is an invitation to identify the existence of information in the content of @earthhourjogja that is packaged in an attractive way so that it can be accepted by the public.

Keywords: Digital content management · Twitter · Social media · Information

1 Introduction

The development of technology and information is increasingly advanced, making the world's nations very literate in developing information to meet their needs [1]. Progress technology development of digital forms of communication and socialization can be called social media. New ways of communicating and socializing by looking at new people to interact with people and audiences [2].

Media management is studied from different perspectives ranging from communication and journalism [3]. Social media has exploded in recent years, as Facebook, Twitter, and youtube are the most visited communication platforms [4]. Social media is an essential part of life, which is relatively and widely accessible to broadcast news information, and knowledge and establish new relationships [5]. A community manages alternative media as a diversity of ownership and the antithesis of mainstream media [6]. Digital content can unleash further creative potential by being creatively more attractive [7].

C. Stephanidis et al. (Eds.): HCII 2022, CCIS 1655, pp. 18–24, 2022.
https://doi.org/10.1007/978-3-031-19682-9_3

Digital content is one of the information-driven concepts for engagement with exchanging ideas [8]. Twitter as a platform for discussion and activity on various social issues. Twitter engages in conversation, sharing resources with the community [9]. The community has researched other online social movements, such as #Iniaksiku. To access social representations related to hashtags [10]. Twitter has spread throughout the world and has become one of the major social networks [5].

It has been confirmed that human activities in the environment have a major impact on the climate [11]. The environment has an essential role in supporting human life. A global environmental crisis includes forest destruction, pollution (soil, water, air), climate change, biodiversity extinction, loss of energy resources, and other environmental damage. All the damage is mainly caused by human activities [12]. Environmental issues that are widely exposed trigger Indonesian citizens to prevent the impact of losses caused by environmental damage [13].

Environmentally friendly is harmony between humans and the environment. It is hoped that this activity can invite the public to be aware of protecting the environment and saving energy. Therefore, it will make content-aware of human behaviour that often ignores the environment and does not save energy by using the hashtag #iniaksiku. So that many people know the importance of protecting the environment and saving energy, it is necessary to have content about an environmentally friendly lifestyle using the hashtag #iniaksiku through the @earthhourjogja twitter account.

2 Literature Review

The rapid development of internet technology provides users with unlimited access to a wide range of information. Management of the planning, organization, direction, and use of organizational resources to achieve the goals set [6]. Content management is a system that provides access to all types of digital content files [14]. Content management is changing or creating, controlling, organizing, compiling, and making accessible digital objects [16]. As a global conversation lately, climate change has confirmed that environmental activities have a profound impact on the environmental climate [11]. The environment is increasingly threatened when there is a world environmental crisis, such as the destruction of forest pollution, pollution (soil, water, air), climate change, biological diversity, and the loss of energy and environmental damage caused by humans [13]. This content management system is used to manage content. This content management can help and solve usability problems, and the concepts that have been implemented into it are shown to users [18].

Social media is a personal communication channel with the capacity to create a conversation with an audience or interact with an audience [19]. Information and communication technology devices and tools are used to communicate, create, manage, store, and disseminate information. Digital content is created and developed using several technologies that increase access [20]. The development of communication and information technology has led to competition in the digital world. Digital uses information technology tools to access, produce and distribute information. Digital content is becoming the current media information [21]. This digital content is related to the speed production process by emphasizing activities in presenting the work to the audience. Messages and information are conveyed that contain important values and must be factual to be interesting for consumption by the audience. Some require efficient and precise stages of production execution [22].

3 Method

To answer the research question, this study uses a qualitative approach to determine the function of social media @erathhourjogja. This method uses the Nvivo 12 Plus tool to describe social media data. The data collection process uses N-capture capturing by retrieving data from the @earthhourjogja social media account. According to [23], Nvivo can translate unstructured data by dividing it into several types according to research needs; in addition, [24] assessing the gradual data translation process helps describe it clearly.

4 Results and Discussions

Content management makes information more interesting so that information affects the audience, in view [16]. This study categorizes several findings that describe the form of digital content from social media Twitter @earthhourjogja. See Fig. 1; the social media account @earthhourjogja provides information with different intensities, in the last seven years the intensity of information from 2015–2017 has increased even though it is fluctuating.

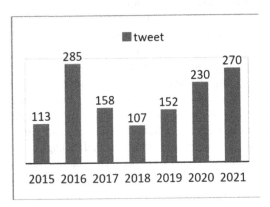

Fig. 1. Twitter account activity @earthhourjogja. (source Nvivo 12 plus Software)

Figure according to M. Kumar and A. Nath [17] The @earthhoujogja account had the highest activity in 2016 which then decreased in 2017 and 2018 after which it rose again in 2019–2021. Account @earthhourjogja every year up and down. This finding shows that digital content and content management are being used to launch a campaign for awareness of climate change with the hashtag #iniaksiku. This content management system is used to manage content. This kind of content management system provides

Table 1. Twitter Account Interaction @earthhourjogja. (source Nvivo 12 plus Software)

Community	Percentage	Campaign team
ehjogja	62%	Non Government
Organitationehindonesia	19%	
wwf_id	6%	
respiration	6%	
ehbalikpapan	2%	
twse_jogja	2%	
earthhour	2%	
fighter	1%	
unisifmyk	100%	Media
warkopbardiman	27%	Local development
playon_jogja	25%	
sheratonjogja	25%	
Malammuseum	23%	

procedures for organization to manage workflow. This step is a form of public awareness with concern for climate change (Table 1).

Table according to Sulianta [21], and it has three interactions: nongovernment organization, media, and local development. The highest level of interaction is in nongovernment organizations, and the lowest is in the media. The non-government organization section mentions the @erthhourjogja account with the highest level of interaction with digital content. The content created when mentioning the @earthhourjogja account is content that is concerned with climate change. Meanwhile, other mentions, such as media and local development, interact and collaborate by using these mentions. The findings above show that digital content focuses on mentioning the @earthhourjogja account.

Information and communication technology tools used to communicate, create, manage, store, and disseminate information. Digital content is created and developed in digital using several technologies that increase access [20].

Table 2. Account communication Twitter@earthhourjogja. (source.Nvivo12 plus Software)

Hastag	Category communication @earthourjogja		
	Content	Information	Media
iniaksiku	✓	✓	✓
jogjapetengan	✓	✓	✓
earthour	✓	✓	✓
connect2earth	✓	✓	✓

Management and digital content use, #jogjapetengan, #earthour, and #connect2earth for each of their content that discusses climate change concerns. The four hashtags used can influence the audience to make climate change, produced by content management. The function of the following table is to find out which one is more in the use of hashtags.

The information category has the intensity in Table 2 according to E. Cuevas-Molano [19], which is often used to categorize climate change concerns. Social media is a personal communication channel with the capacity to create a conversation with the audience or interaction with the audience. The environment is increasingly threatened when there is a world environmental crisis such as the destruction of forest pollution, pollution (soil, water, air), climate change, biological diversity and the loss of energy and environmental damage caused by humans [13]. This research answers about information. The word that is often used shows the amount of digital content on the @aerthhourjogja account that climate change is often discussed.

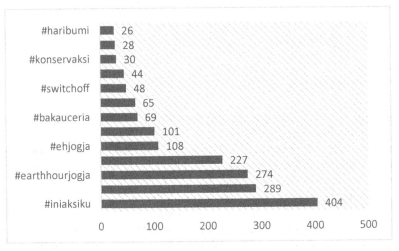

Fig. 2. Hashtag Twitter account @earthhourjogja. (sourceNvivo 12 plus Software)

Figure 2 according to J. A. Ottuh [11]. The image above shows that the category of information can be seen from the hashtag, earthhoujogja provides campaigning on the issue of climate change. Hashtag categories like #iniaksiku, #earthour, #bakauceria, #haribumi. The most used hashtag is #iniaksiku. Climate change has become a global conversation. Lately, it has been confirmed that human activities on the environment profoundly impact the environmental climate. The environment is increasingly threatened when there is a world environmental crisis such as the destruction of forest pollution, pollution (soil, water, air), climate change, biological diversity and the loss of energy and environmental damage caused by humans [13].

Fig. 3. Word frequency about climate change

Figure 3 according to Gordo-Molina Social media is a personal communication channel with the capacity to create conversations with the audience or interact with the audience [19]. The picture above shows that there are still many who use the hashtag, the most important of which is the hashtag #iniaksiku; not only that, there are still many who use the hashtag for climate change movements such as #earthhour, #jogjapetengan. This is one of the movements by using hashtags so that people care about environmental changes.

5   Conclusion

Based on the results of research on the social media Twitter account @earthhourjogja with the hashtag #iniaksiku, it can be concluded that @earthhourjogja has implemented an important aspect in presenting climate change information using the hashtag #iniaksiku. So far, the community has started by doing climate change by going directly in the field by creating content through Twitter social media accounts using the hashtag #iniaksiku, but this has not been able to touch all circles. The content is made consistently using the hashtag #iniaksiku. In managing hashtags, @erathhourjogja is quite good at targeting the community and all walks of life. In managing social media, Twitter @earthhourjogja is enough to manage climate change issues.

References

1. Ismandianto, I., Susilawati, N.S.: Production management of the Riau-KepriTvri religious pulpit program. J. Audience **4**(01), 28–37 (2021). https://doi.org/10.33633/ja.v4i01.4172
2. Rebucas, E.M., Pilayan, J.S., Ramos, I.R.P., Molina, M.A.A., Dugos, C.M.M.: Multifaceted potentials of social media: digital immigrants in focus, April 2021
3. Khajeheian, D.: Nord. J. Media Manag., 1 (2020). https://doi.org/10.5278/njmm.2597-0445.1
4. Maxwell, S.P., Carboni, J.L.: Social media management: exploring Facebook engagement among high-asset foundations. Nonprofit Manag. Leadersh. **27**(2), 251–260 (2016). https://doi.org/10.1002/nml.21232
5. Gomathy, C.K.: The Twitter behavioral analytics, December 2021
6. Saifudin, B.E., Rosilawati, Y.: JawaPos Multi Media (JPM) stream media management in facing competition in the era of digital disruption **1**(2) (2020). https://doi.org/10.18196/ja.12029

7. Ivarsson, F., Selander, L.: Coordinating digital content generation. In: Proceedings Annual Hawaii International Conference on System Sciences, pp. 5811–5820 (2021). https://doi.org/10.24251/hicss.2021.705

8. IO Eshiett: Digital content marketing and customer loyalty in Nigerian University, April 2022

9. Cao, J., Lee, C., Sun, W., De Gagne, J.C.: The #StopAsianHate movement on Twitter: a qualitative descriptive study. Int. J. Environ. Res. Public Health 19(7) (2022). https://doi.org/10.3390/ijerph19073757

10. Vitali, M.M., Presotto, G.C., Gizzi, F., de Andrade Gomes, M., Giacomozzi, A.I.: #Blacklivesmatter: a study of social representations from Twitter. Community Psychol. Globe. Perspective 8(1), 1–19 (2022). https://doi.org/10.1285/i24212113v8i1p1

11. Ottuh, J.A.: Christianity and environmental care in Nigeria: the role of Christians in addressing indiscriminate refuse disposal. Pharos J. Theol. 103, 1–15 (2022). https://doi.org/10.46222/PHAROSJOT.103.015

12. Istiqomah, I., Suwondo, S., Firdaus, L.: Environmental education in forming attitudes of environmental care for students. J. Educ. Sci. 4(1), 200 (2020). https://doi.org/10.31258/jes.4.1.p.200-211

13. Arjani, A., Santoso, S., Muryani, C.: The environmental care level of junior high school students in Surakarta. IOP Conf. Ser. Earth Environ. Sci. 683(1) (2021). https://doi.org/10.1088/1755-1315/683/1/012050

14. Jankulovski, J., Anastoska-Jankulovka, M., Mitrevski, P.: Content management systems – unleashed possibilities, pp. 547–550 (2013)

15. Zain, F.M., Hanafi, E., Don, Y., Yaakob, M.F.M., Sailin, S.N.: Investigating student's acceptance of an EDMODO content management system. Int. J. Instr. 12(4), 1–16 (2019). https://doi.org/10.29333/iji.2019.1241a

16. Hassanzadeh, M.: Editor-in-chief's note digital content management: an amalgam of all disciplines, pp. 1–10, August 2021

17. Kumar, M., Nath, A.: Web content management system (CMS). Int. J. Innov. Res. Adv. Eng. 03, 1–7 (2016). https://doi.org/10.6084/M9.FIGSHARE.3504368.V1

18. Abdullah, E.N., Ahmad, S., Ismail, M., Diah, N.M.: Evaluating E-commerce website content management system in assisting usability issues. In: 2021 IEEE Symposium Engineering Electrons App, ISIEA 2021, pp. 1–6, November 2021. https://doi.org/10.1109/ISIEA51897.2021.9509991

19. Cuevas-Molano, E., Sánchez-Cid, M., Gordo-Molina, V.: Brand strategy and content management on Instagram: scheduling and message length as factors to improve engagement. Commun. Soc. 35(2), 71–87 (2022). https://doi.org/10.15581/003.35.2.71-87

20. Shah, U.A., et al.: Problems and challenges in the preservation of digital contents: an analytical study. Libr. Philos. Pract. 2021(May), 1–12 (2021)

21. Gusti Bobby, M., Bayu Wicaksono, Y., Putri, W.N., Triono, J.: Digital content model development of learning using R&D method to enhanced digital literacy competency. Int. J. Psychosoc. Rehab. (2021). https://doi.org/10.37200/IJPR/V24I1/PR200525

22. Ramadhan, M.F., Kinasih, A.V.Z., Pernikasari, D.A.: Production management of 6 SCTV news broadcasts during the Covid-19 pandemic. J. Audiens 2(2), 227–234 (2021). https://doi.org/10.18196/jas.v2i2.11780

23. Woolf, N.H., Silver, C.: Qualitative analysis using MAXQDA: the five-level QDA® method. In: Qualitative Analysis Using the MAXQDA Five-Level QDA Method, pp. 1–208 (2017). https://doi.org/10.4324/9781315268569

24. Beekhuyzen, J., Nielsen, S., VonHellens, L.: The Nvivo looking glass: seeing the data through the analysis. In: 5th International Conference Qualitative Research IT (2010)

Understanding Users' Deepfake Video Verification Strategies

Dion Hoe-Lian Goh, Chei Sian Lee[✉], Zirong Chen, Xue Wen Kuah, and Ying Ling Pang

Wee Kim Wee School of Communication and Information, Nanyang Technological University, Singapore 637718, Singapore
{ashlgoh,leecs,zchen039,xkuah002,pany0011}@ntu.edu.sg

Abstract. Deepfakes are synthetically generated media that pose as actual video recordings, and are a potential source of fake news or disinformation. Consequently, the ability to detect them is imperative. Although research has been done in creating algorithms for automatic detection, there is little work conducted on how users identify deepfakes. Hence, the present paper fills this gap with a user study. Through semi-structured interviews, participants were asked to identify real and deepfake videos, and explain how they arrived at their conclusions. Seven verification strategies emerged, with the most popular being the use of subtle indictors in the videos suggesting the presence of imperfections. The use of one's social circle to verify a video was the least used. Surprisingly, only half our participants could correctly identify all the videos they watched. Deepfake videos that seemed to portray believable content or were of high quality made participants think they were real.

Keywords: Deepfake videos · Identification · Verification strategies · Authenticity · User study

1 Introduction

Seeking information on social media is a double-edged sword. On the one hand are advantages such as access to a wide variety of information sources and the ability to share and discuss content with other users [17]. On the other hand, are credibility issues regarding the content being shared [16], specifically, whether it is authentic and trustworthy. In particular, recent years has witnessed widespread concern about fake news, which refers to misinformation or disinformation packaged as legitimate news.

In its original conception, fake news is typically text-oriented, such as those found in mainstream news sites. With advancements in technology, fake news has extended to videos as well. The quintessential example is the deepfake video, or simply, deepfake. Deepfakes are synthetically generated media that pose as actual video recordings [5]. A common use is to replace the face of a person in a video with someone else who is originally not in it. The "deep" in deepfakes refer to the use of deep learning and artificial neural networks to generate falsified videos. Deepfakes have been used to create pornography where a hapless victim appears as an actor in the video. Deepfakes are also found in areas such as news, politics and entertainment.

The use of deepfakes as a source of fake news is of concern for a couple of reasons. First, the richness of content in videos when compared to predominantly text-based articles such as news, makes the former more persuasive and hence has the potential to be perceived as more credible [2]. Consequently, the impact of deepfake videos used to disseminate fake news is greater than other media formats [24]. Second, people are increasingly turning to YouTube and Facebook to consume news in the form of videos [3]. Those that are not discerning may thus be persuaded by the content found in deepfakes. Finally, technology advancements have eased the creation of realistic deepfakes, whereas in the past, such videos were limited in number and of dubious quality due to the complexities of producing them [11].

Identification of deepfakes has unsurprisingly garnered much research attention. Current work concentrates mainly on the design, implementation, and evaluation of machine learning algorithms for deepfake detection (e.g. [12]). These algorithms typically aim to spot irregularities in video rendering or unusual behavior of people in the video content (e.g. [25]). Although such research has yielded useful findings, the human perspective of deepfake identification has not yet been investigated sufficiently. More specifically, it is important to understand how people identify the authenticity of a given video, that is, whether it is a deepfake or not. We contend that such investigations are essential because they play complementary roles to algorithmic research, possibly leading to the design of new automated deepfake detection techniques. Further, new insights from user-oriented research would help in the creation of materials to educate people about deepfakes and how to identify them.

Hence, the objectives of the present study are to: (1) uncover the strategies that people undertake to identify deepfakes; and (2) identify the challenges that people face in doing so.

2 Methodology

The present study was qualitative in nature, using semi-structured interviews for data collection. This method was used because there is currently little work done from the users' perspective, and interviews would allow us to gather richer and more in-depth data when compared with questionnaires that collect quantitative data [7].

A total of 20 participants, comprising 11 males and nine females, were recruited for our study using a combination of convenience and snowball sampling. They were between the ages of 21 to 40, and represented a common age group of people who watched videos online. The majority (15 participants) spent at least once a day watching online videos. Participants used nine different platforms to watch videos, comprising Dailymotion, Facebook, Instagram, Tiktok, Twitter, Vimeo, WeChat, Weibo and YouTube. Of these, the most popular platform was Facebook (19 participants).

As part of the study, four videos were prepared, two of which were real, and two were deepfakes. The real videos were: (A) a speech by Mark Zuckerberg supporting the investigation of the Russian government's interference in the 2016 United States presidential election; and (B) a speech by former United States president Barack Obama urging Kenyans to take responsibility in their upcoming national election to make a difference in the nation. The two deepfakes were: (C) a speech by Indian politician, Manoj Tiwari criticizing an opposing political party in English and encouraging people to vote for his party; and (D) a speech by UK politician Jeremy Corbyn encouraging voters to support his opponent, Boris Johnson as UK prime minister.

The procedure of the study was as follows. Each participant independently watched all four videos but were not told which were real and which were fake. The sequence of the videos shown were randomized for each participant to minimize order effects [10]. Participants were allowed to watch each video twice.

After watching the videos, participants were asked a series of questions in the semi-structured interview. These include demographic questions, and those pertaining to video consumption behavior. Next, they were asked to identify which videos were real or fake. Questions were then posed to understand how the participants came their conclusions about the authenticity of the videos. Participants were encouraged to explain their decisions through probing questions. Finally, those who wrongly identified the videos were requested to reflect on why their decisions were incorrect.

Following the study, all interview responses were analyzed to address the research objectives. Specifically, the interview responses were transcribed. Thereafter, two coders inductively created categories independently, focusing on the verification strategies that our participants utilized to identify the real and deepfake videos.

3   Results

3.1   Identification of Videos

Unexpectedly, participants did not fare well in identifying which videos were real or deepfake. Only six of the 20 participants made all correct identifications, with the majority (nine) making only two correct identifications. Four participants correctly identified three videos, while one participant incorrectly identified all videos.

In terms of individual deepfake video identification, Video C (speech by Manoj Tiwari) was correctly identified as a deepfake by 17 of 20 participants. In contrast, Video D (speech by Jeremy Corbyn) was correctly identified by only half (10) of our participants. The real videos fell in-between these two. Video A (speech by Mark Zuckerberg was correctly identified by 14 participants, and Video B (speech by Barack Obama) was correctly identified by 13 participants.

3.2   Verification Strategies

To address the first research objective, an examination of our interview transcripts yielded seven types of strategies used to verify the authenticity of the videos:

1. Subtle indicators. Video imperfections such as facial blurring, shimmer or distortion, inconsistencies in speech and mouth movements, abnormal body movements, lighting inconsistencies, unnatural reflections and shadows, lack of breathing, overly smooth skin, strange behaviors, missing details such as hair and teeth.

2. Context/content of video. Concepts or content presented in a way that appears to be fabricated.
3. Personal knowledge. Participant used his/her knowledge to discern authenticity of a video.
4. Information search. Participant searched online to verify authenticity of a video.
5. Video source. Whether the source of the video was deemed to be credible.
6. Intuition. Use of intuition to determine the authenticity of a video.
7. Social influence. Use of one's social circle to ascertain a video's authenticity.

To provide a finer-grained analysis, we examined participants' verification strategies separately according to the type of video, whether deepfake or real. Table 1 shows the number of participants that employed each strategy that led to correct deepfake identification. The top strategy was the use of subtle indicators, with the context/content of a video coming in second place. Intuition and social influence were the least used, in contrast.

Table 1. Strategies used for correct deepfake identification.

Strategy	Number of participants
Subtle indicators	14
Context/content of video	10
Personal knowledge	3
Information search	2
Video source	2
Intuition	1
Social influence	1

Table 2 shows the number of participants that employed each strategy that led to correct real video identification. The top two strategies were equally used by participants and involved subtle indicators and the context/content of a video. The bottom two strategies were the same as for deepfake identification. In the middle, there were differences in the popularity of the strategies used.

To address the second research objective, we analyzed the interview transcripts to uncover why participants failed to correctly identify the videos they watched. In this regard, six reasons emerged:

1. Realistic footage. Content depicted in the video seemed to present a real event.
2. Video quality. Video and audio were of high quality.
3. Intuition failure. Use of intuition resulted in an incorrect identification.
4. Lack of knowledge. Participant did not have the knowledge to discern a video's authenticity and assumed it was real.
5. Recognizable character. Character appearing in the video was someone whom the participant knows or is aware of.

6. Search failure. Online searches did not yield information about authenticity of a video and participant assumed it was real.

Table 3 shows the number of participants that reported each failure reason. Here, the seemingly realistic footage was the most popular reason, while recognizable characters and search failures were the least.

Table 2. Strategies used for correct real video identification.

Strategy	Number of participants
Subtle indicators	9
Context/content of video	9
Personal knowledge	5
Information search	3
Video source	2
Intuition	2
Social influence	2

Table 3. Reasons for incorrect video identification.

Reason	Number of participants
Realistic footage	7
Video quality	3
Intuition failure	2
Lack of knowledge	2
Recognizable character	1
Search failure	1

4 Discussion

We found it surprising that only a minority (six of 20) of our participants could correctly identify all of their assigned videos as real or deepfake. This is despite the fact that participants were briefed about the nature of the study, and were thus mindful that they could be watching falsified content. One could imagine that in the real world, identification performance would be worse if someone were to stumble upon a deepfake online without prior knowledge that the content could be fake [22].

There could a few reasons for the relatively low identification success rate. One is that increasingly, deepfake creation tools are not only becoming easier to use, but are also containing better quality content [4]. Hence when accompanied with a convincing story, people may more likely believe that a deepfake is authentic. For example, one participant remarked that the *"quality of [deepfake] videos and topics mentioned"* conveyed the impression of authenticity. A second reason surrounds the concept of unfamiliarity, in particular the unfamiliarity of the video's topic and/or the familiarity of the people in the video. For the former, it appeared that participants assumed or randomly guessed a video's authenticity if they were unsure of the content. This is reflected in a participant's comment, *"I would think that the lack of knowledge or following on the current affairs in India presumably was the main reason. I may have remembered wrongly about Obama's ancestry"*. For the latter, one participant claimed that the video was real because it depicted an *"infamous figure"*, but this turned out to be incorrect. A third reason encompasses failures of intuition or information seeking. Here, one participant commented, *"I can't be sure video [A] is fake or not. Just gut feel... So I picked video [A] out as the video feels too clean"*. Note that *"video A"* refers to Mark Zuckerberg's speech which is authentic. Another participant remarked that *"there wasn't any alternate source to cross reference the content"*. As a result, this participant made a wrong guess.

The verification strategies that led to correct deepfake and real video identification were the same, although there were small variations in the number of participants that used them across the video types. Of the seven strategies uncovered, the use of subtle indicators in the videos was the most popular, as exemplified by a participant's comment, *"... Hand movements, body gestures that kept looping, mouth not moving in sync..."*. Notably, these indicators, such as facial distortions, abnormal mouth movements, and strange behaviors, are also employed by current deepfake detection algorithms [21], further justifying their use.

Interestingly, the use of the context and content of a video to ascertain its authenticity could have positive and negative consequences. On the positive side, this strategy could complement someone's personal knowledge to ascertain if a video was a deepfake or not. For example, one participant noticed that the *"scripted speech"* and the *"discussed topic"* were not aligned with what was known about the person in the video. However, our findings also suggest that if falsified content was presented in a way that was realistic enough, it could tilt the balance and persuade people to believe in its authenticity. This is shown in Table 3, where what seems to be realistic content may not always be the case. For example, a participant noted with surprise that *"the footage seems real"*, when told the video was actually a deepfake.

It was heartening to note that our participants used techniques advocated in the literature to ascertain content credibility (e.g. [14, 18]). In the context of this study, these include examining the source of the video (*"the logo/icon of the publisher that was in the video"*), conducting online searches to verify the video content (*"cross reference subject content on different sources/media"*), and consulting one's social network for verification help (*"ask opinion from friends"*). However, what was interesting was that these strategies were not as popular. It appeared that participants would prefer to examine the video and rely on themselves first, rather than utilize external sources such as online searches or other people.

5 Discussion

The present study provides an understanding of how people verify the authenticity of videos in response to the rise of deepfakes on the Internet. Using semi-structured interviews, we elicited verification strategies from participants who watched two real and two deepfake videos, and asked them to ascertain their authenticity. We also uncovered reasons for why participants failed in this identification task.

The following implications may be drawn from this work. First, from the research perspective, we extend prior work in deepfake detection and user assessments of information credibility. In particular, we fill the gap in deepfake research by focusing on users and revealing the strategies they undertake to detect deepfakes. Further, where prior credibility studies examined text-heavy fake news, our work shows how verification is performed differently in the video medium. Second, from a practical perspective, our results suggest potentially useful ways that people could employ to detect deepfake videos encountered online. At the same time, people who attempt to verify the existence of deepfakes should be mindful of the reasons for incorrect video identification that we uncovered from our study. Finally, because people seem to have difficulty in correctly identifying deepfakes, there is a need for more education among Internet users to the dangers of such videos and how to spot them [8]. It should be noted that all our participants watched online videos frequently, were aware of the nature of the study, and would thus have been expected to be more familiar with the deepfake concept. Further it is important to instruct people that the authenticity of a video cannot be simply evaluated based on a single strategy, and for better results, multiple methods should be employed.

Although our study has yielded potentially useful results, care should be taken in generalizing them for the following reasons. One, the qualitative approach meant that we interviewed a small number of participants. Although rich, detailed data was obtained, our findings may not be applicable to the larger population of people who encounter deepfakes. Two, our participant profiles were not sufficiently diverse due to the sampling method used. Hence, future work may consider adopting quantitative methodologies such as large-scale surveys to verify the stability and usefulness of our set of verification strategies. As part of this proposed effort, it would be instructive to recruit participants from a wider range of profiles including age, digital literacy and domain knowledge of video content. Finally, using videos from a greater variety of topics would better improve on the generalizability of our findings.

References

1. Ajder, H., Patrini, G., Cavalli, F., Cullen, L.: The State of Deepfakes: Landscape, Threats, and Impact. Deeptrace, Amsterdam (2019)
2. Ajukhadar, M., Senecal, S., Ouellette, D.: Can the media richness of a privacy disclosure enhance outcome? A multifaceted view of trust in rich media environments. Int. J. Electron. Commer. **14**(4), 103–126 (2010)
3. Anderson, K.E.: Getting acquainted with social networks and apps: combating fake news on social media. Libr. Hi Tech News **35**(3), 1–6 (2018)
4. Chawla, R.: Deepfakes: how a pervert shook the world. Int. J. Adv. Res. Dev. **4**(6) (2019). Article 2

5. Chesney, R., Citron., D.: Deepfakes and the new disinformation war. Foreign Aff. **98**(1), 147–155 (2019)
6. Gieseke, A.P.: "The new weapon of choice": Law's current inability to properly address deepfake pornography. Vanderbilt Law Rev. **73**(5), 1479–1515 (2020)
7. Hennink, M., Hutter, I., Bailey, A.: Qualitative Research Methods, 2nd edn. Sage, New York (2020)
8. Hwang, Y., Ryu, J.Y., Jeong, S.H.L.: Effects of disinformation using deepfake: the protective effect of media literacy education. Cyberpsychol. Behav. Soc. Network. **24**(3), 188–193 (2021)
9. Kietzmann, J., Lee, L.W., McCarthy, I.P., Kietzmann. T.C.: Deepfakes: trick or treat? Bus. Horiz. **65**(2), 135–146 (2020)
10. Lavrakas. P.J.: Encyclopedia of survey research methods. Sage, New York, NY (2008)
11. Li, Y., Lyu, S.: Exposing deepfake videos by detecting face warping artifacts. In: Proceedings of the 2019 Computer Vision and Pattern Recognition Workshop, pp. 46–52. IEEE Press, Piscataway (2018)
12. Lyu. S.: Deepfake detection: current challenges and next steps. In: Proceedings of the 2020 IEEE International Conference on Multimedia & Expo Workshops, pp. 1–6. IEEE Press, Piscataway (2020)
13. Matern, F., Riess, C., Stamminger, M.: Exploiting visual artifacts to expose deepfakes and face manipulations. In: Proceedings of the 2019 IEEE Winter Applications of Computer Vision Workshops, pp. 83–92. IEEE Press, Piscataway (2019)
14. Metzger, M.J., Fanagin, A.J., Zwarun, L.: College student web use, perceptions of information credibility, and verification behavior. Comput. Educ. **41**, 271–290 (2003)
15. Mittal, T., Bhattacharya, U., Chandra, R., Bera, A., Manocha, D.: Emotions don't lie: an audio-visual deepfake detection method using affective cues. In: Proceedings of the 28th ACM International Conference on Multimedia, pp. 2823–2832. ACM Press, New York (2020)
16. Osatuyi. B.: Information sharing on social media sites. Comput. Hum. Behav. **29**(6), 2622–2631 (2013)
17. Shang, S.S.C., Wu, Y.L., Li, E.Y.: Field effects of social media platforms on information-sharing continuance: do reach and richness matter? Inf. Manag. **54**, 241–255 (2017)
18. Shapiro, I., Brin, C., Bédard-Brûlé, I., Mychajlowycz, K.: Verification as a strategic ritual. J. Pract. **7**(6), 657–673 (2013)
19. Sohrawardi, S.J., et al.: DeFaking deepfakes: understanding journalists' needs for deepfake detection. In: Proceedings of the Sixteenth Symposium on Usable Privacy and Security (2020). https://www.usenix.org/system/files/soups2020_poster_sohrawardi.pdf
20. Thaw, N.N., July, T., Wai, A.N., Goh, D.H., Chua, A.Y.K.: Is it real? A study on detecting deepfake videos. Proc. Assoc. Inf. Sci. Technol. **57**(1), e366 (2020)
21. Tolosana, R., Vera-Rodriguez, R., Fierrez, J., Morales, A., Ortega-Garcia, J.: Deepfakes and beyond: a survey of face manipulation and fake detection. Inf. Fusion **64**, 131–148 (2020)
22. Wagner, T.L., Blewer. A.: "The word real is no longer real": deepfakes, gender, and the challenges of AI-altered video. Open Inf. Sci. **3**, 32–46 (2019)
23. Westerlund, M.: The emergence of deepfake technology: a review. Technol. Innov. Manag. Rev. **9**(11) (2019). https://timreview.ca/article/1282
24. Wilding, D., Fray, P., Molitorisz, S., McKewon, E.: The Impact of Digital Platforms on News and Journalistic Content. University of Technology Sydney, NSW (2018)
25. Yang, X., Li, Y., Lyu. S.: Exposing deep fakes using inconsistent had poses. In: Proceedings of the 2019 IEEE International Conference on Acoustics, Speech and Signal Processing, pp. 8261–8265. IEEE Press, Piscataway (2019)

Analysis of News Data on 'Super App' Using Topic Modeling

Sujin Han[1], Xu Li[2], and Hyesun Hwang[2(✉)]

[1] Convergence Program of Social Innovation, SungKyunKwan University, Seoul, South Korea
[2] Consumer Science, SungKyunKwan University, Seoul, South Korea
h.hwang@skku.edu

Abstract. Super apps are applications that allow users to use multiple services in a single app without switching to other apps. As they began to be perceived as a leading future-oriented platform in the industry, global enterprises who are joining this new mobile trend are increasing. In this regard, this study examines the consumers' experience or issues on the platforms, since its evolution, by focusing on KakaoTalk, the characteristic super app in South Korea. For the purpose of this study, Latent Dirichlet Allocation (LDA) analysis was conducted on 4,782 news data that included KakaoTalk in the title, from 2010 to February 26, 2021. Considering the interpretability, nine topics were derived from the LDAvis, and each of the topics was specified as 'industry', 'basic service', 'information service', 'entertainment', 'privacy protection', 'payment service', 'e-commerce', 'extra service', and 'police investigation'. Along with the basic chat services, consumers were found to be enjoying other diverse services including games, e-commerce, and online payment. However, consumers' concerns for personal information were found to be high, in consideration to words, such as phishing/victim, in the topic of 'privacy protection'. This exploratory study showed how KakaoTalk, the super app, is being discussed in Korean society. The study has identified the key functions of the super apps and provided the meaningful basis for the future direction of the app industry.

Keywords: Super app · KakaoTalk · Platform industry · Fintech · Consumer experience

1 Introduction

The radical shift to a digital world has accelerated the emergence of new types of platforms. As the number of mobile app users continues to increase, improving the mobile app environment has become essential in the platform industry. Meanwhile, super apps have emerged as consumer demand for using various services on one mobile app has increased. Super apps provide various services, such as finance, shopping, gaming, and music, within one app. Most super apps adopt a strategy that attracts heavy users using high-frequency core services and then expand their business areas to various services. With this strategy, super app enterprises have accessed abundant user data and have focused on providing various services by combining big data and financial technology

© The Author(s), under exclusive license to Springer Nature Switzerland AG 2022
C. Stephanidis et al. (Eds.): HCII 2022, CCIS 1655, pp. 33–39, 2022.
https://doi.org/10.1007/978-3-031-19682-9_5

(fintech) based on the user data [1]. Mobile apps are relatively acceptable in Asia, which has experienced rapid development; therefore, all apps ranked at the top of the super app trend were released in Asia [2]. Super app research has been conducted in recent years, but it primarily addressed apps from other Asian regions, such as WeChat from China, Gojek from Indonesia, and Grab from Singapore. Digital technology has also developed in Korea. Although Korean super apps have appeared in comparative studies with other super apps, few studies have been conducted with these as independent research subjects. Therefore, this study conducts research on KakaoTalk in accordance with the current situation, where the need for research on domestic super apps is raised. The super app craze, which started in Asia, now greatly influences the Western market, and its influence is expanding. Accordingly, Western companies are also developing parent company app services by referring to Asian super apps [3]. From this perspective, this study provides necessary insights to foreign countries that will develop super apps in the future using Korea's largest super app research. This study aims to determine the characteristics of super apps, focusing on KakaoTalk and experiences of consumers with various services supported by KakaoTalk. Thus, the goal is to ultimately contribute to the development of super apps both domestic and abroad and increase positive consumer experiences.

2   Literature Review

2.1   What is Super App?

A super app allows users to use multiple services in one app without switching to another [1, 4]. Mike Lazaridis, founder of Blackberry, first came up with the idea of the Super App in 2010 [5]. According to him, super apps are an ecosystem where many apps are trapped and platforms that provide efficient experiences to people. Platform services with smart devices have continued to develop since 2010. As such, the timing of the super app's appearance has not been specified but was naturally introduced to the world as the platform developed. China's WeChat, the world's first super app, which began as a social media platform and currently provides public security systems, transportation, tax services, e-commerce, and message functions [6]. WeChat has become a mega platform that connects all services, as the payment system is integrated into the 5th software upgrade. The introduction of the payment system enables access to capital, and the platform continues to grow [7]. Rodenbough [8] stressed that super apps should have direct access to users' wallets. Before the introduction of the super app, consumers were unfamiliar with cash or manganese payment systems. However, SuperApp's payment system assumed control of users' wallets and familiarized them with the online payment system. The introduction of payment systems has become an opportunity for generating new revenue in the digital platform ecosystem and is an important factor in attracting more users [9]. Evidently, the combination with the fintech industry is significant in the super app trend.

2.2   Case Study of KakaoTalk

KakaoTalk has drawn blueprints for users to use KakaoTalk services in every aspect of their daily lives. KakaoTalk goes beyond a simpler instant messaging app. It has now grown into a comprehensive platform that includes multiple services, such as news, e-commerce, payment, music, and sports. Since its deployment in 2010, KakaoTalk has become the most widely used messaging app in South Korea, used by 93 percent of Koreans. According to previous studies, super apps have been developed in accordance with the development of the fintech industry. KakaoTalk went through a process similar to WeChat by launching electronic wallets and digital banks [10]. In 2014, KakaoTalk launched the 'Kakao Pay' service, allowing users to register bank accounts in-app and use various transaction services. KakaoTalk started e-commerce services by offering a banking system and securing user information. A special feature in KakaoTalk e-commerce is that KakaoTalk sends a push notification to each user on their friend's birthday based on the user's friends list. This function naturally induces users to shop on KakaoTalk [11]. In addition, under Korea's transportation regulations prohibiting privately owned vehicles that offer transportation services, KakaoTalk expanded its mobility system, which offers various traveling services, including maps, taxis, airplane/train booking services, and car rental services. KakaoTalk has evolved from a chat app to a super app that supports various services and has become the undisputed top app in the domestic app industry beyond the concept of a simple messenger app. Thus, KakaoTalk, the largest super app in Korea, has all the overall features of a Korean super app and requires continuous research.

3 Methods

Data were collected through BIGKINDS (https://www.bigkinds.or.kr), a real-time big data news analysis service provided by daily newspapers, and broadcasters offered by the Korea Press Foundation.

The data were collected over the last ten years (January 1, 2010, to December 16, 2021). Since 2010, when KakaoTalk was released, this study aimed to discover the changes made to KakaoTalk and how user experience has changed over time. The collected news data for each year were 8,000. Among the 8,000 data, 2,653 were articles without links, deleted articles, or duplicated articles. After the full screening procedures, the finalized data of 5,347 data were used for analysis.

This study used a topic modeling approach to identify hidden themes and discourses in large amounts of unstructured news data. Analysis was performed on the various topic modeling algorithms using the most widely used Latent Dirichlet Allocation (LDA) algorithm. All data handling procedures were executed in Python.

4 Results

4.1 Frequency Analysis

Table 1 lists the top 30 words determined by analyzing the frequency of words appearing in KakaoTalk news data. N is the number of words appearing in the entire document. The most frequently appearing word was service (9,836), followed by user (6,548), use (5,455), message (4,802), offer (4,047), messenger (3,240), enterprise (2,996), smartphone (2,851), friend (2,679), information (2,283), and channel (2,178).

Table 1. Top 30 words derived from frequency analysis

Words	N	Words	N	Words	N
Service	9,836	Smartphone	2,851	Emoji	1,925
User	6,548	Friend	2,679	Chat	1,779
Use	5,455	Information	2,283	Talk	1,721
Message	4,802	Channel	2,178	Platform	1,534
Offer	4,047	Customer	2,045	Version	1,521
Messenger	3,240	Games	1,980	Gift sending	1,393
Enterprise	2,996	Release	1,970	Operation	1,392

4.2 LDA Topic Modeling

Topic modeling was conducted to examine social consensus and perceptions related to the target keyword in more detail. Table 2 lists the keywords for each topic.

Nine topics were derived from the analysis according to their values and interpretability. According to each topic's highest-ranked words, we named the nine topics: Industry, Basic Service, Information Service, Entertainment, Privacy Protection, Payment Service, E-Commerce, Extra Service, and Police Investigation. The nine extracted topics represented the services provided by KakaoTalk as a super app.

Table 2. LDA topic modeling results

Topic	Relevant keywords
1. Industry	Enterprise, service, representative, platform, global, chatbot, marketplace, messenger, new user, business, development, contents, industry, user, Japan, United States, executives, council member, Facebook, public
2. Basic service	User, message, service, use, smartphone, messenger, error, version, transmission, inconvenience, defects, confidential, telecommunication, free, Android, accession, server, data, call
3. Information service	Channel, information, citizen, offer, operation, communication, COVID-19, complaints, voucher, open, Omicron, vaccination, residents, convenience, use, censoring, reinforcement, aged, cyber
4. Entertainment	Chat, games, mode, talk, user, denial, update, delete, technology, upgrade, stock, version, android, lists, chat room, provide, menu, server, device, AniPang
5. Privacy protection	Use, personal information, crime, certification, friend, smartphone, enterprise, send, police, payment, person, local tax, payment, government, purchase, information, phishing, victim, account, account, message

(continued)

Table 2. (*continued*)

Topic	Relevant keywords
6. Payment service	Profile, wallet, interception, video, YouTube, luxury items, image, multi-profile, refunds, small and medium-sized enterprises (SME), execute, bank wallet, package, chat, texts, establishment, person, expression, Instagram, camera
7. E-Commerce	Gift-sending, gift, product, service, payment, advertisement, sale, product, commerce, purchase, brand, sales, offer, delivery, store, release, expansion, platform, pay, online
8. Extra service	Service, offer, use, friend, emoji, customer, search, release, information, channel, make order, character, plus, user, convenience, menu, participation, non-touch, button, store
9. Police investigation	Prosecution, chat, search operation, investigation, police, license, driver's license, proof, student, Seoul, suspicion, identification card, Naver, issues, qualification, information, court, Cheongwadae (Korean presidential house), campaign, school

Topic 1's primary keywords, 'Service,' 'Global,' 'Market,' and 'Platform,' showed the overall issues and new technologies of the platform industry. Moreover, identifying the enterprises and countries that KakaoTalk is industrially connected to is possible.

Keywords such as 'user,' 'message,' 'smartphone,' 'error,' and 'version' appeared in Topic 2. Thus, Topic 2 is assumed to be primarily about the basic chat service, the original KakaoTalk service. Inferring keywords such as 'error,' 'transmission,' and 'message' showed that users felt uncomfortable owing to transmission errors when interacting with other users.

Topic 3 showed issues related to the information service provided by KakaoTalk. Keywords such as 'channel,' 'information,' 'citizens,' and 'communication' show that citizens obtain necessary daily information through KakaoTalk. The words 'COVID-19' and 'Omicron' in Topic 3 show that people primarily used KakaoTalk to obtain information related to COVID-19. Indeed, Koreans are known to typically use KakaoTalk to schedule vaccinations and obtain proofs of vaccination. KakaoTalk also provides government-certified statistical services to facilitate the acquisition of confirmed cases and route information.

Keywords such as 'Chat,' 'Game,' 'Mode,' 'Update,' and 'Device' appeared in Topic 4. Inferring that Topic 4 is particularly related to games was possible. Actively interacting with other users while gaming was revealed to be possible through keywords such as 'chat,' 'talk,' and 'user.' In addition, the keywords 'Device' and 'Android' showed that KakaoTalk provided services suitable for each device.

Topic 5 raised concerns about users' personal information and personal information issues. The primary keywords derived from Topic 5 were 'personal information,' 'crime,' 'payment, 'and 'transmission.' The keywords in Topic 5 show concerns about the misuse of personal information that occurs when using payment systems and chat services. KakaoTalk has been suspected of collecting user cookies several times, including user login status, search history, and frequently visited websites, without permission.

Furthermore, Kakao Pay's security system has been noted to be also poor. Unlike other topics, Topic 5 is particularly meaningful as it presents problems that must be improved to better consumer experiences.

Topic 6 consists of keywords such as 'multi-profile,' 'refund,' and 'bank wallet' related to the payment system. Among these keywords, 'multi-profile' is a service only for loyal customers and function that only Kakao Wallet subscribers can use. Topic 6 shows that people are particularly interested in the services provided by the payment system.

The keywords shown in Topic 7 related to the e-commerce services provided by KakaoTalk. These included keywords such as 'gift,' 'product,' 'e-commerce,' 'delivery,' and 'payment.' Inferring through keywords such as 'delivery' and 'extension,' identifying the current major e-commerce business areas of KakaoTalk was possible. In particular, keywords such as 'gift-sending' and 'gift' showed KakaoTalk's specialized service, a friend list-based gift-sending function, which is widely used. This function is important to investigate, as it is heavily involved with the expansion of the KakaoTalk e-commerce business.

In Topic 8, services appeared in addition to the basic chat service provided by KakaoTalk. The primary keywords were 'emojis,' 'characters,' 'plus,' and 'channels.' As the functions supported by the additional service, 'emojis' can be used to interact with other users smoothly. In addition, users can continue to receive information by adding Kakao channels that suit their interests. As such, Topic 8 introduced additional functions that allow users to enjoy services abundantly, although these are not major functions such as payment or e-commerce services.

Finally, keywords such as 'prosecutors,' 'search operations,' 'investigations,' and 'courts' appeared in Topic 9. Through KakaoTalk, the prosecution's investigation was determined to be underway. KakaoTalk is a message service currently used by 93% of Koreans and representative investigation channel used to track messages when searching for crime routes. In addition, the anonymous-based open chat service provided by KakaoTalk is highly likely to be involved in crimes; therefore, KakaoTalk pays particular attention to solving problems. As various crime-related issues were found in Topic 9, KakaoTalk can be understood to have uses in various fields.

5   Conclusion

This study aims to explore the experiences and significant issues of super app consumers through news data analysis. To this end, 5,347 news articles were used for the analysis, of 8,000 news articles published for ten years from 2010 to 2021. Text-mining methods, such as frequency analysis and topic modeling, were used as analysis techniques. We expect that the results derived from this study can be used as basic data for improving super apps and super app consumer experiences. The primary research results and implications of this study are as follows.

First, as a result of frequency analysis, keywords such as 'service,' 'user,' 'use,' 'message,' and 'provide' were determined to be high. These words roughly show the services provided by KakaoTalk. Next, nine topics, including 'Industry,' 'Basic Service,' 'Information Society,' 'Entertainment,' 'Private Protection,' 'Payment Service,'

'E-commerce,' and 'Expert' were derived from theme modeling. From the topic modeling results, we identified the functions that were mainly used in KakaoTalk. Furthermore, the results derived the positive and negative experiences that consumers experienced while using each service.

The results of this study provide implications for improving the experience of Korean super app users; however, some limitations and suggestions should be addressed in future studies. First, this study investigated the characteristics of super apps and consumer experiences limited to KakaoTalk. In subsequent studies, the subject of the study should be expanded to include more super apps released domestically and abroad to increase the possibility of generalization. Second, obtaining various consumer discourses was difficult by limiting data sources to news data. In a follow-up study, exploring consumers' direct experiences in more depth using various social media platforms such as Twitter, Instagram, and blogs seems necessary. Third, this study attempted to identify discourses hidden in news data through frequency analysis and subject modeling using text mining. However, because inferring people's thoughts using text-mining techniques alone is difficult, supplementing the validity through surveys and interviews is necessary.

References

1. Walsh, C., Grewal, R., Udaskin, J.: SuperApps dominate digital life in Asia. Will they do the same in other markets? CPP Investments (2020). https://www.cppinvestments.com/insights/superapps-dominate-digital-life-in-asia-will-they-do-the-same-in-other-markets
2. BBF Digital: The Rise of SuperApps in Asia. BBF Digital, 14 July 2021. https://bbf.digital/the-rise-of-superapps-in-asia
3. Huang, A., Siegel, M.: Super app or super disruption? KPMG Global (2019). https://home.kpmg/xx/en/home/insights/2019/06/super-app-or-super-disruption.html
4. Infopulse: Introducing super app: a new approach to all-in-one experience. Infopulse, 24 December 2019. https://medium.com/@infopulseglobal_9037/introducing-super-app-a-new-approach-to-all-in-one-experience-8a7894e8ddd4
5. Tu, F.: WeChat and civil society in China. Commun. Public 1(3), 343–350 (2016)
6. Perez, S.: PayPal launches its 'super app' combining payments, savings, bill pay, crypto, shopping and more. TechCrunch, 21 September 2021. https://techcrunch.com/2021/09/21/paypal-launches-its-super-app-combining-payments-savings-bill-pay-crypto-shopping-and-more/
7. Jia, K., Kenney, M.: Mobile internet business models in China: vertical hierarchies, horizontal conglomerates, or business groups. In: Berkeley Roundtable on the International Economy Working Paper, 6 (2016)
8. Rodenbaugh, R.: A deep dive into super apps and why they're booming in the East Tech in Asia (2020). https://www.techinasia.com/deep-dive-super-app-booming-east-not-west
9. Chan, C.: When one app rules them all: the case of WeChat and mobile in China. Recuperado de (2015). http://a16z.com/2015/08/06/wechat-china-mobile-first
10. Kapronasia: Asia's super apps will aim to cash in on fintech in 2021. Kapronasia, 18 February 2021. https://www.kapronasia.com/asia-banking-research-category/asia-s-super-apps-will-aim-to-cash-in-on-fintech-in-2021.html
11. Samsung Securities: The three mobile platform kingdoms: Korea, China, Japan. Global Investment 2.0 Global Research (2019)

Micro-influencer Marketing Beauty Brand on Social Media

Ilma Hanifa Madina[(✉)], Filosa Gita Sukmono, and Fajar Junaedi

Department of Communication, Universitas Muhammadiyah Yogyakarta, Kasihan, Indonesia
`Ilma.hanifa.fisip18@mail.umy.ac.id`

Abstract. This study aims to analyze how influencers affect marketing for beauty products by how micro-influencers spread a message to consumers. The high number of internet users and many beauty product consumers make companies demand to be more innovative in managing social media and forming good relationships with their customers. This research uses a qualitative analysis approach of beauty influencer Twitter account, with Nvivo tools as an analytical tool or Computer Assistant Qualitative Analysis. The research data sources are beauty influencer social media accounts on Twitter; they are @nekoyasaku, @bulbulkun, @glowithven, and @h0neymilktea_. This study answer that beauty influencers have the characteristics of using information; it is based on the ability to create responses through Twitter social media. Furthermore, the micro-scale builds a good relationship pattern with users on Twitter social media. This study answers that the micro-influencers conducted by the 4 Twitter social media accounts have an informational character by using the hashtag and mentions when creating content to influence the target market. This study confirms that the role of a micro-influence is someone who can influence the target market with the content she creates. They spread the message with hashtags and mentions. Moreover, the characteristics of the content created are reviews, recommendations, ratings, and promotions.

Keywords: Micro-influencers · Social media · Brand · Marketing

1 Introduction

Indonesia is a country with the highest number of internet users globally; the number of internet users reached 191.4 million out of 277.7 million. Indonesian health and beauty products are the most popular by consumers when doing online shopping, which is 40.1%. Shopping activity shows that the number of product transactions in the health and beauty category in 2021 increased compared to 2019, only 29.1% [1]. Social media is an intermediary in increasing spending because 37% of internet users claim to find beauty brands through advertisements and 35% through recommendations shared on social media [2]. Social media makes it easy for brands to access large social networks and interact with their audiences [3], this is an excellent opportunity for brands to market their products effectively in a short period.

Twitter is one of the most widely used social media; in October 2021, Indonesia became the sixth-largest Twitter user globally, with 17.5 million [4]. Companies use many Twitter users to launch their promotions through influencer marketing. One study found that consumers have the same level of trust in Twitter influencers as they trust their friends [5]. Through Twitter, influencers share content sponsored by brands, but influencers still prioritize relationships with their followers [6]. If the content created by this influencer is considered attractive by followers, then the post will generate lots of likes, comments, and clicks so that it can increase brand engagement with the sponsoring brand [7, 8]

Of many internet users, 40% look for information on social media about their preferred brand, and 52% of users decide to buy products from that brand online [2]. Because of this, influencers are one of the factors driving the increase in transactions and shopping for beauty brands on social media [9]. In view of Beme [10], influencers have a close relationship with the market. Then Ponirah [11] revealed that Influencer marketing is a very effective marketing strategy used to attract consumers and significantly influences purchasing decisions. Factors that influence followers' trust in influencers are informative content, influencer trust, attractiveness, and similarities between followers and influencers [12]. However, recently brands have started to leave mega-influencers and be replaced by micro-influencers with smaller followers because micro-influencers have a stronger trust relationship with their followers [13].

Scholar has classified the function of micro-influencer marketing to be an essential element in marketing on social media [14]. At the same time, Kay [15] assessed that micro-influencers could increase brand sales by building good relationships with followers. The small number of followers allows micro-influencers to serve and reach more followers so that it can be helpful for brands to convey their message to their target market [13]. According to Alampi [16], micro-influencers can strongly influence the audience and inspire them to make decisions, such as influencing followers to do something, such as buying an item. Therefore Rahmah [17] states that micro-influencers can be relied on to build brand awareness and products, including beauty brands. Based on the explanation above and research on other micro-influencers, this study aims to analyze how the role of micro-influencers affects the market, by looking at how beauty micro-influencers spread messages to consumers and the characteristics of the content shared through Twitter social media.

2   Overview of Literature

Along with the development of technology, social media users have also increased; this is why the marketing industry in social media is growing [18]. Many brands uses sponsored content, but this makes the audience's level of trust in the brand decrease [19]. To overcome this problem, brands use influencers from social media to restore audience confidence in the brand; this is called Influencer Marketing [11].

According to Isyanto [9], influencer marketing is a promotion strategy that uses influential people on social media. The primary purpose of influencer marketing is for brand positioning, brand awareness, and customer acquisition, with the primary objective being to generate revenue gains [20]. Influencers have unique ways and characteristics to attract large audiences and motivate others that can be used to expand their reach exponentially [15]. Consumers consider influencers to have good, authentic, credible, likable, and accessible personalities who happen to have large followers and audiences when advertising products [21]

Factors that influence followers' trust in influencers are personalization, engagement, and authentic relationships through the content created [22]. Influencers usually create content regarding recommendations, reviews, product ratings, and sponsored or promotional content [21]. Usually, brands ask influencers to create content about products in real-life as sponsored content [17]. Through the content, influencers can influence the audience, which increases purchase intention [23].

Brands are increasingly realizing that the number of followers of an influencer is not the main factor. However, the level and quality of engagement they achieve play the most important role [17]. Kay [15] also challenged the assumption that high popularity can lead to more effective marketing, but on the contrary, a small number of followers can be more beneficial for a brand. Therefore, brands prefer micro-influencers with small communities to promote their products [24]. In addition to having a good relationship, the same background between influencers and followers can also increase the trust of a brand promoted by the influencer [9]. Brands are more likely to choose micro-influencers as part of their marketing campaigns because the costs are much lower, and the followers of these micro-influencers have tremendous persuasive [21].

3   Method

This study uses a qualitative approach with computer-assisted data analysis tools Nvivo [25], Nvivo functions to parse unstructured data from social media, and Nvivo functions to translate data sets from Twitter [26]. A qualitative approach using Nvivo aims to describe the role of micro-influencers from the information conveyed through Twitter. The data sources in this study consisted of social media accounts @nekoyasaku, @bulbulkun, @glowithven, and @h0neymilktea_. The data retrieval process used N-capture with pre-determined accounts.

4   Results and Discussions

Micro-influencers have characteristics [15]; these characteristics are to expand the network to influence the target market; these findings categorize the activity of beauty micro-influencer social media accounts on Twitter. Beauty micro-influencer @nekoyasaku, @bulbulkun, @glowithven and @h0neymilktea_ have more than 10.000 followers. Figure 1 shows that the account with the highest intensity is @nekoyasaku, and the account with the lowest intensity is @glowithven.

The intensity of micro-influencers reaches 200 to 1,900 tweets every month. The @nekoyasaku account has the highest activity in February, declining in March and April. The same thing happened to the @bulbukun account. Meanwhile, @glowithven and @h0neymilktea_ their account activity fluctuates every month. The four accounts tweet more often than a retweet. This finding shows that brands can use micro-influencers for product promotion campaigns.

Beauty brands utilize micro-influencers as a marketing medium by creating content about their products so that the content created can reach the brand's target audience

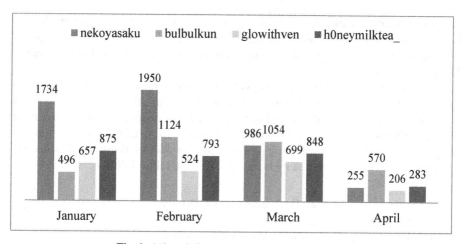

Fig. 1. Micro-influencer activity on social media

[23]. Because of Isyanto [9], This step is a form of promotion to create the trust of the mentioned influencer and brand.

Table 1. Accounts that interact with micro-influencer

Micro account	Account categorization						
	Beauty brand	Total	%	Influencers	Total	%
nekoyasaku	somethinc4u	65	25%	honeymilktea_	39	15%
	rosealldayco	56	21%	orchidpoison	34	13%
	lacoco_id	37	14%	nekoyasaku	33	13%
bulbulkun	azarinecosmetic	46	20%	curadellapelle_	43	18%
	lacoco_id	41	18%	nisynwafer	33	14%
	airinbeautycare	39	17%	nesthir	31	13%
glowithven	lacoco_id	36	11%	mafiaskincare	96	28%
	somethinc4u	29	9%	nna	88	26%
	whitelab_id	27	8%	skinarvelvet	65	19%
h0neymilktea_	lacoco_id	61	19%	nekoyasaku	70	22%
	somethinc4u	42	13%	nna	61	19%
	skingameofc_	30	9%	destryangryana	54	17%

See Table 1; micro-influencer @nekoyasaku has the highest interaction rate with the beauty brand @somethinc4u account and the lowest interaction with influencer account @nekoyasaku. The micro-influencer @bulbulkun has the highest interaction rate with the beauty brand @azarinecosmetic account and the lowest interaction with the @nesthr influencer account. The micro-influencer @glowithven has the highest interaction rate with the @mafiaskincare influencer account and the lowest interaction with the beauty brand @white_lab account. Micro-influencer @h0neymilktea_ has the highest interaction rate with influencer account @nekoyasaku and the lowest interaction with beauty brand account @skingameofc_.

The official beauty brand account with the highest interaction rate with micro-influencers is @lacoco_id, and the lowest is @skingameofc_. The content created when mentioning the official beauty brand account is content about product reviews from that brand. While mentioning other influencers is interacting and also recommending the products they review. The findings above show that micro-influencers influence the target market by mentioning beauty brand accounts and fellow influencers.

Table 2. The hashtag used by micro-influencer

#racuninskincare	This hashtag refers to skincare content
#keeyracunankiara	This hashtag refers to skincare and makeup content
#racuninmakeup	This hashtag refers to making up the content
#racuninbodycare	This hashtag refers to body care content

Table 2 shows that the beauty micro-influencer uses the hashtag #racuninskincare, #keyracunankiara, #racuninmakeup, or #racuninbodycare on any product that discusses beauty products. Micro-influencers discuss the same type of beauty product with various brands in each hashtag. The four hashtags used can influence the audience to make purchases on the content produced. Micro-influencers use hashtags to group the same brand; micro-influencers share information with real-life content [17]. Content such as the results of reviews, recommendations, product ratings, and promotions influence social media users to determine product buying attitudes [15, 16, 17]. In addition, by providing an assessement of the micro-influencer product, it also provides an evaluation of the brand, through hashtags [10], between these functions [6] assessing that micro influencers have a good relationship with social media users. #racuninskincare is widely used by beauty micro-influencers, this can be seen from the many words that are often used.

Meanwhile, Table 3 shows the results of the word frequency analysis by beauty micro-influencer accounts found that #racuninskincare was the word that most often appeared on the accounts @nekoyasaku @bulbulkun and @glowithven. At the same time, the word that often appears on the @h0neymilktea_ account is Serum; this shows that beauty micro-influencers often create content with the #racuninskincare feature, including review content, recommendations, ratings, and promotions.

The information category has intensity. See Table 3-word frequencies often used by micro-influencers to produce content. [22] Social media users respond to the product being promoted so that the product can be categorized through word frequency. According to Goh [19], this step was taken to increase the number of ratings and users of beauty brands, thereby creating trust in the brand [11]. This research answers the information submitted by each micro-influencer account. Words often used show much content related to things often discussed in micro-influencer activities.

Table 3. Categories of words frequency

Category	Words
Review	#racuninskincare, review, serum, kulit, cocok, toner, kering, banyak, lip, cream, tekstur, kulitku, gel, #racuninmakeup, glow
Recommendation	Pakai, coba, cobain, skincare
Rating	Cantik, suka, cakep, bagus, enak
Promotion	Produk, beli, harganya, punya, harganya, dipake

5 Conclusion

This finding confirms the role of influencers with the concept of micro-influencer marketing on beauty brands. The result shows that brands can use micro-influencers for product promotion campaigns because they often interact with beauty brand accounts and other micro-influencers. They use the same hashtag to discuss content related to a beauty product, and they also often create content about beauty products. So the role of micro-influencers on beauty brands on social media is as a marketing medium. Furthermore, the function of micro-influencers is to provide reviews, recommendations, ratings, and make promotions. This function can be seen from the category of information conveyed by influencers to beauty brands through the intensity of posts, mentions, hashtags, and content created. This study also confirms that Nvivo, as an analytical tool, can map and reduce data sets from influencer Twitter accounts to describe data in text, images, charts, and tables.

References

1. Hadya Jayani, D.: Produk Kesehatan dan Kecantikan Paling Laku Saat Pandemi, Databoks 2021. https://databoks.katadata.co.id/datapublish/2021/10/27/produk-kesehatan-dan-kecantikan-paling-laku-saat-pandemi
2. GWI, Indonesia Key Digital Behaviour, Gobal Web Index, pp. 1–6 (2019)
3. Zhu, X., Gan, T., Song, X., Chen, Z.: Sentiment analysis for social sensor In: Zeng, B., Huang, Q., El Saddik, A., Li, H., Jiang, S., Fan, X. (eds.) Advances in Multimedia Information Processing – PCM 2017. PCM 2017. Lecture Notes in Computer Science, vol. 10735, pp. 893–902. Springer, Cham (2018). https://doi.org/10.1007/978-3-319-77380-3_86
4. Statista, Countries with the most Twitter users 2021 (2022). https://www.statista.com/statistics/242606/number-of-active-twitter-users-in-selected-countries/. Accessed 17 Mar 2022
5. Swant, M.: Twitter says users now trust influencers nearly as much as their friends, adweek.com (2016). https://www.adweek.com/performance-marketing/twitter-says-users-now-trust-influencers-nearly-much-their-friends-171367/
6. Wellman, M.L., Stoldt, R., Tully, M., Ekdale, B.: Ethics of authenticity: social media influencers and the production of sponsored content. J. Media Ethics Explor. Quest. Media Moral. **35**(2), 68–82 (2020). https://doi.org/10.1080/23736992.2020.1736078
7. Marques, I.R., Casais, B., Camilleri, M.A.: The effect of macrocelebrity and microinfluencer endorsements on consumer–brand engagement in Instagram. In: Strategic Corporate. Communication. Digital Age, pp. 131–143 (2021). https://doi.org/10.1108/978-1-80071-264-520211008.

8. Endri, E.P., Prasetyo, K.: strategi komunikasi pemasaran produk kopi kawa daun tanah datar dalam membangun brand awareness. J. Audiens **2**(1), 134–142 (2021). https://doi.org/10.18196/jas.v2i1.9836.

9. Isyanto, P., Sapitri, R.G., Sinaga, O.: Micro influencers marketing and brand image to purchase intention of cosmetic products focallure. Syst. Rev. Pharm. **11**(1), 601–605 (2020). https://doi.org/10.5530/srp.2020.1.75

10. Berne-Manero, C., Marzo-Navarro, M.: Exploring how influencer and relationship marketing serve corporate sustainability. Sustain. **12**(11) 2020. https://doi.org/10.3390/su12114392.

11. Ponirah, A.: Influencer marketing as a marketing strategy. J. Econ. Stud. **4**(1), 11–16 (2020). http://www.journal.islamicateinstitute.co.id/index.php/joes/article/view/649/76

12. Lou, C., Yuan, S.: Influencer marketing: how message value and credibility affect consumer trust of branded content on social media. J. Interact. Advert. **19**(1), 58–73 (2019). https://doi.org/10.1080/15252019.2018.1533501

13. Ehlers, K.: Micro-influencers: when smaller is better. Forbes.com. (2021). https://www.forbes.com/sites/forbesagencycouncil/2021/06/02/micro-influencers-when-smaller-is-better/?sh=79c5f7e9539b. Accessed 30 Mar 2022

14. Ashley, C., Tuten, T.: Creative strategies in social media marketing: an exploratory study of branded social content and consumer engagement christy. Psychol. Mark. **32**, 15–27 (2014). https://doi.org/10.1002/mar

15. Kay, S., Mulcahy, R., Parkinson, J.: When less is more: the impact of macro and micro social media influencers' disclosure. J. Mark. Manag. **36**(3–4), 248–278 (2020). https://doi.org/10.1080/0267257X.2020.1718740

16. Alampi, A.: The future is micro: How to build an effective micro-influencer programme. J. Digit. Soc. Media Mark. **7**(3), 203–208 (2019)

17. Rahmah, S., Ren, D.: The impact of micro-influencer marketing on millennials MSC in digital marketing the impact of micro-influencer marketing on millennials purchasing decision Sarah Rahmah & DAN REN Master of Science Digital Marketing, no. September 2019 (2020). https://doi.org/10.13140/RG.2.2.26944.35841.

18. Zietek, N.: Influencer marketing: the characteristics and components of fashion influencer marketing (2016)

19. Goh, K.-Y., Heng, C.-S., Lin, Z.: Social media brand community and consumer behavior: quantifying the relative impact of user-and marketer-generated content. Inf. Syst. Res. **24**(1), 88–107 (2013)

20. R. Alassani and J. Göretz, "Product placements by micro and macro influencers on instagram," *Lect. Notes Comput. Sci. (including Subser. Lect. Notes Artif. Intell. Lect. Notes Bioinformatics)*, vol. 11579 LNCS, pp. 251–267, 2019, doi: https://doi.org/10.1007/978-3-030-21905-5_20.

21. A. T. Silalahi, "MICRO-INFLUENCER CELEBRITY ' S COMMUNICATION STRATEGY IN BRAND PROMOTION," vol. 12, no. March, pp. 21–28, 2021, doi: https://doi.org/10.21512/humaniora.v12i1.6786.

22. Girsang, C.N.: Pemanfaatan micro-influencer pada media sosial sebagai strategi public relations di era digital. Ultim. J. Ilmu Komun. **12**(2), 206–225 (2020). https://doi.org/10.31937/ultimacomm.v12i2.1299

23. Brown, D., Hayes, N., Chu, Y.L.: Influencer marketing: who really influences your customers?, Amsterdam, Netherland. Elsevier/Butterworth-Heinemann (2015).

24. Rakoczy, M.E., Bouzeghoub, A., Lopes Gancarski, A., Wegrzyn-Wolska, K.: In the search of quality influence on a small scale – Micro-influencers discovery. In: Panetto, H., Debruyne, C., Proper, H.A., Ardagna, C.A., Roman, D., Meersman, R. (eds.) OTM 2018. LNCS, vol. 11230, pp. 138–153. Springer, Cham (2018). https://doi.org/10.1007/978-3-030-02671-4_8

25. Woolf, N.H., Silver, C.: Qualitative analysis using MAXQDA: the five-level QDA® method. Qual. Anal. Using MAXQDA Five-Level QDA Method, pp. 1–208 (2017). https://doi.org/10.4324/9781315268569.
26. Kaefer, F., Roper, J., Sinha, P.: A software-assisted qualitative content analysis of news articles: Example and reflections. Forum Qual. Sozialforsch **16**(2), (2015)

Online Trusts; How Media Shaping Student Trust Towards Vaccination News

Alvina Putri Maharani[✉], Fajar Junaedi, and Filosa Gita Sukmono

Department of Communication, Universitas Muhammadiyah Yogyakarta, Yogyakarta, Indonesia
`alvina.putri.fisip18@mail.umy.ac.id`

Abstract. Indonesian government carries out vaccination program as part of the COVID-19 response. This study aimed to determine student responses to the news of COVID-19 vaccination through online media in August 2021. The media plays an essential role in understanding the importance of vaccines for the community. COVID-19 cases in Indonesia; simultaneously, the government pushed for a vaccination program. This study uses a stimulus-organism-response approach, the SOR approach, that looks at the individual's (organism) perception of the message (stimulus) received. The SOR theory looks at the individual's perception of policies through online media; the elements in SOR analysis look at the stimulus through student responses. The study uses descriptive quantitative methods to describe student responses through purposive sampling. The finding of this study show three categories of aspects; appropriate sources, covering both sides, and verification steps. According to this study, students rate vaccination news differently in three categories: first, aspects of appropriate types of media with assessment (32%), second, cover both sides with assessment (33%), and third, verification with assessment (35%) as a result of news broadcast on online news, pupils can get vaccination programs developed by the government to combat COVID-19. This acceptability is shown by a change in the attitude of the respondents, from being confident to being more confident about carrying out the Covid-19 vaccination. This study classifies the role of online media in shaping students' impressions of government policies and initiatives during the COVID-19 time.

Keywords: Vaccination · News · Media · Trust · Content analysis

1 Introduction

Currently, Covid-19 is a health case that has been declared a global pandemic. Coronavirus disease or Covid-19 began with the emergence of a SARS-like virus that was discovered in Wuhan, China in December 2019 [1]. In Indonesia, the first Covid- 19 case was found in Depok with three cases at once on March 1, 2020 as stated by President Joko Widodo [2]. So that various forms of handling Covid-19 have been implemented by the government. Starting from implementing the 3M regulations (washing hands with soap, wearing masks, and maintaining a distance of ± 1 m), 3T (testing, tracing, and treatment), to vaccination [3]. Vaccination policy aims to break the chain of disease transmission and stop the outbreak, as well as eliminate the disease [4]. As of January

C. Stephanidis et al. (Eds.): HCII 2022, CCIS 1655, pp. 48–55, 2022.
https://doi.org/10.1007/978-3-031-19682-9_7

6, 2021, 329.5 million doses of various vaccination brands have arrived in Indonesia. Meanwhile, its implementation will begin in the second week of January 2021 after obtaining permission from BPOM [3].

Massive news about Covid-19 in Indonesia. All media ranging from conventional media to digital media compete with each other in providing the latest information. Digital media is a platform that facilitates audiences to still be able to carry out social communication without having to have personal face-to-face interactions [5]. Every context of mass communication presented in digital media can be accessed online via the internet. Digital media can contain a variety of content at once. Starting from text, audio, images, to video [6]. One of the digital media that provides information and is often accessed by the audience is digital newspapers. Digital newspapers are certainly about how a text message is read, received, understood, and interpreted by its readers. In theory, a media text can only be interpreted when the message is received, that is, when the text message is read, seen and heard [7]. The audience in mass communication is very diverse. So that each audience has differences in responding and reacting to text messages received based on life experiences and life orientation [8].

Junaedi and Sukmono assessed that during covid-19 students were looking for information on social media about social media about Covid-19[9]. Students' responses to media coverage are generally related to what happened. This is as shown in the research by Dicky Oswin Gamaliel [10], his research states that the public's response to media coverage describes the problems that are currently happening in the area [10]. Based on the explanation above, this study aims to determine the response of UMY students to the news regarding the Covid-19 vaccination published in the online media Kompas.com for the period 01–20 August 2021. The reason for UMY is because the university has implemented online learning since 2016 so that students can be considered familiar with digital media [9].

1.1 Over View of Literature

According to Hosland, this SOR theory is based on the assumption that behavior change can occur depending on the quality of the stimulus that communicates with the organism. This means that the quality of communication sources such as credibility, leadership, or speaking style can greatly determine the success of behavior change in a person, group, or society [11]. SOR theory (stimulus-organism-response) is the basis of communication in this study to determine respondents' responses. The elements contained in this theory are message (stimulus), communicant (organism), and effect (response). The purpose of this theory is to find out how the communicant responds to the stimulus [10]. Stimulus conveyed by the media can be accepted or rejected by the communicant. The SOR communication model proves that the communication process is an action-reaction. There are several things that must be considered in order to create a response, namely the stimulus delivered must have several elements, namely attention, understanding, and acceptance [12]. The response generated by the stimulus includes only the cognitive and affective stages because mass media coverage is limited by public opinion. The cognitive stage includes memory, recognition, and knowledge of a message. While the affective stage includes a willingness to seek more information, evaluation of the message, and interest in trying [13].

2 Method

The research method used in this paper is using quantitative research methods. Quantitative research methods are often referred to as traditional research methods, this is because this method has long been used for research. This method uses a positivistic paradigm because it is based on a positivist philosophy [14]. In addition, quantitative methods are able to produce research that is more accurate and the results are more convincing [15].While the type of research used in writing this research is descriptive research with a quantitative approach. Descriptive research seeks to describe various variables related to the object to be studied. Hidayat Syah revealed that this type of descriptive research aims to be able to find the broadest knowledge in a certain period [16] (Table 1).

Table 1. Data type

No	Data type	Results
1	Primer	Questionnaire results
2	Secondary	Article news about Covid-19 on Kompas.com

The object of research used in this research is the active student of Communication Studies at UMY. These UMY students include students majoring in Communication Studies with classification of gender, concentration, already and not vaccinated, as well as responses from UMY Communication Science students. Sources of data obtained through a questionnaire as the primary data source. Questionnaire is one of the data collection in a study. The technique of collecting data using a questionnaire is done by distributing a list of questions that have been compiled by the researcher to the respondents. These questions will be set forth in a questionnaire and then given to the respondents in accordance with this research. After getting primary data through *propose population* then the data is drawn using the linkert scale method to get the primary data results. Linkert scale by setting the highest value 5 and the lowest value 1 [17].

3 Results and Discussion

The findings of the data obtained from the respondents can be described first and then described as research results. This is done so that the discussion can be interconnected as a whole. In this study, the data obtained was drawn using a Likert scale to become an infographic of the population referring to Communication Studies students at UMY who had read news about the Covid-19 vaccination on Kompas.com. In writing this research, there are 3 aspects, namely the use of appropriate sources, the application of *cover both sides*, and the application of verification discipline in loading news. Then the primary data obtained will be identified to find out the response of UMY Communication Science students to the news of the Covid-19 vaccination on Kompas.com.

3.1 Respondent Data Analysis Unit

In this study there were 100 respondents who were UMY students. Primary data regarding the sex of the respondents is obtained, namely respondents with female sex as many as 58 respondents (58%) and male respondents as many as 42 respondents (42%) with 19 years of age as many as 19 respondents (19%), 20 years as many as 31 respondents (31%), 21 years as many as 30 respondents (30%) and 22 years as many as 19 respondents (19%).

3.2 Analysis Unit for Vaccination Reporting in Certain Areas

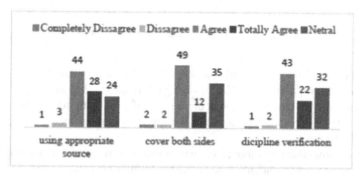

Fig. 1. Vaccination news in certain areas

Based on Fig. 1 above, it shows that 44 respondents (44%) agreed with the use of appropriate sources in reporting. Then in the aspect *of cover both sides*, 49 (49%) respondents agreed, and 43 (43%) respondents agreed with the application of the verification discipline concept in the news.

This data shows that Kompas.com is considered by Communication Studies students to have used the right selection of sources. The news about vaccines on Kompas.com featured sources with the background of the Head of the Bantul Health Office, the Head of the Surveillance and Immunization Section of the Disease Control and Eradication Midwife, and the Head of the Tourism Office. In accordance with the SOR theory, the presence of sources who are in accordance with their credibility has made the public believe in the content of the news. As we know, the source is the who element in the news. The selection of sources by journalists must be in accordance with the factuality of the issues being reported [18]. The respondents of this study were Communication Studies students who had good knowledge of how journalism works. This match is what causes the SOR in this study to appear to work.

3.3 Analysis Unit of Vaccine Required Areas

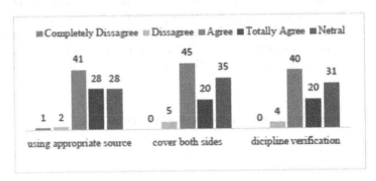

Fig. 2. News of vaccine required areas reporting

Based on Fig. 2 above, it shows that 41 (41%) respondents stated that they agreed with the use of appropriate sources in conveying information. Then as many as 45 (45%) respondents agreed to the application of the concept of cover both sides in the news. And as many as 40 (40%) respondents agree on the application of the concept of verification discipline in the news.

This data shows that news about areas where vaccines are mandatory is considered by Communication Science students as news that has fulfilled cover both side aspects. Cover both sides is the main principle in quality journalism by gathering information from both parties [19]. The background of research informants who come from Communication Studies is an important factor in the running of the SOR theory. Communication Studies students have received Introduction to Journalism courses since semester 3.

3.4 Unit of Analysis of Mass Vaccination Reporting

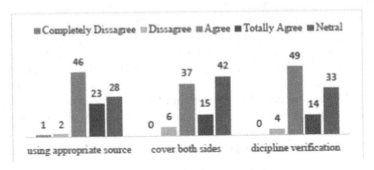

Fig. 3. Mass vaccination news section

Based on Fig. 3 above, it shows that the most data obtained in the news, as many as 46 respondents (46%) agreed to the use of appropriate sources in conveying information.

Then as many as 42 respondents (42%) were neutral on the application of the concept of *cover both sides* in the news. And as many as 49 respondents (49%) agree on the application of the concept of verification discipline in the news.

Verification discipline is an important aspect in reporting. Kompas.com is part of the Kompas Gramedia Group. Kompas.com is the development of Kompas Daily. Kompas Daily is a newspaper that is well known for its verification discipline and high standards of quality journalism [20]. This makes Kompas the largest newspaper in Indonesia. Respondents of this study gave a positive response to Kompas news regarding mass vaccination to prevent Covid-19. The background of the respondent as a Communication Science student encourages this conformity.

3.5 Analysis Unit of Vaccination Reporting for Pregnant Women

Based on Fig. 4 below, it shows that in the news as many as 40 respondents (40%) agreed to the use of appropriate sources in conveying information. Then 47 respondents (47%) agreed with the application of the concept of *cover both sides* in the news. And as much as 47% agree with the application of the concept of verification discipline in the news.

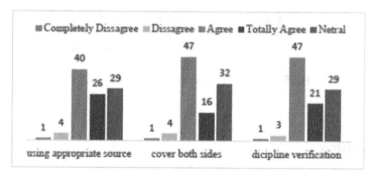

Fig. 4. Vaccination news for pregnant women

The existence of cover both sides in the news about pregnant women shows that research respondents give appreciation for Communication Science students to Kompas.com in maintaining the quality of the news. According to the Covid-19 Handling Committee and National Economic Recovery (KPCPEN) during the Covid-19 pandemic, circulating hoaxes related to vaccines, such as halal-haram vaccines, dangerous ingredients in vaccines, vaccine effectiveness and safety, and so on have become major issues [21]. Kompas.com is considered by Communication Studies students as a media that is determined to maintain the quality of journalism from the threat of hoaxes. Keeping the principle of cover both sides carried out by Kompas.com is to use resource persons from the Ministry of Health and the National Immunization Expert Advisory Committee. According to the SOR theory, there can be a change in the decision by the organism after receiving the stimulus. So that respondents are more confident about the vaccination program after reading the news published in Kompas.com.

3.6   Analysis Unit of Vaccination Target Reporting as of August 2021

Based on Fig. 5 below, it shows that 45 respondents (45%) agreed with the use of appropriate sources in conveying information. Then 45 respondents (45%) agreed to the application of the concept of *cover both sides* in the news. And as many as 50 respondents (50%) agree on the application of the concept of verification discipline in the news.

In this data, respondents agree that the reporting of vaccination targets has been disciplined for verification. Verification discipline is carried out by looking for many witnesses to an event, using as many sources as possible, and collecting different points of view [22]. In the SOR theory, there are various different responses, namely because of the different backgrounds, viewpoints, and living environments of each individual.

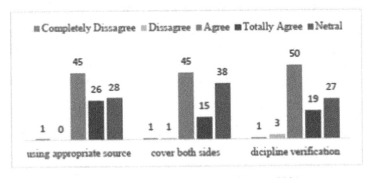

Fig. 5.   Vaccination target news as of august 2021 s

4   Conclusion

Based on the results of research on the online news media Kompas.com it can be concluded that Kompas.com has implemented 3 important aspects in presenting news information which is cover both side, using appropriate source, and discipline verification. Kompas.com has been accordance with the basics of journalism in presenting vaccination news. So that, by looking the response from people, they agree that vaccination news from Kompas.com is online news media that can be trusted with the quality of the news.

References

1. Petropoulos, F., Makridakis, S.: Forecasting the novel coronavirus COVID- 19. PLoS ONE **15**(3), 1–8 (2020). https://doi.org/10.1371/journal.pone.0231236
2. Dwiputra, K.O.: Analisis resepsi khalayak terhadap pemberitaan Covid-19 di. J. Komun. Prof. **5**(1), 26–37 (2021). http://ejournal.unitomo.ac.id/index.php/jkp.
3. Gandryani, F., Hadi, F.: Pelaksanaan Vaksinasi Covid-19 Di Indonesia. vol. 10, no. 23–41, 2021

4. Gurning, F.P., Siagian, L.K., Wiranti, I., Devi, S.: Kebijakan Pelaksanaan Vaksinasi covid-19 Di. vol. 10, no. 1, pp. 43–50, 2021. https://doi.org/10.37048/kesehatan.v10i1.326
5. Reyna, J., Meier, P.: Co-creation of knowledge using mobile technologies and digital media as pedagogical devices in undergraduate STEM education. vol. 28, no. 1063519, pp. 1–14, 2020
6. Syamsul, A., Romli, M.: Jurnalistik Online : Panduan Praktis Mengelola Media Online. Nuansa Cendekia, Bandung (2012)
7. Pertiwi, M., Ri'aeni, I., Yusron, A.: Analisis Resepsi Interpretasi Penonton terhadap Konflik Keluarga dalam Film 'Dua Garis Biru. J. Audiens 1(1), 1–8 (2020). https://doi.org/10.18196/ja.1101
8. Werung, M.Y.: Persepsi Audiens terhadap Tayangan D'Academy Indosiar di Kelurahan Sungai Pinang dalam Kecamatan Sungai Pinang. vol. 3, no. 4, pp. 185–199, 2015
9. Junaerdi, F., Sukmono, F.G.: University Students Behavior in Searching and Disseminating COVID- 19 Online Information Perilaku Mahasiswa dalam Mencari dan Menyebarkan Informasi Covid-19 di Media Sosial. vol. 5, no. 2, pp. 245–253, 2020
10. Gamaliel, D.O.: Si Buncu Pada Surat Kabar Kaltim Pos Di Kota Samarinda (Studi Pada Kelurahan Gunung Kelua Kecamatan Samarinda Ulu. vol. 3, no. 3, pp. 442–451, 2015
11. Effendy, O.U.: Ilmu, Teori dan Filsafat Komunikasi. PT. Citra Aditya Bakti, Bandung (2003)
12. Kurniawan, D.: Komunikasi model Laswell Dan Stimulus-Organism- Response Dalam Mewujudkan Pembelajaran Menyenangkan Laswell Communication Model and Stimulus-Organism-Response for Creatng Fun Learning. vol. 2, pp. 60–68, 2018
13. Nur, E.: Tanggapan Masyarakat Terhadap Pemberitaan Media Provinsi Sulawesi Selatan People Response to Mass Media Transmissions About. J. Penelit. Komun. Dan Pembang. 17(2), 113–126 (2016)
14. Sugiyono, Metode Penelitian Kuantitatif, Kualitatif, R&D. Alfabeta, Bandung (2013)
15. Aedy, H., Mahmudin, H.: Metodologi Penelitian Teori dan Aplikasi Penuntun bagi Mahasiswa dan Peneliti. Deepublish, Yogyakarta (2017)
16. Samsu, METODE PENELITIAN : Teori dan Aplikasi Penelitian Kualitatif, Kuantitatif, Mixed Methods, serta Reseacrch & Development. Pusaka, Jambi (2017)
17. Riduwan, Skala Pengukuran Variabel-variabel Penelitian. Alfabeta, Bandung (2002)
18. Rakhmadani, R.: Objektivitas Media di Tengah Pandemi Covid-19: Analisis Isi Berita tentang Penerapan New Normal di Indonesia pada Media Tirto.id. J. Audiens 1(2) (2020). https://doi.org/10.18196/ja.12030
19. Aslam, M., Hasrullah, H., Bahfiarti, T.: Framing Pemberitaan Kasus Kpk Vs Polri Di Surat Kabar Tribun Timur. KAREBA J. Ilmu Komun. 6(2), 235 (2018). https://doi.org/10.31947/kjik.v6i2.5319
20. Dhiya, A., Fadilah, E.: Transformasi Harian Kompas Menjadi Portal Berita Digita Subscription Kompas. Id, vol. 01, pp. 190–213, 2018
21. Dewi, S.A.E.: Komunikasi Publik Terkait Vaksinasi Covid 19. Heal. Care J. Kesehat. 10(1), 162–167 (2021). https://doi.org/10.36763/healthcare.v10i1.119
22. Kristina, K., Setiawan, B.: Disiplin Verifikasi dalam Jurnalisme Media Online detikcom (Verification Discipline in detikcom Online Media Journalism). J. IPTEKKOM (Jurnal Ilmu Pengetah. Teknol. Informasi), vol. 23, no. 1, pp. 33–48, 2021

Digital Literacy: How Social Media Prevent Misinformation During Pandemic

Mia Tri Nurcahyani[✉], Fajar Junaedi, and Erwan Sudiwijaya

Department of Communication, University of Muhammadiyah Yogyakarta, Kasihan, Indonesia
mia.tri.fisip18@mail.umy.ac.id, {fajarjun,
erwansudiwijaya}@umy.ac.id

Abstract. This research aims determine the literacy practices used by government officials to prevent the spread of hoaxes and misinformation. The pandemic created a crisis that crowded information sources; in that situation, social media users had to decide which information to trust and use as the primary reference. As a result of the Covid-19 cases, the spread of false information has increased. This study employs a qualitative narrative analysis method with the MAXDA software tool to investigate the government's digital literacy function. According to the study's findings, the government used social media under the ministry of information and communication to filter information for social media users. To support this step, the government also campaigned for an electronic transaction law as a preventive measure to prevent the spread of hoaxes on social media. In addition, to create massive information, the ministry of information and communication uses several accounts under the coordination of the ministry to provide information. The findings underline the ability to create digital literacy by the ministry of information and communication through the electronic transaction law. In the last three years, the intensity of tweets by the Ministry of Communication and Information account has increased; this is based on the increase in Covid-19 cases and the implementation of large-scale social distancing policies in Indonesia.

Keywords: Digital literacy · Covid-19 · Social media · Information

1 Introduction

Corona Virus or Covid-19 originating from Wuhan China has spread to Indonesia on March 2, 2020 [1]. Corona viruses are a large family of viruses that cause disease in humans and animals. In humans, it usually causes respiratory tract infections, ranging from the common cold to serious diseases such as *Middle East Respiratory Syndrome*) and *Severe Acute Respiratory Syndrome* (SARS). MERSThe crisis for people's lives is not only a health crisis, but a crisis in every sector so that every individual must be involved in the struggle [3].

This is in line with the growth of social media which creates a rapid spread of news. Based on the results of the 2016 APJII survey, that 97.5% of sharing information is the highest activity in social media. In recent years, the negative impact of social media

C. Stephanidis et al. (Eds.): HCII 2022, CCIS 1655, pp. 56–62, 2022.
https://doi.org/10.1007/978-3-031-19682-9_8

has become uncontrollable. When information is shared or created, it only increases the "status" of sending information. Information sharing activities cause more public anxiety and discomfort. Currently sharing information quickly without the need to filter whether the information is true or not has become a social activity [4].

The level of literacy in Indonesian society is still low, as can be seen from the many discoveries of hoax information, hate speech, and fake news [5]. The spread of false information in the midst of the Covid-19 pandemic caused public unrest [6]. In addition, the widespread spread of hoax news also causes chaos among the public [7]. Knowledge and understanding of digital literacy are the fortresses for selecting information. Not only the information obtained is also used in a healthy, wise, intelligent and careful manner, but also selects information that has the potential to have a negative impact, especially during the Covid-19 pandemic [8].

Previous research has explained that the Directorate General of IKP as the government's public relations officer has carried out in accordance with communication management procedures. However, the implementation is still not optimal due to the unattractive upload quality [9].

Based on the above explanation regarding Digital Literacy, this study examines how digital literacy practices are used by the government to prevent the spread of hoaxes and misinformation related to the Covid-19 pandemic through Twitter social media. The results of this study are expected to be able to understand digital literacy carried out by the government which is produced to prevent the spread of hoaxes.

2 Literature Review

Digital literacy is the ability to understand and use information in various forms from a very wide variety of sources that are accessed through computer devices [10]. Digital literacy involves more "mastery of ideas" not an emphasis. One way that is used to distinguish the set of digital literacy concepts that are currently developing is to describe concepts that emphasize mastery of ideas and emphasize intelligent evaluation of information and analysis [11]. Literacy is defined as reading and writing, along with its development the concept of Literacy began to be defined as the ability to share meaning through a symbol system to fully participate in society [12].

There are nine important elements in digital literacy including social networking, transliteracy, maintaining privacy, managing identity, creating content, organizing and sharing content, reusing/repurposing content, filtering and selecting content, and self broadcasting. In online culture, the most important thing in digital literacy is the ability to use social networking services effectively [13].

There are eight elements that must be known to support the development of digital literacy, including: Cultural, Cognitive, Constructive, Communicative, Confidence and responsibility, Creative, Critical and socially responsible [14]. Digital literacy primarily requires positive content, while The function of positive content in question is informative, educative, and inspiring [15].

3   Method

This research discusses how the government uses Twitter social media as a medium for digital literacy education in preventing hoaxes during the Covid-19 pandemic. This study uses a *content analysis* using a qualitative approach called Q-DAS (Qualitative Data Analysis Software). Q-DAS helps researchers to collect, organize, analyze, visualize, and report data [16]. Nvivo can translate unstructured data by dividing it into several types according to research needs [17]. The data obtained came from the Twitter accounts @kemenkominfo and @djikp as content data obtained.

4   Results and Discussions

The terminology of digital literacy or digital literacy relies on two words, namely literacy and digital which means the ability to read and write [18]. Digital literacy is the ability to understand and use information in various forms from a very wide variety of sources that are accessed through computer devices [10]. This should also go hand in hand with the ability to select and create informative content.

Based on Fig. 1, the social media accounts @djikp and @kemkominfo provide information with different intensities, in the last year the intensity of information provided has increased even though it fluctuates.

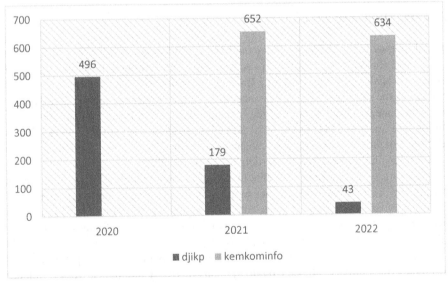

Fig. 1. Activities on social media.

The @djikp account has the highest activity in 2020, while the @kemkominfo account has the highest activity in 2021. This finding shows that social media twitter can be used by the government as a medium to literate users regarding Covid-19 hoax news. 2020–2021 is the year with the highest spike in Covid-19 cases in Indonesia in line with the spread of hoax news about Covid-19 and Covid-19 vaccinations on various social media [19] . Based on data from kominfo.go.id, during the Covid-19 pandemic, almost every day hoax news circulates on social media [4] .

This finding explains that government accounts provide validate information from a wide variety of sources with informative content with different intensities each year.

Table 1. Accounts interacting with DJIKP and Kemkominfo accounts.

Account categorization	djikp	Presentage	kemkominfo	Presentage
Public figures	jokowi	38%	platejohnny	67%
			jokowi	17%
Government	kemkominfo	25%	aduanppi	6%
	bkkbn official	13%	bappenasri	6%
Media	bpipri	13%		
	antaranews	13%	siarandigital	6%

Based on Table 1. It has three interactions, public figures, government, and media. The @platejohnny account has the highest level of interaction with the @kemkominfo account and the lowest interaction is with the @siarandigital media account. The @jokowi account has the highest interaction with the @djikp account and the lowest interaction with the @antaranews media account.

There are nine important elements in digital literacy including social networking, transliteracy, maintaining privacy, managing identity, creating content, organizing and sharing content, reusing/repurposing content, filtering and selecting content, and self broadcasting [13].

The content created when mentioning the accounts of public figures is content about information and webinars related to the Covid-19 pandemic. This finding shows that the accounts of public figures have the highest level of interaction due to the level of trust of net citizens in the facts presented by government accounts. Various calls to wisely absorb information from online media have been echoed by various government agencies [20]. Information submitted by the government will provide feedback in the form of perceptions from the public which can lead to positive and negative stigma [21].

These findings are in line with the theory put forward by Steve about nine important elements in digital literacy, government accounts use these nine elements to create content on Twitter accounts, especially in managing identity as well as possible (Fig. 2).

See Table 1. Content presented by twitter accounts @djikp and @kemkominfo presenting informative messages or information to create smart and healthy netizens. In this case, the @djikp and @kemkominfo accounts use the hashtags #sobatkom, #bersamakominfo, #hoaksvaksin, #digitalliterasi, #makindigital to provide information using valid sources and the information obtained can be accounted for. Digital literacy primarily requires positive content, while The function of positive content in question is informative, educative, and inspiring [15]. This finding explains that through these

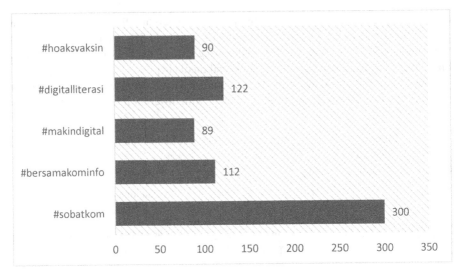

Fig. 2. Hashtag used by @djikp and @kemkominfo

hashtags, the @djikp and @kemkominfo accounts not only educate their readers who are the recipients of the message but also educate their readers who will later become disseminators of information through their informative content.

@kemkominfo   @djikp

Fig. 3. Categories of words that appear frequently

See Fig. 3. Words that government accounts often use to generate content. These captured words became the main topic of conversation, especially during the one month period [22]. In online culture, the most important thing in digital literacy is the ability to use social networking services effectively [13]. This study answers the information submitted by government accounts. The words used indicate the amount of content related to things that are often discussed in digital literacy activities.

5 Conclusion

Based on the above analysis, this study confirms the digital literacy practices used by the government in preventing the spread of hoax news and misinformation related to the Covid-19 pandemic through social media twitter by using nine elements of digital literacy including social networking, transliteracy, maintaining privacy, managing identity, creating content, organizing and sharing content, reusing/repurposing content, filtering and selecting content, and self broadcasting. The digital literacy practice used by the goverment is to validate the findings of hoax news related to Covid-19 cases in the last three years, especially during the social media. This step was taken by government as an effort to campaign for electronic transaction law. The government validates the data using positive, informative, educational and inspiring content.

This study also confirms that Nvivo as an analytical tools is able to prove and reduce data collections from twitter accounts so as to describe data in the form of text, images, charts and tables.

References

1. Tim Detik.com, When Actually Corona for the first time to enter Indonesia? (2020). https://news.detik.com/berita/d-4991485/
2. Ministry of Health, What are Corona Virus and Covid-19? (2022). https://www.kemkes.go.id/folder/view/full-content/structure-faq.html
3. WHO, WHO Director-General's opening remarks at the media briefing on Covid-19, (2020). https://www.who.int/director-general/speeches/detail/who-director-general-s-opening-remarks-at-the-media-briefing-on-covid-19---11-march-2020
4. Sutisna, I.P.G., Digital literacy movement during the covid-19 pandemic. STILISTICS: J. Lang. Arts Educ. 8(2), 268–283 (2020). https://doi.org/10.5281/zenodo.3884420
5. Rochadiani, T.H., Santoso, H., Dazki, E.: Improving digital literacy during the covid-19 pandemic. J. Commun. Serv. 1(1), 11–21 (2020). https://jurnal.pradita.ac.id/index.php/jpm/article/view/124
6. Saputra, D.: A Rumor (Hoax) about Covid-19. Mau'idhoh Hasanah J. Da'wah Commun. Stud. 1(2), 1 (2020). https://doi.org/10.47902/mauidhoh.v1i2.69
7. Solihin, M.M.: The relationship between digital literacy and the behavior of spreading hoax lecturers during the covid-19 pandemic. In: Jurnal Pekommas Special Issue 2021: The Role of Communication and IT against Covid-19, pp. 91–103 (2021). https://doi.org/10.30818/jpkm.2021.2060309
8. Meitania Noor, L.: Digital literacy becomes a fortress of information selection. https://djikp.kominfo.go.id/categories/kabar-djikp/474060/literasi-digital-menjadi-benteng-seleksi-information
9. Munir, K.M., Hamidah, L., Rizky, A.S.: Monitoring and evaluation of government public relations in the use of social media to combat hoaxes. J Commun. Manage. 5(1), 78–95 (2020). http://jurnal.unpad.ac.id/manajemen-komunikasi/article/view/27616/pdf
10. Gilster, P.: Digital Literacy. Wiley, Hoboken (1998)
11. Collin Lankshear, M.K.: Digital Literacy. Peter Lng Publishing, New York (2008)
12. Hobbs, R..: Digital and Media Literacy : A Plan of Action written by (2010). http://mediaeducationlab.com
13. Wheeler, S.: Digital literacies for engagement in emerging online cultures. eLC Res. Paper Ser. 5, 14–25 (2013)

14. Belshaw, D.A.: What is 'digital literacy'? Douglas A. J . Belshaw. Durham E-Theses Online, pp. 0–274 (2012). http://etheses.dur.ac.uk/3446

15. Rahmawan, D., Mahameruaji, J.N., Anisa, R.: Positive content development as part of the digital literacy movement. J. Commun. Stud. 7(1), 31 (2019). https://doi.org/10.24198/jkk.v7i1.20575

16. Lee, H.N.: Resource review. Evid. Based Med. 8(2), 38 (2003). https://doi.org/10.1136/ebm.8.2.38

17. Woolf, N.H., Silver, C.: Qualitative Analysis Using MAXQDA. Abingdon, Oxon; Routledge, New York (2017). Series: Developing qualitative inquiry: Routledge, 2017. https://doi.org/10.4324/9781315268569

18. Bahri, S., Social, M.: Digital literature responding to covid-19 hoax in the media. vol. 10, no. 1, pp. 16–28 (2021)

19. Rizkinaswara, L.: Kominfo removes 5,036 hoaxes regarding covid-19 that are spreading on social media (2021). https://aptika.kominfo.go.id/2021/12/kominfo-hapus-5-036-hoaks-seputar-covid-19-yang-tersebar-di-medsos/

20. Yovita, Netizens Fight Hoax News at #BijakHadapiHoax (2017). https://www.kominfo.go.id/content/detail/8707/netizen-perangi-berita-hoax-di-bijakhadapihoax/0/sorotan_media

21. Putri Pratiwi, V., Rahmawati, D.E., Purwaningsih, T.: BNPB_RI twitter account as a communication media for the indonesian government during the covid-19 pandemic. Soc. Polit. J. 7(2), 212–226 (2021). https://doi.org/10.22219/sospol.v7i2.16116

22. Nurhajati, L., Sukandar, R., Oktaviani, R.C., Wijayanto, X.A.: Conversation on the corona covid-19 issue in online media and social media in Indonesia, Institute for Research, Publications, and Community Service, vol. April, no. Big data analysis, pp. 1–23 (2020)

Social Media Consistency Analysis Ministry of State-Owned Enterprises in Indonesia During the COVID-19 Pandemic

Alfira Nurfitriana[✉], Filosa Gita Sukmono, and Erwan Sudiwijaya

Department of Communication, University of Muhammadiyah Yogyakarta, Kasihan, Indonesia
alfira.n.isip19@mail.umy.ac.id, {filosa,
erwansudiwijaya}@umy.ac.id

Abstract. This study aims to identify shifts in the production of social media information content in the industrial world during the COVID-19 pandemic in Indonesia. Official government social media accounts during the COVID-19 pandemic era experienced significant changes in disseminating information. The research was conducted on the official account @KemenBUMN. Indonesia is a national government agency in charge of fostering and managing state-owned enterprises. This research method uses the Q-DAS approach (Qualitative Data Analysis Software) and NVivo 12. The data source for this research is the official account activity of @KemenBUMN, using NCapture from the Twitter social media activity of the Indonesian Ministry of State-Owned Enterprises. The results found in this study for the production of information content about industrial developments during the COVID-19 pandemic are quite consistent from 2021 to 2022. The amount of content produced during the COVID-19 pandemic was more than 20 tweets in one month for a year starting from March 2021 to March 2022. In the results of Wordcloud analysis, the most widely used keywords are "BUMN" and "Sobat BUMN." The dominant information submitted by the @KemenBUMN account is information about activities and developments from various fields managed by the Ministry of SOEs for one year. The ministry of state-owned enterprises is quite active in greeting their followers with the hashtags # SobatBUMN and #bumnuntukindonesia in each of their tweets strategy for disseminating information during the pandemic by mentioning MNC official accounts in Indonesia. This is evidenced by the widespread use of content with the hashtags #bumnuntukindonesia and #sobatBUMN aimed at partners. That the production of SOE information social media content does not focus on dealing with COVID-19.

Keywords: Social media · Consistency · Twitter · Analysis · COVID-19

1 Introduction

The world is now entering the era of the industrial revolution 4.0 so information technology has become the basis of human life [1]. Responses to events and phenomena in the current digitalization era have proven to be more responsive as a result of the existence of social media (Azmi et al., nd). Communication that occurs between the government and

C. Stephanidis et al. (Eds.): HCII 2022, CCIS 1655, pp. 63–68, 2022.
https://doi.org/10.1007/978-3-031-19682-9_9

citizens must be mutually beneficial since the COVID-19 index case was first published in Wuhan on December 1, 2019 [3].

Indonesia is one of the countries that has been heavily affected by the spread of the virus. ThereSeveral sectors are experiencingisis COVID-19, ranging from the health, economic and political sectors. Not only that, but the information crisis is also experienced by the community due to Covid-19. (book on the dynamics of communication during the covid-19 pandemic). Social media has a big role in today's life, especially during the COVID-19 pandemic when computers are not only a means of entertainment but also a means needed every day for educational needs and communicating with others. [4]. Government social media has an important role in disseminating information and can be used as a way for people to interact with the government or e-government. [5].

As technology develops, the government recognizes its function as a 'useful instrument' or 'activator' rather than a 'driver' of transformation (Lips, in Idris, 2018). There are various types of social media, such as blogs, microblogging, sharing services, text messages, discussion forums, and social networks that can interact directly with their users, are social media that are currently often used by government departments in various countries. [7]. The presence of online dialogues made by government agencies gets more likes and comments compared to all posts without dialogue. Once the government is involved, citizens further engage and respond. [8]. Social media Twitter is one of the media that provides opportunities for agencies and institutions to communicate and build relationships with the community.[9].

In this study, the Ministry of State-Owned Enterprises of Indonesia has disseminated information through social media Twitter during the Covid-19 pandemic. This study uses Q-DAS (Qualitative Analysis Data Software) Nvivo 12 plus to collect data and analyze the consistency of Twitter social media belonging to the Indonesian Ministry of State Enterprises during the Covid-19 pandemic and compare it with years before the Covid-19 outbreak. This study aims to analyze the consistency of the Indonesian government in disseminating information during the covid-19 pandemic and compare it with the activities that occurred on the Twitter account of the Indonesian Ministry of State-Owned Enterprises in previous years. How does the government use social media to interact more closely with the public, by disseminating information through content created by the government? This study will provide analysis results on a comparison of the government's consistency in providing information related to the Indonesian government's business activities during the COVID-19 pandemic.

2   Overview of Literatur

According to [7], social media is currently very influential on social life. Communication through social media can be an advanced method involving multiple stakeholders and public participation and interaction. Dissemination of information through social media has the advantage that the information conveyed quickly spreads and can reach many users [9].

In the research conducted by DePaula and Dincelli, there is a positive interaction of citizens in government dialogue, which can demonstrate the value of government information to citizens through social media [8]. The existence and use of digital platforms continue to grow, the question for the government is how to build operational capabilities to engage with a wide network of interactions among its citizens to best serve the public interest. [5].

One of the digital social media that is currently widely used by the government to get closer to citizens is the social media Twitter. Social media Twitter has a very wide reach and includes many people. The platform is also equipped with features that support interaction with uploaded content. This feature is like, retweet, and comment. If all these things are used, they will automatically appear on the Twitter account timelines of users who follow the Twitter account [9].

On Twitter social media accounts we can upload various things from text, and images to videos. Based on research conducted by Furqon and his friends, posting videos and images tends to get more positive responses than posting text on one of the government's social media to account profiles. [10].

3   Method

This research uses descriptive qualitative research, as well as data analysis sourced from NVivo 12 Plus software. Data retrieval was carried out on the Twitter account of the Ministry of State Enterprises of Indonesia (@KemenBUMN) via NCapture from NVivo 12 Plus via the Google Chrome Website platform.

4   Result and Discussion

The Twitter social media account belonging to the Indonesian Ministry of State-Owned Enterprises has 656,800 followers. This account was created in 2015. In the Twitter account bio of the Indonesian Ministry of State-Owned Enterprises, some information is shown including the address, telephone number, and also the website of the Indonesian Ministry of State-Owned Enterprises (Fig. 1).

Fig. 1. Screenshot of the twitter social media account profile of the ministry of state-owned enterprises of Indonesia (@KemenBUMN). (Source: Nvivo 12 Plus Software)

Before the COVID-19 pandemic, the Twitter account of the Ministry of State-Owned Enterprises (BUMN) which was created in 2015 was not very active in its use to disseminate information to the public. The Twitter account of the Ministry of State-Owned Enterprises (BUMN) became active during the COVID-19 pandemic where we all had to do virtual work from home (WFH) activities to prevent the spread of the COVID-19 virus.

In approximately one year since the COVID-19 pandemic, the Twitter social media account of the Ministry of State-Owned Enterprises has been quite active every month in the production of their Twitter content for the benefit of disseminating information related to Indonesian state-owned businesses (Fig. 2).

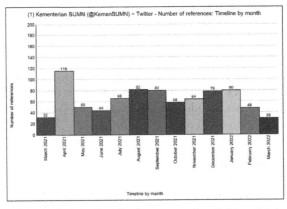

Fig. 2. Bar chart data for total production of twitter content for ministry of state-owned enterprises accounts for 1 year (2021–2022). (Source: Nvivo 12 Plus Software)

The use of hashtags on Twitter social media accounts belonging to the Ministry of State-Owned Enterprises of Indonesia on average shows a greeting to greet followers of the account which aims to provide information about domestic businesses in Indonesia. Hashtag with#SobatBUMN was used the most in every content post created by that account. Within a year, there were 560 tweets with the hashtag #SobatBUMN produced by the Twitter account @KemenBUMN (Fig. 3).

Based on an analysis conducted using Nvivo 12 and NCapture on the Twitter social media account of the Ministry of State-Owned Enterprises (@KemenBUMN), the word BUMN dominates every content post on their account. This of course can affect the public's attention to interact easily with government agencies through social media Twitter (Fig. 4).

It can be seen from the frequency of words that often appear are BUMN and the hashtag #SobatBUMN. Based on this data, the government has been quite active in using Twitter for approximately one year after the COVID-19 pandemic as a means of disseminating information.

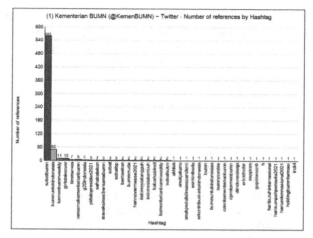

Fig. 3. Percentage of hashtag usage in Indonesia's @KemenBUMN (Ministry of state-owned enterprises) twitter account for 1 Year (2021–2022). (Source: Nvivo 12 Plus Software)

Fig. 4. Word frequency in the twitter account of the ministry of state-owned enterprises (@KemenBUMN) Indonesia for 1 Year (2021–2022). (Source: Nvivo 12 Plus Software)

5 Conclusion

This study found that the analysis of the consistency of social media shown by the Ministry of State-Owned Enterprises regarding the dissemination of information during the COVID-19 pandemic was quite good. Research using analysis through Nvivo 12 shows that after the COVID-19 pandemic, the government is trying to be more open to the public by mingling through various social media platforms. With the use of hashtags that are included in every content uploaded by the government, it will make it easier for the public to search or just looking for information about various things. The Twitter account of the Ministry of State-Owned Enterprises (@KemenBUMN) has a pretty good consistency for disseminating information related to state-owned businesses after the COVID-19 pandemic. The information provided on average is in the form of information on activities carried out by the Ministry of State-Owned Enterprises of Indonesia. Not infrequently this account also uploads greetings for big days such as Christmas, Eid al-Fitr, New Year, and commemorations of other big days. This study also shows that Nvivo is a tool that can analyze various data on Twitter accounts belonging to the Ministry of State-Owned Enterprises of Indonesia (@KemenBUMN) and reduce data in various forms such as text, tables, percentages, and also images.

References

1. Rohida, L., Sos, S., Si, M., Sumber, D., Manusia, D.: Pengaruh Era Revolusi Industri 4.0 terhadap Kompetensi Sumber Daya Manusia (2018)
2. Azmi, N.A., Fathani, A.T., Sadayi, D.P., Fitriani, I., Rayhan Adiyaksa, M.: Social media network analysis (SNA): Identifikasi Komunikasi dan Penyebaran Informasi Melalui Media Sosial Twitter. Jurnal Media Informatika Budidarma. 5, 1422–1430 (2021). https://doi.org/10.30865/mib.v5i4.3257
3. Huang, C., et al.: Clinical features of patients infected with 2019 novel coronavirus in Wuhan, China. The Lancet 395(10223), 497–506 (2020). https://doi.org/10.1016/S0140-6736(20)30183-5
4. Tkáčová, H., Pavlíková, M., Jenisová, Z., Maturkanič, P., Králik, R.: Social media and students' wellbeing: an empirical analysis during the covid-19 pandemic. Sustainability (Switzerland). 13(18) (2021). https://doi.org/10.3390/su131810442
5. Weng, S., Schwarz, G., Schwarz, S., Hardy, B.: A framework for government response to social media participation in public policy making: evidence from China. Int. J. Public Adm. 44(16), 1424–1434 (2021). https://doi.org/10.1080/01900692.2020.1852569
6. Idris, I.K.: Government social media in Indonesia: Just another information dissemination tool. Jurnal Komunikasi: Malaysian J. Commun. 34(4), 337–356 (2018). https://doi.org/10.17576/JKMJC-2018-3404-20
7. Pratama, D., Nurmandi, A., Muallidin, I., Kurniawan, D., Salahudin.: Information dissemination of COVID-19 by ministry of health in Indonesia. In: Ahram, T., Taiar, R. (eds) Human Interaction, Emerging Technologies and Future Systems V. IHIET 2021. Lecture Notes in Networks and Systems, vol. 319, pp. 61–67. Springer, Cham (2022). https://doi.org/10.1007/978-3-030-85540-6_8
8. DePaula, N., Dincelli, E.: Information strategies and affective reactions: How citizens interact with government social media content. First Monday 23(4) (2018). https://doi.org/10.5210/fm.v23i4.8414
9. Solihin, F., Awaliyah, S., Muid, A., Shofa, A.: Pemanfaatan Twitter Sebagai media penyebaran informasi oleh dinas komunikasi dan informatika. Jurnal Pendidikan Ilmu Pengetahuan Sosial (JPIPS) 1(13), 52–58 (2021). http://e-journal.upr.ac.id/index.php/JP-IPS
10. Furqon, M.A., Hermansyah, D., Sari, R., Sukma, A., Akbar, Y., Rakhmawati, N.A.: Analisis jenis posting media sosial pemerintah daerah di indonesia berdasarkan like dan analisis sentimental masyarakat. Jurnal Sosioteknologi 17(2), 177 (2018). https://doi.org/10.5614/sostek.itbj.2018.17.2.1

Health Communication Using Social Media: As Preventive of Suicide Act

Rena Nurhaliza[✉], Adhianty Nurjanah, and Fajar Junaedi

Department of Communication, University of Muhammadiyah Yogyakarta, Kasihan, Indonesia
rena.n.isip18@mail.umy.ac.id, {adhianty,fajarjun}@umy.ac.id

Abstract. Young people, in particular, use social media to express their thoughts and feelings. Young people make up 29.2 percent of social media users in Indonesia. Suicide is common among young people, according to an Infodatin Ministry of Health report, and it is typically communicated through social media. According to the Central Statistics Agency, there have been 5,787 suicides, with social media accounting for 40%. The qualitative content analysis method is used in this study. The education offered by the @IntoTheLightID account, according to content analysis, includes information on suicide prevention, mental health information, and mental health campaign information. Researchers divided the roles of Twitter accounts into two categories: first, offering information on avoiding suicide in themselves and others. Second, as part of suicide prevention and mental health campaigns, offering information about seminars. The community (SP-CARE) emphasizes education with the primary purpose of raising public awareness about suicide prevention. The hashtags #suicidepreventionday, #preventsuicide, #mentalhealth, and #cooperationforthesoul have been used to regularly update education about suicide prevention and mental health on the Twitter account @IntoTheLightID. Twitter users can access information quickly. People's conduct can be changed by using social media, such as hashtags on Twitter, to provide an active response to a situation.

Keywords: Social media · Mental health · Suicide · Communication

1 Introduction

The World Health Organization (WHO) estimates that suicide is the 13th leading cause of death worldwide; more than 700,000 people die from suicide. Suicide is one of the leading causes of death worldwide, more than HIV/AIDS. The Global Health Observatory (GHO) said that in Indonesia, the death rate due to suicide in Indonesia in 2018 reached 265 million people; it can be calculated that the estimated death due to suicide in Indonesia is around 9,000 cases per year. So that preventive measures are needed in anticipating cases of suicide.

This suicide can be anticipated through many things, one of which is through social media. Social media is considered an essential role in suicide prevention. Social media platforms are usually used to express thoughts and feelings, especially by young people. In Indonesia, social media users are dominated by young people reaching 29.2%; from

C. Stephanidis et al. (Eds.): HCII 2022, CCIS 1655, pp. 69–75, 2022.
https://doi.org/10.1007/978-3-031-19682-9_10

a report by Infodatin (Center for Data and Information of the Indonesian Ministry of Health), suicide often occurs in young people and is usually expressed through social media. The 2018 Basic Health Research (Rikesdas) said that more than 19 million people over 15 had mental and emotional disorders, and more than 12 million people over the age of 15 had depression. Moreover, from the WHO Global Health report in 2019, deaths due to suicide reached more than 50,000 people with a vulnerable age group of 15–29 years, which women dominated.

Social media is used by the Company, the Government, and musicians and is also being used by the community to disseminate information and education. Social media has the potential to support suicide prevention and is increasingly seen as an essential tool for public health communication, such as using social media Twitter. Twitter can become a tool detector for national health _ and global, giving correct information to the public or individual. Several studies have analyzed some Twitter content that discusses health, such as breast cancer outbreaks, toothaches, vaccinations, etc. One of the previous studies explained that social media is an effective tool for disseminating information and education. This study discusses how social media Twitter is a means to access information about sexual harassment. This research focuses on how Twitter media is an information tool for trending topics. However, until now, not many studies have analyzed communication on Twitter about mental health, especially mental health and suicide. As is the case in the United States, people with *mental illness* do not get any treatment.

There has not been much research on mental health on Twitter-based suicide prevention, especially in Indonesia. Previous research has shown that suicide is more common due to major depression. This research focuses on how suicide in Gunung Kidul can occur and how to prevent it [9] directly. Instead, this study aims to analyze the use of Community-owned Twitter social media (SP-CARE) as a tool to provide education via the internet. This study has one research question: how is the health communication strategy of Community Twitter social media (SP-CARE) in providing education related to suicide prevention.

2 Overview of Literature

According to Greenhow & Lobelia 2008, social media in teaching and learning environments can generate new forms of inquiry, communication, collaboration, identity work, or have positive cognitive, social, and emotional impacts. Social media is a platform that engages users to participate, comment, and creates content to communicate with their social graph. It can be said that social media is a tool, service, and communication facilitating the connection between colleagues with common interests. One of the social media used as educational media is Twitter. Twitter social media is starting to present much educative content through a post. Besides that, Twitter is also widely used by various groups from abroad, so it contains more comprehensive information. Many parts of Twitter can be used as informal education media for citizens, including education about health. Social media as a form of technology and information development cannot be ignored. Suicide is the leading cause of death among young people. Several factors cause a person to want to commit suicide, such as depression, environmental, social factors, substance abuse, hopelessness, loss of a loved one, *insecurity, bullying,* or even work and financial difficulties.

According to Edwin Seidman, there are three strategies for preventing suicide, including reducing suffering and deep psychological pain, because people who desire to commit suicide must have at least one psychological disorder. Then open a view, such as motivating that there are various options in solving problems other than ending one's life. Furthermore, the last one encourages the person concerned, even if it is only a step away from self-destructive action. Provide information regarding the characteristics of people who have suicidal ideation, provide counseling, and provide education about preventing suicide, either through socialization or through social media. Primary prevention can be in education and the provision of hotlines. In contrast, secondary prevention can be psychosocial and biological management, and tertiary prevention can be in the form of counseling.

3   Method

This study uses a qualitative approach called Q-DAS *(Qualitative Data Analysis Software);* this study aims to analyze how the Community (SP-CARE) uses social media Twitter as an educational medium in preventing suicide. This study uses qualitative analysis, with Nvivo 12 Plus as an analytical tool; the tool in a qualitative approach is called Computer Assistant Qualitative Analysis. Nvivo 12 Plus is a data analysis software that facilitates the collecting, categorizing, mapping, analyzing, and visualization of qualitative data. The research data source is the Twitter social media account @IntoTheLightID.

4   Results and Discussions

In the era of globalization, technology is increasingly advanced. The internet and social media are also increasingly needed in people's lives. Currently, social media is used as an alternative to access and provide information like the Community (SP-CARE), which uses social media as a source of information and education about preventing suicide.

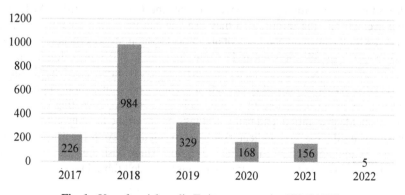

Fig. 1. Use of social media Twitter community (SP-CARE)

The content that has been presented by the Community (SP-CARE) is one of the efforts to help educate the public about the importance of preventing suicide. The following is data regarding the use of Twitter social media by the Community (SP-CARE) (Fig. 1):

The Community Twitter account (SP-CARE) has 19.4 thousand followers and follows 619 users. 984 times. Although it tends to experience ups and downs from year to year, the Community (SP-CARE) remains focused on providing education through Twitter social media, it's just that it may not be as intense as in 2018. The Community (SP-CARE) retweets more than tweets but still only retweets information related to suicide prevention. The Community (SP-CARE) has tweeted 1123 and retweeted 745. In view [11], This step can prove that social media can be used as an educational medium. In order to help spread information about preventing suicides quickly, the Community (SP-CARE) also includes mentions in each of its tweets, such as the accounts below (Fig. 2):

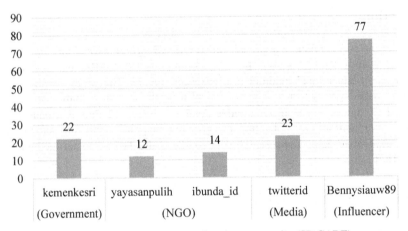

Fig. 2. Account category mentions by community (SP-CARE)

It can be seen that the Community (SP-CARE) made more mentions as much as 52% (77 mentions) on Bennysiauw89's account, which is an influencer in the mental health sector. By mentioning the above account, the Community (SP-CARE) hopes that the account and the information they provide can be spread quickly, and people associated with the account can find out about the Community's existence (SP-CARE). The existence of digitalization makes the Community (SP-CARE) provide education that follows efforts to prevent suicide so that it can be accessed very easily. The Community Strategy (SP-CARE) in providing education includes providing motivational content so that readers avoid the desire to commit suicide, actively retweeting other content related to suicide prevention, and using hashtags on social media. Any content created. The hashtags used have three indicators related to suicide prevention. The indicators in question are campaigns, counseling, and prevention. These hashtags can be a preventive strategy for overcoming various factors that cause suicide (Table 1).

Table 1. Categories of suicide prevention

Hashtags	Categories of Suicide Prevention		
	Campaign	Counseling	Prevention
#corporationforthesoul	☑		
#preventsuicide			☑
#mentalhealth		☑	
#suicidepreventionday	☑		

The community (SP-CARE) uses the hashtags #suicidepreventionday, #mentalhealth, #preventsuicide, and #cooperationforthesoul in their content discussing the prevention of suicide. The four hashtags used can influence the audience to stay away from suicide. The hashtag frequency used was 28 tweets about #suicidepreventionday, then there were 20 tweets about #preventsuicide, #mentalhealth with 10 tweets, and #cooperationforthesoul with 44 tweets with content information that discussed preventing suicide. The hashtags above confirm that indirectly using these hashtags can be part of primary and secondary prevention. This community (SP-CARE) focuses on how they can provide education about suicide prevention through content on social media. In addition to using hashtags, we can also see some frequency words often used by the Community (SP-CARE) to create their content. It can be seen in the image below (Fig. 3):

Fig. 3. Word frequency from community (SP-CARE)

Based on the picture above, it can be seen that the words that appear the most are prevention and suicide. Following this, the Community (SP-CARE) use social media as a medium for prevention education. This step was taken to make it easier for the audience to obtain information related to suicide prevention; this proves a relationship between prevention and suicide with the Community (SP-CARE), which aims to access every audience who wants to access information that can find the information quickly.

5   Conclusion

This finding confirms that suicide is common among young people, and most of them express it through social media. Effective suicide prevention measures for young people can be done through social media. Such as using Community-owned Twitter social media (SP-CARE) to provide education about preventing suicide. The strategy for using social media in providing health education is delivered through content that can be seen from the prevention category based on the hashtags and mentions used. Community (SP-CARE) uses hashtags related to the prevention of suicide, both primary and secondary. In addition, the Community (SP-CARE) also often mentions several accounts to help spread information about their accounts and content. This study also confirms that Nvivo as an analytical tool can reduce data from the Community Twitter account (SP-CARE) to describe data in the form of text, images, charts, and tables.

References

1. Robinson, J., et al.: Social media and suicide prevention: a systematic review. Early Interv. Psychiatry 10(2), 103–121 (2016). https://doi.org/10.1111/eip.12229
2. World Health Organization (WHO), suicide worldwide in 2019: global health estimates (2021)
3. Kementerian Kesehatan Republik Indonesia, Situasi dan Pencegahan Bunuh Diri, Pusat Data dan Informasi, pp. 1–10 (2019)
4. Robinson, J., Rodrigues, M., Fisher, S., Herrman, H.: Suicide and social media, Melbourne, Aust. Young Well Coop. Res. Cent. (2014)
5. Permassanty, T.D., Muntiani, M.: Strategi komunikasi komunitas virtual dalam mempromosikan tangerang melalui media sosial. J. Penelit. Komun. 21(2), 173–186 (2018). https://doi.org/10.20422/jpk.v21i2.523
6. Purnomo, E.P., et al.: How public transportation use social media platform during covid-19: study on jakarta public transportations' Twitter accounts? Webology 18(1), 1–19 (2021). https://doi.org/10.14704/WEB/V18I1/WEB18001
7. Anastasya, R.: Media Sosial Twitter Sebagai Sarana Mengakses Informasi Pelecehan Seksual (Studi Netnografi Thread Korban Pelecehan 'Fetish Kain Bungkus'), Universitas Medan Area (2021)
8. Mcclellan, C., Ali, M.M., Mutter, R., Kroutil, L., Landwehr, J.: Using social media to monitor mental health discussions-evidence from Twitter. J. Am. Med. Inf. Assoc. 24(3), 496–502 (2017). https://doi.org/10.1093/jamia/ocw133
9. Andari, S.: The Suicide Phenomenon in the Gunungkidul Regency. Sosio Konsepsia 7(1), 92–107 (2017)
10. Christine Greenhow, B.R.: Old communication, new literacies : social network sites as social learning resources. J. Comput. Commun. 14, 1130–1161 (2009). https://doi.org/10.1111/j.1083-6101.2009.01484.x
11. Mardiana, H.: Social media and implication for education : casestudy in faculty of technology and science universitas buddhi dharma. Sains Terap. dan Teknol. FST Buddhi Dharma 1(1), 1–12 (2016)

12. Merangin, D.I.D., et al.: Dampak penggunaan Twitter terhadap pembelajaran bahasa inggris (Ditinjau Dari Persepsi Mahasiswa). J. Stud. Lingkung. Assiut **2**(2), 2016 (2018)
13. Apandie, C.: Konstruksi edukasi bagi warga negara muda pada akun media sosial Twitter @asumsico. J. Kewarganegaraan **5**(1), 21–29 (2021). https://doi.org/10.31316/jk.v5i1.1291
14. Zalsman, G., et al.: Suicide prevention strategies revisited: 10-year systematic review. Lancet Psychiatry **3**(7), 646–659 (2016). https://doi.org/10.1016/S2215-0366(16)30030-X
15. M. L, Teori Bunuh Diri, UIN Malang (2014)
16. Supyanti, W., Wahyuni, A.: Pencegahan percobaan bunuh diri pada anak dan remaja dengan gangguan depresi. e-jurnal Med. Udayana**1**(1), 1–10 (2012)
17. Mirjami Pelkonen, M.M.: Suicide in Children and Adolescent. Pelkonen Marttunen **5**(4), pp. 243–263 (2018)
18. Salahudin, S., Nurmandi, A., Loilatu, M.J.: How to design qualitative research with NVivo 12 plus for local government corruption issues in Indonesia? J. Stud. Pemerintah. **11**(3) (2020). https://doi.org/10.18196/jgp.113124

Gender Advocacy, Social Media Campaign to Against Sexual Violence

Sri Suci Nurhayati[(⊠)] and Filosa Gita Sukmono

Department of Communication, Universitas Muhammadiyah Yogyakarta, Yogyakarta, Indonesia
sri.suci.isip19@mail.umy.ac.id, filosa@umy.ac.id

Abstract. This study aims to determine how the use of social media on the Twitter of the National Commission on Violence Against Women in gender advocacy. Based on data from datareportal.com, in 2021, the use of Twitter in Indonesia occupies the fourth position with a percentage of 63.6% of the population of social media users in Indonesia of 170 million users. That means that many Indonesians access Twitter to get information, one of which is about gender advocacy. Based on the National Commission on Violence Against Women report 2021, 338,496 reports gender-based violence against women; this number increased by about 50% from the previous year, which amounted to 26,062 cases. Therefore, Twitter is a place to deliver messages disseminate information and education about gender advocacy in Indonesia. This research method uses Qualitative Data Analysis Software using NVivo. The data source for this research is the official Twitter account @KomnasPerempuan. The data retrieval stage is carried out through N-Capture on tweet and retweet account activities. The findings show that the account has been active for the last three years and the highest percentage was in 2020 during the Covid-19 pandemic. The percentage looks significant from the previous year. Based on the analysis of @KomnasPerempuan's information content regarding gender advocacy, information was found regarding the Ratification of the sexual violence laws. It was also found that there were Twitter tweets regarding gender advocacy in Indonesia with the hashtags #gerakbersama, #sahkanruupks, #jangantundalagi and #kawalsampailegal. The findings show that the Twitter account aims to change policies towards gender equality in Indonesia.

Keywords: Social media · Advocacy · Sexual violence · Gender

1 Introduction

Social media is now an online platform that people use to share content in the form of photos, videos, experiences, and comments. One such online platform is Twitter [1]. With Twitter Information can be shared very quickly and easily, including current issues and news stories. The impact he feels is that the use of Twitter can open up insights and influence people's behavior, one of which is regarding the issue of sexual violence [2]. The rise of the issue of sexual violence in Indonesia has made Twitter one of the strategies to carry out a campaign against sexual violence. Based on the interaction and rapid exchange of information on Twitter, although sometimes conflicting, Twitter

C. Stephanidis et al. (Eds.): HCII 2022, CCIS 1655, pp. 76–82, 2022.
https://doi.org/10.1007/978-3-031-19682-9_11

can also change the structure of gender advocacy to help fight sexual violence. It also helps activists, communities, and organizations working in a similar field, namely gender advocacy that has the same goal [3].

Sexual harassment is a behavior or action such as speech, gesture that is not desired by another party whose direction is sexual which causes one of the parties to feel embarrassed or offended by the behavior. The existence of this definition proves that there are many cases that occur which is also proven by data from KOMNAS Perempuan [4]. Based on the annual record on Gender-Based Violence against Women conducted by the National Commission on Violence against Women (KOMNAS Perempuan) as of March 8, 2022, the dynamics of direct complaints to Komnas Perempuan, service agencies and Badilag were collected as many as 338,496 cases of gender-based violence (KBG) against women with details, complaints to Komnas Perempuan 3,838 cases, service agencies 7,029 cases, and BADILAG 327,629 cases. These figures illustrate a significant 50% increase in KBG for women, namely 338,496 cases in 2021 (from 226,062 cases in 2020). A sharp increase occurred in BADILAG data of 52%, namely 327,629 cases (from 215,694 in 2020) (KOMNAS Perempuan). From the increasing number of cases, KOMNAS Perempuan has taken a way to use social media, one of which is Twitter as a form of disseminating information and education to increase awareness to the public, especially social media users, so that they can jointly help fight against sexual violence as well so that gender advocacy in Indonesia can be done immediately followed up [5].

Sexual violence is a widespread public health problem, with one in five women having experienced or been the victim of rape in their [6]. Sexual violence can happen anywhere, it can be in big cities where the development of technology and culture has advanced or in small towns that still prioritize customs and traditions. Everyone can also be a target of sexual violence, adults and minors. To minimize such cases, it is necessary to have a law that regulates to protect victims from sexual crimes [7]. Indonesia regulates the existence of an article for the protection of every citizen because everyone has the right to obtain legal protection, including in cases of sexual crimes that are rampant today as stated in market 28 D paragraph 1 of the 1945 Constitution which reads "everyone has the right to recognition, guarantees of protection and law, fair certainty and equal treatment before the law" [8]. Not only the law written in the article, other movements to fight against sexual violence have also been carried out, especially by women. For example, in 2017–2019, which was booming on social media, this movement was called #MeToo, a movement on social media that spoke out against sexual harassment, especially in the workplace. This movement was jointly carried out in various countries including the United States with the aim of fighting for the same goal, namely to provide demands for more responsive policy changes in their respective countries. As a result of this movement, many of the victims reported cases related to sexual harassment and crimes that were rampant [9].

For several years, the government has used Twitter as a medium of information and education. The official twitter account @KomnasPerempuan is one of the government organization accounts that is used as a forum for protection from the phenomenon of sexual harassment, sexual violence, and sexual crimes that occur in Indonesia. With a total of 66,541 thousand followers, this @KomnasPerempuan account quotes a lot of links regarding the number of cases of sexual violence in Indonesia every month and year, laws and articles on gender advocacy, education and information for awareness regarding sexual violence issues such as seminars, links and tweets, joint movements., as well as updates on cases of sexual violence that occurred in Indonesia. From this rationalization, it is interesting to do this research on how Komnas Perempuan creates its twitter account pattern in humanitarian action against gender advocacy one of which is sexual violence so that it can be widely known and also gain awareness to the public.

2 Literature Review

The development of technology is currently progressing very rapidly with the influence of technology in various aspects of life. Technological progress is inseparable from the influence of the fast internet. The development of the internet is a factor in facilitating communication access from cellphones to smartphones. The facilities provided by smartphones are various, one of which is social media. Along with the development of society, they began to often use social media in their daily life because of the ease of internet access which facilitates communication and does not know distance or close. [10].Currently the government uses social media as a tool to provide information to the public. One of the social media used is Twitter. Uniquely, Twitter is not only a place of opinion or sharing of information, but it can also be used as a media campaign to uphold justice and fight against sexual violence. The social media campaign on Twitter is one of their main strategies used by organizations that aim to reduce the global problem of gender-based violence [11]. Recent years have seen notable progress on gender and human rights issues in standard setting and to some extent the application of standards through international and domestic law and jurisprudence, and in programming and institutional development. [12]. KOMNAS Perempuan is an independent state institution for upholding the human rights of Indonesian women, KOMNAS Perempuan uses social media twitter with the @KomnasPerempuan account as a medium of information related to cases of sexual violence in Indonesia.

3 Research Method

This study aims to find out how effective the use of social media is in delivering information on the fight against sexual violence that occurs among women in Indonesia using the @KomnasPerempuan twitter account. The research method used in this article is a qualitative approach or also known as Q-DAS (Qualitative Data Analysis Software) to analyze social media data and NvivoPlus12 software to present qualitative descriptive data. This data was taken with the limitation of the year the content was taken from 2019. The source of this research data is the official Twitter account @KomnasPerempuan. The data retrieval stage is carried out through NChapture on tweet and retweet account activities.

4 Result and Discussions

In the era of globalization, the use of social media is an alternative where information and education are delivered to the public. Nowadays, almost everyone has a social media account because it has become a necessity for their life. The government and organizational institutions also take advantage of technological advances with alternatives to convey information to the public, including Komnas Perempuan. The Twitter social media account @KomnasPerempuan has been followed by 66,541 followers. From year to year the @KomnasPerempuan account actively tweets on its twitter in the form of information on the number of cases of sexual violence in Indonesia every month and year, laws and articles on gender advocacy, education and information for awareness regarding sexual violence issues such as seminars, links and tweets, joint movements, as well as updates on cases of sexual violence that occurred in Indonesia. The year 2019 was the lowest year for the activity of using Twitter accounts and in 2020 it was the highest year where in 2020 the COVID-19 pandemic first appeared in Indonesia. During the pandemic, all activities turned to the internet and social media, everyone was also being laid off at that time. As a result, many cases of violence and harassment, especially for women, have increased. The @KomnasPerempuan twitter account provides information on every report that often occurs during the pandemic in 2020 every month as well as education and support for survivors of cases of sexual violence. In 2021 account activity appears to be decreasing, this shows that reports of sexual violence to Komnas Perempuan have effective awareness to the public on issues surrounding gender sexual violence.

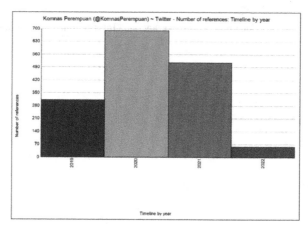

Fig. 1. The activity of using the @KomnasPerempuan Twitter account. (Source: NVivo 12 Plus Software)

The data above is taken from the official account @KomnasPerempuan for the last 3 years. From 2019 to 2020 there was a very significant increase, in that year there were only 320 tweets. The most tweets were in 2020 with a total of 690 tweets, almost double the previous year. However, in 2021 there will be a decrease of only 540 in one year. The twitter activity carried out by Komnas Perempuan is accompanied by hashtags on every content created. The hashtags used are related to indicators of forms of support for justice movers related to gender advocacy, especially for women in Indonesia. These categories relate to education, information, advocacy, and communication.

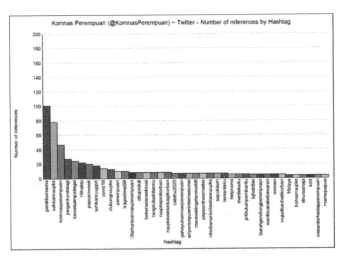

Fig. 2. Twitter Hashtag Activity @KomnasPerempuan. (Source: NVivo 12 Plus software).

Table 1. Hastag sample used by the @KomnasPerempuan account.

Hastag	Category			
	Education	Advocacy	Information	Communication
gerakbersama		✓		
sahkanruupks		✓		
komnasperempuan		✓		
jangantundalagi		✓		
kawalsampailegal		✓		

Komnas Perempuan uses the hashtags #gerakbersama #sahkanruupks #komnasperempuan #jangantundalagi and #kawalsampailegal as the highest percentage of their content. The content is included in the category of gender advocacy regarding sexual violence. The frequency of the hashtag was used as many as 100 tweets about #gerakbersama, 78 tweets about #sahanruupks, then for #komnasperempuan there were 48 tweets, #jangantundalagi there were 23 tweets, and for hastgag #kawalsampailegal there were 20 tweets. The hashtag above confirms that indirectly the use of this hashtag is part of the fight and justice for cases of violence against gender in Indonesia. Komnas Perempuan focuses on how to provide justice and protection against sexual violence in Indonesia through content on social media.

The next analysis uses word frequency, in order to find words that are often used on Twitter accounts. Using the frequency of words makes it easier to conclude the outline of the topic on the Twitter account of the National Commission Against Violence Against Women (Komnas Perempuan).

Fig. 3. Word frequency in the Twitter account @KomnasPerempuan (Source: Nvivi 12 plus).

Based on the word frequency analysis above, it shows that the word violence against women ranks the most frequently used words by the @KomnasPerempuan account. In accordance with the objectives of Komnas Perempuan itself, it is a form of support for anti-violence resistance against women. The word also contains various information, education, advocacy, and communication related to anti-gender violence in Indonesia.

5   Conclusion

The National Commission on Violence against Women (Komnas Perempuan) uses the Twitter social media account @KomnasPerempuan as an advocacy medium for justice enforcement and protection against gender violence in Indonesia. This account is quite active in enforcing advocacy so that justice can be realized in Indonesia. It can be seen from the five hashtags that they are an important category for awareness to the public so that they understand and know more about the issue.

Acknowledgments. This research is supported by the Universitas Muhammadiyah Yogyakarta, Communication Studies Program. The authors would like to thank the review team from The International Conference on Human Interaction & Emerging Technologies.

References

1. Akar, E., Mardikyan, S.: Analyzing factors affecting users ' behavior intention to use social media : Twitter. Int. J. Bus. Soc. Sci. **5**(11), 85–95 (2014)
2. Arciniegas Paspuel, O.G., Álvarez Hernández, S.R., Castro Morales, L.G., Maldonado Gudiño, C.W.: No 主観的健康感を中心とした在宅高齢者における健康関連指標に関する共分散構造分析Title **8**, 6 (2021)

3. Bogen, K.W., Bleiweiss, K.K., Leach, N.R., Orchowski, L.M.: #MeToo: disclosure and response to sexual victimization on twitter. J. Interpers. Violence **36**(17–18), 8257–8288 (2021). https://doi.org/10.1177/0886260519851211

4. Budiman, K., Zaatsiyah, N., Niswah, U., Muhanna, F., Faizi, N.: Analysis of sexual harassment tweet sentiment on twitter in Indonesia using naïve Bayes method through national institute of standard and technology digital forensic acquisition approach. J. Adv. Inf. Syst. Technol. 2(2), 21–30 (2020). https://journal.unnes.ac.id/sju/index.php/jaist

5. Farrior, S.: Human rights advocacy on gender issues: challenges and opportunities. J. Hum. Rights Pract. 1(1), 83–100 (2009). https://doi.org/10.1093/jhuman/hup002

6. Friedman, E. J. (n.d.). The Advocacy Role. Latin American Politics and Society, 90

7. Fulper, R., et al.: Misogynistic language on twitter and sexual violence. Proc. ACM Web Sci. Workshop on Comput. Approaches Soc. Model. (ChASM) **2014**, 6–9 (2015)

8. Handayani, T. A., Prasetyo, T., Rahmat, D.: Legal protection of women victims of sexual harassment in Indonesia. UNIFIKASI : Jurnal Ilmu Hukum, 6(2), 209 (2019). https://doi.org/10.25134/unifikasi.v6i2.1939

9. Huda, M.A.: Sexual Harassment in Indonesia: Problems and Challenges in Legal Protection **7**(3), 303–314 (2021)

10. Kareem, O. L., Akoja, M. I.: Social media and advocacy communication research: trends and implications. Babcock J. Mass Commun., 37–52 (2019)

11. Narida, M. G., Siahaan, C., Sinaga, Y. A., Iswari, L. N., Sihotang, T.: Penyuluhan tentang pencegahan pelecehan seksual dalam media sosial kepada siswa-siswi SMA di Jakarta dan Depok. Jurnal Abdi Masyarakat Indonesia, 2(1), 311–320 (2022). https://doi.org/10.54082/jamsi.187

Utilization of Social Media in Handling and Preventing Violence Against Women and Children Case Study: Indonesia

Ditha Aditya Pernikasari[✉] and Filosa Gita Sukmono

Department of Communication, Universitas Muhammadiyah Yogyakarta, Yogyakarta, Indonesia
dita9729@gmail.com

Abstract. This study aims to determine the Indonesian government's communication strategy in preventing acts violence against women and children. Social media is an important part of providing education through communication of preventive measures and assistance. This study uses QDAS (Qualitative Data Analysis Software) approach using the data source of the Twitter @kpp_pa (KPPA) social media account. The Ministry of Women's Empowerment and Child Protection is an Indonesian government agency that has the authority to handle the empowerment and protection of women and children. Data analysis of this research uses software retrieve data, collect data, and analyze it with a focus on content analysis in communication strategies. The results of the study show social media is part of the Indonesian government's strategy in preventing violence against women and children. KPPA's social media activities in producing information aim to provide education and understanding regarding the protection of women and children. KPPA's communication strategy is carried out through the use of hashtags in each content grouped based on different content related to education and information. The results of the word cloud analysis show that the information conveyed can be distinguished based on the content that educates, informs, entertains, and influences. In addition, the use of these hashtags can be distinguished based on target assisting women or children. Delivery of information on educational messages to women through the use of #Empowered Women, #Advanced Indonesian Women, and #RememberMessenger Ibu. Information.analysis Word frequency show that KPPA in carrying out approach to preventing violence and protecting women, the focus is on communication focused on education and fighting for women's rights. Content to overcome child violence using #AnakTerlindung, #Stop Child Marriage, #AnakTerlindungiIndonesiaMaju. Overall, hashtag communication strategy is an important part in creating a movement to protect children's safety and security, in addition to campaign activities not to marry underage.

Keywords: Communication · Social Media · Prevention · Women · Children

1 Introduction

The phenomenon of violence against women and children is a form of violation of human rights [12]. According to WHO, 30% of women worldwide have been estimated to have

C. Stephanidis et al. (Eds.): HCII 2022, CCIS 1655, pp. 83–88, 2022.
https://doi.org/10.1007/978-3-031-19682-9_12

experienced sexual violence in their lives, both physical and sexual violence [3]. Violence against women can be identified as a result of social structures and ideologies of gender domination [11]. The number of violence against women in 2019 according to Komnas Perempuan was 431,471 [10]. According to Maria Advianti as Deputy Chair of the Child Protection Commission (KPAI), violence against children can occur in the family environment, school environment, and community environment [7]. On the other hand, the causes of violence against children are often found in the family environment. The basis of this treatment is the impact of parental disappointment, so the child becomes one of the targets [2]. Therefore, a preventive action is needed to anticipate cases of violence against women and children.

Anticipation of violence against children and women can be done through many things, one of which is social media. Social media is a platform used to provide information, make it easier for someone to interact, as a means of business, as education [1]. Social media is considered to have an important role in preventing acts of violence against women and children. Quoted from (Jelita and Raya 2021) said that on Instagram accounts there are many institutions that provide educational information about preventing violence against women and children. Apart from Instagram, Twitter is also an account that can handle acts of violence against women and children. Like the Twitter account @kpp_pa (KPPA) which was created specifically with the aim of providing education and understanding about the protection of women and children. The communication strategy contained in the @kppa (KPPA) account is carried out through hastags that are distinguished in each content.

Research on the use of Twitter-based social media in handling and preventing violence against women and children with case studies in Indonesia has not been found. Previous research conducted by Diah Agustina; Ayu Riana Sari; Nita Pujianti; Erma Rahmaniah; Nor Azizah aims to analyze the increase in promotions on Instagram-based social media as well as reporting cases of violence against women and children. Then the research conducted by Rezky Hizriani aims to determine the communication planning of the women and children empowerment office in disseminating programs regarding the prevention of violence against women and children in the city of Pekanbaru. The next research conducted by Murat Meru; Seda Mengu discusses assessing media coverage of news where social media and violence occur simultaneously.

2   Overview of Literature

Social media is an online medium where users can easily participate, share and create content including blogs, social networks, wikis, forums and virtual worlds. According to Puntoadi (2011: 5) social media provides an opportunity for closer interaction with consumers. Social media offers more individualized communication content. Through social media, various marketers can find out the habits of their consumers and carry out a personal interaction and can build a deeper interest. The characteristics of social media according to [8] in Nasrullah include networks, information,archives, interactions (interactivity.

One of the social media used as education is twitter. Quoted from (Simbolon 2021). Twitter is social media with the symbol of a bird with a blue color that has various features such as likes, retweets, and comments. Therefore, a communication strategy is very necessary in managing the content of social media. As said by Wilbur Schramm, the requirements for formulating a communication strategy in order to create messages-Masrifah Cahyani 2020) It is known that in 2021 twitter social media users will increase to 63% to put twitter into the 5th rank as the most frequently accessed social media [9], besides being used by teenagers, Twitter is also cannot be used by Public Relations or Public Relations to convey an Instasi message to the public. Because the most important key in a government-community relationship is information and communication [6].

3 Method

This study discusses the Indonesian government's communication strategy by utilizing social media based on the @kppa (KPPA) twitter account in preventing acts of violence against women and children. The method used in this research is the QDAS (Qualitative Data Analysis Software) approach, then the content analysis is processed using the N-Vivo 13 Plus application.

4 Results and Discussions

Technology has been integrated into social life, the changing times are increasingly advanced and developing. The internet and social media have become a necessity in social life. With social media, it is easier for people to communicate remotely, access news both domestically and abroad and exchange information from various platforms. Through social media, people can find the desired information quickly and easily, the scope of access is also very wide. Users can find information about fashion, the latest news, to the world of entertainment, almost all groups from children to adults feel the impact of modernization who have now turned into social media users. Like the Ministry of Women's Empowerment and Child Protection (KPPA) using social media through the Twitter account @kpp_pa (KPPA as a means of information to prevent acts of violence against women and children. The use of the Twitter social media account @kpp_pa (KPPA) can be seen below:

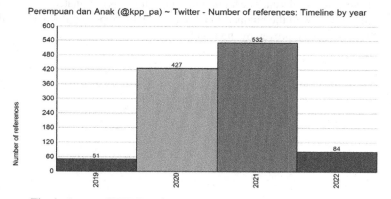

Fig. 1. Image of KPPA's twitter account activity trends for 2019–2022

The Twitter account @kppa pa (KPPA) has 158.9 thousand followers, and follows 242. The account has been actively used since 2019, then from the initial identification results, it shows that the twitter account @kppa_pa (KPPA) always provides education regularly although there is a decline in each year. The Commission for the Protection of Women and Children (KPPA) actively uses Twitter in 2021 with a figure of 532, and the lowest data occurred in 2019 with a number of 51. In addition, the communication strategy carried out by the Commission for the Protection of Women and Children (KPPA) in preventing acts of violence violence against women and children through his twitter account which contains information, education can be seen from the hashtags used.

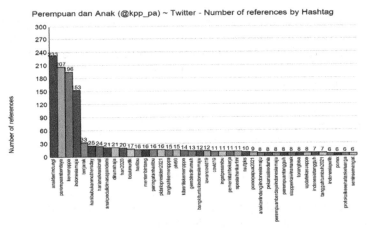

Fig. 2. Image of strategy for using hashtags in preventing violence against women and children

Hashtags are a very important feature in social media. Because of the benefits of hashtags to categorize various types of posts. Like the Twitter account @kpp_ppa (KPPA) using hashtags as an effort to prevent acts of violence against women and children. The information conveyed in the content includes content that educates, informs, entertains, and influences. In addition, the use of these hashtags can be classified based on the target of assisting women or children. The highest hashtag subject is dominated by the hashtag of protected children with the number 233, the hashtag of empowered women with the number 207. This can be proven by the data below:

Table 1. Hastga content in actions to prevent violence against women and children (Source: Author, 2022)

Subjects	Hashtag	%	Content
of Women	#Empowered	207	Motivations
	#Forward Indonesian Women	8	Motivations
	#RememberPesanIbu	11	Motivations
Children's	#AnakTerlindungi	233	Preventive
	#Stop Child Marriage	8	Education
	#AnakTerlindungiIndonesiaMaju	8	Preventive

The results of the analysis show that the use of hashtags has a specific purpose. The results of the analysis are grouped by subject. In the use of hashtags, female subjects have the highest percentage of empowered women with content to influence related to women's motivation. In the subject of the highest hashtag, it is shown in the percentage with a figure of 49% on preventive measures.

Content	Purpose
Motivational	Content on the Twitter account @kppa_ppa (KPPA) aims to build gender equality, so that women can participate in development
Preventive	The preventive content on the @kppa_pa (KPPA) twitter account aims to provide an understanding that children must have their rights such as protection from violence, the right to live, grow, develop, and not receive discriminatory treatment according to the article regulated by Law no. 35 of 2014
Education educational	Content on the Twitter account @kppa_pa (KPPA) aims to prevent early marriage

5   Conclusion

The phenomenon of violence from year to year is increasing. There are many ways to prevent cases of violence against women and children, one of them is by using social media. Twitter account @kpp-pa (KPPA) is an account created specifically to provide the purpose of providing education and understanding about the protection of women and children. The communication strategy carried out on the account is through hashtags. The Twitter account @kpp_ppa (KPPA) every post conveys content that contains information, education, prevention, and entertainment. Then the use of hashtags on the Twitter account @kpp_ppa (KPPA) is distinguished based on the target of assisting women or children. To convey information, educational messages for women can be seen from the use of hashtags #Women Empowerment, #Women Indonesia Maju, and #RememberMessenger Mother, while to protect violence against children it can be conveyed through the use of hashtags #AnakTerlindung, #Stop Child Marriage, #Anak-TerlindungiIndonesiaMaju.

References

1. Amedie, J.: The Impact of Social Media on Society Pop Culture Intersections (2015)
2. Andhini, Dina, A.S., Arifin, R.: Analisis perlindungan hukum terhadap tindak kekerasan pada anak di Indonesia. Ajudikasi: Jurnal Ilmu Hukum 3(1), 41 (2019). https://doi.org/10.30656/ajudikasi.v3i1.992
3. Ellsberg, M., et al.: Prevention of violence against women and girls: what does the evidence say? Lancet 385(9977), 1555–1566 (2015). https://doi.org/10.1016/S0140-6736(14)61703-7
4. Helena, J.: Universitas Palangka Raya. PROSIDING-SEMNAS-PSKM-FK-ULM 2nd (2021)
5. Cahyani, M., Adelia.: Strategi komunikasi humas pemerintah kota surabaya dalam melayani dan menggali potensi masyarakat melalui media sosial. J. Ilmu Komunikasi 10(1), 1–16 (2020). https://doi.org/10.15642/jik.2020.10.1.1-16
6. Permatasari, I.A., Nurmandi, A., Wijaya, J.H.: Kualitas informasi publik dalam twitter: perbandingan pemerintah daerah di yogyakarta dan dki jakarta the quality of public information on twitter: di yogyakarta and dki jakarta regional government comparison. Jurnal Penelitian Komunikasi 24(1), 75–90 (2021). https://doi.org/10.20422/jpk.v24i1.722
7. Praditama, S., Nurhadi., Budiarti, AC.: Kekerasan terhadap anak dalam keluarga dalam perspektif fakta sosial. J. Ilmiah Pend. Sos. Ant 5(2), 1–18 (2015)
8. Setiadi, A.: Pemanfaatan media sosial untuk efektifitas komunikasi. J. Ilmiah Matrik 16(1) (2014)
9. Simbolon, C.A.D.: Penggunaan komunikasi media sosial twitter di kalangan remaja di kecamatan cibinong, kabupaten bogor. JISIP: J. Ilmu Sosial Dan Ilmu Politik 10(3):219–26 (2021)
10. Soleman, N.: Kekerasan berbasis gender online selama pandemi COVID-19 Di Indonesia. J. Kajian Perempuan, Gender Dan Agama 15(1), 49–60 (2021)
11. Solórzano, Navarrete, D.A., Gamez, M.R., Pérez de Corcho, OJ.: Gender violence on pandemic of COVID-19. Int. J. Health Sci. 4(2), 10–18 (2020). https://doi.org/10.29332/ijhs.v4n2.437
12. Suryamizon, Lestari, A.: Perlindungan hukum preventif terhadap kekerasan perempuan dan anak dalam perspektif hukum hak asasi manusia. Marwah: J. Perempuan, Agama Dan Jender 16(2):112 (2017). https://doi.org/10.24014/marwah.v16i2.4135

Investigating Information Cocoon Attitudes in Short-Form Video Applications

Shanjiao Ren, Lili Liu[✉], Suting Yang, and Jiujiu Jiang

College of Economics and Management, Nanjing University of Aeronautics and Astronautics, Nanjing, China

{joy9971,lili85,yst1122}@nuaa.edu.cn, j.tanya@foxmail.com

Abstract. The explosive development of short-form video applications (SVAs) and online recommendation services bring us enjoyable experience in accessing abundant information, and simultaneously create information cocoon. Limited research has paid attention to this phenomenon. To fill the gap, drawing on Dual-factor Theory, this study systematically investigates the enablers and inhibitors in conjunction to measure user attitudes toward information cocoon (both positive and negative attitudes: information cocoon attitude and information cocoon breakthrough attitude, respectively), as well as users' continuance usage intention resulting from information cocoon attitudes. Data was collected from 142 respondents via an online survey, then analyzed with Smart PLS 3.3. Findings reveal that enablers (preference stability and subjective norm) positively affect information cocoon attitude, while the inhibitors (perceived heterogeneity and alternative attractiveness) positively affect information cocoon breakthrough attitude. Furthermore, information cocoon attitude positively affects continuance usage intention. Theoretical and practical implications are discussed.

Keywords: Information cocoon · Short-from video applications · Dual-factor theory

1 Introduction

The explosive development of short-form video applications (SVAs) and online recommendation services bring us enjoyable experience in accessing abundant information, and simultaneously create information cocoon (IC) [29]. IC is first proposed by the Harvard scholar Cass R. Sunstein, indicates a phenomenon that the internet constructs a "communications universe in which we hear only what we choose and only what comfort us" [29]. Under such circumstances, users are exploring the world from a single perspective. That is, instead of being better informed and exposed to ever-broadening viewpoints, research shows that online users are unconsciously more polarized and draw from shrinking pools of information. There is growing research interest in the consequences of IC. For instance, high IC been widely demonstrated to be the best indicator of increased distorted perceptions of public opinion [22] and even the ideological fragmentation of society [25, 30]. On the contrary, IC may improve users' online experience

C. Stephanidis et al. (Eds.): HCII 2022, CCIS 1655, pp. 89–96, 2022.
https://doi.org/10.1007/978-3-031-19682-9_13

by reducing the diversity of information so that users enter the "safe zone". In particular, as a social software for information exchange, SVAs attach great importance to user experience.

SVAs enable users to generate or watch videos that last several seconds to a few minutes [33], including music, talent show, daily life and many other types. After the rapid development in recent years, SVAs are coming to dominate China's social media use. According to China Internet Network Information Center report, the number of SVAs users in China has reached 934 million by the end of December 2021, accounting for 90.5% of the total Internet users [8]. While TikTok has taken the west by storm, its Chinese counterpart Douyin faces a range of rivals (e.g., Kuaishou, the biggest rival of Douyin in China), each vying to take a chunk out of its domestic dominance, indicating ever fiercer competition among SVAs. SVAs are competing for Chinese netizens' leisure hours – a resource that is ultimately finite. Hence, maximizing the retention of existing users and attracting new users become crucial for the sustainable development of SVAs. The fascinating content, personalized recommendation, and immersive experiences afforded by SVAs may tempt users to fall into the "information cocoon" and consume short-form videos excessively [15, 21, 37]. Cass R. Sunstein's description of IC discloses the phenomenon that Internet technology limits the information a netizen may access to some extent [29]. However, users' perception and attitude towards IC changes with the passage of time and the shift of interest [36]. For instance, individuals who feel the presence of IC, may attempt to break through the IC in order to avoid its negative impacts.

Yet to our current knowledge, relatively few studies thoroughly investigate the potential positive consequences of IC (e.g., consumers' continuance usage intention). Furthermore, the attitude of IC can be either positive (IC attitude) or negative (IC breakthrough attitude) [23] and is driven by distinct motives that influence consumer behavior differently. Thirdly, no prior study has separately examined the enablers and inhibitors of IC attitude and IC breakthrough attitude and their association with consumer intentions in the context of SVAs. Therefore, it is necessary to understand the link between the antecedents of IC (which have long been a subject of study for consumer research) and its behavioral consequences.

Drawing on Dual Factor Theory (DFT) [6, 7], we develop a model to link explicitly the antecedents and consequences of IC in the context of short-form video applications. In particular, we aim to bridge these gaps by examining whether and how inhibitors and enablers of SVAs use are associated with IC attitude, and IC breakthrough attitude and how IC attitude and IC breakthrough attitude may, in turn, be associated with continuance usage intention.

2   Theoretical Background

The Dual Factor Theory (DFT) states that enablers and inhibitors are the two distinct sets of antecedents that determining technology usage [6, 7]. Enablers (inhibitors) are the factors encouraging (discouraging) the adoption of a product or service [22]. Enablers and inhibitors co-exist in users' perceptions, resulting in simultaneous product or service evaluations from both negative and positive viewpoints, which are "related in nature but opposite in valance" [7].

DFT is a well-accepted theory and has been applied in various contexts, including social media platforms [28] and non-adoption of technological innovations [35]. Talwar extends DFT by systematically investigating the enablers and inhibitors in conjunction to measure consumer behavior toward mobile wallets, and proves that the antecedents of positive word of mouth are different from those of negative word of mouth [31]. In the present study, we utilize the theoretical lens of DFT to examine the influence of enablers and inhibitors on IC attitude and IC breakthrough attitude toward SVAs, as well as the association of IC attitude and IC breakthrough attitude and continuance usage intention.

3   Research Models and Hypotheses

The research model is illustrated in Fig. 1. Corresponding hypotheses are discussed as followings.

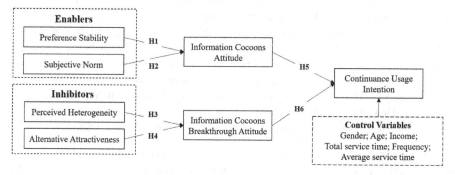

Fig. 1. Research model

Preference stability refers to the choice consistency among options with different attribute values in the same product category [2, 11, 27]. Research suggest that a consumer's subjectively held belief of preference stability may be an important determinant of response to personalized recommendations [26]. For instance, the intensity of information processing is directly related to the need for information, expectancy (i.e., the cognitive association between information processing and the expected goal attainment), and value of the information [5, 34]. Users with high preference stability tend to be consistent in choosing the type of videos recommended by SVAs, may have a stronger need for and expect more benefit from customized recommendations and, therefore, are more likely to be in IC created by personalized recommendation. Consequently, we propose:

H1. Preference stability positively affects IC attitude.

Subjective norm is defined as "the influence of the thoughts of a person who is more important to him on his cognition" [1]. In other words, individuals will pay more attention to their own life or the opinions of people in their social circle, and these opinions will also affect users' attitude toward certain behavior. SVAs as a mobile social media that can make, upload and watch short-from videos, the social attribute is very obvious. Users will involve in the original social circle or formatnew social circles brought about by the network, then will most likely be socially influenced and thus have an impact on t IC attitude. Hence, we hypothesize:

H2. Subjective norm positively affects IC attitude.

Communication on social media tends to be more interactive compared to that on traditional media platforms [9]. People are able to express their own ideas and share their opinions freely and also come across with new and unique pieces of various information frequently via these platforms [20]. Users may encounter opinions contradicting with their own viewpoint, which is defined as perceived heterogeneity in the literature [16]. When the information of different opinions is helpful for future decision-making, users are happy to take advantage of information inconsistent with their own views [10]. Hence, we propose:

H3. Perceived heterogeneity positively affects IC breakthrough attitude.

Alternative attractiveness refers to customers' perceptions regarding the extent to which viable competing alternatives are available in the marketplace' [17]. When an alternative company provides high-quality customer service, consumers may leave their incumbent service provider and switch to it [3, 18, 19]. The same principle is applicable to SVAs, users expect that its information quality can fulfill their needs for socializing and enjoyment [12–14, 32]. When users believe other alternatives can provide more diverse information they are looking for, which cannot be satisfied by current information provider, they will have a strong desire to break through IC and switch to the alternative platforms. Thus, we assume:

H4. Alternative attractiveness positively affects IC breakthrough attitude.

The financial sustainability of any company depends on repeat business [24]. Accordingly, we believe that continuance usage intention is important considerations for SVAs. Attitude has been validated in TAM based studies as an important predictor of intention concerning IS use [4]. Attitude reflects users' subjective psychological status such as like, hate, support or opposition on a particular behavior or event [1]. Attitude towards IC has been divided as positive attitude (IC attitude – to what extent users prefer or accept the recommended information) and negative attitude (IC breakthrough attitude - willingness to break through information limitations, such as avoid drawing from recommended and shrinking pools of information) [23]. Under different context or for different research objects, the influencing intensity of attitude to continuance intention can be different [37]. Therefore, we hypothesize:

H5. IC attitude positively affects users' continuance usage intention.

H6. IC breakthrough attitude negatively affects users' continuance usage intention.

4 Data Collection and Analysis

4.1 Data Collection

We conducted an online survey on Sojump (www.sojump.com) to collect data, then test the proposed research model empirically. All the measurement items were adapted from existing literature and modified to reflect the context of SVAs. Seven-point Likert scale ranging from 1 (strongly disagree) to 7 (strongly agree) were used to measure the items. The target group comprised anybody who has used SVAs. Finally, 142 valid responses were received. Table 1 lists the demographic information of the respondents. To summarize, 42.25% of them were male and 57.75% were female, with ages ranging from 18 to 50.

Table 1. Respondent demographics

Item	Category	Frequency	Ratio (%)
Gender	Male	60	42.25
	Female	82	57.75
Age	<18	1	0.70
	18–25	104	73.24
	26–30	9	6.34
	31–40	18	12.68
	41–50	5	3.52
	>50	5	3.52
Monthly income (CNY)	≤2000	67	47.18
	2001–5000	31	21.83
	5001–8000	15	10.57
	>8000	29	20.42

4.2 Data Analysis

We tested the measurement model and structural model respectively, using Smart PLS 3.3.3. First, we examined the measurement model to assess reliability and validity. For items evaluating each construct, the Cronbach's α values were all above 0.70, the composite reliability (CR) values all exceeded 0.76, and the average variance extracted (AVE) values were all greater than 0.5, all the indicator loadings are above 0.7, suggesting sufficient reliability and validity.

Results of the structural model were shown in Fig. 2, in which the impacts of preference stability on IC attitude ($\beta = 0.413$, $p < 0.001$), subjective norm on IC attitude ($\beta = 0.231$, $p < 0.05$), perceived heterogeneity on IC breakthrough attitude ($\beta = 0.186$, $p < 0.05$), alternative attractiveness on IC breakthrough attitude ($\beta = 0.389$, $p < 0.001$), IC attitude on continuance usage intention ($\beta = 0.658$, $p < 0.001$) were significant. However, ICs breakthrough attitude had no significant impact on continuance usage intention. Hence, H1, H2, H3, H4, and H5 were supported. Besides, among the control variables, usage frequency significantly influenced continuance usage intention ($\beta = 0.268$, $p < 0.001$). Preference stability and subjective norm jointly explained 31.0% variance of IC attitude, perceived heterogeneity and alternative attractiveness jointly explained 22.4%

variance of IC breakthrough attitude, which in turn jointly explained 43.8% variance of continuance usage intention.

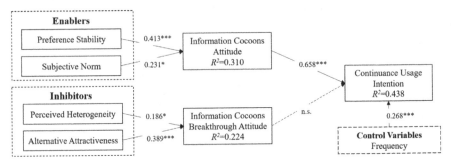

Fig. 2. Structural model

5 Conclusions

We examined user behavior in SVAs by adopting DFT to unite the enablers and inhibitors as antecedents of IC attitude and IC breakthrough attitude. Findings reveal that enablers are positively associated with IC attitude. In comparison, inhibitors are positively associated with IC breakthrough attitude. Furthermore, only IC attitude significantly influence the continued intention to use.

This study has important implications for academics and practitioners. Theoretically, we make three key contributions: (1) in light of the dual-factor theory, identify the enablers and inhibitors of IC in the context of SVAs; (2) verify the impacts of enablers and inhibitors on IC attitude and breakthrough attitude respectively, thus extends existing studies on IC; (3) apply the studies of IC to explain users' continuance intention, which provides solid theoretical basis for investigating the impact of IC on the sustainability of SVAs. Practically, this study provides detailed insight for SVAs developers, that is, how they could effectively encourage users' continuance usage to maintain the sustainable development of SVAs. First, SVAs developers can leverage enablers to get users' IC attitude, and then improve users' continuance intention. Second, the inhibitors (perceived heterogeneity and alternative attractiveness) cause existing users to breakthrough IC. Consequently, SVAs developers should provide diverse information to discourage users from generating negative attitude (i.e., IC breakthrough attitude).

Our study is exploratory in nature, being the first to propose the antecedents and consequences of IC in the context of SVAs. Due to this, the insights offered by the study may be limited. In the future, researchers can expand the list of considered enablers and inhibitors to enrich our findings.

Acknowledgment. This study was supported by the Fundamental Research Funds for the Central Universities No. NR2021003 awarded to the second author.

References

1. Ajzen, I.: The theory of planned behavior. Organ. Behav. Hum. Decis. Process. **50**, 179–211 (1991)
2. Amir, O., Levav, J.: Choice construction versus preference construction: The instability of preferences learned in context. J. Mark. Res. **45**(2), 145–158 (2008)
3. Bansal, H. S., Taylor, S. F., St. James, Y.: Migrating to new service providers: toward a unifying framework of consumers' switching behaviors. J. Acad. Market. Sci. 33(1), 96–115 (2005)
4. Bhattacherjee, A.: Understanding information systems continuance: an expectation-confirmation model. MIS Q., 351–370 (2001)
5. Burnkrant, R.E.: A motivational model of information processing intensity. J. Consum. Res. **3**(1), 21–30 (1976)
6. Cenfetelli, R.T., Schwarz, A.: Identifying and testing the inhibitors of technology usage intentions. Inf. Syst. Res. **22**(4), 808–823 (2011)
7. Cenfetelli, R.T.: Inhibitors and enablers as dual factor concepts in technology usage. J. Assoc. Inf. Syst. **5**(11), 16 (2004)
8. China Internet Network Information Center, http://www.cnnic.net.cn/hlwfzyj/hlwxzbg/hlw tjbg/202109/P020210915523670981527.pdf. Accessed 15 Sep 2021
9. Eveland, W.P.: A"mix of attributes" approach to the study of media effects and new communication technologies. J. Commun. **53**(3), 395–410 (2003)
10. Festinger, L.: A theory of cognitive dissonance, 2nd edn. Stanford University Press, Location (1957)
11. Hoeffler, S., Ariely, D.: Constructing stable preferences: a look into dimensions of experience and their impact on preference stability. J. Consum. Psychol. **8**(2), 113–139 (1999)
12. Hou, A.C., Shiau, W.L.: Understanding facebook to Instagram migration: a push-pull migration model perspective. Inf. Technol. People 33(1), 272–295 (2020)
13. Hsiao, C.H., Chang, J.J., Tang, K.Y.: Exploring the influential factors in continuance usage of mobile social apps: satisfaction, habit, and customer value perspectives. Telematics Inform. **33**(2), 342–355 (2016)
14. Hsieh, J.K., Hsieh, Y.C., Chiu, H.C., Feng, Y.C.: Post-adoption switching behavior for online service substitutes: a perspective of the push–pull–mooring framework. Comput. Hum. Behav. **28**(5), 1912–1920 (2012)
15. Huang, Q., Hu, M., Chen, H.: Exploring stress and problematic use of short-form video applications among middle-aged Chinese adults: the mediating roles of duration of use and flow experience. Int. J. Environ. Res. Public Health **19**(1), 132 (2022)
16. Jeong, M., Zo, H., Lee, C.H., Ceran, Y.: Feeling displeasure from online social media postings: a study using cognitive dissonance theory. Comput. Hum. Behav. **97**, 231–240 (2019)
17. Jones, M.A., Mothersbaugh, D.L., Beatty, S.E.: Switching barriers and repurchase intentions in services. J. Retail. **76**(2), 259–274 (2000)
18. Jung, J., Han, H., Oh, M.: Travelers' switching behavior in the airline industry from the perspective of the push-pull-mooring framework. Tour. Manage. **59**, 139–153 (2017)
19. Keaveney, S.M.: Customer switching behavior in service industries: an exploratory study. J. Mark. **59**(2), 71–82 (1995)
20. Kumar, N.: Facebook for self-empowerment? A study of facebook adoption in urban India. New Media Soc. **16**(7), 1122–1137 (2014)
21. Mou, X., Xu, F., Du, J.T.: Examining the factors influencing college students' continuance intention to use short-form video APP. Aslib J. Inf. Manag. **73**(6), 992–1013 (2021)
22. Neubaum, G., Krämer, N.C.: Monitoring the opinion of the crowd: psychological mechanisms underlying public opinion perceptions on social media. Media Psychol. **20**(3), 502–531 (2017)

23. Peng, H., Liu, C.: Breaking the information cocoon: when do people actively seek conflicting information? Proc. Assoc. Inf. Sci. Technol. **58**(1), 801–803 (2021)
24. Rather, R.A.: Investigating the impact of customer brand identification on hospitality brand loyalty: a social identity perspective. J. Hosp. Market. Manag. **27**(5), 487–513 (2018)
25. Röchert, D., Weitzel, M., Ross, B.: The homogeneity of right-wing populist and radical content in YouTube recommendations. In: International Conference on Social Media and Society, pp. 245–254, Location (2020)
26. Shen, A., Ball, A.D.: Preference stability belief as a determinant of response to personalized recommendations. J. Consum. Behav. **10**(2), 71–79 (2011)
27. Simonson, I.: Determinants of customers' responses to customized offers: conceptual framework and research propositions. J. Mark. **69**(1), 32–45 (2005)
28. Sullivan, Y.W., Koh, C.E.: Social media enablers and inhibitors: understanding their relationships in a social networking site context. Int. J. Inf. Manage. **49**, 170–189 (2019)
29. Sunstein, C.R.: Infotopia: How Many Minds Produce Knowledge. Oxford University Press, Location (2006)
30. Sunstein, C. R.: A prison of our own design: divided democracy in the age of social media. Democratic Audit UK, Location (2017)
31. Talwar, M., Talwar, S., Kaur, P., Islam, A.N., Dhir, A.: Positive and negative word of mouth (WOM) are not necessarily opposites: a reappraisal using the dual factor theory. J. Retail. Consum. Serv. **63**, 102396 (2021)
32. Wang, J.L., Jackson, L.A., Gaskin, J., Wang, H.Z.: The effects of social networking site (SNS) use on college students' friendship and well-being. Comput. Hum. Behav. **37**, 229–236 (2014)
33. Wang, X., Zhao, S., Zhang, M.X., Chen, F., Chang, L.: Life history strategies and problematic use of short-form video applications. Evol. Psychol. Sci. **7**(1), 39–44 (2020). https://doi.org/10.1007/s40806-020-00255-9
34. Wilton, P.C., Myers, J.G.: Task, expectancy, and information assessment effects in information utilization processes. J. Consum. Res. **12**(4), 469–486 (1986)
35. Wolverton, C.C., Cenfetelli, R.: An exploration of the drivers of non-adoption behavior: a discriminant analysis approach. ACM SIGMIS Database: DATABASE Adv. Inf. Syst. **50**(3), 38–65 (2019)
36. Zhang, H.: Research on the formation mechanism and influencing factors of internet users' information cocoon. J. Intell. **40**(10), 166–170 (2021)
37. Zhang, M., Tang, G., Zhang, Y.: Factors influencing mobile search engine users' continuance behavior under the context of service harm crisis event. Int. J. Mobile Hum. Comput. Inter. (IJMHCI) **10**(3), 30–48 (2018)
38. Zhang, X., Wu, Y., Liu, S.: Exploring short-form video application addiction: socio-technical and attachment perspectives. Telematics Inform. **42**, 101243 (2019)

Governing for Free: Rule Process Effects on Reddit Moderator Motivations

Hannah M. Wang[1(✉)], Beril Bulat[1], Stephen Fujimoto[1], and Seth Frey[1,2]

[1] University of California, Davis, Davis, CA 95616, USA
{hawang,bbulat,ssfujimoto,sethfrey}@ucdavis.edu
[2] Ostrom Workshop, Indiana University, Bloomington, IN 47408, USA

Abstract. Developing a strong community requires empowered leadership capable of overcoming governance challenges. New online platforms have given users opportunities to practice governance through content moderation roles. The over 2.8 million "subreddit" communities on Reddit are governed by hundreds of thousands of volunteer moderators, many of whom have no training or prior experience in a governing role. While moderators often devote daily time to community maintenance and cope with the emotional effects of hate comments or disturbing content, Reddit provides no compensation for this position. Thus, moderators' internal motivations and desire to continue filling this role is critical for their community. Drawing upon the relationship between governance procedures and internalized motivation, we investigate how the processes through which subreddit moderators generate community rules increase moderators' motivation through the meeting of social-psychological needs: Procedural Justice and Self Determination, and Self-Other Merging. Preliminary analysis of survey data from 620 moderators across Reddit shows a correlation between moderators' administrative behaviors and the social-psychological needs underpinning their motivations. Understanding these relationships will allow us to empower moderators to build engaging and cooperative online communities.

Keywords: Reddit · Self-governance · Moderation · Online communities · Leadership

1 Introduction

What do volunteer moderators of online communities get out of moderating, and what does it mean for peer production and online collective action? Platforms such as Reddit have captured the attention of HCI scholars interested in applying frameworks of self-governance and cooperative resource management to a multitude of communities run by amateurs. The over 2 million "subreddit" communities aggregated on Reddit.com are each independently managed by a team of volunteer moderators, who are responsible for the creation of community rules and the sanctioning of members who break those rules. While past scholarship has centered around the development of these communities across time, and the relationship between governance and community maturity [10], the

C. Stephanidis et al. (Eds.): HCII 2022, CCIS 1655, pp. 97–105, 2022.
https://doi.org/10.1007/978-3-031-19682-9_14

motivations of moderators to continue developing successful communities are relatively under-researched.

Due to the lack of formal compensation provided to moderators by Reddit, Inc., we propose that internal motivating factors—the satisfaction of social-psychological needs—promote moderators' continual commitment to their community. Our key finding was that the level of hierarchical versus participatory governance in a community is associated with different levels of need fulfillment. More hierarchical structures preserve moderators' sense of Procedural Justice and Self Determination, the belief that the community is run fairly and grants members independence. On the other hand, more participatory structures are associated with higher levels of Self-Other Merging, or the extent to which moderators perceive a cohesive community identity. Understanding the importance of these needs, as well as how governance structures help fulfill them, will allow us to design systems that empower and motivate moderators.

2   Literature Review

There are a variety of communities online where a group of people connect around a shared purpose and interact with each other by following established norms, rules, and protocols [8, 9, 18]. Online communities present an example of information commons, as they provide collective goods such as social network capital and knowledge capital [19] and distribute digital resources such as information and creative content that are produced collectively [11]. An information common can be described as a "highly accessible, self-rising information system in which stakeholders share an overarching goal" [16]. Online communities, being self-rising, rely on voluntary efforts and continuous provision of resources, and require sustainability to realize the community's shared goal. This reliance, however, also brings forward a dilemma, where increased participation in a community can both facilitate and hinder user attention, a scarce resource for online communities, when the increased activity also includes unwanted user behaviors [12, 20]. Thus, effective governance is critically essential to any online community's success and endurance.

Online communities are self-governing social systems where the responsibility of the governing mechanism often lies with community moderators who monitor and regulate behaviors through formal rules and policies. Moderators voluntarily carry the burden of drafting, implementing, and updating community rules as needed, usually with little to no training [2]. Individuals tasked with community moderation not only invest time and energy but also emotional labor in upholding community values against potential aggressors that violate community norms [5]. Despite the significance of their roles in facilitating cooperation and engagement in online communities, very little is known about the motivations that drive moderators to fulfill their voluntary roles in the first place. Previous work on online community moderators have considered how formal leadership and community characteristics affect individuals' leadership efforts [1], how they engage with and develop their communities [21], how they foster public discussion [13], and their engagement in collective action across communities [14]. However, there is a research gap pertaining to internal motivations of community moderators, and how different forms of community governance affect these motivations.

Past scholarship in psychology points to the importance of internal motivation for success in any endeavor. When individuals are motivated by self-fulfillment as opposed to the promise of a reward, they are more enthusiastic about their task and tend to perform it better than their externally motivated counterparts [4]. In a governance setting, citizens only reap the benefits of a participatory structure when the governing body is willing to implement it [24]. Research on local governments highlights the importance of leaders' personal ideologies and motivation for participatory governance in the successful implementation of these structures [23].

More specifically, experimental results from DeCaro and colleagues proposed a set of six social-psychological needs as being strongly associated with internal motivation in the governance of a common-pool resource [3]. The researchers proposed that governance structures promote cooperation through the satisfaction of these needs: Procedural Justice and Self-Determination, Belonging, Competence, Security, Interpersonal Justice, and Self-Other Merging. Using a survey based on established measures, it was found that forms of governance – voting on rules versus having them imposed, enforcement versus lack of enforcement – were associated with different levels of these social-psychological needs, and thus internal motivation.

While DeCaro's experiment looked at social-psychological needs in response to governance methods, he only examined two governance conditions – voting and enforcement [3]. Far truer to the reality of online social systems is a continuum of governance structures from hierarchical (one moderator making all decisions) to participatory (all community members involved in decision-making). A series of structured interviews provides four common processes through which moderators guide their communities through the creation of community rules: one moderator making rules alone, a group of moderators making rules, a small group of community members aiding in rule creation, or the entire community working together to make rules [21]. Furthermore, DeCaro's original experiment did not consider the wealth of community diversity apparent on digital platforms. Communities on Reddit range in complexity from small groups of classmates to worldwide social activism movements, each presenting a unique environment in which moderators may experience different challenges and gratifications.

These results underscore the importance of social-psychological need satisfaction in the development of successful systems of governance, as well as the need to look to additional elements of community context when analyzing these outcomes. Several past studies have researched the impacts of governance systems on online communities, finding that users tend to view democratic systems as more legitimate and/or empowering [6, 7, 17]. But such structural institutional measures disregard moderators' social-psychological need satisfaction, which provide the most micro-level basis for higher-level manifestations of self-governance and institutional support for empowerment. In fact, when interviewed about implementing democratic systems, Reddit moderators were conflicted. While many admire the idea of community participation, moderators question the ability of community members to make wise decisions in the group's best interest [15, 21]. In some cases, moderators felt unsure as to whether to believe in the legitimacy of votes. Since Reddit is a public platform with no way of restricting access to content, votes could easily come from users outside the core community, or users intentionally choosing a less favorable option for humor or mischief [15].

Due to this potential for interference, online community leaders often gravitate to an emergent hierarchical order, in which one or a group of moderators has the final say in community policies or decisions. Findings show that the likely fate of most online communities is one with power concentrated within a small group of leaders who exert control over their communities [22]. However, this is not necessarily a bad thing as some evidence suggests that communities benefit from the control of one or a few strong moderators [9]. In fact, many moderators seem to prefer these hierarchical structures, not necessarily out of megalomania, rather a desire to avoid conflict or chaos. While many researchers are quick to favor democratic forms of governance out of fear for totalitarianism or tyranny, we propose that the "best" form of governance must succeed at preserving moderators' internal motivation via the satisfaction of their social-psychological needs. Such a system promotes their continued willingness to engage in governing on a volunteer basis, regardless of its level of community participation. We propose that there exists a relationship between the level of hierarchy present in a community and the satisfaction of moderators' social-psychological needs, which in turn affects their motivation to continue governing without compensation.

3   Current Study

The aim of the present study is to understand how moderators' social-psychological needs are related to the systems of governance they employ in their communities, namely the level of participatory decision making conceptualized via the four structures described above (the "rule processes"). Due to this work's focus on moderators as opposed to group members, we focused primarily on two social-psychological needs in our analysis. First is Procedural Justice and Self-Determination, the level of perceived fairness and influence the rule processes afford moderators as well as the level to which moderators feel as if they can exercise their "true desires." Second is Self-Other Merging, or the level to which moderators believe the rule processes give their community a cohesive identity [3]. We believe that in the context of moderators, the satisfaction of these two needs is the most critical.

Many moderators are guided by a sense of "responsibility" to their community, finding the most gratification when they are helping the community grow and develop [21]. Thus, we believe that this gratification is best found when moderators feel as if they have the power to cultivate their ideal community environment (Procedural Justice and Self Determination) and when they identify strongly with community members (Self-Other Merging). Additionally, we find that other social-psychological needs can be interpreted rather trivially in the context of being a moderator (ex. One would naturally feel secure in a community they created or help to organize). Following the past scholarship on emergent hierarchy, focusing on these two measures provides the psychological prerequisites for community members to support the sustainable operation of a volunteer-run peer production community.

Furthermore, we added community age and size as moderators in this model, in light of the immense diversity in community context present on Reddit. In general, subreddit moderators displayed a desire to avoid conflict within their communities. Moderators reported feelings of stress upon being in an unfamiliar group and encountering challenges such as increases in spam, misunderstandings, or hate speech [15]. Thus, we believe that the relationship between hierarchical governance and Procedural Justice and Self-Determination is stronger in young communities, where a less-established group is more likely to present moderation challenges and require tighter control. Furthermore, we believe that the relationship between participatory governance and Self-Other Merging is stronger in smaller communities, where moderators are more likely to trust a "tight circle" of community members and feel a more cohesive sense of identity. We do not believe that size would affect moderators' Procedural Justice and Self Determination because while a larger group may have more potential to become unruly, its age will truly dictate how familiar moderators are with keeping it under control. Similarly, we believe age will have little effect on Self-Other Merging as moderators will have more challenges in building the needed social capital to establish a cohesive identity in a larger community, regardless of its age.

Thus, we hypothesize the following:

Hypothesis 1: More hierarchical rule processes will be correlated with greater feelings of Procedural Justice and Self Determination among moderators.

Hypothesis 1a: This relationship is moderated by community age, with the relationship being stronger in younger communities.

Hypothesis 2: More democratic rule processes will be correlated with greater feelings of Self-Other Merging among moderators.

Hypothesis 2a: This relationship is moderated by community size, with the relationship being stronger in smaller communities.

4 Methods

4.1 Participants and Procedure

The survey was hosted on the Qualtrics platform. Participants were directly contacted through Modmail, Reddit's feature for messaging moderators. They were told that the goal of the survey was to "understand the relationship between Reddit use, leadership, and community-building behavior" and were required to provide consent before taking the survey. In addition to core metrics of interest, the survey elicited basic demographic information, questions pertaining to Reddit use and community-building behavior. Participants were incentivized to participate with a small lottery. Upon recruitment, they were also encouraged to share the survey with others. One attention check was contained in the survey; a question asked users to "Please mark 'Strongly Disagree'" and those who did not were omitted. No personally-identifying information was collected or stored.

A total of 2269 respondents took part in the study, however, all but 620 (1649) responses were discarded due to lack of completion, not being a subreddit moderator, or failure to pass the attention check. We suspect that a number of these discarded responses were bots programmed to go through the survey in order to enter the lottery. The 620 remaining participants had a mean age of 31.42 (SD = 10.06), and the majority identified themselves as male (71.09%, n = 450). 45.66% (n = 289) of participants spent less than five hours each week moderating their community. 27.96% (n = 177) spent 5–10 h,

15.01% (n = 95) spent 10–15 h, 4.58% (n = 29) spent 15–20 h, and 6.79% (n = 43) reported spending 20 h or more.

4.2 Measures

Procedural Justice and Self-Determination (PJSD). Four questions in the survey were used to measure the respondent's PJSD score on a 7-point scale. For example: "The procedures used to create rules make me feel as if: I am able to exercise my views and desires." The final PJSD score was the average of the four coded responses (M: 5.89; SD: 1.00; Cronbach's alpha: 0.84).

Self-Other Merging. Self-Other Merging score was also calculated in a similar way, with four items, such as "I feel good about the other people in this community." The final Self-Other Merging score was the average of the coded responses (M: 5.50; SD: 1.12; Cronbach's alpha: 0.89).

Rule Process. The rule process values were coded responses (1 to 4) from one question asking for the response that best matches the way the community decides on rules. The options for this question ranged from most hierarchical (1) to most democratic (4): 1) moderators create rules on their own; 2) a small group of moderators create the rules; 3) moderators work with a small group of community members; and 4) moderators work with the entire community (M: 2.60; SD: 1.13).

Community Age. The survey also asked how old the community is, providing six options (ranging from "less than 6 months" to "10 years or more"); the coded responses to this question (1 to 6 from shortest age to longest age) were used as the values for the community age variable (M: 4.34, corresponding to in between "3–6 years" and "6–9 years"; SD: 1.24).

Size of Active Community. The size of the active community variable was coded responses for the question asking for an estimate of the number of community members who make five or more posts or comments per month (ranging from 0 to "more than a thousand"). This measure of activity, i5, has been used elsewhere to determine user engagement on Reddit communities [10]. The responses were coded from 1 to 8 (M: 4.62, corresponding to in between "11–50" and "51–100"; SD: 2.05).

5 Results

In order to explore our two research questions, we looked at two models. For Hypothesis 1, the model was made up of rule process as the explanatory variable and PJSD scores as the response variable, with community age as the moderator variable. For Hypothesis 2, the second model was made up of rule process as the explanatory variable and Self-Other Merging scores as the response variable, with size of active community as the moderator variable. The explanatory variable and both moderator variables were centered around the mean of each (the mean was subtracted from each value in the variable). To permit data exploration in a way that mitigated the risk of p-hacking, we pursued a semi-self-replication strategy in which we developed our models on a minority of the data (just 292 observations, 47.1% of the data) before freezing the models and running and reporting them on the full dataset of 620 observations.

5.1   Model 1: Procedural Justice and Self-determination Model

Firstly, the model was significant overall ($F(3, 616) = 9.89$, $p < 0.05$). The rule process was negatively associated with PJSD ($\beta = -0.33$, $p < 0.05$): moderators in communities with a more democratic rule-making process reported lower PJSD. The interaction between rule process and community age was not significant.

5.2   Model 2: Self-other Merging Model

The second model was also significant overall ($F(3, 616) = 9.51$, $p < 0.05$). We found a positive association ($\beta = 0.44$, $p < 0.05$) between rule process and Self-Other Merging score meaning that the more democratic the rule-making process, the higher Self-Other Merging was reported. We also found a significant negative interaction between rule process and active community size ($\beta = -0.32$, $p < 0.05$), pointing to the effect of rule process being larger for smaller communities.

6   Discussion

This study explores the reasons why individuals would choose to continue moderating online communities, looking at social-psychological needs in particular as a possible explanation. Using the survey data, the study looked at two hypothesized relationships between rule process and two specific social-psychological needs. The data showed support for most of the two hypotheses.

The first model provided evidence that H1 was correct, showing a significant negative association where the more participatory the rule process reported, the lower the PJSD score was seen overall. This falls in line with the previous findings regarding moderators' preferences for emergent hierarchy. Moderators with more control over their community feel more confident that the procedures used to create the rules are fair because they are protected from users acting outside the community's best interests. The more control they have over their community, the more they feel empowered to act in its best interest. However, the interaction term in Model 1 was not significant and thus H1a could not be supported by the data.

The survey data also showed that democratic rule process was positively correlated with higher Self-Other Merging scores, supporting H2. Such a finding suggests that while they may take away from moderators' sense of justice and fairness, democratic processes do promote a cohesive community identity. This is also important to the social-psychological well-being of moderators, as many align with the philosophy that moderators should act as engaged community members while simultaneously "setting an example" for good behavior [21]. Furthermore, H2a was backed up by the model, with the negative interaction between rule process and active community size being significant. Thus, the sense of cohesiveness that more democratic processes are associated with will likely decrease as the community gets larger.

It may seem provocative to claim that a more hierarchical, less democratic decision structure leads to more "democratic" attitudes of higher Self-Determination, Procedural Justice, and group identity (Self-Other Merging). However, under conditions of an overworked, underappreciated population of volunteer moderators, without whom these communities would not exist, centralization of authority is unarguably pragmatic, and apparently beneficial in such a resource constrained peer production setting.

7 Conclusion

Online platforms provide vast arenas for discussion, collaboration, and the creation of shared meaning. However, the unpaid structure of governance underlying such platforms points to the need for internally motivated community moderators. Although much attention has been given to the community implications of governance structures and practices, it is essential to consider their relationships with moderators' social-psychological well-being. Designing systems to best satisfy moderators' social-psychological needs will allow platforms to be sustained by motivated, engaged moderators acting in the best interests of their communities.

Acknowledgements. The authors wish to thank research assistants Theresa Sims, Jesleyn Gill, Sharon Yoo, Katherine Coviello, Hannah Skepner, Samantha Vigil, Kabir Sahni, Anastacia Dobson Bell, Megan Tsang, Anna Beatrice Ricasata, Sean Abellera, Chengyue Jiang, Evan Brosnan, Yuqi Cheng, Nicole Calbreath, Abigail Endler, Nebiyat Walelign, Harneet Nagra, Alessandra Soto, Mark Murakami, Kelley Ann, Kexin Li, and Yakov Perlov for help with recruitment. Funding for this project was provided by the Provost's Undergraduate Fellowship from the UC Davis Undergraduate Research Center.

References

1. Butler, B., Sproull, L., Kiesler, S., Kraut, R.: Community effort in online groups: who does the work and why. In: Weisband, S.P. (ed.) Leadership at a distance: Research in technologically-supported work, pp. 171–194. Lawrence Erlbaum Associates, Hoboken, NJ (2002)
2. Jie, C., Wohn, D.Y.: Coordination and collaboration: how do volunteer moderators work as a team in live streaming communities? (2022)
3. DeCaro, D.A., Janssen, M.A., Lee, A.: Synergistic effects of voting and enforcement on internalized motivation to cooperate in a resource dilemma. Judgm. Decis. Mak. **10**(6), 511–537 (2015)
4. Deci, E.L., Ryan, R.M.: Intrinsic Motivation and Self-Determination in Human Behavior. Springer Science & Business Media, Berlin (1985). https://doi.org/10.1007/978-1-4899-2271-7
5. Bryan, D., Semaan, B.: Moderation practices as emotional labor in sustaining online communities: The case of AAPI identity work on Reddit. In: Proceedings of the 2019 CHI conference on human factors in computing systems (2019)
6. Fan, J., Zhang, A. X.: Digital Juries: a civics-oriented approach to platform governance. 1–14 (2020). https://doi.org/10.1145/3313831.3376293
7. Forte, A., Bruckman, A.: Scaling consensus: increasing decentralization in Wikipedia governance. In: Proceedings of the 41st Annual Hawaii International Conference on System Sciences (HICSS 2008) (2008). https://doi.org/10.1109/hicss.2008.383
8. Frey, S., Krafft, P. M., Keegan, B.C.: This place does what it was built for: designing digital institutions for participatory change. In: Proceedings of the ACM on Human-Computer Interaction 3, CSCW (2019)

9. Frey, S., Sumner, R.W.: Emergence of integrated institutions in a large population of self-governing communities. PLoS ONE **14**(7), 1–18 (2019). https://doi.org/10.1371/journal.pone.0216335

10. Frey, S., et al.: Governing online goods: maturity and formalization in Minecraft, Reddit, and world of Warcraft communities. In: Proceedings of the ACM on Human-Computer Interaction CSCW (2021)

11. Hess, C., Ostrom, E.: A framework for analyzing the knowledge commons: a chapter from understanding knowledge as a commons: from theory to practice (2005)

12. Kiesler, Sara, et al.: Regulating behavior in online communities building successful online communities: evidence-based social design 1, 4–2 (2012)

13. Mano, M., Dalle, J.-M., Tomasik, J.: The consent of the crowd detected in an open forum. In: Proceedings of the 14th International Symposium on Open Collaboration (2018). https://doi.org/10.1145/3233391.3233538

14. Matias, J. N.: Going dark: social factors in collective action against platform operators in the Reddit blackout. In: Proceedings of the 2016 CHI Conference on Human Factors in Computing Systems, 1138–1151 ACM (2016). https://doi.org/10.1145/2858036.2858391

15. Matias, J. N.: The Civic Labor of volunteer moderators online. Social Media + Society, 5(2), (2019) https://doi.org/10.1177/2056305119836778

16. Mindel, V., Mathiassen, L., Rai, A.: The sustainability of polycentric information commons. MIS Q. **42**(2), 607–632 (2018)

17. Ostrom, E.: Collective action and the evolution of social norms. J. Econ. Perspect. **14**(3), 137–158 (2000). https://doi.org/10.1257/jep.14.3.137

18. Preece, J.: Online Communities: Designing Usability and Supporting Sociability. John Wiley and Sons, New York (2000)

19. Rheingold, H.: The Virtual Community: Homesteading on the Electronic Frontier. The MIT Press, Cambridge (2000). http://www.rheingold.com/vc/book

20. Nathan, S., et al.: Modular politics: toward a governance layer for online communities. In: Proceedings of the ACM on Human-Computer Interaction 5, 1–26. CSCW1 (2021)

21. Seering, J., Wang, T., Yoon, J., Kaufman, G.: Moderator engagement and community development in the age of algorithms. New Media Soc. **21**(7), 1417–1443 (2019). https://doi.org/10.1177/1461444818821316

22. Shaw, A., Hill, B.M.: Laboratories of oligarchy? how the iron law extends to peer production. J. Commun. **64**(2), 215–238 (2014). https://doi.org/10.1111/JCOM.12082

23. Schönleitner, G.: Can public deliberation democratise state action?: municipal health councils and local democracy in Brazil. In: Harriss, J., Stokke, K., Törnquist, O. (eds.) Politicising Democracy. IPES, pp. 75–106. Palgrave Macmillan UK, London (2005). https://doi.org/10.1057/9780230502802_4

24. Speer, J.: Participatory governance reform: a good strategy for increasing government responsiveness and improving public services? World Dev. **40**(12), 2379–2398 (2012). https://doi.org/10.1016/j.worlddev.2012.05.034

Interactive Technologies for Learning

From Data Humanism to Metaphorical Visualization – An Educational Game Case Study

Alessandro Canossa[✉], Luis Laris Pardo, Michael Tran, and Alexis Lozano Angulo

The Royal Danish Academy, 1435 Copenhagen, Denmark
acan@kglakademi.dk

Abstract. When attempting to understand a phenomenon or learn new concepts, we often use data to create models of reality, but "the map is not the territory". We treat these imperfect abstractions as the reality itself, we design standardized dashboards to account for the multidimensional interdependencies of systems, each already complex in its own right. In doing so we fail to acknowledge the importance of emotion in learning and memory. One of the biggest challenges for digitally-mediated learning environments, whether they are serious games or online teaching platforms, is providing feedback to learners. This feedback is often constituted by scores, percentages or quantities in general and it is represented with traditional visualization techniques such as graphs, bar charts or scatter plots. This paper attempts to subvert this approach: it aims at suggesting an alternative framework for visualizing behavioral player data that can provide learners of educational games with timely feedback. This feedback should leverage emotional as well as rational appraisal of information in order to maximize the learning potential. The intended goal is to produce a generalizable framework for feedback to learners; the resulting framework will need to be validated in terms of both rational and emotional impact on the community of learners. This approach, enabled by advances both in learning science and data visualization, has the potential to innovate the emerging landscape of online learning platforms; this field is in fact burgeoning due to the ongoing pandemic and even after the emergency recedes, distance education is expected to keep growing. In this paper we outline the state of the art of humanistic data visualization and other visualization approaches that leverage emotional learning; after that we will suggest strategies for visualizing players' choices and progress. The result is a concrete example for visualizing behavioral user data leveraging emotional appraisal of information.

Keywords: Serious games · Data visualization · Data humanism · Learning games · Player behavior

1 Introduction

Games for a purpose other than entertainment (also called educational games, serious games, transformational games, games for learning, etc.) are currently being used in

© The Author(s), under exclusive license to Springer Nature Switzerland AG 2022
C. Stephanidis et al. (Eds.): HCII 2022, CCIS 1655, pp. 109–117, 2022.
https://doi.org/10.1007/978-3-031-19682-9_15

a number of domains ranging from transferring knowledge to changing behaviors or even changing people's sense of self [1, 2]. The EU funded the Games and Learning Alliance (GALA) under a FP7 Network of Excellence on "Serious Games". GALA produced excellent research on how to design games that have an impact [3–5] as well as on how to validate such impact [6–11]. These learning technologies have for the largest part been designed by leveraging two seminal advances in learning sciences: the Evidence-Centered Design (ECD) framework [12–14] and research on game-based learning [15–20], both branches are deeply rooted in the latest developments of cognitive science. Both ECD and learning science identified "timely feedback" in the form of data visualization as a crucial component of the iterative learning process [21–27]. The majority of educational games routinely present timely feedback to players by visualizing the status of the game/simulation as easily readable data encodings (both categorical and ordinal data types). For example in the game "Darfur is Dying" (TAKE ACTION games, 2006) water and food supply levels are represented with instantly updated blue and green bars (Fig. 1a); in the game "Adopt a planet" [28], items' characteristics are displayed as numbers (Fig. 1b); and in the game "EnergyCat" [29] game variables are represented as bar charts (Fig. 1c).

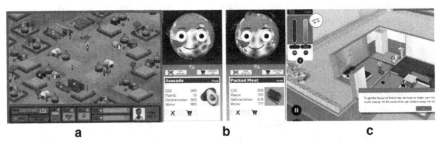

a   b   c

Fig. 1a, 1b and 1c. Darfur is dying, adopt a planet, and EnergyCat.

1.1 Issues with the Current State of Data Visualization

Games, especially serious games, rely consistently on timely rational data visualization to present a myriad of relevant information to players by leveraging the whole array of visual devices employed by data analytics for dashboards and infographics. However, there is mounting evidence, from both cognitive and learning sciences, that a purely rational appraisal of information does not fully engage the brain of the learner [20, 43–45]. Learning activities, in fact, concern the whole brain: the cortex (or "higher" intellectual functions) as well as the amygdala and the limbic system (where emotional life is housed). Emotion appears to be a key source of motivation for driving thinking, learning, and problem solving [30–32, 42]. In parallel, there is a movement within data visualization that attempts to go beyond traditional "rational" dashboards and engage users on a visceral and emotional level.

2 Data Humanism

Giorgia Lupi, one of the main proponents of Data Humanism, suggests that if we move *"past what we can call peak infographics, we are left with a general audience that understands some of the tools needed to welcome a second wave of more meaningful and thoughtful visualization"* [33]. Data humanism proposes a set of principles to visualize data in a more humane way:

Embrace complexity, Lupi suggests avoiding just measuring quantities instead transforming raw information into interconnected knowledge, presenting unexpected parallels and secondary narratives to complement the main story. Visual display of information does not need to provide instant clarity, therefore it is possible to layer multiple visual tales over a main story, providing varied angles where readers can choose the point of view most aligned with their interests in a similar way to nonlinear interactive storytelling. Visualizations can provide an open text for readers to explore individual elements, minor trends and larger vectors within the greater visualization. These dense and granular data visualizations foster a slower consumption pace, contrarily to the norm of providing superficial and instant understanding. If data visualization can encourage careful reading and personal engagement, people will find real value in data and in what it represents.

Move beyond standards, Lupi maintains that creators of business intelligence and dataviz tools have led users to believe that the ideal way to make sense of information is to load data into a tool, pick from among a list of suggested out-of-the-box charts, and get the job done in a couple of clicks. This approach results in not spending enough time framing the question that triggered the exploration in the first place leading to results that are both superficial and often erroneous. Pre-packaged solutions are rarely able to frame problems that are difficult to define, let alone solve. *"Making enticingly accurate infographics requires more than a computer drafting program or cut-and-paste template, the art of information display is every bit as artful as any other type of design or illustration"* [34]. The suggestion is to analyze data to understand what is contained in the numbers and in their structure and how to define and organize those quantities in a visual way to create opportunities to gain insight, Lupi calls it "sketching with data" to arrive at designs that are uniquely customized for the specific type of data problems under examination.

Sneak context in, data is not completely objective, but rather a tool that filters reality; how it is collected, the information included and omitted determines the information conveyed. As theorized by semiotics, context is as important as language when shaping the communication process. This is why Lupi suggest reclaiming a personal approach to how data is captured, analyzed and displayed, acknowledging the role played by context and subjectivity in understanding the world, and people in particular. Only if data is properly contextualized, it can succeed in writing more meaningful and intimate narratives.

Data is Imperfect. Data is primarily human-made and as such it is prone to errors, imperfections, blind spots and does not necessarily portray a universal truth. Data visualization should embrace imperfection and approximation, allowing users to leverage data not just to understand and learn, but also to connect with ourselves, others, and the world at a deeper level. Lupi suggests that putting more efforts in researching and translating data into visualizations allows users to more easily understand and relate to the stories, which analysts tell.

2.1 Steps Towards Data Humanism

To act on these recommendations, radical changes are required in the way information is represented visually. Experts and data analysts should learn how to visualize data in more qualitative and nuanced manner. One of the axioms of serious game design is to present players with clear, transparent data and allow them to make informed choices to learn the principles that regulate the interaction between systems [35]. Designers of serious games should experiment with visualizing uncertainty, possible biases and subjective appraisal of the data in order to pursue a more visceral strategy that allows users to learn both rationally and emotionally. An example of this shift is provided by Meigniez [36]. He designed an alternative to traditional running apps (Fig. 2).

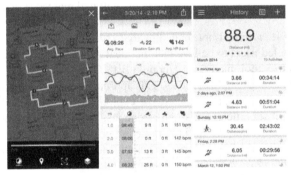

Fig. 2. Traditional running apps showing the trace of the run, pace of movement, track elevation, heartbeat, distance covered and duration of the run.

The redesigned app (Fig. 3a) chose to focus on different metrics such as the dominant colour for each kilometre of the run, the music that the runner was listening to, environmental, physical and psychological feedback, as well as the length of the track and its difficulty. Meigniez also chose to visualize all this information adopting different unconventional strategies and making it interactive.

Another example of the application of these principles to data visualization is Sonia Kuipers' "A view on despair", recipient of the Information is Beautiful Award [37]. Here the designer used abstract imagery to represent people who committed suicide in the Netherlands in the year 2017 (Fig. 3a). These examples show possible avenues to explore when designing feedback systems for learning games. Games represent the perfect artefacts to experiment with metaphoric, visceral, and poetic data visualization because of the intrinsically diegetic nature of the information feedback systems, yet very little work has been done to examine the impact on learning of alternative visualization strategies.

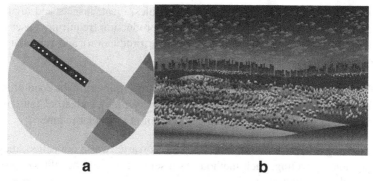

Fig. 3a and 3b. The circle at the left represents a run. The 9 stripes on the right represent the colors seen on that track. The 3 big stipes on the left represent the music listened. The black bar gives details about the state of mind of the runner (Environmental, Physical and Psychological). The rotation of the circle indicates the difficulty (horizontal: easy, vertical: difficult). In the landscape on the right, each element represents a person who committed suicide in the Netherlands in the year 2017.

3 Metaphorical Data Visualization for Learning Games

With this paper we are proposing to explore metaphor-based data visualization to provide learners of an educational game with timely feedback that leverages emotional as well as rational appraisal of information, following the principles proposed by Lupi's Data Humanism. By metaphorical data visualization system we intend a system that leverages metaphors that engage players on a visceral and emotional level.

3.1 The Game: SubSyst Simulator

In this article we utilize the game SubSyst Simulator [39] as a case study to present strategies for metaphor-based visualizations. The game's purpose is to transfer knowledge from subject-matter experts, like the Cities and Circular Economy for Food Report from the Ellen MacArthur Foundation [45] and the Food wastage footprint & Climate Change assessment from the Food and Agriculture Organization of the United Nations (FAO) [46]. Players take the role of food producers, managing resources, securing food for the city and adapting to cataclysms. The game was first showcased at the 13th International Symposium on Visual Information Communication and Interaction (VINCI 2020) [38] and subsequently it received the United Nation student award.

The objective of the game is to increase players' knowledge and awareness of users on complex topics (sustainability and circular economy for food production) by interacting with the simulation. The learning happens not by reading about the subject or by exposition, but by experimenting with the systems and seeing first-hand the outcomes of decisions. Even if players fail at the game they are learning fundamental complex concepts. This decision was taken because there are important lessons in how systems fail. The pillars of the model derived from the literature are the relationships between food production, energy consumption, and waste processing, therefore it was decided to give direct agency to players over these three systems (production variables).

Food Production: There are 4 food types: vegetables, meat, insects and algae. Each food type can be produced in 3 ways: small-scale production (requiring a user to click every time), industrial scale production (automatizing production), and a circular method (minimizing waste production);

Energy Production: Energy can be produced in 3 ways (mirroring the food production methods): small-scale (requiring a user to click every time), industrial (automatizing production) and biogas (utilizing waste instead of oil in a circular manner).

Waste Processing: There are 4 methods to process waste: waste collection, recycling, composting, and upcycling, each method has a set of costs and benefits, unprocessed waste accumulates as pollution.

Additionally there are 2 sets of variables on which players do not have direct agency: *Socio-economic variables*: money, public approval (or number of "likes"), and population count; *Environmental variables*: pollution and unprocessed waste, natural capital, and bee population count. Lastly the simulation includes 12 different cataclysms that are triggered at different thresholds of both production variables (food, energy and waste) and additional variables (socio-economic and environmental). The simulation is fully instrumented, meaning is able to log players' choices and actions, and through a telemetry system can send these anonymized logs to a remote database [40].

3.2   Rational and Emotional Data Visualizations

We wanted the game to be able to visualize the impact of player's choices on the environment according to two distinct strategies: a) leveraging rational appraisal of information, b) relying on emotional triggers based on metaphors. The first strategy was informed by social simulators such as Civilization V and Cities: Skylines. The second strategy was informed by 3 workshops with both domain knowledge experts (N = 9, 5 male, 4 female) and end users (N = 15, male 7, female 8) utilizing the ZMET method [47], conceptual metaphors [50, 51] thematic apperception tests [41] and Kelly repertoire grid [48, 49]. The workshops first introduced participants to metaphorical thinking: *"understanding and experiencing one kind of thing in terms of another"* [50], subsequently participants were asked to freely explore which metaphor to use when representing game events, cataclysms, systems or variables by identifying pictures from the internet. The material was then processed during the course of interviews following the ZMET steps. The first strategy can be seen in Fig. 4a: traditional numeric values, resources represented as flow of packets and bars. The second strategy (seen in Fig. 4b) visualizes the state of the simulation as a living and breathing biome.

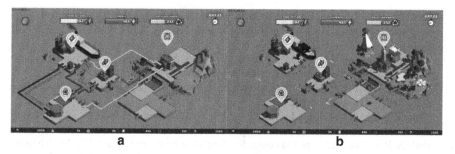

a   b

Fig. 4a and 4b. Rational and emotional visualizations.

4 Conclusions

This project aimed at producing a viable strategy to visualize learners' behavior and performance that can support emotional as well as rational thinking. In order to do so, the serious game Subsyst Simulator was be used as a case study. Three workshops were organized both with domain knowledge experts and end users and design guidelines were produced to visualize the impact on the ecosystem of player choices. What remains is to test ad validate what kind of impact each of the two visualization strategies have on knowledge transfer. The key contribution is to begin establishing procedures, guidelines and frameworks for data visualizations that can support and elicit emotional responses, since overwhelming new research has proven that *"it is literally neurobiologically impossible to build memories, engage complex thoughts, or make meaningful decisions without emotions"* [44].

References

1. Culyba, S.: The transformational framework: a process tool for the development of transformational games (2018). http://lulu.com/
2. Harteveld, C.: Triadic Game Design - Balancing Reality, Meaning and Play. Springer, Heidelberg (2011). https://doi.org/10.1007/978-1-84996-157-8
3. De Gloria, A., Veltkamp, R. (eds.): (2016). Games and Learning Alliance: 4th International Conference, GALA 2015, Rome, Italy, December 9–11, 2015, Revised Selected Papers, vol. 9599. Springer, Heidelberg
4. Dias, J., Santos, P., Veltkamp, R.C.: Games and Learning Alliance. Springer, Lisbon (2017)
5. Marfisi-Schottman, I., Bellotti, F., Hamon, L., Klemke, R.C.: Games and Learning Alliance. Springer, Laval (2020)
6. Olsen, T., Procci, K., Bowers, C.: Serious games usability testing: how to ensure proper usability, playability, and effectiveness. In: Marcus, Aaron (ed.) DUXU 2011. LNCS, vol. 6770, pp. 625–634. Springer, Heidelberg (2011). https://doi.org/10.1007/978-3-642-21708-1_70
7. Zaibon, S.B.: User testing on game usability, mobility, playability, and learning content of mobile game-based learning. Jurnal Teknologi **77**(29) (2015)
8. Moreno-Ger, P., Torrente, J., Hsieh, Y.G., Lester, W.T.: Usability testing for serious games: making informed design decisions with user data. In: Advances in Human-Computer Interaction (2012)

9. Shute, V., et al.: Maximizing learning without sacrificing the fun: Stealth assessment, adaptivity and learning supports in educational games. J. Comput. Assist. Learn. **37**(1), 127–141 (2021)

10. Almond, R., Shute, V.J., Tingir, S., Rahimi, S.: Identifying observable outcomes in game-based assessments. Innov. Psychom. Model. Methods **163** (2020)

11. Shute, V.J., Rahimi, S.: Stealth assessment of creativity in a physics video game. Comput. Hum. Behav. **116**, 106647 (2021)

12. Mislevy, R.J., Almond, R.G., Lukas, J.F.: A brief introduction to evidence-centered design. ETS Res. Rep. Ser. (2003). https://doi.org/10.1002/j.2333-8504.2003.tb01908.x

13. Mislevy, R.J.: Evidence-centered design for simulation-based assessment. Mil. Med. (special issue on simulation, H. O'Neil, Ed.) **178**, 107–114 (2013). https://doi.org/10.7205/MILMED-D-13-00213

14. Arieli-Attali, M., Ward, S., Thomas, J., Deonovic, B., Von Davier, A.A.: The expanded evidence-centered design (e-ECD) for learning and assessment systems: a framework for incorporating learning goals and processes within assessment design. Front. Psychol. **10**, 853 (2019)

15. Gee, J.P.: What video games have to teach us about learning and literacy. Comput. Entertain. (CIE) **1**(1), 20 (2003)

16. Gee, J.P.: Good Video Games+ Good Learning: Collected Essays on Video Games, Learning, and Literacy. Peter Lang, Bern (2007)

17. Squire, K.R.: Game-based learning: present and future state of the field. In: e-Learning Consortium, an X-Learn Perspective Paper, Masie Center (2005). www.masie.com/xlearn/game-based_learning.pdf

18. Squire, K.R., Jenkins, H.: Harnessing the power of games in education. Insight **3**(2004), 5–33 (2004)

19. Shaffer, D.W., Squire, K.R., Halverson, R., Gee, J.P.: Video games and the future of learning. Phi delta kappan **87**(2), 105–111 (2005)

20. Gee, J.P.: Learning and games. the ecology of games: connecting youth, games, and learning. In: Salen, K., John, D., Catherine, T. (eds.) MacArthur Foundation Series on Digital Media and Learning, pp. 21–40. The MIT Press, Cambridge (2008). https://doi.org/10.1162/dmal.9780262693646.021

21. Barsalou, L.W.: Language comprehension: archival memory or preparation for situated action. Discourse Process. **28**(1999), 61–80 (1999)

22. Bereiter, C., Scardamalia, M.: Surpassing Ourselves: An Inquiry into the Nature and Implications of Expertise. Open Court, Chicago (1993)

23. Brown, A.L.: The advancement of learning. Eduational Res. **23**(1994), 4–12 (1994)

24. Brown, A. L., Collins, A., Duguid.: Situated cognition and the culture of learning. Educ. Res. **18**(1989), 32–42 (1989)

25. Bruer, J.T.: Schools for Thought: A Science of Learning in the Classroom. MIT Press, Cambridge (1993)

26. Bransford, J., Brown, A.L., Cocking, R.R.: (2000) How People Learn: Brain, Mind, Experience, and School. National Academy Press, Washington, DC (2000)

27. Sawyer, R.K.: Analyzing collaborative discourse. In: Sawyer, R.K. (ed.) The Cambridge Handbook of the Learning Sciences, pp. 187–204. Cambridge University Press, Cambridge (2006)

28. Klemke, R., Antonaci, A., Limbu, B.: Designing and implementing gamification: GaDeP, gamifire, and applied case studies. Int. J. Ser. Games **7**(3), 97–129 (2020). https://doi.org/10.17083/ijsg.v7i3.357

29. Hafner, R., et al.: Results and insight gained from applying the EnergyCat energy-saving serious game in UK social housing. Int. J. Ser. Games **7**(2), 27–48 (2020). https://doi.org/10.17083/ijsg.v7i2.333

30. Damasio, A.: Descartes' Error: Emotion, Reason, and the Human Brain. Penguin, New York (1994)
31. Damasio, A.: The Feeling of What Happens: Body and Emotion in the Making of Consciousness. Harvest Books, Orlando (1999)
32. Damasio, A.: Looking for Spinoza: Joy, Sorrow, and the Feeling Brain. Harvest Books, Orlando (2003)
33. Lupi, G., Posavec, S.: Dear Data. Princeton Architectural Press, Princeton (2016)
34. Heller, S.: Infographics Designers Sketchbooks. Adams Media (2014)
35. Meyer, S.: Sid Meier's Memoir!: A Life in Computer Games. W. W. Norton & Company, New York (2020)
36. Meigniez G.: Data Humanism—A Case Study (2019). Accessed 01 Apr 2021. https://medium.com/nightingale/data-humanism-a-case-study-c16d0efef533
37. Kujpers, S.: A view on despair (2017). Accessed 01 Apr 2021. https://www.informationisbeautifulawards.com/showcase/4313-a-view-on-despair
38. Angulo, A.L., Pardo, L.L., Canossa, A.: Subsyst simulator: an interactive infographic for knowledge transfer. In: Proceedings of the 13th International Symposium on Visual Information Communication and Interaction, pp. 1–5 (2020)
39. Accessed 14 Mar 2022. https://royaldanishacademy.com/project/subsyst-simulator
40. El-Nasr, M.S., Drachen, A., Canossa, A.: Game Analytics. Springer, London (2016)
41. Morgan, C.D., Murray, H.A.: A method for investigating fantasies: the thematic apperception test. Arch. NeurPsych. 34(2), 289–306 (1935). https://doi.org/10.1001/archneurpsyc.1935.02250200049005
42. Russell, J.A.: A circumplex model of affect. J. Pers. Soc. Psychol. 39(6), 1161 (1980)
43. Tyng, C.M., Amin, H.U., Saad, M.N., Malik, A.S.: The influences of emotion on learning and memory. Front. Psychol. 8, 1454 (2017)
44. Immordino-Yang, M.H., Damasio, A.R.: We feel, therefore, we learn: the relevance of affective and social neuroscience to education. Mind Brain Educ. 1(1), 3–10 (2007)
45. Ellen MacArthur Foundation (2019). Cities and Circular Economy for Food. Ellen MacArthur Foundation. 4 June 2020. https://www.ellenmacarthurfoundation.org/assets/downloads/Cities-and-Circular-Economy-for-Food_280119.pdf
46. Scialabba, N.: Food wastage footprint & Climate Change. Food and Agriculture Organization of the United Nations (2015). Accessed 4 June 2020. http://www.fao.org/3/a-bb144e.pdf
47. Zaltman, G.: How customers think: essential insights into the mind of the market, p. 368. Harvard Business School Press, Boston (2003). ISBN 1-57851-826-1.P
48. Edwards, H M., McDonald, S., Young, S.M.: The repertory grid technique: its place in empirical software engineering research. Inf. Softw. Technol. (2009)
49. Kelly, G.: The repertory test". The Psychology of Personal Constructs. 1. A Theory of Personality. Routledge in association with the Centre for Personal Construct, London Psychology (1991)
50. Lakoff, G., Johnson, M.: Metaphors We Live By. Chicago: Chicago UP (1980)
51. Lakoff, G., Johnson, M.: Philosophy in the Flesh. Basic Books, New York (1999)

Video Conferencing Platforms for Learning: Which is the Best Platform?

Omar Cóndor-Herrera[1] (ID), Mónica Bolaños-Pasquel[2],
and Carlos Ramos-Galarza[1,2(✉)] (ID)

[1] Centro de Investigación en Mecatrónica y Sistemas Interactivos MIST/Carrera de
Psicología/Maestría en Educación Mención Innovación y Liderazgo Educativo, Universidad
Tecnológica Indoamérica, Av. Machala y Sabanilla, Quito, Ecuador
{omarcondor,carlosramos}@uti.edu.ec
[2] Facultad de Psicología, Pontificia Universidad Católica del Ecuador, Av. 12 de Octubre y
Roca, Quito, Ecuador
caramos@puce.edu.ec

Abstract. Due to the COVID-19 pandemic, the education field was forced to develop virtual learning environments on videoconferencing platforms. The most used videoconferencing platforms are Microsoft Teams, Zoom, Google Meet, and WhatsApp. This article aims to identify the perceptions that teachers have when using these platforms to determine which platform is the most optimal for developing the activities.

The study involved 33 male and female teachers working at the high school and university levels. They responded to a survey that evaluated various aspects of four videoconferencing platforms: Microsoft Teams, Zoom, Google Meet, and WhatsApp.

The aspects evaluated were usability, platform design, benefits of the application for learning, and platform reliability.

According to research results, survey participants said that, according to their perceptions, the best videoconferencing platform for the development of online classes is Zoom; WhatsApp, and Zoom are the easiest applications to learn to use; Google Meet is the most difficult to learn to use; and Zoom has the best interface design. The video conference platform that offers the best benefits for the teaching–learning process is Zoom. WhatsApp offers the least benefits in relation to the others.

Based on the results, it can be stated that, according to the perceptions of the teachers surveyed, the platform that offers the best benefits in the areas evaluated is Zoom.

Keywords: Distance learning · Disruptive technology · Electronic learning platform · Virtual learning · Videoconference

1 Introduction

The appearance of the COVID-19 virus generated the greatest global disturbance of educational systems in generations, which largely made it possible for the change to

C. Stephanidis et al. (Eds.): HCII 2022, CCIS 1655, pp. 118–129, 2022.
https://doi.org/10.1007/978-3-031-19682-9_16

online education to occur in an accelerated manner [1], which is why educators migrated teaching to videoconferencing systems. However, a large number of teachers were not familiar with online distance learning before the pandemic [2] in this scenario. Teachers experienced in the use and application of technological resources were identified, as well as teachers with a lower degree of ICT management who were enthusiastic about learning and cautious teachers in ICT management, denoting as the variable that affects the fit of a teacher to online education the level of digital literacy before the crisis [3, 4].

In various educational systems, the absence of a formal digital learning management system (DLMS) was evident, so educational centers around the world adopted social networking sites (SNS) for their academic activities, such as Facebook and WhatsApp, and/or other digital communications platforms, including Microsoft Teams and Zoompara [5], among others.

In addition to hosting a platform that serves as a basis for the development of learning activities, various educational centers face five challenges in the transition process to online education: the integration of synchronous/asynchronous learning tools; access to technology; online competition of faculty and students; academic dishonesty; and privacy and confidentiality. It is also necessary to provide e-learning training support for faculty and students, foster online learning communities, and expand traditional face-to-face course delivery to incorporate more elements of blended learning [6, 7].

In this context, the present investigation aims to provide a vision from the perspective of teachers regarding the various video conference platforms used by teachers for the development of their academic activities. Recent studies that address similar questions point to WhatsApp as one of the most used online platforms during the pandemic because it was the easiest to access and operate, but Zoom stands out when it comes to these tasks [8, 9]. Likewise, among the difficulties that teachers encountered with online platforms, an unstable signal was mentioned, especially in mountainous areas [6]. On the other hand, platforms such as Microsoft Teams, Zoom, Google Meet, and WebEx are found to be the most-used online platforms for conducting classes since they have virtual whiteboard software tools [3, 10].

For the development of this study, teachers evaluated four video conference platforms: Zoom, Microsoft Teams, Google Meet, and WhatsApp. The results, as well as the analysis, are presented below.

1.1 Effects of Online Education Identified

Recent studies have indicated that teacher fatigue is one negative effect of online education. A group of teachers was evaluated in which the composite score of teacher videoconference fatigue was 3.35 over 5, suggesting a moderate level of fatigue.

The most significant predictors of videoconferencing fatigue among teachers include attitude, the feeling of being physically trapped, mirror anxiety, the emotional stability domain of personality, intervals between videoconferences, and the duration of videoconferences [11]. On the other hand, both teachers and students agree that online education is useful during the current pandemic; however, at the same time, according to the perceptions of each one, it is less effective than face-to-face teaching and learning [10], for what is currently necessary to adapt this form of teaching.

1.2   Previous Studies on the Use of Videoconferencing Platforms in Education

Table 1 presents the reader with several recent studies that focus on videoconferencing platforms in the areas of use, advantages, applications, etc.

The research objectives are briefly detailed, as well as the most important results of each investigation, among which the importance of interaction with the platforms, the perception of the different platforms, the perception of perceived usefulness, and ease of use stand out.

The reader is invited to carefully review Table 1.

Table 1. Research on videoconferencing platforms.

Title	Authors	Investigation	Findings
The Acceptance of Learning Management Systems and Video Conferencing Technologies: Lessons Learned from COVID-19	Camilleri, M., Camilleri, A. (2021) [12]	Investigate student perceptions of remote learning through asynchronous learning management systems (LMS) and synchronous video conferencing technologies, such as Google Meet, Microsoft Teams, or Zoom, among others	Findings suggest that research participants accessed asynchronous content and interacted with online users, including their course instructor, in real time
User Experience in Communication and Collaboration Platforms: A Comparative Study Including Discord, Microsoft Teams, and Zoom	Mora-Jimenez et al., 2022 [13]	This research describes the results of an evaluation of the user experience of three widely used platforms: Discord, Microsoft Teams, and Zoom	Discord is better in nontask aspects and provides an above average UX. On the other hand, Zoom excels when it comes to tasks

(continued)

Table 1. (*continued*)

Title	Authors	Investigation	Findings
Students' Perceptions of Using Microsoft Teams Application in Online Learning during the Covid-19 Pandemic	Wea, K., Dua Kuki, A. (2021) [14]	This study aims to determine the perceptions of FKIP students about the use of Microsoft Teams application in online learning during the COVID-19 pandemic	The benefits were primarily self-learning, low cost, convenience, and flexibility. They showed that FKIP UNIPA students had a good perception of the use of Microsoft Teams. Students expect this app to continue to be used during instruction
Review of Online Teaching Platforms in the Current Period of COVID-19 Pandemic	Dash, S. et al. (2021) [15]	This study aims to understand the perspective of usability and practicality of audio and video conferencing platforms in the current situation. A review of various available online platforms was conducted, namely Zoom, Google Meet, Google Classroom, Microsoft Teams, Cisco Webex, GoToMeeting, and Say Namaste	The number of similar platforms to boost online learning is numerous, and the features that each program can provide are somewhat limitless, but the response to a video conferencing service is good
Analysis of the Use of Videoconferencing in the Learning Process During the Pandemic at a University in Lima	A. Rio-Chillcce, L. Jara-Monge y L. Andrade-Arenas,(2021) [16]	The objective of the research is to report on the impact of student learning through the use of the aforementioned videoconferencing tools	Most of the students became familiar with the platforms; however, less than 24% rated that their academic performance has improved. Some teachers still have psychological difficulties due to this new teaching method

(*continued*)

Table 1. (*continued*)

Title	Authors	Investigation	Findings
Video conferencing in the e-learning context: Explaining learning outcome with the technology acceptance model	Bailey, D., Almusharraf, N.,Almusharraf, A, 2022 [17]	Explains how the use of technology influences learning outcomes that emanate from engagement with the Zoom video conferencing platform. Ease includes Perceived Ease of Use (PEoU) and Perceived Usefulness (PU)	PEoU with Zoom strongly affected PU and actual usage. Furthermore, PU with Zoom predicted intentions to use Zoom in the future; however, it failed to influence perceived learning outcomes
Transitioning to E-Learning during the COVID-19 pandemic: How have higher education institutions responded to the challenge?	D. Turnbull, R. Chug y J. Luck (2021) [7]	The objective of this study is to identify the role of educational technologies in the transition from face-to-face to online teaching and learning activities during the COVID-19 pandemic	Identified five challenges to transitioning to online education experienced by higher education institutions: integration of synchronous/asynchronous learning tools, access to technology, online competition of faculty and students, academic dishonesty, and privacy and confidentiality

2   Methodology

For the present investigation, a quantitative investigation was conducted in which a questionnaire was applied to assess four videoconferencing platforms: Zoom, Microsoft Teams, Google Meet, and WhatsApp. Four dimensions of each platform were evaluated: usability, design, benefits of the platform to develop academic activities, and the reliability of each platform.

The survey population consisted of 33 male and female teachers who work in the fiscal education system, of which 13 teachers had fourth-level studies and 20 had third-level studies.

In relation to the information collection instrument, it was a questionnaire that consisted of five questions elaborated on with the Likert scale.

3   Results

Table 2 lists the questions that the teachers were asked to answer.

Table 2. Quiz

	Questions
Q1	In your experience, which do you consider the best platform for the development of online classes?
Q2	How easy is it to learn how to use each app?
Q3	In relation to the platforms listed, how would you rate the aesthetics of the user interface?
Q4	Based on your experience, how would you rate the operation of the tools and functions, such as screen sharing, audio, whiteboard, chat, and creating work rooms offered by the different platforms?
Q5	How would you rate the ability of the platforms to be available when you need to use them?

Participants were asked to state which videoconferencing platform was the best in relation to their experience, to which 81.82% determined that the best platform is Zoom (Fig. 1).

Fig. 1. Results of question 1

Table 3 shows the breakdown of responses to question 1.

Table 3. Numerical breakdown of responses to question 1

In your experience, which do you consider the best platform for the development of online classes?

Zoom	27	81.82%
Microsoft teams	4	12.12%
Google meet	2	6.06%
WhatsApp	0	0.00%
Total	33	100%

Platform Usability Dimension. Figure 2 shows the response percentages to question 2 on how easy it is to learn how to use each app, which indicates that Zoom is the easiest platform to learn to use.

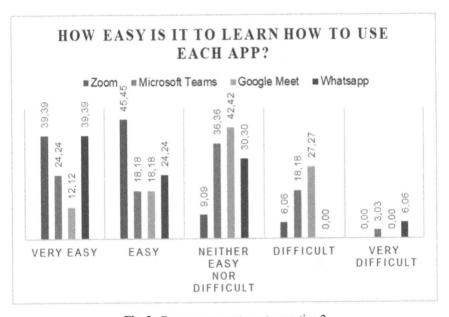

Fig. 2. Response percentages to question 2

Table 4 shows the breakdown of responses to question 2.

Table 4. Numerical breakdown of responses to question 2

How easy is it to learn how to use each app?

Platform	Very easy	Easy	Neither easy nor difficult	Difficult	Very difficult	Total
Zoom	13	15	3	2	0	33
Microsoft teams	8	6	12	6	1	33
Google meet	4	6	14	9	0	33
WhatsApp	13	8	10	0	2	33

Design Dimension of Video Conference Platforms. Figure 3 shows the response percentages to question 3 regarding the platform interfaces, with Zoom and WhatsApp being the platforms that participants indicated as having the best user interface design.

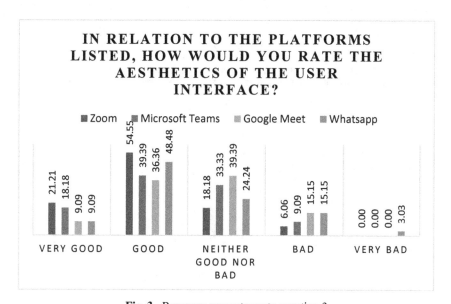

Fig. 3. Response percentages to question 3

Table 5 shows the breakdown of responses to question 3.

Table 5. Numerical breakdown of responses to question 3

In relation to the platforms listed, how would you rate the aesthetics of the user interface?						
Platform	Very good	Good	Neither good nor bad	Bad	Very bad	Total
Zoom	7	18	6	2	0	33
Microsoft teams	6	13	11	3	0	33
Google meet	3	12	13	5	0	33
WhatsApp	3	16	8	5	1	33

Dimension Benefits of the Platform in Developing Academic Activities. Figure   4 shows the response percentages to question 4 regarding the benefits of the platform to develop academic activities, with Zoom considered the platform that provides the best benefits, followed by Teams.

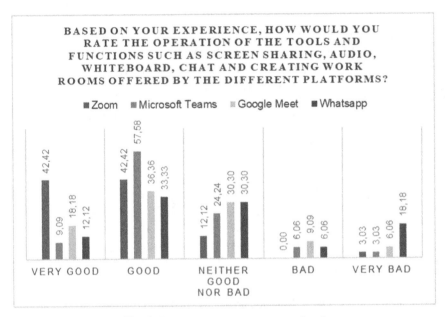

Fig. 4. Response percentages to question 4

Table 6 shows the breakdown of responses to question 4.

Table 6. Numerical breakdown of responses to question 4

Platform	Very good	Good	Neither good nor bad	Bad	Very bad	Total
Based on your experience with the different platforms, how would you rate the operation of the tools and functions, such as screen sharing, audio, whiteboard, chat, and creating work rooms?						
Zoom	14	14	4	0	1	33
Microsoft teams	3	19	8	2	1	33
Google meet	6	12	10	3	2	33
WhatsApp	4	11	10	2	6	33

Platform Reliability Dimension. Figure 5 shows the response percentages to question 5 regarding the reliability of videoconferencing platforms, such as whether they are available when required, with WhatsApp perceived as having the greatest reliability, followed by Zoom.

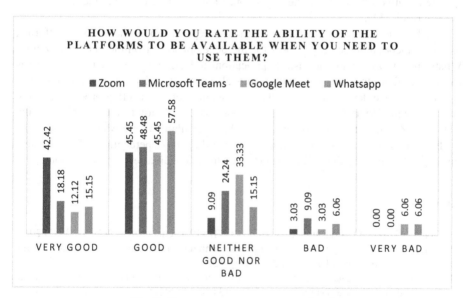

Fig. 5. Response percentages to question 5

Table 7 shows the breakdown of responses to question 5.

Table 7. Numerical breakdown of responses to question 5

How would you rate the ability of the platforms to be available when you need to use them?						
	Very good	Good	Neither good nor bad	Bad	Very bad	Total
Zoom	14	15	3	1	0	33
Microsoft teams	6	16	8	3	0	33
Google meet	4	15	11	1	2	33
WhatsApp	5	19	5	2	2	33

4 Conclusions

Similar studies point to a link between the learning experience and the chosen system. For example, Zoom, Skype, and Teams support screen sharing, app sharing, and in-meeting file transfer, which gives educators a host of ways to exchange and share educational materials [2] and users' intentions to use Zoom in the future. Other studies have pointed out the negative effects of online education, finding that teacher fatigue is the worst adverse result [11].

Finally, based on our research of teacher perceptions about the various platforms, the best videoconferencing platform for the development of online classes is Zoom; WhatsApp and Zoom are the easiest applications to learn to use, while Google Meet is the most difficult to learn. The study results also show that Zoom is perceived to have the best interface design and offers the best benefits for the meeting process teaching learning, while WhatsApp offers the least benefits. In relation to the reliability of the platforms, Zoom and WhatsApp are seen as being available to use when needed.

Based on the results, it can be noted that according to the perceptions of the teachers surveyed, the platform that offers the best benefits in the areas evaluated is Zoom.

References

1. Cóndor-Herrera, O.: Educar en tiempos de COVID-19. Cienciamerica 9(2), 31–37 (2020)
2. Correia, A., Liu, C., Xu, F.: Evaluating videoconferencing systems for the quality of the educational experience. Distance Educ. 41(4), 429–452 (2020)
3. Lee, A., Chan, H.: Challenged by the masses: using microsoft teams live event to moderate large-scale meetings. J. Dental Educ. 85(1), 1134–1135 (2021)
4. Ramos-Galarza, C., Arias-Flores, H., Cóndor-Herrera, O., Jadán-Guerrero, J.: Literacy toy for enhancement phonological awareness: a longitudinal study. In: Miesenberger, K., Manduchi, R., Covarrubias Rodriguez, M., Peňáz, P. (eds.) ICCHP 2020. LNCS, vol. 12377, pp. 371–377. Springer, Cham (2020). https://doi.org/10.1007/978-3-030-58805-2_44
5. Sobaih, A., Salem, A., Hasanein, A., Abu Elnasr, A.: Responses to covid-19 in higher education: students' learning experience using microsoft teams versus social network sites. Sustainability 13(18), 1–12 (2021)
6. Pramana, C., et al.: Virtual learning during the covid-19 pandemic, a disruptive technology in higher education in Indonesia. Int. J. Pharm. Res. 12(2), 3209–3216 (2020)

7. Turnbull, D., Chug, R., Luck, J.: Transitioning to E-learning during the COVID-19 pandemic: how have higher education institutions responded to the challenge? Educ. Inf. Technol. **26**, 6401–6419 (2021)
8. Almahasees, Z., Mohsen, K., Amin, M.: Faculty's and students' perceptions of online learning during COVID-19. Front. Educ. **6** (2021)
9. Dorfsman, M., Horenczyk, G.: The coping of academic staff with an extreme situation: the transition from conventional teaching to online teaching. Educ. Inf. Technol. **27**, 267–289 (2022)
10. Kansal, A., Gautam, J., Chintalapudi, N., Jain, S., Battineni, G.: Google trend analysis and paradigm shift of online education platforms during the COVID-19 pandemic. Infect. Dis. Rep. **13**(2), 418–428 (2021)
11. Oducado, R., Dequilla, M., Villaruz, J.: Factors predicting videoconferencing fatigue among higher education faculty. Educ. Inf. Technol. 1–12 (2022)
12. Camilleri, M., Camilleri, A.: The acceptance of learning management systems and video conferencing technologies: lessons learned from COVID-19. Technol. Knowl. Learn. (2021)
13. Mora-Jimenez, L.D., Ramírez-Benavides, K., Quesada, L., Lopez, G., Guerrero, L.A.: User experience in communication and collaboration platforms: a comparative study including discord, microsoft teams, and zoom. In: Rocha, Á., Ferrás, C., Méndez Porras, A., Jimenez Delgado, E. (eds.) ICITS 2022. LNNS, vol. 414, pp. 52–61. Springer, Cham (2022). https://doi.org/10.1007/978-3-030-96293-7_6
14. Wea, K., Kuki, A.D.: Students' perceptions of using microsoft teams application in online learning during the Covid-19 pandemic. J. Phys. Conf. Ser. **1842**(1), 012016 (2021)
15. Dash, S., Samadder, S., Srivastava, A., Meena, R., Ranjan, P.: Review of online teaching platforms in the current period of COVID-19 pandemic. Indian J. Surg. 1–6 (2021)
16. Rio-Chillcce, A., Jara-Monge, L., Andrade-Arenas, L.: Analysis of the use of videoconferencing in the learning process during the pandemic at a university in lima. Int. J. Adv. Comput. Sci. Appl. **12**(5), 870–878 (2021)
17. Bailey, D., Almusharraf, N., Almusharraf, A.: Video conferencing in the e-learning context: explaining learning outcome with the technology acceptance model. Educ. Inf. Technol. 1–20 (2022)

Effects of Virtual Reality on School Students' Learning in Safety Education: A Meta-analysis

Jen-I. Chiu and Mengping Tsuei[✉]

Graduate School of Curriculum and Instructional Communication Technology, National Taipei University of Education, Taipei, Taiwan
mptsuei@mail.ntue.edu.tw

Abstract. Virtual reality (VR) has been used to create immersive and realistic learning environments. Safety education increases students' awareness of potential hazards. Effective safety education should include a variety of scenarios in which students can practice recognising and responding appropriately to hazardous situations. VR has been shown to benefit students' safety education by increasing their awareness of hazards. This meta-analysis was performed to examine the overall effect of VR use on students' safety education, including safety knowledge, safety behaviour, motivation and presence, compared with control interventions. Locomotion, the input device and the display hardware were examined as moderating variables. Fifteen publications with 39 effect sizes ($n = 2,411$ participants) were included. No publication bias was detected. VR had a significantly positive effect on the overall effect size for safety education compared with control interventions (e.g., educational documents, lectures, animations). Effect sizes were large for motivation, medium for presence and safety knowledge, and small for safety behaviour. Only locomotion (large effect size) had a moderating effect, improving safety education. These findings support the effectiveness of VR use in safety education. Additional research is needed to examine more independent and moderating variables for this educational approach.

Keywords: Meta-analysis · Safety education · Virtual reality

1 Introduction

Accidental injuries pose serious health risks (Murray et al. 2018). The majority of them can be predicted and prevented. Although safety education is widely regarded as an effective and challenging means of injury prevention, traditional training methods (e.g. brochures, lectures, animations) are not considered to be the ideal solution in terms of students' knowledge acquisition and retention (Lovreglio et al. 2021). Physical training, considered to be an effective means of safety education, is difficult to generalise due to the high associated costs (Enz and Taylor 2002). Virtual reality (VR) provides a highly interactive, low-cost learning environment in which students can participate actively in learning contexts. Students who engage in virtual worlds can transfer their virtual behaviour strategies to the real world (Ferretti 2021). Although VR cannot completely

© The Author(s), under exclusive license to Springer Nature Switzerland AG 2022
C. Stephanidis et al. (Eds.): HCII 2022, CCIS 1655, pp. 130–137, 2022.
https://doi.org/10.1007/978-3-031-19682-9_17

replace physical safety training courses due to hardware limitations, it can be used to simulate hazardous situations in a hazardless virtual environment, allowing students to practice repeatedly (Norris et al. 2019).

Research findings regarding the effectiveness of VR in safety education have been inconsistent. Compared with control interventions, some studies support the effectiveness of VR-based approaches in terms of students' motivation (Araiza-Alba et al. 2021), presence (Ahn et al. 2020), safety behaviour (Josman et al. 2008) and safety knowledge (Feng et al. 2021). However, Makransky et al. (2019) found no significant difference in laboratory safety knowledge between students who learned through VR and those who learned using educational documents. Kinateder et al. (2013) also found no significant difference in fire safety behaviours between students who received a VR intervention and those who received no intervention. Hence, we conducted a meta-analysis to examine the overall learning outcomes of VR application in safety education. The mean effects of VR and control interventions on school students' safety learning outcomes were compared, and factors moderating these effects were identified.

2 VR in Safety Education

VR has been shown to facilitate students' safety learning. Çakiroğlu and Gökoğlu (2019) proposed a VR-based behavioural skills training model with an instruction–modelling–rehearsal–feedback structure, and reported that this model motivated students to improve their safety skills in the virtual environment. Nykänen et al. (2019) proposed a model based on planned behaviour and social cognitive theories, and noted that a sense of presence influenced students' safety knowledge during VR training. Primary-school students have been shown to be more motivated to receive VR-based than traditional video and poster–based water safety education (Araiza-Alba et al. 2021). College students showed significantly more presence during VR-based than during smartphone-based flight safety education (Buttussi and Chittaro 2020). Avveduto et al. (2017) found that students who received VR-based construction safety education had more intent to follow safety principles than did those who received a control intervention. Finally, Lovreglio et al. (2021) observed more acquisition and retention of safety knowledge among college students who received VR-based fire safety education than among those who received a video-based intervention.

Students may experience sickness in virtual environments due to hardware limitations, resulting in reduced presence and a greater cognitive load (Somrak et al. 2019). Shu et al. (2019) found no significant difference in the presence of college students receiving VR- and computer game–based earthquake safety education. Makransky et al. (2019) found no significant difference in the safety knowledge of college students receiving VR- and educational document-based laboratory safety education.

3 Method

3.1 Search Strategy and Eligibility Assessment

Relevant studies published between 2008 and 2021 were found by searching the EBSCO-host platform, ACM Digital Library and IEEE Xplore Digital Library. The keywords used were 'virtual reality', 'disaster', 'safety education', 'risk prevention', 'hazardous', 'accident prevention', and 'injury'. Google Scholar was used to retrieve all available identified publications. Researchers first browsed the publications' titles, abstracts and keywords. After reviewing the full text, duplicates and ineligible publications were removed based on the following inclusion criteria: 1) use of VR in safety education; 2) examination of users' presence, motivation, safety behaviour and safety knowledge; 3) use of a (quasi-) experimental research design; 4) inclusion of K–12 and/or college students as participants; 5) publication in English; 6) provision of sufficient statistical data for effect size calculation; and 7) full text availability. This meta-analysis included 15 journal articles published between 2008 and 2021. The total sample comprised 2,411 participants, of whom 1,244 received VR interventions and 1,167 received control interventions. The studies included 39 effect sizes. The sample school students were aged between 7 and 31 and the VR was used for construction, disaster, fire, flight, and laboratory safety education. Control interventions have included computer games, educational documents, lectures, slides, videos, real-life situations and no intervention.

3.2 Coding

Learning outcomes of VR-based safety education were coded as presence, motivation, safety behaviour and safety knowledge. Moderating variables were also coded in this study. Locomotion was defined as the user's ability to perform physical movements in the VR environment. Students who were unable to move or use joystick locomotion were defined as non-locomotion. Input device were coded as no controller, VR joystick and traditional input devices (e.g., keyboard and mouse). Finally, display hardware were coded as immersion VR (HMD VR, projection VR) and non-immersion VR (desktop VR).

3.3 Effect Size Calculation

In calculating effect sizes, the sample size, learning outcome scores, and variance of two groups (VR intervention and control intervention) were used. The comprehensive meta-analysis software version 3.0 (Biostat, Englewood, NJ, USA) was utilized to estimate the overall effect size based on Cohen's d:

$$\text{Cohen's } d = \frac{\overline{X}_1 - \overline{X}_2}{\sqrt{\frac{(n_1-1)S_1^2+(n_2-1)S_2^2}{(n_1+n_2-2)}}}$$

where $\overline{X}_1$ and $\overline{X}_2$ represent the mean scores, n_1 and n_2 represent the sample sizes and S_1^2 and S_2^2 represent the variances of two groups. Hedges' g was used to calculate effect sizes, as the included studies typically had small participant samples. The formula for Hedges' g is:

$$\text{Hedges' } g = \text{Cohen's } d \times \left[1 - \frac{3}{4(N-2)-1}\right].$$

Following Lipsey and Wilson (2001), values ≤ 0.32 were considered to represent small effects, those of 0.33–0.55 were considered to represent medium effects, and those ≥ 0.56 were considered to represent large effects. A random-effects model was used in the overall effect size calculation because of the diversity of publications years and regions. Post-hoc subgroup analyses were conducted using a mixed-effects model (Borenstein et al. 2021).

4 Results

4.1 Overall Effect of VR in Safety Education

The overall effect size was medium ($g = 0.55$; 95% confidence interval, 0.36–0.75; $Z = 5.58$, $p < .001$). Thus, the overall learning outcomes of VR-based safety education were significantly greater than those of the control interventions.

4.2 Publication Bias

We examined publication bias using Egger's test. The result revealed no evidence of publication bias ($p > .05$).

4.3 Effects on Learning Outcomes

The effect size for motivation was large ($g = 0.72$), with significant within-group differences ($Z = 5.21, p < .001$). That for safety knowledge was medium ($g = 0.40$), with significant within-group differences ($Z = 3.05, p < .01$). The effect size for presence was medium ($g = 0.45$) and that for safety behaviour was small ($g = 0.20$), with no significant within-group difference ($Z = 1.53$ and 0.76, respectively; Table 1). The learning outcomes did not moderate the overall effect size ($Q = 4.38$; Table 1).

Table 1. Effects of learning outcomes and moderating variables

	Effect size and 95% confidence interval							Heterogeneity		
	K	g	SE	Lower limit	Upper limit	Z	p	Q	df	p
Overall effect (N = 15)	–	0.55	.10	0.36	0.75	5.58	.00***			
Outcomes										
Motivation	14	0.72	.14	0.45	0.99	5.21	.00***			
Presence	3	0.45	.29	−0.13	1.03	1.53	.13			

(*continued*)

Table 1. (*continued*)

	Effect size and 95% confidence interval							Heterogeneity		
	K	g	SE	Lower limit	Upper limit	Z	p	Q	df	p
Safety behaviour	5	0.20	.26	−0.32	0.72	0.76	.45			
Safety knowledge	17	0.40	.13	0.14	0.65	3.05	.00**			
Total between								4.38	3	.22
Locomotion										
Non-locomotion	37	0.47	.08	0.30	0.63	5.53	.00***			
With locomotion	2	1.59	.46	0.69	2.49	3.47	.00**			
Total between								5.82	1	.02*
Input device										
No controller	10	0.19	.16	−0.13	0.51	1.18	.24			
VR joystick	16	0.58	.13	0.32	0.83	4.42	.00***			
Traditional input devices	13	0.66	.15	0.37	0.95	4.47	.00***			
Total between								5.07	2	.08
Display hardware										
Immersion VR	26	0.43	.10	0.22	0.63	4.13	.00***			
Non-immersion VR	13	0.66	.15	0.37	0.95	4.40	.00***			
Total between								1.62	1	.20

$^* p < .05, ** p < .01, *** p < .01.$

Effects According to Locomotion. The effect size for locomotion was large ($g = 1.59$), with significant within-group differences ($Z = 3.47, p < .01$). The effect size for non-locomotion was medium ($g = 0.47$), with significant within-group differences ($Z = 5.53, p < .001$). Locomotion moderated the overall effect size ($Q = 5.82, p < .05$; Table 1), suggesting that students who performed locomotion in the VR environment had significantly better overall learning outcomes than did students who did not.

Effects According to Input Device. The effect sizes for VR joysticks and traditional input devices were large ($g = 0.58$ and 0.66, respectively), with significant within-group differences ($Z = 4.42$ and 4.47, respectively; both $p < .001$). The effect size for no input device was small ($g = 0.19$), with no significant within-group difference ($Z = 1.18$). The input device did not moderate the overall effect size ($Q = 5.07$; Table 1).

Effects According to Display Hardware. The effect size for non-immersion VR was large ($g = 0.66$), significant within-group differences ($Z = 4.40, p < .001$). That for immersion VR was medium ($g = 0.43$), with significant within-group differences ($Z =$

$4.13, p < .001$). The display hardware did not moderate the overall effect size ($Q = 1.62$; Table 1).

5   Discussion and Conclusions

Previous meta-analyses have found that VR has a significant positive effect on disciplinary knowledge (Merchant et al. 2014). The results of this meta-analysis support the effectiveness of VR use in safety education on overall learning outcomes, especially students' motivation and safety knowledge. Effect sizes for locomotion and non-locomotion in the VR environment were large and medium, respectively. Those for the use of VR joysticks and traditional input devices were large, and that for no input device use was small. Effect sizes for non-immersive and immersive VR were large and medium, respectively.

This meta-analysis contributes to the examination of the effectiveness of locomotion in the VR environment on learning outcomes. Physical movement is considered to have a positive cognitive impact on students (Marsh et al. 2013). Hejtmanek et al. (2020) found that VR with locomotion could slightly increase students' spatial knowledge transfer but also resulted in cybersickness compared to non-immersive VR. Additional empirical studies examining the effectiveness of locomotion in VR learning environments are needed.

This preliminary study of VR use in safety education was limited by the small number of publications included and the focus on traditional school-aged students. We suggest that future research involve the empirical examination of VR-based safety education for adults and the other education-related moderating variables. Overall, this study showed that VR has a significant positive impact on safety education. We recommend that VR developers provide features that allow students to perform locomotion, as this ability improves learning outcomes.

References

Ahn, S., Kim, T., Park, Y.J., Kim, J.M.: Improving effectiveness of safety training at construction worksite using 3D BIM simulation. Adv. Civil Eng. **2020**, 2473138 (2020). https://doi.org/10.1155/2020/2473138

Araiza-Alba, P., et al.: The potential of 360-degree virtual reality videos to teach water-safety skills to children. Comput. Educ. **163**, 104096 (2021). https://doi.org/10.1016/j.compedu.2020.104096

Arbogast, H., Burke, R.V., Muller, V., Ruiz, P., Knudson, M.M., Upperman, J.S.: Randomized controlled trial to evaluate the effectiveness of a video game as a child pedestrian educational tool. J. Trauma Acute Care Surg. **76**(5), 1317–1321 (2014). https://doi.org/10.1097/TA.0000000000000217

Avveduto, G., Tanca, C., Lorenzini, C., Tecchia, F., Carrozzino, M., Bergamasco, M.: Safety training using virtual reality: a comparative approach. In: De Paolis, L.T., Bourdot, P., Mongelli, A. (eds.) AVR 2017. LNCS, vol. 10324, pp. 148–163. Springer, Cham (2017). https://doi.org/10.1007/978-3-319-60922-5_11

Bart, O., Katz, N., Weiss, P.L., Josman, N.: Street crossing by typically developed children in real and virtual environments. Occup. Participation Health **28**(2), 89–96 (2008). https://doi.org/10.3928/15394492-20080301-01

Borenstein, M., Hedges, L.V., Higgins, J.P., Rothstein, H.R.: Introduction to Meta-Analysis. Wiley, Hoboken (2021)

Buttussi, F., Chittaro, L.: A comparison of procedural safety training in three conditions: virtual reality headset, smartphone, and printed materials. IEEE Trans. Learn. Technol. **14**(1), 1–15 (2020). https://doi.org/10.1109/TLT.2020.3033766

Çakiroğlu, Ü., Gökoğlu, S.: Development of fire safety behavioral skills via virtual reality. Comput. Educ. **133**, 56–68 (2019). https://doi.org/10.1016/j.compedu.2019.01.014

Chittaro, L., Buttussi, F.: Assessing knowledge retention of an immersive serious game vs. a traditional education method in aviation safety. IEEE Trans. Vis. Comput. Graph. **21**(4), 529–538 (2015). https://doi.org/10.1109/TVCG.2015.2391853

Enz, C.A., Taylor, M.S.: The safety and security of US hotels a post-September-11 report. Cornell Hotel Restaur. Adm. Q. **43**(5), 119–136 (2002). https://doi.org/10.1177/0010880402435011

Farra, S., Miller, E., Timm, N., Schafer, J.: Improved training for disasters using 3-D virtual reality simulation. West. J. Nurs. Res. **35**(5), 655–671 (2013). https://doi.org/10.1177/0193945912471735

Feng, Z., González, V.A., Mutch, C., Amor, R., Cabrera-Guerrero, G.: Instructional mechanisms in immersive virtual reality serious games: earthquake emergency training for children. J. Comput. Assist. Learn. **37**(2), 542–556 (2021). https://doi.org/10.1111/jcal.12507

Ferretti, G.: A distinction concerning vision-for-action and affordance perception. Conscious Cogn. **87**, 103028 (2021). https://doi.org/10.1016/j.concog.2020.103028

Hejtmanek, L., Starrett, M., Ferrer, E., Ekstrom, A.D.: How much of what we learn in virtual reality transfers to real-world navigation? Multisensory Res. **33**(4–5), 479–503 (2020). https://doi.org/10.1163/22134808-20201445

Joshi, S., et al.: Implementing virtual reality technology for safety training in the precast/prestressed concrete industry. Appl. Ergon. **90**, 103286 (2021). https://doi.org/10.1016/j.apergo.2020.103286

Josman, N., Ben-Chaim, H.M., Friedrich, S., Weiss, P.L.: Effectiveness of virtual reality for teaching street-crossing skills to children and adolescents with autism. Int. J. Disabil. Hum. Dev. **7**(1), 49–56 (2008). https://doi.org/10.1515/IJDHD.2008.7.1.49

Kinateder, M., et al.: Human behaviour in severe tunnel accidents: effects of information and behavioural training. Transport. Res. F: Traffic Psychol. Behav. **17**, 20–32 (2013). https://doi.org/10.1016/j.trf.2012.09.001

Leder, J., Horlitz, T., Puschmann, P., Wittstock, V., Schütz, A.: Comparing immersive virtual reality and powerpoint as methods for delivering safety training: Impacts on risk perception, learning, and decision making. Saf. Sci. **111**, 271–286 (2019). https://doi.org/10.1016/j.ssci.2018.07.021

Lipsey, M.W., Wilson, D.B.: Practical Meta-Analysis. Sage, Thousand Oaks (2001)

Lovreglio, R., Duan, X., Rahouti, A., Phipps, R., Nilsson, D.: Comparing the effectiveness of fire extinguisher virtual reality and video training. Virtual Reality **25**(1), 133–145 (2021). https://doi.org/10.1016/10.1007/s10055-020-00447-5

Makransky, G., Borre-Gude, S., Mayer, R.E.: Motivational and cognitive benefits of training in immersive virtual reality based on multiple assessments. J. Comput. Assist. Learn. **35**(6), 691–707 (2019). https://doi.org/10.1111/jcal.12375

Marsh, W.E., Kelly, J.W., Dark, V.J., Oliver, J.H.: Cognitive demands of semi-natural virtual locomotion. Presence: Teleoperators Virtual Environ. **22**(3), 216–234 (2013). https://doi.org/10.1162/PRES_a_00152

Merchant, Z., Goetz, E.T., Cifuentes, L., Keeney-Kennicutt, W., Davis, T.J.: Effectiveness of virtual reality-based instruction on students' learning outcomes in K-12 and higher education: a meta-analysis. Comput. Educ. **70**, 29–40 (2014). https://doi.org/10.1016/j.compedu.2013.07.033

Murray, M.J., McCunn, M., Kucik, C.J.: Injury prevention. ASA Monit. **82**(1), 40–43 (2018)

Norris, M.W., Spicer, K., Byrd, T.: Virtual reality: the new pathway for effective safety training. Prof. Saf. **64**(06), 36–39 (2019)

Nykänen, M., Salmela-Aro, K., Tolvanen, A., Vuori, J.: Safety self-efficacy and internal locus of control as mediators of safety motivation–randomized controlled trial (RCT) study. Saf. Sci. **117**, 330–338 (2019). https://doi.org/10.1016/j.ssci.2019.04.037

Pham, H.C., et al.: Virtual field trip for mobile construction safety education using 360-degree panoramic virtual reality. Int. J. Eng. Educ. **4**, 1174–1191 (2018)

Rossler, K.L., Ganesh Sankaranarayanan, D., Duvall, A.: Acquisition of fire safety knowledge and skills with virtual reality simulation. Nurse Educ. **44**(2), 88–92 (2019). https://doi.org/10.1097/NNE.0000000000000551

Sacks, R., Perlman, A., Barak, R.: Construction safety training using immersive virtual reality. Constr. Manag. Econ. **31**(9), 1005–1017 (2013). https://doi.org/10.1080/01446193.2013.828844

Shu, Y., Huang, Y.-Z., Chang, S.-H., Chen, M.-Y.: Do virtual reality head-mounted displays make a difference? A comparison of presence and self-efficacy between head-mounted displays and desktop computer-facilitated virtual environments. Virtual Reality **23**(4), 437–446 (2019). https://doi.org/10.1007/s10055-018-0376-x

Smith, S., Ericson, E.: Using immersive game-based virtual reality to teach fire-safety skills to children. Virtual Reality **13**(2), 87–99 (2009). https://doi.org/10.1007/s10055-009-0113-6

Somrak, A., Humar, I., Hossain, M.S., Alhamid, M.F., Hossain, M.A., Guna, J.: Estimating VR Sickness and user experience using different HMD technologies: an evaluation study. Futur. Gener. Comput. Syst. **94**, 302–316 (2019). https://doi.org/10.1016/j.future.2018.11.041

Application of a Mixed Methodology to Evaluate the Interactions of Adolescents with YouTube in the Framework of Comprehensive Sexual Education

Marco Antonio Guzmán Garnica[✉] [iD], Jessica Martínez Herrera[iD],
Adrián Gerardo Mateos Barragán[iD], Rocío Abascal Mena[iD],
Gloria Angélica Martínez De la Peña, and Caridad García Hernández

Master in Design, Information and Communication (MADIC), Universidad Autónoma
Metropolitana, Cuajimalpa, Avenida Vasco de Quiroga 4871, Colonia Santa Fe Cuajimalpa, Del.
Cuajimalpa de Morelos, C.P. 05300 Ciudad de México, Mexico
marcogarnica21@gmail.com, {mabascal,gmartinez,
caridad.garcia}@dccd.mx

Abstract. The article presents the application of a Human-Computer Interaction (HCI) test with teenagers between 15–18 years old in Nezahualcóyotl, Mexico. We aim to identify what steps the teenagers follow to choose information sources coming from digital sources. The main topic is the use and appropriation of communication tools for the resolution of family conflicts with gender perspective in the frame of Comprehensive Sexual Education (CSE) with the aim of creating the frame of reference for the design of a mediation tool based in the principles of Human-Centered Design (HCD). In this document, we describe the stages that constitute the design methodology of Human-Centered Design that allowed us to identify the behavior and interaction that takes place between the teenagers and the digital environment that has the most presence and relevance between them for informing themselves about sexuality. The results obtained of the implementation are as follows: the delimitation of the digital environment with more relevance for teenagers between 15–18 years when they research about sexuality on the internet, the identification of the topic about sexuality that those teenagers search the most and, finally, the understanding of the interaction that takes place between the teenagers and the digital environment so we can design a mediation tool based in the principles of Human-Centered Design.

Keywords: Comprehensive sexual education · Social constructivism · Human-computer interaction · Human-centered design · Digital platform · Youtube

1 Introduction

Comprehensive Sexual Education (CSE) is an educational model that aims to provide teenagers, among other things, with communication tools for the resolution of family

C. Stephanidis et al. (Eds.): HCII 2022, CCIS 1655, pp. 138–145, 2022.
https://doi.org/10.1007/978-3-031-19682-9_18

conflicts with gender perspective [1]. According to the General Law on Children and Adolescents issued in Mexico in 2014, the CSE is a right and, therefore, must be taught in all primary, secondary and high schools in Mexican territory [2].

The CSE model focuses its efforts on seven basic themes, which are: gender, sexual and reproductive health, sexual citizenship, pleasure, violence, diversity and relationships [3]. Another feature of CSE is that it focuses its actions on formal and non-formal education, since according to UNESCO [4] school authorities have the power to regulate various aspects of learning environments and are a meeting place between tutors, students and the community with other services related to the care of children and adolescents. And in non-formal education settings, the international organization states that they "have the potential to reach out-of-school youth and the most vulnerable and marginalized youth populations, especially in countries where school attendance is low or where adequate CSE is not included as part of the national curriculum" [4].

But what happens in densely populated urban environments such as Nezahualcóyotl? That is, in environments where there is educational infrastructure and there are an increasing number of school dropouts, but they are not considered marginalized areas, since even indicators such as internet access or per capita income are high [5]. In addition to the previous context, according to the study Switched on: sexuality education in the digital space carried out by UNESCO, more than 45% of adolescents between the ages of 15 and 18 are informed about sexuality issues on the Internet [6]. All of that has a negative impact on the application of CSE from formal and no-formal education, since digital environments are gaining more relevance. Therefore, it can be said that although the CSE application manuals proposed by international entities and the Mexican government make recommendations for the application of the model through formal and informal education, it is a fact that the new digital information dynamics of young people demand the study of interactions for learning in order to design new implementation strategies through educational tools that contemplate the digital scenarios that are most relevant in contemporary education every day.

In that sense, this research focuses on exploring what adolescent interaction is like for the resolution of doubts about sexuality in digital media to lay the foundations for a design of mediation [7] for learning based on Human-Centered Design [8] and the principles of Human-Computer Interaction [9]. This will allow the implementation strategies of CSE to be opened to social environments that are increasingly relevant among teenagers.

2 Background

Human-Computer Interaction can be understood as the set of actions through which a human use and interacts with a machine [10] or also, as a discipline that deals with the design, evaluation and implementation of interactive computer systems for human use and with the study of the main phenomena that surround it [11]. In this way, both definitions rescue fundamental elements of interaction that help us understand the phenomenon of the digital environments, but above all, the use of devices to meet a particular need in humans.

Something relevant about the HCI is that its principles are based on the HCD, which in turn is based on the understanding and satisfaction of the needs of those who use a product [8] through two central concepts. First, visibility, understood as the relationship between the user's objectives, the actions required and the results in a sensible, meaningful and non-arbitrary way; second, the affordability concept that refers to the properties of objects, that is, what type of operations and manipulations can be allowed to make a particular object [8]. Both pillar concepts of the HCD refer to the construction of objects based on the needs and characteristics of the humans who interact with the object. For this reason, this design perspective is empathetic with the objectives of the CSE, since this model also aims to offer an educational model that respects the psycho-emotional needs of teenagers and responds to the context of people; a context that is currently permeated by digital media.

With regard to pedagogical action, a perspective that is also built from listening to students and recognizes the value of the social context to generate education is social constructivism [7]. This thought perspective establishes that the processes of formation of concepts and new knowledge for daily life are framed by the interaction of students in a social environment, respect for the pedagogical needs of students and the recognition of learning spaces beyond those established within schools. In addition, perspectives for the creation of educational models such as Paulo Freire's [12] also recognize the need to build educational alternatives through dialogue with students, while assessing their information needs and learning dynamics.

For this reason, both social constructivism and the perspectives for the construction of learning tools through dialogue as well as those proposed by Paulo Freire could be the theoretical basis for the application of the HCI tests proposed in this work; since these three perspectives appeal to the understanding of the dynamics of interaction for learning that people have in order to make a design proposal. For its part, the HCD generates user experiences by putting people at the center of the development process and thus, their needs during all stages of it.

With the unification of these four disciplines (HCI, HCD, social constructivism and Paulo Freire's proposal for methodological construction), in the next part of this work will present a proposal of a methodology in order to analyze a digital environment, for the learning of topics related to sexuality in teenagers aged 15 to 18 years of Nezahualcóyotl, Mexico. To achieve this, tests were conducted based on the proposed methodology, with the aim to regard the phenomenon studied in this research, that is, the interaction that the adolescents have in the learning of topics on sexuality by using digital media. Results will lay the foundations for the creation of a mediation design proposal that responds to the new dynamics of search and education from the digital environments of teenagers.

3 Methodological Proposal

Based on Paulo Freire's method of creation through dialogue and the principles of social constructivism that contemplate both the understanding of interaction for learning and the identification of the informative and pedagogical needs of students for the development of mediations that facilitate learning, this methodology proposes the implementation of an instrument for observing interaction integrated by two phases. Prior to the implementation of this methodology, exploratory research was carried out, through in-depth interviews and digital questionnaires, which resulted in two lists. The first of them offers a series of options on digital media that adolescents said they used more frequently to solve their doubts about sexuality; and the other reflects those topics that teenagers look for the most in these platforms. These two lists offer findings that will be the basis of analysis sought by the methodology.

The first phase of the methodology is called delimitation. This first phase is intended to understand which of these topics is of greatest interest to adolescents. Subsequently, this first phase of the methodology will also help to define which is the most relevant platform, with more affinity and most used by adolescents to solve their questions about sexuality, taking into account the list of means proposed by adolescents in that first exploratory research.

The second phase is called interaction comprehension methodology and aims to identify the interaction that teenagers have to satisfy their doubts in the digital platform most used by them in three ways:

- Understanding the way teenagers look for information on the platform.
- The identification of the characteristics in the contents that adolescents consider useful to answer their questions.
- The identification of the affectivity that teenagers have with the digital platform.

The delimitation part is built through a statistical analysis, the recovery of census data on the use of digital platforms in Nezahualcóyotl, Mexico proposed by state agencies of the Mexican government and through the calculation of the penetration rate [13]. While the second part of the methodology is built through HCI tests on a group of nine 15-year-old adolescents living in the region.

4 Discussion

Regarding the delimitation of the topic most asked on digital platforms by teenagers about sexuality, the results were the following: according to the questionnaires and interviews with 20 young people from Nezahualcóyotl that were carried out prior to the HCI test, the following topics are the most sought after: toxic relationships, gender roles, sex-affective orientation, relationships between friends and family life. First, in the HCI test, the nine-young people were asked which of these five topics was the one that generated the most doubts and the results are shown in Fig. 1. As can be seen in Fig. 1, family relationships are the topic that generates more doubts in adolescents, this since as they say "the confinement due to covid-19 made us rethink the way we get along with our families (parents and siblings)".

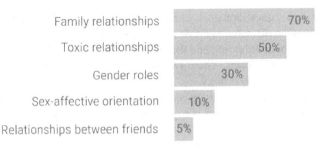

Fig. 1. Topics that students have manifested they search on the internet more frequently in an online survey

Regarding the delimitation of the platform that teenagers use the most to find out about family relationships, the list that emerged from the questionnaires prior to the application of the HCI test was used again. According to questionnaires and in-depth interviews, teenagers use Tik Tok, YouTube and Spotify, but which of these media has the highest penetration rate among users between 15 and 18 years old in Nezahualcóyotl?

According to the penetration rate calculation (number of users on the platform divided by the number of Internet users in Mexico between 15 and 18 years old by 100), YouTube is the medium with the highest penetration in adolescents, both by statistical calculation and by the characteristics of the medium. Since, according to teenagers, YouTube allows them to have an active search attitude through their search bar, there is diversification of specialized channels within the platform and the dynamics of dialogue between communities; they make users see this platform as a good alternative to find content that can be used as a source of first informative contact on the subject.

These characteristics are different in platforms such as Tik Tok or Spotify that, in the words of teenagers "it is a place where I do not look for things, but they come out and it is more about entertainment and not to learn and understand things". The distribution of penetration rate according to the penetration rate calculation and the opinion of adolescents is shown in Fig. 2.

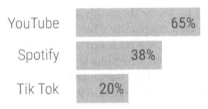

Fig. 2. Penetration rate of the digital media that teenagers said that they used more. This average (the result of calculation of the number of users on the platform divided by the number of Internet users in Mexico between 15 and 18 years old by 100) and the use usage behavior of the users on every platform

During the HCI tests, teenagers were asked what characteristics make YouTube a good space to answer questions about family relationships, in order to reaffirm the statistical data, found in the previous phase. According to the nine teenagers who took part in the interaction tests, what they value about the platform are the video formats, the use of easy-to-understand language, the immediacy of the platform, the practicality of searching thanks to the bar that YouTube has and the informative presentation in a fun and entertaining tone for teenagers.

With these two findings, it was possible to close the first part of the methodological application, since beneficial results were obtained for the investigation in its delimitation phase. These results are as follows: the issue that generates more questions in teenagers related to sexuality is family relationships, this since in the last year and a half they have had to deal with a confinement that exposes them to problems in the family environment. And, regarding the platform with the greatest relevance and usability to resolve doubts on the part of adolescents, the answer is YouTube. This was verified by calculating the penetration rate and the adolescents' verbalization about the characteristics that make this medium an ideal place to seek information at first.

Once the main doubt regarding sexuality and the medium with the greatest relevance was delimited, the second phase of the HCI test was applied. In this phase, the teenagers were asked to search YouTube for any questions they had regarding a topic of sexuality, select the video that best answered their question, and perform a visualization. At the end of the visualization, an interview was conducted with the adolescents to inquire about their experience within the platform and to find some statements about the affectivity they had when in contact with the medium. The results obtained are the following. Regarding the way in which teenagers carry out searches on YouTube, it was observed that six participants in the study did so through a question and another three did so through a keyword or the concept itself. Only one of them went directly to a channel within the platform that he had previously visited and at the time satisfactorily resolved his doubts. The above results show that users interact with the YouTube search engine through questions that have the following structure: "how can I improve my relationship with my parents?", "what is gender identity?" or "how to get out of a toxic relationship?".

Regarding the identification of the characteristics that the contents have that make teenagers consider them relevant and useful to solve their questions, the results are as follows. The covers of the videos, where the presenter shows his face and looks like a specialist, are more attractive to young people. The titles are another important element for them, because in their words they appreciate clear texts that are written in the form of a question and that use plain language. Finally, another important characteristic for the members of the study to consider a video as useful is the information it presents; this must be real, specialized and expressed in common words for adolescents.

Finally, regarding the affectivity that adolescents have with the YouTube platform, the members of the study stated that this medium can present false information, because "many times it is not known if those who are speaking are specialists in the subject"; They also acknowledge that they use the platform as a source of first contact since "the information they consult on YouTube must be verified" and they are grateful that this platform provides them with anonymity since "although I know that YouTube is not the best source, I can access it to resolve complex issues to address with someone".

5 Conclusions and Further Work

Tests to detect the information needs of teenagers regarding sexuality and Human-Computer Interaction show that digital platforms such as YouTube are getting relevance as first-hand information contact points to resolve questions related to sexuality in teenagers; this, since the platform provides anonymity to young people, and is an entertaining, practical and accessible option to find information. Also, we observed that the context of confinement due to Covid-19 modified the behavioral patterns and questions that teenagers have about issues related to sexuality, since according to the results, issues related to family relationships have gained relevance.

The interaction characteristics, the results and the observations that were made, show that teenagers have a great ability to navigate YouTube, search for content within the platform through the search bar and accessibility facilitators through interrogative sentences and the selection of videos through criteria such as immediacy, simplicity in language and attractiveness in the design of the covers.

Regarding the affectivity that teenagers have with YouTube, it was possible to observe that they consider the platform as a good option to access information due to the lack of digital and non-digital media that can provide them with a specialized space on sexuality and that has a fast and immediate user experience. They also considered that this digital platform provides a good experience since they can carry out searches anonymously on topics that are difficult to address with their close social circle.

The findings obtained in the two tests allow to lay the foundations for the design of a digital mediation that responds to the information needs of teenagers within the framework of CSE. The characteristics that are proposed for the design, according to the results, are the following: it must allow anonymous navigation for the users, provide verified information regarding the tools for resolving family conflicts with a gender perspective, present an architecture of information based on frequent asked questions and answers, it must use plain language and enable interaction between users so that, by sharing their experiences, the learning can be collective.

References

1. SALUD: Modelo de Atención Integral en Salud Sexual y Reproductiva para Adolescentes. http://www.cnegsr.salud.gob.mx/contenidos/descargas/SSRA/ModeloAISSRA/web_ModAtnIntSSRA.pdf
2. Diario Oficial de la Federación: Ley General de Niñas, Niños y Adolescentes. https://www.gob.mx/sipinna/documentos/ley-general-de-los-derechos-de-ninas-ninos-y-adolescentes-reformada-20-junio-2018
3. Comisión Nacional de los Derechos Humanos México: El interés superior de niñas, niños y adolescentes una consideración primordial. https://www.cndh.org.mx/sites/all/doc/Programas/Ninez_familia/Material/cuadri_interes_superior_NNA.pdf
4. Organización Mundial de la Salud: La salud sexual y su relación con la salud reproductiva un enfoque operativo. https://apps.who.int/iris/bitstream/handle/10665/274656/9789243512884-spa.pdf
5. Internal Planned Parenthood Federation: Impartir + habilidades. Caja de herramientas: Ampliando la educación sexual integral (ESI). www.ippf.org

6. National Guidelines Task Force: Guidelines for Comprehensive Sexuality Education. https://healtheducationresources.unesco.org/library/documents/guidelines-comprehensive-sexuality-education-kindergarten-through-12th-grade
7. UNESCO: International technical guidance on sexuality education. UNESCO, Francia (2018)
8. Instituto Federal de telecomunicaciones: Uso de las TIC y actividades por internet en México. http://www.ift.org.mx/sites/default/files/contenidogeneral/estadisticas/usodeinternetenmexico.pdf
9. UNESCO: Switched on: sexuality education in the digital space. https://unesdoc.unesco.org/ark:/48223/pf0000372784
10. Vygotsky, L.: Pensamiento y lenguaje. https://abacoenred.com/wp-content/uploads/2015/10/Pensamiento-y-Lenguaje-Vigotsky-Lev.pdf
11. Norman, D.: Diseño emocional, por qué nos gustan (o no) los objetos cotidianos. Paidós, México (2005)
12. Preece, J. (ed.): Human Computer Interaction (ICS). Addison Wesley, Massachusetts (1994)
13. Baecker, R., Buxton, W.: Readings in Human-Computer Interaction: A Multidisciplinary Approach. Morgan Kaufmann, San Mateo (1987)
14. ACM SIGCHI: Curricula for Human-Computer Interaction. https://dl.acm.org/doi/book/10.1145/2594128
15. Freire, P.: Pedagogía del oprimido. Siglo XXI, México (1970)
16. Zambrano, A.: Penetration rate: cómo calcularlo y usarlo para mejorar tu marketing. https://www.sortlist.es/blog/penetration-rate-calculo
17. Dapuez, M., Mariana, M.: Educación Sexual Integral: ¿cómo implementar la ESI con equidad de género? en territorios de educación y salud. Brujas, Córdoba (2019)

The Influence of Phygital Learning: The User Expectations of Perceived Usability of Practical and Theoretical Courses

Shih-Yin Huang[✉] and Shang-Li Chu

Chinese Culture University, Taipei, Taiwan
hsy10@ulive.pccu.edu.tw

Abstract. Recently, due to the coronavirus pandemic, we are experiencing a revolution that is transforming the way, the education has now shifted to an "physical plus digital" or "phygital" multimodal.

This paper analyses the students' behavioral intention to the phygital learning, meaning how students use online learning platform (e.g. Moodle), collaboration application (e.g. Microsoft teams), chat application (e.g. Wechat) and device (e.g. smartphone, laptop) of a course.

For the evaluation purpose is followed by using the Semantic Differential Technique to distinguish the usage attitude of computer and smartphone. The Usage Questionnaire is followed by the System Usability Scale (SUS), which is a Human Computer Interaction (HCI) based approach, and the Technology Acceptance Model (TAM), which is an Information Systems (IS) based approach. The sample size consisted of 68 participants completed the survey questionnaire measuring their responses to perceived usefulness (PU), perceived ease of use (PEOU) and attitudes towards usage (ATU).

Through simultaneously both these instruments in one work for the purpose of usability evaluation. By doing so, this work attempts to streamline and unify the process of usability evaluation. Results that are obtained from a large-scale survey of university students show the attitudes towards usage on phygital learning. Moreover, this work also considers the digital-divide aspect (mobile v.s. web environment) whether it has any effect on the perceived usability. Results show that the multiple education modal could reduce the stress on the learning.

Keywords: Phygital learning · Usability evaluation · System Usability Scale (SUS) · Technology Acceptance Model (TAM)

1 Introduction

Globally, the teaching-learning circumstance is transform from a traditional classroom environment to a mixture of traditional plus online learning. The idea of online learning or e-learning is not new, phygital learning is a concept of a smart learning ecosystem which balances digital contents or online technology-driven experience together with physical or live-contexts. Availability of ubiquitous computing and high-speed Internet

© The Author(s), under exclusive license to Springer Nature Switzerland AG 2022
C. Stephanidis et al. (Eds.): HCII 2022, CCIS 1655, pp. 146–152, 2022.
https://doi.org/10.1007/978-3-031-19682-9_19

access, together with the advances made in cloud technologies have helped to promote the flexibility of the learning procedure and supplement it well to the conventional learning methods [1]. Phygital learning upon internet technologies to increase meaningful and effective interaction among students, teacher, data and environment.

The following research question seeks to examine students' usage of a blend learning situation utilizing the technology acceptance model (TAM): what are individual student's perceptions of usefulness (PU), ease of use (PEOU) and attitude towards usage (ATU) of an phygital learning that inform their behavioral intention. Additionally, which TAM factor (PU or PEOU) has a stronger relation to the measures of perceived usability.

2 Literature Review

The literature review done in this section focuses of two main aspects: (a) the Technology Acceptance Model (TAM) highlighting its similarity to the concept of perceived usability, and (b) the current state of usability evaluation in the phygital learning scenario.

2.1 Phygital Concept

At first, to convergence of physical and digital filed is an extra dimension of interaction and engagement recommended in business. The combination needed to provide a meaningful experience to user, the fundamental concept of phygital at a minimal level is comprised of content, context and consistency [18]. Technology and applications on mobile devices such as quick response (QR), augmented reality (AR), geofencing, iBeacon and Google Glass will blur the boundary between physical and digital and create a new ecosystem [1, 5, 7].

2.2 The System Usability Scale (SUS)

SUS is one of the most popular instruments used for assessing the perceived usability, both in usability related studies and surveys [9–11] by the HCI researchers. Extant research has shown that SUS has got a high degree of reliability (normally the Cronbach's alpha coefficient exceeds 0.90), validity, and can be adapted for different contexts [12]. SUS has 10 items in total, with half of the items having a positive tone (the odd number items), and the other half having a negative tone (the even number items). The response is given on a scale of 1 (strongly disagree) to 5 (strongly agree) for each item. The SUS score ranges from 0 to 100 (higher score meaning a better usability) in steps of 2.5 increments. This scale provides a good way to empirically interpret the meaning of the SUS scores. Table 1 provides a description of this scale.

2.3 The Technology Acceptance Model (TAM)

TAM is one of the most popular and widely used model by IS researchers for predicting the future use of a product or technology. In the TAM context, PU refers to the degree to which a person believes that using technology will improve his/her work performance [3]. Similarly, PEOU is defined as the degree to which a person believes that using technology will be easy and free from any efforts [3]. TAM presumes that behavioral intention is formed as a result of conscious decision making processes [16]. The model specifies three belief factors that are salient in the context of information technology usage and acceptance: perceived usefulness (PU), perceived ease of use (PEOU), and attitude towards usage (ATU) [1, 3]. In TAM, attitude towards usage is referred to as the evaluative effect of positive or negative feeling of individuals in performing a particular behavioral [1] (Fig. 1).

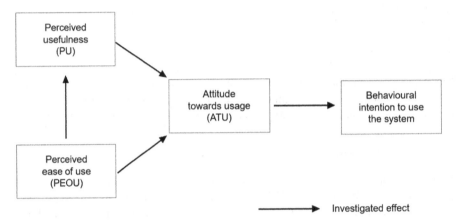

Fig. 1. Conceptual research model [3]

3 Result Analysis

The study adopted an exploratory design approach. Exploratory designs are used to explore research questions and are performed in order to gain a better understanding of a situation, phenomena, community or person [18]. The survey had been sent out to 68 participants, almost 50% of the students' age was 20 or below, with a median age of 20 years. The duration of the classes room around 3 months, and online-learning about 1.5 month. After this period an online survey was conducted for collecting the data.

The participants using their smartphones (mobile-version) or laptops (web-version) and rated their experience accordingly. The questionnaire details for SUS, the participants gave their ratings on a 5-point Likert scale (1 – strongly disagree to 5 – strongly agree). For the TAM, a 5-point Likert scale rating was used (1 – extremely disagree to 5 – extremely agree). All the items of TAM questionnaire positive semantics, and therefore, scores to the right of the scale would indicate a better user experience. In this case also, instead of leaving any question blank, the participants were asked to fill up the mid-value (score of 3), in case of any doubt to keep consistency with SUS.

All the data analysis is done using SPSS version 25.0. Both the SUS and TAM are ratings on a 5-point scale (Likert scale), for get the overall SUS score the sum of the item score contributions is multiplied by 2.5. Therefore, SUS scores range from 0 to 100 in steps of 2.5 points. However, in case of TAM the score calculation is a little bit different as it involves all positively worded items.

For obtaining the overall TAM score, the mean of PU and ATU is computed. This computation process normalizes the SUS and TAM scores in the same range that is used for the purpose of further analysis.

The collection of these questionnaires yielded 51 usable data responses. First, validity of model use in the context of the phygital learning was analyses. Having established validity and robust construct relationships, researchers' data results were then analyses.

According to extant research, concurrent validity is satisfied if the correlation between the different metrics exceeds 0.30 [5]. In Table 1 we present the correlation matrix for all the measures of questionnaire that has been used in this study. Results show that all the values exceed the threshold of 0.30, and are statistically significant (p < 0.05), thereby signifying that concurrent validity is satisfied.

Table 1. Summary of means and standard deviations.

		Statistic
Mean		97.451
95% confidence interval of the difference	Lower	95.892
	Upper	99.009
Median		97.489
Variance		98.000
Standard deviation		30.693
Kolmogorov-Smirnov test	Statistic	0.145
	Df	51.000
	p-value	0.009

As evident form Table 2 the interaction effect between age and phygital learning modal is to be significant is Q4.2 (PU: phygital learning would reduce my stress on the learning.)

Table 2. Independent samples test of age (PU)

	Equal variances assumed	Equal variances not assumed
t	−2.488	−2.498
Df	63.000	60.043
Sig (2-tailed)	0.016	0.15
Mean difference	−0.653	−0.653
Std. error difference	0.263	0.261

Table 3 provides the results with regards to the scores of means, SE, SD, that is obtained from the independent sample test.

Table 3. Group statistics of Q4.2 (PU)

Age	Mean	Std. deviation	Std. error mean
16–20	2.909	1.182	0.206
21–25	3.563	0.914	0.162

Table 4 represents the interaction effect between gender and phygital learning modal is to be significant is Q6.3 (ATU: phygital learning is to be expectant.).

Table 4. Independent samples test of gender (ATU)

	Equal variances assumed	Equal variances not assumed
t	−0.557	−0.57
Df	64	18
Sig (2-tailed)	−0.580	0.574
Mean difference	−0.165	−0.165
Std. error difference	−0.297	0.289

The measurement result of the mean, SE, SD is provided in Table 5 that is obtained from the independent sample test.

Table 5. Group statistics of Q6.3 (ATU)

Gender	Mean	Std. deviation	Std. error mean
Male	3.231	0.927	0.257
Female	3.396	0.968	0.133

4 Discussion and Conclusion

The purpose of this study was presented the usability of phygital learning, use different mobile device (smartphone and laptop) and more than 2 application of communication and learning, through student's behavioral intent evaluation classification four constructs, include the perceived usefulness (PU), perceived ease of use (PEOU), and attitude towards usage (ATU).

For measuring the perceived usability both HCI and IS based approaches are used by taking the SUS and TAM instruments as the baseline measurements respectively. Both the approaches give identical results, consistent with prior research [3, 6], perceived ease of use (PEOU) had a significant effect on attitude towards usage (ATU).

An explanation might be that when students perceive the phygital learning as one that is easy to use and reduce their stress, they may have a positive attitude towards the usefulness of the system. These findings support current research which suggests that user's positive feeling towards the ease of use of technology is associated with sustained use of the technology [18]. The results of the study also showed that perceived ease of use (PEOU) had a significant influence on perceived usefulness (PU).

In general, phygital learning is a complex scenario having multiple factors like the quality of the course contents, quality of the video lectures, the extent of support provided by the system, the UI design of the learning system, interactivity, and learnability of the system that might affect their usage [7].

Although multimodal educational technology usage in learning mothod has increased in recent years, technology acceptance and usage continue to be problematic for educational institutions [2, 4, 14]. Phygital learning is often used to provide more flexible approaches to teaching and student' use of multimodal educational technology in the classroom is extremely varied.

Finally, an understanding of the design of a system can help shift the conventional administrator or faculty mandated design of an phygital learning system towards a student centered design that more closely resonates with students' perceptions of usage and moreover motivation. Usability is just a small part of the overall user experience that the current work tries to capture, while future studies may focus on the broad user experience aspect.

References

1. Ajzen, I., Fishbein, M.: Attitudes and the attitude-behavior relation: reasoned and automatic processes. In: Stroebe, W., Hewstone, M. (eds.) European Review of Social Psychology, pp. 1–331 (2000)
2. Baylor, A.L., Ritchie, D.: What factors facilitate teacher skill, teacher morale, and perceived student learning in technology- USING classrooms? Comput. Educ. **39**(4), 395–414 (2002). https://doi.org/10.1016/S0360-1315(02)00075-1
3. Davis, D.: Perceived usefulness, perceived ease of use, and user acceptance of information technology. MIS Q. **13**(3), 319–340 (1989)
4. Gong, M., Xu, Y., Yu, Y.: An enhanced technology acceptance model for web-based learning. J. Inf. Syst. Educ. **15**(4), 365–373 (2004). http://www.highbeam.com/doc/1P3-793505851.html
5. Hair, J.F., Anderson, R.E., Tatham, R.L., Black, W.C.: Multivariate Data Analysis, 5th edn. Prentice Hall International Inc., New Jersey (1998)
6. Hu, P.J., Chau, P.Y.K., Sheng, O.R.L., Tam, K.Y.: Examining the technology acceptance model using physician acceptance of telemedicine technology. J. Manag. Inf. Syst. **16**(2), 91–112 (1999)
7. Junus, I.S., Santoso, H.B., Isal, R.Y.K., Utomo, A.Y.: Usability evaluation of the student centered e- learning environment. Int. Rev. Student-Centered E-Learn. Environ. **16**(4), 62–82 (2015)

8. Kramer, A.: Retail Business Models for the Future: The Convergence of Physical and Digital Channels Blog post (2014). https://www.capgemini.com/blog/capping-it-off/2014/01/retail-business-models-for-the-future-the-convergence-of-physical-and. Accessed 20 June 2021

9. Lewis, J.R.: Usability: Lessons learned and yet to be learned. Int. J. Hum.-Comput. Interact. **30**(9), 663–684 (2014)

10. Lewis, J.R.: Measuring perceived usability: the CSUQ, SUS, and UMUX. Int. J. Hum.-Comput. Interact. **34**(12), 1148–1156 (2018)

11. Lewis, J.R.: The system usability scale: Past, present, and future. Int. J. Hum.-Comput. Interact. **34**(7), 577–590 (2018)

12. Peres, S.C., Pham, T., Phillips, R.: Validation of the system usability scale (SUS): SUS in the wild. Proc. Hum. Factors Ergon. Soc. **57**(1), 192–196 (2013)

13. Rizki, J.: What is Phygital Marketing? (2014). https://www.quora.com/What-is-Phygital-Marketing. Accessed 20 June 2021

14. Saunders, G., Klemming, F.: Integrating technology into a traditional learning environment. Act. Learn. High. Educ. **4**(1), 74–86 (2003). https://doi.org/10.1177/1469787403004001006

15. Vate-U-Lan, P., Quigley, D., Masouras, P.: Phygital learning concept: from big to smart data. In: The Thirteenth International Conference on eLearning for Knowledge-Based Society, 15 December 2016

16. Venkatesh, V., Morris, M.G., Davis, F.D., Davis, G.B.: User acceptance of information technology: toward a unified view. MIS Q. **27**(3), 425–478 (2003). http://www.jstor.org/pss/30036540

17. Wang, L.Y.K., Lew, S.L., Lau, S.H., Leow, M.C.: Usability factors predicting continuance of intention to use cloud E- learning application. Heliyon **5**(6), e01788 (2019). https://doi.org/10.1016/j.heliyon.2019.e01788

18. Yildirim, S.: Effects of an educational computing course on preservice and Inservice teachers: a discussion and analysis of attitudes and use. J. Res. Comput. Educ. **32**(4), 479–495 (2000)

User-Centered Virtual and Augmented Reality Environments to Support the Classroom Needs of Elementary School Children

Rosa Martinez-Suarez[1] , Francisco Alvarez-Rodriguez[1] ,
Héctor Cardona-Reyes[2](✉) , and Klinge Orlando Villalba-Condori[3]

[1] Universidad Autónoma de Aguascalientes, Aguascalientes, Mexico
al101289@edu.uaa.mx
[2] CONACYT CIMAT Zacatecas, Zacatecas, Mexico
hector.cardona@cimat.mx
[3] Universidad Continental, Arequipa, Peru
kvillalba@continental.edu.pe

Abstract. Virtual reality (VR) and augmented reality (AR) are emerging technologies that in recent years have been the focus of attention in various fields of application. Particularly, in education, they have shown to have a potential in the teaching and learning process allowing students and teachers to have interactive content in which they can explore and discover practically and playfully the topics that are carried out in the classroom. This work focuses on identifying existing educational models in elementary education in order to propose a model that considers VR and AR as part of the activities carried out in the classroom and that allows teachers and students to expand their imagination and creativity and above all to enrich their knowledge by immersing them in activities according to their curricula.

Keywords: Virtual reality · Augmented reality · Learning models · Educacion · Elementary school

1 Introduction

Technology is a tool that day by day becomes indispensable in our daily life activities and that can be directed to different sectors. Particularly in education, technology can be very effective in the classroom learning process, especially in elementary school education with the aim of providing students with technological tools that allow them to capture their interest in a new way in the contents of each of their subjects and that also the learning carried out in the classroom becomes an experience that helps students to understand and comprehend the topics in an interactive and fun way, promoting new ways of learning and achieving a greater educational impact [4].

C. Stephanidis et al. (Eds.): HCII 2022, CCIS 1655, pp. 153–160, 2022.
https://doi.org/10.1007/978-3-031-19682-9_20

In this sense, VR and AR oriented to education can be a factor of interest, since for several years an educational revolution has been taking place, which drives to incorporate of these emerging technologies within the classroom [6].

Learning in the classroom is a process that has been going on for years, the student learns by interacting with books, blackboard, physical objects, videos, etc. In particular, books have been the main source of knowledge transmission.

Currently, there are many alternatives that help and facilitate the transfer of knowledge to students, such as VR and AR that can support the teaching-learning process, since they offer a high degree of interactivity, security and present content in an immersive way that can be adapted to the learning processes of different areas of knowledge [7].

Traditionally the dynamics within the classroom is unidirectional since the teacher explains the topics and the students rarely participate, all this decreases the quality of learning in the classroom and sometimes causes the attitude of the students to be low motivation. Sometimes the student tends to be easily distracted because the content is tedious or irrelevant, the topics of study lose interest and even this can be combined with personal factors where the student is deprived or excluded from the group and tends to participate less, thus affecting their learning process. The use of technological tools can be of utmost importance since the correct and daily use of technology can motivate the student to participate in the acquisition of the expected knowledge.

This paper analyzes traditional educational models to identify opportunities in which VR and AR can be incorporated into classroom activities, particularly in elementary education. Derived from this analysis, a proposed model is presented in which the objective is to design VR and AR solutions to support classroom activities in elementary school children through cognitive tasks, and thus have a variety of applications to be used daily by primary education institutions. The objective is to have didactic content that is also inclusive for all students in the classroom. The model considers the participation of teachers, education specialists, parents and students to produce virtual and augmented reality environments according to the needs of the educational context of the region. It also considers technology adoption factors so that these environments can be accessible and available to both teachers and students [14].

2   Virtual and Augmented Reality in the Educational Context

Utilizing the pedagogical models (see Table 1), the teacher, through didactics, elaborates strategies and methods that allow students to acquire the knowledge that is taught, as well as the process for them to learn [4,7].

Models such as the Constructivist model allow students to develop their learning since the student is responsible for his learning process. It is he who constructs knowledge, who learns. Teaching is centered on the constructive mental activity of the student, he is not only active when he manipulates, explores, discovers, or invents, but also when he reads or listens. As John Dewey [9] said, "we can no longer teach today's students as we taught yesterday's; we rob them of their future".

In another example, the ADDIE model has clearly defined stages that facilitate the implementation of effective training tools, this model allows the redesign of technological tools, such as virtual environments, learning environments, among others the common goal of designing materials to produce learning experiences in students [15].

Design-based learning is a form of reflective teaching, or pedagogy, based on the integration of design thinking and the design process in the classroom [1].

The analysis of pedagogical models allows us to realize that VR and AR oriented to education not only represents a motivational aspect for the student to increase interest in their courses but also to offer dynamics with interactive objects so that they can establish rapid assimilation of knowledge. Turning learning into a game, discovery, challenge or adventure so that they can acquire skills such as confidence, responsibility, communication and relationship between the students themselves as well as with the teacher [5]. In addition, VR and AR applications can be designed to support learning related to disciplinary content, and also allows to take into account other types of skills such as critical thinking, collaboration, teamwork, information sharing, analysis [3].

3 Proposed Model

This section presents a model in Fig. 1 that considers VR and AR as a technological tool to support the activities carried out within the classroom. This model is based on the analysis of existing pedagogical models presented in Table 1.

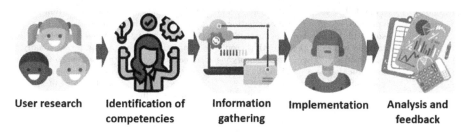

| User research | Identification of competencies | Information gathering | Implementation | Analysis and feedback |

Fig. 1. Model proposed that considers VR and AR as a technological tool to support the activities carried out within the classroom.

This model is mainly user-centered [2,8], in which students are previously identified based on characteristics determined by educational experts, teachers and staff of the educational institution. The main objective is to provide a method for teaching enriched with the proposed VR and AR tools even allowing to address important issues within the classroom such as inclusion, promotion of values adapted to cross-cutting activities. The following is a description of each of the 5 stages that make up the model in Fig. 1.

Table 1. Analysis of educational models and their characteristics relevant to learning.

	Traditional training [10]	Constructivist Model [13]	ADDIE Model [11]	Design-based learning [12]
Form of learning	Typical class session. Classes taught in a unidirectional way. Repetitive support tools (books, whiteboard, videos, etc.)	The student follows his own learning process, constructing new knowledge from previous teachings. Learning is active and participatory	E-learning learning experiences aimed at enhancing students' skills and knowledge	Its way of teaching is reflective or pedagogy. Based on the integration of design thinking and the design process in the classroom
Academic Program (Approach)	The priority is that the student is taught the subjects according to the curriculum	The teacher is responsible for mastering the physical and mental activities so that the student thinks for himself, reflects and interprets reality	An institutional process is designed where the results of the evaluation of each phase may cause the teacher to return to any previous phase	Uses learning strategies and tools
Assessment Strategies	There is more value in rote tests	The way to evaluate is through the learning process. It looks for the student to be responsible and to control the teaching-learning process	It has no technological guidelines or evaluation strategies to follow beyond the framework itself	It favors the design of different ways of integrating work inside and outside the classroom
Promotes Values	They follow the curriculum and sometimes forget to include values in the core subjects. They are educated as a class subject	Student participation is encouraged by creating groups where everyone interacts and shares information and ideas. Values are promoted and lived in the classroom on a daily basis due to the high degree of interaction	Its implementation design can be adapted to e-learning, content can be created to promote values	The acquisition of knowledge, beliefs, values and ways of acting professionally is possible to the extent that one participates in meaningful activities
Transversal Activities	Disciplinary content is not always planned	The student acquires knowledge just as important as the development of skills and attitudes	Its implementation design can be adapted to e-learning, a transversal activity content can be created	—

3.1 User Research

At this stage, the knowledge of VR and AR available to teachers and students is identified by means of questionnaires to determine their mastery of these technologies. This allows from the beginning to propose strategies for the adoption of VR and AR within the classroom context.

3.2 Identification of Competences

At this stage, with the help of teachers and education specialists, an identification of the competencies that will be taken to a VR or AR context is made. The skills of the students and the learning objectives to be achieved with the use of these applications are also identified. As an initial part of this stage, a user profile is defined for which the proposed VR and AR applications will be targeted. Figure 2 shows an example of proposed contents to be used as a complement to classroom activities. It also identifies each of the students' abilities, what type of activities they like, what types of socio-affective behaviors they have, and the learning model that fits their identified profile. The user profile identified are children in 2nd grade of primary school in Mexico and the topic to be evaluated is the knowledge of the environment, specifically that the student identifies and knows the aquatic animals.

Fig. 2. Example of 2nd grade elementary education learning content selected to be supported by VR and AR applications.

3.3 Information Gathering

Once the information from the previous stages is available, a search for VR and AR applications according to the learning needs and objectives can be performed. The user profile identified is important because it allows selecting the technological platform to be used. For example, smartphones or tablets in the case of AR applications or viewers ranging from Cardboard to Oculus Quest. In addition to defining the degree of interaction that the user will have with these applications. For the example given in the previous step, a search was made in GooglePlay and Oculus Quest libraries for applications related to aquatic animals and 2 applications were proposed, one in VR, Ocean Rift[1] for Oculus Quest and another in AR for smartphones called Ocean View AR - Underwater Exploration[2].

3.4   Implementation

The implementation stage consists of proposing a strategy for teachers and students to incorporate the use of the identified VR and AR applications into their classroom activities in order to reinforce knowledge and offer a playful and interactive alternative in which students can build their learning through interaction. These proposed applications can be used inside the classroom or at home. As presented in the example in Fig. 3, the elementary education student uses the two types of applications OceanRiftVR and Ocean View AR as part of feedback of the learning carried out in the classroom.

Fig. 3. Elementary education student using the proposed VR and AR applications as a complementary part of the learning process carried out in the classroom under the theme of aquatic animals.

3.5   Analisys and Feedback

In this stage, evaluation mechanisms are proposed to obtain relevant information from the previous stage. These evaluations can consist of evaluations designed

---

[1] https://www.facebook.com/OceanRiftVR/.

[2] https://vurrealgames.com/.

by the teachers to know the learning of the proposed contents. User experience evaluations to know the degree of student acceptance to the use of VR and AR applications. They can also be focused on teaching and obtain the percentage of interest and use of the students and know if there was a noticeable increase in motivation and learning by proposing these applications as part of the learning carried out in the classroom. As part of the previous example, the 2nd-grade student after using both applications was evaluated by the teacher through an in-class workbook activity and a homework assignment related to the topic as shown in Fig. 4.

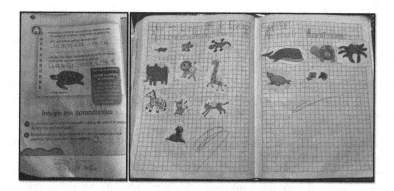

Fig. 4. Example of assessments made by the teacher after using the VR and AR applications as part of the aquatic animals topic within the classroom.

4   Conclusions

This work highlights the importance of introducing and adopting VR and AR as part of classroom activities in basic education as well as in the use of classroom content, in order to achieve a positive impact on student achievement. A method is proposed to support the acquisition of learning within the classroom and thus promote benefits at the intellectual and personal development level in students when using these technologies. Adopting VR and AR can help students and teachers to participate in real-world experiences and interactions, allow them to understand concepts that are difficult for them and thus capture their attention by providing them with a realistic experience. As future work, it is proposed to iterate the proposed model and identify new stages for the adoption of VR and AR within the context of basic education, and that these stages can be easily integrated with existing educational models, as well as identify new user-profiles and strategies for adoption and evaluation of the proposed content.

References

1. Abásolo Guerrero, M.J., et al.: Realidad aumentada, realidad virtual e interacción tangible para la educación. In: XIX Workshop de Investigadores en Ciencias de la Computación (WICC 2017, ITBA, Buenos Aires) (2017)

2. Altay, B.: User-centered design through learner-centered instruction. Teach. High. Educ. **19**(2), 138–155 (2014)
3. Arpentieva, M., Retnawati, H., Akhmetova, T., Azman, M., Kassymova, G.: Constructivist approach in pedagogical science. In: Challenges of Science, vol. Issue IV, pp. 12–17 (2021). https://doi.org/10.31643/2021.02
4. Banchoff Tzancoff, C.M., Fava, L.A., Schiavoni, M.A., Martin, E.S.: Realidad aumentada y realidad virtual: experiencias en diferentes ámbitos de aplicación. In: XXII Workshop de Investigadores en Ciencias de la Computación (WICC 2020, El Calafate, Santa Cruz) (2020)
5. Bernabeu, N., Goldstein, A.: Creatividad y aprendizaje: el juego como herramienta pedagógica, vol. 144. Narcea Ediciones (2016)
6. Fernández, D.A., et al.: Tendencias y tecnologías emergentes en investigación e innovación educativa, vol. 4. Graó (2018)
7. Fernandez, M.: Augmented virtual reality: how to improve education systems. High. Learn. Res. Commun. **7**(1), 1–15 (2017)
8. Kahraman, Z.E.H.: Using user-centered design approach in course design. Procedia Soc. Behav. Sci. **2**(2), 2071–2076 (2010). https://doi.org/10.1016/j.sbspro.2010.03.283. https://www.sciencedirect.com/science/article/pii/S187704281000323X. Innovation and Creativity in Education
9. Gónzalez Hermoso de Mendoza, A.: Transformar la educación (2013)
10. Merina, Á.: Métodos de enseñanza. Revista digital: innovación y experiencias educativas, pp. 2–4 (2009)
11. Morales-González, B., Edel-Navarro, R., Aguirre-Aguilar, G.: Modelo addie (análisis, diseño, desarrollo, implementación y evaluación): Su aplicación en ambientes educativos. Los modelos tecno-educativos, revolucionando el aprendizaje del siglo XXI, pp. 33–46 (2014)
12. Neira, M.A.R., De la Hoz, L.A.G., Jiménez, H.A.F., Zuñiga, A.M.H.: Aprendizaje basado en problemas para la enseñanza de diseño experimental. Inge Cuc **12**(2), 86–96 (2016)
13. Requena, S.H.: El modelo constructivista con las nuevas tecnologías: aplicado en el proceso de aprendizaje. RUSC. Univ. Knowl. Soc. J. **5**(2), 26–35 (2008)
14. Salvador, T.C.C.: La realidad virtual y realidad aumentada usada como herramienta en la educación para la visualización de la historia de la forma de la tierra. In: [2017] Congreso Internacional de Educación y Aprendizaje (2017)
15. Sánchez Espinoza, J., García Herrera, C., Juárez López, Y., Sánchez Espinoza, S.: Diseño instruccional addie como metodología pedagógica para la enseñanza-aprendizaje a través de realidad aumentada. Tecnologías y aprendizaje, pp. 491–499 (2018)

HCI Strategies for Informing the Design of a Teacher Dashboard: How Might Real-Time Situational Data Determine the Potential for Technological Support in the Classroom?

Elsy Meis[1]([✉]), Samuel Pugh[1], Rachel Dickler[1], Mike Tissenbaum[2], and Leanne Hirshfield[1]

[1] University of Colorado Boulder, Boulder, CO 80309, USA
elsy.meis@colorado.edu
[2] University of Illinois Urbana-Champaign, Champaign, IL 61820, USA

Abstract. As AI Technologies become more prevalent in the classroom, there has been an increased interest in teacher dashboards in fields such as computer science and the learning sciences. While extensive research has highlighted potential metrics of interest for teacher dashboards, little work has prioritized the interactivity of the teacher and dashboard in conjunction with students and other responsibilities. There is little knowledge of educators' availability to pay attention to a dashboard when working with students, often under time constraints and various levels of stress. Accordingly, there is a need for stronger HCI research integration during the design and development of teacher dashboards. Specific methods targeted at end-user experiences can inform and validate future iterations by defining what navigation and information teachers consistently utilize based on their priorities in the classroom. To bridge the gap between an ideal dashboard and ideal teacher-dashboard integration, the aim of this research was to design a 1 button, simplified dashboard that seeks the answers to questions best answered in real-time, in-situ contexts, such as when a teacher needs or wants assistance. Dashboard-Zero is a simple and customizable model of a teacher dashboard, inspired by the Staples "easy" big red button, that acts as an input device for gathering situational data to frame the user story during design and development of the teacher dashboard. The goal of Dashboard-Zero is to supplement and validate surveys and interviews at early stages of design.

Keywords: HCI · Teacher dashboard · Storytelling · UX design · UX research · Co-design · Dashboard-zero

1 Introduction

The direction towards AI has, at this point, grabbed the attention of all fields, from the social sciences to STEM to fine arts. This is no less true for the learning sciences. Based on the rising standards for STEM education in primary and secondary schools, it is becoming increasingly difficult for educators to meet these growing expectations while maintaining

C. Stephanidis et al. (Eds.): HCII 2022, CCIS 1655, pp. 161–168, 2022.
https://doi.org/10.1007/978-3-031-19682-9_21

an effective learning environment. There is a need for technological support for teachers in scaffolding their students in STEM practices [4]. Teacher dashboards for facilitating learning in the classroom have been extensively researched for decades [12]. There are a number of possible dashboard metrics that can support teacher orchestration, such as status of on and off task discussion, task progress, and task completion for individual, group, and whole class settings. By co-designing with partnering schools and teachers, researchers in the computer sciences and learning sciences have included the end-user in each step of the design process [7]. With the intention of being teacher-centric at all stages of dashboard design, researchers have strategized interviews and surveys based on each iteration of the interface designs [9]. They have used these interviews and surveys to inform the metrics to measure for display, as well as the visual components displaying said metrics. However, there are limitations to relying only on survey and interview data during dashboard design.

Although extensive research has highlighted potential metrics of interest for teacher dashboards, little work has prioritized the interactivity of the teacher and dashboard in conjunction with students and other responsibilities. There is a lack of research considering educators' ability to pay attention to a dashboard while attending to the intensive tasks involved with classroom orchestration. There is a need for stronger HCI research integration during the design and development of teacher dashboards that takes these time pressures and task complexities into account. Specific methods targeted at end-user experiences can inform and validate future iterations by defining what navigation and information teachers consistently utilize based on their priorities in the classroom. To bridge the gap between an ideal dashboard and ideal teacher-dashboard integration, the aim of this research is to design a 1 button, simplified dashboard that seeks the answers to questions best answered in real-time, in-situ contexts, such as when a teacher needs or wants assistance. 'Dashboard-Zero' is a simple and customizable model of a teacher dashboard, inspired by the Staples "easy" big red button, that acts as an input device for gathering situational data to frame the user story during design and development of the teacher dashboard. The goal of Dashboard-Zero is to supplement and validate surveys and interviews at early stages of design.

2   Background and Literature Review

2.1   Lack of HCI Integration in Early Stages of Design

The data informing the direction of a design and development of a product should be the foundation on which every piece stands. Ez-Zaouia [5] has defined a process framework by which teacher dashboard design should be followed. It encompasses four iterative steps: (1) Situate, (2) Ideate, (3) Develop, and (4) Evaluate. The first step, Situate, is where the research for this paper is focused. It states the importance surrounding the phenomena that goes into building a digital or physical artifact. It describes the situations and stories that make up the domain space. It is these stories that inform the rest of the process. Hence, initial research lays the foundation on which the teacher dashboards are built. The data and analysis of dashboards are crucial, and must be explored from various perspectives, with every detail in mind. User interviews and surveys should be expanded on for several reasons. The questions asked of interviewees must be strategically written and ordered without bias or a push towards a specific answer. Researchers may subconsciously be prone to priming teachers to answer questions in a way that already aligns with their vision or expectations [8]. As humans, bias is almost impossible to avoid. Teachers, as well, must put themselves in a position to honestly answer each question, which is a challenge. The way they interpret each question is influenced by many external factors, such as their mood or a recent experience that came to mind. To avoid human error, researchers' questions would best be answered in real-time, when the situation is current, and the answer is instinctual. There is great potential for integrating technology in order to collect real-time data for dashboard design.

2.2 Methods of Early Design in HCI

When it comes to designing the user experience of a teacher dashboard, much of the work is done before development begins, in the Situate stage [5]. According to Ez-Zaouia [5], this stage includes the phenomena surrounding the situation relevant to the product, such as facts, tasks, activities, and values. The process begins with figuring out the users' needs, then understanding where the product fits into their "story." This story is the key to understanding the big picture, and informs further design, development, and implementation of the user experience. In the design of teacher dashboards, the teacher's story should be at the forefront of every decision. Interdisciplinary research, especially, can benefit from the utilization of storytelling as a basis for understanding the user as well as in building credibility for the design [1]. Uncovering the user's needs followed by a detailed user story informs the user flow, metrics, and navigation of the dashboard. This includes initial interviews as well as outside research on what has been done, what has worked, and what has not. The pursuit of the user's story is crucial for a successful design.

2.3 Storytelling as a Means for Informing Design

A story involves true human attributes, emotions, and processes in the design of a product. It helps to hold the designers and researchers accountable for creating a product for "human." A story paints a picture that helps to inform how and where the product fits in, not vice versa. The details used in crafting user stories are very important and should be backed up by valid, unbiased data. Surveys and initial user interviews do not hold strong enough data to inform an entire technological system. They induce biases, rhetorical situations, and are informed by external measures. Predicting future actions involves making guesses which can cause errors in judgment [8]. Survey and interview data have a high chance of being skewed. They are not uninformative or useless, however. There is a need for further initial user research that supplements and validates interviews and surveys. By asking questions in the form of in-situ prompts, interviewees answer questions instinctively, without a push towards a specific answer or idealized situation. It is more reliable and realistic; this is where Dashboard-Zero is useful.

2.4 Related Work

BROMP. The Baker Rodrigo Ocumpaugh Monitoring Protocol (BROMP) 2.0 is a method for gathering quantitative student-affect data in order to obtain ground truth labels for Educational Data Mining research [10]. Trained researchers individually assess each student in real time and determine their engagement or affect with a momentary time sampling method. This means that the student's engagement is recorded for every twenty seconds of an activity [2]. BROMP supports automated intervention and teacher reporting as well as data-mining models used to inform constructs.

Similar to BROMP, Dashboard-Zero is a method for gathering quantitative data in real-time. Its extensive use has proven the need for gathering data in-situ. The design, like Dashboard-Zero, seeks to determine the user's states holistically with great attention to detail. While BROMP requires extensive training and certification on the coded model for researchers to determine student emotions, Dashboard-Zero allows the user (teacher) to answer based on a single prompt. The proven track record of BROMP suggests the need for a holistic approach to real-time quantitative data gathering.

Lumilo Co-design Case Study. In this case study, the LATUX workflow was used for the co-design and development of Lumilo, a real-time wearable learning analytics tool for teachers working in AI-supported classrooms [7]. The LATUX workflow was a set of phases that each encompassed a unique research methodology to inform the design of Lumilo. The designers of Lumilo believed that the co-design of Learning Analytics (LA) technology needed to include stakeholders from the very beginning. Including users after a first prototype was already too late; by then the pedagogical goals had already been decided on [7, 11]. This is a principle Dashboard-Zero was designed for, as well.

Like Dashboard-Zero, LATUX emphasizes the importance of storytelling to inform design. Early in the co-design process, methods for directed storytelling helped to shape the goals of Lumilo before its inception. They also included various design activities such as card sorting and semi-structured interviews with teachers [7]. Dashboard-Zero recognizes the importance of the early design stages, and seeks to accomplish what LATUX did for Lumilo in a real-time, efficient manner.

3   Inspiration Behind Dashboard-Zero

Storytelling is a key element to building a robust design. However, past and current methods of producing these stories are not meeting the standards they could be. Dashboard-Zero has the potential to amplify the outcomes of initial user-oriented design by backing theories with more detail-oriented and unbiased data. It presents questions in the form of simple prompts, allowing the users to build their stories. Before describing Dashboard-Zero, we first describe the inspiration behind the design.

3.1   Inspiration for Design

Researchers from the University of Wisconsin at Madison in conjunction with other Universities in the NSF AI Institute on Student-AI Teaming conducted a participatory design study for a teacher dashboard based on interviews done with teachers in the Madison area in November of 2021. The inspiration for Dashboard-Zero came from the design process used to conduct this study [3]. The goal of the study was to identify key metrics to include as features in a teacher dashboard. To ensure relevant information was being displayed, researchers included teachers in their co-design through a set of interviews regarding a mid-fidelity prototype of potential interface options. The researchers followed a user-centered design approach to inform their design decisions. The Feigh et al. [6] Adaptive System Framework, based on the three AI processing states of sensing, assessing, and acting, framed their research questions. The acting state includes the user-interface, which is what the teacher interacts with. The interviews with teachers sought to discover what content to show, when to show it, who should see certain information, and how the information should be shown.

A navigable set of screens were reviewed by each teacher who participated in the study. Their review was followed by a set of questions regarding the who, what, when, and how framework. For example, to address the "when" question, teachers were asked "Would you use this information before, during, or after class?". While the teachers' responses were excellent for informing future iterations of the teacher dashboard design, the answers would have benefited from real-time data that includes the actual classroom context, versus only relying on rhetorical scenarios.

By having questions answered in real-time in classroom situations, a breadth of knowledge can be discovered related to the realities of the classroom in order to optimize the dashboard's user experience. By reducing the load of interview questions to a single factor, simplifying the way each question is answered, and having them answered in-situ, implementing Dashboard-Zero into the classrooms would have answered many of the interview questions while also accounting for contextual impacts of the classroom. Further, it would have provided a prompt for an unbiased real-time, situational answer.

Dashboard-Zero (iPad/tablet) could be given to each of the teachers before the school day with a prompt for clicking the button. To prove or discover the most important research question, "will a teacher dashboard be useful," the first prompt would have been, "Click every time you need more information regarding what is happening in each student group to move forward in the lesson efficiently." From there, supplemental interviews regarding the physicality of carrying a dashboard and what exactly teachers were experiencing each time they "clicked" would provide data to consider in the next steps of building the dashboard.

4 Dashboard-Zero

This paper proposes a method for gathering qualitative and quantitative situational data at early stages of design. With the goals of exploring the domain space from every angle, and of informing every detail of the design, the proposed method incorporates a simple technology that supplements, validates, and potentially replaces early surveys and interviews in a co-design process. Dashboard-Zero is a one click input-only application that stores click counts and their timestamps as an indicator of a significant moment in a class period or time of day. It also acts as a placeholder for a future dashboard in terms of a physical handheld device as a "feeler" for teachers. Throughout the school day, teachers will click the button each time they find themselves in a particular situation (as specified by a prompt provided by the researchers). For instance, at a very early stage in design, the researcher may ask the teacher to "click when you wish you knew more about each group's progress but could not address all of them." This simple prompt informs further questions and decisions about the situations in which a group progress metric would be relevant, how often the situations arise, and why the situations should be explored in greater detail. On the other hand, another early prompt regarding the physical carrying of the tablet would be, "click each time this dashboard is distracting or taking away from your time with students." Throughout the design process, prompts can continue to be made more specific to answer sub questions and find overlapping data. If researchers noticed the teacher clicking frequently when students were doing group work at the beginning of a new lesson, the next prompt could, for example, be "click each time you are unsure of the specific parts of a new lesson to re-address for more student understanding." Prompts should be decided by researchers at every stage in order to best inform their research questions. To further investigate, recordings of class periods could be reviewed by researchers with the teacher in order to ask more about why they clicked when they did. Dashboard-Zero is useful in making the co-design process more efficient and detail-oriented by getting the internal state of each teacher involved. It builds the foundation for each user story vital to the design of a teacher dashboard. This paper proposes the design of Dashboard-Zero.

Dashboard-Zero is an intentionally limited dashboard for understanding teachers' thoughts and processes in the classroom domain. It informs a more robust design plan because it gathers honest feedback and data in real-time and in the correct context (in-situ). By reducing the load to a single factor, each research question can be explored in greater detail. Supplemented by classroom recordings, teachers are prompted to click a button each time they experience a specific emotion, situation, or challenge. With the in-situ data, researchers can go back and study the contexts surrounding each time the prompt was relevant as well as review the internal feelings with the teachers.

4.1 Technical Definition

Dashboard-Zero is a one-screen, one-button application that stores input "click" data. Each time the button is pressed, a timestamp is logged, and the count of "clicks" is increased by an increment of one. In the case of an accidental "click" there is an option to delete it in the interface immediately. Physically, Dashboard-Zero embodies the size and feel of carrying a dashboard around the classroom. It forces users to have it on hand and pay attention to it when relevant, which is essential to the embodiment of a teacher dashboard. Hence, Dashboard-Zero helps to answer physical implications of teachers having an extra artifact to pay attention to in a class period and throughout the school day. For researchers, it gathers real-time data based on a prompt that answers questions to inform metrics and the situations in which they arise (Fig. 1).

Depending on the research team, data will be logged in their system (Google Sheets is a simple option otherwise) automatically based on the prompt. Data will not include deleted "clicks."

Data:

- Prompt
- Press count
- Time pressed

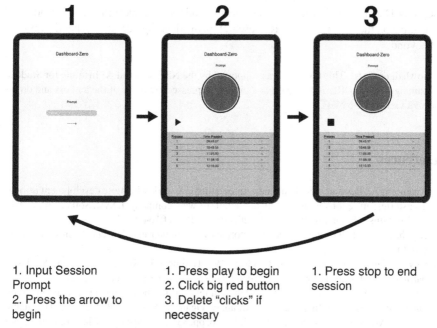

1. Input Session Prompt
2. Press the arrow to begin

1. Press play to begin
2. Click big red button
3. Delete "clicks" if necessary

1. Press stop to end session

Fig. 1. The design of Dashboard-Zero was done in Figma, with the intent of passing on to a development team to incorporate into their research software. Above is the interface as seen by teachers while using it. This was intentionally designed as a very simple and customizable dashboard, so that research teams can adjust it to their needs

5   Limitations, Future Work, and Conclusion

Dashboard-Zero is limited in that it can only be used to its fullest potential if it is supplemented by classroom recordings. It does not take any microphone or video data of its own. Additionally, while there is a strong argument for the potential of Dashboard-Zero to be used in initial studies for teacher dashboard designs, there is a lack of "active" evidence of its benefit. Dashboard-Zero should soon be implemented into classrooms gathering data for an AI device that informs the metrics for the dashboard. These classroom sessions must be recorded, and Dashboard-Zero will act as a supplement for interpreting the data gathered, and framing the user story during dashboard design.

Dashboard-Zero also holds significant potential in other domains, such UX research for B2B and B2C applications. Exploration into how a single-red-button interface could be used in various testing scenarios, including UX research and design of IT solutions and interfaces (mobile or for web), has many opportunities in both academia and industry domains. The goal is to explore this theory further both in the teacher dashboard and other designs.

Teacher dashboard design holds strong ties to AI and learning science research. However, it lacks in HCI research. Creative HCI methods can help to inform the designs of teacher dashboards by building a strong foundation of user-experiences and user stories. This theory has been proven by extensive research using BROMP and the Lumilo case study. Dashboard-Zero provides a novel method for initial design practices and a new perspective on the integration of HCI research in the development of teacher dashboards and beyond.

Acknowledgements. This research was supported by the NSF National AI Institute for Student-AI Teaming (iSAT) (DRL 2019805). The opinions expressed are those of the authors and do not represent views of the NSF.

References

1. Ananieva, A., Persson, J.S., Bruun, A.: Integrating UX work with agile development through user stories: an action research study in a small software company. J. Syst. Softw. **170**, 110785 (2020). https://doi.org/10.1016/j.jss.2020.110785. ISSN 0164-1212
2. Bosch, N., et al.: Detecting student emotions in computer-enabled classrooms. In: IJCAI (2016)
3. Dey, I., Dicker, R., Hirshfield, L. Goss, W., Tissenbaum, M., Puntambekar, S.: Using participatory design studies to collaboratively create teacher dashboards (2021)
4. Dickler, R.: An intelligent tutoring system and teacher dashboard to support mathematizing during science inquiry. In: Isotani, S., Millán, E., Ogan, A., Hastings, P., McLaren, B., Luckin, R. (eds.) AIED 2019. LNCS (LNAI), vol. 11626, pp. 332–338. Springer, Cham (2019). https://doi.org/10.1007/978-3-030-23207-8_61
5. Ez-Zaouia, M.: Teacher-centered dashboards design process. In: 2nd International Workshop on Explainable Learning Analytics, Companion Proceedings of the 10th International Conference on Learning Analytics & Knowledge LAK20. Frankfurt, Germany, ffhal-02516815f (2020). https://doi.org/10.35542/osf.io/p7cdv
6. Feigh, K.M., Dorneich, M.C., Hayes, C.C.: Toward a characterization of adaptive systems: a framework for researchers and system designers. Hum. Factors **54**(6), 1008–1024 (2012). https://doi.org/10.1177/0018720812443983
7. Holstein, K., McLaren, B.M., Aleven, V.: Co-designing a real-time classroom orchestration tool to support teacher-AI complementarity. J. Learn. Anal. **6**(2), 27–52 (2019). https://doi.org/10.18608/jla.2019.62.3
8. Hufnagel, E.M., Conca, C.: User response data: the potential for errors and biases. Inf. Syst. Res. **5**(1), 48–73 (1994). https://doi.org/10.1287/isre.5.1.48
9. Matuk, C.F., Linn, M.C., Eylon, B.-S.: Technology to support teachers using evidence from student work to customize technology-enhanced inquiry units. Instr. Sci. **43**(2), 229–257 (2015). https://doi.org/10.1007/s11251-014-9338-1
10. Ocumpaugh, J.L., Baker, R.S., Rodrigo, M.T.: Baker Rodrigo Ocumpaugh Monitoring Protocol (BROMP) 2.0 Technical and Training Manual. Academia, San Francisco (2015)
11. Triana, M.J.R., et al.: Monitoring, awareness and reflection in blended technology enhanced learning: a systematic review. Int. J. Technol. Enhanced Learn. **9**(2/3), 126 (2017). https://doi.org/10.1504/ijtel.2017.084489
12. Verbert, K., et al.: Learning dashboards: an overview and future research opportunities. Pers. Ubiquit. Comput. **18**(6), 1499–1514 (2013). https://doi.org/10.1007/s00779-013-0751-2

Methodological Strategies to Potentiate the Teaching-Learning Process in Virtual Modality of Business Administration Students

Evaristo Navarro[1]($\boxtimes$), Milagro Villasmil[2], and Alfredo Perez-Caballero[3]

[1] Universidad de la Costa, 58 Street #55 66, Barranquilla, Colombia
enavarro3@cuc.edu.co
[2] Universidad Libre de Colombia, 51B street #135 – 100, Barranquilla, Colombia
[3] Universidad Libre de Colombia, 177 Street 30 #20, Cartagena, Colombia

Abstract. This study is developed to identify the methodological strategies used in the business administration program of a private university located in the region of the Colombian Caribbean Coast to promote the teaching-learning process in virtual modality of students. At the methodological level it is developed as a field research, quantitative, non-experimental research, which data was collected during the first semester of 2021 from a sample of 28 university professors who teach in the administration program of a university located on the Colombian Caribbean Coast, to which a survey was applied consisting of 13 items divided into five dimensions: competences, teaching, pedagogical strategies, meaningful learning, and education quality. The presentation of the results that underpins the authors' research to diagnose and evaluate data sources is formulated so it can assure efficient support that allows maximum theoretical advantage. The results show important shortcomings within the institution under study related to the recognition of practical elements of meaningful learning in virtual media. It is concluded that education in recent years has undergone extremely important changes; therefore, universities must adapt to these new dynamics with new educational proposals that allow to maintain quality standards in higher education.

Keywords: Methodological strategies · Teaching-learning process · Virtual modality

1 Introduction

The development of society has been extremely accelerated in recent years as a result of the entry of new technologies based on the Internet; which have made it possible to significantly reduce the existing gaps in the world; especially in terms of communication and improvement of processes that occur in various institutions, whether private or public [1–4].

It is undeniable to recognize how the new information and communication technologies, the tools based on the internet of things and the expansion of the capacity of devices such as computers or smartphones create an innovative environment that allows

C. Stephanidis et al. (Eds.): HCII 2022, CCIS 1655, pp. 169–174, 2022.
https://doi.org/10.1007/978-3-031-19682-9_22

all the processes that take place within society to be enhanced [5–7]. In this way, the great impact of these new trends and tools within the educational environment should be highlighted; which has significantly changed their thinking and actions towards the training of students [8].

In this sense, the teaching-learning process is one of the fundamental axes of teaching action and this is significantly enhanced through the application of strategies formulated by the teacher and supported by the institution [9]. However, it should be mentioned that the contextual jump from attendance to virtuality has represented a great challenge for the entire modern educational system. Certainly, using a pedagogical strategy in the face-to-face environment is not comparable to using it within the virtual environment [10, 11].

For the present study, the objective is to identify the methodological strategies used in the business administration program of a private university located in the region of the Colombian Caribbean Coast to promote the teaching-learning process in virtual modality of students. It should be noted that this subject was previously taught in a mixed way (virtual and presence) and for the completion of the study in 2021 it is developed in a 100% virtual way.

2 Materials and Method

This study is formulated in order to identify the methodological strategies used in the business administration program of a private university located in the region of the Colombian Caribbean Coast to promote the teaching-learning process in virtual modality of students.

To achieve this, an instrument of a quantitative nature is proposed based on a questionnaire with three options: Yes, No and Sometimes. This instrument is developed with a total of 13 indicators, which are the following (Table 1):

Table 1. Instrument indicators

Item	Indicator
1	Student performance
2	Role of the teacher in the teaching process
3	Application of technological tools for the development of classes
4	Guides and study materials originated from technological elements are developed
5	Guides and study materials developed from technological elements are provided
6	Application of innovative theories in training practice
7	Agile methodologies present in the training process
8	Impart knowledge based on synchronous and asynchronous communication tools
9	The institution provides technological equipment for the development of their classes

(continued)

Table 1. (*continued*)

Item	Indicator
10	The institution trains him in new educational models based on technology
11	Inquiry into the technological skills of students
12	Promotes in students the use of technological tools to answer the subjects
13	Allows new proposals from students to respond to the subject

In this way, the population under study consists of the teachers who teach classes in the business administration career of the private University under study located in the Colombian Caribbean region. The study sample is made up of a total of 28 teachers who are selected through a non-probabilistic convenience sampling. For the reliability of the research, Cronbach's alpha is used, which shows a reliability of 0.79; value which is considered reliable.

The analysis tool taken into consideration for the research is descriptive statistics, from which the statistics of frequency and relative frequency are used. All the information is processed directly in the SPSS statistical software through data extracted from virtual forms in the first semes.

3   Results

The results of the developed investigative process are shown below (Table 2):

Table 2. Tabulation of teacher surveys I.E.D Juan Manuel Rudas

Y_i	F_i	FR	F_i	FR	F_i	FR	Total F_i	Total Fr
Indicator	Yes	Yes	No	No	Sometimes	Sometimes		
1	27	0,96	1	0,04	0	0,00	28	1
2	28	1,00	0	0,00	0	0,00	28	1
3	27	0,96	1	0,04	0	0,00	28	1
4	15	0,54	5	0,18	8	0,29	28	1
5	4	0,14	0	0,00	24	0,86	28	1
6	28	1,00	0	0,00	0	0,00	28	1
7	0	0,00	19	0,68	9	0,32	28	1
8	15	0,54	1	0,04	12	0,43	28	1
9	16	0,57	0	0,00	12	0,43	28	1
10	23	0,82	0	0,00	5	0,18	28	1

(*continued*)

Table 2. (*continued*)

Y$_i$	F$_i$	FR	F$_i$	FR	F$_i$	FR	Total F$_i$	Total Fr
Indicator	Yes	Yes	No	No	Sometimes	Sometimes		
11	11	0,39	17	0,61	0	0,00	28	1
12	13	0,46	0	0,00	15	0,54	28	1
13	0	0,00	7	0,25	21	0,75	28	1

When reviewing the table shown above, it is possible to observe how in the Student Performance result there is a positive response in a frequency of 27 teachers; evidencing how these keep track of academic performance in virtual educational models, the indicator of the teacher's role in the teaching process shows a totality in the Yes alternative, evidencing how teachers identify the importance of the teacher's role in the virtual training process.

Next, it is observed how with respect to the Application of technological tools for the development of classes, said indicator is fulfilled with 96% of the totality. On the other hand, on the development of Guides and study materials developed from technological elements, a frequency of 15 teachers is given and on the provision of Guides and study materials developed from technological elements, a 14% compliance is observed together with a 86% of the *Sometimes* option.

On the processes of Application of innovative theories in the training practice, it is observed how this is fulfilled 100% based on the contributions of the teachers. While the indicator of agile methodologies present in the training process shows 68% of teachers who do not apply it and 32% who sometimes link them. Regarding the indicator of whether the teacher imparts knowledge based on synchronous and asynchronous communication tools, where 54% take advantage of both tools, while 43% sometimes carry out said action. On the other hand, 57% consider that the institution provides technological equipment for the development of their classes.

Regarding whether the institution trains them in new educational models based on technology, it is highlighted that this is 82% complete according to the contributions of the teachers surveyed. The Inquiry of the technological competences of the students shows a 39% presence, while 61% shows an absence of it. With respect to the indicator of Promotes in students the use of technological tools to respond to the subjects, it has a 46% presence and 54% in turn, Finally, in the indicator of allows new proposals from students to respond to the subject there is an absence of 25% and it is highlighted that this is sometimes present in 75%. These results by frequency can be observed in a summarized way in the following graph (Fig. 1):

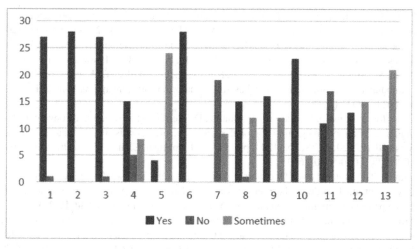

Fig. 1. Total results

4 Conclusions

Taking into consideration the empirical results of the study, it is possible to recognize how the linking of new technologies is extremely pertinent due to its objective of training students in a more effective way; where the use of ICT-based tools and constant feedback appear as two of the fundamental elements of the training process in the new reality. It is in education where this support becomes a fundamental concept that allows responding more effectively to the approaches required by the comprehensive training of students with learning difficulties through interactive work between the student and the teacher.

In this same sense, strengths related to the work developed by the teacher are observed, but a weakness is visualized in the process of linking students as a fundamental part of the process, who are also able to contribute to the training process and making this much more dynamic.

Thus, the University must become the headquarters of educational creation for the development of cognitive abilities and transform it into skills, based on the social and personal development of a critical, participatory, supportive learner and thus prevent possible learning difficulties. Finally, it is recommended that this type of educational institutions at the professional level organize pedagogical workshops where teachers attend to enrich their personal training and socialize the various forms of student learning; especially taking advantage of new strategies for effective training and the use of agile methodologies.

References

1. Pérez Zúñiga, R., Mercado Lozano, P., Martínez García, M., Mena Hernández, E., Partida Ibarra, J.Á.: La sociedad del conocimiento y la sociedad de la información como la piedra angular en la innovación tecnológica educativa. RIDE. Revista Iberoamericana para la Investigación y el Desarrollo Educativo **8**(16), 847–870 (2018)

2. Flores-Cueto, J., Hernández, R., Garay-Argandoña, R.: Tecnologías de información: acceso a internet y brecha digital en Perú. Revista Venezolana de Gerencia **25**(90), 504–527 (2020)
3. Almenara, J., Ruiz-Palmero, J.: Las Tecnologías de la Información y Comunicación para la inclusión: reformulando la brecha digital. IJERI: Int. J. Educ. Res. Innov. **1**(9), 16–30 (2018)
4. Alam, M., Malik, H., Khan, M., Pardy, T., Kuusik, A., Le Moullec, Y.: A survey on the roles of communication technologies in IoT-based personalized healthcare applications. IEEE Access **6**, 36611–36631 (2018)
5. Parra, M., Marambio, C., Ramírez, J., Suárez, D., Herrera, H.: Educational convergence with digital technology: integrating a global society. In: Stephanidis, C., Antona, M., Ntoa, S. (eds.) HCII 2020. CCIS, vol. 1294, pp. 303–310. Springer, Cham (2020). https://doi.org/10.1007/978-3-030-60703-6_39
6. Brey, P.: The strategic role of technology in a good society. Technol. Soc. **52**(C), 39–45 (2018)
7. Lay, N., et al.: Uso de las herramientas de comunicación asincrónicas y sincrónicas en la banca privada del municipio Maracaibo (Venezuela). Revista Espacios **40**(4) (2019)
8. Moreno, M., Duran, S., Parra, M., Hernández-Sánchez, I., Ramírez, J.: Use of virtual resources as a tool for teaching language skills at the Colombian Caribbean region primary basic level. In: Stephanidis, C., Antona, M., Ntoa, S. (eds.) HCII 2021. CCIS, vol. 1499, pp. 286–293. Springer, Cham (2021). https://doi.org/10.1007/978-3-030-90179-0_37
9. Granda-Asencio, L., Espinoza Freire, E., Mayon-Espinoza, S.: Las TICs como herramientas didácticas del proceso de enseñanza-aprendizaje. Conrado **15**(66), 104–110 (2019)
10. Herrera, H., Barrera, A., Ballestas, M., Ballestas, I., Schnorr, C.: Virtual classrooms for the development of practical laboratories in a Colombian higher education institution. In: Stephanidis, C., et al. (eds.) HCII 2021. LNCS, vol. 13096, pp. 417–425. Springer, Cham (2021). https://doi.org/10.1007/978-3-030-90328-2_27
11. Wut, T.-M., Xu, J.: Person-to-person interactions in online classroom settings under the impact of COVID-19: a social presence theory perspective. Asia Pac. Educ. Rev. **22**(3), 371–383 (2021). https://doi.org/10.1007/s12564-021-09673-1

Innovative ICT-Based Strategies Used by Teachers for the Development of Social Competences in Business Administration Students

Evaristo Navarro[1]([✉]), Marlene Ballestas[2], Ismael Alvarez[1], and Johny García-Tirado[3]

[1] Universidad de La Costa, 58 Street #55 66, Barranquilla, Colombia
enavarro3@cuc.edu.co
[2] ITSA, 18 Street # ##39-100, Soledad, Colombia
[3] Corporación Universitaria Taller Cinco, Km 19, Chía, Colombia

Abstract. This study is developed with the aim of diagnosing the innovative strategies based on ICT used by teachers for the development of social skills in business administration students; which were applied during the COVID 19 pandemic as a response to the change of modality launched by higher education institutions. In this case, the present study was located in the positivist paradigm, with a descriptive level, with a non-experimental, transactional field design. The sample is taken from a group of 25 teachers, who teach in the business administration program of a private university located in the city of Barranquilla, Colombia. A questionnaire consisting of a total of 15 items applied to this sample, which was validated by experts and its reliability was determined by means of the Cronbach's Alpha coefficient, yielding a value of 0.87. As a result, an average of 2.86 was obtained in the variable strategies for the development of social competences; located in the category neither appropriate nor inappropriate. These results show an important level of shortcomings in the implementation of innovative strategies based on ICT used by teachers for the development of social skills in business administration students.

Keywords: Innovative strategies · Information and communication technologies · Social competences

1 Introduction

Throughout history, education has gone through different stages, in which various strategies, methodologies and models have been implemented that are consistent with the needs and demands of the current contexts at the time. Currently we have faced the COVID-19 pandemic, which has generated changes in mobility, in social interactions, in the daily routine and above all in our work and academic activities. To counteract the adversities caused by this, digital tools have been implemented for the normal continuity of our lives. In relation to the health emergency, students and teachers of higher education have chosen to use Information and Communications Technology (ICT). This

C. Stephanidis et al. (Eds.): HCII 2022, CCIS 1655, pp. 175–183, 2022.
https://doi.org/10.1007/978-3-031-19682-9_23

has caused challenges in its use, in addition to marking the digital gaps that mark the economic and social inequalities that exist in our world [1, 2].

It is in this way that the pandemic and preventive isolation allowed the strengthening of technological resources applied to an educational field, granting, from a progressive point of view, the appropriation of technological skills, opening a door to the opportunity of spaces to train the higher education institutions. In the social aspect, the so-called ICTs have been associated as an important learning tool to educational methods. Due to this, during the last years significant social changes have been seen where education has had a transformation in the educational system. These offer simulations and models that cause students to be more active, because they have the possibility of recreating learning situations, thus stimulating them to challenge their own understanding [1, 3].

In recent years there has been continuous work with a systemic educational model, but this in turn has been evolving in such a way that it is essential to have knowledge of technology in this era, because it is seen as an opportunity for pedagogical restructuring. Within an organizational framework of curricular adaptation, which can help overcome difficulties and social conflicts that lead to the improvement of training processes, through interactions between students and teachers of the student community.

The use of these technologies implies that teachers present new roles, approaches and pedagogies, which depend clearly on their skills and abilities for the structuring of learning environments, in favor of developing socially active spaces where collaborative learning, interaction cooperative and teamwork. This is why it can be confirmed that ICTs are a current trend in the education sector as support for learning and teaching processes, where teachers and students learn and use them to acquire and put into practice skills in the effective use of technologies. Digital versus modern society [4–6].

As study centers, private universities are linked to educational dynamics such as the production of knowledge, for which the preparation and training of their students is essential for a more developed and competitive service to society. This is why they adjust to technological innovations, in this sense, higher educational institutions, taking into account their cultural, economic and technological characteristics, have welcomed educational reforms for their integration with new technologies. In this way, higher education institutions have the duty to offer an effective and efficient academic system that can fully guarantee the quality of education and that in turn captures the needs of society [7, 8].

At the global level, there has been an impact of technologies that have been evolving day by day in such a way that in this new era there is the ability to search for and implement information, taking into account the quantity and quality of the sources. These technologies are considered as an end and not as a means, because it can still be applied with a traditional pedagogy, which allows the combination of strategies and techniques such as collaborative learning that is based on the interaction with the participants, that allows the construction of communication routes [9, 10].

The university student has a fundamental role in the construction of knowledge, because their behavior leads to results in the learning process. Knowledge is acquired in such a way that the interaction with the environment helps him to transform the reality around him and in this case given the evolution of education at a technological level, the student through interaction with this perceives the information of a faster, and pleasant way, achieving changes in the development of social competences [11]. This article focuses on the use of ICT as a tool through strategies for the development of social skills in business administration students at a private university in the city of Barranquilla.

2   Materials and Method

The research is carried out in a private university institution, located in the city of Barranquilla, Atlántico, Colombia. For the subsequent development of this, it was necessary to use different methods and tools to measure and evaluate the variables and dimensions to be studied. The sample delimitation was the following:

Table 1. Delimitation of the Study Sample

Universe	Universities that teach the career of business administration
Target Population	Teachers who teach in the business administration program of a private university located in the city of Barranquilla, Colombia
Sample	Group of 25 professors from the university under study

In this sense, the sampling for the research was voluntary, in which 25 professors from the private university in the area of business administration were provided with a material that they had to answer, which was composed of 15 items, or indicators., through which they allow us to have a wide repertoire of information to be able to carry out the respective analysis. For the reliability of the research, Cronbach's Alpha is used, which shows a reliability of 0.87.

3   Results

Next, the results obtained from the surveys carried out on the sample population are presented, taking into account that the analysis is carried out based on measurement scales, which function as an aid for the classification of the variables studied. The validity and reliability of the measurement of a variable are subject to the choices made to operate and achieve a suitable understanding of the criterion, avoiding inaccuracies and ambiguities. It is relevant to mention that the factors analyzed set the guidelines to influence the integration of the work team, the identification and commitment with the university to achieve high quality indices. Initially, the variables of Strategies for the development of social competences are studied as shown in Table 2, the results obtained from the application of the instrument on it are presented.

In this table you can see the different indicators such as Acceptance, Communication, Self-esteem, Encouragement and Affectivity. Where each of them obtained a respective weighting of 2.96, 2.78, 2.89, 3.10 and 2.97. These results are located each within the scale intended for this purpose, as follows:

Table 2. Strategies used by teachers for the development of social skills.

	INDICATOR 01 ACCEPTANCE			INDICATOR 02 COMMUNICATION			INDICATOR 03 SELF-ESTEEM (ITEMS)			INDICATOR 04 STIMULUS			INDICATOR 05 AFFECTIVITY		
	1	2	3	4	5	6	7	8	9	10	11	12	13	14	15
Average	2.96			2.78			2.89			3.10			2.97		

Total, average dimension 2.94

Table 3. Categorization of the Scale of the dimension, strategies used for the development of social competences.

Indicator	Measure	Scale Categorization
Acceptance	**2.96**	Neither Appropriate nor Inappropriate Level of Development of Social Competencies that Promote Student Success in School
Communication	**2.78**	Neither Appropriate nor Inappropriate Level of Development of Social Competencies that Promote Student School Success
Self-Esteem	**2.89**	Neither Appropriate nor Inappropriate Level of Development of Social Competencies that Promote Student Success in School
Stimulus	**3.10**	Neither Appropriate nor Inappropriate Level of Development of Social Competencies that Promote Student Success in School
Affectivity	**2.97**	Neither Appropriate nor Inappropriate Level of Development of Social Competencies that Promote Student Success in School

These strategies for the development of social skills using ICT, have as their purpose the academic success of university students, their function is to mediate between the educational project and the recipients. By implementing these strategies, progress can be made in the different items of acceptance, communication, self-esteem, encouragement and affectivity. When measuring these indicators, it is evident that the appropriate level is not reached in the implementation of strategies for the development of social competences in the university environment, which can be carried out through the characteristics of the Colombian educational model that gives priority to development of academic content, leaving aside fundamental elements related to the attitudinal field, which are part of the repertoire of social, civic, civic and other skills, which are closely linked to the full development of the personality.

This is why higher education entities, including students, must unify in order to redesign institutional educational projects in order to fulfill the task of providing comprehensive training in these scenarios for future business managers in the country. After the use of new strategies, teachers are the ones who must lead the learning process through the implementation of ICT, without neglecting that teaching practice involves a diverse and complex network of relationships between people, and from this perspective relationships with students constitute the fundamental link around which ties are established with other people.

In this Table 2, there are the items that respond to the Acceptance indicator, which, as can be seen, resulted in the specific percentages for each alternative, which are presented below:

- Item 1; Develops student skills by analyzing their potential.
- Item 2; Instill values of acceptance among students to develop in them a critical personality.
- Item 3; He believes that it is important to develop a comprehensive education that leads to renewal and changes for the benefit of the common good.

Acceptance refers to the teacher as a human being, whose practice is also human, given his individuality, the decisions he makes in his professional work acquire a particular character. From the perspective of this research, the particular importance of developing cognitive and procedural skills to the detriment of attitudinal skills (social and axiological) can be appreciated, which undoubtedly calls into question the slogan of comprehensive education. (See in Table 2, indicator 1).

Table 2 also shows the results in specific percentages for each alternative of the Communication indicator, which are presented below:

- Item 4; Perceives that parents and representatives show the quality of attention and listening with their children.
- Item 5; Observes that parents and representatives collaborate in the educational process of their children with clear and sincere communication.
- Item 6; Believes that assertive communication generates energetic and critical personalities who perceive things as they are.

With this study, it was possible to establish the breakdown of the parent-university bond, which is corroborated by observing the results obtained by items 4 and 5. (See Table 2, indicator 2). Continuing with the analysis of Table 2, which shows the results in specific percentages for each alternative of the Self-esteem indicator, which are presented below:

- Item 7; Observes that in the classroom the conditions are favored to form an adequate self-esteem in children and adolescents.
- Item 8; Perceives in the classroom children or adolescents who withdraw to themselves and maintain an isolated attitude with the rest of the group.
- Item 9; He believes that social and school stimulation contributes positively to confronting personality patterns in students.

Self-esteem from the strategies used by teachers for the development of social skills, is based on the relationships of the actors involved in the educational task: students, teachers, directors, mothers and fathers. These relationships are complex, since the different educational actors have a great diversity of characteristics, goals, interests, conceptions, beliefs, etc., which makes the institutional climate difficult. From the present investigation, the lack of social stimuli from the classroom is observed, which contribute to significantly favor the formation of a self-esteem appropriate to the characteristics of the students. (See in Table 2, indicator 3).

The analysis of this dimension also supposes a reflection on the spaces of internal participation and communication styles; the types of conflicts that arise and the ways to solve them, the type of coexistence of the school and the degree of satisfaction of the different actors regarding the relationships they maintain, since all these factors ultimately have repercussions on the good development of the Institution. The results of the frequencies, in Table 2, show the specific percentages for each alternative of the Stimulus indicator, which are presented below:

- Item 10; Reinforce positive student behaviors.
- Item 11; Equitably rewards the progress made by students, in coexistence, in knowledge and in educational praxis.
- Item 12; Stimulates leadership potential in the classroom.

Regarding the analysis of the stimulus indicator, in teaching practice it refers to the set of relationships that has to do with the way in which each teacher perceives and expresses their task as an educational agent whose task is to reinforce and allow their students to reach the proposed goals. in different personal, social, academic or other orders. The result established that the teacher rarely reinforces positive behaviors, including leadership, however, on a regular basis, he fairly rewards academic achievement. (See in Table 2, indicator 4). Concluding with the analysis of Table 2, in relation to the affectivity indicator, the results are found in specific percentages for each alternative, which are shown below:

- Item 13; Believes that the affectivity of parents towards their children affects their behavior.
- Item 14; Considers that human development is stimulated by the people with whom affective ties are maintained.
- Item 15; Carry out contextualized activities with the representatives to promote the confidence and affective security of children and adolescents.

Finally, reference is made to the Affectivity indicator, which can be defined based on people's positive expressions of affection, in such a way that it enables rapprochement with their parents, peers, teachers and other members of the community, strengthening ties of fraternity, love, tolerance, respect and trust, etc. In the context under study, it can be seen that the teacher does not consider it significantly important to establish affective ties as a behavioral modeling factor, as shown in the results obtained (See Table 2, indicator 5).

4   Conclusions

Taking into account the previous results, the use of ICT-based strategies for the development of social competences is essential, it is concluded that at present the didactic and technological methodology allows a greater reception of the topics treated, in addition to have an impact on different aspects such as academic and socio-personal factors, taking into account each of the evaluated indicators that reflect the knowledge and attitudes of teachers in the face of different situations and stimuli that are related to these [12].

From the types of strategies, it is concluded that the model to be implemented must be clear in order to achieve greater academic success in the training of students, this was measured by instructional indicators. Which demonstrate that the use of technologies allows to form and maintain links with students, parents and teachers through communication, in addition to being able to influence students to trace a path to achieve the proposed objectives, formulating in this way new challenges and allows the student to self-evaluate in a way that takes into account their degree of progress. In conclusion, the implementation of ICTs as teachers' tools for the development of social competence is viable, can be successful and effective as long as the strategies to be implemented are assertively structured, taking into account not only the advances technological, but the academic and socio-personal factors, in favor of achieving academic success in business administration students of the universities of our country [12].

In this way, it is possible to recognize how the current changes have caused a significant impact on the various levels of society; especially in educational organizations which constantly innovate to improve their training processes at various levels [13, 14]. Certainly it is undeniable to recognize how the empirical evidence demonstrates the relevance of ICTs for society and the interaction of its actors [15].

References

1. Ortiz Záccaro, Z.: Uso del tic como herramienta de aprendizaje en tiempos de aislamiento social. Universidad de la costa (2021)
2. García, L.: Coronavirus. Educación y uso de tecnologías en días de pandemia. Ciencia UNAM (2022)
3. Mujica-Sequera, R.M.: La Enseñanza Tecno emocional en la Educación del Siglo XXI. Revista Tecnológica-Educativa Docentes 2.0, 9(2), 71–78 (2020)
4. Cortés, R.: Prácticas innovadoras de integración educativa de TIC que posibilitan el desarrollo profesional docente. Un estudio en Instituciones de niveles básica y media de la ciudad de Bogotá (Col). Universidad Autónoma de Barcelona (2016)
5. Laiton Zarate, E., Gómez Ardila, S., Sarmiento, P.R., Mejía Corredor, C.: Competencia de Prácticas Inclusivas: las TIC y la Educación inclusiva en el desarrollo profesional docente. Sophia 13(2), 82–95 (2017)
6. Pineda-Castillo, K.: Uso de Tecnología como Recurso Preponderante en el Aprendizaje a Distancia en tiempos de Confinamiento Social. RTED 11(1), 89–98 (2021)
7. Cruz Rodríguez, E.: Importancia del manejo de competencias tecnológicas en las prácticas docentes de la Universidad Nacional Experimental de la Seguridad (UNES). Revista Educación 43(1), 196–218 (2018)
8. Gamboa, P.A.: Las TIC en la gestión del proceso de enseñanza-aprendizaje en el área Comunicación Organizacional: licenciatura en Ciencias de la Comunicación. RIDE Revista Iberoamericana para la Investigación y el Desarrollo Educativo 8(16), 764–788 (2018)
9. Mayor Paredes, D.: El aprendizaje-servicio como estrategia metodológica innovadora para el desarrollo de competencias digitales y ciudadanas. Revista Internacional de Tecnología, Ciencia y Sociedad 7(2), 57–67 (2019)
10. Fernández M.D., González, A.S.: Estrategias didácticas creativas en entornos virtuales para el aprendizaje. Actualidades Investigativas en Educación, 9(2), 9521 (2011). https://doi.org/10.15517/aie.v9i2.9521
11. Pinillos, H., Terán, F.: Constructivist methodologies in higher education: divergent thinking drivers. Revista de Educación 23, 221–241 (2021)
12. Parra, M., Marambio, C., Ramírez, J., Suárez, D., Herrera, H.: Educational convergence with digital technology: integrating a global society. In: Stephanidis, C., Antona, M., Ntoa, S. (eds.) HCI International 2020 – Late Breaking Posters. Communications in Computer and Information Science, vol. 1294, pp. 303–310. Springer, Cham (2020). https://doi.org/10.1007/978-3-030-60703-6_39
13. Picalúa, V.P., Payares, K.M., Navarro, E.J., Hurtado, K.: Gestión de la experiencia de las unidades principales de internacionalización en las instituciones de educación superior. Formación universitaria 14(2), 37–46 (2021)

14. Moreno, M., Duran, S., Parra, M., Hernández-Sánchez, I., Ramírez, J.: Use of virtual resources as a tool for teaching language skills at the colombian caribbean region primary basic level. In: Stephanidis, C., Antona, M., Ntoa, S. (eds.) HCI International 2021 - Late Breaking Posters. Communications in Computer and Information Science, vol. 1499, pp. 286–293. Springer, Cham (2021). https://doi.org/10.1007/978-3-030-90179-0_37

15. Lay, N., et al.: Uso de las herramientas de comunicación asincrónicas y sincrónicas en la banca privada del municipio Maracaibo (Venezuela). Revista Espacios **40**(4) (2019)

Workids: Kids Homework Planner to Enhance Learning and Motivation in a Meaningful Way

Melina Avila Cruz[1,2] , Monica Gonzalez Garduño[1,2(✉)] ,
Diana Luz Peña Dominguez[1,2] , and Rocio Abascal Mena[1,2]

[1] Master in Design, Information and Communication (MADIC), Universidad Autónoma
Metropolitana, Cuajimalpa, Mexico
monica.gonzalezg@gmail.com, mabascal@cua.uam.mx

[2] Avenida Vasco de Quiroga 4871, Colonia Santa Fe Cuajimalpa, Del. Cuajimalpa de Morelos,
Ciudad de México C.P. 05300, México

Abstract. School activities had to be moved to a virtual environment in order
to keep the population safe from Covid-19. However, even though educational
platforms proved to be rather useful during this episode by allowing classes to
continue; one must not overlook the fact that these platforms were hardly adapted
for the most elementary levels. Moreover, when children enter school, they need
a lot of support from both parents and teachers. Then again, they also need to
eventually develop autonomy and ownership on their school assignments. During
lockdown, the by-product of homework became more complicated due to the
need to upload exercises done on paper to an online space. Therefore, following
a human-centered approach, this project pursues the goal of helping school-age
children achieve more independence when doing homework incorporating digital
tools.

Keywords: Elementary School · Children · Homework · Autonomy ·
Motivation · User-Centered Design

1 Introduction

It is a well-known fact that schools, like other social institutions, faced a transition
towards an online modality due to the forced lockdown caused by the Covid-19 pandemic.
In Mexico City, this meant that around thirteen million children in elementary school had
to attend classes from home [11]. Higher education institutes have worked on keeping
learning and evaluation processes through an online modality [7]. Nonetheless, there has
been little research concerning the adequate use and a pertinent interface of e-learning
tools adapted to elementary school students.

Unlike other countries, in Mexico the lockdown lasted more than two years and so,
social restrictions are slowly being lifted and establishments are opening once again. In
a similar fashion, schools have begun their return to onsite classrooms. However, the
reincorporation process of the kids stands as a worrying problem due to the differences
in learning styles, knowledge and motivation. Another key consideration is that these

C. Stephanidis et al. (Eds.): HCII 2022, CCIS 1655, pp. 184–190, 2022.
https://doi.org/10.1007/978-3-031-19682-9_24

children have spent two years of school at home through a virtual format conceived for adults.

On the other hand, in recent years computers have been replaced by mobile phones and tablets in frequency of use [3]; according to INEGI, smartphones are the main means of access to the internet in Mexico. As for 2020, almost 70% of children between the ages 6 and 11 in urban areas were already users of this technology [4]. Thus, some schools have adopted educational platforms and have decided to continue using them not only inside the classroom but to provide assignments and additional material. In fact, there has always been a debate about homework and its benefits since children may struggle to incorporate learning strategies at home. Nonetheless, homework is a practical exercise which helps students revise and deepen what they have learned [2].

2   Pedagogical Research on Homework

With this panorama and the post-pandemic situation in mind, children who send their homework on digital platforms need to be assisted by their parents due to the lack of a clear and intuitive display. This inadequacy of learning tools widens the competence gap related to digital skills of students to properly make use of those platforms for a successful performance [6]. The confusing arrangement causes the children to find it difficult to turn in their assignments into the respective section or to miss the due date. While this situation is constantly repeated, it produces great frustration in the children, who grow to dislike doing homework even more.

Cheung *et al.* [1] say that there are theoretical arguments backing that home learning activities and autonomy support provided by parents can also contribute to children's school liking. This may help explain how the home learning environment benefits children's achievement given the importance of school liking in the development of pre-academic skills [1]. On that matter, our design team found a great area of opportunity in working with kids on the conception and development of a digital homework diary in order to enhance children's autonomy.

Although the central user is the child, by making it easier for them to do homework on their own, it also eases the need for intervention of both parents and teachers. Students who do more homework are supposed to have better achievements [2]. The parents' involvement in homework is essential to learners of this age in order to enhance their school performance. According to Hurwitz and Schmitt [8], parents can establish greater mediation on the use of digital tools at an early age. However, younger children tend to show less autonomy and parents cannot be with their kid all the time. And so, the main objective of this project is to encourage the autonomy of the children as specified previously in the need statement.

3   Methodology

To this end, the starting point of this project was the study case of the mainstream e-learning app Google Classroom at a private elementary school on the West side of Mexico City. The present work is based on the User-Centered Design (UCD) process which outlines the phases throughout the analysis, design and life-cycle development while focusing on the understanding of the user needs. Hence, our first approach was getting to know about the interaction of the children with Google Classroom in their context of use when doing homework.

The analysis phase consisted of brief interviews and an ethnographic study in order to detect the needs of students aged from 6 to 11 at a private elementary school in Mexico City. The ethnographic study implied the observation as the main activity to analyze the ways in which Google Classroom was used at home. Understanding autonomy support as the practices of fostering children's ability to plan and regulate their own behaviors [12], we identified the need for raising the autonomy of elementary school children to do their assignments while avoiding confusion about due dates and mixing subjects up.

We realized that as the kids grow older, they become more able to finish and submit their assignments on their own. Thus, we wish for our solution to accompany them along this journey to become more independent on this matter. With this insight in mind, we framed the various stages of this progress by age. In order to analyze the viable solutions, three user profiles were defined. Then again, some identified concerns were related to the time it takes them to turn in their work. Another important pain point was the obvious dislike for this school activity in general.

The following steps in the design process involved a storyboard, which is a technique focused on building a scenario by identifying tasks (actions) that will help users solve their needs (see Fig. 1). It should be noticed that users will always appear and participate along the process. Secondly, a pretype was presented to the kids in order to confirm the relevance of the problem [13]. Once the idea was approved, in a further stage, a low-fidelity prototype of a preliminary solution was built.

Fig. 1. Individual storyboards as a first approach

In this first round of ideation, the design team considered it important to encourage ownership on homework in order to properly cultivate autonomy. We must not forget that our main objective is to enable the kids to feel confident, responsible and autonomous in completing their homework at the same time they find it fun. For that purpose, a progress section with stimulating elements within the app, such as the accumulation of star-shaped emblems, was included (see Fig. 2). By creating a motivating environment, learners can gain relatedness, competence, and autonomy [9].

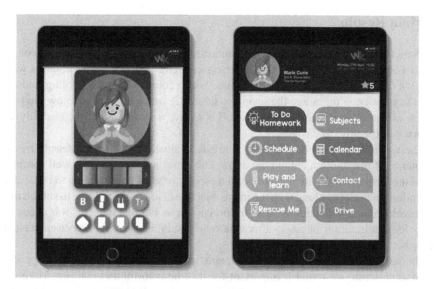

Fig. 2. Screenshots of avatar and home pages

These rewarding elements can be earned when submitting the work on time or used to access a backup of the material in case the kid forgets the textbook (see Fig. 3). Some restrictions were also considered in order to truly encourage the kids to assume the consequences of their misses. However, this kind of feature does not seek to incite comparison or unhealthy rivalry among the peers. On the contrary, we hope to open a communication channel where classmates can collaborate in teamwork assignments. Fardoun *et al.* [5] state that communication tools as technological resources must support the teaching-learning process and allow meaningful learning through peer cooperation.

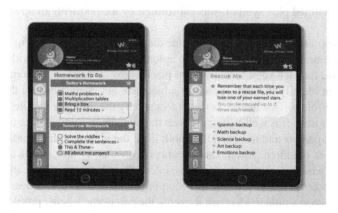

Fig. 3. Screenshots showing both cases when stars are earned and redeemed

4 Main Results

The prototype was presented to six kid students from the same traditional school and were asked to put it to the test, both in person and remotely. In order to obtain a wider source of feedback, the model was also shared with a couple of homeschooling students. In the same way, at this stage the team considered it was important to know the point of view of parents and teachers. The overall objective was to evaluate the usability and adequacy of the proposed solution.

The test phase was followed by a heuristic evaluation [10] of the feasibility and acceptance of the solution among the users. The concept in general was well accepted. Out of the ten principles, the most important aspect we must pay attention to is the error prevention since it goes along with the main objective of allowing children to submit their homework on their own with the least friction possible. For that purpose, it is necessary to provide confirmation messages after a successful submission or an easy-to-understand alert when a problem occurs.

On that same line, regarding the minimalistic design principle, since it is a product aimed at children, we found it important for it to be colorful and inviting. Moreover, a lively interphase proved to be stimulating and was well received. The children felt specially empowered by the avatar feature. They seemed eager to customize it, even though it was not fully developed. Thus, the mock elements caused the youngest users to lose interest pretty quickly. Similarly, the introduction of a communication channel among peers really got them excited.

On the other hand, from the test with the homeschooling kids, some contexts of use that were not considered before appeared as well. For instance, in case a family has two or more children, but they have to share devices, it would require the inclusion of a setting that allows more than one student account and be able to switch from one to another keeping both separated. Likewise, some improvements must be made on the icons in order to make them more intuitive, such as the different subjects and calls to action. In particular, the icon indicating to upload and to submit an assignment. The original icon, which was a circled plus symbol, was substituted by a cloud with an upward-pointing arrow.

An incorporated update was an aid frame displayed on camera (see Fig. 4) when the kids take a picture of the work they want to upload. The app will also provide a ready-to-print QR code for each subject that will be placed next to the sheet of homework. This code will then identify the corresponding subject and automatically save the archive in the respective folder. This feature is meant to simplify the fitting of the sheet in order to capture a clear image; as well as helping with the organization and finding of those files.

As for the parents and teachers, they both liked the idea of a platform that connects the three actors (children, parents and teachers) considering their needs as secondary users. This is when we confirmed that these interactions between central and peripheral users also foster the kids' process in becoming more autonomous. Hence, a further development stage would work on establishing the parent and teacher profiles. However, at present these features are not a priority and will have to be put on standby.

Regarding information architecture, we can work on clearer categories and address some aspects on the display in order to reduce the number of elements presented on the home page. The corrected version might be shared once more with our users in

Fig. 4. Kid user trying the guide frame on camera to upload her homework

order to get new insights that can help us build a more functional version. Although not completely refined, the results at this stage are promising since kids have shown interest in adopting Workids as a tool to help them with their schoolwork in this digital era.

5 Conclusions

To sum up, the starting point of this project was the identification of a lack of age-adapted educational platforms in elementary levels widely incorporated during lockdown and kept even afterwards. Since the first years of education are crucial for kids to get used to new responsibilities and digital devices are becoming a more common tool in school activities, especially homework, an interesting opportunity was found in this intersection.

The axis of the project was the UCD process. In the user research stage, we resorted to several methods in order to know the needs and pain points of our little users. One of them being the kids' dislike towards homework due to the difficulties they face when submitting it in a virtual space. From then, it was established that the main objective of the project was to encourage them to become more independent in this specific task. Likewise, a secondary objective was to provide a fair source of motivation and collaborative learning while they grow ownership of their assignments.

Hence, a rewarding system was featured in order to keep track of their progress. A guiding frame on camera was also placed to make it easier to take cleaner shots of the work on paper. Two prototypes were built and tested directly with the users. Some of the improvements were related with the icons and the setting of the user profile.

All in all, the results have been encouraging so far despite being at an early stage in the development. Among the many improvements left unattended, there is the development of the account version for parents and teachers. We feel very pleased by the enthusiasm shown by the users towards the product. But it only shows the exciting potential this solution may have.

References

1. Cheung, S.K., Cheng, W.Y., Cheung, R.Y., Lau, E.Y.H., Chung, K.K.H.: Home learning activities and parental autonomy support as predictors of pre-academic skills: The mediating role of young children's school liking. Learn. Individ. Differ. **94**, 102127 (2022)
2. Chophel, T., Choeda, U.: Impact of Parental Involvement in Homework on Children's learning. J. Educ. Soc. Behav. Sci. **34**(6), 35–46 (2021)
3. Dirección General de Planeación, Programación y Estadística Educativa. Principales Cifras del Sistema Educativo Nacional 1 ed. Mexico City: Secretaría de Educación Pública (2020). https://www.planeacion.sep.gob.mx/Doc/estadistica_e_indicadores/princi pales_cifras/principales_cifras_2019_2020_bolsillo.pdf
4. Encuesta Nacional sobre Disponibilidad y Uso de Tecnologías de la Información en los Hogares (ENDUTIH) INEGI (2020). https://www.inegi.org.mx/contenidos/saladeprensa/bol etines/2021/OtrTemEcon/ENDUTIH_2020.pdf
5. Fardoun, H., González, C., Collazos, C.A., Yousef, M.: Estudio exploratorio en Iberoamérica sobre procesos de enseñanza-aprendizaje y propuesta de evaluación en tiempos de pandemia. Educ. Knowl. Soc. (EKS) **21**, 9 (2020). https://doi.org/10.14201/eks.2353
6. Enguita, M.F.: Cuaderno de campo: Una pandemia imprevisible ha traído la brecha previsible. Blog Enguita. Blogger 31 Mar 2020. http://bit.ly/2VT3kzU
7. Hodges, C., Moore, S., Lockee, B., Trust, T., Bond, A.: The difference between emergency remote teaching and online learning. Educause Review (2020)
8. Hurwitz, L.B., Schmitt, K.L.: Can children benefit from early internet exposure? Short-and long-term links between internet use, digital skill, and academic performance. Comput. Educ. **146**, 103750 (2020). https://doi.org/10.1016/j.compedu.2019.103750
9. Knopik, T., Oszwa, U.: Self-determination and development of emotional-social competences and the level of school achievements in 10–11-year-old Polish students. Education 3–13, **48**(8), 972–987 (2020). https://doi.org/10.1080/03004279.2019.1686048
10. Nielsen, J.: 10 usability heuristics for user interface design. Fremont: Nielsen Norman Group (1995).
11. Principales Resultados del Censo Población y Vivienda 2020. SEDECO (2021). https://www.sedeco.cdmx.gob.mx/storage/app/media/uploaded-files/resultados-del-censo-pob-y-viv-2020-1.pdf
12. Ryan, R.M., Deci E.L., Grolnick, W.S., La Guardia J.G.: The significance of autonomy support in psychological development and psychopathology. In: Cicchetti, D., Cohen, D.J. (eds.) 2nd ed. Developmental psychopathology, vol. 1, John Wiley & Sons Inc. (2006)
13. Savoia, A.: Leader summaries (2003).https://www.pretotyping.org/uploads/1/4/0/9/140 99067/pretotype_it_2nd_pretotype_edition-2.pdf

Exploring Information Retrieval for Personalized Teaching Support

Nanjie Rao(✉) ⑩, Sharon Lynn Chu⑩, Zeyuan Jing⑩, Huan Kuang⑩,
Yunjie Tang⑩, and Zhang Dong

University of Florida, Gainesville, FL 32611, USA
{raon,slchu,jingzeyuan,huan2015,yunjie.tang,zdong}@ufl.edu

Abstract. The outbreak of Covid-19 challenged the education system
and caused more disconnections than ever between instructors, students,
and content. Having instructors use personal information relevant to their
students within a lesson would create a more personalized lesson that
could resonate with the students and facilitate their participation in the
classroom. However, teaching is already a complex and challenging job
as teachers must multitask in delivering content and fulfilling students'
needs. To encourage and support instructors to integrate the personal
experiences of students during their lessons, we propose an approach based
on a speech-recognition-based personal information retrieval pipeline. We
designed and developed PRIS, a personalized, real-time teaching support
system, as an exemplar of the approach. This paper presents a small-scale
within-subjects study comparing the use of PRIS and typical notecards to
assess the impact of the proposed approach on teaching. Results showed
that the PRIS condition has better usability, imposes lower cognitive load
on the teacher, and leads to more frequent personalized teaching behaviors compared to the notecard condition. We discuss the implications for
the design of personalized teaching support systems.

Keywords: Personal relevant information · Information retrieval ·
Teaching support

1 Introduction

In an era where online and distant learning is becoming increasingly important,
grabbing students' attention has never been so crucial and challenging. Technological distractions can hardly be avoided, and methods are urgently needed
to enhance students' engagement and performance. In previous research, it has
been found that the implementation of relevant information in a lesson can have
positive effects on learning [2,6]. A more personalized lesson could resonate with
the students. Therefore, having teachers use information personally relevant to

Supported by National Science Foundation Grant #1942937 *CAREER: Bridging Formal and Everyday Learning through Wearable Technologies: Towards a Connected
Learning Paradigm*

their students within a lesson could thus improve students' perceived closeness to the teacher [9], which could lead students to engage more deeply in class. However, teaching in the classroom is already a complex and challenging process as teachers must multitask in delivering content and fulfilling students' needs. If not supported, requiring teachers to make use of the personal experiences of the learners could overwhelm the teachers during teaching.

To tackle this challenge, recent years have seen increased interest in the design of technologies to support personalized teaching in real-time [1]. Support systems have been developed across disciplines and in various forms. To encourage and support teachers in making use of the personal experiences of the learners during instruction, this paper introduces PRIS (Personally Relevant Instruction System), a real-time personalized teaching support system that uses speech recognition to retrieve previously stored information related to specific individual students and presents it to the teacher during teaching. We present a study that compares the use of the PRIS approach and typical notecards in an online teaching scenario. Our work proposes novel directions for future research on the design of personalized teaching support systems.

2   Background and Related Work

Prior work has addressed the need to build rapport between teachers and students. Including information that relate students' individual experiences will result in better study motivation and results for students [6], where focusing on Yupik culture incorporated into a math lesson resulted in improved learning. Also, connecting science to social context can support science teaching in urban settings [2]. Real-world problems and school-community partnerships were used as contextual scaffolds to bridge community and school-based knowledge. Students learned more key concepts and were more apt to discuss what they learned with their family.

However, teaching is already a multitasking job by itself [3] and is increasing in complexity and intensity. Requiring attention from teachers for the purpose of personalized learning can be tricky. In order to scaffold teaching activities in real-time and not overwhelm the teachers, the supporting system needs to be automatic enough to not burden teachers with additional tasks [1]. Moreover, the cognitive load aspect should be carefully considered in the design of the system for avoiding the interruption to teachers' nomadic workflows.

3   Research Questions and Study Design

Our research investigated the impact of using PRIS or not for retrieving students' personal information to support personalized teaching. In a personalized teaching scenario, we addressed the following research questions:

Are there significant differences between teacher's use of PRIS as opposed to notecard in terms of:

RQ1: teacher's perception, operationalized as perceived usability, importance, and competence?;

RQ2: cognitive overload of the teacher?; and

RQ3: frequency of personalized teaching behaviors?

To answer these research questions, we designed a within-subjects study with *Using PRIS system or not* as the single independent variable with two conditions - 'PRIS' condition and 'notecard' condition. For the PRIS condition, participants used the real-time personalized teaching support system developed by us, based on a speech-recognition-based personal information retrieval pipeline. For the notecard condition, participants used a Word document that contains the same information as it would be in the PRIS system to serve as teachers' notecards while they were teaching. Examples of participant's screens when doing PRIS condition on the topic of Christmas and notecard condition on the topic of sleep are shown in Fig. 1. Our dependent variables (DV) are: (1) teacher's perception (perceived usability, importance, and competence), (2) cognitive overload of the teacher, and (3) frequency of personalized teaching behaviors.

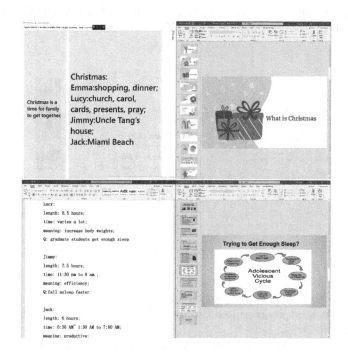

Fig. 1. Examples of participant's screen for 2 conditions

4   System and Study Description

PRIS - the real-time personalized teaching support system designed and developed by us, is based on a speech-recognition-based personal information retrieval pipeline. The system design is flexible, meaning it can easily be deployed to run on any platform with any device and any language. The kernel of the system consists of a local client program and a cloud service. Most computation-heavy tasks are processed in the cloud in order to not pose any demand for teachers and students' machines. And the local client program basically serves as a teleprompter to display the dictation and students' personally relevant information to the teacher while also offers easy copy-and-paste manipulation on contents (before class) and freedom to select the language to teach in. During the online class, the local client program collects voice signals from the teacher's microphone and sends processed data to the cloud service. The speech recognition engine in the cloud service converts and transcribes the audio and returns the corresponding text. Then the keyword matching function in the local client program searches through the text and pulls out related contents according to customized keywords set by the teachers before class. Microsoft Azure API was adopted in our study for speech recognition. However, it can be substituted for any other resources. This hardware requirement of the PRIS system is just a basic setup of online learning equipment which most laptops or Chromebooks would do. How our setup was in a Virtual Zoom Study is shown in Fig. 2.

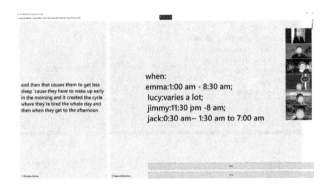

Fig. 2. Example of PRIS setup in a Zoom Study

We had a total of 8 study participants (5 male, 3 female). All participants were university students recruited through university listservs, and compensated with course credit.

Each participant went through both PRIS and notecard in a 60-minute study session. The order of the two conditions and two topics was counterbalanced across participants.

In our study, during the first 10–15 minutes, each participant was given a detailed explanation and instruction about this study. They had 5 min to prepare their teaching of the first topic and 10 min to teach the first topic, with or without the assistance of the PRIS system depending on their assigned order. And then they spent 5–10 minutes to answer the survey on Qualtrics. For the 2nd condition, they had 5 min to prepare another topic and 10 min to teach the second topic without or with the PRIS system. And then they spent 5–10 minutes to answer the survey again but based on their experience of their 2nd condition.

The two topics were the Christmas holiday and sleep and chosen in the manners that: (1) It's familiar yet everyone would have their own experiences and opinions. Both common and uncommon knowledge can be taught. (2) Whichever the topic appears in what condition or what order, there will not be learning effects of carry-on knowledge from the previous topic. For a simulated online teaching setup, every participant was assigned a role as the teacher and 4 of our researchers acted as students. Simulated students were trained so that for each different teacher, they always had a similar behavior pattern.

5   Measures and Data Collection

The participants filled out 3 questionnaires after each condition: (1) Post Study System Usability Questionnaire (PSSUQ) [5], to measure teacher's perceived usability about the system - DV1; (2) Intrinsic Motivation Inventory (IMI) [8], to measure teacher's perceived importance, choice, and competence - DV1; and (3) NASA Task Load Index (TLX) [4], to measure the cognitive overload of the teacher, - DV2. The frequency of personalized teaching behaviors from recorded teaching sessions was the normalized count of the behaviors (per minute). It was counted by 2 counters following a simple rubric: The words said by the teacher were intended to connect specific student(s) to the learning content. The inter-coder agreement was 87.93%. An agreement level of at least 70% is typically deemed acceptable [7]. And the 2 counters subsequently agreed on the final count.

6   Data Analysis and Results

Paired-samples t-tests were conducted to compare perceived usability, importance and competence, cognitive overload, and frequency of personalized teaching behaviors.

Results showed that there were statistically significant differences between the PRIS section and the notecard section on perceived usability (t $(119) = -1.69$, p $< .05$), cognitive overload (t $(47) = 2.37$, p $< .05$), and frequency of personalized teaching behaviors (t $(7) = 7.89$, p $< .05$). There was no significant difference in importance and competence from IMI.

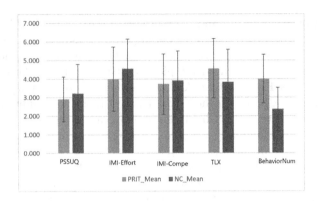

Fig. 3. A bar chart of our results

From PSSUQ, PRIS (M = 2.91, SD = 1.21) was perceived more usable than notecard (M = 3.23, SD = 1.57).

From NASA-TLX, PRIS (M = 4.56, SD = 1.60) has lower cognitive load than notecard (M = 3.83, SD = 1.75).

From normalized count of the behaviors, PRIS (M = 4.00, SD = 1.31) has more frequent personalized teaching behavior than notecard (M = 2.38, SD = 1.16).

7   Discussion and Limitations

As seen in Fig. 3, almost all aspects met our expectations except for perceived effort and competence from IMI. PRIS prompted the teachers to lead personalized teaching almost twice as often as a notecard. These findings matched the basic premise of cognitive load theory, which is learners have a working memory with very limited capacity when dealing with new information [10], as the PRIS system retrieved the relevant information when needed automatically, and this saved the effort of the teacher searching through the notecard. As it's more convenient and easier for the teacher to use PRIS than notecard, they tend to engage in more personalized teaching. This could lead to the enhanced performance of both teachers and students and improved class quality.

For perceived effort and competence, there was no significant difference between PRIS and notecard. This finding might seem surprising at first, but it's also understandable because of 2 reasons, the participants never used the PRIS system before and most of them don't have teaching experience. Another limitation is that our sample size is small. Future work could take a deeper look at methods of preserving students' privacy and better ways to deliver personally relevant information.

8   Conclusion

We designed and developed PRIS - a real-time personalized teaching support system based on a speech-recognition-based personal information retrieval pipeline. This paper presents a within-subject study comparing using PRIS and normal notecards to assess its impact on teaching. Our results showed that the PRIS condition did get better usability, the lower cognitive load on the teacher, and more frequent personalized teaching behaviors compared to the notecard condition. Our work paves the way for needed future research on the design of a personalized teaching support system.

Acknowledgments. This research supported by National Science Foundation Grant #1942937 *CAREER: Bridging Formal and Everyday Learning through Wearable Technologies: Towards a Connected Learning Paradigm*

References

1. An, P., Holstein, K., d'Anjou, B., Eggen, B., Bakker, S.: The ta framework: designing real-time teaching augmentation for k-12 classrooms. In: Proceedings of the 2020 CHI Conference on Human Factors in Computing Systems, pp. 1–17 (2020)
2. Bouillion, L.M., Gomez, L.M.: Connecting school and community with science learning: real world problems and school-community partnerships as contextual scaffolds. J. Res. Sci. Teach. Official J. Nat. Assoc. Res. Sci. Teach. **38**(8), 878–898 (2001)
3. Brante, G.: Multitasking and synchronous work: complexities in teacher work. Teach. Teach. Educ. **25**(3), 430–436 (2009)
4. Hart, S.G., Staveland, L.E.: Development of NASA-TLX (task load index): results of empirical and theoretical research. In: Advances in Psychology, vol. 52, pp. 139–183. Elsevier (1988)
5. Lewis, J.R.: Psychometric evaluation of the post-study system usability questionnaire: the PSSUQ. In: Proceedings of the Human Factors and Ergonomics Society Annual Meeting, vol. 36, pp. 1259–1260. SAGE Publications Sage CA: Los Angeles, CA (1992)
6. Lipka, J., Illutsik, E.: Transforming the culture of schooling: teacher education in southwest Alaska (1999)
7. Lombard, M., Snyder-Duch, J., Bracken, C.C.: Content analysis in mass communication: assessment and reporting of intercoder reliability. Hum. Commun. Res. **28**(4), 587–604 (2002)
8. McAuley, E., Duncan, T., Tammen, V.V.: Psychometric properties of the intrinsic motivation inventory in a competitive sport setting: a confirmatory factor analysis. Res. Q. Exerc. Sport **60**(1), 48–58 (1989)
9. Opdenakker, M.C., Maulana, R., den Brok, P.: Teacher-student interpersonal relationships and academic motivation within one school year: developmental changes and linkage. Sch. Eff. Sch. Improv. **23**(1), 95–119 (2012)
10. Paas, F., Renkl, A., Sweller, J.: Cognitive load theory and instructional design: recent developments. Educ. Psychol. **38**(1), 1–4 (2003)

INTELIAPP: An Application to Detect the Different Intelligence and Cognitive Abilities in Public High School Students to Develop a Better Appropriation of Knowledge

Orlando Arturo Rizo Mendoza[1,2] (ID), Daniel Sánchez Fuentes[1,2] (ID),
Alvaro Josias Ornelas Medina[1,2(✉)] (ID), and Rocío Abascal Mena[1,2] (ID)

[1] Master in Design, Information and Communication (MADIC), Universidad Autónoma
Metropolitana, Cuajimalpa, Mexico
`alvarojosias@gmail.com, mabascal@cua.uam.mx`
[2] Avenida Vasco de Quiroga 4871, Colonia Santa Fe Cuajimalpa, Del. Cuajimalpa de Morelos,
Ciudad de México C.P. 05300, México

Abstract. Education plays a fundamental role in social mobility and equal opportunities. However, after two years of a pandemic, the differences between the students are bigger. Traditional education has always been given to all without taking
into account the cognitive and intellectual differences of the students. Nonetheless,
the task of making individual material or detecting these differences is not trivial
for the teachers. A quote that appears on the Plan and study programs section on
the Mexico City Government website exemplifies the above: "In this sense, the
teacher assumes a role of companion in the process of discovery, exploration, and
development of the possibilities of their students" [5]. This implies that teachers
have a great responsibility. Yet, it is difficult for them to achieve this function
because there are several factors that affect their work. In this article, we seek to
delve into two elements, which are currently having a great presence in educational centers: we will refer to the irruption of mobile technologies in classrooms
and to the theory of multiple intelligences. The fundamental part of this work will
consist of the research, development and creation of the prototype of an educational app developed based on its applicability and relevance. In this way, we take
into account the user profile and their needs.

Keywords: Multiple intelligence · Education · User-Centered Design · Teacher ·
Digital app

1 Introduction

Teachers are appreciated because they play a fundamental role in society; however,
at times the job is frustrating. In early stages of our research, we discovered that, for
different reasons, teachers lack the material needed to teach their classes; that public
high schools in Mexico usually have more than 40 students per classroom, and that

C. Stephanidis et al. (Eds.): HCII 2022, CCIS 1655, pp. 198–204, 2022.
https://doi.org/10.1007/978-3-031-19682-9_26

teachers need and want more training in order to accomplish their professional goals. Also, something that we realized in this research was that teachers are really interested in having tools that help them improve the quality of their classes.

On the other hand, according to the 2019 PISA test result [11], out of all the 15 years old Mexican high school students: 45% do not achieve sufficient learning in Reading, 56% in Mathematics, and 47% in Science. Furthermore, 17% of students say they feel lonely at school. These results show that learning occurs unequally in public high schools in Mexico City. The process of learning and practicing these cognitive abilities has many variants to take into account.

We found in the multiple intelligence theory, developed by Howard Gardner, a viable way to help teachers to fulfill their objectives [4]. Teachers know about this theory and some of them use it actively in their classes [7]. But not all of them, because they find it difficult to develop a kind of individual planning for each student when they have more than 40 per classroom. We identified that this was a breach where we can do something to help.

The concept of intelligence has changed rapidly since it was perceived as static, innate, and influenced by heredity and culture [3]. In this sense, Gardner's theory of multiple intelligences proposes a plural vision of intelligence, recognizing in it various facets, thus deducing that each person has different cognitive potentials [2]. In the educational field, this theory provides relevant information on learning styles, helping to perceive students as entities that learn in different ways, which should generate diverse methodological strategies for the same content, empowering the student with the possibility of recognizing and using their cognitive abilities to the fullest. Although the Theory of Multiple Intelligences was formulated in the 1980s, there are currently few valid, reliable, and easy-to-apply tools to assess Multiple Intelligences.

The objective of the present article is to explain the process we took to provide high school teachers in Mexico with a digital tool that allows them to: diagnose the multiple intelligences that each of their students and groups, plan classes based on that diagnosis, and create a community with other teachers to share experiences related to its implementation.

The organization of the paper is divided into four parts. In Sect. 2, we will be able to compare the tools, systems, or applications that already exist and that partially solve the same problem as the one we are posing. In the third section, we will describe the methodology used and each of the parts of the project development process. Later, in Sect. 4, we will show our results through a digital prototype. And, in the end, we will conclude with what are the steps to follow to give continuity to the project.

2 Related Work

In this part of the research process, we look at existing digital and non-digital projects that will come close to what we are looking for. As a premise, we had lesson planning and multiple intelligences.

As for tools that make it easier for teachers to plan and manage the content of classes, there are several such as Kahoot[1], which is a tool of innovation in upgrading the teaching

---

[1] https://kahoot.com.

and learning method to students. It is game-based learning that allows students to explore different parts of the game as a form of learning to help them improve their skills or achieve specific learning outcomes [1].

Google Classroom[2], is another application used by schools to provide a central site to help teachers and students to communicate with each other [13]. It helps teachers to manage groups and create collaborative networks; among other digital tools that allow the creation of collaborative networks such as Slack[3], which is an application that permits communications inside teamworks [6].

There are several online tests to identify the multiple intelligences but that stand out in each person. The result of these is only informative, there is no link to another tool that shows how to apply it to a specific situation or that can process groups intelligences.

We also found some offline resources, such as the book "El genio que llevas dentro"[4] (The genius you have inside), which approaches the multiple intelligences theory of Howard Gardner with concepts and activities that teachers and parents can follow in order to develop their children's different intelligences.

Most of the online systems mentioned above have to be accessed through a browser, few offer an app; hence the relevance of our proposal. In addition, there is no technological outlet that provides, within a single product (in this case an app), tools to manage classes based on the result of a multiple intelligence test.

3   Development Process

The present work uses the User-Centered Design (UCD) methodology in order to create a solution based on the main characteristics, goals, and needs of the teachers of public high schools in Mexico City. The process followed to design a mobile application to help teachers detect intelligence abilities and plan their classes was composed of 6 iterative phases:

Analysis: composed of interviews and an ethnographic study in order to detect the needs of teachers at the public high schools. Based on the results of the interviews with teachers (we interviewed three high school teachers), we detect one main problem: teachers lack the necessary tools to plan their classes according to their students' multiple intelligences. We also identified three main obstacles to achieving it: high school teachers have huge student groups, which make it very difficult to identify their multiple intelligences; also, they don't have easy access to information about activities they can include in their planning; and there is a lack of time to plan classes considering the multiple intelligence theory.

Brainstorm: this means a generation of words, images, sentences, and concepts that could help to get inspiration from the world so the construction of an appropriate design could take into account the opportunities that surround the users. In order to work with an objective in mind, the design team defined the next point of view: Public high school teachers have very large groups, which makes it difficult to identify the multiple

---

[2] https://classroom.google.com.

[3] https://slack.com.

[4] https://acortar.link/7YQQwK.

intelligences of their students and can frustrate them. However, if their planning is made easier, they could be motivated and reach more students to encourage better learning, and reduce frustration and the rate of failure.

Storyboard: consists of simulating a scenario where a task is required to be done. It helps to show the experience of the user and what has to be done to complete the task in a successful way. This part of the process was helpful in prioritizing one single need, which was to identify the multiple intelligences by student groups and to offer information about how to develop them.

Pretotype: By using the Pinocchio method, this step consisted of making a video with a non-operative version of the product explaining the general idea of it, and receiving feedback from potential users [14]. The video was uploaded to YouTube and was shown to twelve different teachers who subsequently conducted an evaluation through a Google Form. In the video we show the steps to follow to use the app: registration and profile generation, filling in information about the groups, how to share the content with others, see results and tips. With the virtual questionnaire ready, we share the link via WhatsApp to twelve public high school teachers to obtain relevant data for our proposal. This stage helped our team to confirm that we were on the right track as we received positive feedback from the potential users to whom we showed the pretotype.

Digital prototype: the digital prototype contains the structure and organization of the information (text, images, buttons, among other elements); the arrangement of those elements on the screen; the simulation of the actions performed by the buttons with the execution of certain tasks and their results, which is very useful for the first test with users (see Fig. 1). The contribution of this stage was the user's interaction design with the application, which allowed the team to correct some design assumptions that were made during the pretotyping step.

Evaluation: the digital prototype was tested with high school teachers according to the ten usability heuristics for user interface design defined by Jacob Nielsen [8, 9].

4 Main Results

In this first evaluation, we obtained information that allows us to make the necessary adjustments to advance to the current phase of the project. For example, teachers told us that it was necessary to have more basic information about the multiple intelligence theory and exposed their need of having a way to interact and exchange best practices with teachers from other schools, a function that we included in the following prototype.

With the sum of teachers needs and observations, inspiration and interaction design, we developed Inteliapp, a mobile app prototype that serves to facilitate the identification of multiple intelligences at the individual and group level; provides tips for lesson planning based on the findings; and facilitates the exchange of information between teachers from different schools. The proposal considers teachers who have difficulties with the use of technologies, so it will provide options to facilitate their use.

The app provides a test that will permit teachers to know the details about the different abilities of their pupils. Moreover, it provides ideas and activities that teachers can implement in the classroom. This section will be fed by professors who want to share their success experience with others.

After this research, we believe that Inteliapp has a great potential to help teachers' communities in Mexico. The project is still in the prototype phase and has called the attention of every individual that has participated in the process of developing it.

Fig. 1. Main screens of Intelliapp

5 Conclusions and Further Work

We believe that the use of mobile devices, as shown by different studies, can substantially improve the quality of teaching processes, especially if they are directly related to theories that facilitate learning, such as the case of multiple intelligences [12]. In this way, the present project manifests genuine interest in the teachers and other people involved, showing that the proposed solution addresses the correct motivations and needs.

Further work includes new evaluations with the users since we have noticed that the development of educational apps and their use with mobile devices constitutes a broad, flexible and versatile context; and enables learning and access to content inside and outside the classroom. So, there is a need to evaluate the application in different contexts, not only in the classroom.

It is necessary to point out the importance of the theory of Multiple Intelligences in education since the use of different didactic strategies and the use of various resources and styles to develop the curriculum will undoubtedly enhance the creative capacity of children and adolescents. In this sense, it would be interesting for further work to explore other education trends that are being used in the classrooms, such as those coming from neuroscience, in order to include more contents and advices that will be useful for teachers.

On the one hand, the application of the theory of multiple intelligences proposes that our students can learn in different ways, which means that we can, in some way, personalize their preferences and abilities. On the other hand, the implementation of an educational app and its use with mobile devices constitutes a broad, flexible and versatile context that enables learning [10].

References

1. Aishah, A., et al.: Students' acceptance towards Kahoot application in mastering culinary terminology. Jurnal Pendidikan Teknologi dan Kejuruan. **27**, 1–6 (2021). https://doi.org/10.21831/jptk.v27i1.38391
2. Altan, M., . Intelligence reframed: multiple intelligences for the 21st century. TESOL 2. Quar. **35**, 204 (2002). https://doi.org/10.2307/3587873
3. Cascón-Pereira, R.: Mentes creativas: una anatomía de la creatividad vista a través de las vidas de Sigmund Freud. In: Einstein, A., Picasso, P., Stravinsky, I., Eliot, T.S. (eds.) Marta Graham y Mahatma Gandhi. Barcelona: Ediciones Paidós Ibérica. Revista Internacional de Organizaciones, 155 (2016). https://doi.org/10.17345/rio16.155-157
4. Gardner, H.: Estructuras de la Mente. La Teoría de Las Inteligencias Multiples. Fondo de Cultura Economica USA (2017)
5. de Mexico, G.: (n.d.) Planes y programas SEP. Accessed 05 May 2022. https://www.planyprogramasdestudio.sep.gob.mx/
6. Menzies, R., Zarb, M.: Professional communication tools in higher education: a case study in implementing slack in the curriculum. In: 2020 IEEE Frontiers in Education Conference (FIE) (2020). https://doi.org/10.1088/1742-6596/1175/1/012165/meta
7. Nalda, F., Campión, R., Tourón, J.: Opinions from teachers in the Fresno area of Central California regarding the influence of mobile technology on their students' learning. RELIEVE - Revista Electrónica de Investigación y Evaluación Educativa **19** (2014). https://doi.org/10.7203/relieve.19.2.3148

8. Nielsen, J.: Enhancing the explanatory power of usability heuristics. Proc. ACM CHI'94 Conf. Boston, MA, April 24–28, 152–158 (1994a)
9. Nielsen, J.: Heuristic evaluation. In: Nielsen, J., Mack, R.L. (eds.) Usability Inspection Methods, John Wiley & Sons, New York, NY (1994b)
10. Parsons, D., Ryu, H.: A framework for assessing the quality of mobile learning. In: 11th International Conference for Process Improvement, Research and Education (INSPIRE) (2016). https://www.researchgate.net/publication/250715030_A_Framework_for_Assessing_the_Quality_of_Mobile_Learning
11. PISA Rankings---PISA Results---PISA Ranking 2019. (2020, February 8). Reviews of International Schools. Accessed 05 May 2022. https://schoolinreviews.com/pisa-results-publis hed-in-dec-2019-which-countries-score-the-highest-and-why/
12. Campión, R.S., Filvà, D.A., Ochoa, A.D.: Can educational mobile apps strength multiple intelligences development? Edutec. Revista Electrónica De Tecnología Educativa 47 (2014). https://doi.org/10.21556/edutec.2014.47.63
13. Sudarsana, I.K., Putra, I.B.M.A., Astawa, I.N.T., Yogantara, I.W.L.: The use of Google classroom in the learning process. J. Phys. Conf. Ser. 1175 (2019). https://doi.org/10.1088/1742-6596/1175/1/012165/meta
14. Savoia, A.: Pretotype It: make sure you are building the right it before you build it right (2011). https://www.pretotyping.org/uploads/1/4/0/9/14099067/pretotype_it_2nd_pretotype_edition-2.pdf

Design of a Virtual Laboratory for Practical Learning of Environmental Management and Industrial Safety

Pablo Ron-Valenzuela[1]([✉]) [iD], Diana Vargas[2] [iD], and Lizeth Medina[3] [iD]

[1] SISAu Research Group, Facultad de Ingeniería y Tecnologías de La Información y Comunicación, Universidad Tecnológica Indoamérica, Quito, Ecuador
pron@indoamerica.edu.ec
[2] Tesquimsa S.A, Quito, Ecuador
[3] Mienium S.A, Quito, Ecuador

Abstract. At present, the world has experienced great and serious problems with the arrival of the COVID-19 pandemic and, of course, among the sectors that present the most inconveniences is face-to-face university education; therefore, higher education centers seek teaching methodologies to put students into practice. For this reason, the creation and implementation of the virtual laboratory is an alternative solution to this problem; For this, technical criteria were proposed that were evaluated through weighted factors and the analysis of three alternatives that can contribute to the design of the virtual laboratory was carried out; these are Second life, Unity 3D and Virtual plant, selecting the most appropriate tool that responds to the needs of use. Unity 3D is the tool that best contributes to each of the proposed criteria, obtaining a virtual environment for practical learning of students through a virtual tour of a simulated industrial company for the artisan manufacture of chocolates with the SKETCHUP tool, during their journey through an avatar in the company the student interacts and finds questions based on the actual exposure of the avatar to occupational hazards and the environmental management that must be fulfilled within the company with response options based on knowledge learned in class, thus achieving content feedback and decision-making in the face of physical and environmental occupational risks.

Keywords: Environmental management · Industrial safety · Virtual laboratory

1 Introduction

1.1 Background

For a long time, the use of technologies such as virtual laboratories have aroused the interest of teacher's students and students because its use favors theoretical-practical learning. Due to the increase in technology educational institutions are making their students a computer society and that can they are able to adapt to the digital age and implement virtual laboratories within their areas of study. Each activity that is carried

C. Stephanidis et al. (Eds.): HCII 2022, CCIS 1655, pp. 205–212, 2022.
https://doi.org/10.1007/978-3-031-19682-9_27

out within the virtual environment such as simulation laboratories, have the same or even better results than a conventional laboratory.

The universities face adverse situations for the students since they did not have TIC´s in academically or at work, many people have had to learn new technological tools to interact from home with the outside world, therefore education requires complementing the teaching process - learning with the design and generation of virtual laboratories that allow to put into practice the theoretical knowledge acquired and be introduced to simulations in virtual environments. The training project of Environmental Management and Industrial Safety, are theoretical subjects that require to be applied in the labor fields, with the purpose of contributing to the improvement of the environment, care of the personnel and help to the quality of the education that must be imparted in the universities; for this you must use the innovation of teaching-learning methods and techniques.

1.2 Works Related to the Subject of Study

The present work has been carried out with the objective of making known the relevance in both the development and application of virtual environments for the learning of practical subjects in the educational systems of the superior. Currently in the world different computer skills and abilities have been developed, mainly due to technological development and evolution in the way of perceiving and interpreting the environment in which they interact.

With the help of human ingenuity and boundless creativity, the creation of informative systems has been achieved. Complex thought by programming in software that help students improve the co theoretical and practical knowledge [1]. In general, a virtual laboratory has been defined as a scheme of reality, governed by laws of a scientific nature, which has patterns and codes that when processed in a computer, it provides a response that resembles reality [2]. Several countries have seen the need to implement the technological resources at their disposal to improve the environments educational programs that are currently handled, for this purpose different code programming languages are used (LMS Moodle) such as: HTML (Hyper Text Markup Language), JavaScript CSS and (Cascading Style Sheets) [3]. Several universities in Ecuador have systems that allow them to have a silver virtual form, likewise they work with different software for the development of virtual laboratories that allow learning to be more efficient and faster, so that students have an experience similar to real life under virtual conditions [4]. The virtual laboratories were designed as a complement to learning and education, the advancement of virtual environments has been possible thanks to the advancement of information technologies, and this has increased its relevance due to the confinement conditions caused by the Covid-19 pandemic [5], this interaction alternative technology complements face-to-face practices and facilitates access to them remotely [6]. According to Sánchez [7], remote access to laboratories provides flexibility and versatility at low costs, thus. This way allows to improve the learning of the students in those institutions that implement it as Practical tools at a low cost. Additionally, profits could be obtained by offering solutions professionals from consultancy to cases presented by external users. On the other hand, Torres [8] explains that the virtual recreation of a real environment helps students to deepen the knowledge acquired theoretically in a simulated scenario similar to reality. Once the programming there is the possibility of executing said simulation on different platforms without the need to start from zero. Virtual labs provide opportunities that might not otherwise be counted in the environment educational because you can find different scenarios where you need to identify problems, and develop environmental solutions whether they are soil issues, water treatment, gas emissions, or any other scenario that arises; facilitating the understanding of the theory to put it into practice [9]. The labors Remote offices are virtual environments that, in addition to having a computer system structured in the web, they have the necessary tools that allow the control and access to physical equipment. Mind on the premises [10]. This modality offers the possibility of manipulating the real equipment in a virtual, managing to enrich the learning process and take advantage of the available resources [11]. They have developed several virtual environments focused on laboratory practice simulators, in addition to have made environments under the modality of Virtual Reality (VR), with the help of Unity 3D software, this way it is possible that the users, in this case the students, can not only observe and interact with the developed environment but also have a first-person perspective to experience the activities and develop practices in greater detail. [12].

2   Methods

2.1   Analysis

This research is part of the educational use of virtual laboratories within higher education in Ecuador, the training projects of Environmental Management and Safety are taken as an example. Industrial Authority of the Industrial Engineering career at the Universidad Indoamérica, for this it was established the following operating model (Fig. 1).

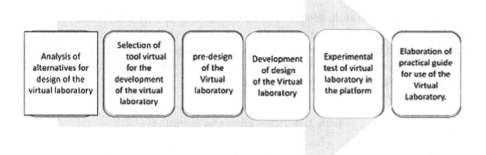

Fig. 1. Development of activities for the operating model of the virtual laboratory

2.2 Analysis of Alternatives for the Design of the Virtual Laboratory

For this analysis, several technical criteria are determined, which are analyzed through a matrix of weighting, in which their relationship and the importance between them is considered to select the option that best suits established considerations such as language, visibility, interaction, innovation, costs and use; In this way, the best option for the analysis of alternatives, the mentioned criteria are shown below (Fig. 2):

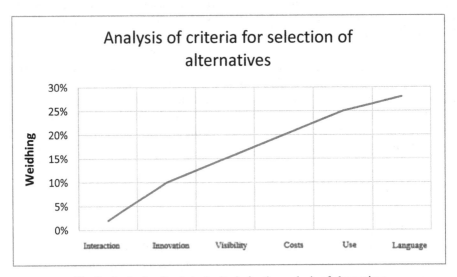

Fig. 2. Analysis of technical criteria for the analysis of alternatives

2.3 Selection of the Virtual Tool for the Development of the Virtual Laboratory

Once the criteria to be evaluated have been defined, a comparative table is made between the 3 alternatives to consider, taking into account the most relevant aspects of technological platforms, it is given a eighting to each one and an algebraic sum is performed which will show the alternative with the highest score and that will be the defined alternative to use, then the comparison table is presented (Table 1).

Table 1. Selection criteria for alternatives

Alternatives Criteria	Virtual Plant	Second Life	Unity 3D
a) Concept	Modeling in third dimension	Design your daily life in virtual	Real-time 3D animations and visualization

(*continued*)

Table 1. (*continued*)

Alternatives Criteria	Virtual Plant	Second Life	Unity 3D
b) Language	Dialect of the CMAScript standard, based on an HTML	The structure of the LSL is based on Java and C	The language is called C# Scripting languages are used for objects, they have syntax
c) Visibility	The 3D options are limited	Create video game effects, images, videos and sounds	2D and 3D Effects, avatars can be integrated, interactions
d) Interaction	It is a platform for individual use	It is a platform for individual use	Add questions with assessment to given answers
e) Innovation	It is a formal platform inwhich the planned cycle is fulfilled	It is considered as (gamification), in which users interact	It integrates avatars, sounds, videos and interaction through questions
f) Costs	Economic agreement with the University	It has a cost of $12.99 per month	It is free to use
g) Use	It runs in any web browser	Free downloadable application	Public use, through a downloadable link or document

Once the analysis has been carried out according to the importance of each criterion, it is obtained that the most suitable for the development of the virtual laboratory of Industrial security is Unity 3D. Because it meets with the proposed parameters and is considered more feasible and economical to apply. Programming to using will be easier to understand thanks to the built-in Unity library. The idea is to be able to integrate gamification in the development of the proposal and in turn evaluate the knowledge of the student who will enter to the virtual tour. The advantage of this tool is that it can be given personal use and relate your content nested with the professional practices developed by an Industrial Engineering student applying knowledge industrial safety and environmental management training.

3 Results

3.1 Development of the Virtual Laboratory Design

The virtual tour carried out in the SKETCHUP tool consists of several areas such as: Grinding of cocoa, Roasting oven, Cocoa husk, Milk tank, Chocolate bar production line, cocoa injection machine, Finished merchandise, Control area, Maintenance area, al raw material storage, finished product storage area, transportation area and waste management area; in these areas the students have interactivity with an avatar the same as runs with movements and directionality given by the student through the keyboard of his computer and you will find questions regarding the occupational risk present in each area and the environmental management that must be observe the student (Fig. 3).

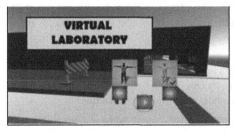 

Fig. 3. Virtual laboratory avatar selection for industrial safety or environmental management

3.2 Programming Language in UNITY 3D

UNITY 3D uses the "C SHARP" programming language, which is developed by Microsoft with the goal for developers to create a multitude of applications, since it is a simple language, with security and oriented to the desired objectives, it is very easy to understand and consists of libraries to use either installable as is the one used for UNITY 3D, it can be combined with other types of languages to be supplemented. The scripts are the part behind the visual part, it is what is shown in the simu travel lation.

The programming carried out for the different actions to be carried out is presented below. Realize.

- Programming for time, the function of timing the time.
- Function for the user to exit the virtual tour,
- Function is used for the storage of the user, that is, it saves the answers given.
- Function that grants the configuration of selecting the answers and using buttons to continue the re ran
- Gives instructions to help the user to have a 360° visibility of the entire structure of the company
- Set of instructions given to the program is to use the movement keys, that is, arrows or letters that are identified so that the user can move the avatar in different directions.
- Functions used to take a tour of the entire infrastructure of the company, visiting the
- different areas of the laboratory.
- As a final result, a virtual laboratory was obtained aimed at the practical theoretical teaching of management. Environmental and Industrial Safety. The novelty of the virtual laboratory is the implementation of two avatars that give orientation to the area of industrial safety and environmental management. Dialog boxes that indicate the steps to follow within the route to solve the questions raised during the development of this practice. Next, statistical evidence of students who carried out the simulation is presented virtual laboratory setting (Table 2).

Table 2. Results of the virtual laboratory survey.

Questions	Answers	Regularly	Good	Very Good	Excellenttnte
1. What did you think of the simulation in the software?		0	1	14	9
2. Are the questions in the virtual laboratory consistent with the knowledge acquired throughout your professional training as an Industrial Engineer?		0	0	6	18
3. What degree of utility do you give to the virtual laboratory?		0	5	7	12
4. How interactive or friendly did you find the interface of the simulation program?		0	0	6	18
5. Do you think that virtual laboratories are a good alternative to learn about labor risks and environmental management that occurring within companies?		0	0	10	14
6. How functional do you think this software can be for people who are not related to the industrial environment?		0	0	8	16

Given the survey of 24 students, after performing the simulation, it is concluded that the design of the Virtual Laboratory, is very practical, and interactive giving a great approach to the professional profile of an Industrial Engineer, becoming a practical tool for the student.

4   Conclusions

The implementation of a virtual laboratory provides greater educational support for universities, due to interaction and practical theoretical mastery of learning, providing greater satisfaction to students and allowing you to make decisions based on evidence.

The virtual tour offered by the laboratory designed in UNITY 3D allows an interaction between the student and the industrial sector, offering the possibility of finding labor and environmental risks in order to relate them to the contents learned in the classroom.

The virtual laboratory designed in this research complies with the design parameters, taking into account different previous investigations such as having a virtual environment, being flashy, having sound, interaction, images, and color; which allows to increase the educational performance of the students and contribute to the development of their capacities and decision-making.

References

1. Vázquez, A.: El uso de los laboratorios virtuales en la asignatura Bioquímica como alternativa para la aplicación de las tecnologías de la información y comunicación, Red de Revistas Científicas de América Latina, el Caribe, España y Porugal (2019)
2. Noboa, J.: Laboratorios virtuales una alternativa para mejorar el rendimiento de los estudiantes y la optimización de recursos económicos. INNOVA Res. J. Guayaquil (2020)
3. Vargas, G.: Diseño y gestión de entornos virtuales de aprendizaje, Cuad. Hosp. Clín. **62**(1), 80–87 (2021). La Paz
4. Zúñiga A., Jalón, E., Albarracín, L.: Laboratorios virtuales en el proceso enseñanza-aprendizaje en Ecuador, Revista Dilemas Contemporáneos: Educación, Política y Valores, Junio (2019)
5. Triana, C., Herrera, D., Mesa, W.: Importancia de los laboratorios remotos y virtuales en la educación superior, ECBTI Working Papers (2020)
6. Zaldívar, A.: Laboratorios reales versus laboratorios virtuales en las carreras de ciencias de la computación. IE Revits Inv. Educativa La REDIECH **10**(18), 9–10 (2019)
7. Sanchez, C.: Laboratorio Virtualy Remoto, Aprendiendoa Través de la Experimentación. Universidad Tecnológica Nacional, Resistencia (2017)
8. Torres, M.: Diseño de entornos virtuales para el desarrollo de clases prácticas y seminarios en la temática de sostenibilidad ambiental, Granada (2021)
9. Chimbo, L.: El laboratorio virtual como estrategia didáctica para el aprendizaje de biología molecular en los estudiantes de cuarto semestre de la carrera de biología química y laboratorio, período enero-agosto 2017. Universidad Nacional de Chimborazo, Riobamba (2017)
10. Zamora, R.: Laboratorios remotos: Análisis; características y su desarrllo como alternativa a la práctica en la Facultad de Inngenieria. In: INGE CUC, pp. 281–290 (2017)
11. Canu, M., Duque, M., Paris, F.: Laboratorios Remotos: ¿Qué Interés Pedagógico?, de Encuentro Internacional de Educacíon en Ingeniería ACOFI, Bogotá (2017)
12. Rocha, A., Baborza, B., Segundo, A., Guerra, J.: Capacitación Mediante Visitas y Prácticas En Talleres y Laboratorios Virtuales

"I CAN Do This!": Teaching Introductory Programming in Face-to-Face vs. Online Classes

Simona Vasilache(✉)

Faculty of Engineering, Information and Systems, University of Tsukuba, Tsukuba, Japan
simona@cs.tsukuba.ac.jp

Abstract. Programming courses are becoming increasingly popular with students from all kinds of majors; however, often students studying humanities are more pessimistic in their ability to master even basic programming skills. This poster will highlight some of the experiences of a group of social sciences students with an introductory programming course. The face-to-face format and the online format will both be analyzed and the instructor's empirical observations, along with data gathered from questionnaires administered to students will be presented.

Keywords: Introductory programming · Online learning · Emergency remote teaching

1 Introduction

Introductory programming courses are offered all around the world in higher-education institutions. Computer programming has often been framed as "computational literacy" (e.g. in [1]). A lot of times students involved in so-called "humanities" studies feel that they should learn programming in order to be able to use various tools that support their academic research. At the same time, many of these students are reluctant to enroll in such courses, perceiving them as too difficult and imagining programming skills as unattainable.

There is a wide variety of approaches and formats for teaching introductory programming courses in different academic institutions. Until 2020, in Japan, the traditional delivery method was face-to-face. The Covid-19 pandemic changed that, forcing many higher education institutions all over the world to cancel their face-to-face classes and suddenly switch to online courses. The new "emergency remote teaching" (ERT) term was coined, highlighting the current pressing teaching and learning conditions [2].

Based on the author's experience of teaching an introductory programming course for several years at a national university in Japan, this poster will highlight the perceptions of students with regard to this course in two types of classes: face-to-face (until 2019) and online (after 2020). The conclusions and lessons learned by the author are based on empirical observations gathered during classes, and on data obtained from questionnaires created by the instructor and administered to students during and at the end of the course, as well as the university mandated end-of-course evaluation questionnaires.

C. Stephanidis et al. (Eds.): HCII 2022, CCIS 1655, pp. 213–218, 2022.
https://doi.org/10.1007/978-3-031-19682-9_28

2   Course Description and Evolution

2.1   General Course Description

The observations and lessons described in this work are based on empirical observations and data collected by the author within the last 3 years during a course titled "Introduction to programming" (the course was first held almost 10 years ago). This is an elective undergraduate course at the University of Tsukuba in Japan, mainly aimed at students in the undergraduate English programs. The lectures use Python as a first programing language, and they teach introductory concepts, like basic data structures and algorithms, functions, recursion etc. The course targets students with no previous programming knowledge and, although it was introduced in the social sciences department, students from life and environmental sciences often enroll in it, as well. In terms of format, until 2019, the course was held face-to face; starting with 2020, the course has been held in an online environment.

The most important merit of this course is that it offers students with no previous programming knowledge the tools they need to embark on a learning journey, in a field they often imagine as very difficult to understand. The pace of the course is relatively slow and the instructor takes all the time needed in order to make sure that (most) students understand every new concept taught. The first lecture emphasizes the importance of patience and high levels of concentration, along with the need to practice writing simple programs which become more and more complex as the course progresses. Throughout all the years that this course was taught, a large number of students admitted that before enrolling in the class they believed that programming is more suitable for those with a strong background (and interest) in mathematics in general. At the end of the course, many of these students found themselves confident and with a new passion for learning programming further.

2.2   Course Evolution – Changes in Numbers and Format

The evolution of the course structure, with changes in numbers and format, is shown in Fig. 1. Before 2016, the students were taught BASIC and their numbers were usually below 30. From 2016, the number of students fluctuated (22 in 2016, 36 in 2017, 42 in 2018 and 37 in 2019), and the language used to introduce programming concepts was changed to Python. In 2020, with the sudden transition to the newly named Emergency Remote Teaching format (brought upon by the Covid-19 pandemic), the class was moved from the spring semester to the fall semester; it was held online, with a rather low number of students (i.e. 15 participants). For the following year (2021), the timing of the class was reverted to spring; however, a decision was made to not hold it that year (mainly due to the instructor's high hopes that the face-to-face classes would be resumed soon; at the time, she also strongly believed that the online format was not as beneficial for an introductory programming course). As of 2022, the class is still held in an online format, with 22 students enrolled in it (at the time of writing this paper, the course is in its 6th week).

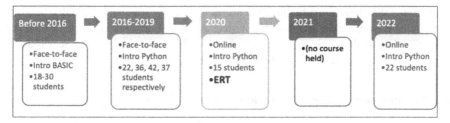

Fig. 1. Programming course change over the years

3   Face-to-Face Classes and Online Classes

3.1   Face-to-Face Courses

Before the sudden changes in the academic world brought by the Covid-19 pandemic, the introductory programming course was held in a classical lecture style, face-to-face. The instructor would introduce new concepts, demonstrate them, and the students would reproduce the programs, create new versions and solve exercises during class. The course would take place in a computer room; each student was seated in front of a computer, where they could try out their programs in real time. As mentioned earlier, many students generally lacked confidence in their ability to easily learn programming. However, as the class progressed, most of them experienced a growth in enthusiasm and enjoyment of the classes.

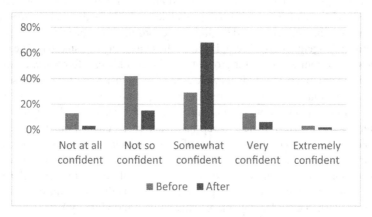

Fig. 2. Confidence in advancing skills before and after the face-to-face course

Figure 2 highlights the students' level of confidence in advancing their programming skills, by comparing their perceptions before the course started and after the end of the course. We can observe that the number of students who considered themselves "not at all confident" or "not so confident" decreased after they took part in the course. Also, data shows that, before the class began, 62.5% of students thought that the class would be either difficult or very difficult; at the end of the course, only 37.5% of students thought that the class was difficult (with no student seeing it as very difficult). In terms of enjoying the course, before the class started, about 28% assumed that they would not enjoy the class at all or enjoy it very little. At the end of class, this percentage was down to 0 – a remarkable result, as seen by the instructor.

3.2 Online Course Effects: Observations and Discussion

In 2020, a number of only 15 students enrolled in the course, representing the lowest number since the establishment of the course about 10 years ago. The instructor believes that this is due to the suddenly adopted online format; the course is an elective one and, generally, only students interested in acquiring programming skills decide to join it. The idea of learning how to program "remotely", without the instructor being present and being able to actively help the students while implementing their programs, discouraged many students from enrolling in the course. There were numerous uncertainties with regard to class structure, flow, evaluation etc. and they all contributed to the reluctance of enrolling in courses offered online only.

During its first online edition, in 2020, the students participated from various locations, inside and outside Japan. Some of them were either stuck in their home countries after the spring holidays (due to pandemic related restrictions, they could not return in time for their classes) or they simply decided to remain in their home countries (since all the classes were taking place online). (The 2022 edition of the course has 22 students enrolled in the class, 20 are in Japan and only two are still outside the country.)

The introductory programming classes were held synchronously, online, using the Zoom platform [4]. The lectures were recorded almost in their entirety; the recordings were placed on Microsoft Stream [5] and then made available for the students to watch on-demand. All the class materials and the links to recordings were provided in *manaba* [6] (the learning management system employed by the University of Tsukuba). The breakout room feature of Zoom was used for group work: during classes, after a new concept was introduced and practiced, the students were given a short task to perform in these groups. Participants were placed in different breakout room during different classes (but the same breakout room componence was maintained during one lecture). The online platform proved very useful in offering these group-based activities, considering that the students were located in different countries. The use of breakout rooms, where collaborative work was required, provided an environment where class participants could feel that they are part of the same group, that they can communicate in real time with their colleagues. (It is worth noting that there were no group activities in past editions of the course; if given a task during class, the students would usually solve it individually.)

At the end of the course, the instructor administered a short survey, in which she attempted to find out the students' perceptions of the difficulty of the class, the level of enjoyment and their confidence levels. The participants were asked to rate how they felt before the course started (in October) and how they felt at the end of the course (in December). Figure 3, for instance, illustrates this comparison in terms of the students' level of confidence. Whereas the percentage of "very confident" participants remained about the same, we can observe that students who felt "not at all confident" greatly reduced in number. Unfortunately, the number of "not so confident" students increased after the end of the course, but so has the number of those "somewhat confident" (although with a smaller percentage).

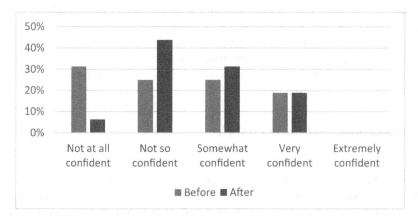

Fig. 3. Confidence in advancing skills before and after the online course

With regard to how difficult the class was perceived to be, the situation was almost unchanged at the end of course vs. at the beginning. The same results were obtained in relation to the level of enjoyment in class: almost no change between the two different moments in time (i.e. before and after the course). These results show that there is a certain difference between the face-to-face classes and the online classes (naturally, the groups of students were different, so a rigorous comparison was not possible).

Furthermore, as per university rules, at the end of each course, the students must provide feedback through an evaluation questionnaire, in which they rate how well the class was prepared and conducted etc. To give only two examples, most of the participants either agreed or strongly agreed that they were satisfied with the course; similarly, the majority of the students felt that they achieved the course's objectives. When asked what they liked about the course, the responses included: "The class is highly interactive, even though it was set on online setting", "This class really help me to solve problems from the view of a programmer". One class participant gave a longer response, as follows: "Sensei explained very detail on each content of the topic we had been covered. She gave time for us to ask questions and provided back the answer. Also, we could talk in small group of the class on the problems that are given. Assignment parts were very helpful to fulfill our understanding on the topic both after and before the lecture."

With regard to improvements that could be made, several students stated their preference for a face-to-face class, in various forms, e.g. "It would be much better if we could do [...] face-to-face classes", "Hopefully things return to normal so online classes will not be the last resort in the future", "I think it is very hard for the professor to do this so I would say it is not better to do it online".

As mentioned previously, the group activities were introduced in the online format (they did not exist in the face-to-face one). They seem to have been successful with some of the students, who emphasized that "I think the group work part is a good idea" and "I really enjoy the discussion part with other classmates, so I suggest that this kind of activity is still obtain in the future.". However, the students understood the importance of individual participation (e.g. "This online class was good, break out rooms [were] sometimes a bit useless though, if other people don't talk").

Last, but not least, the students were asked how effective they believe an online programming class can be. 50% stated that it can be equally effective to a face-to-face class, almost 37.5% believed that it is less effective, whereas the remaining 12.5% believed that online classes can be more effective than face-to-face classes (unfortunately, the students did not provide specific reasons for the increased effectiveness in an online format).

4 Conclusions and Future Work

This poster highlighted the experiences of a group of social sciences students enrolled in an introductory programming course. The data gathered through questionnaires, as well as the instructor's observations, showed that, in case of face-to-face classes, the students' enjoyed the courses to a higher extent than they thought they would and they perceived the classes as less difficult than their expectations before enrolment. In case of online classes, these two aspects were unchanged between the beginning and the end of the course. However, in both face-to-face and online classes, confidence in the students' acquired programming skills increased. Overall, despite the initial low expectations (both on the instructor's side and on the students' side), the online classes proved to be almost as successful as the face-to-face classes. However, a certain reluctance of enrolling in online classes, especially where a computer is needed for classwork, seems to remain. As part of our future work, we intend to gather more quantitative and qualitative data which could help in finding the most effective method of teaching programming concepts to absolute beginners, particularly those in the field of humanities.

References

1. Vee, A.: Understanding computer programming as a literacy. Literacy Compos. Stud. **1**(2), 42–64 (2013)
2. Hodges, C., Moore, S., Lockee, B., Trust, T., Bond, A.: The difference between emergency remote teaching and online learning. Educause Rev. **27**, 1–12 (2020)
3. Chat, Meetings, Calling, Collaboration | Microsoft Teams. https://www.microsoft.com/en-us/microsoft-365/microsoft-teams/group-chat-software. Accessed 17 May 2022
4. Zoom: Zoom Meetings & Chat. https://zoom.us/meetings. Accessed 17 May 2022
5. Microsoft Stream. https://www.microsoft.com/en-us/microsoft-365/microsoft-stream. Accessed 17 May 2022
6. Manaba Homepage. https://manaba.jp/products/. Accessed 17 May 2022

3D Printing for STEAM Education

Mireya Zapata-Rodríguez[1]([✉]) [iD], Hugo Arias-Flores[1] [iD], and Jorge Álvarez-Tello[2] [iD]

[1] Centro de Investigación en Mecatrónica y Sistemas Interactivos – MIST, Universidad Tecnológica Indoamérica, Machala y Sabanilla, 170103 Quito, Ecuador
{mireyazapata,hugoarias}@uti.edu.ec
[2] Centro de Transferencia de Tecnología e Innovación – CTTI, Universidad Tecnológica Indoamérica, Machala y Sabanilla, 170103 Quito, Ecuador
jorgealvarez@uti.edu.ec

Abstract. 3D printing has been considered a disruptive technology and its impact on education with the generation of educational resources that increase student engagement and improve STEAM learning by promoting their creativity, collaborative work, attention and participation in class, strengthening the development of their skills. This paper discusses the different applications that can be given to rapid prototyping through 3D printing in education and how it can influence the STEAM skills acquired by students.

Keywords: STEAM education · 3D printer · Education

1 Introduction

The STEAM methodology is based on the integrated learning process of Science, Technology, Engineering, Arts, and Mathematics disciplines in an interdisciplinary framework. The curricula and teaching methods grow faster in academia, searching for new pedagogical strategies for the planning and learning concepts for the educators [1]. Since the industry needs to integrate creativity and innovation through the 3D print technology to answer the market growth for the current Pandemia. The energy storage devices, the materials for the design and construction of the key applications and the rapid prototyping methods brings a wide future perspective [2, 3] for the integration of new and disruptive technology that could be validate with the early customers and future pioneers of the knowledge production.

Education seeks to promote the transversality of knowledge in children and young people to guarantee meaningful learning. It also involves the development of skills and types of thinking such as scientific, quantitative, visuospatial processing, among others. Its fundamental principle is experience-based learning, combined with project-based learning witch represent an innovative approach to teaching. It involves the integration of learning with TICs, also the appropriation of knowledge in scientific areas promotes creative capacity and imagination. In this sense, the learning spaces generated are collaborative places called co-working, which provide the conditions to develop mathematical thinking, computational thinking, and emotional management skills in young people and enhance communication skills with their peers.

C. Stephanidis et al. (Eds.): HCII 2022, CCIS 1655, pp. 219–224, 2022.
https://doi.org/10.1007/978-3-031-19682-9_29

Under this framework, 3D printing technology now more accessible and within the reach of children in educational institutions, allows venturing into rapid prototyping for the generation of physical models and the practical consolidation of ideas, achieving more interesting classes for students. Thus, three-dimensional printing technology is being used more and more in education at all levels.

In the technological development, the 3D technology needs techniques according the manufacturing facilities for complexes structures [4]. The material for the 3D print technology is the gap for the industry as well for the Academy, to promote the design integrating and the low cost simulation models for the training in several fields of the knowledge production as the medicine, aeronautics, and defense as referents sectors for the childhood [5].

The challenge for the STEAM fields is to complement the curriculum with tools and rapid manufacturing facilities to solve real world situation [6] with scale models and teams interaction to promote the integration of the community as well. In this sense, the knowledge production as an answer of the experience in the Labs, requires an advanced and accessible research with technology and innovation. Figure 1 shows the Hype Cycle curve in its 5 phases for 3D Printing, where various applications and their location on the growth curve are analyzed. It can be seen how 3D bioprinting for organ transplantation has grown faster compared to the printing of consumable products. This is due to its potential benefit in people's lives. The applications that have reached the productivity plateau are related to services where the adoption of this technology is beginning to be widespread.

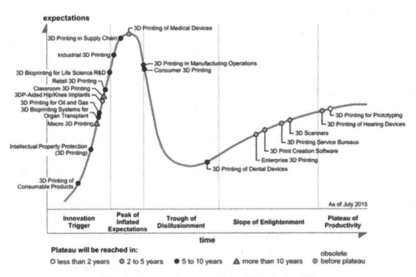

Fig. 1. Gartner hype cycle for 3D printing [7]

The implementation of innovation places contribute for the agile projects developing student's proposal based on modeling processes, methods and technological solutions co-designing with the final customers. The conceptualization for the challenges combines topics and tendencies as the 3D print origami structures and renewable energy has practices, as shows the K-12 next generation Science [8].

The acceptance of the 3D solutions are the first step for the emotional and team organization, where the teaching and interactive methods examine the potential of the students in comparison with pre-COVID methods applied.

The workflow of the design task has at the modelling, design tools and programs according with the paths for the rapid prototyping, needs a technological environment assisted of 3D print to integrated models of self-designed ones. On the other hand, the maker culture is a do yourself (DYS) trend that explore emerging technology from the perspectives of learning, instruction and assessment to provide an integration space for further research and knowledge production [9].

Integrating these references and aspects, the 3D print technology has an enormous potential for the development of new methodology for the teaching and working for children and young with real-society problems associated with the rapid prototyping.

1.1 Rapid Prototyping and Production

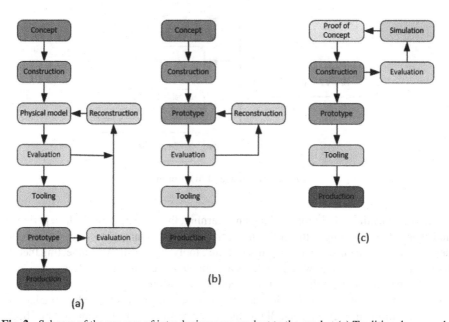

Fig. 2. Scheme of the process of introducing new product to the market (a) Traditional approach (b) Rapid prototyping (c) new proposal model for rapid prototyping. Image modified from [10]

The models for the rapid prototyping have an evolution in the last 5 years. It is a tool that seeks to create prototypes of a preliminary version of the final product, based on putting ideas into action in a simple and fast way, generating tangible results, using basic materials and elements. Its objective is to obtain a material object in the shortest time possible to analyze concepts such as volume ratio, ergonomics, assembly and other product characteristics. Figure 2 shows a comparison between the conventional prototyping approach and rapid prototyping presented in [10]. In addition, a reduced proposal is presented by inserting phases of proof of concept and simulation in a cyclical process seeking the constant product improvement.

1.2 3D Printing

3D printing, also called additive manufacturing (AM) allows create an object using different methods, however Fused Deposition Modeling is the most widely used due its relative low cost. It consists of a thermoplastic filament heated until its melting point and then extruded creating layer by layer a 3D model.

This technology became more accessible in 2009 when patent for material extrusion was released, and with this, the development of desktop size printers. The AM became an efficient alternative for many applications in education and rapid prototype design, replacing milling and turning traditional techniques [11]. Figure 3 shows advantages of this technology.

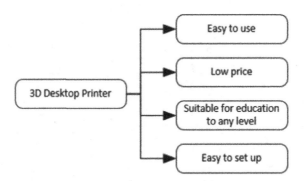

Fig. 3. Advantage of 3D printing

In the educational field for teaching and learning, their use requires little experience and it is relatively simple to do the first jobs in a few hours, since they have been designed for regular users with easy-to-configure tools; its use allows connecting theory with practice in a fast way where students are able to materialize their ideas.

The ultimate goal of education is to produce professionals who enter the job market with the most up-to-date skills and the ability to acquire new knowledge to adapt to new innovations in their careers. 3D technology together with 3D printing have been established as teaching strategies in areas related to science, technology, engineering, art and mathematics (STEAM). Educational institutions can get benefits such as:

- The physical representation of a solid can provide a better setting for its characterization and unravel scientific concepts.
- Students are more attracted to tangible results that provide them with knowledge based on experience. 3D printing is a tool that allows, from a digital design that can

be generated as a result of the application of theoretical concepts, to obtain a physical element that allows rapid feedback of the result obtained.

● Students feel more motivated and enthusiastic when they manage to obtain a palpable object, as well as their interest to continue experimenting with 3D designs.

Despite the obvious advantages, educational institutions must face the costs related to the acquisition of equipment, its maintenance and the cost of materials, software, as well as having trained teachers who are willing to adapt this technology as an educational strategy in the classroom.

Table 1. 3D software, comparison table [12].

Software	Free	Desktop	Online	Previous skills	3D model quality
Sketch up	Yes	Yes	No	No	High
SolidWorks	No	Yes	No	Recommended	High
TinkerCAD	Yes	No	Yes	No	Limited
Open SCAD	Yes	Yes	Yes	Recommended	High

Table 1 shows a comparison table of 3D modeling software, with some useful features to select the appropriate tool, it should be noted that the higher the application level at the engineering level, the more powerful tools will be required to be able to carry out specialized designs, while at the basic one of the main criteria is that it be open access software.

2 Conclusions

At present, the speed at which technological advances appear is increasingly accelerated, even more so when compared to the development of academic content. The need to develop new methodological strategies that allow new professionals to be prepared for the current challenges of the industry is imperative. 3D printing is a disruptive technology alternative that offers several advantages in the educational field given its accessibility and relatively easy handling. This is an alternative that allows innovation and should be used as a tool to produce educational resources to support teaching-learning processes.

References

1. Pikkarainen, A., Piili, H.: Implementing 3d printing education through technical pedagogy and curriculum development. Int. J. Eng. Pedagogy **10**(6), 95–119 (2021)
2. Alghamdi, S.S., John, S., Choudhury, N.R., Dutta, N.K.: Additive manufacturing of polymer materials: progress, promise and challenges. Polymers **13**(5), 1–39 (2021). https://doi.org/10.3390/POLYM13050753

3. Saleh, E.: 3D and 4D printed polymer composites for electronic applications. 3D and 4D Printing of Polymer Nanocomposite Materials: Processes, Applications, and Challenges, pp. 505–525 (2019). https://doi.org/10.1016/B978-0-12-816805-9.00016-8

4. Deshmukh, K., Muzaffar, A., Kovářík, T., Křenek, T., Ahamed, M.B., Pasha, S.K.K.: Fundamentals and applications of 3D and 4D printing of polymers: challenges in polymer processing and prospects of future research. In: 3D and 4D Printing of Polymer Nanocomposite Materials: Processes, Applications, and Challenges, pp. 527–560 (2020). https://doi.org/10.1016/B978-0-12-816805-9.00017-X

5. Lichtenberger, J.P., Tatum, P.S., Gada, S., Wyn, M., Ho, V.B., Liacouras, P.: Using 3D printing (additive manufacturing) to produce low-cost simulation models for medical training. Mil Med. 183(suppl_1), 73–77 (2018). https://doi.org/10.1093/milmed/usx142

6. Bicer, A., Nite, S.B., Capraro, R.M., Barroso, L.R., Capraro, M.M., Lee, Y.: Moving from STEM to STEAM: The effects of informal STEM learning on students' creativity and problem solving skills with 3D printing. In: Proceedings - Frontiers in Education Conference, FIE, 2017-Octob, pp. 1–6 (2017). https://doi.org/10.1109/FIE.2017.8190545

7. Assante, D., Cennamo G.M., Placidi L.: 3D printing in education: an European perspective. In: 2020 IEEE Global Engineering Education Conference (EDUCON), 2020, pp. 1133–1138, doi: https://doi.org/10.1109/EDUCON45650.2020.9125311

8. Kennedy, J., Lee, E., Fontecchio, A.: STEAM approach by integrating the arts and STEM through origami in K-12. In: Proceedings - Frontiers in Education Conference, FIE, 2016-Novem, 2–6 (2016). https://doi.org/10.1109/FIE.2016.7757415

9. Glaser, N.J., Schmidt, M.: Usage considerations of 3D collaborative virtual learning environments to promote development and transfer of knowledge and skills for individuals with autism. Technol. Knowl. Learn. 25(2), 315–322 (2018). https://doi.org/10.1007/s10758-018-9369-9

10. Szulżyk-Cieplak, J., Duda, A., Sidor, B. 3D printers – new possibilities in education. Adv. Sci. Technol. Res. J. 8, 96–101 (2014). https://doi.org/10.12913/22998624/575

11. Kirchheim, A., Dennig, H.-J., Zumofen, L.: Why education and training in the field of additive manufacturing is a necessity. In: Meboldt, M., Klahn, C. (eds.) AMPA 2017, pp. 329–336. Springer, Cham (2018). https://doi.org/10.1007/978-3-319-66866-6_31

12. Papp, I., Zichar, M.: 3D modeling and printing interpreted in terms of cognitive infocommunication. In: Klempous, R., Nikodem, J., Baranyi, P.Z. (eds.) Cognitive Infocommunications, Theory and Applications. TIEI, vol. 13, pp. 365–389. Springer, Cham (2019). https://doi.org/10.1007/978-3-319-95996-2_17

Digital Transformation in Business, Government, and Organizations

Moral and Political Concerns About Patents: A Cross-Cultural Perspective

Benedicto Acosta[(⊠)]

Instituto Universitario de Estudios de la Ciencia y la Tecnología, University of Salamanca,
Salamanca, Spain
bneacosta@usal.es

Abstract. The aim of this contribution is to address some issues concerning moral and political limitations to patentability. Although patents are rights that States protect in their territory, there are certain globally shared points on what constitutes a patent and what does not. These limitations can be of a technical nature, such as the novelty or commercial application of the invention, or of a moral and political nature. Almost all countries restrict inventions that affect national security and those that are contrary to morality or ordre public. I will show that, although these assumptions are shared by the different States, they are specified in a different way depending on social and cultural factors.

Keywords: Ethics · Patentability · Ordre public

1 First Section

Most patent codes recognize cases in which patentability would not be possible -or rather the disclosure of patents- due to "external" reasons, namely moral, social, and not just because of the "internal" characteristics of the invention (i.e., lack of novelty or lack of inventive step).

There are usually two types of external limits: exceptions for inventions that violate *ordre public* or moral, and secret patents. The former prohibits patentability, while the latter simply keep secret existing patents that jeopardize national security.

There are authors who consider that these limitations of the States are reactive [1], since they only prevent certain technologies from being marketed or disclosed, but do not necessary generate a social value in return, something that would presuppose a more active component.

The "generation" of social value occurs, for instance, in patents that seek a more sustainable, more accessible technology or that aim to end inequalities, poverty, etc. Whereas these reactive limitations, which I have identified as "external", would only prevent immoral technologies or those that compromise national security (such as certain weapons or human cloning technologies), from going through the usual patent channel. The former generates public value because it has a positive impact on society, while the latter would only have a negative social value, which is given by the fact that they do not appear on the market or are not published. A similar relation is recently proposed

C. Stephanidis et al. (Eds.): HCII 2022, CCIS 1655, pp. 227–231, 2022.
https://doi.org/10.1007/978-3-031-19682-9_30

by Umbrello and van de Poel [2] when they distinguish between values promoted and values respected by technology.

Although cases involving social value in patents are increasingly studied in current literature [1, 3], not so those that have to do with external limitations, as they are considered to be very scarce. However, while there are certainly few patents that are not published or commercialised due to moral or political reasons, they represent a symptom of the way in which technologised societies attempt to regulate science and technology, and therefore represent a very fruitful field of study for the sociology of science and STS and, more specifically, for the study of the relation we aspire to have with biotechnologies, computers, artificial intelligence or disruptive technologies.

The main objective is to analyse certain cases and to show that, although these limitations are shared by the legislations of the various States, they are specified in a different forms depending on social and cultural factors. In what follows I try to show this very briefly through the limitations to patentability for reasons of *ordre public* or moral, in the first place. Next, I address the case of secret patents and, finally, I discuss the challenge that all these limitations pose to the harmonization of patent systems.

2   Proposal

Like any other kind of property, patents are limited by States. Limitations on inventions that affect *ordre public* and morality are some of the most common figures in patent codes. One of the difficulties that some authors have pointed out when studying them is that, apart from their rarity, it is difficult to distinguish the morality clause from the ordre public clause in patents [4].

The reason is not only the heterogeneity of interpretations that countries make of these assumptions, a reason that *prima facie* supports the argument that external limitations are context-dependent, but the very interdependent nature of what is immoral for a society and what represents a public disorder for that society.

A great part of the studies on these two limitations of patents is related to biotechnologies and health. For example, a very large group of authors study how the monopoly conferred by patents on certain technologies affects prices and how this impacts the access to technologies [5]. Another group of scholars also problematizes the patentability of health inventions, analysing for example treatments protected by patents that have been publicly funded [6].

An example of a recent debate in this regard is the COVID-19 vaccines´ controversy [7]. However, a more established and more evident proof of the cultural dependency of these limitations may be the use of surveys in previous biomedical controversies, to better specify what is immoral or unfair for a population. Shobita Parthasarathy [8] shows how, in the famous case of oncomouse in 1993, opponents of patents on genetically modified animals offered the eurobarometer to the EPO as a proof that Europeans, so concerned about animal pain, would be against the genetic modification of animals for the express purpose of developing cancers.

Other scholars, like Justine Pila, have even encourage to take this social representation to a more decisive role: "the opportunity for public representation in the process of negotiating them should be increased beyond its currently limited degree, and assessments of the moral and public policy implications of patenting inventions be expanded accordingly" [9].

This dependency or interrelation of the technical-legal nature of patents with the social and political dimension is also complemented by the historical nature *ordre public* expression has. For example, during the last century many Offices were concerned about nuclear technology, within the framework of the Cold War, but after the fall of the USSR, the concern shifted to technologies that could be used by terrorist groups, such as biological weapons [10]. Here, in turn, this *ordre public* clause is interrelated with secret patents, a case that we will mention at the end.

The other external limitation is related to patents that are contrary to morality. Although this a topic analogous to the previous one, it is also conceptually separable. As the inclusion of contextual criteria seems evident in moral issues, we will outline a single example.

Objects that probably best exemplify this context-dependency are sex toys. The reason here is not only that all cultures understand these artifacts in a different way, sometimes even prohibiting their use, but also the existence of a historical variable, related to this cultural journey that each nation has experienced. Many countries that are permissive nowadays with the use of those artefacts and allow their patentability used to prohibit it in the past. Many perspectives, such as gender, also join these considerations. For example, the Indian Patent Office recently rejected the application to patent an anal sex toy invoking the section of the Penal Code that criminalises gay sex [11].

And these moral changes are sometimes fluctuating. In 2014, for example, the United Kingdom restricted certain pornographic sexual practices considered indecent or violent [12]. Although it remains to be studied how this affects a country's patents, it is clear that moral considerations do not follow a linear trajectory, towards a pre-established final objective, but rather mutable. A more extensive relationship on the subject can be found in the book "Biotechnological Inventions. Moral Restrictions and Patent Law", by Oliver Mills.

However, these patents that violate what each State understands to be its moral or *ordre public* only affect commercialization. But limitations can go further. Disclosure of technological and commercial information, a fundamental part of the so-called "social contract of patents", may also be limited. This is the case of secret patents.

Many laws order secrecy for patent applications that affect national security, most of which are relevant to defence: missiles, radar weapons, biotechnologies... Although it is clear that these procedures are very jurisdiction dependent [13], there is evidence that suggest that reasons for secrecy are not limited to the legislation of each country.

There are countries like the US that decide, after a certain time, to declassify many of their secret patents. By contrast, in other countries like the United Kingdom the number of secret inventions is higher. In fact, secret patents in UK have been accumulating and come to exceed those of the US by three [14], although British arms industry is less powerful. In some other nations, like Spain, there is no even a record of secret patents that have ever revealed.

What happens then? It seems that some middle-ranking military powers do not declassify their patents, but other major powers do, so these very similar codes sometimes cannot explain the situation, and neither can the resistance to maintain the power of the arms industry: there must be a different way of understanding industrial property in each case.

Sometimes codes can certainly differ, as we have pointed out. Unlike European laws, article 1395 of the Russian Civil Code states that secrecy over patents can cover every invention that affects a state secret, and thus, that concerns Russian defence, economy, policy and even politics, in contrast to the more restrictive European formula of "national security" or "national defence". The point here is that even in these cases, the contrast between codes may be based on differences in political traditions and patent cultures.

Therefore, it seems interesting to focus on this culture of intellectual property when studying how patents are the result of the social and political interests of certain nations. The case of secret patents gives a good account of this, and also represents one of the least studied external limitations.

I hope to have explained in this brief analysis that the clauses of secret patents, such as those of *ordre public* and morality, although shared by the States, are interpreted and applied in a different way by each one of them. These differences do not always lie in legislation, but are sometimes based on deeper differences, which have to do with culture and society in a broader sense.

3   Discussion and Final Remarks

It is not so clear that these external limitations have to be contextual in nature, since the harmonization of patent systems is, although imperfect, a real tendence in some regions of the world, such as Europe. But it seems that, although there are similar or even common procedures, different cultures - also including intellectual property cultures, as in the case of secret patents- lead to differences the way such clauses are interpreted and applied.

It is also important to leave open for discussion the question of whether the harmonization of patent systems should be an irremediable trend. It seems that unless we want to subsume or reduce the external limitations and the social value of patents in the purely economic value, cases where there is a strong social influence should also be considered in their own. Karen Walsh defends the benefits of keeping both spheres separate: "When it comes concerning issues, for example, morality, human dignity, and public order, this scope for divergence needs to exist. Judges in all jurisdictions ought to be able to go against the majority if there is such a reason to do so. It is important that these types of issues remain open to debate and that national diversity remains, given the importance of these topics, the different views involved, and the changing nature of technology" [15].

This should certainly lead us to reflection. In this vein, it would also be appropriate to review the dichotomy between reactive limitations and positive generation of value. What is clear is that precisely because different cultures matter, there is a need for study. In these few pages I have tried to exemplify it, but greater efforts are needed in the future.

References

1. Ribeiro, B., Shapira, P.: Private and public values of innovation: a patent analysis of synthetic biology. Res. Policy **49**(1), 103875 (2020)
2. Umbrello, S., van de Poel, I.: Mapping value sensitive design onto AI for social good principles. AI and Ethics **1**(3), 283–296 (2021). https://doi.org/10.1007/s43681-021-00038-3
3. Giménez, G.: The impact of the patent system on the social welfare: a critical view. Intangible Capital **14**(2), 253–269 (2018)
4. Lai, J.: A comparative examination of the socio-political-moral lives of patents. J. Responsible Innov. **6**(1), 109–113 (2019)
5. Biddle, J.: Can patents prohibit research? On the social epistemology of patenting and licensing in science. Stud. History Philos. Sci. Part A **45**, 14–23 (2014)
6. Dutfield, G.: Intellectual Property Rights and the Life Science Industries A Twentieth Century History. Routledge, Abington (2003)
7. McMahon, A.: Global equitable access to vaccines, medicines and diagnostics for COVID-19: the role of patents as private governance. J. Med. Ethics **47**(3), 142–148 (2020)
8. Parthasarathy, S.: Whose knowledge? what values? the comparative politics of patenting life forms in the United States and Europe. Policy Sci. **44**(3), 267–288 (2011)
9. Pila, J.: Reflections on a post-pandemic European patent system. Eur. Intellect. Prop. Rev. **42**(9), 530–535 (2020)
10. Ramcharan, R.: Intellectual property and security: a preliminary exploration. Contemporary Security Policy **26**(1), 126–159 (2005)
11. BBC. India rejects patent plea for 'immoral' sex toy. https://www.bbc.com/news/world-asia-india-45179057. Accessed 03 Mar 2022
12. The Guardian. The UK pornography law: a scientific perspective. https://www.theguardian.com/culture/2014/dec/02/pornography-law-bans-list-sexual-acts-uk-made-online-films. Accessed 03 March 2022
13. Rassenfosse, G., Higham, K.: Decentralising the patent system. Gov. Inf. Q. **38**(2), 101559 (2021)
14. The New Scientist. UK keeps three times as many patents secret as the US. https://www.newscientist.com/article/dn18691-uk-keeps-three-times-as-manypatents-
15. Gooday, G., Wilf, S.: Diversity versus harmonization in patent history. In: Gooday, G., Wilf, S. (eds.) Patent Cultures Diversity and Harmonization in Historical Perspective, pp. 3–88. Cambridge University Press, Cambridge (2020)
16. Walsh, K.: Promoting Harmonisation Across the European Patent System Through Judicial Dialogue and Cooperation. IIC 50, 408–440 (2019)

Automation of an Electro-Hydraulic Test Bench Using a Weitek CMT3092 HMI- PLC

Diego Altamirano-Haro[1] , Patricio Eduardo Sánchez-Díaz[1] , Jorge Buele[2,3] , and Manuel Ayala-Chauvin[2(✉)]

[1] Carrera de Ingeniería Industrial, Facultad de Ingeniería y Tecnologías de la Información y la Comunicación, Universidad Indoamérica, Ambato 180103, Ecuador
{diegoaltamirano,patriciosanchez}@uti.edu.ec
[2] Centro de Investigaciones de Ciencias Humanas y de la Educación CICHE, Universidad Indoamérica, Ambato 180103, Ecuador
{jorgebuele,mayala}@uti.edu.ec
[3] Department of Electronic Engineering and Communications, University of Zaragoza, 44003 Teruel, Spain

Abstract. The industrial environment demands mean that future professionals must acquire more and more technical skills. However, this represents a high investment that many higher education institutions cannot afford. Therefore, the laboratory equipment is updated, and this study begins with the automation of an electro-hydraulic test bench that was manual. For this, a PLC - Weintek was selected, whose programming was carried out in ladder language using CODESYS as a development platform, using an open Modbus programming code through the SFD block language. A human-machine interface (HMI) on a touch screen in the system allows user input (with various hierarchies) and operations control. The operator can also store data for later analysis. Finally, the validation of this proposal is carried out with the respective experimental tests, obtaining a significant reduction in the execution time of the three proposed tasks and improvement of learning conditions.

Keywords: Automation · Engineering laboratory · PLC

1 Introduction

Nowadays, companies are trying to replace mechanical equipment to reduce accident rates, manual failures, and similar problems. Having automatic equipment raises productivity, efficiency and quality levels, which competes better in the market [1]. With Industry 4.0, the digitization and interconnection of equipment have become a necessity. The most common control units in industrial environments are logic programmers (PLC). Also, the application of sensors and pneumatic, hydraulic and robotic actuators has increased the use of databases and other tools for the storage and processing of information [2].

The education of future engineering professionals requires new approaches that are in line with Industry 4.0. High-tech equipment and machinery are needed to contribute

© The Author(s), under exclusive license to Springer Nature Switzerland AG 2022
C. Stephanidis et al. (Eds.): HCII 2022, CCIS 1655, pp. 232–239, 2022.
https://doi.org/10.1007/978-3-031-19682-9_31

to their skills and knowledge. Equipping students with these tools increase their employability and performance [3]. The technical skills of professionals develop in universities through exercises and practices in laboratories, workshops and complementary activities; however, the increase in engineering students makes it difficult to meet their expectations of practical training. In this sense, laboratories have an obvious need to have adequate equipment for their needs and that performs well. Therefore, an analysis of the laboratories' current situation must propose actions that allow them to be improved, as presented in [4]. It is necessary to carry out a functional diagnosis of each machine, robot or teaching station. In this regard, Educational centers are innovating their engineering laboratories, as shown in [5], where applied surveys show their usefulness in improving technical skills.

The Internet of Things (IoT) and machine learning are tools to improve the teaching-learning process [6]. In [7], a server-based application to automate the computer networking laboratory improved the efficiency of the processes. However, this is a challenge for universities in Latin America, where budget allocation is low. Many educational centers must make a heavy economic investment independently, seek financing or request support from private companies. Therefore, improving or upgrading existing equipment is a good solution. In [8], it proposes to implement an electro-pneumatic test bench, which contributes to student learning. In this way, it encourages students and gives them access to tools that are not available in a classroom. Something similar is presented in [9], where a didactic system using PLC will use for training in industrial automation topics for manual and automatic use. While in [10], a pneumatic training system and a series of laboratory activities to teach essential PLC programming complement what students learn in class.

Today's laboratories must be for comprehensive engineering education, where students can develop vocational skills relevant to an industry that is constantly updating. In this sense, as an initial part of a project to improve the engineering laboratories of a university in Ecuador, the automation of a previously manual test bench is proposed. With this equipment upgrade, changes in the practical modules of the curriculum and complementary activities propose to improve the learning processes. The following is a brief description of the hardware and software changes to the case study. Also, the respective validations that allow the use of this machine in academic training are present.

The distribution of this document is in 4 sections, including the introduction in Sect. 1. Secttion 2 presents the materials and methods used in the structure of the electrohydraulic bench. Section 3 shows the tests and results of the runtime measurement and their respective analysis. Finally, the conclusions obtained in Sect. 4.

2   Materials and Methods

2.1   Materials

Electro-hydraulic test bench. It is a machine-made project by the students of the industrial engineering course, consisting of two mobile benches: On the first bench are mounted mechanical commands and electro-hydraulic actuators: piston A, piston B and hydraulic motor. The second bench mounts the hydraulic part, including a hydraulic pump, storage tank, accumulator, tamping valves, pressure valve and a pipeline. Therefore, it can be appreciated the need to automate it since, at present, it can work in a semi-autonomous way. Figure 1 shows the electro-hydraulic station.

Fig. 1. Electro-hydraulic test bench that was automated.

The improvement process implements some automation components among which a PLC-Weintek stands out. This 4.0 technology device use to control different electrome-chanical elements autonomously. There is also a Weintek TocuhPanel, which facilitates the interaction and control of the elements through a touch interface. Here an HMI inter-face is developed to visualize and program the virtual controls of a piece of equipment or process. Finally, a router allows various devices connected by cable, ADSL, or Wi-Fi to access the Internet. Figure 2 shows the general diagram of the automation proposal.

Fig. 2. Schematic of the developed system.

2.2 Method

As part of the applied method, lifting the electrical circuits that are currently manually operated was carried out. It begins by verifying the electrical connections. Then, the electrical wiring and the connections of the mechanical and electronic components are modified—subsequently, the labelling and coding of the cables to identify the actuators, sensors and control valves. The next point was to develop the station's layout, which has been provided in the following link: https://indoamerica-my.sharepoint.com/:f:/g/ personal/diegoaltamirano_uti_edu_ec/Erz138roX_BFki_-F_YTiJcBaiIa8ikmMm3YX 58rATvT3w?e=dJQehD. On the other hand, parallel, the Weinktek PLC and the box are assembled in control, in which the control modules, power source, control breaker and touch panel install. Finally, the power supply of the test bench is connected.

2.3 Voltage Supply Scheme

The programming was developed in ladder language, which can be seen in the following link: https://indoamerica-my.sharepoint.com/:b:/g/personal/diegoaltamirano_uti_ edu_ec/EWmpJJLbrWRFnJV83F2OfzUBF3JiCvZ7dw-j9HoNyFAMFQ?e=PWP. This algorithm was uploaded to the PLC via an RJ45 Ethernet cable. In addition, the HMI - PLC connection with the Touch Panel was managed using an RJ45 cable and a T-LINK router that will be connected to the internet. After the complication of the program and the respective tests will be continued.

3 Results

3.1 Execution Time

Validation is conducted to monitor the experiment manually and automatically and verify each computational execution time. In order to know the number of samples required, the formula described in (1) is as follows. Preliminarily, $n = 10$ measurements are made, with a reliability of 95%, equivalent to $z = 1.96$. Task 1 involves the movement of a hydraulic arm. The next one is similar but with another arm. The last one is turning a motor clockwise for half the time and changing the turn for the rest. The formula defines 20, 16 and 13 measurements for tasks 1, 2 and 3, respectively. Table 1 describes the data obtained from the experiments.

$$N = \left(\frac{z\sqrt{n\left(\sum x^2\right) - \left(\sum x\right)^2}}{k * \sum x} \right)^2 \tag{1}$$

With the automatic mode, task 1 has an execution time of 9.23 s; however, when compared with the manual mode, it can be seen that there is a great deal of variation. The relative error calculated ranges between 0.76% and 51.68%, and this is because the execution time is proportional to the period during which the student keeps the respective button pressed. This practice in the industrial sector symbolizes a waste of time and inefficient use of resources that could be avoided by taking appropriate actions. In the case of task 2, the execution time in automatic mode is 11.612 s, while for task 3, it is 20.215 s. For the first case, the error is between 1.45% and 20.57%, while the error reaches 17.24% in the following case. The trend is the same in tasks 2 and 3, and the times remained oscillating.

Table 1. Execution times of the tasks developed.

Item	Task 1			Task 2			Task 3		
	M	AE	RE [%]	M	AE	RE [%]	M	AE	RE [%]
1	11,90	2,670	28,927	13,55	1,938	16,690	21,81	1,595	7,890
2	11,81	2,580	27,952	12,92	1,308	11,264	20,42	0,205	1,014
3	9,04	0,190	2,059	13,12	1,508	12,987	17,30	2,915	14,420
4	11,10	1,870	20,260	9,88	1,732	14,916	20,42	0,205	1,014
5	13,00	3,770	40,845	12,87	1,258	10,834	23,70	3,485	17,240
6	11,15	1,920	20,802	12,92	1,308	11,264	23,00	2,785	13,777
7	11,00	1,770	19,177	14,00	2,388	20,565	19,55	0,665	3,290
8	10,32	1,090	11,809	12,36	0,748	6,442	19,93	0,285	1,410
9	14,00	4,770	51,679	12,46	0,848	7,303	18,50	1,715	8,484
10	11,25	2,020	21,885	12,16	0,548	4,719	19,57	0,645	3,191
11	10,80	1,570	17,010	13,12	1,508	12,987	20,03	0,185	0,915
12	10,61	1,380	14,951	12,16	0,548	4,719	19,73	0,485	2,399
13	10,55	1,320	14,301	12,34	0,728	6,269	20,32	0,105	0,519
14	10,50	1,270	13,759	12,72	1,108	9,542			
15	10,22	0,990	10,726	12,58	0,968	8,336			
16	9,91	0,680	7,367	11,78	0,168	1,447			
17	9,30	0,070	0,758						
18	9,36	0,130	1,408						
19	9,47	0,240	2,600						
20	9,21	0,020	0,217						

M = Measure, AE = Absolute error, RE = Relative error.

3.2 Satisfaction Analysis

This section executes a satisfaction analysis of the automated system to determine user satisfaction. The aim is to ensure that the student experience is adequate. Evaluating their satisfaction is an essential part of identifying flaws in the design, implementation and validation. For this purpose, an online questionnaire was implemented, found at the following address: https://forms.gle/YmP9K9YssaXeLKuV8. A Likert scale uses 1 symbolizes strong disagreement and 5 symbolizes total agreement. The results can see in Table 2.

In this way, it is possible to know the additional needs that the participants might have. For example, the question with the highest average (4.42 ± 0.674) mentions a need for automation of more machinery in the laboratory. The disputed interface scored high for being intuitive for the user (3.84 ± 0.586). The results of question 3 (3.89 ± 0.788) corroborate what was previously analyzed, i.e., there is a reduction in execution times in automatic mode. Whereas the score of 3.84 ± 0.933 (Q11) describes that the

Table 2. Participant satisfaction results.

Pt	Questions										
	Q1	Q2	Q3	Q4	Q5	Q6	Q7	Q8	Q9	Q10	Q11
1	4	4	4	4	4	4	4	4	3	3	3
2	4	3	4	3	4	5	4	3	3	5	5
3	3	4	3	4	5	3	1	1	4	1	3
4	4	4	4·	4	4	4	4	4	5	4	4
5	3	2	4	3	4	5	4	1	2	3	3
6	4	4	4	4	3	4	3	1	4	4	4
7	4	3	4	4	5	4	5	1	3	3	3
8	4	3	3	3	3	5	3	3	3	3	3
9	3	4	4	4	4	4	3	2	3	4	3
10	3	4	3	3	3	5	5	1	3	4	2
11	4	4	4	4	4	4	4	4	4	4	4
12	5	4	4	4	4	5	4	4	4	5	4
13	4	5	5	5	4	5	4	4	4	5	5
14	4	4	5	4	3	5	2	4	4	4	5
15	5	4	2	3	3	4	3	4	3	5	5
16	2	3	4	4	5	5	5	5	4	4	4
17	3	4	5	4	3	5	4	3	4	4	5
18	3	4	5	5	3	5	5	4	3	3	5
19	4	3	3	4	3	3	4	3	4	4	3
A	3,68	3,68	3,89	3,84	3,74	4,42	3,74	2,95	3,53	3,79	3,84
TD	0,73	0,65	0,79	0,59	0,71	0,67	1,02	1,32	0,68	0,95	0,93

Pt = Participant, A = Average, TD = Typical deviation.

knowledge and skills of the participants increased with this exercise. Finally, the lowest score of 2.95 ± 1.317 (Q8) shows that the students did not use the equipment before automation. Therefore, their skills in hydraulics were reduced and lost in this specific period without tools for the work.

3.3 Discussion

Engineering laboratories must be constantly renewed, following the learning needs of their students and the needs of the industry. The maintenance and renewal of equipment is a valid option that allows for preserving the physical characteristics of the hardware available. In Palmer's work [7], were made changes in the network laboratory at Solent University. Although he mentions that productivity improved, he does not specify what percentage or how this was validated; therefore, it cannot be compared with our work.

At the same time, Rojas-Suarez et al. [8] developed an electro-pneumatic test bench for undergraduate practice. This proposal is similar to the one we have done; however, it does not incorporate an intuitive HMI interface that motivates students.

Similarly, Sukir et al. [9] have built a training system using PLC, but they have not incorporated a display for process visualization. Alavizadeh & Mikhail [10] built a training system incorporating pneumatic elements connected to a computer; they have not performed validation tests. Finally, Topçu [11] proposes a methodology focused on teaching control systems using an electrohydraulic system, but its design does not show to replicate it. None of the described researchers has executed a satisfaction survey that evaluates their perception of the participants regarding the developed or improved equipment.

4   Conclusions

This study proposes a modification of a previously manual electro-hydraulic test bench. The methodology used focuses on automating the internal processes of this didactic station used for educational purposes. The results showed that before, there was a significant oscillation in the execution times of the three tasks that this machine has. Now the times are static and standardized, which demonstrates to users the advantages of automation in a tangible way. Experimental tests show a reduction of up to 50% in the relative error obtained before implementing this proposal. In addition, the time saved can now be used for other activities in the laboratory.

The current design of this hydraulic network allows students to perform tests involving the use of PLCs. In addition, being in a controlled environment provides the student with the assurance that the errors made are part of their academic training and the experimentation they must perform in the training stage. The updating of the engineering laboratories allows for better dissemination of practical knowledge. It also promotes the development of research projects that improve the skills of future professionals who will work in an industrial environment. Moreover, according to the satisfaction questionnaire, these initiatives are massively supported.

In future work, it proposes implementing a control algorithm that improves the current design and execution times. Also, plan to continue with the improvement of the engineering laboratories to promote better teaching of engineering careers.

Acknowledgments. Universidad Tecnológica Indoamérica, for its support and the financing of the project "Big data analysis and its impact on society, education and industry".

References

1. Saá, F., Varela-Aldás, J., Latorre, F., Ruales, B.: Automation of the feeding system for washing vehicles using low cost devices. In: Botto, M., León-, J., Díaz Cadena, A., Montiel Díaz, P. (eds.) ICAETT 2019. AISC, vol. 1067, pp. 131–141. Springer, Cham (2020). https://doi.org/10.1007/978-3-030-32033-1_13

2. Varela-, J., Chávez-Ruiz, P., Buele, J.: Automation of a lathe to increase productivity in the manufacture of stems of a metalworking company. In: Botto, M., Zambrano, M., Torres--Tobar, P., Montes León, S., Pizarro Vásquez, G., Durakovic, B. (eds.) ICAT 2019. CCIS, vol. 1195, pp. 244–254. Springer, Cham (2020). https://doi.org/10.1007/978-3-030-42531-9_20

3. Cox, D.: Development of hands-on laboratory resources for manufacturing engineering. In: Annual Conference and Exposition, Conference Proceedings, 2017, June 2017. https://doi.org/10.18260/1-2--28172

4. Kuric, I., Císar, M., Tlach, V., Zajačko, I., Gál, T., Więcek, D.: Technical diagnostics at the department of automation and production systems. In: Burduk, A., Chlebus, E., Nowakowski, T., Tubis, A. (eds.) ISPEM 2018. AISC, vol. 835, pp. 474–484. Springer, Cham (2019). https://doi.org/10.1007/978-3-319-97490-3_46

5. Wang, L., Wang, J.: Design of laboratories for teaching mechatronics/electrical engineering in the context of manufacturing upgrades. Int. J. Electr. Eng. Educ. (2019). https://doi.org/10.1177/0020720919837856

6. Buele, J., et al.: Interactive system to improve the skills of children with dyslexia: a preliminary study. In: Rocha, Á., Pereira, R.P. (eds.) Developments and Advances in Defense and Security. SIST, vol. 152, pp. 439–449. Springer, Singapore (2020). https://doi.org/10.1007/978-981-13-9155-2_35

7. Palmer, N.: Work in progress - Automation of a computer networking laboratory. In: IEEE Global Engineering Education Conference EDUCON, pp. 348–353, April 2015. https://doi.org/10.1109/EDUCON.2015.7095995

8. Rojas Suárez, J.P., Pabón León, J.A., Orjuela Abril, M.S.: Development of an electro-pneumatic system for the practical training of pneumatic processes in the university environment. J. Phys. Conf. Ser. **2073**, 012016 (2021). https://doi.org/10.1088/1742-6596/2073/1/012016

9. Sukir, S., Hartoyo, S., Saifullizam, B.P.: Performance of trainers kits for industrial automation based on programmable logic 1. Sukir, Sa'adilah, Hartoyo, Sunaryo, Saifullizam, B.P.: Performance of Trainers kits for Industrial Automation Based on Programmable Logic Controllers. J. Phys. Conf. Ser. J. Phys. Conf. Ser. **2111**, 012040 (2021). https://doi.org/10.1088/1742-6596/2111/1/012040

10. Alavizadeh, A., Mikhail, M.: Design and development of portable pneumatic trainers to teach basic PLC wiring and programming. In: ASEE Annual Conference and Exposition, Conference Proceedings (2019). https

11. Topçu, E.E.: PC-based control and simulation of an electro-hydraulic system. Comput. Appl. Eng. Educ. **25**, 706–718 (2017). https://doi.org/10.1002/cae.21831

Apply the M/M/C Model of Queuing Theory in a Service System Based on FlexSim Simulation in the Post-COVID

Ana Álvarez Sánchez[(✉)] 🆔 and Alexis Suárez del Villar Labastida 🆔

Grupo de Investigación en Sistemas Industriales, Software y Automatización SISAu, Facultad de Ingenierías, Industria y Producción, Universidad Tecnológica Indoamérica, Ambato, Quito, Ecuador
{anaalvarez,asuarez}@indoamerica.edu.ec

Abstract. The study includes a literature review, modeling and simulation concepts, applications, FlexSim characterization, and the M/M/C model, i.e., multiple channels. Customer service processes with Coronavirus Disease 2019 (COVID-19) have been affected by dissimilar reasons among them the distancing that causes queues to become longer and the set of operations to be carried out with the same personnel, being this a not so satisfactory experience for the customer. The article addresses key concepts related to the use of FlexSim software within a simulation model in a service process where decisions can be made based on the study of queuing theory. After performing the Poisson goodness-of-fit test, it was determined that the distribution of hourly queue arrivals does meet a Poisson-type distribution since its Chi-square test reaches a value of 0.92 which is well above the coefficient of 0.5. Therefore, the exact probability of finding n arrivals during a given time T can be found, if the process is random, as is the case of the cooperative. The average number of customers in the queue waiting to be served, gives a reduction from 1.04 to 0.14 customers, so it is understood that, if the increase of servers in the cooperative were applied, this would cause queues to be generated in the system, since its L_q is 0.14 customers.

Keywords: Customers · Distribution · Model · Simulation · Queuing theory

1 Introduction

Queuing theory is a fundamental topic in Operations Research, as part of the approach to models that allow the efficient management of these lines, whether for products, people, materials, among others [1]. As part of a company's strategic plan, the customer's perspective and one of its main variables, "customer satisfaction", must be taken into account [2]. Queuing theory emerged at the beginning of the 20th century, when the problem of traffic congestion in telephone networks was first studied from a scientific approach by the Danish Agner Kraup Erlang. Since then, this theory has been applied to a multitude of real-life problems, such as those mentioned above [3], It is a collection of mathematical models that describe waiting line systems. Such models serve to find

© The Author(s), under exclusive license to Springer Nature Switzerland AG 2022
C. Stephanidis et al. (Eds.): HCII 2022, CCIS 1655, pp. 240–247, 2022.
https://doi.org/10.1007/978-3-031-19682-9_32

a balance between the cost of the service and the cost associated with waiting for that service [4].

To describe the service system to be modeled, we used Kendall's extended notation, through which we specify: the probability distribution of the inter-arrival times, the probability distribution of the service times, number of servers, maximum number of simultaneous users allowed in the system, and queue discipline, respectively [7]. The simulation starts with a model. A model is a physical or mathematical description of a system and usually represents a particular point in time [8]. A system is a complex, integrated set of interconnected elements, which is part of a higher-order system and is composed of higher-order systems [9]. The level of abstraction is difficult because most real systems are too complex for analytical evaluations, so systems must be studied by simulation [10]. In 2003, FlexSim software was released, which proved to be substantially different from previous simulators in both its simulation language and architecture [8]. The object under investigation is a small financial cooperative that analyses its current customer service queue in the post-COVID stage using operations management tools and statistics to facilitate decision making to reduce its operational expenses. Therefore, it seeks to answer the following questions: ¿How would it affect the queue if I add one more customer service window and the arrival rate is expected to increase to more than 18 per hour? ¿What effect will this have on the number of people in the queue?

1.1 Method

This Cooperative has a Poisson distribution for the arrival of customers, with an exponential service pattern, the queue has a PEPS discipline which means the first in is the first out, which are served by 2 employees. The FlexSim 2020 3D modelling allowed to analyse, visualise and improve the case to be solved in a suitable way, for its analysis. It also makes use of statistical tools such as: Goodness of fit test, chi-square test, exponential distribution and as a fundamental point of the work, mathematical modelling of waiting rows. This research was able to carry out 200 systematic observations.

1.2 Results

The starting point was to find out how the co-operative operates, customer behaviour and waiting times. Users arrive at the cooperative every day of the week during the cooperative's working hours (8:00 am to 16:00). (8:00 am to 16:00). As is usual for the type of queues that financial institutions generally manage, these are managed with an irregular timetable of arrival to the queue. The agency currently has 4 servers, which rotate in 2 shifts of 4 h each, which means that they are always operating the 2 windows that are available to the public.

The cooperative's customer population is much larger in number than the number of servers at the counters, so for practical purposes it is considered to be an infinite population [11]. The arrival rate, which is the same as the number of units per period, must be established, so FlexSim 2020 software is used to simulate the counters and arrival times. As shown in Fig. 1.

By simulating the process, it has been possible to obtain the following database on the number of customer arrivals in the queue, their waiting time and the time it takes to

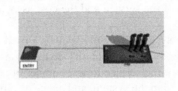

Fig. 1. Simulation of queue arrivals.

serve each customer. For a total of 67 hours, the number of customers arriving in the queue every hour is observed, see Table 1.

Table 1. Frequency of arrivals at the queue every hour.

N° Arrivals at the queue every hour	Frequency
12	14
13	6
14	8
15	9
16	7
17	7
18	5
19	11

It was determined whether the distribution of the hourly arrival time at the queue complies with a Poisson distribution, so a good-ness-of-fit test for Poisson was performed, where the results in Tables 2, 3 and 4were obtained.

Table 2. Descriptive statistics.

N	Mean
67	15,2687

Table 3. Observed and expected counts for N° Arrivals at the queue every hour.

N° Arrivals to the queue every hour	Probability of Poisson	Count observed	Count expected	Contribution to chi-square
<=12	0,245951	14	16,4787	0,372855
13	0,092053	6	6,1675	0,004551
14	0,100395	8	6,7264	0,241135
15	0,102193	9	6,8469	0,677068
16	0,097521	7	6,5339	0,033244
17	0,087590	7	5,8685	0,218164
18	0,074299	5	4,9780	0,000097
>= 19	0,199999	11	13,3999	0,429829

1 (12, 50%) of expected counts are less than 5.
Null hypothesis H_0: The data follow a Poisson distribution.

Table 4. Chi-square test.

GL	Chi-sq	p-Value
6	1,97694	0,922

Alternative hypothesis H_1: The data do not follow a Poisson distribution.

Fig. 2. Row arrival properties in Flexsim

Figure 1 shows the relationship between the observed values of the number of hourly arrivals at the cooperative's queue, where it can be seen that the highest expected value is found in the bar of less than 12 people per hour arriving at the queue. After performing the goodness-of-fit test for Poisson, it was determined that, the distribution of hourly arrivals to the queue does meet a Poisson-type distribution because its Chi-square test reaches a value of 0.92 which represents that it is well above the coefficient of 0.5. So the exact probability of finding n arrivals during a given time T can be found, if the process is random as in the case of the cooperative, then the Poisson distribution is formulated as follows:

$$P_t(n) = \frac{(\lambda T)^n e^{-\lambda t}}{n!} \tag{1}$$

With all the above said, we proceed to simulate in FlexSim 2020 and take the queue arrival time by customers at the customer service counters expressed in minutes, following a Poisson distribution, a total of 400 observations are taken. This results in the database for the first 200 shown in Table 5, and the second 200 observations in Table 6.

Table 5. Customer arrival time to queue (minutes) First 200 observations.

3,09	3,27	4,93	4,05	3,83	4,91	4,5	3,25	3,82	4,66	3,91	4,35
3,19	3,38	3,92	4,89	4,3	4,45	3,05	3,36	3,59	4,98	3,23	3,72
3,83	4,34	4,83	3,29	4,28	4,87	4,4	3,15	3,79	4,32	4,26	3,11
4,4	3,68	4,82	4,22	4,18	4,21	3,88	4,96	3,75	4,63	4,43	4,61
4,97	4,56	3,1	3,48	4,12	4,75	3,76	3,3	3,01	3,69	3,97	4,29
3,97	3,07	4,91	4,99	3,38	4,52	3,08	3,96	3,49	4,14	4,81	3,76
3,5	3,58	4,93	4,02	3,83	3,71	4,51	4,52	3,24	4,61	4,21	4,82
4,91	4,18	3,35	3,83	3,75	3,48	4,5	3,17	4,59	3,06	3,34	3,36
4,94	4,73	4,08	4,95	4,67	4,04	4,41	4,07	3,99	3,14	4,09	3,33
4,47	4,96	4,01	3,16	4,09	3,5	3,95	4,5	3,98	4,95	4,81	3,38
3,27	4,29	3,14	4,61	3,57	4,95	3,52	4,87	3,36	3,04	4,9	4,97
4,2	4,19	3,84	4,45	4,61	3,16	4,96	4,64	3,86	3,34	3,57	4,29
3,79	3,55	3,59	4,41	4,39	4,5	3,08	4,46	4,71	3,04	4,15	3,61
3,57	3,57	4,4	4,0	3,84	4,41	3,43	4,76	4,26	4,19	4,77	3,31
3,53	3,06	4,96	4,1	4,36	3,49	3,26	3,69	4,86	3,89	4,55	3,33
4,06	3,68	4,79	4,08	4,16	3,79	4,76	3,21	3,53	4,66		
3,92	3,05	3,4	3,32	4,6	4,16	3,03	3,07	3,1	4,43		

For the simulation in FlexSim 2020 the properties for the simulation are expressed as shown in Fig. 2.

Table 6. Customer arrival time to queue (minutes). Second 200 observations.

5,17	6,25	6,31	5,1	5,53	6,97	6,2	5,38	6,04	5,49	6,25	5,24
6,71	6,3	5,78	6,76	6,07	6,96	6,83	5,96	6,74	6,53	5,4	6,77
6,92	5,54	5,41	5,45	5,45	5,82	5	6,4	6,97	5,16	5,59	5,87
5,73	5,52	5,04	6,08	5,13	5,46	6,08	6,77	5,42	5,43	5,36	5,46
6,21	5,23	5,46	6,11	5,18	6,47	5,62	6,07	6,47	5,6	5,73	5,36
5,2	6,83	6,46	6,14	5,25	5,74	6,39	6,24	6,08	6,05	6,61	6,67
6,83	5,46	6,76	6,41	7,0	6,7	6,19	5,67	5,24	6,21	6,18	6,9
5,02	5,24	5,95	5,59	5,68	5,11	5,8	5,0	6,71	5,53	6,29	5,33
5,6	5,97	6,57	6,01	6,47	5,74	5,04	6,29	5,32	5,49	5,95	5,45
6,49	5,76	5,59	5,83	6,14	6,21	5,55	6,04	5,76	6,72	5,22	5,32
6,7	5,51	6,18	6,67	5,8	5,47	5,09	6,67	6,55	5,5	6,11	6,68
6,63	6,42	5,6	5,1	6,83	6,64	6,35	6,77	5,27	6,89	6,72	6,89
6,72	6,98	5,34	5,86	5,91	5,85	5,37	5,34	5,54	5,8	5,11	6,82
6,48	5,48	5,25	6,81	6,62	5,01	6,03	5,01	5,12	5,52	5,76	6,25
6,11	5,93	6,75	6,82	6,17	5,84	5,59	5,69	5,63	6,58	5,53	5,01
5,64	5,19	6,74	6,07	5,06	6,22	6,35	5,66	5,38	6,89	5,82	6,48
6,21	6,41	6,15	5,63	6,52	6,77	5,46	6,21				

Table 7. Comparison of results with one more server.

	2 servers	3 servers
0	20,28%	25,64%
()	2,36	1,47
()	1,04	0,14
()	10,63	6,59
()	4,67	0,63

The cooperative has 2 counters at the time of diagnosis, which operate throughout the 8 h working day, so, as explained above, their customer service time differs from one customer to another and, as usual, an exponential distribution is used to simulate this type of cases, as explained by Chase et al. [11]. Therefore, the following data are obtained.

The sample mean is 5.9591 min. For the simulation in FlexSim 2020, the properties for the simulation considering the above are expressed as shown in Fig. 3 in the case of counter service.

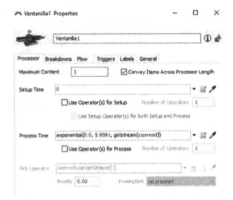

Fig. 3. Attention properties at the counter in FlexSim.

1.3 Model M/M/C

In the diagnosis it was obtained that the λ: Average arrival rate in time unit = 0.222 customers/minute, 1λ: Time between customer arrivals = 4.496 min, μ: Average service rate = 0.222 customers/minute, 1μ: Service time = 5.9591 min and c: Number of servers = 2. The following were calculated:

$$P_0 = \frac{1}{\left[\sum_{n=0}^{c-1} \frac{1}{n!}\left(\frac{\lambda}{\mu}\right)^n\right] + \frac{1}{C!}\left(\frac{\lambda}{\mu}\right)^c \frac{c\mu}{c\mu-\lambda}} \text{ for } c\mu > \lambda \tag{2}$$

Probability that there is no customer in the system, $P_0 = 20, 28\%$

$$L_s = \frac{\lambda\mu\left(\frac{\lambda}{\mu}\right)^c}{(c-1)!(c\mu-\lambda)^2}P_0 + \frac{\lambda}{\mu} \tag{3}$$

Average number of customers in the system. $L_s = 2{,}36$ customers

$$L_q = L_s - \frac{\lambda}{\mu} \tag{4}$$

Average tail length, $L_q = 1{,}038$ customers

$$Ws = \frac{L_s}{\lambda} \tag{5}$$

Average customer waiting time in the system, $Ws = 10.63$ minutes.

$$Wq = \frac{L_q}{\lambda} \tag{6}$$

Average waiting time for each customer in the queue, $Wq = 4.67$ minutes.

The cooperative intends to implement one more post COVID window in its customer service system, therefore, we proceeded to apply the M/M/C Model for 3 servers with the same data obtained previously, since it will be applied to the same financial entity, only the number of servers would change, which is the value of c. This is done so that the cooperative can observe what would happen if one more employee would be added to the customer service line and so the administrators of the cooperative have a back-up to make decisions. In order to compare how the cooperative's queuing system would look like if one more counter were added, the following comparison table was designed.

2 Conclusions

With the increase of one server in the credit union's customer service system in the post-COVID stage, according to the M/M/C method, there is an increase of approximately 5% in the probability that there will be no customers in the system with respect to the waiting queue with 2 servers, which is logical since, if one more window is increased, this would cause the credit union to run out of customers at some point since it caters to everyone. On the other hand, the average number of clients in the system was reduced to 1.47 clients. The same is true for the average number of customers in the queue waiting to be served, since it was practically reduced to zero customers, so it is understood that, if the increase in servers were applied in the cooperative, this would cause no queues to be generated in the system, since its Lq is 0.14 customers. The average time spent by the client in the system was reduced from 10.63 min to 6.59 min due to the increase of one more server, the same happened with the average time spent by the client in the queue, since this decreased considerably from 4.67 min to 0.63 min, this happens because the client population is well supplied by the servers since 3 customer service windows would be enabled and therefore no queues would be generated and if there were, it would be in a minimum amount and with a very low waiting time.

References

1. Hillier, F., et al.: Introducción a la investigación de operaciones, p. 778. McGraw-Hill, México D.F (2019)
2. Kaplan, R.S., Norton, D.P.: Cuadro de Mando Integral. Gestión, Barcelona (2000)
3. W WL. "Investigación de Operaciones. Aplicaciones y Algoritmos". 4ta ed, Stamford: Thomson Internacional (2017)
4. Shortle, J.F., et al.: Fundamentals of Queueing Theory, New York (2017)
5. Allen, A.: Probability, Statistics, and Queueing Theory. Academic Press, New York (2016)
6. A S. Applied Probability and Queues. Springer, New York (2019)
7. Haghighi, A.M., Mishev, D.P.: Delayed and Network Queues. Wiley, New York (2018)
8. Beaverstock, W.M., et al.: Applied Simulation Modeling and Analysis using FlexSim. FlexSim Software Products, Orem USA (2017)
9. Owen, D.G., Tocher, K.D.: The automatic programming of simulations. In: Proceedings of the Second International Conference on Operational Research, pp. 50–68 (1960)
10. L A M and W D A. Simulation Modeling and Analysis, 4a ed., Tucson, Arizona, U.S.A: McGraw – Hill, p. 1–273 (2017)
11. Jacobs, R.F., et al.: Aquilano, Administración de operaciones producción y cadena de suministros. McGraw-Hill, México D.F. (2019)
12. Zárate-Cruz, R., Díaz-Martínez, M.A.: Simulación con Flexsim, una nueva alternativa. Científica **22**(2), 97–104 (2018)

Evaluation Methods Review of the Innovation Capacity of Companies Based on Knowledge Management

Jorge Álvarez-Tello[2]([⊠]) [iD], Jenny Martínez-Crespo[3] [iD],
and Mireya Zapata-Rodríguez[1] [iD]

[1] Centro de Investigación en Mecatrónica y Sistemas Interactivos – MIST, Universidad Indoamérica, Av. Machala y Sabanilla, 170103 Quito, Ecuador
mireyazapata@uti.edu.ec
[2] Centro de Transferencia de Tecnología e Innovación – CTTI, Universidad Indoamérica, Av. Machala y Sabanilla, 170103 Quito, Ecuador
jorgealvarez@uti.edu.ec
[3] Facultad de Ciencias Administrativas y Económicas – FACAE, Universidad Indoamérica, Av. Bolívar y Guayaquil, Ambato, Ecuador

Abstract. The knowledge economy and the improvement of efficiency in the dissemination and promotion of the achievements of innovation from the knowledge generated in the organization is relevant. The value chain of knowledge allows absorbing and making the most of new knowledge useful to improve competitiveness opportunities for business competitiveness. The relevant elements that evaluate the innovation of organizations based on knowledge management are delimiting through the bibliographic review in the Scopus and Google Scholar databases, using Boolean search formulas. About evaluation methods nearly to 40% work in organizational strategy, in approx. 25% include in region cluster and industry for the optimization. Hence the preponderance of topics related to knowledge optimization and innovation, decision making, value generation and knowledge supply chains. Finally, all models have limitations that must be considered, in relation to the cultural context where they are applied and the human-organizational phenomenon present. They should also consider the limitations in the use of quantitative techniques, leaving aside the richness of qualitative constructs in the analysis and strategic decision-making for a technological evolution of organizations.

Keywords: Knowledge-management · Making decisions · Innovation

1 Introduction

The knowledge economy and the improvement of efficiency in the dissemination and promotion of innovation achievements from the knowledge generated in the activities defined in the organization in the virtual and real value chain supported by Big Data [1], make knowledge management become increasingly important in the development

C. Stephanidis et al. (Eds.): HCII 2022, CCIS 1655, pp. 248–257, 2022.
https://doi.org/10.1007/978-3-031-19682-9_33

of business and industry. The integration of knowledge acquires greater relevance in research, in the field of knowledge management, for its effects on the improvement of the levels of knowledge management (acquisition, storage, application and innovation of knowledge) according to Cong, [2], the improvement in the capacity for methodological and technological innovation, in the formation of competitive advantages in organizations [3], in the configuration of an organizational knowledge value chain [4] and of a knowledge supply chain [5].

Therefore, knowledge management improves the effectiveness and efficiency of knowledge, while at the same time it can improve the decision, application and production capacity of technological innovation [6]. The ability to innovate and to acquire knowledge necessary to support the innovation process determine the success of an organization [7]. The knowledge value chain is important for the company, to the extent that it allows absorbing and making the most of new knowledge, taking advantage of useful knowledge to improve competitiveness [8]. The integration of technology to information management includes the implementation of methodologies such as AHP, as well as clustering assisted by the development of neural network architecture or genetic algorithms, through which knowledge sharing in the organization can be evaluated [9].

For the development of the information architecture, on which the exchange of knowledge generated from each of the links in the value chain in organizations is based, there are evaluation methods for the development of knowledge management and innovation generated in organizations. The analysis of the bibliographic review will allow to answer in an exploratory way which methods are frequently used to improve the performance of knowledge management in organizations in relation to innovation processes and capabilities?

2 Method

In the period of 2018–2022, through the bibliographic review of 20 articles from the Scopus databases, and Google Scholar, also through the Publish or Perish and Dimensions application. To better filter the information, Boolean search formulas are used (knowledge management, innovation, evaluation methods), the information is systematized to identify articles related to knowledge management in terms of innovation capacity in the organization to determine the relevant variables of the methods that evaluate the innovation of organizations based on knowledge management, which delimit the opportunities for business development and competitiveness that constitute value co-creation systems and dynamism the value chains of organizations.

3 Results

This evaluation helps the management departments of organizations to dimension the capacity of the research and development (R&D) area in relation to the exploration and exploitation of knowledge, as well as the expansion of the company in the market, against its own development potential to integrate innovation as a catalyst for knowledge management. Under this scenario, knowledge management becomes a fundamental element for the generation of innovation processes and the articulation of work and knowledge

Table 1. Elements of analysis of the selected papers on knowledge management and innovation in organizations (Source: Authors)

n°	Author (year) [nn]	Elements			Innovation Impact
		Evaluation methods	Ecosystems building	N° helices	
1	Tang (2020) [1]	Big data analysis	Enterprise ocean informatization	3	Creation and appreciation of the value of information
2	Cong, Liu, Zhang, Zhao y Wang (2020) [2]	Comprehensive assessment using AHP and cloud modeling	Power Design Engineering Team - Case Study	2	Optimizing the knowledge base
3	Guang (2018) [6]	Shared organizational mental model	Paper industry	4	Added value of knowledge
4	Lin, Yu, Wu y Cheng (2018) [10]	Intellectual capital valuation model	Construction industry	4	Improving decision making in intellectual capital management
5	Yu & Yang (2018) [11]	Bibliometric	Knowledge-intensive construction industry	4	Evolution of knowledge management in the construction industry
6	Robescu, Fatol, Baesu, Draghici (2020) [12]	ROI, NWW analytics	Big multinational production company NWW	3	Identification of critical capabilities for innovation
7	Xiaoping (2020) [13]	BIM and Bayesian network	Safety in construction projects	4	Improving the safety of construction projects
8	Wang (2022) [14]	BPNN enhanced BPNN with PSO (PSO algorithm and BP neural network)	Industry-University-Research Alliance	4	Valuation of shared knowledge

(continued)

Table 1. (*continued*)

n°	Author (year) [nn]	Evaluation methods	Ecosystems building	N° helices	Innovation Impact
9	Yu, Hu, Li & Xiao (2022) [15]	Enhanced entropy-TOPSIS method	Case study Chongquing University, China	3	Decision making
10	Zhang (2022) [16]	Neural net-work (NN) model	Technology Enterprise case study	3	Virtual team knowledge transfer value chain
11	Jun & Kim (2022) [17]	Corporate Open Innovation Attitude Assessment (COIAA) scales and Test for Delphi Survey	SMEs and large local and foreign firms (Korean Management Association)	4	Organizational attitude evaluation scale
12	Silverstein, Benson, Gates y Nguyen (2022) [18]	Logic Model and the Kirkpatrick Model	Baylor College of Medicine International Pediatric AIDS Initiative (BIPAI)	4	Reducing professional isolation, strengthening peer relationships and improving the knowledge and practices of health professionals.
13	Liu, Yang, Zheng, Xiao, Gao y Lu (2022) [19]	PVAR model and Monte Carlo method	Provinces of China	4	Improving the GTIE of developing countries
14	Trstenjak, Opetuk, Cajner y Hegedic (2022) [20]	Analytic hierarchy process (AHP method)	Case study of a metal machining company	3	Making decisions support
15	Durand, Ricardo, Beaudet, Fortin-Pellerin, Morales y Tremblay (2022) [21]	General Estimating Equations	Health care practice (Canada)	4	Collaboration, psychological safety and engagement in the community of practice

(*continued*)

Table 1. (*continued*)

n°	Author (year) [nn]	Elements			
		Evaluation methods	Ecosystems building	N° helices	Innovation Impact
16	Liu y Zhang (2022) [22]	Intelligence-based knowledge management fuzzy evaluation algorithm (intelligent algorithm and neural network algorithm)	16 universities	3	Making decisions and knowledge management innovator
17	Pei (2022) [23]	Entropy weighting method and fuzzy integral evaluation method	Four provinces in China	4	Innovation performance in companies
18	Han & Gu (2022) [5]	Analytic hierarchy process (AHP) and data envelopment analysis (DEA algorithm)	Yangtze River Delta region (includes four provinces in China)	4	Efficiency in the knowledge supply chain
19	Szczekala y Stadnicka (2022) [24]	Bibliometric	Bibliometric analysis in databases	-	Effective implementation of knowledge management in manufacturing areas
20	Bao y Wang (2022) [25]	Neural network and information transmission model	Business clusters in various regions of China	4	Transformation of innovative knowledge flow

networks that facilitate the generation of value and the construction of differentiating factors that allow the sustainability and growth of the organization. The following Table 1 gives a summary of all elements.

The following Table 2 gives a summary of the color legend indicators for the interpretation of the Table 1.

Table 2. Color legend indicator (Source: Authors)

n°	Elements					
	Evaluation methods		Ecosystems building		Innovation Impact	
1	Organizational and strategy	40%	Enterprises	20%	Value generation	15%
2	Big data	10%	Building industry	15%	Optimization	35%
3	Neuronal network	25%	Education sector	15%	Making decision	20%
4	Hierarchic	15%	Regions, Clusters, Industry	25%	Personal value	15%
5	Bibliometric	10%	Health	10%	Knowledge supply chain	15%

It is interesting the combination of methods and their enrichment to design and evaluate QA and innovation assessment models, as well as to ensure that the results not only meet the conditions of methodological validity and reliability, but also respond to the needs and requirements of organizations and different industry sectors. This can be seen in the breadth of use of the models, whether in small and medium-sized companies, or large companies in various industries, in different sectors of the economy, manufacturing, construction, engineering, health. In this sense, ecosystems are being worked on in some research from two/three helixes, when they are case studies, which develop models within organizations in relation to governmental impositions and the market, including competition. In other studies, usually focused on regions, provinces, industries and clusters, it is possible to identify the presence of the four helixes of the ecosystem, the business environment, the governmental environment, the competitive environment and the civil society.

4 Discussion

The literature review allows us to identify three elements of analysis related to culture, (infra)structure and strategic direction or business model. In relation to culture, it is possible to talk about management styles, communication processes, values related to trust, recognition, and valuation of personnel dedicated to R&D, all of them different depending on the region, the sector of the economy and the industry in which the analysis is made. In terms of strategy, the role of the leader or manager to promote and facilitate the flow of knowledge in a value chain and permanent supply in the organization, as well as the policies and incentives related to R&D results and products, the capabilities and knowledge of personnel, researchers and managers, as well as the focus of the business and the area of the economy in which it operates, which makes the processes more or less stable and change (innovation) becomes a constant or not of survival. It also includes bets on sustainability and green economies, which, in the current economic scenario, are differentiating elements that the market rewards. In relation to infrastructure, access to technology, the relationship between financing, technology and knowledge, as well as leverage and the potential for generating profits and value from knowledge and innovation.

On the other hand, it is important to recognize that organizations have elements that condition their capacity for innovation based on knowledge management, which establish conditions for evolution in the field of technological integration in the value chain of organizations, factors such as human talent, research, infrastructure, market exploration and development, as well as sustainable and sustainable business development are part of the relevant factors to have triggers for processes that promote innovation. Knowledge transfer barriers are also identified in relation to economic, legal and cultural perspectives. Cultural issues are the most complex to overcome, although they have been identified. The evaluation models used provide us with an image of organizational complexity, in which the development relationship of organizations depends on the ecosystemic relationship and social integration for the development of collective dimensions of knowledge that relates the design, creation and networks for knowledge and technology transfer, with the use of capabilities and their development in organizations internally and externally. It can be noted that most evaluations are based on perception through strategic analysis of databases in the cloud, as well as resorting to simulation in the systems for their optimization and the generation of information that allows you to make decisions in real time, assertively.

Evaluating the innovation capacity of organizations in a particular sector, in relation to knowledge management, involves making use of statistical approaches that make it possible to assess which variables interact with others and what the results of these interactions are. Neural networks, factorial analysis, fuzzy logic, among others, are statistical approaches/analyses that allow finding which elements interact with others and which ones influence more in one process than in another. Statistical methods allow understanding phenomena that are governed by multiple endogenous and exogenous factors, which can find correlations between the different factors being analyzed and their perturbations, in a multivariate phenomenon. Deciding which model (statistical or non-statistical) is the most appropriate for organizations is complex, and the literature reviewed reports various models that can be applied to the phenomenon under study: entropic models, cloud models, big data, value chain, organizational shared mind model, organizational knowledge acquisition assessment (OKA) model, algorithms and fuzzy models, particle swarm optimization method; fuzzy border number analytical method, catastrophe progression method, Fuzzy neural network, fuzzy comprehensive evaluation, Fuzzy clustering analysis, neural network, among others.

Expanding the indicators and analysis variables, as well as using evaluation methods that combine qualitative and quantitative methods, is recommended to overcome the limitations of the models, variables and indicators selected. Complementing the information from questionnaires or surveys with in-depth interviews, focus groups, meetings with experts, as well as the review of relevant literature on the subject, is an element to be taken into account to improve the evaluation models of the relationship between knowledge management and technological innovation in organizations, especially if it is desired to evaluate this relationship in terms of value generation, decision making, strategic positioning and sustainability over time.

5 Conclusions

This article, through the literature review, identifies the most significant articles on the subject of study in the period 2018–2022 and reviews both their analysis models, as well as the relationship of their variables and categories, the most important conclusions reached in relation to the use of each method and their possible uses in organizations. This information will allow decision makers to select the tool and model (or even build a hybrid model) that best meets their objectives and particularities. In innovation in the articles reviewed, the optimization of both knowledge management and innovation itself have the greatest coverage, followed by the contribution to organizational decision making, in third place are the generation of value from knowledge and innovation, the generation of value from subjects and teams, and the knowledge value chain. The models present us with a path of evolution and maturation of the construction of information for decision making in real time, by building with bibliometric a knowledge base and indicators for the strategy and the collection of quality data that allow, in a hierarchical way, the construction of neural networks for decision and assistance for decision making at the executive level. In the construction of ecosystems, the focus on regions, clusters and industry in general is very relevant, followed by case studies in companies, also relevant is the focus on the construction industry and the education sector, ending with the health sector. This leads to the conclusion that the evaluation of knowledge management as a fundamental support for organizational innovation is a highly relevant topic in all sectors of the economy, from companies to industry, from clusters to regions, and in different countries. The limitations of the studies reviewed in general are associated with cultural elements, in relation to their application and validity in cultural contexts in other regions of the world, outside the countries analyzed, particularly China, Korea, Canada and India.

Finally, organizations and businesses engaged in different activities in the market scenario can select the model that best suits their needs, understanding the uses of each of them and their results, as well as their limitations. The articles reviewed maintain the semantic line on the subject and are the most current in the discussion proposed here, in such a way that it is possible to have an approximation to the way in which the models of evaluation of the innovation capacity of organizations have been changing from knowledge management.

References

1. Tang, H.: The value creation path and effect evaluation of enterprise marine informatization project in the context of big data (2020). https://doi.org/10.2112/JCR-SI112-114.1
2. Cong, R., et al.: Evaluation of Engineering Team's Knowledge Base Management Capability Based on Cloud Model (2020). https://doi.org/10.1109/ICEMME51517.2020.00011

3. Shao, W., Feng, X., Zhu, M., Tao, R., Lv, Y., Shi, Y.: Fuzzy evaluation system for innovation ability of science and technology enterprises. In: Uden, L., Ting, I.-H., Wang, K. (eds.) KMO 2021. CCIS, vol. 1438, pp. 147–159. Springer, Cham (2021). https://doi.org/10.1007/978-3-030-81635-3_13

4. Zhang, A.: The application of virtual teams in the improvement of enterprise management capability from the perspective of knowledge transfer. PLoS ONE 17(3), e0264367 (2022). https://doi.org/10.1371/journal.pone.0264367

5. Han, H., Gu, X.: Evaluation of innovation efficiency of high-tech enterprise knowledge supply chain based on AHP-DEA. J. Math. 2022, 1–9 (2022). https://doi.org/10.1155/2022/3210474

6. Guan, H.: Research on performance evaluation model of papermaking enterprise innovation management based on organizational shared mental model (2018). https://www.scopus.com/record/display.uri?eid=2-s2.0-85059179848&origin=inward&txGid=07ffe4f76fdd2dff7e a65c7c98204c15&featureToggles=FEATURE_NEW_DOC_DETAILS_EXPORT:1#met rics

7. Li, Y., Wang, S.-S., Wang, Y.-H.: The appraisal and empirical study on the knowledge management running performance of High-tech industrialization (2014). https://doi.org/10.1109/ICMSE.2014.6930345

8. Chun-Yu, Z.: Research on enterprise knowledge value chain model (2011). https://doi.org/10.1109/CCDC.2011.5968697

9. Sonj, L., et al.: A study on performance evaluation model of individual knowledge-sharing (2010). https://doi.org/10.1109/CSCWD.2010.5471974

10. D Lin, W.Yu., Wu, C., Cheng, T.: Correlation between intellectual capital and business performance of construction industry–an empirical study in Taiwan (2018). https://doi.org/10.1080/15623599.2017.1315528

11. Yu, D., Yang, J.: Knowledge management research in the construction industry: a review. J. Knowl. Econ. 9(3), 782–803 (2016). https://doi.org/10.1007/s13132-016-0375-7

12. Robescu, D., Fatol, D., Baesu, V., Draghici, A.: Conceptual knowledge sharing model to support organizational performance development. Expanding Horizons: Business, Management and Technology for Better Society, ToKnowPress (2020). https://ideas.repec.org/h/tkp/mkl p20/255-262.html

13. Xiaoping, B., Tao, P.: Strategic Learning and Knowledge Management of Technological Innovation in Safety Evaluation Planning of Construction Projects (2021). https://doi.org/10.1177/21582440211061536

14. Wang, L.: Performance evaluation of knowledge sharing in an industry-university-research alliance based on PSO-BPNN. Comput. Intell. Neurosci. 2022, 1–9 (2022). https://doi.org/10.1155/2022/1283588

15. Yu, X., Hu, D., Li, N., Xiao, Y.: Comprehensive evaluation on teachers' knowledge sharing behavior based on the improved TOPSIS method. Comput. Intell. Neurosci. 2022, 1–8 (2022). https://doi.org/10.1155/2022/2563210

16. Zhang, H., He, Y.: Manufacturing knowledge management performance evaluation based on grey fuzzy evaluation (2010). https://doi.org/10.1109/ESIAT.2010.5568310

17. Jun, Y., Kim, K.: Developing an open innovation attitude assessment framework for organizations: focusing on open innovation role perspective and locus of activity. Behav. Sci. 12(2), 46 (2022). https://doi.org/10.3390/bs12020046

18. Silverstein, A., Benson, A., Gates, C., Nguyen, D.: Global community of practice: a means for capacity and community strengthening for health professionals in low- and middle-income countries. J. Glob. Health 12, 04034 (2022). https://doi.org/10.7189/jogh.12.04034

19. Liu, Y., Yang, Y., Zheng, S., Xiao, L., Gao, H., Lu, H.: Dynamic impact of technology and finance on green technology innovation efficiency: empirical evidence from China's Provinces. Int. J. Environ. Res. Public Health 19(8), 4764 (2022). https://doi.org/10.3390/ije rph19084764

20. Trstenjak, M., Opetuk, T., Cajner, H., Hegedić, M.: Industry 4.0 readiness calculation—transitional strategy definition by decision support systems. Sensors **22**(3), 1185 (2022). https://doi.org/10.3390/s22031185
21. Durand, F., Richard, L., Beaudet, N., Fortin-Pellerin, L., Hudon, A.M., Tremblay, M.-C.: Healthcare professionals' longitudinal perceptions of group phenomena as determinants of self-assessed learning in organizational communities of practice. BMC Med. Educ. **22**(1), 75 (2022). https://doi.org/10.1186/s12909-022-03137-9
22. Liu, R., Zhang, H.: Artificial-intelligence-based fuzzy comprehensive evaluation of innovative knowledge management in universities. Math. Probl. Eng. **2022**, 1–11 (2022). https://doi.org/10.1155/2022/5655269
23. Pei, S.: Research on innovation performance of regional industrial enterprises above scale based on fuzzy comprehensive evaluation. In: 2022 7th International Conference on Big Data Analytics (ICBDA), pp. 349–354 (2022). https://doi.org/10.1109/ICBDA55095.2022.9760308
24. Szczekala, Ł., Stadnicka, D.: Knowledge management as a sustainable development supporting method in manufacturing organizations – a systematic literature review. In: Batako, A., Burduk, A., Karyono, K., Chen, X.W.R. (eds.) Advances in Manufacturing Processes, Intelligent Methods and Systems in Production Engineering. Lecture Notes in Networks and Systems, vol. 335, pp. 431–459 (2022). https://doi.org/10.1007/978-3-030-90532-3_34
25. Bao, Z., Wang, C.: A multi-agent knowledge integration process for enterprise management innovation from the perspective of neural network. Inf. Process. Manage. **59**(2), 102873 (2022). https://doi.org/10.1016/j.ipm.2022.102873

Intelligent Dashboard to Optimize the Tax Management in a Town Municipal Government

Franklin Castillo[(✉)], José A. Oleas-Orozco, Fernando Saá-Tapia,
and Carlos Mena-Navas

SISAu Research Group, Facultad de Ingeniería y Tecnologías de la Información y La
Comunicación, Universidad Tecnológica Indoamérica, Ambato 180103, Ecuador
franklincastillo@uti.edu.ec

Abstract. During the pandemic period, the tax collection in the Municipal Governments in Ecuador held a considerable decrease in money income, suffering
reductions in budgets that finance the institutional works in the towns. With several taxes, existence becomes challenging to know which are the ones that citizens
stop paying. With the purpose of solving this difficulty, in this work, we developed an intelligent dashboard by using the CRISP methodology. As a first step,
we evaluated the tax collections information from the Town Cevallos' municipal government in Ecuador through the management of administrative processes.
The information was obtained from the municipality's official digital databases,
documentary collections, and interviews with the departments involved in tax collection. The information released helps us determine the need for an intelligent
automated tool to optimize the tax collection process.

The tool allowed the understanding of the know-how of the tax collection process in the municipality and the paradigm of information storage. Thus, the tool
allows us the detection of errors in databases and the collaborative construction
of interactive reports for the management staff. The dashboard implementation
allowed to optimize the information management, the depuration, and correction
of inconsistent data. In consequence, the time used for this process was 40% compared to the time employed without the dashboard. Finally, the intelligent dashboard gives great support. It reduces the global response time by 87%, obtaining
several scenarios based on information entered into the database, contributing to
the correct decision-making based on graphical reports.

Keywords: Business intelligence · Dashboard · Data processing · Tax
application

1 Introduction

The dashboard is an intelligent computer solution used as a tool for visualizing statistical
data that allows for determining the performance of a company [1]. The data from
Physical or digital databases are the primary source or supply of information with which
intelligent systems are nourished [2]. The dashboards summarize the key performance
metrics of the organizations [3], with this shows the evolution of the business, if there are

© The Author(s), under exclusive license to Springer Nature Switzerland AG 2022
C. Stephanidis et al. (Eds.): HCII 2022, CCIS 1655, pp. 258–264, 2022.
https://doi.org/10.1007/978-3-031-19682-9_34

problems and what are the new business trends. To do this, it transforms large amounts of information into quality information for decision making. [4, 5]. The importance of the investigation in the context of municipal tax collections lies in the information that is generated from the data stored by the computer systems [6], by integrating the historical data of several dependencies in a single report [7] that presents the information with interactive visualizations with the perspective of studying critical data [8].

When reviewing related jobs, a smart dashboard has been made that helps students make decisions on how to make adjustments to their learning habits [9]. Another study indicates that business intelligence software tools are essential to analyze corporate information effectively [10]. Data analysis is applied in various fields, such as data collected by georeferencing tools that seek to create public policies to minimize criminal acts [11].

In public administration, there is a variety of data that can be treated through dashboard methodologies; however, the application of these techniques in municipal governments is still pending execution. For this, a control panel was cre-ated using business intelligence software tools with the purpose of optimizing the income of economic resources to municipal governments. Therefore, the practical case study is taken in the Municipal of Cevallos town.

The present study develops an intelligent control panel for the collection of taxes of the Municipal of Cevallos town, which is manipulated from a personal computer that is connected with the data generated by the computer systems of the institution. For this propose, in the first part is presented the introduction to the general topic part two is made up of the tools used as well as the methodology that was used for the development of the final product, in the third part are presented the results obtained, and finally the conclusions obtained at the end of the work.

2   Materials and Methods

Power BI was used to develop this product, a software that generates business intelligence solutions. The tool integrates the information generated in the institution's daily transactions over the course of several years; which is stored in a computer system as a result of the activities generated on a day-to-day basis through an ETL process (Extraction, Transformation and Loading) that extracts the information from the databases, so that these are transformed into a structured format that optimizes the loading of data to the Business Intelligence software, which carries out the pertinent filters that allow analyzing the information from various points of view, as support for decision-making based on the taxes collection more effectively.

CRIPS was used, since it is an agile methodology applied in projects that require Business Intelligence. It has a series of steps that facilitate the processing of data and the understanding of the business with a single common objective, allowing the explanation in each of the steps, which facilitates the understanding of the tasks done. The methodology details are included in the Fig. 1.

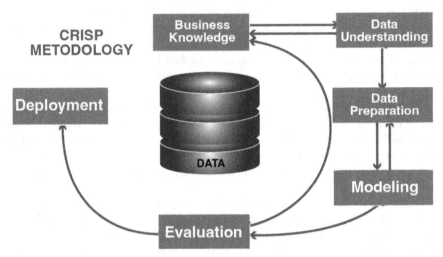

Fig. 1. Stages of the CRISP Methodology, which are used for the Development of Smart Panels, based on historical business data

2.1 Business Understanding

This phase describes the first interaction of the technician with the municipality of Cevallos town to understand the movements of the tax collection process and the survey of the requirements that will later become the reason for the data analysis. In the Subsequent paragraphs, however, they are indented.

2.2 Data Analysis

After understanding the information contained in the database, it is essential to carry out an analysis and cleaning of the data obtained. In this process, inconsistent data is eliminated, where invalid data is identified, typing errors in the entry of data generate inconsistencies in the information. With this input, we proceed to the debugging and correction of errors at the database level.

2.3 Modeling

The evaluation was carried out in collaboration with the head of technologies of the Municipal of Cevallos town, contrasting the information obtained in the panel with physical reports requested from the officials who generate the information that was stored in the database. These results allow the verification of the complete database debugging when a difference in values is found. A new data cleaning is carried out. This process is repeated from the first phase until the tool returns the expected results.

2.4 Deployment

For the visualization of information, it was implemented the Dashboard executable on a desktop computer.

3 Results

3.1 Reason for Collection with the Most Incidence in the year

Based on Fig. 2 the collection that generates the most income for the Municipality is the values issued from the Property Registry tax. Therefore, it is necessary to consider strategies that help collect taxes. The other taxes.

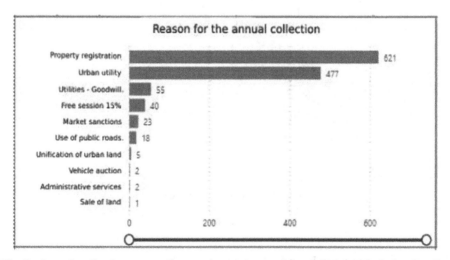

Fig. 2. Annual collections, according to the category of municipal taxes of the Cevallos Municipality.

3.2 Values that Were Collected in a year

The Fig. 3 shows the taxes of title state collected from citizens per year. From 2004 to 2020. The graph includes the taxes pending to collect and the eliminated register.

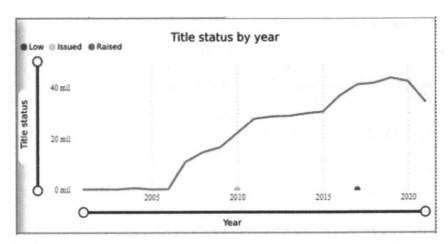

Fig. 3. Representation of financial collection in annual periods until 2020

3.3 Values that Were Collected in a year

In Fig. 4 the total money collected until 2021 is graph, with the possibility of reviewing the values collected for each year using the existing control panel filters.

Fig. 4. Total money raised over time

3.4 Values Received by Each Collector

In Fig. 5 the total of money collected by the personnel is presented, essential information to measure the productivity of the officials who work in that area, as well as control the economic items that enter the Municipality verifying with the physical documents issued in the financial department.

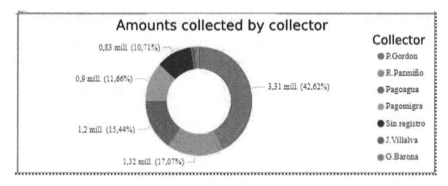

Fig. 5. Values registered by collector

4 Conclusions

With the implementation of the dashboard in the Cevallos' Municipality, the collection of taxes is centralized into two taxes, the others taxes do not contribute significantly to the annual budget. The filters used show detailed information by tax and by year, which allows the visualization of various scenarios for decision making and thereby generating strategies that increase tax collection and, therefore the economic resource for the institution.

References

1. Román-Mendoza, E.: Aprender a aprender en la era digital: Tecnopedagogía crítica para la enseñanza del español LE/L2. Routledge (2018)
2. Benítez, Y.L.: Business intelligence. ADGG102PO. IC Editorial (2019)
3. Ganapati, S.: Use of Dashboards in Government, p. 5 (2011)
4. Azevedo, A., Azevedo, J., Hayakawa, M.: Designing and implementing a dashboard with key performance indicators for a higher education institution. In: Proceedings of the 13th International Conference on Computer Supported Education, Online Streaming, --- Select a Country ---, 2021, pp. 165–172. https://doi.org/10.5220/0010539501650172
5. Escudero, P., Alcocer, W., Paredes, J.: Recurrent neural networks and ARIMA Models for euro/dollar exchange rate forecasting. Appl. Sci. **11**, 5658 (2021). https://doi.org/10.3390/app11125658
6. Matheus, R., Janssen, M., Maheshwari, D.: Data science empowering the public: data-driven dashboards for transparent and accountable decision-making in smart cities. Govern. Inf. Quart. **37**, February 2018. https://doi.org/10.1016/j.giq.2018.01.006
7. Maheshwari, D., Janssen, M.: Dashboards for supporting organizational development: principles for the design and development of public sector performance dashboards. In: Proceedings of the 8th International Conference on Theory and Practice of Electronic Governance, New York, NY, USA, oct. 2014, pp. 178–185. https://doi.org/10.1145/2691195.2691224
8. «Praxis_and_Politics_of_Urban_Data_SSRN.pdf». Accedido: 16 de mayo de 2022. [En línea]. Disponible en. https://www.northeastern.edu/visualization/wp-content/uploads/2016/04/Praxis_and_Politics_of_Urban_Data_SSRN.pdf
9. Susnjak, T., Ramaswami, G.S., Mathrani, A.: Learning analytics dashboard: a tool for providing actionable insights to learners. Int. J. Educ. Technol. High. Educ. **19**(1) (2022). https://doi.org/10.1186/s41239-021-00313-7

10. Mamani-Coaquira, Y.: Business Intelligence: herramientas para la toma de decisiones en procesos de negocio (2018)
11. Castillo, F., Naranjo-, H., Buele, J., Varela-, J., Amaguaña, Y.D., Salazar, F.W.: Interpreting felony acts using georeferenced data. Case study in Ambato, Ecuador. In: Botto, M., Montes León, S., Camacho, O., Chávez, D., Torres-, P., Zambrano, M. (eds.) ICAT 2020. CCIS, vol. 1388, pp. 44–54. Springer, Cham (2021). https://doi.org/10.1007/978-3-030-71503-8_4

Idea Management in SMEs – Design Principles for Collaboration in Idea Management Systems

Andreas Hermann$^{(\boxtimes)}$, Torsten Gollhardt, Paul Kruse, Ann-Kristin Cordes, and Jörg Becker

European Research Center for Information Systems (ERCIS), University of Münster, Münster, Germany
{andreas.hermann,torsten.gollhardt,paul.kruse,
ann-kristin.cordes,becker}@ercis.uni-muenster.de

Abstract. To improve Digital Transformation efforts in SMEs, the application of dedicated Idea Management Systems that involve the collaboration with external supporters is promising. In this context, scientific contributions that structure underlying design knowledge appear to be scarce. Addressing this gap, this paper proposes eleven Design Principles that prescribe the collaboration between SMEs and external supporters in Idea Management Systems. These Design Principles have been derived retrospectively from a previous Action Design Research endeavor. Ultimately, they inform the implementation of solution instances.

Keywords: Digital transformation · Idea management · Collaboration · Small and medium-sized enterprise · External support unit

1 Motivation

Organizations, regardless of size or sector, are confronted with the ever-present dynamics brought along by Digital Transformation (DT) [23]. This ongoing process is associated with both valuable opportunities as well as great challenges and complexity for organizations [3,20]. In particular, Small and Medium-sized Enterprises (SMEs) seem to struggle with the complexities and hurdles of DT [9,31]. SMEs' nature in terms of restricted financial resources and presumable knowledge gaps further reinforces this situation [2,5]. An often overlooked practice that moderates DT success and aims to bring structure to the early phase of DT is Idea Management (IM) [8,10,28,32].

Organizations which properly integrate IM practices are more likely to navigate DT successfully [10,28]. However, multiple studies have revealed that SMEs, in particular, tend to perform IM rather ad hoc and rarely follow elaborate DT plans. [27, 28, 30, 32]. In an attempt to solve this problem, governmental authorities have established publicly-funded External Support Units (SUs) [3] that, among others, are designed to support SMEs' IM [2, 18].

The use of adequate software appears to be beneficial in the context of collaborative IM, involving both SMEs and SUs [10, 14]. Against this backdrop, scholars have proposed dedicated software concepts or implemented solutions that support collaborative IM (e.g., [1, 19, 24, 26, 33]). Those propositions often focus on providing a ready-to-use solution instance (cf. [11]). In this sense, existing software artifacts offer solutions for the practice-inspired problem of SMEs requiring IM support. However, a distinct focus on enacting design knowledge for collaborative Idea Management Systems (IMS) for SMEs that involve external supporters is seemingly rare in the literature [22]. From reviewing the literature from this and adjacent fields, only a couple of contributions stand out. For instance, scholars have presented Design Principles and requirements for DT methods [2, 16], IM processes [4, 15], DTs software tools for SMEs [10, 14], or IMS [13, 22]. Throughout those contributions, a focus on collaborative aspects and the users' roles appears underrepresented.

To address this gap, this paper proposes a set of *Design Principles prescribing the collaboration between SMEs and SUs in the context of IMS*. According to the involved roles in the envisioned IMS, the final set of Design Principles is structured into the three categories, *collaboration principles*, *SME principles*, and *SU principles*.

2   Research Method

To achieve the research objective, the Design Principles (DPs) are retrospectively derived from an *Action Design Research (ADR)* endeavor [25] along three externally supported digital innovation projects in German SMEs (see [10]). This research approach is inspired by Hönigsberg et al. [16], who have demonstrated its effectiveness in a similar context.

Following Gregor and Hevner [12], DPs are *"[n]ascent design theory–knowledge as operational [principles]"* which help in particularizing design knowledge [11]. DPs prescribe how a solution artifact can be constructed to achieve a specified goal (per principle). In this sense, they mediate the communication between researchers and potential implementers of respective IT artifacts [11].

To ensure a standardized structure, the multi-level schema for formulating DPs by Gregor et al. [11] is applied. Their proposed template is adapted and transferred to the observed practical problem space. The schema suggests that a DP for instantiation by the implementer should consist of a context, a mechanism, and a rationale for that mechanism. Here, the context is represented by the collaborative IM environment containing *"boundary conditions, implementation settings, [or] further user characteristics"* [11]. The mechanism represents the sort of *"acts, activities, processes, [...]"* [11] that need to be conducted. Each DP requires a rationale that justifies achieving the aim in a specific context through the mechanism applied.

3   Design Principles

By following the guidelines as outlined in the previous method section, we identified eleven DPs in three categories: five *collaboration principles*, three *SME principles*, and three *SU principles*. The DPs are not presented in any particular order and are considered equally important for collaborative IMS as such. The descriptive knowledge will provide the theoretical basis for the design of practical and valuable artifacts [12]. Overall, the DPs aim to prescribe the logic of the class of IMS under analysis [11]. In the following, with the term IMS, we refer to collaborative IMS involving both SMEs and SUs. The presented DPs can be instantiated as actual system features. Each category is shortly described as to what associated principles prescribe. Subsequently, containing DPs are presented in detail. For each DP, a condensed aim is presented in Tables 1, 2 and 3.

DPs of the cluster *collaboration principles* capture how a system should support the interaction between SMEs and SUs in the context of IM. That is, these principles prescribe necessary system mechanisms that enable collaboration between SMEs and SUs while taking the differences between their roles and responsibilities into consideration (see Table 1). Contrary, *SME principles* focus solely on the demands of SMEs that are imposed on a system's design (see Table 2). In the same way, *SU principles* prescribe required system mechanisms that fulfill the requirements of SUs (see Table 3).

Collaboration Design Principles

Principle of Communication (DP$_{C1}$): An IMS must integrate effective and efficient communication mechanisms to facilitate virtual collaboration between SMEs and SUs. In many collaborative contexts, the involved parties require convenient ways to communicate, especially when performing IM activities together [21]. SMEs, for instance, may need advice for particular activities, which can be readily provided by SUs via adequate communication mechanisms. To fulfill such requirements, an IMS should integrate well-established communication features, such as instant messaging or voice calling (e.g. [13]).

Principle of Coordination (DP$_{C2}$): An IMS should address the needs for coordination between SMEs and SUs. Coordination is important whenever either of both parties requires the information or action of the other party to perform some IM task. For instance, involved SME staff may deem it necessary to conduct an idea generation workshop together with external supporters. For that, an IMS should integrate mechanisms that allow SME staff to proactively contact SU staff to coordinate planned IM activities (e.g. [13]). The possibility for SMEs to reach out to SUs could diminish potential concerns of SMEs to collaborate with external supporters [17].

Principle of Convenience (DP$_{C3}$): Regardless of IM-related matters, an IMS should be perceived as convenient by its users. The differences and peculiar needs of SMEs and SUs should be reflected in the IMS and its features (e.g. [13]). This is essential to emphasize the intended role of both parties and improve their understanding of the system's purpose. For instance, SMEs require an IMS to integrate mechanisms that convey a sense of comfort and safety as SMEs open their organizational boundaries for external supporters [17].

Principle of Variable Guidance (DP$_{C4}$): An IMS should allow its users to control for the degree of guidance provided by the system when engaging in system-supported collaboration activities. In other words, SMEs and SUs should be able to choose from different system modes, which reflect their collaboration as it happens in on-site settings (e.g. [13]). This principle emerges from the importance of perceiving an IMS as an Information System. In this sense, an IMS is meant to support the performance of tasks for concerned actors [29]. Here, those tasks are IM activities in collaborative settings, which may differ with regard to the degree of guidance provided by SUs.

Principle of Role Differentiation (DP$_{C5}$): The unique setting of the focused class of IMS is characterized by the involvement of SMEs and SUs as two distinct roles. Correspondingly, a system of that class should reflect the differences of these roles. To achieve that, an IMS should embed role-related differences into the various system features [7,13]. For instance, system components could be instantiated so that both SMEs and SUs have different views or permissions. Through such role-specific system differences, users should be supported in the fulfillment of their tasks.

Table 1. Overview of Collaboration Design Principles (DPs)

Design Principle	Aim
DP$_{C1}$ – Principle of Communication	Allow for effective and efficient communication between SMEs and SUs
DP$_{C2}$ – Principle of Coordination	Allow for effective and efficient coordination between SMEs and SUs
DP$_{C3}$ – Principle of Convenience	Enable for SMEs and SUs to perceive the usefulness of the IMS beyond IM-related matters
DP$_{C4}$ – Principle of Variable Guidance	Allow for SMEs and SUs to control the degree of guidance provided by an IMS
DP$_{C5}$ – Principle of Role Differentiation	Allow for users to clearly distinguish their roles

SME-related Design Principles

Principle of Self-directed Usage (DP$_{SME1}$): While the intended class of IMS shall support collaboration, such systems must also ensure to be used in a non-collaborative, self-directed manner by SMEs to implement IM. Support provided by SUs is planned and time-limited [2]. Therefore, an IMS should be built in a way that its features support IM for SMEs regardless of the involvement of SUs. Correspondingly, features need to be easily understandable and self-explanatory, e.g., through the integration of user guides.

Principle of Organizational Integration (DP$_{SME2}$): For an IMS to leverage IM performance for SMEs in the long term, it must be integrated into the particular organizational context. For that, an IMS needs to integrate mechanisms that ensure, among others, easy accessibility and degrees of customizability to an SME's preferences. Furthermore, such an IMS needs to have a clearly defined scope as to which business tasks it supports and which it does not [29]. On the contrary, if a system disregards those aspects, its overall value for improving SMEs' IM activities is diminished.

Principle of Ownership (DP$_{SME3}$): In the context of collaborative IM, SMEs are put into a position that requires them to share sensitive information with external supporters. This setting, however, can lead to SMEs having concerns about the effectiveness and efficiency of external IM support [17]. In other words, SMEs may question the permanent collaborative setting facilitated by such an IMS. Thus, an IMS should embed mechanisms that aim to convey a sense of ownership and control for SMEs in those collaborative contexts. For instance, an IMS could treat external supporters as IM advisors whose access to a confined company space and involvement in IM is governed by the SME.

Table 2. Overview of SME-related Design Principles (DPs)

Design Principle	Aim
DP$_{SME1}$ – Principles of Self-directed Usage	Facilitate for SMEs to continuously use the IMS in a self-directed fashion
DP$_{SME2}$ – Principle of Organizational Integration	Facilitate for SMEs to integrate the IMS into their current system landscape and daily organizational routines
DP$_{SME3}$ – Principle of Ownership	Achieve for SMEs to perceive a sense of ownership and system control

SU-related Design Principles

Principle of Intervention Support (DP$_{SU1}$): An IMS must not only provide value for involved SMEs but also for SUs. In their standard on-site environment, SUs act as IM facilitators and follow an intervention-based approach [2,6]. A virtual system environment needs to allow SUs to perform their role as usual. For that, an IMS must provide mechanisms that support known interventions formats (e.g., workshops) and prescribe dedicated intervention points (e.g., provision of recommendations).

Principle of Onboarding Support (DP$_{SU2}$): Despite the professional knowledge of SUs to support IM, new SME contexts require an understanding of the initial situation. In fact, a solid understanding of an SME's situation is a prerequisite for SUs to provide adequate IM support [2]. For that, IMS must integrate features that support the onboarding of SUs in new SME contexts. More specifically, those features should help SUs acquire an understanding of, e.g., company goals, business models, or prevalent challenges.

Principle of Administration Support (DP$_{SU3}$): In addition to providing IM support for SMEs, SUs are usually obligated to fulfill certain administrative duties. For instance, when SUs are publicly-funded, the funding initiative might request reports and proof about performed activities. For that, an IMS must feature mechanisms that support SUs in their administrative work, e.g., automatically generating export-ready reports from workshops.

Table 3. Overview of SU-related Design Principles (DPs)

Design Principle	Aim
DP$_{SU1}$ – Principles of Intervention Support	Enable for SUs to implement effective and efficient interventions
DP$_{SU2}$ – Principle of Onboarding Support	Enable for SUs to readily begin with providing IM support by integrating effective onboarding mechanisms
DP$_{SU3}$ – Principle of Administration Support	Enable for SUs to fulfill their tasks and responsibilities in terms of administrative work

4   Conclusion

One success factor for DT in SMEs is to perform IM in a structured manner. However, SMEs often perform such activities rather on an ad hoc basis. Information Systems may support IM in such contexts, but respective instance solutions [11] tailored to the needs of SMEs are still missing.

Thus, in this paper, we derive eleven DPs based on a retrospective analysis of a former ADR endeavor. The DPs prescribe collaborative aspects of corresponding IMS for SMEs. In particular, the proposed DPs inform the design of IMS that involve SUs to facilitate IM in SMEs.

Scholars gain a better understanding of collaboration potentials for IM in an SME context. The DPs shed light on how SUs can be integrated into IM-related activities in SMEs. Moreover, the DPs may help practitioners, i.e., SMEs as well as SUs, to better understand the collaboration with their respective counterparts, leading to better informed DT initiatives. Finally, we hope that the proposed design knowledge motivates further research on the elaborated phenomenon as well as helps researchers and practitioners provide corresponding IT support.

References

1. Baez, M., Convertino, G.: Innovation cockpit: a dashboard for facilitators in idea management. In: Proceedings of the 2017 ACM Conference on Computer Supported Cooperative Work and Social Computing, CSCW, pp. 47–48 (2012)
2. Barann, B., Hermann, A., Cordes, A.K., Chasin, F., Becker, J.: Supporting digital transformation in small and medium-sized enterprises: a procedure model involving publicly funded support units. In: Proceedings of the 52nd Hawaii International Conference on System Sciences, pp. 4977–4986. Wailea, HI (2019)
3. Barthel, P.: What is Meant by Digital Transformation Success? Investigating the Notion in IS Literature. In: Proceedings of the 16th International Conference Wirtschaftsinformatik (WI 2021), pp. 167–182 (2021)
4. Boeddrich, H.J.: Ideas in the workplace: a new approach towards organizing the fuzzy front end of the innovation process. Creat. Innov. Manag. **13**(4), 274–285 (2004)
5. Brunswicker, S., Ehrenmann, F.: Managing open innovation in SMEs: a good practice example of a german software firm. Int. J. Ind. Eng. Manag. **4**(1), 33–41 (2013)
6. Chrisman, J.J., McMullan, W.E.: A preliminary assessment of outsider assistance as a knowledge resource: the longer-term impact of new venture counseling. Entrep. Theory Pr. **24**(3), 37–53 (2000)
7. Ebel, P., Bretschneider, U., Leimeister, J.M.: Leveraging virtual business model innovation: a framework for designing business model development tools. Inf. Syst. J. **26**(5), 519–550 (2016)
8. Gerlach, S., Brem, A.: Idea management revisited: a review of the literature and guide for implementation. Int. J. Innov. Stud. **1**(2), 144–161 (2017)
9. Goerzig, D., Bauernhansl, T.: Enterprise architectures for the digital transformation in small and medium-sized enterprises. Procedia CIRP **67**, 540–545 (2018)
10. Gollhardt, T., Hermann, A., Cordes, A.K., Barann, B., Kruse, P.: Design of a software tool supporting orientation in the context of digital transformation. In: Proceedings of 55th Hawaii International Conference on System Science (HICSS 2022), pp. 4859–4868. Maui, HI [virtual conference] (2022)
11. Gregor, S., Chandra Kruse, L., Seidel, S.: Research perspectives: the anatomy of a design principle. J. Assoc. Inf. Syst. **21**(6), 1622–1652 (2020)
12. Gregor, S., Hevner, A.R.: Positioning and presenting design science research for maximum impact. MIS Q. **37**(2), 337–355 (2013)
13. Hermann, A.: Design and implementation of a collaborative idea evaluation system. In: 24th International Conference on Human-Computer Interaction (HCII 2022) (2022)
14. Hermann, A., Gollhardt, T., Cordes, A.K., Kruse, P.: PlanDigital: a software tool supporting the digital transformation. In: Chandra Kruse, L., Seidel, S., Hausvik, G.I. (eds.) 16th International Conference on Design Science Research in Information Systems and Technology (DESRIST 2021), pp. 356–361. Kristiansand, Norway [hybrid conference] (2021)
15. Herrmann, T., Binz, H., Roth, D.: Necessary extension of conventional idea processes by means of a method for the identification of radical product ideas. In: Proceedings of International Conference on Engineering Design ICED, vol. 8 (2017)
16. Hönigsberg, S., Dias, M., Dinter, B.: Design principles for digital transformation in traditional SMEs - an antipodean comparison. In: Chandra Kruse, L., Seidel, S., Hausvik, G.I. (eds.) DESRIST 2021. LNCS, vol. 12807, pp. 375–386. Springer, Cham (2021). https://doi.org/10.1007/978-3-030-82405-1_36

17. Mole, K., North, D., Baldock, R.: Which SMEs seek external support? Business characteristics, management Behaviour and external influences in a contingency approach. Environ. Plan. C Gov. Policy **35**(3), 476–499 (2017)
18. Müller, E., Hopf, H.: Competence center for the digital transformation in small and medium-sized enterprises. In: FAIM 2017–27th International Conference. Flexible Automation and Intelligent Manufacturing, vol. 11, pp. 1495–1500. Modena, Italy (2017)
19. Murah, M.Z., Abdullah, Z., Hassan, R., Bakar, M.A., Mohamed, I., Amin, H.M.: Kacang cerdik: a conceptual design of an idea management system. Int. Educ. Stud. **6**(6), 178–184 (2013)
20. Orji, C.I.: Digital business transformation: towards an integrated capability framework for digitization and business value generation. J. Glob. Bus. Technol. **15**(1), 47–57 (2019)
21. Price, M.: Scientists discover upsides of virtual meetings. Science **368**(6490), 457–458 (2020)
22. Reibenspiess, V., Drechsler, K., Eckhardt, A., Wagner, H.T.: Tapping into the wealth of employees' ideas: design principles for a digital intrapreneurship platform. Inf. Manag. **59**(3) (2020)
23. Reis, J., Amorim, M., Melão, N., Matos, P.: Digital transformation: a literature review and guidelines for future research. In: Rocha, Á., Adeli, H., Reis, L.P., Costanzo, S. (eds.) WorldCIST'18 2018. AISC, vol. 745, pp. 411–421. Springer, Cham (2018). https://doi.org/10.1007/978-3-319-77703-0_41
24. Röltgen, A.T., Bernardy, V., Müller, R., Antoni, C.H.: Entwicklung, Einsatz und Evaluation eines Tools für digitales Ideenmanagement. Ein Fallbeispiel Anna. Grup. Interaktion. Organ. Zeitschrift fur Angew. Organ. **51**(1), 49–58 (2020)
25. Sein, H.: Purao, Rossi, lindgren: action design research. MIS Q. **35**(1), 37–56 (2011)
26. Sint, R., Markus, M., Schaffert, S., Kurz, T.: Ideator - A collaborative enterprise idea management tool powered by KiWi? In: CEUR Workshop Proceedings, vol. 632, pp. 41–48 (2010)
27. Soluk, J., Kammerlander, N.: Digital transformation in family-owned Mittelstand firms: a dynamic capabilities perspective. Eur. J. Inf. Syst. **30**(6), 676–711 (2021)
28. Stevanovic, M., Marjanović, D., Štorga, M.: A model of idea evaluation and selection for product innovation. In: Proceedings of the 20th International Conference on Engineering Design (ICED 15), pp. 193–202 (2015)
29. Teubner, R.A.: Organisations- und Informationssystemgestaltung. Deutscher Universitätsverlag (1999)
30. Tiwari, R.: The early phases of innovation: opportunities and challenges of public private partnership. Asia Pacific Tech Monit. **24**(1), 32–37 (2007)
31. Van Goolen, R., Evers, H., Lammens, C.: International innovation labs: an innovation meeting ground between SMES and business schools. Procedia Econ. Financ. **12**, 184–190 (2014)
32. Wagner, S., Bican, P.M., Brem, A.: Critical success factors in the front end of innovation: results from an empirical study. Int. J. Innov. Manag. **25**(04), 2150046 (2021)
33. Westerski, A., Iglesias, C.A., Nagle, T.: The road from community ideas to organisational innovation: a life cycle survey of idea management systems. Int. J. Web Based Commun. **7**(4), 493–506 (2011)

Human Interface and Competitive Intelligence in Management of Business Science Teaching Research

César Eduardo Jiménez-Calderón$^{(\boxtimes)}$ (ID), Petronila Liliana Mairena-Fox (ID), and Giancarlo Mariano Mancarella-Valladares (ID)

César Vallejo University, Lima, Peru
cesarjimenez.investigacion@gmail.com

Abstract. The development of a competitive intelligence plan facilitates the management of a research group. Complementarily, the design of an organizational structure for the management of teaching research in business sciences not only facilitates the integration of researchers to scientific production, but also the organization of their own finances, marketing, and the dynamics of the staff. The aim of the study is to draft a system to be implemented based on human interface and competitive intelligence that leads to the management of business science research in higher education, Lima, Peru. Every dimension of the draft will be discussed through the descriptive comparative method between the statements and the evidence from the research group practice. The presentation language from a computer to a human being and the action language from him to a computer will be measured as fulfilled hypotheses on a Likert Scale to construct an analytical road map to make decisions. In conclusion, the development of a competitive intelligence plan in the administration of teaching research, combined with the design of the organizational structure, will allow the staff create a management control model for a research group in business sciences in Lima.

Keywords: Management · Competitive intelligence · Human interface device

1 Organizational Purpose and Scope

1.1 Aims

The research group has a clear definition of its aims and goals and plans the academic, scientific, and economic management of its program [1].

Indicator. The device presents a consistent list of aims aligned with the research group mission and projects (Yes. /No.). The user answers the questions about the process of achieved goals (strongly disagree, disagree, neither agree nor disagree, agree, strongly agree).

1.2 Profile

The research group demonstrates its ability to comply with its regulations, obligations, and scientific offer [2].

Indicator. The device presents the regulations that regulate the act of the teaching, technical and administrative staff (Yes. /No.). The user answers the questions about the process of achieved regulations and interests (strongly disagree, disagree, neither agree nor disagree, agree, strongly agree).

1.3 Accountability

The information (scientific, administrative, and financial) that is disseminated about the projects is specific, timely and faithful to its reality [3].

Indicator. The device presents reliable information related to the project execution, properly registered and including mechanisms of feedback (Yes. /No.). The user answers whether the information is timely available to the public to correct possible errors in the records (strongly disagree, disagree, neither agree nor disagree, agree, strongly agree).

2 Organizational Substructure

2.1 Staff

The research group has sufficient and suitable scientific staff to fully comply with all planned activities towards the achievement of the researcher profile [4].

Indicator. The device presents the profiles of qualified and competent researchers (Yes. /No.). The user assesses the disciplines and research training of staff as appropri-ate (strongly disagree, disagree, neither agree nor disagree, agree, strongly agree).

2.2 Finance

The research group has financial resources for projects and provision [5].

Indicator. The device presents total resources available per project (Yes/No). The user evaluates the budget and follow up (strongly disagree, disagree, neither agree nor disagree, agree, strongly agree).

2.3 Scientific Production

The research group encourages its researchers to publish scientific papers with positive impact on society, economy, and environment [6].

Indicator. The device publishes or exhibits scientific works and methodologies in achieving the profile of staff (Yes/No). The user assesses the impact of research works (strongly disagree, disagree, neither agree nor disagree, agree, strongly agree).

Indicator. The device presents scientific materials that will contribute to the scientific program (Yes/No). The user evaluates the materials and transcendence of them (strongly disagree, disagree, neither agree nor disagree, agree, strongly agree).

Indicator. The device presents basic research articles, research materials and book chapters from staff (Yes/No). The user perceives the utility of research materials (strongly disagree, disagree, neither agree nor disagree, agree, strongly agree).

Indicator. The device presents applications related to new technologies or processes (Yes/No). The user judges new work methods to impact society (strongly disagree, disagree, neither agree nor disagree, agree, strongly agree).

2.4 Marketing

The research group is challenged to meet the demands and needs of consumers in a highly digitized world, where technology is present in almost every aspect of their lives [7].

Indicator. The device presents relations with centers, groups, networks, or programs dedicated to research in the disciplinary field (Yes/No). The user validates the use-fulness of research group relationships (strongly disagree, disagree, neither agree nor disagree, agree, strongly agree).

3 Linking Competitive Intelligence

3.1 Environmental Surveillance

The research group focuses its study on environmental topics that make up the framework of competition.

Indicator. The device presents a list of activities that the organization carries out related to environmental actions (Yes/No). The user evaluates the environmental conditions and impact of research group actions (strongly disagree, disagree, neither agree nor disagree, agree, strongly agree).

3.2 Business Surveillance

The research group promotes transparency as well as equal trading rules [8].

Indicator. The device presents project beneficiaries (Yes/No). The user evaluates business transparency and equity (strongly disagree, disagree, neither agree nor disagree, agree, strongly agree).

3.3 Competitive Surveillance

The research group analysis and monitors current and potential competitors and those substitute products.

Indicator. The device presents data to configurate the strategy of research projects (Yes/No). The user evaluates the quality of data and projects (strongly disagree, dis-agree, neither agree nor disagree, agree, strongly agree).

3.4 Technology Surveillance

The research group monitors the state-of-the-art update for positioning projects and opportunities.

Indicator. The device presents captured information from outside / inside organization on science and technology (Yes/No). The user converts useful information into knowledge to diminish risk and increase changes (strongly disagree, disagree, neither agree nor disagree, agree, strongly agree).

4 Outcomes, Quality Management and Competitiveness

4.1 Outcome Impact

The research group records the scientific performance and progress of its members.

Indicator. The device presents important results from actions and projects on society, science, and technology (Yes/No). The user evaluates the information available for the design and implementation of continuous improvement actions (strongly disagree, disagree, neither agree nor disagree, agree, strongly agree).

4.2 Quality Management

The research group has a self-assessment process with the participation of internal and external core informants. The self-assessment report is known by stakeholders and community [9].

Indicator. The device presents the reached goals and gaps established within the development quality plan of staff (Yes/No). The user assesses the quality of research provided by staff to community (strongly disagree, disagree, neither agree nor disagree, agree, strongly agree).

4.3 Competitiveness

The research group determines actions, facts and evidence based on current or prospective strategies about industry and competitors, considering the evaluation criteria issued by accreditation [10].

Indicator. The device presents appropriate facts and improvement items for competitiveness status (Yes/No). The user identifies the responsible parties, risks, and opportunities of the research projects (strongly disagree, disagree, neither agree nor disagree, agree, strongly agree).

References

1. Takebayashi, Y., Doi, M.: Multimodal human computer interaction research at Toshiba research and development center. In: Conference on Human Factors in Computing Systems - Proceedings, pp. 79–80. Association for Computing Machinery, Atlanta (1997)
2. Tarrayo, V.N., Hernandez, P.J.S., Claustro, J.M.A.S.: Research engagement by English language teachers in a Philippine University: insights from a qualitative study. Asia Pac. Soc. Sci. Rev. **21**(3), 74–85 (2021)
3. Samsonova-Taddei, A., Turley, W.S.: Accountability in an independent regulatory setting: the use of impact assessment in the regulation of financial reporting in the UK. J. Bus. Ethics **155**(4), 1053–1076 (2017). https://doi.org/10.1007/s10551-017-3527-1
4. Kekäle, J.: Proactive strategic recruitment in research groups. Tert. Educ. Manag. **24**(2), 144–153 (2017). https://doi.org/10.1080/13583883.2017.1407439
5. Souza, T.A., Antunes, L.G.R., Azevedo, A.S., Angélico, G.O., Zambalde, A.L.: Innovative performance of Brazilian public higher educational institutions: analysis of the remuneration of research groups and companies. Innov. Manag. Rev. **16**(4), 323–343 (2019)
6. Castro Maldonado, J.J., Patiño Murillo, J.A., Gómez López, C.: Procesos de I+D+i en el Centro de Servicios y Gestión Empresarial del Servicio Nacional de Aprendizaje SENA 2015–2017. Espacios **39**(20), 21–27 (2018)
7. Castro, M.V.M., de Araújo, M.L., Ribeiro, A.M., Demo, G., Meneses, P.P.M.: Implementation of strategic human resource management practices: a review of the national scientific production and new research paths. Revista de Gestao, **27**(3), 229–246 (2020)
8. Galindo-Melero, J., Sanz-Angulo, P., De-Benito-Martín, J.J.: Need to establish a methodological philosophy of Competitive Intelligence in SMEs and research groups based on patent analysis. In: 9th Iberian Conference on Information Systems and Technologies (CISTI), pp. 1–6. Association for Computing Machinery, Spain (2014)
9. Sahu, A.K., Kumar, A., Sahu, A.K., Sahu, N.K.: Need to establish a methodological philosophy of competitive intelligence in SMEs and research groups based on patent analysis. TQM J. ahead-of-print No. ahead-of-print (2020)
10. Thyagaraju, P.H., Momaya, K.S.: Flow of spin-off technologies from Bhabha atomic research Centre: A technology management perspective. In: 28th International Conference for the International Association of Management of Technology. IAMOT, pp. 317–326. Excel India Publishers, Mumbai (2019)

Risk Training Tool on Structured Knowledge for Risk Management

Noriyuki Kushiro[1] and Toshihiro Mega[1,2(✉)]

[1] Kyushu Institute of Technology, Iizuka Fukuoka 820-8502, Japan
[2] Mitsubishi Electric Building Solutions, Arakawa Tokyo 116-0002, Japan
kushiro@mx1.ttcn.ne.jp

Abstract. In this paper, fundamental issues with legacy risk trainings for occupational accidents were discussed on the results of experiments for totally 22 actual field supervisors. The risk training tool was proposed to solve the fundamental issues and applied to 7 field supervisors to validate effectiveness of trainings. As a result, we confirmed that the training tool was succeeded in teaching structured knowledge and procedural knowledge required for field supervisors.

Keywords: Risk training tool · Knowledge structure for risk recognition · Tool for extracting latent knowledge · Tool for visualizing structure of knowledge

1 Introduction

Approximately, 130 thousand workers have been exposed to serious occupational accidents every year in Japan [1]. To prevent occupational accidents, almost every company provides "work procedure manual" and conduct "risk perceiving training" regularly to all the workers. Nevertheless, the number of occupational accidents are increasing [1]. We suspect that there are fundamental issues with current risk trainings.

At the first step of the study, the fundamental issues with legacy risk training were clarified through experiments for 22 actual field supervisors. To fulfill the experiments, a tool for promoting verbalization of latent knowledge with eye tracking sensor, and a tool for visualizing logical structure of risk knowledge involved in field supervisors' utterances with natural language processing technique were developed (Sect. 2).

At the second step, a new risk training tool with VR technology was proposed to solve the issues, and the tool was applied to risk trainings for 7 field supervisors to estimate effectiveness of the training tool (Sect. 3).

2 Issues with Legacy Risk Trainings

The following two kinds of risk trainings were conducted regularly to prevent occupational accidents in most companies:

C. Stephanidis et al. (Eds.): HCII 2022, CCIS 1655, pp. 278–285, 2022.
https://doi.org/10.1007/978-3-031-19682-9_37

- Periodic review on "work procedure manual", which contains proper instructions for typical tasks, and dos and don'ts lists
- Regularly training on "risk perception training", like "KYT (Japan)" and "JSA (USA)" etc., which utilizes an illustration containing risk scenes as a training material.

The following tools were developed to clarify fundamental issues with the legacy risk trainings experimentally:

- A Tool for eliciting risk knowledge from workers with eye tracking sensor
- A Tool for visualizing structure of risk knowledge with natural language processing techniques

2.1 Tools for Clarifying Issues with Legacy Risk Trainings

Overviews of the tools to extract latent risk knowledge from workers are explained in the sections.

Tool for Eliciting Risk Knowledge with Eye Tracking Sensor [6,7]. Knowledge for risk perception is regarded as a kind of tacit dimension of knowledge [2], so that the workers felt difficulties to verbalize their own knowledge explicitly without help. The tool to promote verbalization of worker's knowledge was indispensable to conduct the examinations. The compositions and functions of the tool are illustrated in Fig. 1. The tool is composed of a PC, an eye tracking sensor, a motion sensor, a monitor, and a head mount display. The PC provides training videos, including 360∘ multi-view video, both in the monitor and in the head mount display. The eye tracking sensor accumulated trainee's trajectory of eyes, and the motion sensor also preserved trainee's utterances during training. The transitions of eyes and gazed objects are presented to the trainee after their trainings, so as to facilitate verbalization of risk knowledge by explaining reasons for their own eye movements and transition of gazing objects during training.

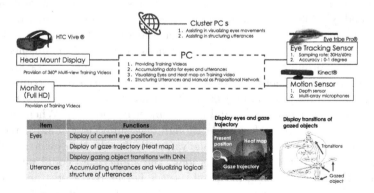

Fig. 1. Tool for eliciting risk knowledge from workers with eye tracking sensor

Tool for Visualizing Structure of Risk Knowledge with Natural Language Processing Techniques. [8,9] The tool for visualizing logical structure of risk knowledge was developed to clarify which kinds of knowledge is essential to decrease occupational risks. Furthermore, indexes of risk skills were defined on the results of visualization. Algorithms for identifying logical structure in texts were implemented with natural language processing techniques (Fig. 2).

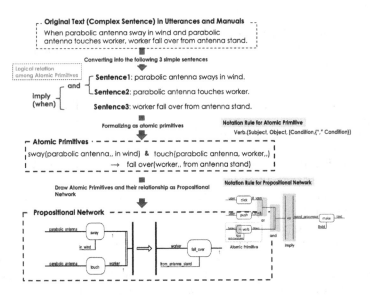

Fig. 2. Tool for visualizing structure of risk knowledge

Texts, containing compound and complex sentences, are divided into simple sentences, and each sentence is formalized as an atomic primitive [3] on "cases" and "cases frame", extracted through the analysis with parsers, e.g. Stanza [4] in English, and KNP [5] in Japanese. Simultaneously, the tool also identifies logical relations among atomic primitives based on the rules, which were established through authors' surveying features of sentences in technical documents [10].

The atomic primitives are regarded as basic components of risk knowledge and the propositional network, in which atomic primitives are connected by logical relations: and, or and imply etc., is regarded as field supervisors, reasoning process behind their perception and management of the risks. When the width of the propositional network is wide enough, the supervisor could detect risks from a variety of events, and could take various risk reduction behaviors for the risks. When the length of network is long, the supervisors could perceive the risks from the former events, and could select better risk-averse behaviors for the risks. The width and length of the propositional network could be utilized as indicators of capability of risk perception and management.

2.2   Issues with Legacy Risk Training

As a result of experiments for 22 actual field supervisors, the following issues were confirmed through the examinations [7]:

1. Risk knowledge of experts (skilled field supervisor) has an unique structure composed of 5 elements (Fig. 3), and the procedure of risk assessment is constrained strongly by the structure of their knowledge
2. As the structured risk knowledge is distributed widely along spatial and in temporal axes in video, the illustrations used in legacy risk perception training (KYT or JSA) has limits to express risk knowledge dispersed widely
3. For preventing the accidents, primary role of filed supervisors is to detect omens increasing probability of risks and impediments scenarios. However, the legacy manual is devoted to describe risks and risk reduction behaviors, not to mention the omens increasing the probability of the risks

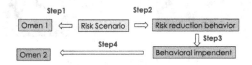

Fig. 3. Logical structure for risk perception and management

3   Proposal for Risk Training Tool Based on Issues

A risk training tool was designed to solve the issues.

3.1   Risk Training Tool on Structured Knowledge

The following concepts were set for a risk training tool on the issues:

1. To learn structured risk knowledge composed of 5 elements (Fig. 3)
2. To learn domain knowledge and meta-knowledge (procedural knowledge) for risk perception and management concurrently
3. To learn risk knowledge heuristically along with the reason why to do so, so as to be applied the acquired knowledge in practice

Based on the concepts, we designed and implemented a risk training tool with the following two learning modes (Fig. 4):

1. Risk knowledge discovery mode (Mode1)
   - Risk knowledge uttered by the trainees is placed on 360o panoramic moving picture as an annotation with voice recognition technology
   - VR technology allows the trainees to move freely to the point where they want to look, and makes it possible to train tasks in narrow space
2. Risk knowledge structuring mode (Mode2) (Fig. 5)
   - Risk knowledge annotated during Mode1 allocates onto the risk knowledge structure with "reasons" why they should do them
   - Samples of risk knowledge in the manual and in experts, are stored in the tool and reused to compensate missing knowledge of trainees

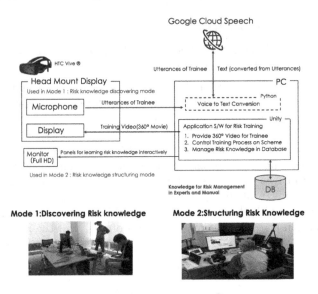

Fig. 4. Risk training tool

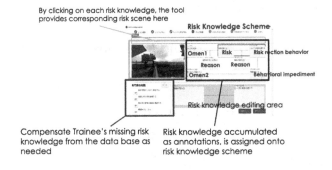

Fig. 5. Panel for risk knowledge structuring mode

3.2 Effectiveness of Risk Training with Proposed Tool

The experiments to validate effectiveness of the proposed tool were conducted on the following steps for 7 field supervisors:

Step1: Each trainee was trained on the legacy risk training method with the illustration (**KYT1**)

Step2: Each trainee was trained on the proposed risk training tool

Step3:: Each trainee was trained again on legacy risk training method with the illustration, which contained same risks and objects in KYT1 (**KYT2**)

By comparing the results of trainings on KYT1 and 2, the effectiveness of risk training on the proposed risk training tool was validated. Capability of risk perception and management for each trainee was scored with the following

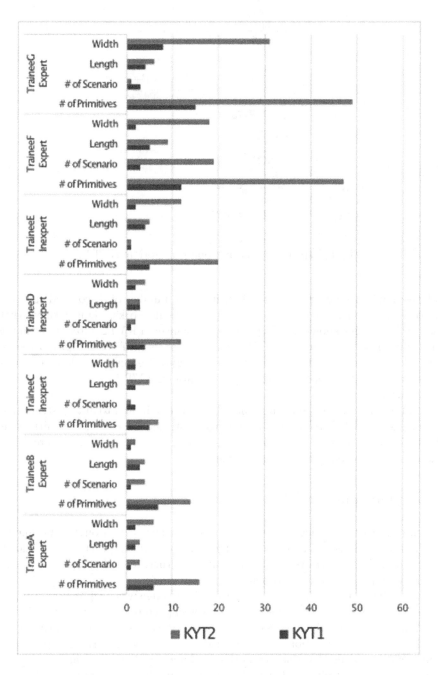

Fig. 6. Effectiveness of training on proposed risk training tool

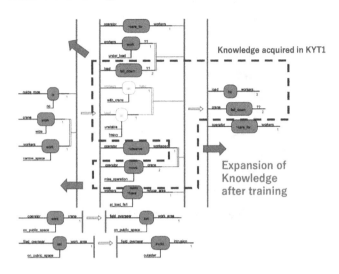

Fig. 7. Expansion of propositional network in KYT2

indexes: number on extracted atomic primitives, number of discovered risk scenario, maximum length and width of propositional networks. Figure 6 shows that the number of risk knowledge increased significantly in KYT2, after the training on the proposed training tool. The "length" and "width" of the propositional network also increased for almost trainees. Figure 7 is an example of propositional networks for risk knowledge elicited through KYT 1 and 2 of the trainee A (expert).

On these results, we confirmed that the tool contributed to obtain structured knowledge for risk perception and management, and we can also confirm that the tool was succeeded in providing procedural knowledge for risk perception and management besides domain knowledge.

4   Conclusion

Fundamental issues in legacy risk trainings were clarified through experiments for 22 field supervisors in the study. The tools for eliciting practical risk knowledge from field supervisors and for visualizing structure of risk knowledge were developed for the above experiments.

The risk training tool on structured risk knowledge was proposed and implemented to solve the above issues. The tool was applied to risk trainings for 7 field supervisors and the effectiveness of risk training was estimated quantitatively. As the results of evaluation, we confirmed that the tool contributed to obtain structured knowledge for risk perception and management. In near feature, the proposed training tool is going to be brushed up through applications to risk training in actual field.

References

1. Labor Ministry of Health and Welfare in Japan: Occupational Accidents Incident (2022)   https://www.mhlw.go.jp/bunya/roudoukijun/anzeneisei11/rousaihassei/. Accessed 20 May 2022
2. Polanyi M.: Tacit Dimension, Reissue edn. University of Chicago Press, Chicago (2009)
3. Rolland, C., Achour, C.B.: Guiding the construction of textual use case specifications, Data Knowl. Eng. **25**(12), 125160 (1998)
4. Manning, C.D., Surdeanu, M., Bauer, J., Finkel, J., Bethard, S.J., McClosky, D.: The stanford CoreNLP natural language processing toolkit in Association for Computational Linguistics (ACL) system demonstrations, In: Proceedings of 52nd Annual Meeting of the Association for Computational Linguistics: System Demonstrations, pp. 55–60 (2014)
5. Kawahara, D. and Kurohashi, S.: A fully-lexicalized probabilistic model for Japanese syntactic and case structure analysis, In: Human Language Technology Conference of the North American Chapter of the Association of Computational Linguistics, Association for Computational Linguistics. pp. 176–183 (2006)
6. Kushiro, N., Nishinaga, K., Mega, T.: Training Tool on Structured Knowledge for Risk Management with VR Technology, HCI International 2021, Springer, Cham, pp. 262–281 (2021). https://doi.org/10.1007/978-3-030-90963-5_21
7. Kushiro, N., Aoyama, Y., Mega, T.: Extracting and structuring latent knowledge for risk recognition from eyes and utterances of field overseers. In: Stephanidis, C., Duffy, V.G., Streitz, N., Konomi, S., Krömker, H. (eds.) HCII 2020. LNCS, vol. 12429, pp. 509–528. Springer, Cham (2020). https://doi.org/10.1007/978-3-030-59987-4_36
8. Kushiro, N., Ogata, Y.: Supporting test case design on reasoning scheme with natural language processing technique, In: 2021 IEEE International Conference on Big Data (Big Data), pp. 3472–3479 (2021). https://doi.org/10.1109/BigData52589.2021.9671718
9. Kushiro, N., Ogata, Y., Aoyama, Y.: Visualizing schemes and logics among sentences in paragraph. In: 25th International Conference on Knowledge-Based and Intelligent Information & Engineering System, Procedia Computer Science, vol. 192, pp. 3030-3039 (2021). https://doi.org/10.1016/j.procs.2021.09.075
10. Aoyama, Y., Kuroiwa, T., Kushiro, N.: Executable test case generation from specifications written in natural language and test execution environment. In: 2021 IEEE 18th Annual Consumer Communications and Networking Conference(CCNC), pp. 1–6 (2021)

Chrono-Spatialism. Introducing a Time-Based Approach for Retail Space Design in the Digitalized Scenario

Yuemei Ma[(⊠)] 🆔 and Anna Barbara 🆔

Politecnico di Milano, 20158 Durando 10, Milan, Italy
Yuemei.ma@polimi.it

Abstract. In the future the important criterion to evaluate market participants, will be the proportion of its products and services in 24 h a day of consumers [1]. Thanks to the media and digital revolution, time became portable and elastic, a temporal form Agger (2011) designated as iTime. And in a culture dominated by the use of smartphones, iTime dissolved the boundaries between day and night, work and leisure, and space and time [2]. As retail activities become more accessible at any time and from any location, and as omni-channel retailing disrupts retail stores' monopoly on shopping activities, brick and mortar retailers face the threat of online shopping and must transform in this context. Within the theory of urbanism, the concept of chrono-urbanism is proposed as a key step to question in depth our lifestyles, production and consumption, to be aware of the existing dissociation between space and time. From the perspective of sociology and design disciplines, a time-based design approach proposes a response to this phenomenon, where interior design could no longer be the same as before, because the fluidity of time would have reshaped the space. By extension, it might also be thought of as chrono-spatialism when considering the design of time in interior spaces. This paper explores the temporality, proximity and engagement of human-centered approaches to retail store design in the digitized scenario through the lens of urbanism, marketing, interior and service design. This study utilizes literature and case studies in order to understand the impact of time, consumer shopping behavior and experience on the changing of retail spaces.

Keywords: Retail · Digitalization · Temporality · Spatial user experience · Interior design

1 Introduction

While the advent of mobile devices was celebrated for the numerous possibilities it brought in terms of communication, online trading and social class association, it has had numerous documented negative impacts on the physical retailing. Thanks to the media and digital revolution, time became portable and elastic, a temporal form Agger (2011) designated as iTime. And in a culture dominated by the use of smartphones, iTime dissolved the boundaries between day and night, work and leisure, and space and

C. Stephanidis et al. (Eds.): HCII 2022, CCIS 1655, pp. 286–295, 2022.
https://doi.org/10.1007/978-3-031-19682-9_38

time [2]. Online retailing has led to the demise of many brick-and-mortar retail stores due to its "anytime" accessibility and "anywhere" convenience that dissolves the time and space limitations of traditional retail stores.

The financial crisis, the competitive pressure of the society and the social media, which is the fruit of the new technologies of our new era, and surely the pandemic have varied the scale of priorities and values. The act of shopping in the new society is moving on a time-space axis with a somewhat easily trustable in the future. The retail system could be considered as a faithful mirror of the society. By analyzing it, it can see that they have both been in a process of slow, but continuous, transformation [3].

It is also a moment that prompted us to focus on the significance of the time variable in the spatial design of retail. While in the history of design, spatial qualities have been central in the search for techniques and tools, but temporal qualities in spatial and interior design have not been given enough attention, yet temporal qualities may be capable of deforming, compressing, reconfiguring spaces and supporting new ways of living [4].

2 Introducing Time-Based Design Approach

Many scholars [4–7] are becoming aware of the importance of considering time, spatio-temporal interactions, and its representation as a fourth dimension in urban and spatial planning and design.

The complexity of exploring the impact of time-based design on retail spaces needs to be considered from the integrated perspective of multiple disciplines. Zygmund Bauman (2007) introduced the concept of 'liquid modernity', he launched a deep reflection on the spatial-temporal morphology of places, on relationships and technologies, which is still ongoing. The rationalized control of time and space is being reimagined as the nonlinear and placeless means of decision-making, relating and exploiting in the multiple dimensions of an emerging digitized world. Where space and time were treated as differentiated in early modernity, they are dedifferentiated in a digitized modernity-as is also the case in a liquefied modernity [8].

From the perspective of urbanism, since Moreno proposed the concept of the 15-min city in 2016, which sparked discussions in other global cities, there have been emerging variations of the concept that seem to portray the same principle of "chrono-urbanism" while supporting the need for proximity-based indicators to better service urban areas. These approaches of chrono-urbanism are in line with studies underlining the importance of urban rhythms in order to understand the quality of life in cities: especially space is relevant only as it is coupled with temporal dimension [9, 10].

Although this is a larger scale space and does not seem to be applicable to theoretical systems for smaller scale spaces or interior design, the challenges posed by social media and digitalization for retail stores are not only internal but also external. Digital communication weaves an invisible network to connect each individual, which will also drive retail stores to coordinate, or complement, online retail by developing different types of stores to build offline retail networks to serve different purposes for consumers, and retailers need to analyze the purpose and function of retail store networks for cities and surrounding communities based on their location.

This leads to an important concept of proximity in spatio-temporal design. Manzini (2022) addressed in Livable Proximity to investigate the qualities of time, the kind of hybrid proximity which helps to construct communities in different dimension, a place where encounters occur in the physical world, but that could not exist if they were not supported by what happens in the digital world.

Among the external factors of retail space design, the definition of the location variables is fundamental for both the retailer and the consumer, the most important variables to take into account are the geographical location and the type of structure. The choice of the venue includes the decision about the urban location of the retail point: city center or outskirt, commercial or residential district, etc. The typology can be: stand-alone store, shop within a commercial center, and so on. Every decision involves many trades off, such as the size of the location, the occupancy cost, the customer traffic (pedestrian and vehicular) and the consequent convenience for customers, the potential restrictions placed on the location, etc.

From the point of view of spatial design, the "time-based" [11] concept was borrowed from the video and movie world because it introduces, in design, the tools for a dynamic control of form and time. From the moment Bauman introduces the concept of "liquid modernity", interior design could no longer be the same as before, because the fluidity of time would have reshaped the space as well. The spaces weren't the frame, the reference set, of human actions but instead became one of the possible media able to allow adaptability and flexibility, in a continuous flow of changes characterized by an endemic uncertainty. The revolution introduced by the smart technologies has led to a further possible scenario in the time-based design, related to the mediation, between humans and spaces, that these devices perform in acceleration, compression, time overlap. They are able to accommodate temporal and functional instances in continuous mutation within real spaces [12]. The smart technologies reshape spaces, interiors, architecture, buildings, infrastructures according to the needs, desires, environmental conditions, as well as customize experience [13].

3   Digital Influences on Retail Space Changes

In retailing, consumers' shopping behavior has grown with no more time-limited as a result of the rise of online shopping. The retail space, for instance, with the innovation of marketing events and activities, a large number of pop-up stores were emerged. Temporality, compression and instability enable retail to exist in more creative, dynamic and experimental forms. Besides, the time consumer spent in space differs greatly due to their different shopping journeys, the space design should respond to the variety based on time. Hence, the brick and mortar stores should consider consumers' shopping and the relations of time, such as entity retail shopping can get real advantage, self-service store provides 24-h convenience service, flagship store to create more experience for consumers to spend more time in the store, temporary spaces like pop-up and mobile stores, and so on. Retailers must consider what their target consumers are looking for through the experience. Thus, physical retail space should be defined by thinking about the relationship between people, products, places and time.

The search for time-based retail space design cannot be separated from the impact of digital in its implementation. In the past, the success of a store from a business perspective was measured by using the tool of "Sales per unit area [14]" to calculate the space efficiency of retail. However, advances in technology and the development of omni-channel retailing have made it possible to link shopping activities online and offline, with many retailers introducing click and collect services, a model that involves creating an order online and then picking up the product directly from the nearest physical store. With for instance of this phenomenon, the spatial value of physical retail needs to be redefined.

In terms of store time efficiency, one of the metrics of store success used to be increasing the length of time customers spent looking at displays or staying in a specific area, known as "dwell time [15]". This is believed as an essential retail metric for analyzing shopping behavior and increasing customer spending. Applications such as video sensing systems that can track people's paths through a store and the time they spend in different areas are now being used to create heat maps that show retailers and spatial designers the layout of store spaces that can be improved by calculating the time spent. In addition, online shopping offers convenience, easy payment solutions and a wider range of choices at customers' fingertips, while traditional retail represents a physical experience of products, personal service and trust. In-store shopping and online shopping have different advantages that can be enhanced by combining the two pathways through ingenious innovation. Some retailers are introducing digital, interactive gaming devices in their stores through emerging technologies such as voice user interfaces (VUIs), artificial intelligence (AI) and augmented reality (AR), for example, the Decathlon connect store in Munich is equipped with a video game unit in the retail space where customers can enter a game box and experience an immersive riding game, which the retailer uses to provide and prolong positive experience to motivate users.

In addition to extending the experience and dwell time in the store, another type of time in the store needs to be reduced, namely queuing time. According to a report by Capgemini [16], 60% of shoppers are irritated with long checkout lines, and 57% of people think long hold times are a disappointing. Some retailers are reducing consumer wait times by applying self-checkout solutions. Amazon opened its cashier-less, checkout-less store Amazon Go, Nike is using instant checkout in its House of Innovation 000 store, where consumers can install an app on their smartphones to scan a barcode or through in-store sensor to self-checkout and avoid queuing in the store. Furthermore, some retailers have chosen to place pickup lockers in or near their stores, where consumers can place orders from their digital devices anywhere and go to their nearest pickup locker to collect their orders, thereby saving roaming time in the store and waiting time at home.

In spite of the purchasing function, retail stores also have another dimension of social mission, that is to be a destination for social activities. Shopping has become a leisure activity as part of our daily life. Shopping is not only a functional activity anymore, but it has become a goal in itself with hedonic value [17]. Digital media and online retail have created communities for consumers to communicate in virtual spaces, and physical stores have become communities of activity for consumers. For instance, the Calories Department Store opened in Beijing by online fitness community Keep, through a temporary pop-up form in a department store, has designed a variety of fitness games in the store space to attract consumers from nearby communities who can win prizes by earning account points in their smartphones for their exercise performance of playing the games in the store. The value of the store space at this point is no longer the immediate consuming value, but the brand value of building a bridge between the retailer and the consumer as well as the social value of the incentive campaign.

4   Chrono-Spatialism. Time Qualities for Spatial Transformation of the Shopping Journey

The complexity of time-based retail space design in the digital scenario is that it cannot only be considered from the context of interior design theories, but also from the multi-disciplinary perspective of urbanism, sociology, experience design and service design, etc. In service design theories, a perspective of the qualities of time on the evaluation of chrono-urbanism is proposed, is that it requires developing a new vision of time: the single, accelerated time of modernity must be transformed into the plural time of the caring city; a plural time, because it does not exclude fast time, but recognizes and appreciates also, and perhaps above all, slow time [6]. Digital technologies in retail compress the waiting time for the consumers, on the other hand, it prolongs the time of their experiences. To explore the qualities of time in retail spaces, two case studies are selected: Nike House of Innovation 000 store in New York and Lululemon flagship store in Chicago.

The selection of the cases was based on several criteria. Firstly, they are stores that opened within five years, because the lifespan of most retail interiors is said to be five years or less [19]. Secondly, they are located in modern cities with regionally important retail activity. Thirdly, in each project, digital retail tools are applied. Fourthly, in each case study, we can recognize multiple temporal and experiential journeys in the same store.

Data were collected through reviewing professional publications, observing photos or watching videos of designer interviews. Borrowing the user journey map tool from experience design, we developed a spatial experience model to understand shoppers' spatio-temporal interactions in the store as a way to measure different temporal and spatial journeys in the store (see Fig. 1, 2, 3).

Case Study 1: Nike House of Innovation 000, New York
Nike House of Innovation 000 is a full-category independent flagship store with a total space of 6 floors and an area of 6,400 m^2. Start with athletes, sneaker lab, museum, immersive experience. Which located in 5th avenue street in New York. Designed by Nike team and released in November 2018.

Compared of the last generation of Nike flagship store, Nike Town, the new flagship store adopted the technology elements to establish new shopping experiences. But also, the brand has broken the tradition of dividing sports brands by categories, but by gender, dividing male and female collections into different floors to serve consumers with different aims.

Flagship store
Nike House of Innovation 000 (New york)

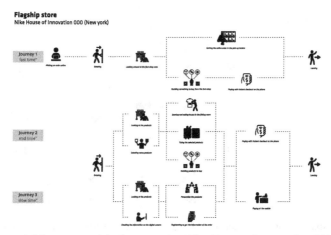

Fig. 1. Time-spatial journey model of case study: Nike House of Innovation 000, New York. Made by Yuemei Ma.

Journey 1: Fast Shopping and Pick up the Online Order in the Speed Shop

Locating in the basement, consumers can go through a dedicated entrance from the ground floor to enter the Speed Shop. The Speed Shop allows consumers to quickly select their favorite items. The brand automatically identifies local consumers' favorite products based on online sales data and displays them in this area. It allows customers to reserve products online to try on in-store. More specifically, customers can arrive in this floor to find a locker with their name on, which can be unlocked via their smartphone. This is designed for local consumers to get what they want to improve the shopping efficiency and saving time.

Journey 2: Shopping in Store

The ground floor is Nike Arena where the brand displays seasonal items and host temporary installations. There is a service desk will allow consumers to book appointments with store employees.

Above this level is designated floor for genders. In the store, outfits dressing mannequins can easily be purchased through a "Shop the Look" feature. Merchandise is fitted with a QR code for the brand members to scan with their app, either to purchase immediately or have the items sent to a fitting room to try on. Another digital aspect is the Scan & Pay, which allows app members to buy products on their phone and avoid long queues.

Journey 3: Personalization

The third and fourth floors host the Sneaker Lab and design studio, which is used for one-to-one sessions with store staff to help customers to find suitable products or provides the customization services.

Case Study 2: Lululemon Flagship Store, Chicago

Lululemon flagship store in Chicago's Lincoln Park neighborhood which was opened in 2019. Besides of merchandise, the 1860 m^2 space hosts dining area, meditation rooms and workout studios for fitness classes for the consumers in neighboring communities.

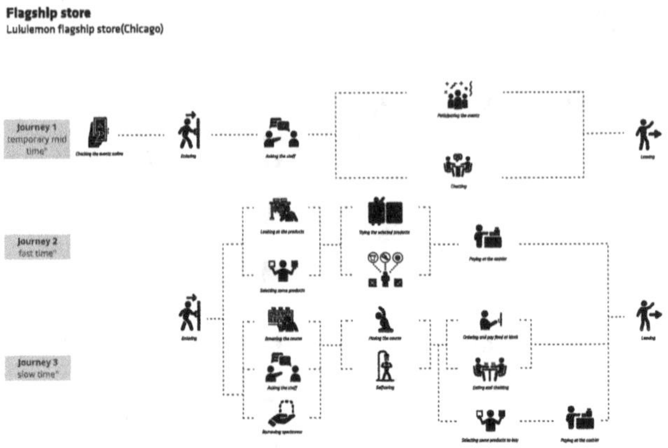

Flagship store
Lululemon flagship store(Chicago)

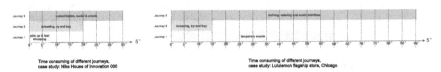

Fig. 2. Time-spatial journey model of case study: Lululemon flagship store, Chicago. Made by Yuemei Ma.

Journey 1: Shopping in Store
The shopping area is divided on the first and second floor by genders, which keeps the original function of displaying and purchasing for consumers.

Journey 2: Fitness Lessons Experience and Catering Service
The second floor also locates two workout studios and a meditation space. Additionally, the upper wing features a dining area to provide healthy food for consumers. The opening of training and catering service can be looped in with the emerging trend of retailers who are attempting to attract more customers to their stores as more and more sales continue to happen online. The restaurant features digital kiosks to reducing the waiting time of ordering and paying. The dining tables sit in front of two fitness studios. Sweaty customers can grab food immediately after classes. They'll sit on seats and couches in a space called the "connection room" which creates an area for promoting the customers' social activities and healthy lifestyle.

Journey 3: Temporary Events
The brand is also spotlighting local businesses with an area on the ground floor dedicated to a rotating cast of retailers. Movie screenings and mini- concerts will be held periodically, as the company aims to solidify its place in the community.

The experiential model has increasingly been taken on in the digital era, when companies are throwing more money behind a fusion of retail and entertainment offerings instead of just selling products.

Fig. 3. Comparing time consuming of different journeys of case studies. Made by Yuemei Ma.

By evolving hybrid experiences and different time qualities in the stores, retailers and brands are trying to redefine the value of physical retail spaces by blending experiences, communications, interactions with the consumers to build the connections and communities both online and offline.

Gwiazdzinski [5] defined "chrono-urbanism" would be "the ensemble of plans, schedules, and agendas that coherently act upon space and time, enabling the optimal organization of technical, social, and aesthetic functions in the city, in an attempt to create a more human, more accessible, welcoming city". By extension, we propose the concept as chrono-spatialism when as a time-based approach in evaluating and measuring the design of time in retail spaces.

5   Conclusion and Discussion

The inadequacy of the spaces where we live, purchase, work, is accentuated by the most significant technologies today, which are those of:

mobility, distorting the perception of space and time;
communication, redefining the interaction between chronemics and proxemics;
sharing, encouraging the flexibility, transformability and availability of spaces.

In the field of mobility, telecommunications often play an average role of coordination and orientation between individuals located in distant areas [19]. It is evident that the interaction between physical and digital places is primarily a time-based relationship. The temporal experience expands and contracts the experience inside the spaces depending on the simultaneity of physical actions and digital interactions. This interaction can in turn alter the form of spaces that result from this chrono-spatiality approach, and not vice versa.

In fact, if a single real and digital chronotope is designed that includes the sequence of actions, or the simultaneity and duration of activities, it is evident that the spaces generated by a temporal approach reconfigure the spaces themselves, as well as the behaviors and activities that are dependent on the simultaneity of physical actions and digital interactions. This interaction, rather than the other way around, can change the shape of the environments that come from this chrono-spatiality approach.

Cellphones and media have changed our relationship with physical space and with people in presence. They change the forms of time by encouraging multi-temporality, simultaneity, etc. But above all, they manipulate the distances between things and people, they redefine the organization of time in the spaces, in the relationships and in the processes.

Retail, which has a clear measure of the surface area/productivity ratio, thus becomes a territory for experimentation with the new parameters. Shops in recent years have been the ones that have most begun to consider the impact of digital on their spaces and to realize that new services, new forms of shops and new experiences would result from this interaction, "instead of thinking of places as areas with boundaries around, they can be imagined as moments articulated in a network of established social relations [20]".

In fact, the time paradigm introduces other key performance indicators (KPI) that are measurable, customizable, logistically efficient and energy-saving. In terms of measurability, the interaction with digital enables the estimation of the time spent in different spaces or areas and the understanding of whether surfaces are over - or under - estimated and the reconfiguration of quantities according to actual needs or even the controlled adaptation of layouts as required.

The impact of digital technologies on time-based design affects not only the production and construction of spaces and their performance, but also the possibility that through the media of communication, the space "can be controlled, actuated, and animated by digital means [21]". The user/digital relationship allows one to change the hierarchy and size of certain areas of the store, as well as their quality, making them more experiential than functional.

Depending on the involvement, the experience can be:

immersive if it involves only the user, but excludes those present;
pervasive if it pushes those present in the background;
conjunctive if it involves all those present.

Even today, smart devices are mainly used:

– to protect and build around yourself a **cocoon** able to exclude the context and ensure a portable reality consistent with your emotional state, with your needs of the moment;
– to connect to a network of digital belonging, occupying temporarily the spaces, **camping**, setting up and using smart infrastructure able to rebuild anywhere our digital, productive, existential habitat;
– to share information and traces of our movements and lives, leaving a **footprint**, able to increase our visibility, orientation, but also, from the point of view of the network, to control our lives and those of others [22].

This interaction also shows potential in defining customer journeys that can change not only according to users, but also according to days or seasons. Through digital control, the front-end/back-end relationship can be managed and the proportion between spaces can change.

Finally, within the SDGs (Sustainable Development Goals) a temporal interaction reduces energy waste in favor of greater sustainability, because spaces are adjusted on actual use and not on the statistical average of presence. Thus, digital interaction becomes an efficiency tool, and one could speculate that in the future, each user could even personalize their relationship with the store not only online, but by profiling the space.

References

1. Zhang, T.: Future Retail: New Strategic Thinking in the Digital Era. Deloitte (2018)
2. Lee, R.L.: Time, space, and power in digital modernity: From liquid to solid control. Time Soc. **31**(1), 69–87 (2022)

3. Barbara, A., Ma, Y.: Extended Store How Digitalization Effects Retail Space Design, 1st edn. FrancoAngeli Edizioni, Milan (2021)

4. Barbara, A.: Temporal dimensions in the mediation between machines, humans and spaces. SPOOL **7**(3), 5–13 (2020)

5. Gwiazdzinski, L.: Redistribution des cartes dans la ville malleable. Espace Popul. Sociétés **3** (2007)

6. Manzini, E.: Livable Proximity Ideas for the City that Cares. Egea, Milan (2022)

7. Moreno, C., Allam, Z., Chabaud, D., Gall, C., Pratlong, F.: Introducing the "15-Minute City": sustainability, resilience and place identity in future post-pandemic cities. Smart Cities **4**(1), 93–111 (2021)

8. Bauman, Z.: Liquid Modernity. Polity, Cambridge (2000)

9. Mulíček, O., Osman, R., Seidenglanz, D.: Urban rhythms: a chronotopic approach to urban timespace. Time Soc. **24**(3), 304–325 (2015)

10. Neuhaus, F.: Urban rhythms. In: Emergent Spatio-Temporal Dimensions of the City: Habitus and Urban Rhythms, pp. 1–11. Springer, Cham (2015). https://doi.org/10.1007/978-3-319-09849-4

11. Leupen, B.R.H., Heijne, R., van Zwol, J.: Time-Based Architecture. 010 Publishers, Rotterdam (2005)

12. Hassanein, H.: Utilization of 'multiple kinetic technology KT' in interior architecture design as concept of futuristic innovation. ARChive, Forthcoming (2017)

13. Carpo, M.: The Second Digital Turn: Design Beyond Intelligence, 1st edn. The MIT Press, Cambridge (2017)

14. En-Academic. https://en-academic.com/dic.nsf/enwiki/944520

15. Retail Sensing. https://www.retailsensing.com/people-counting/retail-dwell-time-metric/

16. eMarketer. https://www.emarketer.com/chart/233465/leading-pain-points-shopping-in-store-according-adults-worldwide-oct-2019-of-respondents

17. Christiaans, H.H.C.M., Almendra, R.A.: Retail design: a new discipline. In: 12th International Design Conference, pp.21–24, The Design Society, Dubrovnik, Croatia (2012)

18. Douglas, J.: Building Adaptation, 2nd edn. Elsevier, Oxford (2006)

19. Castells, M.: The informational City: Information Technology Economic Restructuring and the Urban-Regional Process. Blackwell Publishers, Oxford (1989)

20. Massey, D.: Space Place and Gender. University of Minnesota Press, Minneapolis (1994)

21. Bier, H., Knight, T.: Digitally-driven architecture. Footprint **06**, 1–4 (2010)

22. Ling, R., Campbell, S.W.: The reconstruction of space and time: mobile communication practices, 1st edn. Routledge, Oxfordshire (2010)

Transformation of the Australian VET Sector: Investigations into the Key Competencies Required of the Australian Workforce in the Era of Industry 4.0 Technologies

Shisir Prasad Manandhar[1], Abhishek Sharma[2]([✉]) [iD], and Kunnumpurath Bijo[3]

[1] Healthovation, Health Careers International, Melbourne, Australia
`shisir@healthcareers.edu.au`
[2] Swinburne University of Technology, Melbourne, Australia
`sharmaabhishek570@gmail.com`
[3] Healthovation, Health Careers International, Melbourne, Australia
`bijo@hcigroup.com.au`

Abstract. With the commencement of the Fourth Industrial Revolution, the future of new jobs, worker skills, and competencies appears to be a major concern for the Australian economy. There is widespread agreement that the current revolution (i.e., Industry 4.0) will impact both labour force transformation and future worker education. As a result, it is of high importance for researchers and practitioners in the Australian vocational and educational training (VET) sector to investigate the skills and abilities that will serve as the foundation for jobs in the third millennium. Hence, this paper aims to provide a scoping review of the skills and competencies needed in the Australian workforce in light of the Industry 4.0 revolution. Besides this, the paper offers knowledge-based contributions for all stakeholders to encourage and facilitate the transition of Australian businesses and workers to the Industry 4.0 revolution.

Keywords: Industry 4.0 · Australian VET sector · IoT · Skills collaboration · Competence's profilessss

1 Introduction

Global labour markets are undergoing massive transformations, with business and workforce profile changes accelerating in recent years (Payton and Knight 2018; Maisiri et al. 2019; Prikshat et al. 2020; Rainnie and Dean 2020; Sharma 2021). Within these transformations, technological innovation is seen as a driver of both productivity growth and long-term economic development (Bongomin et al. 2020; Payton and Knight 2018). These developments are the result of the introduction of the so-called fourth industrial revolution–also known as Industry 4.0–which began with the preliminary deployment of artificial intelligence and automation in a variety of different sectors (Tommasi et al. 2020; Adepoju and Aigbavboa 2021). Additionally, the implementation of Industry 4.0 has had a global impact, affecting all sectors and industries.

© The Author(s), under exclusive license to Springer Nature Switzerland AG 2022
C. Stephanidis et al. (Eds.): HCII 2022, CCIS 1655, pp. 296–310, 2022.
https://doi.org/10.1007/978-3-031-19682-9_39

In this vein, considering the implications of Industry 4.0, VET researchers and practitioners are concerned as to how and to what extent Industry 4.0 will affect worker's skills and competencies. More specifically, there is a lack of a comprehensive understanding of how the Australian workforce will be able to sustain current workforce demand in terms of the skills and abilities required in the light of Industry 4.0 transformations. Based on these assumptions, the paper investigates how the Australian VET sector can meet the existing workforce skill shortages caused by the implications of the Industry 4.0 phenomenon. As a result, the goal of this paper is to present a scoping literature review to answer the following questions:

a) To investigate the interaction between disruptive technologies and skill development needs in the Australian VET sector from the standpoint of industry.
b) Investigating key international and national best practices in a variety of Australian vocational education industries to show how business and workforce transformation can be accomplished.
c) Identifying guiding principles and recommendations for business and workforce transformation resulting from the impacts of Industry 4.0 in the Australian vocational education sector.

2 Background

2.1 Overview of the Emerging Skills Due to Industry 4.0

With Industry 4.0 comes increased disruption and risk and a broader range of social concerns (Seet et al. 2018). Given such a fundamental shift, it is critical to understand what kind of training and qualifications are required within the Australian workforce to meet this demand. While these emerging skillsets are not necessarily new skills, they are becoming increasingly in demand in the workplace. Recent research done by White (2018) explored the employability skills that employers have demanded over the last four years. Based on the employability skills, it is found that communication skills, detail orientation, collaboration skills, problem-solving, time management skills, research and digital literacy skills are some of the most demanded within the industry (Seet et al. 2018; Hernandez-de-Menendez et al. 2020; Rampersad and Zivotic-Kukuloj 2019; Gekara et al. 2019; Prikshat et al. 2020). Further, Table 1 summarises the disruptive technologies that have been implemented in a variety of industries, with the argument that the Australian workforce lacks the necessary skills and competencies to work in these sectors.

Currently, there is a lack of agreement on the potential magnitude of job losses caused by disruptive technologies. Furthermore, a growing body of research focusing on the relative vulnerability of specific skills and occupations has questioned the high proportion of jobs at risk due to the Industry 4.0 revolution (Hernandez-de-Menendez et al. 2020). To these discussions, Prikshat et al. (2020) added that

"Australia must develop its education system to effectively respond to technological change and develop the skills required for a labour force to initiate innovation and growth. It is advocated that this includes increasing the availability of skilled ICT graduates

Table 1. Disruptive technologies and skills shortage domains within industry 4.0

Disruptive technologies	Research study
Internet of Things (IoT)	(Bongomin et al. 2020; Sharma 2021; Yousif et al., 2021; Javaid and Khan, 2021, Umair et al. 2021)
Big Data (Data Mining and Data Analytics)	(Persaud 2020; Li et al. 2021; Priyanka and Thangavel, 2020; Lee et al., 2018; Ibarra et al., 2018)
Additive Manufacturing (3D Printing and Scanning)	(Li et al., 2021; Leitão et al., 2020; Sepasgozar et al., 2020; Jemghili et al., 2021)
Cloud Computing	(Li et al., 2021; Bongomin et al., 2020; Adepoju and Aigbavboa, 2021)
Autonomous Robots (Industrial Robots)	(Radhakrishnan et al., 2021; Bongomin et al., 2020; Mittal et al., 2018)
Virtual Reality (VR) and Augmented Reality (AR)	(Radhakrishnan et al., 2021; Lu, 2017; Bongomin et al., 2020; Lopez et al.)
Cyber-Physical Systems (CPS)	(Rampersad, 2020; Bongomin et al., 2020; Rho et al., 2016; Waschull et al., 2020)
Artificial Intelligence and Machine Learning	(Engelhart and Mupinga, 2020; Radhakrishnan et al., 2021; Bongomin et al., 2020)
Smart Sensors	(Radhakrishnan et al. 2021; Agarwal 2018; Bongomin et al. 2020)
Advanced Simulation	(Udwadia 2021; Bongomin et al. 2020; Korčok 2016)
Nanotechnology	(Zeidan and Bishnoi 2020; Bongomin et al. 2020)
Drones, UAV, RPA	(Pathak et al., 2020; Finn and Donovan, 2016; Bongomin et al. 2020)
Biotechnology	(Chand and Tung, 2019; Abe et al. 2021; Cerna and Czaika, 2021; Bongomin et al. 2020)
Blockchain (Bitcoin, Cryptocurrency)	(Sharma and Kumar, 2020; Bongomin et al. 2020; Mulaji and Roodt, 2021)
Industrial Internet of Things (IIoT)	(Adepoju 2022; Bongomin et al. 2020; Ercan and Kutay, 2022)
Cybersecurity	(Thake, 2021; Bongomin et al. 2020; Adepoju, 2022)
Smart Factory and Intelligent Factory	(Alam and Dhamija, 2022; Bongomin et al. 2020)

(*continued*)

Table 1. (*continued*)

Disruptive technologies	Research study
Internet of Services (IoS)	(Brucker Juricic et al. 2021; Bongomin et al. 2020)
Vertical and Horizontal (V&H) System Integrations	(Morgan et al. 2021; Saxena et al. 2020; Bongomin et al. 2020)
Machine to Machine Communication (M2M)	(Anderson, 2015; Bongomin et al. 2020)
5G Network (Advanced Network Technology)	(Haider et al. 2020; Afaq et al. 2021; Bongomin et al. 2020)
Information & Communication Technology (ICT)	(Duell, 2020; Wright and Constantin, 2021; Bongomin et al. 2020)
Quantum Computing	(Venegas-Gomez, 2020; Bongomin et al. 2020; Prewett et al. 2020)
Manufacturing Execution System (MES) & SCADA	(Mir and Ramachandran, 2021; Ngambeki et al. 2021; Bongomin et al. 2020)
Neurotechnology	(Maiti and Ghosh, 2021; Shmatko and Volkova 2020; Bongomin et al. 2020)
Advanced Human to Machine Interface (HMI)	(Shmatko and Volkova, 2020; Hartlieb et al. 2020; Bongomin et al. 2020)
Materials Science	(Hariri et al. 2020; Bongomin et al. 2020)
Internet of data (IoD)	(Nagy, 2022; Bongomin et al. 2020)
Internet of Energy (IoE)	(Arcelay et al. 2021; Bongomin et al. 2020)
Flexible Production System (FMS)	(Marinas et al. 2021; Bongomin et al. 2020)

to work in "emerging technologies and growth areas, such as AI and cyber security" (Prikshat et al. 2020. p. 372).

To date, research has been carried out to determine the various work-ready competencies that employers seek in their employees. According to reports, relevant competencies and skillsets enhance the performance of tasks, which in turn results in improved job performance (Sousa and Rocha 2019). Australian graduates are supposed to gain these competencies during their studies and training as these skills are critical for employment within industry sectors in the face of increased global competition. However, the skills and competencies required within the industry sector are always listed within the skill shortages list but seem to lack clarity on their categorisation and prioritisation. As a result, this paper aims to outline a strategy for providing future workers with the competencies and skills required in the immediate wake of the industrial revolution.

2.2 Australian VET Sector

Australia's vocational education and training (VET) sector is a riddle wrapped in a mystery. Vocational Educational and Training (VET) is one of the essential components of the Australian education system that is designed to provide workplace-specific skills and knowledge-based competencies (Payton and Knight 2018; Knight and Mlotkowski 2009). Despite its importance, it remains arguably one of the least known and invisible areas of the sector.

The importance of the VET system is illustrated by the fact that the technical and trade sector employs over 1.2 million people, accounting for more than 13% of the total Australian workforce (Payton and Knight 2018). Specifically, the national VET system is industry-driven and client-focused to ensure that education and training are flexible, relevant, and responsive. However, there have been growing discussions on the importance of transferable skills for economic prosperity and social well-being, which is well established in international literature; however, many countries struggle to develop these skills. One major reason for this failure has been suggested to be a lack of basic definition and conceptualisation, i.e., what is a transferable skill and how can it be developed.

Additionally, the rapid change occurring due to the disruptive technologies are changing the demand for skills and abilities in a wide range of occupations, with a decrease in demand for some talents associated with everyday work and an increase in demand for knowledge and skills related to the development of the digital economy. Several researchers have discovered that the adoption of disruptive technologies has changed the nature of some existing jobs and, as a result, increased the variety of duties, such as problem-solving and teamwork, necessitating the acquisition of new skills and knowledge. Furthermore, the Industry 4.0 agenda predicts that, while some skills and the education and training that supports them will become obsolete, the demand for digital skills and capabilities will skyrocket, necessitating the adoption of programme offerings by education and training providers to meet this demand.

There has been a great deal of discussion about technological disruption's impact on the Australian workforce. A recent paper by the National Center for Vocational Education Research (NCVER 2017) examines how the advancement of technology is reshaping the labour market, the workforce, and the nature of jobs (Seet et al. 2018). Despite the uncertainty about the scope and nature of the impact, there is growing consensus that Australia's tertiary education system must change to meet the needs of a future labour force focused on innovation and creativity. Hence, this research examines the relationship between emerging – or disruptive – technologies and the skills required, emphasising the anticipated, necessary skills from the perspectives of both innovators (technology producers) and industry (technology users) within the Australian VET industry.

3   Literature Review

To meet the above-mentioned objectives, an extensive review search is conducted using databases such as EbscoHost, ProQuest, and Google Scholar. Based on this review, articles are chosen that reveal key insights into the skills that Australian graduates lack in order to be workforce ready in the industry.

3.1 Challenges with Required Skills and Competencies in the Industry and Existing VET Sector

Graduate work readiness (GWR) is a key factor that every employer in the industry looks for in recent graduates (Prikshat et al. 2020). Several researchers, however, have noted that a lack of graduate work readiness appears to be a major concern in employing Australian graduates in the existing workforce industry. Given the impending Fourth Industrial Revolution (4IR), this is extremely concerning, which will affect workplaces and occupations through artificial intelligence (AI), robotics, and machine learning. These revolutions will undoubtedly put routine and unskilled jobs at risk, and the challenge will be to develop efficient skill transition and preparation strategies (Prikshat et al. 2020; Maisiri et al. 2019; Tommasi et al. 2020).

As a result, the essential skills for Industry 4.0 were extracted from research papers that met the eligibility criteria for this scoping review paper (see Fig. 1). All of the skills deemed necessary for Industry 4.0 were taken into account, resulting in a diverse set of skills. Each skill category was subdivided into sub-categories, which then displayed the skills required along with the relevant references (see Table 2).

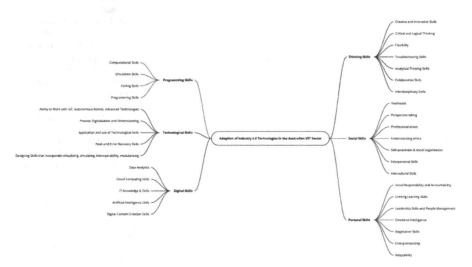

Fig. 1. Australian graduate workforce skill deficiency map

Table 2. Australian workforce skill set requirements in light of industry 4.0 transformations

Skills deficit category	Skills deficit sub-category	Skill set requirements	Relevant literature
Technical skills	Lack in programming skills	Computational skills Simulation skills Coding skills Cybersecurity analytics skills Enhance user experience skills Machine learning skills Networking skills Cloud computing skills Technical support skills Database administration skills Data visualisation skills Data science Big data Automation skills	(Payton and Knight 2018; Zoellner 2012; Sharma and Yarlagadda 2018; Rampersad and Zivotic-Kukolj 2018; Hernandez-de-Menendez et al. 2020) (Seet et al. 2018; Osborne et al. 2020; Winterton and Turner 2019; Hernandez-de-Menendez et al. 2020) (Esposto and Meagher 2002; Ejsmont 2021; Hernandez-de-Menendez et al. 2020) (Gekara and Snell 2018; Prikshat et al. 2020; Offner et al. 2020; De Zan 2019) (Patterson and Erturk 2015; Maisiri et al. 2019) (Prikshat et al. 2020; Seet et al. 2018; Dudyrev et al. 2019; Molla and Cuthbert 2019) (O'Dwyer 2021; Maisiri et al. 2019; Rampersad and Zivotic-Kukolj 2018; Hernandez-de-Menendez et al. 2020) (Seet et al. 2018; Gekara and Snell 2018; Mosely et al. 2020; Li et al. 2021) (Maisiri et al. 2019; Tommasi et al. 2020; Rampersad 2020; Rampersad and Zivotic-Kukolj 2018; Hernandez-de-Menendez et al. 2020) (Venkatraman et al. 2018; Li et al. 2021; Hernandez-de-Menendez et al. 2020) (Venkatraman et al. 2019; Li et al. 2021) (Li et al. 2021; Maisiri et al. 2019; Tommasi et al. 2020) (Tommasi et al. 2020; Maisiri et al. 2019; Prikshat et al. 2020) (Payton and Knight 2018; Gekara and Snell 2018; Sharma et al. 2016)

(continued)

Table 2. (*continued*)

Skills deficit category	Skills deficit sub-category	Skill set requirements	Relevant literature
	Lack in technological skills	Interoperability skills Modularising and decentralising capabilities Ability to work with IoT, autonomous robots, 3D printing and advanced technologies	(Gekara and Snell 2018; Babacan and McHugh 2020) (Myconos 2019) (Maisiri et al. 2019; Seet et al. 2018; Bongomin et al. 2020)
	Lack in digital skills	Data analytics and data processing skills Cyber security skills Digital content creation skills	(Venkatraman et al. 2019; Li et al. 2021; Tommasi et al. 2020; Rampersad 2020; Hernandez-de-Menendez et al. 2020) (De Zan 2020; Scanlan et al. 2020; Griffin et al. 2021; Gekara and Snell 2018) (Gekara and Snell 2018; Gekara et al. 2019)
Non-technical skills	Thinking skills	Creativity and innovation skills Flexibility at workplace skills Technical and literate communication skills Collaborative skills	(Prikshat et al. 2020; Maisiri et al. 2019; Seet et al. 2018; Verma et al. 2018; Hardy et al. 2018; Hernandez-de-Menendez et al. 2020) (Maisiri et al. 2019; Esposto and Meagher 2002; Prikshat et al. 2020; Rook and Sloan 2021; Abelha et al. 2020; Hernandez-de-Menendez et al. 2020) (Maisiri et al. 2019; Esposto and Meagher 2002; Prikshat et al. 2020; Creely et al. 2021; Nankervis et al. 2018; Zenner-Höffkes et al. 2021) (Maisiri et al. 2019; Esposto and Meagher 2002; Verma et al. 2018; Pham et al. 2019; Hernandez-de-Menendez et al. 2020)

(*continued*)

Table 2. (*continued*)

Skills deficit category	Skills deficit sub-category	Skill set requirements	Relevant literature
	Social skills	Teamwork skills Professional ethics Interpersonal skills	(Prikshat et al. 2020; Esposto and Meagher 2002; Payton and Knight 2018; Verma et al. 2018; de Lange et al. 2022; Rook and Sloan 2021; Hernandez-de-Menendez et al. 2020) (Prikshat et al. 2020; Esposto and Meagher 2002; Payton and Knight 2018; Nankervis et al. 2018; Jackson 2019) (Prikshat et al. 2020; Esposto and Meagher 2002; Payton and Knight 2018; Pham et al. 2019; Jackson 2019; Verma et al. 2018; Winterton and Turner 2019; Hernandez-de-Menendez et al. 2020)
	Personal skills	Social responsibility and accountability skills Lifelong learning skills Leadership skills Negotiation skills Entrepreneurship skills Adaptability skills	(Prikshat et al. 2020; Seet et al. 2018; Abe et al. 2021; Nankervis et al. 2018; Hernandez-de-Menendez et al. 2020) (Prikshat et al. 2020; Seet et al. 2018; Nankervis et al. 2018) (Prikshat et al. 2020; Seet et al. 2018; Abe et al. 2021; Verma et al. 2018; Nankervis et al. 2018) (Prikshat et al. 2020; Payton and Knight 2018; Rook and Sloan 2021; Pham et al. 2019; Hernandez-de-Menendez et al. 2020) (Prikshat et al. 2020; Seet et al. 2018; Payton and Knight 2018; Hernandez-de-Menendez et al. 2020) (Prikshat et al. 2020; Abe et al. 2021; Payton and Knight 2018; Verma et al. 2018; Rook and Sloan 2021; Winterton and Turner 2019; Jackson 2019; Hernandez-de-Menendez et al. 2020)

4   Conclusion and Key Recommendations

Australia has one of the world's most advanced vocational education and training (VET) programmes. VET prepares Australian and international students for careers in a variety of industries, including agriculture, food processing, health care, community services, and several others. However, several skill competencies in Australian graduates must be improved for them to fit into the existing workforce, which is rapidly evolving with the industry. 4.0 revolution (Guthrie and Waters 2022). Industry 4.0 is not about replacing people with intelligent machines; instead, workers will be tasked with more complex duties. Hence, the Australian VET system should train people for the future economy while also allowing Australian firms to compete globally. As a result, the below-mentioned recommendations are suggested to be implemented within the Australian VET sector.

1. Incorporate the use of cutting-edge technology in the development of a curriculum and course instruction design in the Australian VET sector.
2. Invest in the establishment of in-house innovation centres within the Australian VET sector to improve learning methodologies (such as problem-based learning), which is expected to produce graduates with a diverse set of skills and talents.
3. Integrate the Australian VET sector curriculum with qualification systems and student work placements integrated with industry to contribute to innovation and up to date with the latest trends and technology.
4. Focus on understanding the future of vocational education learning and the future VET instructor in Australia. As a result, a future learning strategy would be required to attract and retain high-quality VET instructors and teachers.

References

Abe, E.N., Abe, I.I., Adisa, O.: Future of work: skill obsolescence, acquisition of new skills, and upskilling in the 4IR. In: Future of Work, Work-Family Satisfaction, and Employee Well-Being in the Fourth Industrial Revolution. IGI Global, Hershey (2021)

Abelha, M., et al.: Graduate employability and competence development in higher education—a systematic literature review using PRISMA. Sustainability 12, 5900 (2020)

Adepoju, O. 2022. Reskilling for construction 4.0. In: Re-skilling Human Resources for Construction 4.0. Springer, Cham (2022). https://doi.org/10.1007/978-3-030-85973-2_9

Adepoju, O.O., Aigbavboa, C.O.: Assessing knowledge and skills gap for construction 4.0 in a developing economy. J. Public Aff. 21, e2264 (2021)

Afaq, A., Haider, N., Baig, M.Z., Khan, K.S., Imran, M., Razzak, I.: Machine learning for 5G security: Architecture, recent advances, and challenges. Ad Hoc Netw. 123, 102667 (2021)

Agarwal, V.: Smart sensors for structural health monitoring-overview, challenges and advantages. Sens. Transd. 221, 1–8 (2018)

Alam, S., Dhamija, P.: Human resource development 4.0 (HRD 4.0) in the apparel industry of Bangladesh: a theoretical framework and future research directions. Int. J. Manpower. A head of print (2022)

Anderson, J.: The impact of machine to machine communication on the dairy industry in New Zealand (2015)

Arcelay, I., et al.: Definition of the future skills needs of job profiles in the renewable energy sector. Energies 14, 2609 (2021)

Babacan, H., Mchugh, J.: Re-thinking agricultural supply chains in Northern Australia. Aust. J. Reg. Stud. 26, 239–268 (2020)

Bongomin, O., et al.: Exponential disruptive technologies and the required skills of industry 4.0. J. Eng. 2020, 1–17 (2020)

Brucker juricic, B., Galic, M., Marenjak, S.: Review of the construction labour demand and shortages in the EU. Buildings **11**, 17 (2021)

Cerna, L., Czaika, M.: Rising stars in the global race for skill? A comparative analysis of Brazil, India, and Malaysia. Migrat. Stud. **9**, 21–46 (2021)

Chand, M., Tung, R.L.: Skilled immigration to fill talent gaps: a comparison of the immigration policies of the United States, Canada, and Australia. J. Int. Bus. Policy **2**(4), 333–355 (2019). https://doi.org/10.1057/s42214-019-00039-4

Creely, E., Chowdhury, R., Southcott, J.: Academics' understandings of the literacy needs of international graduate students. Qual. Rep. **26**, 3787–3804 (2021)

de Lange, P., O'Connell, B.T., Tharapos, M., Beatson, N., Oosthuizen, H.: Accounting graduate employability: employer perspectives on skills and attributes of international graduates. Acc. Educ. **2022**, 1–29 (2022)

De Zan, T.: Mind the gap: the cyber security skills shortage and public policy interventions (2019)

De Zan, T.: Future research on the cyber security skills shortage. In: Cyber Security Education: Principles and Policies, pp. 194–207. Routledge, New York (2020)

Dudyrev, F., et al.: Worldskills approaches to comparable skills assessment in vocational education. In: Современная аналитика образования, pp. 5–44 (2019)

Duell, N.: Skills shortages and labour migration in the field of information and communication technology in Canada, China, Germany and Singapore (2020)

EJsmont, K.: The impact of industry 4.0 on employees—insights from Australia. Sustainability **13**, 3095 (2021)

Engelhart, M., Mupinga, D.: Essential employability skills as perceived by employers: implications for technical and vocational education and training. Int. J. Voc. Educ. Train. **25** (2020)

Training professional smart city workforces through a partnership with technology firms. In: Smart Cities Policies and Financing, pp. 181–196. Elsevier, Amsterdam (2022)

Esposto, A., Meagher, G.: The future demand for employability skills and the implications for the VET system. Idea **11** (2022)

Finn, R., Donovan, A.: Big data, drone data: privacy and ethical impacts of the intersection between big data and civil drone deployments. In: Custers, B. (eds.) The Future of Drone Use. Information Technology and Law Series, vol. 27. T.M.C. Asser Press, The Hague (2016). https://doi.org/10.1007/978-94-6265-132-6_3

Gekara, V., Snell, D.: Designing and delivering skills transferability and employment mobility: the challenges of a market-driven vocational education and training system. J. Voc. Educ. Train. **70**, 107–129 (2018)

Gekara, V., Snell, D., Molla, A., Karanasios, S., Thomas, A.: Skilling the Australian Workforce for the Digital Economy. Research Report. National Centre for Vocational Education Research (NCVER) (2019)

Griffin, A.J., Johnson, N.F., Valli, C., Vernon, L.: The impact of twenty-first century skills and computing cognition cyber skills on graduates' work readiness in cyber security. In: Daimi, K., Arabnia, H.R., Deligiannidis, L., Hwang, M., Tinetti, F.G. (eds.) Advances in Security, Networks, and Internet of Things. TCSCI, pp. 213–221. Springer, Cham (2021). https://doi.org/10.1007/978-3-030-71017-0_15

Guthrie, H., Waters, M.: Delivering high-quality VET: what matters to RTOs? Research Report (2022)

Haider, N., Baig, M.Z., Imran, M.: Artificial intelligence and machine learning in 5g network security: opportunities, advantages, and future research trends. *arXiv preprint* arXiv:2007. 04490 (2020)

Hardy, D., Myers, T., Sankupellay, M.: Cohorts and cultures: developing future design thinkers. In: Proceedings of the 20th Australasian Computing Education Conference, pp. 9–16 (2018)

Hariri, N., Nader, R.B., Haykal, S.: Technological change and future skill-shortages in engineering and architecture education: lessons from Lebanon. In: Bach Tobji, M.A., Jallouli, R., Samet, A., Touzani, M., Strat, V.A., Pocatilu, P. (eds.) ICDEc 2020. LNBIP, vol. 395, pp. 38–50. Springer, Cham (2020). https://doi.org/10.1007/978-3-030-64642-4_4

Hartlieb, P., et al.: A comprehensive skills catalogue for the raw materials sector and the structure of raw materials education worldwide. Min. Technol. **129**, 82–94 (2020)

Hernandez-de-menendez, M., et al.: Competencies for industry 4.0. Int. J. Interact. Des. Manuf. **14**, 1511–1524 (2020)

Ibarra, D., Ganzarain, J., Igartua, J.I.: Business model innovation through Industry 4.0: a review. Procedia Manuf. **22**, 4–10 (2018)

Jackson, D.: Student perceptions of the development of work readiness in Australian undergraduate programs. J. Coll. Stud. Dev. **60**, 219–239 (2019)

Javaid, M., Khan, I.H.: Internet of Things (IoT) enabled healthcare helps to take the challenges of COVID-19 pandemic. J. Oral Biol. Craniof. Res. **11**, 209–214 (2021)

Jemghili, R., Taleb, A.A., Khalifa, M.: A bibliometric indicators analysis of additive manufacturing research trends from 2010 to 2020. Rap. Protot. J. A head of print (2021)

Knight, B., Mlotkowski, P.: An Overview of Vocational Education and Training in Australia and Its Links to the Labour Market, ERIC (2009)

Korčok, D. Industry 4.0: the future concepts and new visions of factory of the future development. In: Sinteza 2016-International Scientific Conference on ICT and E-Business Related Research, 2016. Singidunum University, pp. 293–298 (2016)

Lee, M., et al.: How to respond to the fourth industrial revolution, or the second information technology revolution? Dynamic new combinations between technology, market, and society through open innovation. J. Open Innov. Technol. Mark. Comp. **4**, 21 (2018)

Leitão, P., Geraldes, C.A., Fernandes, F.P., Badikyan, H. Analysis of the workforce skills for the factories of the future. In: 2020 IEEE Conference on Industrial Cyberphysical Systems (ICPS), vol. 1, pp. 353–358. IEEE (2020)

LI, G., Yuan, C., Kamarthi, S., Moghaddam, M., Jin, X.: Data science skills and domain knowledge requirements in the manufacturing industry: a gap analysis. J. Manuf. Syst. **60**, 692–706 (2021)

Lopez, J., Bhandari, S., HAllowelL, M.R. Virtual reality and construction industry: review of current state-of-practice and future applications. In: Construction Research Congress 2022, pp. 174–184 (2022)

Lu, Y.: Industry 4.0: a survey on technologies, applications and open research issues. J. Ind. Inf. Integr. **6**, 1–10 (2017)

Maisiri, W., Darwish, H., Van dyk, L.: An investigation of Industry 4.0 skills requirements. S. Afr. J. Ind. Eng. **30**, 90–105 (2019)

Maiti, M., Ghosh, U.: Next generation Internet of Things in fintech ecosystem. IEEE Internet of Things J. Early Access (2021)

MArinas, M., Dinu, M., Socol, A.G., Socol, C.: The technological transition of European manufacturing companies to industry 4.0. Is the human resource ready for advanced. Econ. Comput. Econ. Cybern. Stud. Res. **55** (2021)

Mir, A.W., Ramachandran, R.K.: Implementation of security orchestration, automation and response (SOAR) in smart grid-based SCADA systems. In: Dash, S.S., Panigrahi, B.K., Das, S. (eds.) Sixth International Conference on Intelligent Computing and Applications. AISC, vol. 1369, pp. 157–169. Springer, Singapore (2021). https://doi.org/10.1007/978-981-16-1335-7_14

Mittal, S., Khan, M.A., Romero, D., Wuest, T.: A critical review of smart manufacturing & Industry 4.0 maturity models: implications for small and medium-sized enterprises (SMEs). J. Manuf. Syst. **49**, 194–214 (2018)

Molla, T., Cuthbert, D.: Calibrating the PhD for Industry 4.0: global concerns, national agendas and Australian institutional responses. Policy Rev. Higher Educ. **3**, 167–188 (2019)

Morgan, J., Halton, M., Qiao, Y., Breslin, J.G.: Industry 4.0 smart reconfigurable manufacturing machines. J. Manuf. Syst. **59**, 481–506 (2021)

Mosely, G., Wrigley, C., Key, T.: White spaces for innovation in tertiary education: Australian public provider perspectives. Int. J. Train. Res. **18**, 191–210 (2020)

Mulaji, S.S., Roodt, S.S.: The practicality of adopting blockchain-based distributed identity management in organisations: a meta-synthesis. Secur. Commun. Netw. (2021)

Myconos, G.: VET: The International Context. Australia: Brotherhood of St Laurence Research and Policy Centre (2019)

Nagy, R.: A literature review of contemporary industrial revolutions as decision support resources. J. Agric. Inform. **13** (2022)

Nankervis, A., Prikshat, V., Cameron, R.: Graduate work-readiness in Asia pacific economies: a review of the literature. In: Cameron, R., Dhakal, S., Burgess, J.: Transitions from Education to Work: Workforce Ready Challenges in the Asia Pacific, pp. 16–42. Routledge, London (2018)

Ngambeki, I., et al.: Creating a concept map for ICS security–a Delphi study. In: 2021 IEEE Frontiers in Education Conference (FIE), pp. 1–7 (2021)

O'dwyer, L.: Review of Employment-Based Training Models. National Centre for Vocational Education Research (NCVER) (2021)

Offner, K., Sitnikova, E., Joiner, K., Macintyre, C.: Towards understanding cybersecurity capability in Australian healthcare organisations: a systematic review of recent trends, threats and mitigation. Intell. Natl. Secur. **35**, 556–585 (2020)

Osborne, K., Ackehurst, M., Chan, L., Polvere, R.A.: Work-Based Education in VET. National Centre for Vocational Education Research (NCVER) (2020)

Pathak, H., Kumar, G., Mohapatra, S., Gaikwad, B., Rane, J.: Use of Drones in Agriculture: Potentials, Problems and Policy Needs. ICAR-National Institute of Abiotic Stress Management (2020)

Patterson, E., Erturk, E.: An Inquiry into Agile and Innovative User Experience (UX) Design. New Zealand: Eastern Institute of Technology, Napier (2015)

Payton, A., Knight, G.: Skills for a Global Future (2018)

Persaud, A. 2020. Key competencies for big data analytics professions: a multimethod study. Inf. Technol. People (2020)

Pham, T., Tomlinson, M., Thompson, C.: Forms of capital and agency as mediations in negotiating employability of international graduate migrants. Glob. Soc. Educ. **17**, 394–405 (2019)

Prewett, K. W., Prescott, G.L., Phillips, K.: Blockchain adoption is inevitable—barriers and risks remain. J. Corp. Acc. Finan. **31**, 21–28 (2020)

Prikshat, V., Montague, A., Connell, J., Burgess, J.: Australian graduates' work readiness–deficiencies, causes and potential solutions. Higher Educ. Skills Work-Based Learn. (ahead-of-print 2020)

Priyanka, E., Thangavel, S.: Influence of Internet of Things (IoT) in association of data mining towards the development s mart cities-a review analysis. J. Eng. Sci. Technol. Rev. **13** (2020)

Radhakrishnan, U., Koumaditis, K., Chinello, F.: A systematic review of immersive virtual reality for industrial skills training. Behav. Inf. Technol. **40**, 1310–1339 (2021)

Rainnie, A., Dean, M.: Industry 4.0 and the future of quality work in the global digital economy. Labour Ind. **30**, 16–33 (2020)

Rampersad, G.: Robot will take your job: innovation for an era of artificial intelligence. J. Bus. Res. **116**, 68–74 (2020)

Rampersad, G., Zivotic-kukolj, V.: Work-integrated learning in science, technology, engineering and mathematics: drivers of innovation for students. Int. J. Work-Integr. Learn. **19**, 193 (2018)

Rampersad, G.C., ZIvotic-kukuloj, V.: Future of work: innovation skills as the missing link for employability. In: Proceedings of the Australian Conference on Science and Mathematics Education, pp. 129–135 (2019)

Rho, S., Vasilakos, A.V., Chen, W.: Cyber Physical Systems Technologies and Applications. Elsevier, New York (2016)

Rook, L., Sloan, T.: Competing stakeholder understandings of graduate attributes and employability in work-integrated learning. Int. J. Work-Integr. Learn. **22**, 41–56 (2021)

Saxena, P., Papanikolaou, M., Pagone, E., Salonitis, K., Jolly, M.R.: Digital manufacturing for foundries 4.0. In: Tomsett, A. (ed.) Light Metals 2020 the Minerals, Metals & Materials Series TMMMS, pp. 1019–1025. Springer, Cham (2020). https://doi.org/10.1007/978-3-030-36408-3_138

Scanlan, J., et al.: Neurodiverse Knowledge, Skills and Ability Assessment for Cyber Security. Australasian Conference on Information Systems (2020)

Seet, P.-S., Jones, J., Spoehr, J., Hordacre, A.-L. The Fourth Industrial Revolution: The Implications of Technological Disruption for Australian VET. NCVER (2018)

Sepasgozar, S.M., Shi, A., Yang, L., Shirowzhan, S., Edwards, D.J.: Additive manufacturing applications for industry 4.0: a systematic critical review. Buildings **10**, 231 (2020)

Sharma, A.: The role of IoT in the fight against Covid-19 to restructure the economy. In: Stephanidis, C. (ed.) HCII 2021. LNCS, vol. 13097, pp. 140–156. Springer, Cham (2021). https://doi.org/10.1007/978-3-030-90966-6_11

Sharma, J., Yarlagadda, P.K.: Perspectives of 'STEM education and policies' for the development of a skilled workforce in Australia and India. Int. J. Sci. Educ. **40**, 1999–2022 (2018)

Sharma, K., Oczkowski, E., Hicks, J.: Skill shortages in regional Australia: a local perspective from the Riverina. Econ. Anal. Policy **52**, 34–44 (2016)

Sharma, M.G., Kumar, S.: The implication of blockchain as a disruptive technology for construction industry. IIM Kozhikode Soci. Manag. Rev. **9**, 177–188 (2020)

Shmatko, N., Volkova, G.: Bridging the skill gap in robotics: global and national environment. SAGE Open **10**, 2158244020958736 (2020)

Sousa, M.J., Rocha, Á.: Skills for disruptive digital business. J. Bus. Res. **94**, 257–263 (2019)

Thake, A.M.: Dependency on Foreign Labor in the Information and Communication Technology Sector of the Maltese Economy. Contemporary Issues in Social Science. Emerald Publishing Limited, Bingley (2021)

Tommasi, F., Franceschinis, I., Perini, M., Sartori, R.: A systematic scoping review on skills variety for VET in the industry 4.0. In: Proceedings of the International Conference on Education and New Developments (END), 2020, pp. 474–476 (2020)

Udwadia, T.E.: Training for laparoscopic colorectal surgery creating an appropriate porcine model and curriculum for training. J. Min. Access Surg. **17**, 180 (2021)

Umair, M., Cheema, M.A., Cheema, O., Li, H., Lu, H.: Impact of COVID-19 on IoT adoption in healthcare, smart homes, smart buildings, smart cities, transportation and industrial IoT. Sens. Actuat. **21**, 3838 (2021)

Venegas-gomez, A.: The quantum ecosystem and its future workforce: a journey through the funding, the hype, the opportunities, and the risks related to the emerging field of quantum technologies. PhotonicsViews **17**, 34–38 (2020)

Venkatraman, S., De Souza-Daw, T., Kaspi, S.: Improving employment outcomes of career and technical education students. High. Educ. Skills Work-Based Learn. (2018)

Venkatraman, S., Overmars, A., Wahr, F.: Visualization and experiential learning of mathematics for data analytics. Computation **7**, 37 (2019)

Verma, P., et al.: Graduate work-readiness challenges in the Asia-Pacific region and the role of HRM. Equal. Diver. Incl. Int. J. **37** (2018)

Waschull, S., Bokhorst, J.A., Molleman, E., Wortmann, J.C.: Work design in future industrial production: transforming towards cyber-physical systems. Comput. Ind. Eng. **139**, 105679 (2020)

Winterton, J., Turner, J.J.: Preparing graduates for work readiness: an overview and agenda. Educ. Train. **61**(5), 536–551 (2019)

Wright, C.F., Constantin, A.: Why recruit temporary sponsored skilled migrants? A human capital theory analysis of employer motivations in Australia. Aust. J. Manag. **46**, 151–173 (2021)

Yousif, M., Hewage, C., Nawaf, L.: IoT technologies during and beyond COVID-19: a comprehensive review. Fut. Internet **13**, 105 (2021)

Zeidan, S., Bishnoi, M.: An effective framework for bridging the gap between industry and academia. Int. J. Emerg. Technol. **13**, 454–461 (2020)

Zenner-höffkes, L., Harris, R., Zirkle, C., Pilz, M.: A comparative study of the expectations of SME employers recruiting young people in Germany, Australia and the United States. Int. J. Train. Dev. **25**, 124–143 (2021)

Zoellner, D.: Dualism and vocational education and training: creating the people who require training. Int. J. Train. Res. **10**, 79–93 (2012)

Virtuality in Non-governmental Organizations: An Analysis from Working Conditions

Davidson Martínez[1]([✉]), Jose Ramírez[1], Angiee Carbonó-Mercado[2],
Osvaldo Arevalo[2], Margel Parra[3], and Daniel Viloria[4]

[1] Fundación de Pana que Sí, 65 Street #84-120, Barranquilla, Colombia
dandresmartinez@mail.uniatlantico.edu.co
[2] Universidad de La Costa, 58 Street #55 66, Barranquilla, Colombia
[3] Corporación Universitaria Reformada, 42F Street #80-117, Barranquilla, Colombia
[4] Universidad del Atlántico, 30 Street #8-49, Puerto Colombia, Colombia

Abstract. Nowadays, organizations' dynamics have resulted in a migration towards organizational models based on remote work, which significantly changes the working conditions of diverse organizations such as non-governmental organizations, which are often responsible for providing advisory and support services to populations in vulnerable situations. In this sense, this study is aimed at identifying the conditions and context of virtual work within a non-governmental organization focused on the attention of the Venezuelan population residing in Colombia. A questionnaire of Likert scale answers is taken as a reference, consisting of a total of 47 questions, broken down into 11 items: Working conditions, Supervision, Recognition, Transcendence, Independence and/or autonomy, Communication with other areas, Career Growth, Technology Resources, Job Performance, Work/Life Balance and Health Conditions. The items in each section are ordinal scale response items (Likert scale) with 4 answer options, categorized from 1 to 4, where category 1 (Very dissatisfied) indicates lower satisfaction and category 4 (Very satisfied) indicates greater satisfaction. The instrument was applied to 30 individuals linked to the administrative and project management areas of the organization, it is observed that the working conditions correspond to 1.65 which indicates that on average people show some degree of high dissatisfaction with their working condition, related to noise, lighting, space, among other factors. As for the supervision item, 2.29 is noted, which means that workers are dissatisfied with the control applied by their boss and the way in which their performance is evaluated, however, the recognition category presents a 3.72 which is a high level of satisfaction and refers to the rewards for the achievement of the objectives and the recognition of their boss. The transcendence item that is related to the possibilities of creativity offered by the work, denotes 2.84 a moderate level of satisfaction, as well as Life/Work Balance, Health conditions with a 3.17 and 3.06 respectively. The items Independence/autonomy, Communication with other areas, Career growth, Technological resources, denote high levels of satisfaction, which means, that workers have the ability to freely decide aspects relating to their job, participate in the decisions of their working group and have opportunities to participate in calls or promotion to other projects. Finally, the item work performance has 2.69 a moderate level of satisfaction, which is related to the tasks and activities that must be performed at work and the times of fulfillment (time available to finish tasks).

© The Author(s), under exclusive license to Springer Nature Switzerland AG 2022
C. Stephanidis et al. (Eds.): HCII 2022, CCIS 1655, pp. 311–316, 2022.
https://doi.org/10.1007/978-3-031-19682-9_40

Keywords: Working conditions · Virtuality · Remote work · Non-governmental organizations

1 Introduction

Virtuality is present in all areas that surround human beings. Historically we have been walking into the digital age, and today it is a reality that has been established in the educational, social, financial, recreational and above all labor field [1–3]. It is difficult in the present, to try to be competitive without being accompanied and endowed with skills for this environment, already at this point, it is a necessity to be familiar with technological and digital tools that make our lives easier. Under this panorama, the public health contingency experienced in 2020 due to the SARS-CoV-2 virus (Covid-19) is included within this context, because it forced social distancing and also quarantine periods that generated dependence on remote work and/or teleworking [4].

Although teleworking is not something new in history, the current reality has allowed organizations to focus their gaze on this modality of work to avoid stopping economical activities or venturing into labor inclusion. However, during the pandemic, this migration to the virtual work happened all of a sudden, which could be represented as a disadvantage, due to the minimal development of programs for teleworking in accordance with the particular needs of the company or entity and its collaborators [5].

From this perspective, it is pertinent to mention that the dynamics of virtuality represent a cumulus of interactions, where the work ecosystem enters the personal and family ecosystem; in turn, lighting conditions, equipment, internet, delegation of functions, working hours, recognition, and emotional salary, etc., generate a teleworking experience that can translate into job satisfaction or dissatisfaction. Focusing on the above, it should be clarified that the term employee satisfaction at work is a psychological disposition of the subjects to their work and this implies a set of attitudes or feelings [6].

Consequently, the permanence of a collaborator within an organization, regardless of their activity or position, depends to a large extent on their level of job satisfaction, guaranteeing their permanence within the company [7]. In this way, virtuality and distancing could also be affected by the organizational commitment of the collaborator, since the lack of personal interaction with the work team directly affects motivation, and emotional health if this modality is not carried out with follow-up plans [8].

Under this panorama, this article studies virtuality as a modality of work in non-governmental organizations in order to make an analysis from the working conditions under the variable of job satisfaction. The article seeks to identify the conditions and context of virtual work within a non-governmental organization who work with the Venezuelan migrant population; which is recognized as a highly vulnerable group [9, 10]; which makes the contribution of this entity much more relevant due to its contribution to the aforementioned group.

Currently it is important to recognize how organizations must migrate from traditional organizational culture strategies to others where not only the face-to-face ecosystem is evaluated, but also virtuality in order to adapt to the requirements of the environment where these organizations develop and this in turn, affects competitiveness and achievement of results. Specifically, referring to non-governmental entities such as those in the following study, which are not far from this reality in search of fulfilling action plans, objectives, and projects for which they need human talent and their workforce in order to be competitive with other organizations. This competitiveness is reflected in the right decision-making, their growth and strengthening, allowing them to position themselves and thus expand the beneficiary population for the application of social improvement projects [11].

2   Materials and Method

For the estimation of the sample, it was chosen to work with a non-governmental entity located in the city of Barranquilla, called "FUNDACIÓN DE PANA QUE SI", focused on the attention of the Venezuelan migrant population and Colombian returnees residing in the city and its metropolitan area, with a sample of 30 people linked to the administrative and project management areas of the organization. To respond to the purpose of the development of this study, a probabilistic sampling of population census has been carried out where the total sample of all the collaborators who work under the virtual modality is taken (Table 1).

Table 1. Delimitation of the study sample

Universe	Non-governmental organizations in the city of Barranquilla
Objective population	"FUNDACIÓN DE PANA QUE SI"
Sample	(30) Collaborators who work under the virtual modality

For data collection process, a quantitative structured questionnaire with responses on the Likert scale is taken as a reference, which seeks to measure the level of job satisfaction in teleworkers, this consists of a total of 47 questions, broken down into 11 items: Working conditions, Supervision, Recognition, Transcendence, Independence and/or autonomy, Communication with other areas, Career growth, Technological resources, Work performance, Work balance and health conditions. The items in each section are ordinal scale response (Likert scale) with 4 answer options, categorized from 1 to 4, where category 1 (Very dissatisfied) indicates lower satisfaction and category 4 (Very satisfied) indicates greater satisfaction. In general, this index is high as long as a group of items explores a common factor [12].

3   Results

The results obtained from the surveys carried out on the sample population are presented, the following analysis is carried out from measurement scales, which allow the classification of the variables studied. The validity and reliability of the measurement of the variables are subject to the choices that are made to operate it, and these will be analyzed independently and also correlated with the overall satisfaction to determine to what extent these variables affect or not in the organization.

It is of the utmost importance to mention that the factors analyzed set the guidelines to influence the integration of the work team, the identification and commitment to the foundation for the achievement of high-quality indexes in the care provided to the migrant population. The variables of working conditions, supervision, recognition, transcendence, independence and/or autonomy, communication with other areas, career growth, technological resources, work performance, life/work balance and health conditions. As can be seen in Table 2, the results obtained from the application of the instrument are presented.

Table 2. Average results for each indicator

Ítems	Indicators	Mean
1	Working conditions	1,65
2	Supervision	2,29
3	Recognition	3,72
4	Transcendence	2,84
5	Independence/autonomy	3,64
6	Communication with other areas	3,56
7	Career growth	3,36
8	Technological resources	3,58
9	Work performance	2,69
10	Work/life balance	3,17
11	Health conditions	3,06

In order to obtain results on working conditions, and the development of social skills using ICT, the description of the selections is presented.

For item 1, it is observed that the working conditions correspond to 1.65 which indicates that on average people show some degree of high dissatisfaction with their working condition, related to noise, lighting, space, among other factors. Then for Item 2, Supervision is noted on 2.29 which means that workers are dissatisfied with the control exercised by their boss and the way in which their performance is evaluated. Meanwhile item 3, the Recognition category presents the 3.72 a high level of satisfaction, which refers to the rewards for the achievement of the objectives and recognition of their boss.

The Transcendence item that is related to the possibilities of creativity offered by work itself, denotes 2.84 a moderate level of satisfaction, as well as Life/Work Balance, Health Conditions with a 3.17 and 3.06 respectively.

Detailing in the items 5, 6, 7, 8 these that represent respectively: Independence/autonomy, Communication with other areas, Career growth, Technological resources; denote high levels of satisfaction (3,64, 3,56, 3,36, 3,58), which means that workers have the ability to freely decide aspects related to their work, participate in the decisions of their working group, and have opportunities to participate in calls or promotion to other projects.

Finally, the item Work performance (9) has 2.69 a moderate level of satisfaction, around the tasks and activities that must be performed at work and the times of fulfillment.

The results of this research reveal that the use of technological tools facilitates the analysis and access to information: technological resources, such as business software and social networks, offer them data and specific information on beneficiaries, donors, volunteers, and trends of new calls, which allows a more accurate decision making, demonstrating the little valuation of the effort around the processes, giving preference to the final result.

It is important to explain that in order to carry out the analysis of the instrument it was necessary to adjust the mean obtained in the overall satisfaction of each item. This is because the questions were measured based on a Likert scale.

4   Conclusions

This analysis allows qualitative and quantitative measurement, which produced results in which certain deficiencies in the processes were perceived, it is considered that it is worth measuring the work environment, even in teleworking, since it is proven that it is a determining factor in the productivity of the foundation. However, the most appropriate thing to do it effectively in remote teams is to constantly obtain information and promote a culture of self-evaluation and assertive communication to take prompt action [13].

A lot of practical creativity is required and in some cases some investment to maintain the activities that previously generated disruption, recreation, and integration; since, the involvement of the leadership of the organization is always a cornerstone.

In conclusion, the implementation of ICT as a tool for the development of social competence is viable, it can be successful and effective as long as you manage to structure in an assertive way the strategies which they want to implement considering not only technological advances [14], but the labor and socio-personal factors, in favor of achieving the success of the programs and fulfillment of the objectives of the foundation. Other studies show that organizations are currently generating innovation focused on the development of the quality of life of their staff; being these the fundamental axis of the development of the same [15]. It is undeniable to recognize how new technologies have marked a before and after in organizational processes, not only bringing important benefits but changing the dynamics to a new environment of the 4.0 era [16, 17].

References

1. Parra, M., Marambio, C., Ramírez, J., Suárez, D., Herrera, H.: Educational convergence with digital technology: integrating a global society. In: Stephanidis, C., Antona, M., Ntoa, S. (eds.) HCII 2020. CCIS, vol. 1294, pp. 303–310. Springer, Cham (2020). https://doi.org/10.1007/978-3-030-60703-6_39
2. Parejo, I., Nuñez, L., Nuñez, W.: Análisis de la transformación digital de las empresas en Colombia: dinámicas globales y desafíos actuales. Aglala 12(1), 160–172 (2021)
3. Handke, L., Klonek, F., Parker, S., Kauffeld, S.: Interactive effects of team virtuality and work design on team functioning. Small Group Res. 51(1), 3–47 (2020)

4. Teleworking during and after the COVID-19 Pandemic: A Practical Guide. International Labour Organization (2020)
5. Carrasco-Mullins, R.: Telework: advantages and disadvantages in organizations and collaborators. faecosapiens **4**(2), 1–14 (2021)
6. Schultz, D.: Psicología Industrial. McGraw-Hill, México (1991)
7. Orhan, M.A., Rijsman, J., van Dijk, G.: Invisible, therefore isolated: comparative effects of team virtuality with task virtuality on workplace isolation and work outcomes. J. Work Organ. Psychol. **32**(2), 109–122 (2016)
8. Herrera.: The impact of telework on the work and family environment and the effects on the worker. Int. Compar. J. Labor Rrelation. Employ. Law **9**, 250–271 (2021)
9. Ramírez, J., Ballestas, M., Herrera, H., Ballesta, I.: Factores asociados al desempleo de los migrantes venezolanos en la ciudad de Barranquilla en el año 2020. Revista de Ciencias Sociales **28**(2) (2022)
10. Garcés, H.: Identificación de prejuicio del docentes en estudiantes migrantes venezolanos en Perú: un abordaje interpretativo. Revista Educare-Upel-IPB-Segunda Nueva Etapa 2.0 **25**(1), 102–127 (2021)
11. Brito, I.: Labor productivity of human talent: criteria to be considered in social intervention foundations in Colombia. Consensus **4**(3), 69–90 (2020)
12. Campo-Arias, A.: Uses of Cronbach's alpha coefficient. Biomedica **26**(4), 585 (2006). https://doi.org/10.7705/biomedica.v26i4.327
13. Hacker, J.V., Johnson, M., Saunders, C., Thayer, A.: Trust in virtual teams: a multidisciplinary review and integration. Aust. J. Inf. Syst. **23** (2019)
14. Davidavičienė, V., Al Majzoub, K., Meidute-Kavaliauskiene, I.: Factors affecting knowledge sharing in virtual teams. Sustainability **12**(17), 6917 (2020)
15. Mendoza-Ocasal, D., Castillo-Jiménez, R., Navarro, E., Ramírez, J.: Measuring workplace happiness as a key factor for the strategic management of organizations. Polish J. Manag. Stud. **24**(2), 292–306 (2021)
16. Pita, G.: Las TICs en las empresas: evolución de la tecnología y cambio estructural en las organizaciones. Dominio de las Ciencias **4**(1), 499–510 (2018)
17. Lay, N., et al.: Uso de las herramientas de comunicación asincrónicas y sincrónicas en la banca privada del municipio Maracaibo (Venezuela). Revista Espacios **40**(4) (2019)

Effects of Teleworking on the Body Mass Index of the Teachers of an Educational Institution

Victor Moreno Medina$^{(\boxtimes)}$ ⓘ, Luis Bermudez ⓘ, and Andrés Lara-Calle ⓘ

SISAu Research Group, Facultad de Ingeniería y Tecnologías de la Información y la, Comu-Nicación, Universidad Tecnológica Indoamérica, Ambato 180103, Ecuador
{victormoreno,luisbermudez}@uti.edu.ec

Abstract. In recent years overweight and obesity are a public health problem, this attention to the integrity of diverse types of professions where the work context from home and interaction with computer equipment are part of the new work models. Currently part of these jobs with a high prevalence of these work characteristics are teachers, the problem lies in an inadequate intake of food and little physical activity because of their work. Hence, assessing nutritional status based on body mass index in teachers of an educational institution in three academic periods, including a period of teleworking. For this, anthropometric indicators and statistical analysis based on a spreadsheet are used, this descriptive cross-sectional study was conducted with the data of forty-five teachers, of which 27% were men and 73% were women. Data were described using mean and confidence intervals, with comparative analysis by sex. Among the main results, it was determined that there was a prevalence of overweight of 42% and obesity of 18.0%, being more critical for men. In the end, it can be concluded that there is no malnutrition or underweight, but that overweight and obesity were highly prevalent, and that two-thirds of 60% of the teachers of the educational unit suffer from them, that is, they are slightly higher than those reported for the country (62.8%), in the National Health and Nutrition Survey in 2012.

Keywords: Body mass index · Education · Teleworking · Obesity

1 Introduction

In recent years, the world has suffered a pandemic related to the coronavirus, the same one that was determined as COVID 19, was unpredictable and being of respiratory origin, exceeded epidemiological control affecting the entire world. The pandemic must be studied through probabilistic and variable analysis to determine the scope and the control that can be maintained over them. In Ecuador, the first case according to the media was registered on February 14, 2020, in Guayaquil, they conducted tests that showed positive for coronavirus, but it was announced on February 29, 2020, by the Ministry of Public Health of Ecuador, being the third country in the region to present cases.

More than 1 billion adults worldwide are overweight, and at least 300 million are clinically obese [1] there is still no consensus to define telework, due to the use of various definitions, depending on the workplace, use of ICT, and the adequate distribution of hours between the office and home., greatly promoting a sedentary lifestyle, which is associated with chronic diseases such as obesity, cardiac pathologies, hypertension, etc.), activities aimed at teleworking during the pandemic period in the educational field are mainly academic, intellectual, mental, most often sitting, in Latin America, several studies have been conducted with various groups, but there are not many studies on teachers of basic and secondary education in Ecuador. The latest study carried out by the National Health and Nutrition Survey of the Ecuadorian State – ENSANUT, describes the health situation related to chronic non-communicable diseases, the nutritional situation, the situation of food consumption, the state of micronutrients, access to food supplementation programs and prophylactic supplementation, physical activity, considering geographical differences, demographic, ethnic, social, economic, gender and age specificities [2].

According to the WHO, physical inactivity is the fourth most important risk factor for mortality worldwide and causes 6% of all deaths on the planet, causing an increase in noncommunicable diseases, caused by poor nutrition and lack of physical activity, most often affecting people in production stages. The prevalence of obesity is over 20%, in 17 of the 20 countries in Latin America, and is significantly higher in women. [3] The ages of the overweight are from 18 to 49 years, being similar in men, attributing the high risk to present cardiovascular pathologies, metabolic, hypertension, diabetes, cancer, etc. [4, 5].

Overweight and obesity is multicausal and considered the determinants that influence such as lack of physical activity, sedentary lifestyle, and excess caloric intake (tabletop potato syndrome). This high is related to the ease and access to obtain food at all times during the working day, leading to a lack of control in food intake and variations in nutrients, that generally in the face-to-face working hours specific hours are assigned for food, the relationship between the syndrome of the desktop potato, the sedentary lifestyle influences the presentation of obesity and overweight, making it one of the determinants to present these pathologies [6]. Currently, teachers are teleworking, so it is urged to conduct a study to determine groups of teachers of secondary and basic education who are overweight and obese, during the period 2018–2021.

This study aims to establish the relationship between the muscle mass index (BMI), and the feeding factors together with the physical activity inside and outside the work, of the teachers of the educational unit.

2   Materials and Methods

This study presents a non-experimental, prospective, cross-sectional, correlational, and descriptive design, in which forty-five teachers participated, (twelve men and thirty-three women), located in urban areas of the city of Ambato, an inclusion criterion was that they have continuity during the years that the study was conducted (2020–2018).

The participation of the teachers was resolved and agreed upon through an informed consent document the same that was voluntary, information was provided before the medical evaluation, which was based on taking anthropometric data, weight kg, height cm, age, and sex, it was indicated that they wear light clothing during the evaluation to establish normal weight levels, overweight, obesity type 1, 2, 3, was compared with the values dictated by the American Heart Association (AHA) [5].

The analysis of the results was conducted using statistical methods and variables such as anthropometric measurements, height in centimeters and weight in kilograms, and data collection on the type of food and eating habits while they were teleworking which were correlated in a spreadsheet in the Microsoft Office Excel 2010 program.

The variables of the study are the body mass index BMI was created to evaluate and classify data ranging from overweight, to obesity type 1,2,3, with the following formula BMI = (weight-kg/height-m^2). Entities such as the World Health Organization report that a BMI greater than 25 means a moderate risk overweight, a BMI greater than 30 high risks of obesity, a BMI greater than 30 to 34.0 obesity type 1, a BMI greater than 35 to 39.9 obesity type 2, a BMI greater than 40 obesity type 3, the data were taken during the days of medical evaluation of the teachers were monitored and a statistical calculation was carried out in Excel.

The procedure of collecting data such as weight in kilograms was performed with a mechanical balance of the DETECTO platform calibrated before the process, with a capacity of 175 kg, for the collection of size data the tall meter of the DETECTO brand was used, all these procedures were performed and registered by the medical staff of the educational institution. It took into consideration the ethical principles of the Declaration of Helsinki of the World Medical Association, ensuring the confidentiality and safeguarding of student patient data.

3 Results

The particularity of the data of the group of teachers evaluated indicates that the age varies between 20 and 80 years, being the average of 31–40 years with 35.4%, for men, for women of 41–50 years with 30% of years. The average BMI (body mass index) for teachers was 0% for a BMI equivalent to thinness, 40% for an index equivalent to a normal weight, 42% for an index BMI equivalent to overweight, 16% for a BMI equivalent to grade 1 obesity, 1% for a BMI index for obesity type 2 and finally for a BMI index of obesity 31% of the population, as presented in Table 1 and Graf. 1.

Table 1. Classification weight, overweight, obesity Type 1, 2, 3 according to BMI

Variable	Body mass index (BMI)	Men				Women				Total	%
		2018	2019	2020	2021	2018	2019	2020	2021		
Thinness	−18	0	0	0	0	0	0	0	0	0	0%
Normal	18–24,9	4	4	4	4	21	18	8	9	72	40%
Overweight	25–29,9	6	6	5	5	11	14	15	14	76	42%
Obesity 1	30–34,9	2	2	2	2	1	1	10	8	28	16%
Obesity 2	35–39,9	0	0	0	2	0	0	0	0	2	1%
Obesity 3	+40	0	0	1	0	0	0	1	0	2	1%

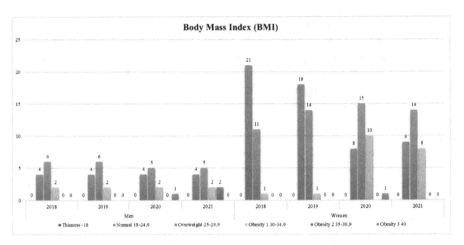

Fig. 1. (Classification weight, overweight, obesity Type 1, 2, 3, according to BMI)

When asked if the docents exercise at least three times a week, we observed that 45% of the participants answered affirmatively while 55% answered that they did not perform many types of exercise and/or some type of physical activity, as presented in Table 2.

Table 2. (Weekly physical activity frequency).

Engages frequently in physical activity (3 days a week)	Men	Women	Total	%
Yes	8	12	20	45%
No	4	21	25	55%

Table 3. Consumption of unhealthy foods (snacks, candies, soft drinks, etc.)

Unhealthy foods	Men	Women	Total	%
Yes	8	12	20	45%
No	4	21	25	55%
Total	**12**	**33**	**45**	**100%**

When asked if they consume foods between meals, breakfast, lunch, or dinner, which contain ingredients high in fat, carbohydrates, energy drinks, carbonated drinks, sweets, or unhealthy snacks (defined as unhealthy foods), 45% of the participants commented that if they do, while 55% of the participants mention that they do not, as presented in Table 3.

4 Discussions

The international labor organization defined the concept of telework as "the form of work carried out in a place far from the central office or the production center and that implies a new technology that allows separation and facilitates communication". [7] teleworking facilitates sedentary behaviors or low physical activity that in the future are harmful to the health of the teacher, increasing the risk of developing chronic pathologies, hypertension, diabetes, obesity, overweight, etc., due to this it is meritorious to have projects that help reduce the number of teachers who are at cardiovascular risk is associated with BMI (overweight and obesity), in that sense, Ecuador reveals 72% for the occurrence of deaths from non-communicable diseases, and of these, 45% corresponds to premature deaths (between 30 and 69 years), within which Cardiovascular Diseases and Diabetes Mellitus occupy the first five places (WHO 2018), with overweight and obesity in 6 out of 10 people, mostly between 40 and 50 years and in the female sex (65.5%), whose onset occurs from the age of 18 so they are considered a public health problem [8].

After the evaluation and the data taken from the teachers of the educational unit, a high average of cardiovascular risk was observed with the data taken, and based on the BMI, and the parameters indicated by the World Health Organization, the teachers present in the ranges of moderate risk to present cardiovascular pathologies, the male teachers in the educational unit are in a lower range due to the average related to the BMI.

In the 4 years where the samples were taken for the present study, the statistics indicate that in the present study the teachers who present a normal BMI (normal weight) are 40% being men with 16 samplers and women with 74 samples, the prevalence of overweight according to BMI are 42%, being 22 samples for men and 54 samples in women, the values of obesity type 1,2,3 according to BMI are 18%, being 11 samples for men and 21 samples for women the data found in this study agree with studies carried out at the national level such as the one carried out by the ASNUT (National Health and Nutrition Survey) of the Ecuadorian State, which describes the situation of food and complementary consumption.

5 Conclusions

It can be concluded that the evidence collected on the effects of teleworking, sedentary lifestyle, obesity, and the consequences on the health of teachers, is prejudicial depending on factors such as age, personal characteristics, chronic diseases, eating habits, physical habits, and the management that is had on them.

According to the results of this study, it can be evidenced that, of the forty-five teachers, 27% were men and the remaining 73% were women, there it was determined that there was a prevalence in the presence of overweight at 42% and obesity at 18.0%, being more critical for men. A point that contributes significantly to weight gain is the intake of unhealthy foods, such as foods rich in fats, carbohydrates, energy drinks, and carbonated drinks, between the three main meals (breakfast, lunch, and dinner), at this point, it could be evidenced that 55% of the teachers who participated in the study do not consume this type of food, while 45% if they consume them. While a differentiating point in the fight against overweight is physical activity, the same as it is advisable to do it on a minimum of 3 occasions during the week, exercises such as walking, running, and practicing some type of sport such as football, which could help burn calories, in addition to helping to prevent symptoms of acute stress product of sedentary and monotonous workdays, at this point, it can be observed that of the total number of participants, 55% of the participants do not practice or perform the activity. Physical more than three times during the week, while 45% of participants responded that if they perform such physical activities during the week.

References

1. Rodríguez, E., Oramas, A., Rodríguez, L.: Stress in basic education teachers: case study in Guanajuato. Mexico. Salud los Trab. **15**, 2–16 (2007)
2. Saá, F., Caceres, L., Fuentes, E.M., Varela-Aldás, J.: Teaching-learning in the industrial engineering career in times of COVID-19. In: Zaphiris, P., Ioannou, A. (eds.) HCII 2021. LNCS, vol. 12784, pp. 517–530. Springer, Cham (2021). https://doi.org/10.1007/978-3-030-77889-7_36
3. Braguinsky, J.: Prevalencia de obesidad en América Latina. An. Sist. Sanit. Navar. **25**, 109–115 (2002). https://doi.org/10.23938/ASSN.0819
4. Goodpaster, B.H., et al.: Obesity, regional body fat distribution, and the metabolic syndrome in older men and women. Arch. Intern. Med. **165**, 777–783 (2005). https://doi.org/10.1001/ARCHINTE.165.7.777
5. Carnethon, M.R., Loria, C.M., Hill, J.O., Sidney, S., Savage, P.J., Liu, K.: Risk factors for the metabolic syndrome: the Coronary Artery Risk Development in Young Adults (CARDIA) study, 1985–2001. Diabetes Care **27**, 2707–2715 (2004). https://doi.org/10.2337/DIACARE.27.11.2707
6. Bernardina, M., Fabregat, A., Cifre Gallego, E.: Teleworking and health: a new challenge for up-to-date psychology. **83**, 55–61 (2002)
7. OIT: Convention C177 Convention on homework (2000). https://www.ilo.org/dyn/normlex/es/f?p=NORMLEXPUB:12100:0::NO::P12100_INSTRUMENT_ID:312322
8. Bertheau, E.L., Cruz-Quintana, F., Pappous, A., Rio-Valle, J.S.: Explicit and implicit attitudes towards obesity in students of physical culture. Rev. Psychol. del Deport. **25**, 91–96 (2016)

How Effective is the Octalysis Gamification to Design Satisfying Electronic Wallet Experiences?

Kwan Panyawanich[✉], Martin Maguire, and Patrick Pradel

Loughborough University, Epinal Way, Loughborough LE11 3TU, UK
k.panyawanich@lboro.ac.uk

Abstract. The purpose of this paper is to investigate recent research on the effectiveness of gamification as a design strategy in the development of financial application. This paper briefly introduces the eight Octalysis gamification core drives and how applying gamified principles with the design thinking process can effectively increase user engagement and motivation for services. This paper will refer to works of literature discussing gamification found in services and will provide examples of cases where gamification was incorporated into electronic wallets. The ambition of this research will centre on the creation of electronic wallet prototypes for universal usage.

Keywords: Octalysis gamification · Gamification · Design experience · Design thinking process

1 Introduction

With the expansion of services in the digital platform-commerce, electronic wallets will rapidly become a common financial payment method. Recent COVID 19 outbreaks highlighted the importance of new technology for long-term societal implications. Thailand, the United Kingdom, and China are all going to transition to a cashless society. During the pandemic period (2017–2020), the number of Thais downloading electronic wallets (True Money) increased significantly. The percentage of users using digital and mobile wallets in the UK's e-commerce landscape remains the highest of all payment types. In 2020, China's mobile payment users will exceed 852 million, placing it first in the world.

A primary concern is that not everybody is comfortable using the electronic wallets. Because of the differences in lifestyles and priorities, there are differences in technology usage behavior among age groups. Older generations follow their old habits, making it difficult to adapt to new technology. Senior citizens suffer from "technology anxiety" or "technophobia." Because of a lack of technological fluency, they are frequently skeptical of using latest technology [16]. Therefore, the goals of this study are to determine whether Octalysis Gamification would be a design strategy in developing the experiences of using electronic wallets, to address the current pain point in existing e-wallets, and to produce

C. Stephanidis et al. (Eds.): HCII 2022, CCIS 1655, pp. 323–331, 2022.
https://doi.org/10.1007/978-3-031-19682-9_42

a universal design that is approachable and satisfying to users of all ages. This paper is aims to demonstrate the most recent literature review evaluation of gamification and electronic wallet knowledge.

1.1 Electronic Wallets

Electronic wallet is a type of E-money server-based financial services that allows businesses and users to process fast transactions without having physical cash on hand [13]. The system protects users' confidential information while preventing financial risks [1, 4, 14]. Prior to registering to use an electronic wallet, it is necessary to download the application via the App Store for iOS Apple devices or the Play Store for Android devices by searching for the application's name.

1.2 Gamification

According to Forbes Global, nearly 70% of businesses have considered incorporating gamification principles into their operations, with gamification anticipated to grow to $11.10 billion by 2020. Specifically, the application of game design elements in non-game contexts. To support the creation of value in services for users as part of the marketing strategy [3].

Numerous studies have explained gamification, it is the incorporation of game mechanisms into non-gaming contexts to driving behavior on using specific services. Chou (2019), the Octalysis gamification model (see Fig. 1) explains eight human core drives to trigger human motivation on using designated services;

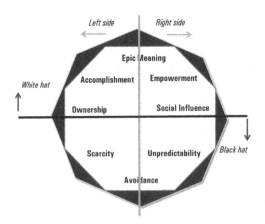

Fig. 1. Octalysis Gamification model [17]

Epic Meaning and Calling: a person felt important and needed to be a part of something special and meaningful, to be a part of heroine story. For example, creating a narrative mission to reduce spending or a financial management mission.

Development and Accomplishment: Motivate because a person is improving, learn, level up, and achieve new skills, milestone, and challenges. Making progress. For example, displaying the progress bar level to become the platform's customer loyalty.

Empowerment of Creativity and Feedback: Motivates a person to feel engaged in a creative process where he or she can express creativity, try new experiences in different combinations, received feedback and adjustment strategies. For example, boosters and unlock milestones be able to use new application features.

Ownership and Possession: Motivates a person to feel in control, possession, and protection of something; enhances this extrinsic possession. Controlling one's own virtual wallet, for example.

Social Influence and Relatedness: motivates a person to influence what other people do and think? An inspiration from the actions and thoughts of others, the connectedness, comparison, or emotional association Mentorships, group quests, and exchange digital gifting are some examples.

Scarcity and Impatience: a desire for something rare, exclusive, or available for a limited time that is normally unattainable or difficult to obtain. For example, a discount voucher for using an e-wallet at a participating merchant.

Unpredictability and Curiosity: a person who felt engaged in something and was eager to learn the unknown outcome, uncertainty that arouses curiosity. For example, mystery boxes and easter eggs.

Loss and Avoidance: a person chooses to avoid or avoid being in a negative situation because they are afraid of losing. For example, countdown timers and progress loss [6, 9].

The logic, calculations, and ownership-related or identified as extrinsic motivators are on the left side of the Octalysis model. The intrinsic motivators on the right side are related to creativity, self-expression, and social aspects. The model's top core drives represent positive White Hat Gamification motivators, while the bottom ones represent negative Black Hat Gamification motivators [6, 9]. The model can be used for developing gamification design to provide quantitative and qualitative feedback.

When illustrating gamification in the context of designing experiences, it is about defining a clear goal, understanding the user's feelings, motivations, and engagement with the overall system and function of the service. Gamification uses human value creation toward a service. Effective gamification integration in design is not equivalent to inserting gaming elements where necessary such as points, scores, badges, and medals to the service. But rather, placing gamified mechanisms in the appropriate context of the service that facilitates user engagement with the technology and has the potential to improve the learning process by facilitating the service experience [6, 16].

Effective gamified design should utilise gaming elements with the purpose of encouraging psychological needs and enjoyable experiences for users, by understanding the value that motivates users and harmonizing the appropriate type of motivators to the correct people. It is advised to maintain a simple mechanism that is ease-of-use, and effortless by also including a non-gamified element in designing especially for senior applications [9]. If a gamified design is integrated to no user value or does not commit a systematic user-focus analysis, the added game-based element may lack acceptance from intended users which leads to demotivation or distraction. This is because products and services have not been obtained as useful [12]. Users will behave in an undesired way, lose performance, and decline in using gamified elements [3, 7]. Whereas, successful gamification services will show understanding of their users, provoke motivation and eventually persuade behavioural changes [12, 15].

Gamified designs are associated with the younger generation. In fact, gamified techniques are effective with senior citizens because they influence their decision to use technology by providing a user-friendly interface and have a positive impact on cognitive, motivational, and behavioral learning [9]. The stickiness strategy used by WeChat Pay, one of China's leading electronic wallet providers, applied gamified embracing the cultural practice of red packets (Hongbao) monetary gifting. It is customary for older adults to send gifts in red envelopes to younger family members and friends during Chinese New Year, birthdays, and weddings. The red envelope represents prosperity and good fortune, and Chinese people enjoy receiving and sending this game mechanism of gift exchange. This feature activates not only WeChat Pay but also the social networking features of WeChat messaging. As a result, senior adult subscriptions to WeChat Pay have soared [16]. Furthermore, scholars have investigated the impact of gamification on accelerating behavioral change through various contexts of designs found in consumer's innovative products that trigger favorable responses to smartphone marketing tactics for example advertising and loyalty schemes [5, 16]. Cultural traditions are no longer a barrier to using new technology as it is confirmed by the design of WeChat Pay that technology can optimize the traditional culture with the technology. Western culture can adopt a similar culture on special occasions and digitalize gifting behaviours such as Christmas, birthdays, and weddings. A cultural practice that technology developers can pay attention to that is consistent with traditional norms means that people are more likely to accept innovative services [16].

2 Future Development

The future research will apply the design thinking process (see Fig. 2), which is a human-centered approach to innovation that prioritises the needs of the user [10]. From the stage of empathize to the test of prototype application.

To understand the research gaps emerged from the literature review, future research will use a mixed-method approach for its secondary and primary study, which will include literature review, survey, social media searching, interviews, and usability testing. The understanding phrase will conduct user research by launching surveys and conducting interviews in order to understand the market size of electronic wallet users and the pain-point of unpleasant experiences while using electronic wallet services. The Ideate phases will integrate the insights/responses of participants into the Octalysis Gamification context. Usability studies will be conducted by testing various designs of electronic wallets during the prototype and testing phases. Targeted sampling will be based on Thailand, United Kingdom and China.

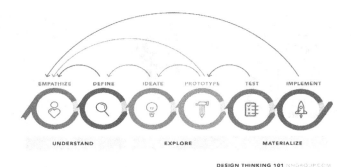

Fig. 2. Design Thinking process [10]

3 Literature Discussion

This paper discusses the use of gamification in three different design types: website, process-related, and socially related game components [3], as well as cases of electronic wallet gamified design that increase psychological needs. A website component is a functional part of gameplay that includes a visual character. It refers to the ability to complete specific game achievements. Badges, for example, are an indicator showing the status of achieving a goal or completing an activity. The process-related components display a visual progress bar to provide information about the user's progress of achieving a goal [3]. Percentage progress a sample indicator can be found in a customised money-saving application. The sample supported the behavioural economics, "endow progress effect" because people feel motivated to achieve goals when they had given opportunity to achieve [5].

Social components deal with the interaction between game players, such as cooperation, teamwork, or sending digital gifts to peers. Fun experiences will be shared with other users and social influence is an important factor in increasing motivation [3]. Gan and Li (2018) explains further that self-documentation and information sharing as utilitarian factors play an important role in influencing user behaviour intention. Social presence will drive users to form personal connections with others. This aligns with the social comparison theory, which referred that people learn by comparing themselves to others to evaluate or improve some aspect of themselves. Nevertheless, some people avoid sharing their goal progress with others and refuse to receive information from others by distancing themselves [3].

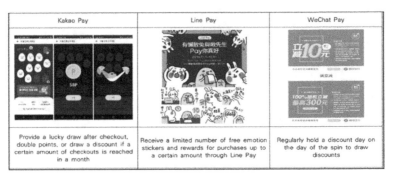

Kakao Pay	Line Pay	WeChat Pay
Provide a lucky draw after checkout, double points, or draw a discount if a certain amount of checkouts is reached in a month	Receive a limited number of free emotion stickers and rewards for purchases up to a certain amount through Line Pay	Regularly hold a discount day on the day of the spin to draw discounts

Fig. 3. Rewards and feedback [5]

Gamification in financial services goes beyond entertainment. It is used for marketing purpose to increase customer loyalty by achieving customer demand, and desires. Four design cases that induce psychological needs include fun and interaction, a scenario-creating mini-game in the application to actively increase participation based on curiosity drive. Kakao Pay a ladder game or a money-spraying game to win the top prizes in a first-come, first served competition. Rewards and feedback are received (see Fig. 3) using a compensation mechanism to receive points and a discount when paying with an electronic wallet only at checkout [5].

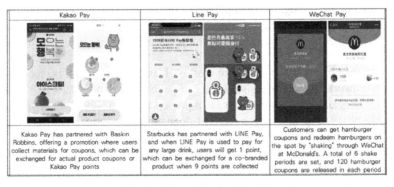

Kakao Pay	Line Pay	WeChat Pay
Kakao Pay has partnered with Baskin Robbins, offering a promotion where users collect materials for coupons, which can be exchanged for actual product coupons or Kakao Pay points	Starbucks has partnered with LINE Pay, and when LINE Pay is used to pay for any large drink, users will get 1 point, which can be exchanged for a co-branded product when 9 points are collected	Customers can get hamburger coupons and redeem hamburgers on the spot by 'shaking' through WeChat at McDonald's. A total of 6 shake periods are set, and 120 hamburger coupons are released in each period

Fig. 4. Win—win situation [5]

The win-win situation is how mobile payment companies collaborate with other companies to create promotions that maximise mutual benefit from using the service. For example, WeChat Pay (see Fig. 4) has a membership system in partnership with McDonald's where users can play the WeChat Pay shake game to claim coupons [5].

The relationship-up type (see Fig. 5) payment services are combined with a social messaging app to create a relationship mechanics game [5].

Previous studies asserted that people value their autonomous motivation because it helps them improve their competence. For example, gamified features in financial management application; the real-time finance tracking, a displayed progression chart monitoring ongoing financial goals, a feedback alert, and a notification indicating account

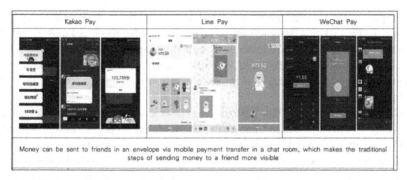

Kakao Pay	Line Pay	WeChat Pay

Money can be sent to friends in an envelope via mobile payment transfer in a chat room, which makes the traditional steps of sending money to a friend more visible

Fig. 5. Relationship-up type [5]

balances so that when goal is achieved, it triggers autonomous motivation. Financial management application displays financial data in progress bars and other performance graphs, allowing users to compare and share their financial situation or goals with other users [2].

Prior studies surprisingly noted the importance of non-gamified designs, particularly for senior users. Application-based services need to offer to customise display settings to be able to adjust the font size, contrast, interaction speed, gamification deactivation, regular activities, a manageable set of rules, and goal visualisation, to fulfil satisfaction [9]. Bitrián, Buil, and Catalán (2021) agreed that a personalised profile and activity will increase motivation by allowing users to be in control of their accounts. Simulation-based game designs are not preferred for senior adults; however, the interactive element of communication between friends and acquaintances is important because they value social contacts more than at younger ages. Collaboration, cooperation features, and cognitive-promoting activities are preferable for senior adults. It is recommended to deliver a positive experience, and avoid using competition as a strategy to provoke motivations and time constraints when designing services for senior users [9].

3.1   Why Gamification Design Must Combine with Design Thinking?

Gamification and design thinking together in the service development process help in connecting ideas and making those ideas more visible. Having both concepts ensures that the innovation process is manageable. Gamification improves the effectiveness of design thinking by providing structure coordinating different functions, assisting in goal setting, and incorporating social aspects to drive user engagement and flow [11, 12]. Gamification will be used primarily in the ideation phases and provide a clearer link between thinking and doing. Incorporating game mechanics in the design thinking processes will improve ideas, modify the risk, assist decision-making, and position the product centre to the users. The gamified procedure focuses on the outcome, which helps to develop goal-setting and multidisciplinary engagement [11, 15].

Gamification brings the co-creation of new solutions, brainstorming from the chosen idea, deepening ideation in the design thinking process and building upon other ideas, and collectively improving ideas that may be generated individually. Gamification makes ideation phases easier to understand by identifying what is the goal of this design process? mapping out the task that designers must do, including what resources must be involved and what changes needed to be done. Design thinking and gamification both led to a data-driven, action-oriented, iterative, cyclical, and insights-driven strategy. A well-rounded description of an idea will improve decision-making and reduces the risk of failed prototyping [11].

When using only design thinking to develop products and services, the method brainstorms only user personas, needs, and goals. The guideline proposes a design mechanism for analysing relevant motivational factors which are just the subset of relevant variables [12]. Non-design thinking routes will not be highlighted, the psychological areas that will improve the functionalities of the service or the social matters where users use products and services to accomplish their goals. On the other hand, if implementing only gamification into products and services, there will be no iterative process, the phases of testing finished prototype to real users. The purpose of this phase is to develop and validate the prototype to see whether products and services meet the user requirements [12, 15].

Gamification matches persona problems to the design features, the specifications of the technological solution. Prototype developers will be able to analyse, select the easiest and the most suitable gamification element that serves the requirement, and discard conflicted ones. Gamification is useful for projects with conceptualising architecture because solutions can be discovered by defining specification needs. It is a decent strategy for creating new products because it examines the entire process whilst also focusing on externalising characteristics needs and requirements [11].

3.2 Limitations/Opportunity

Previous studies have looked at gamification in the context of education, learning, health application, marketing, consumer behaviour, and the analysis of existing financial services [9, 11]. The majority of literature analyses services are based on eastern cultural services and choose specific gamification features [16]. There are still a few publications that focus on the Octalysis gamification model to use in the development of financial services. Future study will take a different approach to implement Octalysis gamification. The Octalysis Gamification model will be used as a design skeleton in conjunction with the design thinking process to create an electronic wallet prototype. The octagon models will be drawn after completing primary and secondary user research to empathize with user values before building the actual prototype.

4   Conclusion

The purpose of this prospective study is to understand the Octalysis gamification as a design strategy, perhaps to identify current research gaps and propose future research directions for a project developing an electronic wallet. The idea is to produce a universal prototype that consider users' needs and problems, allowing designers to create application prototypes that emotionally satisfying for people of all ages and nationalities. People who are not technologically savvy will, hopefully, use electronic wallets more in the future.

References

1. Boonloy, P., Tangpattanak, J.: Factors affecting decision making to use electronic true money wallet of students of kasetsart university si racha campus chon buri province. UBRU Int. J. **1**(2), 1–10 (2021)
2. Bitrián, P., Buil, I., Catalán, S.: Making finance fun: the gamification of personal financial management apps. Int. J. Bank Mark. (2021)
3. Bayuk, J., Altobello, S.A.: Can gamification improve financial behavior? The moderating role of app expertise. Int. J. Bank Mark. **37**(4), 951–975 (2019)
4. Chauhan, M., Shingari, I.: Future of e-wallets: a perspective from under graduates. Int. J. Adv. Res. Comput. Sci. Softw. Eng. **7**(8), 146 (2017)
5. Chen, T.-Y., Pan, Y.-H.: A study on the implementation of gamification in mobile payment services. J. Korea Convergence Soc. **13**(4), 213–226 (2022)
6. Chou, Y.-K.: Actionable Gamification: Beyond Points, Badges, and Leaderboards. Packt Publishing Ltd. (2019)
7. Fischer, H., Heinz, M., Schlenker, L.: Gamifying higher education. Beyond badges, points and Leaderboards. In: Workshop Gemeinschaften in Neuen Medien (GeNeMe) (2016)
8. Gan, C., Li, H.: Understanding the effects of gratifications on the continuance intention to use WeChat in China: a perspective on uses and gratifications. Comput. Hum. Behav. **78**, 306–315 (2018)
9. Gellner, C., Buchem, I., Müller, J.: Application of the octalysis framework to gamification designs for the elderly. In: Proceedings of the 15th European Conference on Games-Based Learning (2021)
10. "Was is Design Thinking? - Design Thinking" Hasso-Plattner-Institut (2022). https://hpi.de/school-of-design-thinking/design-thinking/was-ist-design-thinking.html
11. Patrício, R., Moreira, A.C., Zurlo, F.: Enhancing design thinking approaches to innovation through gamification. Eur. J. Innov. Manag. (2020)
12. Piras, L., Dellagiacoma, D., Perini, A., Susi, A., Giorgini, P., Mylopoulos, J.: Design thinking and acceptance requirements for designing gamified software. In: 13th International Conference on Research Challenges in Information Science (2019)
13. Soegoto, D.S., Tampubolon, M.P.: E-wallet as a payment instrument in the millennial era. In: IOP Conference Series: Materials Science and Engineering, vols. 879, no. 1 (2020)
14. Upadhayaya, A.: Electronic commerce and E-wallet. Int. J. Recent Res. Rev. **1**, 37–41 (2012)
15. Villegas, E., Labrador, E., Fonseca, D., Fernández-Guinea, S., Moreira, F.: Design thinking and gamification: user centered methodologies. In: International Conference on Human-Computer Interaction (2019)
16. Wong, D., Liu, H., Meng-Lewis, Y., Sun, Y., Zhang, Y.: Gamified money: exploring the effectiveness of gamification in mobile payment adoption among the silver generation in China (2021)
17. Freitas, S.A.A., Lacerda, A.R., Calado, P.M., Lima, T.S., Canedo, E.D.: Gamification in education: a methodology to identify student's profile. In: Frontiers in Education Conference (FIE) (2017)

Impulsive Purchase in Agricultural Products Livestreaming: An ELM Model

Suting Yang, Lili Liu[(⊠)], Jiajia Xu, Jiaqi Zhang, Jiaqi Wang, Yun Lu,
and Chuanmin Mi

College of Economics and Management, Nanjing University of Aeronautics and Astronautics,
Nanjing, China
{yst1122,lliliu85,jiajiaxu,jiaqizhang,jiaqiwang,luyun0214,
Cmmi}@nuaa.edu.cn

Abstract. Despite impulsive purchase in livestreaming has aroused great attention among scholars, research on Agricultural Products Livestreaming is still limited. To fill this gap, this study aims to explore the factors that determine consumers' impulsive purchase behavior in the context of APLS. Based on the Elaboration Likelihood Model and trust transfer theory, this paper investigates how the central path factors (product quality and price incentives) and peripheral path factors (professionalism and para-social) affect consumers' impulsive purchase intention, which is mediated by trust (trust in product and trust in broadcaster). Data were collected from 253 respondents and analyzed with smartpls3.0. Findings show that product quality and price incentives positively affect trust in product, professionalism and para-social positively influence trust in broadcaster, both trust in product and broadcaster positively affect consumers' impulsive purchase intention in APLS. Besides, trust in broadcaster is positively correlated with trust in product. Potential theoretical and practical contributions are discussed.

Keywords: Agricultural products livestreaming · Elaboration likelihood model · Impulsive purchase intention

1 Introduction

Since the outbreak of COVID-19 in 2020, livestreaming commerce has become a new normal in advertising and marketing [25]. Due to the epidemic prevention and control, sales of fresh agricultural products such as vegetables and fruits have faced regional and phased unsalable dilemma. A large backlog of agricultural products, unstable sales channels and prices falling below the cost line have appeared in some areas. Fortunately, Agricultural Products Livestreaming (APLS) could effectively solve the problem. On one hand, APLS lively and directly displays the respective advantages of agricultural products in front of consumers, eliminates the information asymmetry. It breaks through the time and space constraints, meets people's diversified needs for fresh agricultural products, and enriches consumers' shopping experience [26]. On the other hand, APLS has a high degree of informatization, which can integrate and optimize the allocation of resources, greatly reducing the waste of resources. In 2020, the number of APLS reached 4 million and the total sales reached 93.8 billion in China, with a year-on-year increase of 31% [11]. By 2022, it is expected that 110,000 farmer broadcasters will do livestreaming on Taobao, further promoting the sales of agricultural products to exceed 5 billion CNY [20]. APLS has obtained certain achievements in the sales of agricultural products and has good development prospects in the future.

However, the business model of livestreaming commerce is still in its infancy, facing many severe challenges in its development process [27]. Researchers barely pay attention to this business mode, we know little about customer purchase behavior in APLC. To fill this gap, drawing on Elaborative Likelihood Model, this study seeks to investigate how central path factors (product quality and price incentives) and peripheral path factors (professionalism and para-social) affect consumers' impulsive purchase intention in the context of APLS. Besides, in light of the trust transfer theory, product trust and broadcast trust are identified as mediators.

2 Theoretical Background

Elaboration Likelihood Model (ELM) is a dual-process theory that explains how the process of persuasion affects an individual's attitude change through two different information processing routes: central and peripheral [19]. The degree of elaboration effort individuals spend on information processing will affect which route they choose. ELM has been extensively applied in studies of social psychology [4], marketing [5], revealing the importance of the moderating variables, such as potential consumers' motivation and ability to elaborate on informational messages [19]. For instance, Chen et al. apply ELM to livestreaming commerce and show two different routes through which consumers' trust can be built to affect their purchase intention and willingness to pay more [2]. Trust transfer theory indicates that one's trust in a known target can transfer to an unknown target [21], which implies trust can be explored from different dimensions. Thus, in this study, we divided trust into trust in product and trust in broadcaster in the context of APLS.

Based on ELM and trust transfer theory, we develop a conceptual model to investigate the effects of central route factors (product quality and price incentive) and peripheral route factors (professionalism and para-social) on consumers' impulsive purchase behavior via the mediation of two types of trust in the context of APLS.

3 Research Model and Hypotheses

Our research model is depicted in Fig. 1. Corresponding hypotheses are discussed respectively in following section.

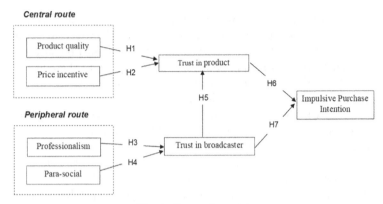

Fig. 1. Research model

3.1 Central Route Attributes: Product Quality and Price Incentive

Product quality refers to the characteristics of the agri-product which meet specified requirements [3]. Previous studies indicate that product quality is an important determinant of consumers' trust and willingness to buy [12]. In this study, if quality of agri-products is good, consumers are more likely to be satisfied and develop trust towards these products. We thus propose:

H1. Product quality is positively related to consumer's trust in product.

Price incentive refers to promotional methods such as discounts offered [24]. Price incentive could stimulate consumers' trust in products in online purchase [8]. In APLS, broadcasters always give gifts to consumers, such as discount coupons. Normally, these discounts or lower prices are time-limited and Livestreaming-only, which is difficult to obtain out of the livestreaming. If consumers want to enjoy the price incentives, they have to instantly establish trust toward the products and complete the purchase. Thus, we assume:

H2. Price incentive is positively related to consumer's trust in product.

3.2 Peripheral Route Attributes: Professionalism and Para-Social

Professionalism is evaluated by broadcaster's ability to introduce agricultural products in a convincing manner [1, 23]. Consumers are more likely to trust broadcasters who are knowledgeable about the products and who can provide precise information about the product, to eliminate the uncertainty of making purchase decisions [22]. If the broadcaster is an expert in the agri-products, who is able to calmly deal with various questions raised by consumers during the APLS, consumers will trust this broadcaster. Therefore, we propose:

H3. Professionalism is positively related to consumer's trust in broadcaster.

Para-social refers to consumers' perception of intimacy with the broadcaster [17]. Online social presence is positively associated with consumers' relatedness and stickiness, which is a vital factor influencing trust [7]. In APLS, para-social between consumers and broadcasters will bring a feeling of real-time interaction to consumers, generating more positive impressions toward broadcasters, such as trust. Thus, we assume:

H4. Para-social is positively related to consumer's trust in broadcaster.

3.3 Trust and Impulsive Purchase Intention

Based on the trust transfer theory, Stewart states that trust in a known entity or context can be transferred to unknown target when they are related [21]. Park and Lin demonstrate that consumers' positive attitude towards broadcasters will be transferred to their endorsed products [18]. In this study, if consumers trust broadcasters, they are more likely to trust the agri-products recommended by the broadcasters. Hence, we propose:

H5. Consumer's trust in broadcaster is positively related to their trust in product.

Impulsive purchase intention is an unplanned intention in which the consumer has a sudden, strong and sustainable desire to buy products [15]. Marketing literature has demonstrated the positive relationships between trust and favorable behaviors [13, 16]. In online transactions, trust is an important predictor of consumer behavior [10, 14]. In this study, consumers' trust in product and broadcaster could reduce consumers' concerns about the agri-products, and finally encourage impulse purchase. Thus, we argue:

H6. Trust in product is positively related to consumer's impulsive purchase intention.

H7. Trust in broadcaster is positively related to consumer's impulsive purchase intention.

4   Research Methodology

4.1   Data Collection

We designed an online survey to collected data via Sojump (https://www.wjx.cn/, one of the largest professional data collection websites in China), in order to test the research model and corresponding hypotheses. All the measurement items were adapted from existing studies, tested with a Likert Seven-level scale, ranging from 1 (strongly disagree) to 7 (strongly agree). Individuals who had experiences of watching APLS were selected as targeted population. In total, 253 valid responses were received.

40.7% of our respondents were male and 59.3% were female. 61.3% of the samples were between 26 and 35 years old. In addition, majority of the respondents were bachelors (82.6%). More than 50% respondents' monthly income were above 6000 CNY. Majority (71.1%) of the respondents had spent less than 1000 CNY on APLS. Detailed demographical information was shown in Table 1.

Table 1. Demographics of respondents

Item	Options	Frequency	Percentage (%)
Gender	Male	97	44.9
	Female	119	55.1
Age	Under 18	2	0.8
	19–25	62	24.5
	26–35	155	61.3
	36–45	31	12.3
	46 and above	3	1.2
Educational level	High school or below	1	0.4
	College	21	8.3
	Bachelor	209	82.6
	Master and above	19	7.5
Monthly income	Below 2000 CNY	5	2.0
	2000–4000 CNY	53	20.9
	4000–6000 CNY	68	26.9
	6000–8000 CNY	70	23.7
APLS purchase consumption	Above 8000 CNY	67	26.5
	Below 500 CNY	83	32.8
	500–1000 CNY	97	38.3
	1000–1500 CNY	51	20.2
	Above 1500 CNY	22	8.7

4.2 Data Analysis and Results

SmartPLS3.0 was used to analyze data. First, we tested the reliability and validity of measurement model by checking Cronbach's Alpha values, factor loadings, composite reliability and Average Variance Extracted (AVE). The Cronbach's Alpha values and factor loadings were greater than the recommended value of 0.70, suggesting sufficient reliability [6, 9]. All composite reliability values were above 0.70 [9], and all AVE exceeded 0.5 [9], indicating good convergent validity.

We then tested the structural model. Findings indicated that all of the hypotheses were supported: (1) product quality and price incentive were positively associated with consumers' trust in product ($\beta = 0.442$, $t = 6.578$; $\beta = 0.195$, $t = 3.156$); (2) professionalism and para-social had positive impacts on consumers' trust in broadcaster ($\beta = 0.402$, $t = 6.567$; $\beta = 0.426$, $t = 7.492$); (3) consumers' trust in broadcaster positively affected their trust in product ($\beta = 0.234$, $t = 2.081$); (4) consumers' trust in product and broadcaster were positively associated with impulsive purchase intention ($\beta = 0.220$, $t = 3.629$; $\beta = 0.313$, $t = 3.151$). Moreover, central route factors jointly explained 53.8% variance of trust in product, while peripheral route factors explained 52.8% variance of trust in broadcaster, which in turn jointly explained 23.0% variance of impulsive purchase intention (see Fig. 2).

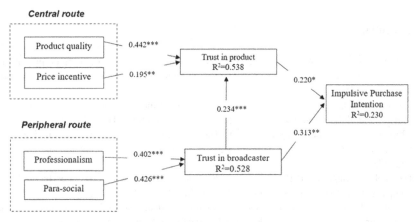

Fig. 2. Structural model

5 Conclusions

We apply ELM to explore the impulsive purchase intention of consumers in APLS. Results show that consumers can build trust via two different routes in APLS, which in turn affect their impulsive purchase intention. Besides, trust in broadcaster is positively related with trust in product. Therefore, in APLS, better product quality and more favorable price, professional broadcaster and strong perceived interaction, will help to strengthen consumers' trust in the broadcaster and products, and ultimately motivate their purchase behavior.

It is worth noting that our study is one of the earliest empirical studies that apply the ELM model to investigate consumers' impulsive purchase intention in APLS, which expands our knowledge on APLS. Secondly, we identify "para-social" instead of "interactivity" as one of APLS's attributes. In addition, our research roots in "impulse purchase intention", which is a relatively new in the context of APLS. In practice, the findings of this study provide useful enlightenment for livestreaming platform and broadcaster of APLS. First, providing more price incentives for agri-products is helpful to attract consumers. Secondly, in order to increase consumers' trust in broadcaster and agricultural products, we should not only select broadcasters with positive image, but also pay attention to the quality control of agricultural products (e.g., products with positive WOM). Third, broadcasters should be knowledgeable on agricultural products, to ensure that they are capable to timely and accurately answer the questions from consumers during APLS. They should have good skills in communication, interacting with consumers as much as possible to make consumers feel involved and cared. There are limitations in the study. For instance, respondents' age and education level were not evenly distributed, which could be solved by future study by expanding the sample size.

Acknowledgment. This study was supported by the Fundamental Research Funds for the Central Universities No. NR2021003 awarded to the second author.

References

1. Agnihotri, R., Rapp, A., Trainor, K.: Understanding the role of information communication in the buyer-seller exchange process: antecedents and outcomes. J. Bus. Ind. Mark. **24**(7), 474–486 (2009)
2. Chen, C.D., Zhao, Q., Wang, J.L.: How livestreaming increases product sales: role of trust transfer and elaboration likelihood model. Behav. Inf. Technol. **41**(3), 558–573 (2020)
3. Chinomona, R., Okoumba, L., Pooe, D.: The impact of product quality on perceived value, trust and students' intention to purchase electronic gadgets. Mediterr. J. Soc. Sci. **4**(14), 463–472 (2013)
4. Davis, F.D., Bagozzi, R.P., Warshaw, P.R.: User acceptance of computer technology: a comparison of two theoretical models. Manag. Sci. **35**(8), 982–1003 (1989)
5. Dennis, A.R.: Information exchange and use in group decision making: you can lead a group to information, but you can't make it think. MIS Q. **20**(4), 433–457 (1996)
6. Fornell, C., Larcker, D.F.: Evaluating structural equation models with unobservable variables and measurement error. Market. Res **18**, 39–50 (1981)
7. Gao, W., Liu, Y., Liu, Z., Li, J.: How does presence influence purchase intention in online shopping markets? An explanation based on self-determination theory. Behav. Inform. Technol. **37**(8), 786–799 (2018)
8. Gu, R., Oh, L., Wang, K.: Developing user loyalty for social networking sites: a relational perspective. J. Electron. Commer. Res. **17**(1), 1–21 (2016)
9. Hair Jr, J.F., Black, W.C., Babin, B.J., Anderson, R.E., Tatham, R.L.: Multivariate Data Analysis. Auflage, Upper Saddle River (2006). https://scholar.google.com.hk/scholar?hl=zh-CN&as_sdt=0%2C5&q=+Multivariate+Data+Analysis.+Auflage%2C+Upper+Saddle+River+&btnG=
10. Jarcenpaa, S., Tractinsky, N., Vitale, M.: Consumer trust in an Internet store. Inform. Technol. Manag. **1**, 45–71 (2000)
11. Jiao, Q.: Live broadcasting to help agriculture: a new model of poverty alleviation through ecommerce. Central China Normal University (2021)
12. Li, X., Hess, T.J., Valacich, J.S.: Using attitude and social influence to develop an extended trust model for behaviour & information technology 13 information systems. Database Adv. Inf. Syst. **37**(2–3), 108–124 (2006)
13. Liang, T.P., Wu, P.-J., Huang, C.C.: Why funders invest in crowdfunding projects: roles of trust from the dual-process perspective. Inf. Manag. **56**(1), 70–84 (2019)
14. Lu, B., Fan, W., Zhou, M.: Social presence, trust, and social commerce purchase intention: an empirical research. Comput. Hum. Behav. **56**, 225–237 (2016)
15. Lo, L.Y.S., Lin, S.W., Hsu, L.Y.: Motivation for online impulse buying: A two-factor theory perspective. Int. J. Inf. Manag. **36**(5), 759–772 (2016)
16. Morgan, R.M., Hunt, S.D.: The commitment trust theory of relationship marketing. J. Mark. **58**, 20–38 (1994)
17. Ou, C.X., Pavlou, P.A., Davison, R.: Swift guanxi in online marketplaces: the role of computer-mediated communication technologies. MIS Q **38**(1), 209–230 (2014)
18. Park, H.J., Lin, L.M.: The effects of match-ups on the consumer attitudes toward internet celebrities and their live streaming contents in the context of product endorsement. J. Retail. Consum. Serv. **52**, 101934 (2020)

19. Petty, R.E., Cacioppo, J.T., Goldman, R.: Personal involvement as a determinant of argument-based persuasion. J. Pers. Soc. Psychol. **41**, 847–855 (1981)
20. Shang, W.: By 2022, there had been 110000 farmer anchors on Taobao livestreaming platform, with more than 2.3 million broadcasts, driving the sales of agricultural products to exceed 5 billion yuan. ChinaDaily (2022). https://cn.chinadaily.com.cn/a/202201/19/WS61e77ecaa3107be497a02e0c.html
21. Stewart, K.J.: Trust transference on the world wide web. Organ. Sci. **14**(1), 5–17 (2003)
22. Suh, K.-S., Chang, S.: User interfaces and consumer perceptions of online stores: the role of telepresence. Behav. Inf. Technol. **25**(2), 99–113 (2006)
23. Szymanski, D.: Determinants of selling effectiveness: the importance of declarative knowledge to the personal selling concept. J. Mark. **52**, 64–77 (1988)
24. Wang, E.P., Ni, Z.Y.: Research on the preference characteristics of agricultural products online consumers—based on the analysis of "Jingdong" sales apple online review data. Price Theory Pract. **02**, 120–123 (2020)
25. Wei, L., Zhang, X.: Current situation, problems and reflection of online live broadcast with goods marketing in the post epidemic era. Media **22**, 85–87 (2021)
26. Yin, H.Y., Zhu, Z.G.: Analysis on the development of e-commerce of fresh agricultural products in China under the background of COVID-19. Agricultural Outlook **17**(07), 129–132 (2021)
27. Zhao, S.M., Liang, B.: Characteristics, challenges and development trend of live broadcast with goods. China's Circ. Econ. **35**(08), 61–71 (2021)

Follow Others: A Study of the Influence of Herd Behavior on Customer Experience in Group-Buying

Kaiyan Zhu[(✉)] [iD]

RMIT University, Melbourne, VIC, Australia
kaiyan.zhu@student.rmit.edu.au

Abstract. Herd behavior refers to the consumer choosing to follow the others in one collective, in instance where consumer information is incomplete. This research aims to understand herd behavior in the context of group-buying and its influence on the customer experience (CX), ultimately a key precursor of consumer purchase decisions. Based on 17 semi-structured interviews with consumers who shopped from one leading Chinese e-commerce group-buying platform - Pinduoduo, this study identifies that group-buying employs multiple media types to encourage an increase in three-way interactions between the seller, the focal customer, and other consumers. Among these are co-ordering, co-reviewing, commenting, sharing, liking, and gifting. In addition, a relationship of circular causality exists in herd behavior, CX, and group-buying interaction. Specifically, herd behavior within a collective can influence the focal customers' experience, which contributes to the focal customer's interaction and intention. Last but not least, the author has adapted the existing measures by combining the research findings in order to assist future quantitative studies to examine the causal relationship between herd behavior, interaction, and CX.

Keywords: Herd behavior · Customer experience · Group-buying · Three-way interaction · Social commerce

1 Introduction

There has been a rising research stream on group-buying recently [1, 2]. Group-buying enables individual customers to enjoy sizeable bulk purchase discounts by cumulating orders together on specific e-commerce platforms, such as Groupon and Pinduoduo. Pinduoduo is a leading group-buying e-commerce platform in China. 868.7 million active buyers placed 61 billion orders on Pinduoduo in 2021 [3]. As one type of social commerce, user-generated content (UGC) is also widely used in group-buying to facilitate interaction that influence the customer purchase decision [4]. The interactions on conventional online shopping mainly refer to enabling customers to comment on and review products. By comparison, Chinese group-buying is able to utilize more UGC and even power the real-time based interactions (e.g., DanMu-enabled videos), facilitated by the large online shopper population and advanced technologies such as 5G. It is no secret that consumers need to have a good customer experience prior to making a purchase decision. Pinduoduo helps emphasize "richer" and "fun" CX by providing virtual games with product rewards (e.g., Duoduo Orchard with real fresh food rewards), and selecting a social media influencer to livestream the product.

However, given this growing trend, there seems to be a lack of research in both East and West about investigating the influence of other consumers on the focal customer in group-buying. Focal customer refers to the consumers who want to buy the product and will actively seek out the information about the product. Whereas other consumers relate to individuals or, in aggregate, influence a focal customer's decision journey at the various stages, while also being influenced by that customer [5]. Hajli [6] pointed out three key constructs of social commerce - ratings and reviews, recommendations and referrals, and forums and communities. All three relate to other consumers. Among the existing literature on group-buying, only deal popularity received attention from academia, as one variant represents co-ordering made by the other consumers [2, 7]. No study explored other herd behavior, such as commenting on product reviews and its influence on the focal customer is unknown. Considering the CX occurred prior to purchase intention and happened through the whole customer shopping journey, the present study focused on exploring "what" is herd behavior in group-buying and "how" it influences the CX.

2   Literature Review

2.1   Herd Behavior and CX

Herd behavior, or follow others' behavior, originates from the animal cluster behavior and was analyzed as an investor behavior in the financial market. It refers to the consumer choosing to follow the others in a collective when consumers trust other consumers based on their incomplete information and situational factors. In terms of the UGC features applied by e-commerce platforms, herd behavior can include co-ordering, co-reviewing, commenting, sharing, liking, and gifting. For instance, co-viewing would occur when more than one individual is exposed to the same media message during the same period, such as livestream [8]. Furthermore, herd behavior exerts different influence levels with regards to the product nature and customer characteristics. Jing and Xie [9] noted that group-buying would benefit a market where the seller faces new/novice consumers or the consumers' product valuation is low. Over-high deal popularity probably would trigger a negative network externality effect in the scope of service product selling on group-buying. Deal popularity relates to the visually displayed information on the number of deals sold to other consumers.

The CX is motivated by interaction and contributes to all customer intentions and behaviors. The CX is a customer's "journey" with a seller over time, during the purchase cycle across multiple touchpoints [10]. Touchpoints represent the "interaction" between the focal customer, other consumers, and the seller. Similarly, The CX refers to all interactions with the focal firm, including its servicescape, employees, and potentially other customers, through face-to-face, electronic, and other channels [11]. Therefore, the overall CX is cumulated by multiple sub-CX. Online CX relevant studies have been emerging from the past two decades, when e-commerce started to spread [12]. Measuring

CX through the customers' cognitive, affective, social, and sensory dimensions is one complete approach confirmed by multiple studies [13, 14]. Sensory relates to the five human senses: sight, sound, smell, taste, and touch.

2.2 Group-Buying

Conventional online stores continue to be where the majority of shopping happens, while group-buying captures the consumers who seek product/service items at a better price. Successful online group-buying APP - Groupon, allows consumers to shop for intangible items – i.e., local services, and redeem them in physical stores later. Pinduoduo re-invented the group-buying by launching a dynamic pricing feature. Pinduoduo shoppers share products with their friends, family members, or social media friends to cumulate orders together. Once the order size achieves a specific minimum number set up by the sellers within a specific period, such as 24 h, the shopper can purchase the item with a significant discount [15]. Among the limited studies in the group-buying field, multiple have already proved that interactions between the focal customer and other consumers can influence purchase intentions. To be specific, textual comments [16]; virtual community [17]; the number of previous buyers [18]; e-WOM [15]; mass media and interpersonal communication [19]; the number of people who have bought a deal and information on friends who "like" a deal [20]; customer referral intensity and group consumption [7]; and online consumer reviews [21]. For instance, Kuan et al. [20] noted that the interaction between the focal customer and other consumers serves as an important signal or information for group-buying consumers.

3   Research Methodology

A semi-structured interview-based qualitative study was conducted through WeChat voice calls with 17 Chinese consumers who shopped products from Pinduoduo at least twice within the recent six months. Purposive sampling was selected by approaching the current group-buying major customer groups, which include millennials (born between 1981 and 1996) (n represents the number of interviewed consumers, hereinafter, n:8), Generation Z (born after the late 1990s) (n:4); and Generation X (born between 1965 and 1980) (n:5). Female consumers dominated the samples (n:16 vs. 1). Ten among those lived in the first or second tiered cities (e.g., first tiered: Beijing; second tiered: Hangzhou). 12 out of 17 consumers only shopped low to medium price fashion items from group-buying (unit prices ranged between about AU$2.1 and AU$42.5). Five consumers purchased from Pinduoduo platform at least five times each week. Interviewee consent and the ethics approval from RMIT university ethics review committee were obtained in advance of the interviews. Both deductive and inductive reasoning tools were utilized [22]. In light of the paucity of research on group-buying, some interview questions were adapted from broader online shopping literature, in order to explore whether the responses in relation to group-buying match the existing CX theoretical knowledge.

Each interview lasted for 60–90 min. Chinese speech recognition program iflyrec was used to transcribe recorded audios into text, which was manually checked by one researcher with native Chinese speaker background. The collected interview data were analyzed through thematic analysis, which focuses on identifying patterned meaning across a dataset. All emerging themes were interpreted into English.

4   Findings and Discussion

The group-buying consumer interviews indicate that a CX-centered circular causality conceptual model exists in group-buying as Fig. 1 shows. Specifically, herd behavior enables three-way intention from other consumers influence the focal customer's CX, which also can further convince the focal customer choosing herd behavior.

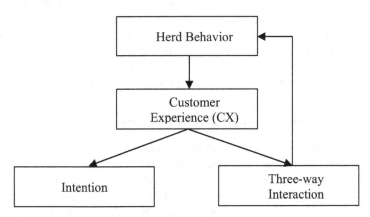

Fig. 1. The circular causality conceptual model of customer experience in group-buying.

4.1   Herd Behavior, the CX, and Three-Way Interaction

Herd behavior varies in the context of Pinduoduo group-buying based on the utilized media type, e.g., co-viewing occurs once the seller adopting livestream media type. Herd behavior can impact the CX to make customers feeling "hot selling" (consumer Jin), "sociable" (consumer Wang), and "trustworthy" (consumer Ping). From one aspect, all those positive herd behaviors were recognized by the interviewed consumers as a kind of social real-time information to reflect the level of social approval and conformity associated with the product item [2]. The information asymmetry between suppliers and consumers commonly exists in the context of online purchase [23]. For instance, consumers who have already purchased can post interactive product review videos and interact with other consumers on the product purchase page. Consumer Dou often participated in this interaction because these interactions made her feel "informative" and "useful" while evaluating items, which can drop to the cognitive dimension of the CX [13]. Further, some of those interactions also made consumers feel "interesting" (e.g., consumer Tong), "connecting with some friends" (e.g., consumer Wang), and even "entertaining". New shoppers started to use group-buying by playing interactive games embedded in Pinduoduo or helping their friends to bargain the price (i.e., price chop).

Consequently, this suggests that people are likely to be influenced by herd behavior from the other consumers and decide to follow it. From the other aspect, the focal customer probably will "jump off the bandwagon" or generate other intentions (e.g., give-up) if she/him perceives the herd behavior is negative, such as "no interest", "low reliability". This finding noted that the focal customer relies on the herd behavior to make inferences and develop beliefs about the product item and its sellers.

The CX triggers the three-way interaction while becoming influenced by the herd behavior. The causal relationship between the CX and interaction has already been proved [10]. CX relates to the "interactive" touchpoints throughout the whole consumer shopping journey. Interaction is everywhere in group-buying, which is consistent with the concept of sub-CX. The collected interview data illustrated that Pinduoduo enables customers to access all relevant product information through blending multiple media types: text + image, short videos, livestreams, animated GIFs, online games, and customer review videos. The ability to blend different media types and enable a three-way interaction on a real-time basis, as media richness [24], interactivity [25], is the important information cue for customers to "paint" the product picture.

4.2   Three-Way Interaction Motivates Herd Behavior

The interactions from other consumers that occurred on Pinduoduo can motivate the focal customer to follow other consumers' behaviors, such as co-viewing (i.e., viewing the same livestream), commenting (i.e., posting real-time comments). Filieri et al. [26] proved that people conform to "anonymous" crowds when they are uncertain about a product or service. For instance, consumer Ya responded that she only selected to follow other customers to purchase the items with high-volume sales. Consumer Hai engaged in following others to ask the group seller's live streamer to introduce items of interest, gifting, or click livestream embedded "Like it" or "Follow it" button. Furthermore, interview results show that interaction with key opinion customers (KOCs) or close friends' participation can more easily trigger the focal customer to follow. For example, consumer Kun mentioned that she often watches Xiaohongshu for seeking purchase inspirations where customers posted product reviews about Pinduoduo product, particularly some influenced consumers. This interaction is so-called parasocial interaction, representing an emotional relationship where the form tends to be a one-way bond and usually occurs between individuals and their idols. In summary, herd behavior is triggered by oscillating three-way interaction in group-buying, creating collective customer behavior.

5   Implications and Conclusion

The research findings yield the following two main implications. First, the author noted that the concept of herd behavior is more appropriate in group-buying as it absorbs the other similar concepts, including bandwagon effect, customer crowding, and joint consumption. For example, product popularity takes place in the form of herd behavior in group-buying circumstance but not in the other aforementioned concepts. Second, this research is one of the first studies exploring the influence of herd behavior on the CX in group-buying. The identified conceptual model laid the foundation for future studies which focusing on examining the causal relationship. Considering three-way interaction is more related to the capability that the seller or the hosted e-commerce platform enables, the author suggests utilizing the scales of media richness and interactivity. The other suggested scales are CX [13] and herd behavior [27] (Appendix). Notwithstanding, a large sample size is necessary for future quantitative studies. Ultimately, this research confirmed that enhancing herd behavior is a practical pathway for forming a better CX in group-buying.

Appendix

CX [13].
Information obtained from group-buying is useful.
I learned a lot from using group-buying.
I think the information obtained from group-buying is helpful.
Shopping fashion products from group-buying: not fun/fun; not enjoyable/enjoyable; not at all entertaining/very entertaining.
There is a sense of human contact in group-buying.
There is a sense of human warmth in group-buying.
There is a sense of human sensitivity in group-buying.
The product presentation on group-buying is lively.
I can acquire product information on group-buying from different sensory channels (e.g., imagery, auditory).
Group-buying contains product information exciting to senses.
Herd Behavior [27].
It seems that group-buying is the dominant type of shopping; therefore, I would like to use it as well.
I follow others in accepting group-buying.
I would choose to accept group-buying because many other people are already using it.
If I were to use group-buying, I would not be making the decision based on my own research and information.
Media Richness [24].
Group-buying allows to tailor my messages to my own personal requirements (e.g., virtual gifts, emojis).
Group-buying can communicate a variety of different cues in the messages (such as emotional tone, attitude, or formality) compared to buying from a website.
Group-buying allows all participants to use rich and varied language within the shopping journey (e.g., multiple perspective, text + image; short videos; livestream videos; animated GIFs; catwalk videos; customer review videos; augmented reality product view; avatars; descriptive videos; haptic feedbacks).
Interactivity [25].
I have a lot of control over my experience while using group-buying.
While using group-buying, I can freely choose what I want to see.
Group-buying facilitates three-way communication among the sellers, other customers, and me.

Group-buying sellers give me the opportunity to provide real-time feedback.
Group-buying sellers respond to my questions very quickly.
I can get information from the group-buying sellers and other customers very rapidly.

References

1. Cao, E., Li, H.: Group buying and consumer referral on a social network. Electron. Commer. Res. **20**(1), 21–52 (2019). https://doi.org/10.1007/s10660-019-09357-4
2. Chow, C.W.C., Chow, C.S.F., Lai, J.Y.M., Zhang, L.L.: Online group-buying: the effect of deal popularity on consumer purchase intention. J. Consum. Behav. **21**, 387–399 (2022)
3. Pinduoduo Inc. 2021 Annual Report. https://investor.pinduoduo.com/financial-information/annual-reports/3. Assessed 20 May 2022
4. Li, C.-Y.: How social commerce constructs influence customers' social shopping intention? An empirical study of a social commerce website. Technol. Forecast. Soc. Chang. **144**, 282–294 (2019). https://doi.org/10.1016/j.techfore.2017.11.026
5. Yin, S.: A study on the influence of e-commerce live streaming on consumer's purchase intentions in mobile internet. In: Stephanidis, C., et al. (eds.) HCII 2020. LNCS, vol. 12427, pp. 720–732. Springer, Cham (2020). https://doi.org/10.1007/978-3-030-60152-2_54
6. Hajli, N.: Social commerce constructs and consumer's intention to buy. Int. J. Inf. Manag. **35**, 183–191 (2015). https://doi.org/10.1016/j.ijinfomgt.2014.12.005
7. Luo, X., Andrews, M., Song, Y., Aspara, J.: Group-buying deal popularity. J. Mark. **78**, 20–33 (2014). https://doi-org.ezproxy.lib.rmit.edu.au/10.1509/jm.12.0422
8. Fang, J., Chen, L., Wen, C., Prybutok, V.R.: Co-viewing experience in video websites: the effect of social presence on e-loyalty. Int. J. Electron. Commer. **22**, 446–476 (2018). https://doi.org/10.1080/10864415.2018.1462929
9. Jing, X., Xie, J.: Group buying: a new mechanism for selling through social interactions. Manag. Sci. **57**, 1354–1372 (2011). https://www.jstor.org/stable/25835785
10. Lemon, K.N., Verhoef, P.C.: Understanding customer experience throughout the customer journey. J. Mark. **80**, 69–96 (2016). https://www.jstor.org/stable/44134974
11. De Keyser, A., Lemon, K.N., Klaus, P., Keiningham, T.L.: A framework for understanding and managing the customer experience. MSI Working Paper No. Marketing Science Institute, Cambridge, MA, pp. 15–121 (2015)
12. Koufaris, M.: Applying the technology acceptance model and flow theory to online consumer behavior. Inf. Syst. Res. **13**, 205–223 (2002). https://doi-org.ezproxy.lib.rmit.edu.au/10.1287/isre.13.2.205.83
13. Bleier, A., Harmeling, C.M., Palmatier, R.W.: Creating effective online customer experiences. J. Mark. **83**, 98–119 (2018). https://doi.org/10.1177/0022242918809930
14. Chen, J.-S., Le, T.-T.-Y., Florence, D.: Usability and responsiveness of artificial intelligence chatbot on online customer experience in e-retailing. Int. J. Retail Distrib. Manag. **49**, 1512–1531 (2021). https://doi.org/10.1108/IJRDM-08-2020-0312
15. Cheng, H.-H., Huang, S.-W.: Exploring antecedents and consequence of online group-buying intention: an extended perspective on theory of planned behavior. Int. J. Inf. Manag. **33**, 185–198 (2013). https://doi.org/10.1016/j.ijinfomgt.2012.09.003
16. Kauffman, R.J., Lai, H., Ho, C.-T.: Incentive mechanisms, fairness and participation in online group-buying auctions. Electron. Commer. Res. Appl. **9**, 249–262 (2010). https://doi.org/10.1016/j.elerap.2008.11.009
17. Tsai, M.-T., Cheng, N.-C., Chen, K.-S.: Understanding online group buying intention: the roles of sense of virtual community and technology acceptance factors. Total Qual. Manag. Bus. Excell. **22**, 1091–1104 (2011). https://doi-org.ezproxy.lib.rmit.edu.au/10.1080/14783363.2011.614870

18. Coulter, K.S., Roggeveen, A.: Deal or no deal? How number of buyers, purchase limit, and time-to-expiration impact purchase decisions on group buying websites. J. Res. Interact. Mark. **6**, 78–95 (2012). https://doi.org/10.1108/17505931211265408
19. Zhou, G., Xu, K., Liao, S.S.Y.: Do starting and ending effects in fixed-price group-buying differ? Electron. Commer. Res. Appl. **12**, 78–89 (2013). https://doi.org/10.1016/j.elerap.2012.11.006
20. Kuan, K.K.Y., Zhong, Y., Chau, P.Y.K.: Informational and normative social influence in group-buying: evidence from self-reported and EEG data. J. Manag. Inf. Syst. **30**, 151–178 (2014). https://www.jstor.org/stable/43590187
21. Shi, X., Liao, Z.: Online consumer review and group-buying participation: the mediating effects of consumer beliefs. Telematics Inform. **34**, 605–617 (2017). https://doi.org/10.1016/j.tele.2016.12.001
22. Gaudet, S.R.D.: Theorizing and Presenting the Results In: A Journey Through Qualitative Research: From Design to Reporting. SAGE Publications Ltd (2019). https://dx.doi.org/10.4135/9781529716733
23. Schlosser, A.E., White, T.B., Lloyd, S.M.: Converting web site visitors into buyers: how web site investment increases consumer trusting beliefs and online purchase intentions. J. Mark. **70**, 133–148 (2006). https://www.jstor.org/stable/30162091
24. Tseng, C.-H., Wei, L.-F.: The efficiency of mobile media richness across different stages of online consumer behavior. Int. J. Inf. Manag. **50**, 353–364 (2020). https://doi.org/10.1016/j.ijinfomgt.2019.08.010
25. Dong, X., Wang, T., Benbasat, I.: IT affordances in online social commerce: conceptualization validation and scale development. In: Twenty-Second Americas Conference on Information Systems, San Diego, American, pp. 1–10 (2016)
26. Filieri, R., McLeay, F., Tsui, B.: Antecedents of travellers' satisfaction and purchase intention from social commerce websites. In: Schegg, R., Stangl, B. (eds.) Information and Communication Technologies in Tourism 2017, pp. 517–528. Springer, Cham (2017). https://doi.org/10.1007/978-3-319-51168-9_37
27. Erjavec, J., Manfreda, A.: Online shopping adoption during COVID-19 and social isolation: extending the UTAUT model with herd behavior. J. Retail. Consum. Serv. **65**, 102867 (2022). https://doi.org/10.1016/j.jretconser.2021.102867

Automated Driving and Urban Mobility

How Should Automated Vehicles Approach Pedestrians? – The Influence of Different Approximation Behaviors & Driver Visibility on Perceived Situation Criticality

Valeria Bopp-Bertenbreiter[1]([⊠]) [iD], Denise Pottin[2] [iD], and Verena Wagner-Hartl[2] [iD]

[1] University of Stuttgart, Nobelstraße 12, Stuttgart, Germany
valeria.bopp-bertenbreiter@iat.uni-stuttgart.de

[2] Faculty Industrial Technologies, Campus Tuttlingen, Furtwangen University, Kronenstraße 16, 78532 Tuttlingen, Germany

Abstract. To ensure acceptance and conformity to society's expectations for Automated Vehicles (AV), not only objective, but also subjective measures of safety in encounters between AV and Vulnerable Road Users (VRU) must be investigated. Objective safety of a traffic situation can be measured using Inoue et al.'s Safety Cushion Time (SCT) [8], which describes the additional braking distance available due to preventive driver actions.

Method. This work describes an online study (within-subject design) with videos of different traffic scenarios with N = 36 participants. This study measured the influence of visibility of a driving person (yes/no) and Safety Cushion Times (1.5 s/ 2 s/ 2.5 s) on pedestrian's perceived safety. Outcome variables included perceived safety, acceptance, conformity of vehicle behavior to pedestrians' expectations, and emotional reaction.

Results & Conclusion. Low SCT values (= high acceleration combined with late braking) resulted in a low subjective safety assessment of a situation, low acceptance of vehicle behavior and negative emotional reaction of pedestrians. High SCT values (=low acceleration and early braking) resulted in high subjective safety ratings, high acceptance, and high conformity to expectations, thus resulting in a positive emotional reaction.

Visibility of a driving person had a lower influence on ratings of subjective safety. Therefore, it is recommended to incorporate our findings into a model for driving behavior for AV if the AV needs to be seen as considerate and subjectively safe.

Keywords: Automated driving · Subjective criticality · Human-vehicle interaction · Experimental study

1 Introduction

Until now, research on automated driving focused primarily on technical feasibility and the associated increased objective safety of vehicles [1]. However, the subjective feeling of safety is essential for users' acceptance of automated driving [2]. Subjective safety is defined as the individual's assessment of their own safety or risk [3], acceptance in the context of automated driving is defined as the willingness of a single person or society to accept an automated system by using the automated vehicle (AV) directly or indirectly [4, 5]. Therefore, the behavior of AVs must feel safe to users [6], not only to those inside the AV, but also vulnerable road users, e.g., pedestrians [2].

In previous studies, Pillai [6] and Yang [7] show that visibility of a driving person [7] and different approach behaviours of an AV [3] have an impact on the hazard perception and emotional response of pedestrians. Based on these insights, this study investigates whether driver visibility and Safety Cushion Time (SCT) [8] as a measure of objective safety have an impact on subjectively perceived safety.

1.1 Influence of the Visibility of a Person in the Driver's Seat on Pedestrians' Perceived Safety

The progression of automated driving means that the detachment of the human driver from the actual driving task is increasing [9]. This detachment of drivers from the driving task means that users can turn to other activities, so called secondary activities, such as reading or sleeping, while driving [1]. The impact of these drivers' secondary activities on other road users, particularly with respect to the perceived safety of pedestrians, has not been adequately studied at present [7]. Against this background, it is now important to investigate how the visibility or absence of a person in the driver's seat of an AV influences pedestrians' subjective perception of safety.

Yang's [7] study ($N = 40$) investigated whether visibility or behavior of a person in the driver's seat of an AV affects pedestrians' perceived safety and emotional reaction. Participants watched videos of approaching vehicles and were then shown pictures of different behaviors of the person in the driver's seat (e.g., sleeping or talking on the phone). The Self Assessment Manikin [10] was used to assess emotional reaction. Subsequently, an interview was conducted. Yang's [7] results indicate that the visibility of a person in the driver's seat positively affected pedestrians' perceived safety and trust in AV when crossing a road.

1.2 Influence of Different Approximation Behaviors of an AV on Pedestrians' Perceived Safety

In a study ($N = 15$), Pillai [6] (2017) investigated how different approximation behaviors of a vehicle influences the extent to which pedestrians can infer the intentions of a person in the driver's seat. The approximation behaviors differed in terms of velocity and acceleration/deceleration behavior. Pillai used a VR-setup followed by an interview. Participants in Pillai's study rated a slow approaching behavior (60km/h) with even braking as most pleasant. Participants perceived late deceleration behavior (70km/h) as unpleasant as well as a very slow approaching behavior (30km/h).

1.3 Safety Cushion Time (SCT)

Inoue et al. [8] developed the concept of a Safety Cushion as a measurement of criticality for traffic situations. A Safety Cushion describes the additional braking distance available due to preventive driver actions [11]. The Safety Cushion Time (SCT) for determining the additional braking distance is composed of the distance between the vehicle and the opponent (e.g., pedestrian), the vehicle's speed, the maximum braking acceleration, and the reaction time of the vehicle's system [8]. In this work, different SCT values were used as a predictor variable, to objectively operaterationalize the safety of a traffic situation.

1.4   Outcome Variables: Perceived Safety, Acceptance, Conformity of Vehicle Behavior to Pedestrians' Expectations, and Emotional Reaction

The presented work investigates the influence of visibility of a person in the driver's seat and of different SCTs on several outcome variables: Most importantly, perceived safety. Since trust in and conformity of the AVs behavior to pedestrians' expectations are crucial for the subjective assessment of a potentially critical situation and the associated safety [6, 12], these aspects should also be considered in the criticality assessment. Acceptance is an essential aspect, especially regarding introduction of AVs [13] as too little acceptance may result in the rejection of AVs by other road users. The emotional reaction of pedestrians towards a crossing situation with an AV is important for pedestrians' perceived safety in the situation, as shown by Yang [7]. Yang's study, however, did not investigate a possible connection between the emotional reaction and acceptance of AVs. Therefore, the presented study investigates the influence of different SCTs and the visibility of a driving person on perceived safety, acceptance, conformity of vehicle behavior to pedestrians' expectations, and emotional reaction.

2   Method

A within-subjects design with randomized order of six different scenarios (see Fig. 1) investigated the influence of the scenarios on outcome variables (Fig. 2). The driving simulator software SILAB was used to create the videos of the six different traffic scenarios (see Fig. 1). In all scenarios, a vehicle approaches a crosswalk. The participants saw the videos from the point of view of a pedestrian standing at the cross walk. In all scenarios, the same locations were used for beginning of deceleration as well as stand still of the vehicles.

		Safety Cushion Time		
		SCT high (< 2.5 s), velocity low	SCT medium (< 2 s), velocity medium	SCT low (< 1.5 s), velocity high
Visability of a driving person	Driving person visible	traffic scenario 1	traffic scenario 3	traffic scenario 5
	Driving person not visible	traffic scenario 2	traffic scenario 4	traffic scenario 6

Fig. 1. Combination of predictors.

An examiner questioned the subjects after each video of the scenarios. LimeSurvey was used to create an online questionnaire which also included the videos of the scenarios. Outcome variables as described above were operationalized as depicted in Fig. 2.

The sample included $N = 36$ subjects (50% female) aged from 18 to 59 years ($M = 38.14$, $SD = 13.49$).

Subjective hazard perception	1 Perceived danger	Verbal Scale ranging from 0 ("Harmless") to 10 ("Dangerous")	Adapted from Neukum et al., 2008 [14]
	2 Trust	Verbal Scale ranging from 0 ("Trust") to 10 ("No Trust")	
	3 Conformity of expectation	Verbal Scale ranging from 0 ("Expected") to 10 ("Not Expected")	
Acceptance	4 Acceptance	Verbal Scale ranging from -2 ("Pleasant") to 2 ("Unpleasant")	Acceptancescale; Subscala: Satisfaction (Van der Laan et al., 1997) [5]
		Verbal Scale ranging from -2 ("Nice") to 2 ("Annoying")	
		Verbal Scale ranging from -2 ("Irritating") to 2 ("Likeable")	
		Verbal Scale ranging from -2 ("Undesirable") to 2 ("Desirable")	
Emotional Reaction	5 Pleasure	Verbal Scale ranging from 1 ("Happy") to 9 ("Unhappy")	Self-Assessment-Manikin (Bradley & Lang, 1994) [10]
	6 Arousal	Verbal Scale ranging from 1 ("Relaxed") to 9 ("Excited")	
	7 Dominance	Verbal Scale ranging from 1 ("Dominant") to 9 ("Submissive")	

Fig. 2. Outcome variables: scales for subjective hazard perception adapted from Neukum et al. [14]; acceptance scale, subscale: satisfaction from Van der Laan et al. [5]; Self-Assessment-Manikin from Bradley and Lang [10]

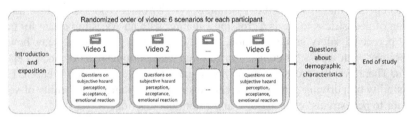

Fig. 3. Procedure of the study.

Figure 3 describes the procedure of the study in detail. IBM SPSS Statistics 25 was used for the statistical analysis of the quantitative data. For every outcome variable, a univariate repeated measures analysis of variance (ANOVA) with a significance level of 5% was conducted.

3 Results and Conclusion

For better interpretability, only the significant ANOVAs' results are reported. Significant differences in post-hoc tests are represented by box brackets and marked with an Asterix *, meaning $p \leq .05$. All other effects did not reach the level of significance.

3.1 Perceived Danger and Trust

Regarding perceived danger of the situation, results of an ANOVA with repeated measures showed a significant main effect of "traffic scenarios" (see Fig. 4a), $F_{HF}(3.40, 139.85) = 24.27$, $p \leq .0001$, $\eta^2_{part} = .409$. Regarding trust in the vehicle in the situation, results of an ANOVA with repeated measures showed a significant main effect of "traffic scenarios" (see Fig. 4b), $F_{HF}(3.83, 133.99) = 20.48$, $p \leq .0001$, $\eta^2_{part} = .369$.

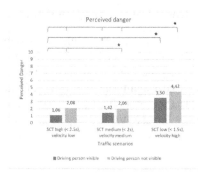

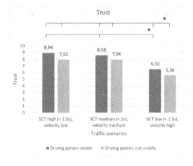

Fig. 4. a) Influence of *SCT values* and *visibility of person in driver's seat* on *perceived danger* of pedestrians in a crossing situation. Perceived danger is the contrary of perceived safety. b) Influence of *SCT values* and *visibility of person in driver's seat* on *trust in the vehicle behavior* of pedestrians in a crossing situation. Significant differences in post-hoc tests are represented by box brackets and marked with an Asterix *, meaning $p \leq .05$.

3.2 Conformity of Vehicle Behavior to Pedestrians' Expectations

Regarding conformity of vehicle behavior to pedestrians' expectation, results of an ANOVA with repeated measures showed a significant main effect of "traffic scenarios" (see Fig. 5a), F_{HF} (3.34, 116.91) = 16.85, $p \leq .0001$, η^2_{part} = .325. Regarding acceptance of vehicle behavior, results of an ANOVA with repeated measures showed a significant main effect of "traffic scenarios" (see Fig. 5b), F_{HF} (3.71, 129.66) = 21.23, $p \leq .0001$, η^2_{part} = .378.

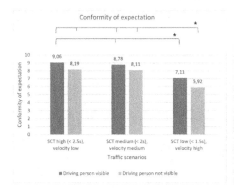

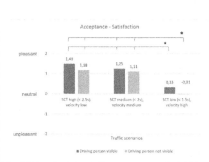

Fig. 5. a) Influence of *SCT values* and *visibility of person in driver's seat* on *conformity of vehicle behavior to expectations* of pedestrians in a crossing situation. b) Influence of *SCT values* and *visibility of person in driver's seat* on *acceptance of vehicle behavior* of pedestrians in a crossing situation. Significant differences in post-hoc tests are represented by box brackets and marked with an Asterix *, meaning $p \leq .05$.

3.3 Emotional Reaction to the Situation (Valence, Arousal, and Dominance)

Regarding the subscale valence of the SAM, results of an ANOVA with repeated measures showed a significant main effect of "traffic scenarios" (see Fig. 6a), F_{HF} (4.09, 143.26) = 15.81, $p \leq .0001$, $\eta^2_{part} = .311$. Regarding the subscale arousal of the SAM, results of an ANOVA with repeated measures showed a significant main effect of "traffic scenarios" (see Fig. 6b), F_{HF} (4.25, 148.64) = 16.09, $p \leq .0001$, $\eta^2_{part} = .315$. Regarding the subscale dominance of the SAM, results of an ANOVA with repeated measures showed a significant main effect of "traffic scenarios" (see Fig. 7), F_{HF} (4.13, 144.51) = 9.38, $p \leq .0001$, $\eta^2_{part} = .211$.

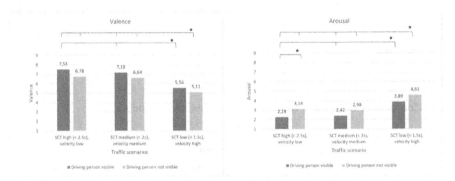

Fig. 6. a) Influence of *SCT values* and *visibility of person in driver's seat* on *emotional reaction – subscale valence* of pedestrians in a crossing situation. b) Influence of *SCT values* and *visibility of person in driver's seat* on *emotional reaction – subscale arousal* of pedestrians in a crossing situation. Significant differences in post-hoc tests are represented by box brackets and marked with an Asterix *, meaning $p \leq .05$.

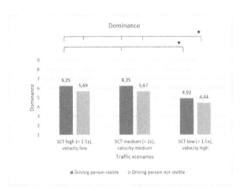

Fig. 7. Influence of *SCT values* and *visibility of person in driver's seat* on *emotional reaction – subscale dominance* of pedestrians in a crossing situation. Significant differences in post-hoc tests are represented by box brackets and marked with an Asterix *, meaning $p \leq .05$.

4   Discussion

The presented study revealed significant effects between the combinations of predicator variables SCT and visibility of a driving person on outcome variables.

The results indicate that varying SCT values has a major influence on subjective safety assessment of a situation, acceptance of vehicle behavior and emotional reaction of pedestrians.

Traffic scenarios with a lower SCT were rated as negative overall. Pedestrians felt less safe subjectively when vehicles approached with a high velocity and braked abruptly, thus confirming Pillai's results [6]. Overall, this vehicle behavior led to a low conformity of vehicle behavior to pedestrians' expectations and thus results in pedestrians misinterpreting the situation. Consequently, pedestrians' emotional reaction was also negative. This driving behavior of the vehicle entails in a low acceptance of the AV, which might result in an overall rejection of the technology as described by Lee and See [12].

By contrast, participants rate traffic scenarios with medium and high SCTs (=medium and low velocity) more positively, because the vehicle approaches slower and brakes early. This driving behavior of the vehicle is evaluated as conform to pedestrians' expectations, thus, perceived safety and acceptance of vehicle behavior increase.

Visibility of a driving person affects perceived safety, acceptance, and emotional reaction only marginally, results are similar with and without a visible driving person regarding conformity of vehicle behavior to participants' expectations and acceptance of vehicle behavior. Therefore, the lack of interaction between person in the driver's seat and pedestrians seems to be a challenge of automated driving in general. Overall, participants found it hard to correctly assess the vehicle's intentions and to perceive the vehicle's next actions if no driving person is visible. This results in uncertainty and low levels of trust on the pedestrians' site.

Our study also shows that general trust in AV is rather low, mainly because a representative sample of society (as used in this study) is rather uninformed and uneducated regarding the topic of "automated driving" at the time of publication.

5   Conclusion and Outlook

The results of the presented study indicate that a slow approximation behavior combined with an early deceleration of a vehicle (= high SCT value) is critical for a driving behavior of AV that conforms to pedestrians' expectations. Such driving behavior positively affects not only perceived safety, but also pedestrians' acceptance and emotional reaction towards a vehicle in a crossing situation. Visibility of a person in the driver's seat, however, only has a minor influence on perceived safety of pedestrians.

Based on these findings, it is recommended to include high SCT values into a model of considerate and anticipatory driving behavior for AV to increase trust in AV and perceived safety of pedestrians in traffic. In the future, the results will be incorporated into virtual test scenarios for AV to promote road safety and AVs' acceptance.

References

1. Matthaei, R., et al.: Autonomes fahren. In: Winner, H., Hakuli, S., Lotz, F., Singer, C. (eds.) Handbuch Fahrerassistenzsysteme. A, pp. 1139–1165. Springer, Wiesbaden (2015). https://doi.org/10.1007/978-3-658-05734-3_61
2. Zwicker, L., Petzoldt, T., Schade, J., Schaarschmidt, E.: Kommunikation zwischen automatisierten Kraftfahrzeugen und anderen Verkehrsteilnehmern - Was brauchen wir überhaupt [Communication between Automated Vehicles and Other Road Users - What Do We Need Anyway]. In: Bruder, R., Winner, H. (eds.) Hands off, Human Factors off? - Welche Rolle spielen Human Factors in der Fahrzeugautomation, pp. 47–57. Universitäts- und Landesbibliothek Darmstadt, Darmstadt (2019)
3. Schewe, S.: Subjektives Sicherheitsgefühl [Subjective feeling of safety]. In: Lange, H.-J., Gasch, M. (eds.) Wörterbuch zur Inneren Sicherheit, 1st edn., pp. 322–325. VS Verlag für Sozialwissenschaften, Wiesbaden (2006)
4. Fraedrich, E., Lenz, B.: Gesellschaftliche und individuelle Akzeptanz des autonomen Fahrens [Social and individual acceptance of autonomous driving]. In: Maurer, M., Gerdes, J.C., Lenz, B., Winner, H. (eds.) Autonomes Fahren, pp. 639–660. Springer, Heidelberg (2015). https://doi.org/10.1007/978-3-662-45854-9_29
5. Van der Laan, J.D., Heino, A., De Waard, D.: A simple procedure for the assessment of acceptance of advanced transport telematics. Transp. Res. Part C Emerg. Technol. 5(1), 1–10 (1997)
6. Pillai, A.K.: Virtual reality based study to analyse pedestrian attitude towards autonomous vehicles. Master's thesis, KTH Royal Institute of Technology (2017). http://urn.fi/URN:NBN:fi:aalto-201710307409
7. Yang, S.: Driver behavior impact on pedestrians' crossing experience in the conditionally autonomous driving context. Master's thesis, KTH Royal Institute of Technology (2017). https://www.diva-portal.org/smash/record.jsf?pid=diva2:1169360
8. Inoue, H., El-Haji, M., Freudenmann, T., Zhang, H., Raksincharoensak, P., Saito, Y.: Validation methodology to establish safe autonomous driving algorithms with a high driver acceptance using a virtual environment. In: Proceedings of the 5th International Symposium on Future Active Safety Technology Towards Zero-Traffic Accident (FAST-zero 2019), Blacksburg, Virgina, USA (2019)
9. Färber, B.: Kommunikationsprobleme zwischen autonomen Fahrzeugen und menschlichen Fahrern. In: Maurer, M., Gerdes, JChristian, Lenz, B., Winner, H. (eds.) Autonomes Fahren, pp. 127–146. Springer, Heidelberg (2015). https://doi.org/10.1007/978-3-662-45854-9_7
10. Bradley, M.M., Lang, P.J.: Measuring emotion: The self-assessment manikin and the semantic differential. J. Behav. Ther. Exp. Psychiatry 25(1), 49–59 (1994). https://doi.org/10.1016/0005-7916(94)90063-9
11. Saito, Y., Inoue, H., El-Haji, M., Freudenmann, T., Raksincharoensak, P.: Context-sensitive hazard anticipation based on driver behavior analysis and cause-and-effect chain study. In: Keqiang Li (ed.), Proceedings of the 14th International Symposium on Advanced Vehicle Control. AVEC 2018, Beijing, China, 16–20 July 2018 (2018)
12. Lee, J.D., See, K.A.: Trust in automation: designing for appropriate reliance. Hum. Factors (2004). https://doi.org/10.1518/hfes.46.1.50_30392
13. Rupp, J.D., King, A.G.: Autonomous Driving - A Practical Roadmap. SAE Technical Paper 2010-01-2335 (2010). https://doi.org/10.4271/2010-01-2335
14. Neukum, A., Lübbeke, T., Krüger, H.-P., Mayser, C., Steinle, J.: ACC-Stop&Go: Fahrerverhalten an funktionalen Systemgrenzen [ACC-Stop&Go: Driver behavior at functional system limits]. In: Maurer, M., Stiller, C. (eds.) 5. Workshop Fahrerassistenzsysteme - FAS 2008, pp. 141–150 (2008)

A Study on the Differentiation of User Emotional Experience of Electric Vehicle Charging Products from a Comparative Perspective

Yuchao Cai[1], Jie Zhang[1(✉)], Xiaojun Lin[2], and Mi Tian[1]

[1] School of Art Design and Media, East China University of Technology, No. 130, Meilong Road, Xuhui District, Shanghai, People's Republic of China
zhangjietianru@163.com

[2] Shanghai Yizhu Architectural Design Engineering Co., Ltd., No. 1518, Xikang Road, Putuo District, Shanghai, People's Republic of China

Abstract. According to different scenarios, electric vehicle charging products can be divided into household and social public. It is necessary to analyze the differences of emotional experience between the two types of products from the perspective of users, so as to better guide the design. This paper selects the TLED public charging pile and PRTDT household charging pile as research cases, takes the online comment data as the object, uses the TF-IDF and K-means clustering algorithm, and uses the methods of text analysis, emotion analysis and social network analysis to mine and compare the emotional themes of the two kinds of charging product comments. For users of public charging piles, charging equipment is cheap and easy to use, parking is convenient and cheap, and the quality of surrounding environment is high, which will have a positive impact; The impolite occupation of charging parking space by fuel vehicles, the waste of time and resources, the loss of cost and the obstacle of finding the way are the important reasons for negative emotion. For household charging pile users, professional sales and on-site installation services, ease of use and durability of products have a positive impact on their emotions; Use risk and design defects such as size, appearance and weight are the key reasons for negative emotions. Based on this, the future design and research of public charging piles should focus on a series of public services associated with charging products, while the design and research of household charging piles should focus on product appearance design and value-added services.

Keywords: Online reviews · Charging pile · Emotional analysis · Cluster analysis · Text mining · Comparative analysis · Social network analysis

1 Introduction

Charging products based on electric vehicle charging piles are an important part of the construction of China's new infrastructure system and an important foundation for the healthy development of the new energy vehicle industry. The charging pile is not only a single product, but also constitutes different application scenarios in the form of networks, groups, and sites. The objects to be studied are charging products based on charging piles and areas for charging vehicles. Therefore, classification according to usage scenarios is more suitable for the dual attributes of products and facilities of charging piles. At present, China's electric vehicle charging products are mainly divided into two basic types of scenarios: households and public use. Residential household charging piles are mostly set up in residential areas for private use and are not-for-profit. Social public charging piles are mostly combined with demand centers such as shopping malls, public buildings, industrial parks, etc., which are used by the public and are profitable. At present, the insufficient number of public electric vehicle charging piles has become a major obstacle to the further growth of electric vehicle sales [1], and its construction is an important way for the government to promote the adoption of electric vehicles [2]. Meanwhile, private charging piles are widely adopted in major cities and partially change the charging behavior of EV users [3]. In actual use, both types of charging piles expose many problems such as difficult use, small number, and poor experience for customers, which bring bad emotional experience to electric vehicle owners. So, what is the emotional experience generated by users in the process of using these two charging pile products? What are the thematic factors associated with positive and negative sentiment? Is there a difference? Where is the difference? How does this difference guide us to design charging pile products that adapt to different scenarios of domestic and public use?

2 Literature Review

Research in the field of electric vehicle charging mainly focuses on infrastructure such as charging stations and charging points, and there are few researches on products such as charging piles. From the perspective of domestic research in China, most researches simply abstract charging products into points, and have not systematically paid attention to the user, product, and environmental attributes they are attached to. Judging from the retrieval content of the SCI database, most of the research is carried out from the perspective of the positive configuration of the government and enterprises, and less research is carried out from the user's use of reverse feedback. Judging from the content retrieved from the SSCI database, most of the research starts from the rational and logical perspective of construction, operation and maintenance, and less research is carried out from the perspective of users' emotional psychology. Some scholars have studied attitudes and responses to plug-in battery electric vehicle charging from the perspective of electric vehicle drivers [4], and others have studied the extent to which experience influences individual preferences for specific EV characteristics, and individual preferences for the environment. Attitude [5], and some scholars evaluate the charging reliability of new energy vehicle charging stations by establishing an index system to reflect the user's charging experience [6]. In addition, mining of social media third-party comment data with the help of machine learning-based natural language processing methods also revealed users' negative sentiment towards electric vehicle charging facilities [7]. However, none of the above studies separates public charging products from household charging products, lacks the exploration of charging experience from the perspective of charging product user reviews, and lacks excavation on the theme of emotional polarity.

Therefore, the article selects the TLED public charging pile with a high share of the chinese charging market and the PRTDT household charging pile with good online sales as research cases, and uses online comment data mining as a method to analyze the emotions of the two types of charging pile products. The thematic factors and constituent relationships are summarized and compared.

3   Research Design and Methods

3.1   Research Framework

The research is based on the online review data mining of two types of charging piles to form a text set of charging piles. With the help of word segmentation tools, the review text set is preprocessed, including deduplication, cleaning, automatic word segmentation, and manual word segmentation, to obtain a charging pile comment corpus composed of comment numbers and comment content. Based on this, the sentiment polarity analysis of each comment is carried out with the help of sentiment analysis tool, and the sentiment score of each comment is obtained. Further carry out the word frequency analysis of positive and negative emotional feature words, cluster analysis of subject words, and visual comparison of the social network of subject words under different product types, and compare the analysis results (Fig. 1).

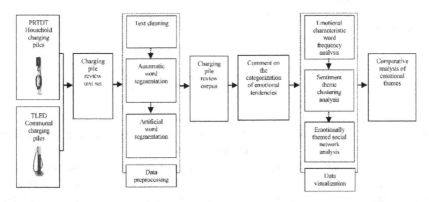

Fig. 1. Technology roadmap

3.2   Research Methods

The first step, Octopus Web Data Collector is a simple and powerful web crawler tool. With the help of Octopus Web Data Collector, 17142 public charging pile comment data were obtained from the TLED online platform, and 2594 PRTDT household charging pile comment data were obtained from JD.com. Step 2: ROST CM 6 is the only large-scale free social computing platform in China developed by Professor Shenyang of Wuhan University. Using the ROST general line processing tool, combined with manual cleaning, the data were processed by de duplication, de English and deletion of blank lines, and 9962 valid data of public charging pile comments and 2145 valid data of household charging pile comments were obtained. The third step is to use the ROST word segmentation tool to segment the effective data, observe the word segmentation that is not in line with the actual situation, summarize a total of 1209 fixed words, enter a user-defined vocabulary, and complete the secondary word segmentation based on this to form a comment corpus. Step 4: both ROST CM 6 and Gooseeker have emotion analysis modules. Gooseeker is a famous online platform for big data analysis in China. This paper compares the effect of emotion analysis between ROST tool and Gooseeker platform. The emotion analysis results derived from the former take the text as the object for scoring; The latter will cut the text into single sentences, score each sentence first, and then weight the results of all sentences together through the algorithm to get the emotional score of the text. In contrast, the result visibility of the latter is better than that of the former, which is convenient for manual item by item proofreading. Therefore, this time, Gooseeker platform is used to carry out emotional analysis on the corpus obtained from word segmentation (as shown in Table 1): in the comment data of public charging point, 3219 comments are positive emotions and 1070 comments are negative emotions; In the household charging point comment data, 1675 comments were positive emotions and 470 comments were negative emotions.

Table 1. Commenting on the division of emotional tendencies

Comment ID	Body	Score
1	The discount is very good and worth recommending	2
...	...	...

The fifth step is to use the ROST Chinese word frequency statistics tool, select Baidu stop word list as the filter word list, and de duplicate and screen all the words, remove the unintentional words and obtain the characteristic word thesaurus. Among them, there are 769 positive comment feature words and 842 negative comment feature words of public charging pile; There are 748 positive comment feature words and 358 negative comment feature words. Step 6: TF-IDF is a statistical algorithm, which is often used for keyword mining. There are a large number of literatures on the principle and formula of TF-IDF algorithm. This paper is limited to space and will not be repeated. The word frequency, the number of text containing characteristic words and the number of words in comment text required in the algorithm can be realized by COUNTIF function and COUNTA function in Excel. Use Excel function to classify and calculate the TF-IDF value of feature words, sort them from large to small, select the top 60 words as the key feature words on the basis of synonym merging [8], and establish TF-IDF matrix with the comment text (see Table 2) to realize the structure of the comment text.

Table 2. Feature word TFIDF matrix

Comment ID	Occupancy	Charging	Fuel vehicles	Parking	Fault	Charging parking	...
4	0	0	0	0	0.420951	0	...
...	...	...	...	...	...	...	...

In the seventh step, with the help of SPSS tool, the characteristic word TF-IDF matrix is imported for K-means cluster analysis. Cluster 9 times according to k = 2~10, and calculate the SSE coefficient of each cluster. According to the elbow theory, the SSE coefficient is compared and the most reasonable number of clusters is determined to be 8. Based on this, the comment text clustering of public charging pile positive comments, public charging pile negative comments, household charging pile positive comments and household charging pile negative comments is completed respectively. Step 8: select the words with the weight value in the top 5 in each cluster center feature word sequence as the subject words, import them into Gooseeker platform, and obtain the subject word co-occurrence matrix (see Table 3). Step 9: UCINET is the most well-known and frequently used comprehensive analysis program for processing social network data and other similarity data. According to the topic clustering results of feature words, the co-occurrence matrix of each topic word is imported into UCINET software, and the centrality index is calculated to form a topic based social network analysis system. Step 10: carry out comparative analysis based on the above analysis results.

Table 3. Co-occurrence matrix of subject words

	Electric pile	Parking	Environment	Smooth	Charging station	Fast charging	...
Electric pile	223	29	21	24	10	8	...
...	...	...	...	...	...	...	...

4 Results and Discussion

4.1 Word Frequency Analysis and Comparison

High frequency characteristic words of positive emotion of public charging pile: environment, smooth, parking, speed, price, location, fast, parking space, fuel vehicles and place. High frequency characteristic words of positive emotion of household charging pile: installation, charging, quality, speed, fast, logistics, price, service, simplicity, customer service, packaging, delivery and master (Fig. 2). Considering the high similarity of the top ten positive and negative high-frequency words of household charging products, in order to achieve better visual comparison effect, some of the same words are not displayed. The high-frequency characteristic words of negative emotions of public charging piles are: space occupation, charging, fuel vehicles, waste, hour, parking space, security, location, parking fee and fast charging. The high-frequency characteristic words of negative emotion of household charging pile are: installation, charging, speed, quality, master, logistics, delivery, service and customer service (Fig. 3). From the analysis results of positive emotional word frequency, in addition to conventional factors such as charging speed and charging price, public charging pile customers also pay great attention to the environmental quality and traffic facilities around the charging pile, and have high requirements for the accessibility and easy location of the charging pile. Customers of household charging piles mainly pay attention to the supporting and follow-up of product installation, logistics and other services, and pay great attention to the ease of use and durability of charging piles. From the analysis results of negative emotion word frequency, customers of public charging pile are very sensitive to whether the charging parking space is occupied by fuel vehicles, and are unhappy with the waste of time, resources and cost loss. The negative emotions of household charging pile customers are mainly concentrated in online shopping links such as product delivery, logistics, installation, use and after-sales. Both types of charging piles pay attention to price and speed. Public charging pile customers pay more attention to charging cost and charging speed, and household charging pile customers pay more attention to product pricing and installation and delivery speed.

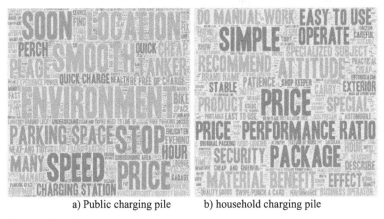

a) Public charging pile   b) household charging pile

Fig. 2. Comparison of word frequency of positive comment feature words

4.2 Subject Analysis and Comparison

The positive emotional experience themes of public charging pile users include: queuing order theme, parking convenience theme, environmental quality theme, practical parity theme, cost preference theme, sufficient parking space theme, equipment stability theme and complete supporting theme. The positive emotional experience themes of household charging pile users include: good function theme, product durability theme, shopping

a) Public charging pile   b) household charging pile

Fig. 3. Comparison of word frequency of negative comment feature words

experience theme, cost performance theme, affordable theme, simple and easy-to-use theme, regular channel theme and installation professional theme. The themes of negative emotional experience of users of public charging piles include site closure theme, slow speed theme, bad attitude theme, use fault theme, management missing theme, location failure theme, fuel vehicle occupancy theme and road finding obstacle theme. The themes of negative emotional experience of household charging pile users include service behind theme, appearance ugly theme, product weight theme, use risk theme, space occupation theme, insufficient configuration theme, poor matching theme and misleading consumption theme.

From the results of thematic cluster analysis, the mood of users of public charging piles may be affected by 10 factors, such as time, accessibility, environment, price, parking space, equipment, supporting facilities, opening, service, management and identification. Among them, the theme of parking convenience is the most important in the clustering of positive emotional themes of public charging piles, and the theme of road finding obstacle is the most important in the clustering of negative emotional themes of public charging piles. The top three weights in the subject words of positive emotion of public charging pile are: free parking, practicality and queuing order; The top three weights in the negative emotion subject words of public charging pile are: environment, difficult to find and time. The emotion of household charging pile users may be affected by 13 factors, such as function, durability, sales, price, ease of use, brand, installation, appearance, weight, safety, volume, configuration and matching. Product durability theme and use risk theme are the most important topics in the clustering of positive and negative emotional themes of household charging piles respectively. Among the positive emotion subject words of household charging pile, the top three are: durability, genuine products and cost performance; Among the negative emotion subject words of household charging pile, the top three are: site, appearance and weight. In contrast, public charging pile users focus on a series of public services centered on charging products, while household charging pile users focus on the function and appearance design of the product itself.

4.3 Social Network Analysis and Comparison

From the results of analysis, for public charging products, the five themes of practical parity, preferential fees, sufficient parking spaces, stable equipment and environmental quality are closely linked. The theme words with high centrality in each theme are: environment, place, fast, smooth, electric pile, cheap, parking and space occupation. Keywords with high collinearity times are: "surrounding-environment", "parking-price" and "cheap-easy to use" (Fig. 4-a). For household charging products, the three themes of professional installation, easy to use and good function are closely related. The theme words with high centrality in each theme are: easy to use, price, customer service, charging, high quality and low price, genuine, durable and fast. Keywords with high collinear times are: "professional-installation", "professional -master", "professional-charging", "charging-effect" and "installation-effect" (Fig. 4-b).

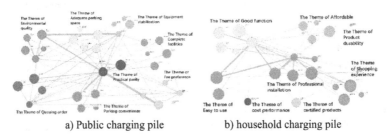

a) Public charging pile   b) household charging pile

Fig. 4. Social network analysis of positive comment subject words

From the results of analysis, for public charging products, the three themes of slow speed, site selection failure and oil truck occupation are closely related. The theme words with high centrality in each theme are: oil truck, slow charging, charging, waste, parking, space occupation, security, hard to find. Keywords with high collinearity times are: "charging-occupancy", "charging-parking space", "oil truck-charging", "oil truck -parking space" and "oil truck-occupancy" (Fig. 5-a). For household charging products, the two themes of backward service and misleading consumption are closely related. The key words with high centrality in each theme are: charging, hardware, appearance, quality, model and performance. Keywords with high collinearity are: "charge-speed", "charge-installation", "speed-installation", "speed-delivery" and "speed -logistics" (Fig. 5-b).

From the social network analysis results of the positive emotion theme words, the charging equipment is cheap and easy to use, the parking price is standardized, and the quality of the surrounding environment is high, which is expected to have a great impact on the positive emotions of customers of public charging products; Professional on-site installation personnel and good charging function effect may have a positive impact on the positive emotion of customers of household charging products. From the social network analysis results of negative emotion theme words, the impolite occupation of charging spaces by fuel vehicles may be an important reason for the negative emotional

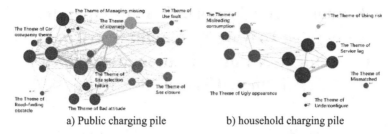

a) Public charging pile   b) household charging pile

Fig. 5. Social network analysis of negative comment subject words

experience of public charging products. The poor speed and timeliness of charging, installation and delivery may be one of the reasons for the negative emotions of household charging products.

5 Conclusion

The comparative study of public charging pile and household charging pile shows that the characteristics of users' emotional needs under the two most basic scene conditions are different, and the requirements for the appearance, function module, interactive interface, logo and environmental design of charging pile will also be different. To sum up, the design and research of public charging piles in the future should focus on charging products and station design, connect users' demand cognition, charging product design and public scene application system, and enhance the benign interaction between "owner-pile" and "pile-scene". The design and research of household charging pile should emphasize the combination of "charging product" and "owner service", and provide customers with complete and sustainable household charging solutions with the help of product service system design means.

References

1. Wu, S., Yang, Z.: Availability of public electric vehicle charging pile and development of electric vehicle: evidence from China. Sustainability **12**, 6369 (2020)
2. Ma, S.-C., Fan, Y.: A deployment model of EV charging piles and its impact on EV promotion. Energy Policy **146**, 111777 (2020)
3. Chen, J., Li, F., Yang, R., Ma, D.: Impacts of increasing private charging piles on electric vehicles' charging profiles: a case study in Hefei City, China. Energies **13**, 4387 (2020)
4. Bunce, L., Harris, M., Burgess, M.: Charge up then charge out? Drivers' perceptions and experiences of electric vehicles in the UK. Transp. Res. Part A Policy Pract. **59**, 278–287 (2014)
5. Jensen, A.F., Cherchi, E., Mabit, S.L.: On the stability of preferences and attitudes before and after experiencing an electric vehicle. Transp. Res. Part D: Transp. Environ. **25**, 24–32 (2013)
6. Zheng, W., Li, Y., Zhang, M., Shao, Z., Wang, X.: Reliability evaluation and analysis for NEV charging station considering the impact of charging experience. Int. J. Hydrogen Energy **47**, 3980–3993 (2022)
7. Shu, T., Wang, Z., Lin, L., Jia, H., Zhou, J.: Customer perceived risk measurement with NLP method in electric vehicles consumption market: empirical study from China. Energies **15**, 1637 (2022)

Human Factor Issues in Remote Operator of Automated Driving System for Services - One Operator to N Units of Automated Vehicles in Automated Vehicle Services -

Naohisa Hashimoto[✉], Yanbin Wu, and Toshihisa Sato

National Institute of Advanced Industrial Science and Technology, Tsukuba 305-8560, Ibaraki, Japan
{naohisa-hashimoto,mwu.yanbin,toshihisa-sato}@aist.go.jp

Abstract. Vehicle automation is expected for future society. Automated driving systems will be implemented in mobility services including public transport. In this study, we focus on automation for mobility service and don't deal with automation for privately owned vehicles. If level 4 automation is used, no drivers on board can be realized. Considering automated vehicle services, level 4 automated vehicles should be monitored by remote operators, and remote operators are expected for managing automated vehicles. One operator should manage more than two vehicles for the cost benefit. On managing or operating, there are interactions between a remote operator and an automated driving system. Human factor issues and adequate human machine interface between a remote operator and the system should be considered. Thus, we exposed the issues related to human factor between them by categorizing the number of vehicles. We are working on social implementation of automated vehicle services, which has been supported by the government in Japan. Also, we have a plan to do the experiments with real automated bus and a remote operation system, which were developed in order to clarify these human factors.

Keywords: Automated vehicles · Human factors · Mobility as a Service (MaaS) · Remote operator

1 Introduction

Vehicle automation is expected for future society [1–8]. The automation will contribute to social issues such as reducing traffic accidents and congestion, providing greater mobility for vulnerable road users in local communities and in aging society, and solving the shortage of drivers in the logistics industry field, and finally ensuring safe and comfortable mobility [9]. The operational domain of automated driving will be extended from highways to public roads, and automated driving systems will be implemented in mobility services including public transport and logistic operations [9]. In this study, we focus on automation for mobility service or logistics, and don't deal with automation for privately owned vehicles.

C. Stephanidis et al. (Eds.): HCII 2022, CCIS 1655, pp. 368–374, 2022.
https://doi.org/10.1007/978-3-031-19682-9_47

If level 4 automation is used, no drivers on board can be realized [10]. Considering automated vehicle services, level 4 automated vehicles should be monitored by a remote operators, and remote operators are expected for managing automated vehicles [10]. If one operator manages only one vehicle, there are less cost benefit, which means this situation is same with that a bus driver is on the bus. So, one operator should manage more than two vehicles. On managing or operating, there are interactions between a remote operator and an automated driving system, shown in Fig. 1. Human factor issues and adequate human machine interface between a remote operator and the system should be considered. Thus, we exposed the issues related to human factor between them by categorizing the number of vehicles, and what should be clear, which will be explained the next chapter.

Now, we are constructing the plan for investigate each human factor's research by discussing with a bus operator in the national project, which was supported by the government in Japan. All over the world, the researches on automated vehicle including the remote system for remote operation, remote control or surveillance are being on-going and also the discussion are being active in ISO standard [11–15]. We started to doing the experiments with real automated bus and remote operation system, which were developed and are shown in Fig. 2 and Fig. 3. In remote operation system, the several features of a remote operator can be measured for investigate the status of the remote operator including brain waves, eye, light of sight and body and head movement.

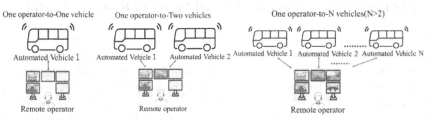

Fig. 1. Remote operator for automated vehicle (From left: one operator to one vehicle, one operator to two vehicles, one operator N vehicles)

Fig. 2. Automated bus

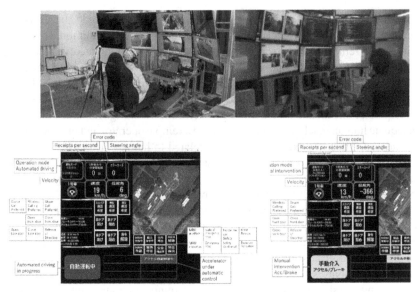

Fig. 3. Remote operation center for experiments (Top) and human machine interface for remote operator (bottom left: automated driving in progress, bottom right: Manual intervention)

2   Human Factor Issues and Related Issues in Remote Operation

Table 1 shows the human factor issues related issues in one operator to one automated vehicle. The basic factors in remote operation are exposed. Comparing to the automation for privately owned vehicles, condition and environment of automation for mobility services are limited. Thus, we considered the mobility services as a first step, and we already realized level 3 vehicle automation in service in Japan and in this study, the assumption of vehicle speed is low. In this breakout paper, it is impossible to explain all factors in detail. Hence, each task should be clarified with scientific evidence, which are from conducted experiments prove with real subjects and vehicles.

Table 2 shows the human factor issues with two automated vehicles. In this situation, if a remote operator is on the duty of handling one automated vehicle, for example, remote control or concentrating the task of the vehicle, other automated vehicle must be stopped. Thus, in level 2 automation, it is impossible that one remote operator does two automated vehicles.

Table 3 shows human factor issues, which expanded to N units and were generalized from 2 unites. It will be important that 1 remote operator can manage how many automated vehicles in vehicle services. By considering previous experience [11], this N number depends on the tasks for remote operator. Thus, it is necessary that the tasks for a remote operator should be exposed, how much time a remote operator need to respond and handle the task, and the frequency of all tasks are cleared. Rogers also pointed out that switching cost for the task should be considered [16], thus task switching should be considered [17, 18].

Table 1. Human factor issues and related issues in one operator to one automated vehicle

Correspondence table （Assumptions of remote, low speed, cart）

		A （e.g. Undetected or false positive by the system）	B （e.g. Detection of the track obstacle by the system）	C （e.g. Traveling within expectations inside the track）
		System operation： No MRM activation in exceptional incidents that can be expected to be out of ODD	System operation： Preconfigured to be out of ODD, MRM activated （cart stop automatically）	System operation： System running in ODD
		Role of Remote operator： The operator has to constantly monitor and handle exceptional incidents by him/herself.	Role of Remote operator： The operator has to handle by him/herself after MRM (cart stop).	Role of Remote operator： The operator only monitors （does nothing）
One operator-to-One vehicle	Ability of remote operator to grasp the situation (understanding the system state and behavior)	Understanding the surrounding traffic condition	Understanding the surrounding traffic situation after MRM	Trust in the system
		• Understanding the current state and future behavior of the system • Status of autonomous vehicle (vehicle speed, GPS position, route, etc.) • Condition of on-board crew		
	Understanding the system function for remote operator	Understanding the exceptional incidents (undetected or false positive targets by the system)	Understanding ODD	
	HMI(input into the system)	Quick manual operation (takeover)	Manual operation after MRM	
		Switching from manual to automatic operation		
	HMI(display information)	Display of targets that the system is able to detect	HMI with MRM activated (display modality, display location, display timing)	Information of system operating status
		Display of surrounding condition to assist grasping the situation		
	Remote operator state	Detection of awakening decline, wandering consciousness and side-eye	Detection of awakening decline	
		How to maintain proper remote operator status		
	State transition method	Remote operator-led transition	• System-led transition • Whether or not there is a warning that the MRM will be activated.	
	Value in the remote operator	• Reduce fatigue and burden • Comfort Improvement		
	External HMI(effect on traffic flow)	**External HMI to inform the takeover**	**External HMI to inform others of MRM activation**	Smooth operation management
		Communication between automated vehicles and other vehicles		
	Social acceptability	Frequency of the takeover to remote operator （Too often is unacceptable?→Discussion on cost of services related）		Trust in the system
	License and Education System	Training of the takeover	Training of the remote manual operations (including semi-automatic)	License of Remote monitoring operator (License as a servicer)

Table 2. Human factor issues and related issues in one operator to two automated vehicles

Correspondence table （Assumptions of remote, low speed, cart）

		A （e.g. Undetected or false positive by the system）	B （e.g. Detection of the track obstacle by the system）	C （e.g. Traveling within expectations inside the track）
		System operation： No MRM activation in exceptional incidents that can be expected to be out of ODD	System operation： Preconfigured to be out of ODD, MRM activated （cart stop automatically）	System operation： System running in ODD
		Role of Remote operator： The operator has to constantly monitor and handle exceptional incidents by him/herself.	Role of Remote operator： The operator has to handle by him/herself after MRM (cart stop).	Role of Remote operator： The operator only monitors （does nothing）
One operator-to-Two vehicles	Same challenging items as one operator-to-one vehicle	• **How difficult is "remote operator's ability to grasp the situation" and "remote operator's understanding of the system function" in one operator-to-one vehicle to be in one operator-to-two vehicles?** • **How can HMI (input to system) and HMI (information display) in one operator-to-two vehicles support the above?** • **Importance of "detection items and accuracy of the remote operator status", "value in the remote operator", "social acceptability" and "education system" compared to one operator-to-one vehicle**		
	Optimal backup system （When additional operators are required due to emergency handling）	Need for additional operators when one cart is in the takeover		
	Ability to grasp the situation of a remote operator for two carts	• Determining which cart requires the takeover • Decision to handle when both carts require the takeover	• Determining which cart activated the MRM • Decision to handle when both carts activated the MRM	
	HMI (input to system) in case of emergency	Appropriate operation for the cart requiring the takeover	Operation of one cart while the other activated the MRM	
		Appropriate manual operation after both carts have stopped (order of start traveling, time from manual to automatic)		
	HMI (information display) in case of emergency	When one cart is in the takeover, the status of the other cart is displayed. Depending on the backup system		
	Emergency external HMI (display of information to surroundings)	When one cart is in the takeover, alert surroundings the other cart		

AorB When 1 cart is in the takeover, it is necessary to determine whether the One-to-One will continue as 2 sets after all.

Table 3. Human factor issues and related issues in one operator to N units of automated vehicles

Correspondence table （Assumptions of remote, low speed, cart）

		A （e.g. Undetected or false positive by the system）	B （e.g. Detection of the track obstacle by the system）	C （e.g. Traveling within expectations inside the track）
		System operation : No MRM activation in exceptional incidents that can be expected to be out of ODD	System operation : Preconfigured to be out of ODD, MRM activated （cart stop automatically）	System operation : System running in ODD
		Role of Remote operator : The operator has to constantly monitor and handle exceptional incidents by him/herself.	Role of Remote operator : The operator has to handle by him/herself after MRM (cart stop).	Role of Remote operator : The operator only monitors (does nothing)
One operator-to-N vehicles(N>2)	Same challenging items as one operator-to-one vehicle	• **How difficult is "remote operator's ability to grasp the situation" and "remote operator's understanding of the system function" in one operator-to-one vehicle to be in one operator-to-two vehicles?** • **How can HMI (input to system) and HMI (information display) in one operator-to-N vehicles support the above?** • **Importance of "detection items and accuracy of the remote operator status", "value in the remote operator", "social acceptability" and "education system" compared to one operator-to-one vehicle**		
	Same challenging items as one operator-to-two vehicles	• **How difficult is "Ability to grasp the situation of a remote operator for 2 carts", " HMI (input to system) in case of emergency" and "HMI (information display) in case of emergency" in one operator-to-N vehicles compared to one operator-to-two vehicles?** • **Emergency external HMI (display of information to surroundings) : How many carts (up to N-1) should alert surroundings the other carts when one cart is in the takeover?**		
	Optimal backup system （when additional operators are required due to emergency handling）	**How many additional operators (up to N-1 carts) are required when one cart is in the takeover?**		

AorB   When 1 cart is in the takeover, It is necessary to determine whether to continue as one operator-to-one vehicle and one operator-to-(N-1) vehicles after all.

3   Summary and Future Work

The human factors issues in detail were exposed and explained by categorizing the number of automated vehicles, which should be monitored. This paper deals with the on-going research, thus with respect with these issues, it is difficult to evaluate these issues at this moment, but these issues should be cleared with using real experiments in order to realize automated vehicle services with remote operators.

As a future work, we have a plan to do experiments in order to clarify the human factor issues, which are exposed and explained in Sect. 2. In the experiments, we will use the automated vehicles and remote operation system with real subjects in the test track and real world.

Acknowledgement. This project has been supported by Ministry of Economy Trade and Industry, and Ministry of Land Infrastructure Transport and Tourism in Japan.

References

1. US. DOT. http://www.its.dot.gov/automated_vehicle/index.htm. Accessed 23 May 2022
2. ITS Japan. http://www.its-jp.org/english/files/2015/04/SIP_Worlshop2015_leaflets_e_2015 0326.pdf. Accessed 23 May 2022
3. European Commission. IOT Large Scale Pilot 5 Autonomous Vehicles in a Connected Environment. https://www.ertrac.org/uploads/documents_publications/2015%20ART%20Info% 20Day/IoTPilot-autonomous%20vehicle-nov5.pdf. Accessed 23 May 2022
4. Aeberhard, M., et al.: Experience, results and lessons learned from automated driving on Germany's highways. IEEE Intell. Transp. Syst. Mag. **7**, 42–57 (2015)
5. Shladover, S.: Challenges to evaluation of $CO2$ impacts of intelligent transportation systems. In: Presented at 2011 IEEE integrated and sustainable transportation system, Vienna (Austria) (2011)
6. Tsugawa, S., Jeschke, S., Shladover, S.: A review of truck platooning projects for energy savings. IEEE Trans. Intell. Veh. **1**, 68–77 (2016)
7. Hashimoto, N., Takinami, Y., Yamamoto, M.: Experimental study on different types of curves for ride comfort in automated vehicles. J. Adv. Transp. (2021)
8. Hashimoto, N., Thompson, S., Kato, S., Boyali, A., Tsugawa, S.: Necessity of automated vehicle control customization: Experimental results during lane changing. Transportation Research Record 2672 (22), 1–9
9. NEDO. SIP Automated Driving for Universal Services (SIP-adus) R&D Plan, https://www. nedo.go.jp/content/100887563.pdf. Accessed 15 Apr 2022
10. SAE J3016TM levels of driving automation. https://www.sae.org/binaries/content/assets/cm/ content/blog/sae-j3016-visual-chart_5.3.21.pdf. Accessed 15 Apr 2022
11. Hashimoto, N., et al.: Introduction of prototype of remote type automated vehicle system by using communication between operator and vehicles in real environment. In: Proceedings of 2018 16th International Conference on Intelligent Transportation Systems Telecommunications (ITST) (2018)
12. Dawson, J., Garikapati, D.: Extending ISO26262 to an operationally complex system. In: 2021 IEEE International Systems Conference (SysCon), pp. 1–7 (2021). https://doi.org/10. 1109/SysCon48628.2021.9447146
13. Neumeier, S., Facchi, C.: Towards a driver support system for teleoperated driving. In: 2019 IEEE Intelligent Transportation Systems Conference (ITSC), pp. 4190-4196 (2019). https:// doi.org/10.1109/ITSC.2019.8917244
14. Xiong, G., Chen, H., Gong, J., Wu, S.: Development and implementation of remote control system for an unmanned heavy tracked vehicle. In: 2007 IEEE Intelligent Vehicles Symposium, pp. 663–667 (2007). https://doi.org/10.1109/IVS.2007.4290192
15. Juang, R.-T.: The implementation of remote monitoring for autonomous driving.. In: 2019 4th Asia-Pacific Conference on Intelligent Robot Systems (ACIRS), pp. 53–56 (2019). https:// doi.org/10.1109/ACIRS.2019.8935978
16. Rogers, R.D., Monsell, S.: Costs of a predictible switch between simple cognitive tasks. J. Exp. Psychol. Gen. **124**(2), 207 (1995)
17. Suzuki, S.: Visualization of task switching strategy of machine operation. In: 2009 International Conference on Networking, Sensing and Control, pp. 513–518 (2009). https://doi.org/ 10.1109/ICNSC.2009.4919329
18. Zhao, G., Liu, Y.-J., Shi, Y.: Real-time assessment of the cross-task mental workload using physiological measures during anomaly detection. IEEE Trans. Hum.-Mach. Syst. **48**(2), 149–160 (2018). https://doi.org/10.1109/THMS.2018.2803025

Is This My Ride? AV Braking Behavior from the Perspective of Waiting Ride Hailing Customers

Fabian Hub[1]([✉]), Silvio Heß[2], Marc Wilbrink[2], and Michael Oehl[2]

[1] German Aerospace Center (DLR), Rutherfordstraße 2, 12489 Berlin, Germany
`fabian.hub@dlr.de`
[2] German Aerospace Center (DLR), Lilienthalplatz 7, 38108 Braunschweig, Germany
`{silvio.hess,marc.wilbrink,michael.oehl}@dlr.de`

Abstract. In virtual stop (vStop) pick-up scenarios the shared automated vehicle's (SAV) approaching behavior as implicit communication to the awaiting customer is an important factor to build trust in the vehicle. Identifying the SAV timely could also help users getting ready for boarding and foster a positive perception of the automated service. An online study was conducted to identify trust building, information enhancing and collaboration fostering vehicle braking dynamics from the perspective of waiting customers. 102 participants viewed videos with three different SAV longitudinal braking dynamics in combination with three different conventional light signals. Results showed a user preference for defensive braking to approach flexible pick-up locations curbside. This complements the vehicle passengers' desires for smooth driving dynamics. Additionally, turn indicator light signals as explicit communication received significantly higher ratings than only implicit communication in the pick-up scenario. Findings add value to understanding SAV behavior when approaching vStops and help designing coherent explicit and implicit communication of SAVs when interacting with surrounding traffic participants in pick-up scenarios.

Keywords: Shared automated vehicles · Vehicle dynamics · Approaching behavior · Implicit communication · Trust · vStop

1 Introduction

In combination with on-demand ride pooling algorithms shared automated vehicles (SAV) are likely to be a promising alternative to conventional fixed route public transportation. Deployed in large scale it shows great potential in terms of reduced resource consumption, traffic congestion, flexibility and convenience for its customers [1, 2]. However, in order to realize the benefits wide spread user adoption and commercial success are crucial. Hence, overall user experience (UX) in the novel mobility service are key factors when developing the vehicle automation [3]. From a user's perspective, one of the first (as booking is done digitally via smartphone) physical touch points with the automated on-demand mobility service is recognizing the SAV approaching the flexible pick-up location. In contrast to conventional bus stops, curbside stopping at virtual stops (vStop) isn't supported by physical cues in the street environment. Furthermore, the absence of a driver requires an approaching behavior which is sufficiently intelligible by customers waiting curbside [4]. On the one hand, by recognizing the vehicle's intention could help identifying the ride timely to prepare for vehicle boarding and speed up the pick-up process. A stopping maneuver perceived as too risky on the other hand could potentially worry users about having an uncomfortable or unsafe ride. Accordingly, the SAV's dynamic human-machine-interface (dHMI) used for implicit communication (i.e., kinematic cues and especially braking dynamics in the pick-up scenario) plays an important role with regard to how users perceive the overall service quality and build trust in the vehicle automation. In combination with intuitively comprehensible light signals used for explicit communication (i.e., conventional light signals like turn indicators or even additional novel external human-machine interfaces (eHMI)) SAV behavior could contribute positively to an efficient pick-up process and high UX which benefits users and traffic flow [5, 6].

This experimental study tries to gain understanding about the SAV's implicit communication in terms of braking behavior from a waiting customer's perspective. Goal of this study was to investigate especially the effect of dHMI and the use of conventional light signals on customers perceived UX ratings, such as quality of information, preparation for boarding, trust in the automated vehicle, and trust in the mobility service during pick-up scenarios. AVs' braking behavior, as part of the dHMI, has been topic to latest research. However, studies mostly focused on AV yielding behavior in pedestrian street crossing scenarios [7, 8]. Overall defensive AV driving styles seem trust building for in-vehicle passengers and pedestrians [9, 10]. However, SAV stopping maneuver has yet to be investigated from an awaiting customer's perspective. By focussing on the dHMI as implicit communication in pick-up scenarios this work gives first insights about vStop approaching maneuvers for SAVs. Aspects of explicit communication were considered as well, addressing specifications by German legislation and also accounting for conventional light signal strategies which don't need to be unfavorable compared to distinct eHMIs [11]. Holisticly, vehicle's implicit and explicit communication needs to be complementary so customers, passengers, and surrounding traffic participants can understand the vehicle's intention most effectively in future stopping scenarios and have positive attitudes towards automated mobility and to ensure safe interaction with the SAV.

2   Method

2.1   Participants and Recruiting

N = 102 participants (44 female) at ages between 19 and 82 years (M = 37.30; SD = 15.17) were recruited by means of volunteer databases, social media and personal contact. Participants had to be at least 18 years old to participate. Scores on the affinity for technology questionnaire (ATI) [12] resulted in a higher than average M = 4.15 (SD = 1.05), based on a 6-point Likert scale (from 1 = "completely disagree" to 6 = "completely agree"). 94% of the participants were familiar with the topic of automated driving. The study was conceptualized and realized in accordance with the declaration of Helsinki.

Informed consent was obtained from all participants before the online experiment. All participants volunteered and had the chance of winning a 25€ universal voucher in a raffle.

2.2 Video Stimuli

Video footage was prepared. Each clip was of high resolution (1920 x 1080 p) and lasted approx. 15 s. All videos showed the same urban environment with a sidewalk and a wide two-lane straight road (Fig. 1). A SAV (a customized driverless shuttle bus with initial speed of 30 km/h) approached the viewer from a distance of approximately 80 m. Perspective of the videos was set to the field of view of a potential SAV customer waiting for pick-up. Videos ended always with the SAV stopping right next to the participants point of view at the same spot (Fig. 1, right).

Fig. 1. The approaching SAV's braking behavior from the participant's perspective exemplary in three stages: Initiation of deceleration at -1 m/s^2 condition (left), While decelerating at -1 m/s^2 using turn signal (middle), final position curbside (right).

2.3 Independent Variables

The experimental online study followed a 3×3 mixed design. A vehicle's braking maneuver on a straight road can be characterized substantially by the vehicle's changes in longitudinal position over time [13]. Hence, *longitudinal deceleration* was chosen as the first independent variable (within factor). From the holistic perspective it seemed reasonable to choose a range of deceleration values perceived as rather comfortably by on-board passengers at low speeds [14, 15]. Thus, *longitudinal deceleration* as within-subjects factor contained the levels "defensive braking" (-1 m/s^2), "moderate braking" (-2 m/s^2) and "strong braking" (-2.5 m/s^2). Due to uniform deceleration, braking distance varied accordingly from 34.72 m (defensive braking) to 17.36 m (moderate braking) and 13.89 m (strong braking) as the vehicle would always stop at the same spot. Lateral dynamics as kinematic cue was kept to a minimum as approaching curbside was designed linearly throughout the whole braking distance.

German legislation (StVO) does not regulate the use of light signals for stopping maneuvers curbside explicitly. Nevertheless, turn indicator is considered the most common light signal by human drivers to indicate approaching a stop. For service buses it is mandatory to use turn indicators when stopping (§7 StVO). Hazard lights can be used by service buses when approaching a stop at specific locations (§16 StVO). Hence, it seemed reasonable to control for these specific conventional light signals. Therefore, as a second independent variable, the between-subjects factor *light signal* with the levels "no light signal", "turn signal" and "hazard lights" was applied.

2.4 Dependent Variables

UX ratings from a waiting customer's perspective were measured by a set of dependent variables. *Trust in automation* regarding the approaching SAV's behavior was measured by a modified version of the "Understanding/Predictability" subscale of the standardized TiA questionnaire [16]. The four items were adapted accordingly ("The behavior of the shuttle was always clear to me", "I was able to understand why things happened" alternating by the inverse items "The shuttle reacted unpredictably" and "It's difficult to identify what the shuttle will do next"). A 6-point Likert scale (from $1 =$ "completely disagree" to $6 =$ "completely agree") was used. The mean across all four items served as *trust in automation* score. *Perceived quality of information* was retrieved by "How well did you feel informed about the shuttle's behavior in this situation?", based on a 7-point Likert scale (from $1 =$ "very bad" to $7 =$ "very good").

Additionally, an item was included to capture whether the shuttle's stopping maneuver would be helpful regarding customers' *readiness for boarding* ("The shuttle's stopping maneuver helps me to prepare for boarding.") so that an efficient pick-up situation would be promoted. Finally, the influence of the SAV's braking behavior in building *trust in the automated mobility service* ("The shuttle's stopping maneuver is conducive to my trust in the automated mobility service.") was captured. Both items were measured by a 6-point Likert scale (from $1 =$ "not true at all" to $6 =$ "completely true").

2.5 Procedure

The online study was set up in SoSci Survey. Participants completed the survey using their own computer, tablet or smartphone. Participants gave their consent to the data processing (DSGVO compliant) and assured that they were at least 18 years old. Subsequently, they tested the video streaming and connectivity. Then the traffic situation was introduced by showing the SAV prior to initializing a braking maneuver. Participants were informed about the scenario in which they had booked a shuttle ride and now are waiting curbside to be picked up at a vStop. Participants viewed the video clips in a 3 × 3 mixed design and rated the SAV's behavior each time. Each participant viewed three different videos including all levels of longitudinal deceleration (-1 m/s^2, -2 m/s^2 and -2.5 m/s^2) in combination with one light signal (no light signal, turn signal or hazard lights) and filled out a set of questions. Order of presentation was fully balanced. Finally, demographic data was captured.

3   Results

For data analysis repeated-measures analyses of variance (ANOVA) with the within-subjects factor *longitudinal deceleration* and the between-subjects factor *light signal* was conducted. Level of significance was set to .05. Pairwise comparisons were computed using Bonferroni correction throughout. Effect sizes (partial η^2) were interpreted as small (.01 to .05), medium (.06 to .13), or large ($\geq$.14) according to Cohen [17]. If sphericity wasn't met, Huynh-Feldt correction was executed. Assumptions of normal distribution and to some extend variance homogeneity were violated, which can be neglected due to ANOVA is considered to be robust against such violations, especially when group sizes are equal, which applied for *light signal* conditions at 34 participants each [18].

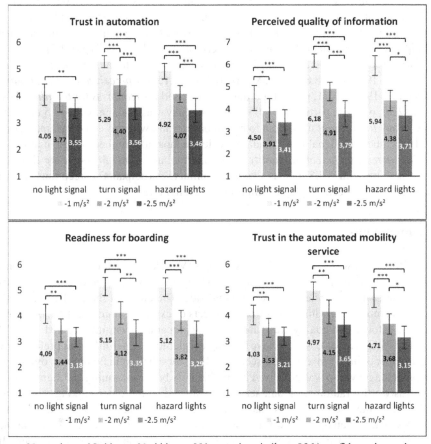

Notes: * p < .05; ** p < .01; *** p < .001; error bars indicate 95 % confidence interval.

Fig. 2. UX ratings in dependence of longitudinal deceleration and conventional light signal including pairwise comparisons for each light signal condition (Bonferroni-correction applied).

A significant main effect was found for *longitudinal deceleration* regarding *trust in automation*, F(1.95, 193.29) = 95.46, p < .001, partial η^2 = .49, *perceived quality of information*, F(2, 198) = 91.33, p < .001, partial η^2 = .48, *readiness for boarding*, F(2, 198) = 66.97, p < .001, partial η^2 = .40, and *trust in the automated mobility service*, F(2, 198) = 57.80, p < .001, partial η^2 = .37, each showing large effects. Pairwise comparisons revealed that a lower *longitudinal deceleration* resulted in significantly higher ratings for *trust in automation, perceived quality of information, readiness for boarding*, and *trust in the automated mobility service* (all p < .001). Figure 2 shows more detailed pairwise comparisons for each light signal condition.

Light signal also had a significant effect on *trust in automation*, $F(2, 99) = 3.96$, p < .05, partial $\eta^2 = .07$, *perceived quality of information*, $F(2, 99) = 6.17$, p < .01, partial $\eta^2 = .11$, *readiness for boarding*, $F(2, 99) = 4.56$, p < .05, partial $\eta^2 = .08$, and *trust in the automated mobility service*, $F(2, 99) = 4.46$, p < .05, partial $\eta^2 = .08$, each showing medium effects, which resulted particularly from significantly higher ratings for "turn signal" compared with "no light signal" for all dependent variables (all p < .05). Additionally, *perceived quality of information* was rated significantly higher when participants were shown "hazard lights" instead of "no light signal" (p < .05).

A *longitudinal deceleration* x *light signal* interaction was found for *trust in automation*, $F(3.91, 193.29) = 8.83$, p < .001, partial $\eta^2 = .15$, for *perceived quality of information*, $F(4, 198) = 4.71$, p < .01, partial $\eta^2 = .09$, and for *readiness for boarding*, $F(4, 198) = 2.76$, p < .05, partial $\eta^2 = .05$. When the SAV was braking with -2.5 m/s^2 the usage of any *light signal* turned out to be minor relevant, whereas at a deceleration rate of -1 m/s^2 the turn signal in particular revealed comparably higher ratings in terms of *trust in automation, perceived quality of information,* and *ready for boarding* (Fig. 2). Strong braking with -2.5 m/s^2 is likely to dominate participants' perceptions so that light signals don't seem to play an important role anymore.

4 Conclusion

Goal of this work was to identify UX fostering SAV braking dynamics as implicit communication in combination with explicit communication via conventional light signals to awaiting customers when approaching curbside. The effect of three different dHMI levels, in combination with three different aspects of explicit communication, on users' perceived information quality, trust, and boarding preparation was investigated. Over all examined categories of UX, defensive braking deceleration at -1 m/s^2 was preferred by the participants in the investigated scenario. The smoothest vehicle braking dynamics in approaching a vStop was perceived as significantly better informing and significantly more trustworthy (automation and service) compared to the other braking dynamics. Furthermore, the use of a turn signal was found to significantly increase all UX ratings, especially when the SAV was braking cautiously. Hence, the results of this online study give clear advice on how SAVs should approach a vStop to pick-up customers. It was shown that turn indicator and defensive braking dynamics is a user-friendly way of approaching customers waiting curbside. From a holistic perspective of SAV's implicit and explicit communication to surrounding traffic participant and in-vehicle passengers, findings are in line with previous research. Realization of smooth driving dynamics in combination with matching light signals ought to be favorable for clear and safe interaction with a SAV in future automated mobility scenarios. Further research should focus on additional forms of light signals on SAVs, such as specific eHMI concepts to gain deeper understanding on how exactly customers' UX could be fostered in pick-up scenarios. Additionally, findings from this study should be reevaluated by conducting an in-field study to address the limitations of the online video study design. By this approach SAV interaction and acceptance of automated mobility could be enhanced.

Acknowledgements. This research was funded by the German Federal Ministry for Digital and Transport within the research project "ViVre" (Grant no.: 01MM19014A).

References

1. Martinez, L.M., Viegas, J.M.: Assessing the impacts of deploying a shared self-driving urban mobility system: an agent-based model applied to the city of Lisbon, Portugal. Int. J. Transp. Sci. Technol. **6**(1), 13–27 (2017). https://doi.org/10.1016/j.ijtst.2017.05.005
2. Herminghaus, S.: Mean field theory of demand responsive ride pooling systems. Transp. Res. Part A: Pol. Pract. **119**, 15–28 (2019). https://doi.org/10.1016/j.tra.2018.10.028
3. Niculescu, A.I., Dix, A., Yeo, K.H.: Are you ready for a drive? In: Mark, G., et al. (eds.) Proceedings of the 2017 CHI Conference Extended Abstracts on Human Factors in Computing Systems. CHI '17: CHI Conference on Human Factors in Computing Systems, Denver Colorado USA, 06 05 2017 11 05 2017, New York, NY, USA, pp. 2810–2817. ACM (2017). doi: https://doi.org/10.1145/3027063.3053182
4. Kemper, A., Bubb, I., Kriebel, E., Müller, A.: Identifikation von kritischen Interaktionen des bedarfsgerechten ÖPNV mit autonom betriebenen Fahrzeugen [Identification of Critical Interactions in Demand Responsive Public Transport with Autonomously Operated Vehicles]. In: 66. Frühjahrskongress der Gesellschaft für Arbeitswissenschaft 2020 (2020)
5. Al-Turki, M., Ratrout, N.T., Rahman, S.M., Reza, I.: Impacts of autonomous vehicles on traffic flow characteristics under mixed traffic environment: future perspectives. Sustainability **13**(19), 11052 (2021). https://doi.org/10.3390/su131911052
6. Hub, F., Wilbrink, M., Kettwich, C., Oehl, M.: Designing ride access points for shared automated vehicles - an early stage prototype evaluation. In: Stephanidis, C., Antona, M., Ntoa, S. (eds.) HCII 2020. CCIS, vol. 1294, pp. 560–567. Springer, Cham (2020). https://doi.org/10.1007/978-3-030-60703-6_72
7. Risto, M., Emmenegger, C., Vinkhuyzen, E., Cefkin, M., Hollan, J.: Human-vehicle interfaces: the power of vehicle movement gestures in human road user coordination. In: Proceedings of the 9th International Driving Symposium on Human Factors in Driver Assessment, Training, and Vehicle Design: driving assessment 2017. Driving Assessment Conference, Manchester Village, Vermont, USA, 26 June 2017–29 June 2017, pp. 186–192. University of Iowa, Iowa City, Iowa (2017). https://doi.org/10.17077/drivingassessment.1633
8. Bazilinskyy, P., Sakuma, T., de Winter, J.: What driving style makes pedestrians think a passing vehicle is driving automatically? Appl. Ergon. **95**, 103428 (2021). https://doi.org/10.1016/j.apergo.2021.103428
9. Jayaraman, S.K., et al.: Pedestrian trust in automated vehicles: role of traffic signal and AV driving behavior. Front. Robot. AI **6**, 117 (2019). https://doi.org/10.3389/frobt.2019.00117
10. Ekman, F., Johansson, M., Bligård, L.-O., Karlsson, M., Strömberg, H.: Exploring automated vehicle driving styles as a source of trust information. Transport. Res. F: Traffic Psychol. Behav. **65**, 268–279 (2019). https://doi.org/10.1016/j.trf.2019.07.026
11. Lee, Y.M., et al.: Understanding the messages conveyed by automated vehicles. In: Proceedings of the 11th International Conference on Automotive User Interfaces and Interactive Vehicular Applications. AutomotiveUI 2019: 11th International Conference on Automotive User Interfaces and Interactive Vehicular Applications, Utrecht Netherlands, 21 09 2019 25 09 2019, New York, NY, USA, pp. 134–143. ACM (2019). https://doi.org/10.1145/3342197.3344546

12. Franke, T., Attig, C., Wessel, D.: A personal resource for technology interaction: development and validation of the affinity for technology interaction (ATI) scale. Int. J. Hum.-Comput. Interact. **35**(6), 456–467 (2019). https://doi.org/10.1080/10447318.2018.1456150

13. Dietrich, A., Maruhn, P., Schwarze, L., Bengler, K.: Implicit communication of automated vehicles in urban scenarios: effects of pitch and deceleration on pedestrian crossing behavior. In: Ahram, T., Karwowski, W., Pickl, S., Taiar, R. (eds.) IHSED 2019. AISC, vol. 1026, pp. 176–181. Springer, Cham (2020). https://doi.org/10.1007/978-3-030-27928-8_27

14. Ackermann, C., Beggiato, M., Bluhm, L.-F., Löw, A., Krems, J.F.: Deceleration parameters and their applicability as informal communication signal between pedestrians and automated vehicles. Transport. Res. F: Traffic Psychol. Behav. **62**, 757–768 (2019). https://doi.org/10.1016/j.trf.2019.03.006

15. Scherer, S., Schubert, D., Dettmann, A., Hartwich, F., Bullinger, A.C.: Wie will der" Fahrer" automatisiert gefahren werden? Überprüfung verschiedener Fahrstile hinsichtlich des Komforterlebens [How Does the Driver Want to Be Driven? An Evaluation of Different Driving Styles Regarding the Experienced Driving Comfort]. Tagungsband 32. VDI/VW-Gemeinschaftstagung Fahrerassistenzsysteme und automatisiertes Fahren **8**, 2016 (2016)

16. Körber, M.: Theoretical considerations and development of a questionnaire to measure trust in automation. In: Bagnara, S., Tartaglia, R., Albolino, S., Alexander, T., Fujita, Y. (eds.) IEA 2018. AISC, vol. 823, pp. 13–30. Springer, Cham (2019). https://doi.org/10.1007/978-3-319-96074-6_2

17. Cohen, J.: Statistical Power Analysis for the Behavioral Sciences. Routledge (2013)

18. Pagano, R.R.: Understanding Statistics in the Behavioral Sciences, 10th edn. Wadsworth Cengage, Australia (2013)

The Sound of Travelers: Analysing Online Travel Podcasts Interest Communities

Leonor Lima(✉) ⓘ and Maria João Antunes ⓘ

Department of Communication and Art, University of Aveiro, Campus Universitário de, Santiago, 3810-193 Aveiro, Portugal
{leonorslima,mariajoao}@ua.pt

Abstract. Podcasts increased its popularity in recent years, and the niche of travel podcasts wasn't an exception. Travel podcasts present stories about trips, about people that travelers meet during their trips, and give helpful tips to help other people with the same travel interests. The purpose of this paper is to identify what features make travel podcasts attractive to listeners, and how podcasts listening influence travel decisions. In terms of methodology, quantitative data (surveys to 36 travel podcasts listeners) and qualitative data (analysis of 50 travel podcasts) were collected. Results show that the analysed podcasts have a very inconstant publication periodicity, do not have a specific page on social networks but are publicize on Instagram profile of the organization/person that promotes it. Most respondents prefer travel podcasts of short duration, interviews with guest(s) about a specific destination, and independently produced. Many respondents follow their favorite podcasters on social networks. Furthermore, all respondents say that travel podcasts influence their travel decisions.

Keywords: Online special interest communities · Travelers · Podcasts

1 Introduction

Tourism is addressed in different social networks. According to statistical data, 51,0% of respondents use the internet to get inspiration for future trips, and 16,0% rely on information shared by celebrities and/or digital influencers to choose the destination of their next trip [1]. Some authors [2] concluded that sharing experiences in the context of travel with friends and/or family, having fun, and social appreciation are relevant factors that condition adherence and permanence in social networks.

Regarding consumers' adherence to social networks in the context of tourism, it is important that user's individual gratifications are achieved, to guarantee the continuity of their online presence and consequent participation in the exchange of information about travel [2]. In addition, adherence to online travel communities derives from psychological factors, such as discovery/learning gratifications and the creation of social relationships based on motivations to travel [2]. The scope of these rewards conditions membership in these communities and influences the desire to share information, and to adopt electronic-Word-of-Mouth (eWOM) [2].

C. Stephanidis et al. (Eds.): HCII 2022, CCIS 1655, pp. 383–390, 2022.
https://doi.org/10.1007/978-3-031-19682-9_49

With the growing relevance of podcasts, an online podcaster community has emerged. In addition to great support among its members, content is also made available to encourage the creation of new podcasts, including travel podcasts. A search for the terms "how to create a travel podcast" brings up various contents such as guides, tips, or articles that highlight reasons to create a travel podcast, mostly focused on the accessible nature of this medium. These guides cover the different phases involved in a podcast creation: market and audience research; equipment and space to be used; recording techniques to adopt; definition of a format and schedule; podcast cover design; hosting; procedures that must be adopted to publicize the content; dissemination of the podcast on social networks; tips to keep the audience; or how to monetize the podcast.

Transition to digital and constant evolution of social networks culminated in their monetization, thus witnessing the emergence of new terms and roles in the area. The creation of the term "influencer marketing" is observed, whose professionals hold the title of "digital influencer". A digital influencer is characterized as a daily internet user, with a high number of followers, who shapes the attitudes of their audience through the content published on their social networks [3, 4]. Digital influencers are quite present in the context of tourism. The content they share positively affects the intention of their followers to visit a specific location [5]. Trust in digital influencers plays a key role in the main stages of the travel purchase process, and it is possible to highlight its influence on the pre-purchase state of a trip [6]. In addition, it is also possible to understand that users who trust digital influencers and feel the desire to visit a destination recommended by them, are more likely to seek information about the same destination [6]. For this reason, it is possible to say that digital influencers exert a positive influence on the desire to visit a certain destination [6].

In this paper the patterns of travel podcast production and influence were examined, and some interesting findings are presented. The next section describes the research methodology followed for data collection. Once the methodology is introduced, the paper presents its main results. The paper ends presenting the final remarks and the limitations of the study.

2   Methodology

This study aims to answer the following research questions: What characteristics make travel podcasts attractive to listeners? What is the influence of these podcasts on the interest in traveling? To find an answer to the research questions, two data collection strategies were used: i) a questionnaire survey carried out with listeners of travel podcasts; ii) observation of a set of travel podcasts. The analysis of the collected data was carried out separately and then combined, to provide an extensive view about the phenomenon. This methodology fits into the convergent design developed by [7]. This design is based on the synchronous collection of quantitative and qualitative data, carried out through separate data collection methods, a subsequent merging of the results, and a joint analysis of the collected information.

Data were collected in April and May 2022. Thirty-six (36) questionnaires to Portuguese listeners of travel podcasts were applied, and 50 international and national travel podcasts with a high number of reproductions were observed using an observation grid.

In the questionnaire survey, the following data were collected: Age group; Gender; Frequency of podcast consumption; Most used platform for podcast listening; Preferred episode format; Preferred episodes length, Preferred periodicity of publication, Production; Social media following habits; Relevance of video version of episode; Influence of travel components and travel podcast influence in travel decision. In the observation of travel podcasts, the following aspects were considered: Platforms on which it is available; Periodicity of publication; Number of hosts; Presence of guests; Social media presence and website existence.

3 Findings

Results presentation is organized according to the topics introduced in the previous section.

3.1 Quantitative Data: Questionnaire

Concerning quantitative data, questionnaires respondents are mainly women (75,0%). 47,0% of the sample have between 17 and 24 years old, 33,3% between 25 and 34 years, 8,3% between 46 and 54 years, 5,6% 55 or more years, and 2,8% have between 35 and 45 years old. The same percentage (2,8%) have 16 years old or a younger age. Respondents podcast consumption habits are presented in Table 1, and listeners preferred characteristics in terms of travel podcasts are presented in Table 2.

Table 1. Consumption habits of podcasts.

Topics analysed	%
Frequency of podcast consumption	
Sporadically	16,7
Less than 1 time per week	16,7
Between 1 and 4 times per week	58,3
More than 5 times per week	8,3
Most used platform for podcast listening	
Spotify	72,2
Youtube	19,4
Others	8,4

Regarding the podcast consumption habits, this study shows that the majority of the respondents (66,6%) are frequent podcast users: 58,3% listen to podcasts between 1 and 4 times a week, while 8,3% listen more than 5 times a week. On the other hand, 16,7% listen less than a time a week and 16,7% only listen to podcasts sporadically. According to the findings, the most used platform for podcast listening is Spotify, followed by Youtube.

Table 2. Travel podcast listeners' preferred features.

Topics analysed	%
Preferred episode format	
Host's monologue	11,1
Interview with a guest about a specific destination	50,0
Interview with a guest about travel habits	33,3
Listeners questions and hosts' answers	5,6
Preferred episodes length	
Up to 15 min	8,3
Between 15 and 30 min	36,1
Between 30 and 45 min	30,6
Between 45 min and 1 h	19,4
No preference	5,6
Preferred periodicity of publication	
Weekly	63,9
Fortnightly	30,6
Monthly	2,8
No preference	2,8
Production	
Independent	80,6
Dependent	19,4
Social media following habits	
Follow most podcast hosts on social media	44,5
Follow some podcast hosts on social media	30,5
Does not follow podcast hosts on social media	25,0
Importance of a video version of the episode	
Preference for video episodes	50,0
Preference for audio-only episodes	25,0
No preference	25,0
Influence of travel components	
Destination image	91,6

(continued)

Table 2. (*continued*)

Topics analysed	%
Intention to visit	80,5
Attractions to visit	83,3
Type of travel	66,6
Accommodation	55,5
Trip's duration	55,5
Travel Logistics	50,0

Concerning the listener's preferred features of travel podcasts, the findings of this study show that interview format is the favorite amongst its users. Regarding its length, smaller episodes - between 15 and 45 min - are preferred. According to the results, it is also possible to identify that the preferred periodicity of episodes' publication for travel podcasts is one episode per week. In regards to the production of travel podcasts, independent podcasts, without sponsorship or connection to brands, are considered to be more pleasant for the users. Regarding social media following habits, respondents tend to follow their favorite hosts on social media. When questioned about the importance of travel podcasts having a video version available, half of the respondents claim to prefer those who do.

The findings of this study point out that four main travel components are influenced by travel podcasts: destination image, intention to visit, attractions to visit and type of travel. The first one, "destination image", defined by the author [8] as the sum of impressions, ideas, and beliefs that persons create about a destination, is considered to be the one in which travel podcasts have the most significant influence. Secondly, "intention to visit", is related to the listener's desire to visit, or not, a certain destination. Afterwards, "attractions to visit", concerning the influence of travel podcasts when deciding which points of interest are worth visiting or which activities to perform while travelling. Lastly, "type of travel", is related to the traveler's taste, budget or even mindset. Can be considered types of travel, for example, backpacking, solo travel, luxury travel, and adventure travel.

On the other hand, the travel components that are less influenced by travel podcasts were also identified: accommodation, trip duration and travel logistics. These are the most related to the listener's personal preference components and can be considered very specific.

It was also discovered that the pre-purchase/research phase is the stage of the booking process in which travel podcasts have the most notable influence. According to the respondents, travel podcasts influence their listeners by making them search online for the destinations mentioned on podcasts. Contrarily, it was also understood that travel podcasts do not influence the listeners to book or cancel an already booked trip. When asked, 100% of respondents considerer that travel podcasts influence their travel decisions.

3.2 Qualitative Data: Observation Grid

An observation grid was designed to collect the qualitative data for this study. This grid consisted of an in-depth analysis of 50 national and international travel podcasts, which allowed patterns to be identified and, therefore, conclusions to be reached. The results show that the most significant patterns concern the following indicators: platforms in which the podcast is available, periodicity of publication, number of hosts and presence of guests (Table 3).

Table 3. Collected data from the observation grid.

Topics analysed	%
Platforms in which the podcast is available	
Soundcloud	4,0
Spotify	100,0
Apple Podcasts	100,0
Google Podcasts	96,0
Podbean	96,0
Youtube	20,0
Castbox	100,0
TuneIn	52,0
Periodicity of publication	
Twice a week	10,0
Weekly	38,0
Fortnightly	10,0
Monthly	8,0
Variable	34,0
Number of hosts	
1	58,0
2	34,0
3 or more	6,0
NA	2,0
Presence of guests	
With guests	82,0
Without guests	18,0
Social media presence	
Dedicated Instagram account	28,0

(*continued*)

Table 3. (*continued*)

Topics analysed	%
Publicized on the profile of the organization/host	42,0
Twitter account	22,0
Facebook account	36,0
Website existence	
Dedicated website	26,0
Page/section inside a main website	46,0

Regarding the first, every podcast is available on 3 platforms: Spotify, Apple Podcasts and Castbox. Furthermore, almost every podcast (96,0%) is available on Google Podcasts and Podbean. In contrast, very few podcasts are available on Soundcloud (4,0%) and Youtube (20,0%).

From the perspective of periodicity of publication, it was detected that the most common is for episodes to be published weekly. Interestingly, almost the same percentage of travel podcasts do not have a fixed periodicity of publication, which is coherent with the sense of freedom commonly associated with the traveler's lifestyle.

Regarding the number of fixed hosts in travel podcasts, the findings of this study manifest that the majority (58,0%) are led by only one host. Additionally, almost every podcast (82,0%) has the presence of guests. From these results, it has been understood that even though there is only one fixed host in most podcasts, he/she is rarely presenting the episode alone.

Concerning the online presence of travel podcasts, two main indicators were analysed: social media presence and website existence. Firstly, results indicate that travel podcasts do not tend to have a substantial presence on social media. Only 28,0% of travel podcasts have a dedicated Instagram account, while 42,0% are publicized on the profile of the organization/person that promotes and/or produces it. Therefore, 30,0% of travel podcasts are not present on Instagram. Regarding Twitter and Facebook, the same scenario is noticed. Only 22,0% of the analysed podcasts have a Twitter account and 36,0% have a Facebook account.

Regarding website existence, the results show that only 26,0% of travel podcasts have a dedicated website. On the other hand, 46,0% have a dedicated page or section inside a main website. Thus, only 28,0% of travel podcasts have no website or dedicated page on another website.

4   Final Remarks

This study aimed to identify the characteristics that make travel podcasts attractive to their listeners and comprehend what influence they have when making travel decisions. Quantitative and qualitative data were collected. Thirty-six travel podcast listeners partook in a questionnaire and, through an in-depth observation grid, 50 travel podcasts were analysed. The results indicate that travel podcast listeners prefer episodes between 15 and 45 min in length, published weekly, independently produced, and non-branded. Regarding the impact of travel podcasts, it was identified that the most influenced travel components when booking a trip are "destination image", "intention to visit", "attractions to visit" and "type of travel". Contrarily, the least influenced travel components are "accommodation", "trip's duration" and "travel logistics", which can be considered the ones that are most related to the listener's personal preferences.

The study has limitations inherent to the chosen methodology and the analysis performed: the sample of travel podcast listeners', consisting in 36 Portuguese individuals, are small, and only 25% of respondents are male. Nevertheless, this is an exploratory study, so the results are now indicative and not conclusive.

References

1. Statista - Sources of vacation inspiration preferred by travelers worldwide as of July 2020. https://www.statista.com/statistics/1239121/main-sources-of-vacation-inspiration-worldwide/. Accessed 10 Feb 2022
2. Chavez, L., Ruiz, C., Curras, R., Hernandez, B.: The role of travel motivations and social media use in consumer interactive. Behaviour: a uses and gratifications perspective. Sustainability **12**(21), 8789 (2020)
3. Abidin, C.: Communicative intimacies: influencers and perceived interconnectedness. Ada: J. Gender, New Media Technol. **8** (2015)
4. Freberg, K., Graham, K., McGaughey, K., Freberg, L.A.: Who are the social media influencers? A study of public perceptions of personality. Publ. Relat. Rev. **37**(1), 90–92 (2011)
5. Xu (Rinka), X., Pratt, S.: Social media influencers as endorsers to promote travel destinations: an application of self-congruence theory to the Chinese Generation Y. J. Travel Tourism Mark. **35**(7), 958–972 (2018)
6. Pop, R.A., Săplăcan, Z., Dabija, D.C., Alt, M.A.: The impact of social media influencers on travel decisions: the role of trust in consumer decision journey (2021). https://doi.org/10.1080/13683500.2021.1895729
7. Creswell, J.W., David Creswell, J.: Research Design: Qualitative, Quantitative, and Mixed Methods Approaches. SAGE, Los Angeles (2018)
8. Crompton, J.L.: An assessment of the image of Mexico as a vacation destination and the influence of geographical location upon that image. J. Travel Res. **17**(4), 18–23 (1979)

Towards a Universal Explicit Communication Design of External Human-Machine Interfaces (eHMI) for Differently Sized Highly Automated Vehicles Evaluated by Different Pedestrian Age Groups

Michael Oehl[1]([✉]), Merle Lau[1], Laura Gehreke[2], and Marc Wilbrink[1]

[1] German Aerospace Center (DLR), Lilienthalplatz 7, 38108 Braunschweig, Germany
{michael.oehl,merle.lau,marc.wilbrink}@dlr.de
[2] Institute of Psychology, Technical University of Braunschweig, Spielmannstraße 19, 38106 Braunschweig, Germany
laura.gehreke@web.de

Abstract. This research deals with the design of external human-machine interfaces (eHMI) for two differently sized highly automated vehicle types (passenger car vs. bus) focusing on the interaction between highly automated vehicles (HAVs) and pedestrians of different age groups. Research has shown that at least in some situations HAVs need to be able to communicate explicitly via an eHMI with their surrounding traffic environment ensuring a safe and accepted interaction among all traffic participants (TPs), e.g., pedestrians. Therefore, their messages should be universally understood. The question that arises is how TPs' information needs may differ for different vehicle types, how this needs to be considered in the eHMI design and if different TP age groups, especially elderly, need other information for a safe and accepted interaction. However, little research addressing this question was done so far. Results of our current experimental online study (N = 321) in a shared space setting revealed that especially explicit communication via an eHMI is beneficial for interaction. Furthermore, results indicated an overall good implementation of the explicit eHMI communication strategies. Pedestrians felt safer, better informed, and indicated a more positive affective valence in interaction with HAVs with dynamic eHMI vs. static eHMI vs. no eHMI. In terms of a universal design, this was true for all age groups. As vehicle type had a significant effect on the pedestrians' feelings of safety and their perceived affective valence in interaction, eHMI might have an especially beneficial effect when interacting as a pedestrian with a large vehicle.

Keywords: Highly automated driving · External human-machine interface · Universal design · User study

C. Stephanidis et al. (Eds.): HCII 2022, CCIS 1655, pp. 391–398, 2022.
https://doi.org/10.1007/978-3-031-19682-9_50

1 Introduction

This research paper deals with the design of external human-machine interfaces (eHMI) for two differently sized highly automated vehicles (car vs. bus) focusing on the inter-action between highly automated vehicles (HAVs) and pedestrians as vulnerable road users in a shared space traffic setting and is evaluated by different age groups from the pedestrian's perspective. HAV will be introduced into future mixed traffic environments and therefore they will interact with different traffic participants (TP), e.g., pedestrians. With higher automation levels, the driver's role will change from an active driver to a more passive on-board user. Regardless of the availability of a human driver, HAVs need to be able to communicate with their surrounding traffic environment. An eHMI seems to be a promising solution to transmit explicit information to other TP and to enable an adequate communication with the traffic environment [1]. Furthermore, the use of an eHMI could improve safety, acceptance, and traffic flow even before it is actually necessary [1]. In general, the overall aim is to design eHMIs that communicate clearly with other TPs in mixed traffic environments [1]. Several eHMI design approaches have been developed [1]. As the most promising one, light-based eHMI designs have been shown to transmit explicit communication signals to other TPs based on different light patterns in a safe and efficient way.

The question that arises is how TPs' information needs may differ for different vehicle types and how this needs to be considered in the eHMI design and if different TP age groups, especially elderly, need more information for a safe and accepted interaction compared to younger TPs. So far, most studies have been including only rather younger participants. With regard to the effect of vehicle size, results by Rasouli and Tsotsos [2] indicated that pedestrians tend to be more careful when interacting with a larger vehicle. However, little research focusing on the design of eHMI for different vehicle types is existing so far [3]. Therefore, the presented study deals with the question of how eHMI communication with means of a 360° LED light-band [3, 4] should be designed for differently sized vehicles, i.e., a highly automated car and a highly automated bus, and with a special focus on the question if these eHMI communication designs are suitable for different age groups in terms of an attempt towards a universal eHMI design. Thus, this study examines pedestrians' information needs by taking subjective measurements into account.

2 Method

2.1 Participants

A total of $N = 321$ participants (154 women) aged 16–74 years ($M = 45.31$, $SD = 18.13$) responded to the survey. Participants were split into four age groups: (1) 16–24 years (n $= 49$, $M = 18.96$, $SD = 3.26$), (2) 25–49 years (n $= 124$, $M = 35.13$, $SD = 8.26$), (3) 50–64 years (n $= 82$, $M = 56.77$, $SD = 4.15$), and (4) 65–74 years (n $= 66$, $M = 66.88$, $SD = 2.87$). Participants' interests in HAVs were measured using a 5-point Likert scale ($1 =$ "not at all" to $5 =$ "strong interest"). This showed the participants' overall mean interest $M = 3.43$, $SD = 1.27$ (age group 1 $M = 3.73$, $SD = 1.00$, age group 2 $M = 3.94$, $SD = 1.10$, age group 3 $M = 2.91$, $SD = 1.33$, age group 4 $M = 2.89$, $SD = 1.23$) in HAVs and for all age groups at least average or above mean ratings. In addition, technology affinity was assessed using the standardized Affinity for Technology Interaction Questionnaire (ATI) [5]. The ATI consist of nine items measuring the user's personality when using technologies on a 6-point Likert scale (1 = "completely disagree" to 6 = "completely agree"). The ATI revealed the participants' overall mean technology affinity of M = 3.98, SD = 1.05. With respect to the different age groups, nonsystematic significant differences (p < .05) were found with regard to the overall ATI score between age group 1 (M = 4.11, SD = 0.80) vs. age group 3 (M = 3.55, SD = 1.28), age group 2 (M = 4.31, SD = 0.88) vs. age group 3, and age group 2 vs. age group 4 (M = 3.77, SD = 0.99) showing mean ratings for all age groups at least on average or above and highest ratings for age group 2 and lowest for age group 3. Participants were acquired via the DLR's test driver database and social networks. Participation in the study was in line with the Declaration of Helsinki, voluntary, and subject to prior consent by the participants. Participants could end the survey at any time without negative consequences. At the end of the study, participants had the opportunity to take part in a raffle for vouchers each 25 Euros worth. For this purpose, the participants provided their e-mail address, which was stored independently of the trial data.

2.2 Study Design and Independent Variables

This experimental video online study followed a $4 \times 3 \times 3 \times 2$ mixed design. The variable age group (V1) consisted of four different age groups: age group 1 (16–24 years), age group 2 (25–49 years), age group 3 (50–64 years), and age group 4 (65–74 years). The richness of information of the eHMI communication as second factor (V2) included three levels: "No eHMI" means that the HAV does not communicate any explicit information to the pedestrian. "Static eHMI" implies that the vehicle is equipped with a 360° LED light-band as eHMI in the color cyan, which lights up continuously to signal the vehicle automation status (VAS), and the "dynamic eHMI" presented explicit information to the pedestrian in three different ways as third factor (V3). For V3 the "VAS + intention" variant, the LED light-band pulses at a slow frequency (0.5 Hz), which shows the brake intention. The light-band pulses until the vehicle comes to a stop. The "VAS + perception" variant presents a light segment on the LED light-band, which follows the pedestrian when crossing the street. The "VAS + Intention + Perception" variant combines the two previously described variants of dynamic eHMI. Also, two differently sized vehicles were presented in the videos as fourth factor (V4). The car presented was a BMW model i3 and the bus was a Mercedes-Benz future bus. The different vehicle and eHMI types are presented in Fig. 1.

Fig. 1. Intention-based (left) and perception-based (right) 360° LED light-band eHMI communication strategies for the car and bus

2.3 Dependent Variables

Perceived information quality ("How well did you feel informed?") was measured using a 7-Likert scale (1 = "very poor" to 7 = "very good"). Perceived safety ("For my personal safety, I perceived the vehicle's behavior to be conducive to safety") was also measured with a 7-Likert scale (1 = "strongly disagree" to 7 = "strongly agree"). In addition, the Self-Assessment Manikin (SAM) questionnaire [6] was used to measure affective valence felt in the interaction with the HAVs. It measures participants' subjective assessments of affective valence on a 9-point Likert scale ranging from 1 = "unpleasant" to 9 = "pleasant".

2.4 Video Stimuli

Videos with a length of 50 s in which pedestrians interacted with a HAV (car vs. bus), were used as stimulus material. The videos were made from an ego centered perspective. The HAVs approached the pedestrian from the left-hand side. Traffic environment was a shared space, i.e., only a few traffic regulations exist and all TPs have the same rights without being segregated by specific lanes etc. Videos were produced with means of virtual reality using the software "Unreal Engine" (version 4.24.2). In total, the participants watched six videos (car without eHMI, bus without eHMI, car with static eHMI, bus with static eHMI, car with dynamic eHMI, bus with dynamic eHMI) in which the deceleration process and the speed of the vehicle were presented in a standardized manner. In all experimental conditions, the vehicle slowed from 20 km/h (12.43 mph) to 5 km/h (3.12 mph) in 12.08 m distance, from 5 km/h (3.12 mph) to 0 km/h in 9.29 m distance and stopped in 7.38 m distance. When an eHMI was presented, it started at a distance of 15.99 m from the pedestrian.

2.5 Procedure

Participants began the study by clicking on the link provided. At the beginning of the study, participants received information on the background of the study, the further processing of the data, and the privacy policy. In addition, instructions were given on how to conduct the study, e.g., that the study should not be conducted on a cell phone.

Subsequently, participants were randomly assigned to one of the three dynamic eHMI variants (V3). The demographic data were requested and the participants were informed about the different eHMI variants. Then, the participants were asked to darken their test environment and a test video followed. The smooth presentation of the video must be confirmed by the participants. Then the actual experiment starts, in which the six videos are presented to the participants. The "no eHMI variant" was always presented as the baseline. It was followed by a randomized presentation of the static and dynamic eHMI variants. In all videos, the pedestrian stood on the same position. The HAV approached the pedestrian from the left. After the vehicle had stopped, the pedestrian crossed the road and turned to face again the passing vehicle. At the end of each video, the dependent variables had to be rated. At the end of the study, participants were asked to provide an assessment of the diligence of their study processing and were given the opportunity to participate in the raffle of the vouchers. The total duration of the study was approximately 20 min.

3   Results

Mixed analyses of variance (ANOVAs) were calculated with the variables age group, information richness, dynamic eHMI, and vehicle size as independent variables. The assumption of a normal distribution can be assumed due to the sample sizes of the experimental groups [7]. If sphericity was not given, Greenhouse-Geisser corrections were applied [7]. Moreover, pairwise comparisons were conducted with Bonferroni correction. The effect sizes were reported with eta quadrat (η_p^2) and interpreted as followed: up to .01 (small effect), between .06 to .13 (medium effect), and .14 and above (large effect).

For perceived information quality, significant main effects for age group [$F(3, 309) = 4.75, p < .01, \eta_p^2 = .044$], information richness [$F(1.91, 590.91) = 184.28, p < .001, \eta_p^2 = .374$] and vehicle size [$F(1, 309) = 22.12, p < .001, \eta_p^2 = .067$] were found. Post-hoc comparisons revealed significant differences between the age groups 16–24 years vs. 25–49 years and the age groups 25–49 years vs. 65–74 years (both p's < .01; see Fig.). Furthermore, participants perceived a higher information quality for the dynamic eHMI compared to static eHMI and no eHMI (p < .001) and, additionally, perceived a higher information quality when there was no eHMI vs. static eHMI (p < .001; see Fig.). Regarding the vehicle size, participants felt better informed with automated car (M = 4.66, SD = 1.28) vs. automated bus (M = 4.49, SD = 1.28; p < .001). Additionally, there were significant interactions between vehicle size and information richness [$F(1.87, 577.53) = 14.03, p < .001, \eta_p^2 = .043$], vehicle size and age group [$F(3, 309) = 2.76, p < .05, \eta_p^2 = .026$], and information richness and the age group [$F(5.74, 590.91) = 4.05, p < .01, \eta_p^2 = .038$], and information richness and dynamic eHMI [$F(3.83, 590.91) = 11.75, p < .01, \eta_p^2 = .024$]. Overall, the found interactions underlined the interpretability of the main effects of age group, information richness and vehicle size (Fig. 2).

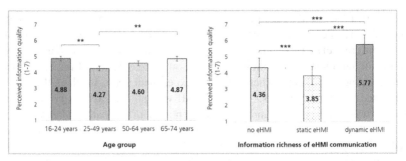

Fig. 2. Pairwise comparisons with Bonferroni-correction for age group (left) and information richness of eHMI communication (right) for perceived information quality. Error bars: ±1 SE. *** p < .001 ** p < .01 * p < .05

For the perceived safety, a significant main effect for age group [F(3, 309) = 3.53, p = .02, η_p^2 = .033] was found indicating that the 16–24 years old participants felt safer compared to all other age groups, i.e., vs. 25–49 years old (p < .05) vs. 50–64 years old (p < .01) vs. the 65–74 years (p < .05; see Fig. 3). Moreover, a significant main effect for information richness showed that the perceived safety differed for the dynamic eHMI vs. static eHMI vs. no eHMI [F(1.94, 598.09) = 166.82, p < .001, η_p^2 = .351]. Post-hoc comparisons showed that participants felt safer with the dynamic eHMI compared to static eHMI and no eHMI (p < .001). A significant main effect for vehicle size was found [F(1, 309) = 48.64, p < .001, η_p^2 = .135] indicating that participants felt safer with the automated car (M = 4.83, SD = 1.28) vs. the automated bus (M = 4.58, SD = 1.37; p < .001). Furthermore, the interactions between vehicle size and information richness [F(1.87, 577.53) = 14.03, p < .001, η_p^2 = .043], vehicle size and age group [F(3, 309) = 3.14, p = .03, η_p^2 = .030], and information richness and age group [F(5.81, 598.09) = 4.28, p < .001, η_p^2 = .040] emphasized the interpretability of the main effects.

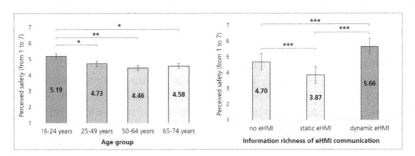

Fig. 3. Pairwise comparisons with Bonferroni-correction for age group (left) and information richness of eHMI communication (right) for perceived safety. Error bars: ±1 SE. *** p < .001 ** p < .01 * p < .05

Regarding participants' ratings of affective valence, significant main effects for information richness [F(1.93, 596.62) = 90.05, p < .001, η_p^2 = .226] and vehicle size [F(1,

309) $= 71.94$, $p < .001$, $\eta_p^2 = .189$] were found. Post-hoc comparisons revealed that participants indicated a more positive affective valence with the dynamic eHMI vs. static eHMI vs. no eHMI ($p < .001$; see Fig. 4). Additionally, participants perceived a more positive affective valence with the automated car ($M = 5.93$, $SD = 1.83$) compared to the automated bus ($M = 5.43$, $SD = 1.86$; $p < .001$). Furthermore, there were significant interactions between vehicle size and information richness [$F(1.84, 569.94) = 12.37$, $p < .001$, $\eta_p^2 = .038$], vehicle size and age group [$F(3, 309) = 4.23$, $p < .01$, $\eta_p^2 = .039$], age group and information richness [$F(5.79, 596.62) = 4.59$, $p < .001$, $\eta_p^2 = .043$], and information richness and dynamic eHMI [$F(3.86, 596.62) = 3.61$, $p < .01$, $\eta_p^2 = .023$]. All other comparisons were not significant ($p > .05$).

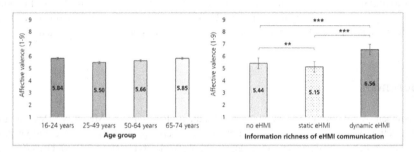

Fig. 4. Pairwise comparisons with Bonferroni-correction for age group and information richness of eHMI communication for affective valence. Error bars: ± 1 SE. *** $p < .001$ ** $p < .01$ * $p < .05$

4 Conclusion

By comparing different eHMI communication strategies for differently sized highly automated vehicles, explicit eHMI communication designs with a higher information richness were preferred over no eHMI or a mere mode awareness conveyed by the 360° LED light-band for both vehicle sizes (car and bus). This was true for all age groups. Pedestrians were found to feel better informed, safer, and showed more positive affective valence with a dynamic eHMI with high information richness vs. static eHMI vs. no eHMI. For perceived information quality and safety, especially younger participants (aged 16–24) were found to feel safer and rated the information quality higher, but the elderly participants aged 65–74 showed high and positive ratings, too. The results indicate an overall good implementation of the eHMI communication strategies that have been previously developed and evaluated for a car [4] for a highly automated bus as well and confirm the findings by Lau et al. [3], here in this study with a larger sample size and an additional focus on different age groups. In terms of an attempt towards a universal eHMI design this was true for all age groups. As vehicle size had a significant effect on the feeling of safety and the affective valence in interaction, eHMI might have an especially beneficial effect when interacting as a pedestrian with a large vehicle, i.e., here with a bus. Following studies will definitely have to examine even older TPs

(75 + years) and take objective measurements (e.g., timing of the crossing decision) and behavioral measures (e.g., crossing initiation, to investigate not only pedestrians' crossing intentions but also the execution of the crossing) into account to go beyond these current findings in an online study in order to ensure a universal eHMI design. As this study was conducted as an online study, technical understanding was necessary for all participants, including the older participants. Interaction with the HAVs is also limited to prerecorded video sequences. Subsequent studies should be given more immersive and offline experimental conditions (e.g., VR environment or field studies) to support these results. Furthermore, future studies should consider cultural differences and individuals with special needs to pursue a universal eHMI communication design.

Acknowledgements. This research was funded by the German Federal Ministry for Economic Affairs and Climate Action within the project @CITY: Automated Cars and Intelligent Traffic in the City, grant number 19A17015B. The authors are solely responsible for the content.

References

1. Schieben, A., Wilbrink, M., Kettwich, C., Madigan, R., Louw, T., Merat, N.: Designing the interaction of automated vehicles with other traffic participants: design considerations based on human needs and expectations. Cogn. Technol. Work 21(1), 69–85 (2018). https://doi.org/10.1007/s10111-018-0521-z
2. Dey, D., et al.: Taming the eHMI jungle: a classification taxonomy to guide, compare, and assess the design principles of automated vehicles' external human-machine interfaces. Transp. Res. Interdiscip. Perspect. 7, 100174 (2020). https://doi.org/10.1016/j.trip.2020.100174
3. Rasouli, A., Tsotsos, J.K.: Autonomous vehicles that interact with pedestrians: a survey of theory and practice. IEEE Trans. Intell. Transp. Syst. 21(3), 900–918 (2020). https://doi.org/10.1109/TITS.2019.2901817
4. Lau, M., Jipp, M., Oehl, M.: One solution fits all? Evaluating different communication strategies of a light-based external human-machine interface for differently sized automated vehicles from a pedestrian's perspective. Accid. Anal. Prev. 171, 106641 (2022). https://doi.org/10.1016/j.aap.2022.106641
5. Wilbrink, M., Lau, M., Illgner, J., Schieben, A., Oehl, M.: Impact of external human-machine interface communication strategies of automated vehicles on pedestrians' crossing decisions and behaviors in an urban environment. Sustainability 13(15), 8396 (2021). https://doi.org/10.3390/su13158396
6. Franke, T., Attig, C., Wessel, D.: A personal resource for technology interaction: development and validation of the affinity for technology interaction (ATI) scale. Int. J. Hum.-Comput. Interact. 35(6), 456–467 (2019). https://doi.org/10.1080/10447318.2018.1456150
7. Bradley, M.M., Lang, P.J.: Measuring emotion: the self-assessment manikin and the semantic differential. J. Behav. Ther. Exp. Psychiatry 25(1), 49–59 (1994). https://doi.org/10.1016/0005-7916(94)90063-9
8. Field, A.: Discovering Statistics Using SPSS, 3rd edn. Sage Publications, London (2009)

ICT as a Resource for the Professional Training of Drivers. Education and Training School for Professional Drivers, Pelileo-Ecuador

Jose A. Oleas-Orozco(✉), Franklin Castillo, Fernando Saá-Tapia,
and Pablo Barrera-Urbina

Universidad Tecnológica Indoamérica, Ambato, Ecuador
joleas@indoamerica.edu.ec

Abstract. This project is framed educational analysis in the education and training resources by professional drivers in Ecuador and use of ICT (Information and Communication Technologies). The study was developed in *Escuela de Formación y Capacitación de Choferes Profesionales de Pelileo-Tungurahua.*

The study starts with a knowledge of reasons that cause traffic accidents on Ecuadorian roads, among which the conditions of the vehicles at the time of driving and foreseeable mechanical damage can be mentioned. The research consists of two moments, the first stage consists of an analysis of the learning resources that are used by the training centers in driving vehicles at a professional level, through a mixed methodology, with a quantitative section through surveys carried out on students. of the vehicle training center, to find out the level of interaction with ICTs, use of educational APPs and activity time on mobile devices. In the qualitative part, interviews were carried out with the instructors, from which it was possible to obtain information regarding teaching-learning techniques and resources, recurrent and necessary topics in the training of professional drivers. The second stage, based on the results of the first, determined the need to use technological tools for learning content for the training of drivers.

Through the design of multimedia applications, content related to basic vehicle maintenance was configured, with multimedia elements (images, videos, animations, audio, etc.) contained in an APP for mobile devices. Subsequently, the application was tested on the students of the training center, to evaluate the effectiveness and capacity as a teaching-learning tool. The test obtained a positive perception of 99%, relevant content of 80%, usability of 90%.

Keywords: ICT · Basic vehicle maintenance · Web applications · Educational APP

1 Introduction

In Ecuadorian territory, traffic accidents are a phenomenon of extensive analysis. The media reports daily accidents on highways and cities [1]. Among traffic accidents causes, can be mentioned: lane losses, speeding, mechanical failures and others.

C. Stephanidis et al. (Eds.): HCII 2022, CCIS 1655, pp. 399–412, 2022.
https://doi.org/10.1007/978-3-031-19682-9_51

According to WHO, traffic accidents are one of ten main causes of declines worldwide among people aged 15 to 29 years. For this reason, countries are invited to apply measures to improve safety on streets and highways. However, in developing countries, mortality rates double, which is a disproportionate relationship to their motorization level [2]. In Ecuador, according to ANT (National Transit Agency, by its acronym in Spanish) statistics at 2018, 85% of accidents are due to mechanical failures, with a five-year mortality rate of 1,058 deaths in 12,460 accidents [3].

At this scenario, studies have been documented on the social and legal need to regulate the traffic law, in relation to driving schools and the capacity of their drivers as professional and non-professional driver trainers [4]. Likewise, in academic studies, traffic accidents caused by human factors have been documented in specific places in the Ecuadorian capital [5]. At the regional level, external factors by causality of accidents can be mentioned, mainly due to use of mobile phones [6]. Based on the analysis and possible solutions to described problem [7], the AGV proposal, automatically guided vehicle, is presented, a simulation of traffic routes through an algorithm to avoid collisions. Regarding studies and analyzes of driving and transit factors, at regional level, Sagbini, Ramírez-Guerrero, Castañeda y Toro [8] and Ydrogo Ramírez [9], on control of public transport routes through use of technological tools, mobile applications for this purpose. Likewise, Cadena and Martínez [10], propose a mobile application to reinforce road culture. Also, there is Guzmán and Chaparro [11], with urban mobility digital applications.

ICT and Education. In relation to technological multimedia or ICT resources and their usefulness for education, can be mentioned the studies by Oleas, Padilla and Cayambe [12] on language learning, English, with multimedia resources, also Navas, Oleas and Zambrano [13] on the relevance of textbooks with augmented reality AR or Oleas, Mena and Ripalda [14] and Jadán-Guerrero, Arias-Flores and Altamirano [15], who analyze the ICT applicability in teaching resources and their usefulness in educational scenarios, training for special abilities people. Equally, the entry of digital technologies into teaching processes in educational contexts has been analyzed by Castro, Guzmán and Casado [16], by virtue of the concept use in teaching-learning processes. Likewise, the perspectives of these resources' usage, have been studied by Hernández [17]. In addition, there is documentation on use of ICT in university education scenario, such as those of Gargallo Castel [18]. Also, the use of ICT and mobile applications by Zambrano, Rey, Zambrano and Rodríguez [19] and Mangisch and Mangisch [20]. Likewise, is necessary to cite Cruz-Barragán and Barragán-López [21] and Garay [22] investigation work, who have documented research in university careers in health areas about to learning, its resources and tools of drivers, Antoñanzas, Salavera, Sisamon and Bericat [23], analyze the human factor in driving and licenses cancellation.

Regarding the driver training processes in Ecuador, there are 142 non-professional training schools for obtaining driver's licenses at the national level and 177 for the delivery of professional accreditations [24]. In relation to this volume of study and accreditation centers, academic studies that refer to training methods are still under development.

Research and Experimentation. The research is based on the mixed, qualitative and quantitative modality [25], within the study scenario of drivers training schools in Pelileo city. Also, the research consists of two stages: an exploratory phase and an experimental phase.

In the first phase, exploratory phase, through qualitative interviews with driver training school teachers, it was possible to obtain training content given to students and which of these are suitable for ICT adaptation. The information obtained determined the need for a mobile application or APP. For the second stage, experimentation stage, usefulness of APP in students, the contents relevance, the perception and its potential as an educational tool were tested.

Exploratory Qualitative Stage. The exploratory stage of qualitative research, semi-structured interviews were carried out with directors and teachers of Training School for Professional Drivers of the Pelileo Canton, as detailed in following Table 1:

Table 1. Professional driver trainers

Interviewees	Positions	Subject
Carlos Rolando Vargas	Automotive Engineer	Basic Mechanics
Patricio Ortega	Industrial Engineer	Basic Mechanics
Diego Mazón Cueva	Lawyer	Vial education
Carlos Hernández	Driving instructor	Driving

The semi-structured interviews were focused on themes of teaching processes, resources and teaching materials that are used in institution. This from teacher's perspective is presented in (Table 2):

Table 2. Teaching methods

Main query topic	Answer
Pedagogical methods	Classes and sessions (theoretical and practical) are based on printed material (brochures) provided by the institution
Resources for teaching classes	The resources used are brochures and practical classes in the cars, which are the essential resource for training
Teaching tools	About theoretical subjects, the resources are traditional ones such as posters, blackboards and markers. Technological resources such as projectors and computers
ICT usage in driving training	ICT use to teach classes at the institution has been sporadic. However, the occasions in which they have been used have been of great help, because the results in evaluations are of top rated
Predisposition to digital technological tools	The general consensus, teachers expresses their approval and predisposition to use digital technologies. Digital technologies use is common in both, teachers and students. This would serve as a face-to-face learning tool, such as autonomous reinforcement
Subjects prone to ICT use	The subjects taught in training school, such as driver education, traffic signs, car operation, among others, have their own teaching material. However, the practice topics, such as vehicle maintenance, do not have their own material, since they only depend on the face-to-face practices

Thus, it was possible to obtain the subject is difficult to teach, is vehicle mechanical maintenance, because the knowledge is not preserved after the practices.

Diagnostic Quantitative Stage. The Training School for Professional Drivers of Pelileo receives an average of 150 students in each training period. Also, work was carried out in its last face-to-face 2019 period, prior to global isolation, with the 150 students enrolled, a survey was applied, which is summarized in the following Table 3.

Table 3. Quantitative Results

Query topic	Results
Mobile, technological or digital devices use	80% of those surveyed said they have a smartphone, personal computer or Tablet/iPad
Technological devices time of use	95% of students responded, they use smartphone, personal computer or Tablet/iPad between 1 to 4 h a day
APP type on mobile devices	Only 2% indicated having an application to learn a specific topic. The remaining 98%, referred to entertainment, news and social networks
Learning predisposition through APP	91% of students agree with having an APP with learning resources
Preferred technological device	68% of response indicates their preference use of smartphones, another 11% prefer tablets or computers
Tendency to use vehicle maintenance APP	91% of students responded, they agree with use of this APP type

In diagnostic stage, it was possible to determine the need to use digital technological resources framed in ICT, because the teaching class methods and driving issues training continue to be traditional. Likewise, the necessary reinforcement content for learning in relation to vehicle maintenance. Likewise, it was possible to obtain data about mobile devices use, time of use and APP type for training school students.

With the information obtained, proceeded an App to design and production with vehicle maintenance content. Maintenance is: "A set of operations and necessary care so that facilities, buildings, industries, etc., can continue to function properly" [26]. In the automotive area, it refers to lubricating, adjusting and replacing elements or parts to keep a car running efficiently and thus prevent premature wear. In the automotive area, it refers to lubricating, adjusting and replacing elements or parts to keep a car running efficiently and thus prevent premature wear. This is divided into three types: preventive, to prevent any type of damage, predictive, to detect the origin or fault, and corrective, to help repair any fault in the automotive [27].

APP Design. For the APP design, the process proposed by Cuello and Vittone [28], is followed, which ranges from the conception of the idea to the analysis of utility and its publication, through simultaneous and coordinated work.

2 Conceptualization

The basic vehicle maintenance APP proposal, is conceived to contribute to learning of basic vehicle maintenance for professional drivers with multimedia content (Fig. 1).

Fig. 1. Image 1. Training school students in basic mechanics classes

3 Definition

3.1 Users Definition

See Fig. 2.

Target: Training School for professional drivers of Pelileo students.

User journey: User navigation to satisfy a need through the APP.

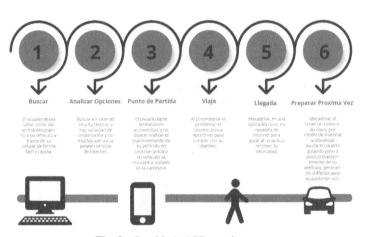

Fig. 2. Graphic 1. APP user journey

Functional Definition
App Role: Basic vehicle maintenance with topics user guide:

- **ENGINE:** Oil change, spark plug replacement and hydraulic fluid change.
- **ELECTRICAL:** Charge battery, change battery and top up battery fluid.
- **TIRES:** Inflation and air pressure, change and rotation of tires.
- **BRAKES:** Pad change and brake regulation.
  Additional Functions.
- Contact guide: tow truck request or mechanical service.
- Gallery of tools: necessary tools images gallery.

4 Information Architecture

See Fig. 3.

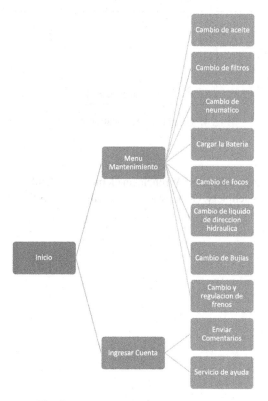

Fig. 3. Graphic 2. Application map chart

5 Design

Idea conception in graphic form until the application final design.

a) **Wireframe:** Simplified presentation of application screens. Shows items and information organization (Fig. 4).

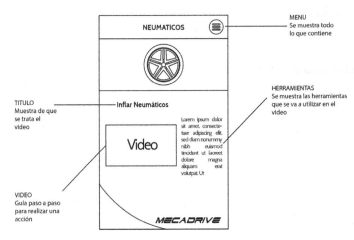

Fig. 4. Graphic 3. Application wireframe

b) **Prototype**: Brand conception. Wrench, an element that symbolizes the maintenance of engines and machinery. Gear lever, connotes the cars and their mechanics (Fig. 5).

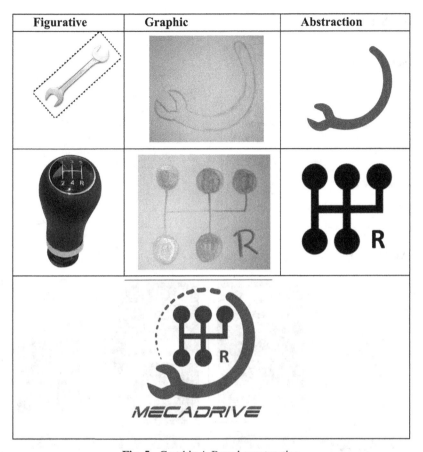

Fig. 5. Graphic 4. Brand construction

Screen Design

APP Screens (Fig. 6)

Screen Design.

APP Screens.

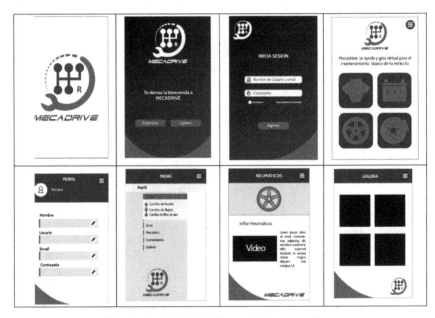

Fig. 6. Graphic 6. APP Screen design examples

6 Developing

Programming of code lines for APP execution, it joins with the graphic part. The design joins with the programming and a functional APP is obtained (Fig. 7).

Fig. 7. Image 2. APP programming

7 Publication

The APP publication can be load directly in the digital stores. However, direct transmission and installation on mobile devices in a student focus group from driver training school has been the option implemented (Fig. 8).

Fig. 8. Image 3. APP test

8 Experimental Stage

The MECADRIVE APP was tested in 40 students focus group from the Pelileo Training School for Professional Drivers. The APP was installed on their mobile devices. Using non-participant observation techniques [29], it was possible to verify the usefulness of the technological resource and subsequently a survey was applied to the test group. The results are summarized in the following Table 4:

Table 4. APP test results

Query topic	Results
APP usefulness of the contents within	85% of respondents mentioned that the contents are very useful for their learning
Application usability and navigability	90% of the students in test group said they had no difficulties using the APP
Other content for driver training	85% of students indicate that it would be appropriate to include content from other subjects, for example, road culture, traffic signs, engine repair
APP recommendation with other users	95% of students indicated the application is highly recommended to other users

9   Conclusions

The professional drivers training, employs similar processes to those used in secondary and college education based on theoretical and practical classes. However, it suffers from similar problems in teaching content, as they continue to use traditional teaching tools. Equally, the practical classes lack autonomous reinforcement for the students. In the described scenario, resources framed in ICT, multimedia and audiovisual content, adapted to mobile devices, are the tools that deliver positive results in educational places. About professional drivers training, like other people, the mobile devices use, tablets and computers is common, for this reason, their usage in learning is by highly support. About the contents, vehicle maintenance is a practical learning subject that is reinforced with digital tools. Thus, the APP has shown considerable effectiveness and willingness to employ in students to be required as a tool in other professional training subjects for drivers.

References

1. Menéndez, T.: Jugada, PRIMICIAS, 24 marzo 2022. [En línea]. https://www.primicias.ec/noticias/sociedad/muertes-accidentes-transito-impunidad-ecuador/. [Último acceso: 01 abril 2022]
2. OMS: Global status report on road safety 2015 (2015). [En línea]. https://contralaviolenciavial.org/uploads/file/DOCUMENTOS/GLOBAL%20REPORT%202015.pdf
3. Cruz, E.: El Universo, 17 AGOSTO 2018. [En línea]. https://www.eluniverso.com/noticias/2018/08/17/nota/6908768/tasa-mortalidad-accidentes-transito-ecuador-ha-aumentado-2018
4. Castillo Cevallos, O.M.: Necesidad de normar en la ley de transito y transporte terrestre, la operatividad de las escuelas de conducción, en cuanto a los instructors. Loja, Loja: Universidad Nacional de Loja (2011)
5. Constante Tipán, N.V.: Accidentes de tránsito producidos por imprudencia y negligencia de conductores y peatones en la avenida Simón Bolívar del DMQ, Año 2016. Proyecto de investigación previo a la obtención del Título de Abogada. Carrera de Derecho. Quito: UCE., Quito (2017)

6. Agüero, D., Almeida, G., Espitia, M., Flores, A., Espig, H.: Uso del teléfono celular como distractor en la conducción de automóviles. Salus **18**(2), 27–34 (2014)

7. Pedroza Reyes, A.S.L.C.R.M.H.U.: Control De Un Vehículo Guiado Automáticamente (AGV). Conciencia Tecnológica [en linea], n° 34, 10–15 (2007)

8. Sagbini, K., Ramírez-Guerrero, T., Castañeda, L., Toro, M.: Aplicaciones Móviles para la Evaluación de Conductores y Usuarios en Sistemas Estratégicos de Transporte Público. de *Desafíos en Ingeniería: Investigación Aplicada*, Medellin, Fundación Universitaria Antonio de Arévalo (2019)

9. Ydrogo Ramírez, E.: Desarrollo de un aplicativo móvil para el registro del cumplimiento y desempeño de líneas de transporte público en la ciudad de Lima, Huancayo: Universidad Continental-Facultad de Ingeniería (2020)

10. Cadena Jaramillo, J., Martínez Oviedo, J.: Aplicación movil encaminada al fortalecimiento de la cultura vial, a personas entre edades de 18 a 30 años de la ciudad de San Juan de Pasto, San Juan de Pasto: Universidad de Nariño-Facultad de Ciencias Naturales y Exactas (2019)

11. Guzman Diaz, N., Chaparro Ariza, M.: Desarrollo de aplicación movil de transporte entre la comunidad universitaria con capacidad de geolocalizacion para el proyecto Ud sobre ruedas., Bogotá: Universidad Distrital Francisco José de Caldas- Facultad Tecnológica Ingeniería en Telecomunicaciones (2017)

12. Oleas-Orozco, J., Padilla-Padilla, N., Cayambe-Palacios, Á.: Multimedia en la enseñanza de vocabulario de idiomas,» de Aportes de ingeniería para desarrollo regional, Ibarra, Universidad Técnica del Norte, pp. 421–427 (2017)

13. Navas, E., Oleas, J., Zambarano, M.: Augmented Reality to facilitate the process of Teaching - Learning in school textbooks. de 2021 Fifth World Conference on Smart Trends in Systems Security and Sustainability (WorldS4), pp. 316–321

14. Oleas-Orozco, J.A., Mena, A., Ripalda, D.: Hearing loss, mobile applications and inclusive social environments: approach to learning sign language for children without disabilities. de Intelligent Human Systems Integration (IHSI 2022) Integrating People and Intelligent Systems, Venecia, (2022)

15. JadánGuerrero, J., AriasFlores, H., Altamirano, I.: Q'inqu: inclusive board game for the integration of people with disabilities. In: BottoTobar, M., ZambranoVizuete, M., TorresCarrión, P., MontesLeón, S., PizarroVásquez, G., Durakovic, B. (eds.) ICAT 2019. CCIS, vol. 1193, pp. 85–94. Springer, Cham (2020). https://doi.org/10.1007/978-3-030-42517-3_7

16. Castro, S., Guzmán, B., Casado, D.: Las TIC en los proecesos de enseñanza y aprendizaje. Laurus. Revista de Educación **13**(23), 213–234 (2007)

17. Hernandez, R.M.: Impacto de las TIC en la educación: Retos y Perspectivas. Propósitos y Representaciones **5**(1), 325–347 (2017)

18. Gargallo Castel, A.F.: La integración de las TIC en los procesos educativos y organizativos. Educar em Revista **34**(69), 325–339 (2018)

19. Rodríguez Zambrano, A., Rey, E.R., Zambrano Cedeño, V., Rodríguez Arieta, G.: TICS y aplicaciones móviles en la educación superior; del dicho al reto. Revista Atlante: Cuadernos de Educación y Desarrollo (2019)

20. Mangisch Moyano, G.C., Mangisch Spinelli, M.D.R.: El uso de dispositivos móviles como estrategia educativa en la Universidad. RIED. Revista Iberoamericana de Educación a Distancia **23**(1), 201–216 (2020)

21. Cruz-Barragán, A., Barragán-López, A.D.: Aplicaciones Móviles para el Proceso de Enseñanza-Aprendizaje en Enfermería. Salud y Administración **1**(3), 51–57 (2014)

22. Garay Núñez, J.R.: Aplicaciones de dispositivos móviles como estrategia de aprendizaje en estudiantes universitarios de enfermería. Una mirada desde la fenomenología crítica. Ride. Revista Iberoamericana para la Investigación y el Desarrollo Educativo **10**(20) (2020)

23. Antoñanzas Laborda, J.L., Salavera Bordas, C., Sisamon Marco, M.C., Bericat Alastuey, M.C.: Las estrategias de aprendizaje de los conductores sin puntos y los profesionales. Securitas Vialis **8**, 1–6 (2016)

24. ANT: Listado de escuelas de capacitación,» Agencia Nacional de Transito del Ecuador - ANT, S.F.. [En línea]. https://www.ant.gob.ec/?page_id=2567. [Último acceso: 18 Abril 2022]

25. Hernandez-Sampieri, R., Mendoza Torres, C.P.: Metodología de la Investigación. Las rutas cuantitativa, cualitativa y mixta, McGraw Hill (2018)

26. Real Academia Española RAE. Diccionario de la lengua Española. RAE 2022. [En línea]. https://dle.rae.es/mantenimiento. [Último acceso: 20 febrero 2022]

27. Ramírez Arteaga, G.V.: Proyecto de modernización para el Tecnicentro Ing. Vinicio Ramirez y CIA. LTDA, Guayaquil: Universidad Internacional del Ecuador-Facultad de Ingeniería Automotriz (2012)

28. Cuello, J., Vittone, J.: Diseñando apps para moviles, José Vittone — Javier Cuello (2013)

29. Angrosino, M.: Etnografía y observación participante en investigación cualitativa. Ediciones Morata, S. L, Madrid (2014)

Research on Information Design of Intelligent Vehicle System Interface Based on Driver Trust

Guo Qi[✉]

East China University of Science and Technology, Shanghai, China
deng2020@ecust.edu.cn

Abstract. The human-machine interface is the main channel of human-vehicle communication in the process of human-machine co-driving. The display form of the interface information affects the driver's perception of the current driving status, which in turn generates a different state of trust. Therefore, this paper takes improving user's driving trust as the research basis and intelligent vehicle system interface information requirements as the research content, through users' subjective scoring of different driving trust levels presented by the interface information, the scored interface information is clustered and analyzed, and finally a driving trust-oriented intelligent system interface information priority design framework is constructed, which provides a theoretical reference and basis for solving the interface design of intelligent vehicle system for the purpose of trust calibration. It provides a theoretical reference and basis for solving the interface design of intelligent vehicle system for trust calibration.

Keywords: Intelligent vehicle · Driver trust · Interface design

1 Introduction

In response to the rapid development of autonomous technology, the National Highway Traffic Safety Administration (NHTSA) and the International Society of Automation Engineers (SAE) have classified the level of intelligence of autonomous vehicles into five levels (L0–L5) according to the degree of automation. However, at present, the driver and the autonomous driving system still need to control the vehicle together in order to cooperate in the driving task, as fully autonomous driving technology has not yet been achieved. In other words, autonomous driving is currently at the stage of human-machine co-driving(Fig. 1) [1]. Human-machine co-driving is the process of human-vehicle cooperation, and driver trust is a necessary condition for human-vehicle cooperation [2].

How to avoid trust deficit and trust excess during human-machine co-driving and over-trust in the process of human-machine co-driving, and to achieve the driver's trust calibration is an important issue that needs to be solved in the field of human factors research for autonomous driving [3]. The problem of trust calibration in human-machine co-driving is an important issue that needs to be solved.

© The Author(s), under exclusive license to Springer Nature Switzerland AG 2022
C. Stephanidis et al. (Eds.): HCII 2022, CCIS 1655, pp. 413–417, 2022.
https://doi.org/10.1007/978-3-031-19682-9_52

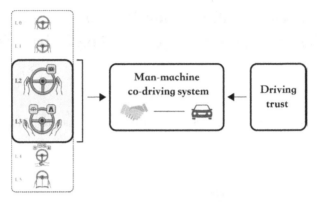

Fig. 1. The relationship between human-machine collaboration and driver trust.

Trust plays an important role in the process of human-machine co-driving, and the trust state of the driver in the process of autonomous driving determines the efficiency of human-machine cooperation and driving safety. Therefore, how to avoid under-trust or over-trust in the human-machine co-driving process and how to achieve driver trust calibration are important issues to be addressed in the field of autonomous driving research. Similar to interpersonal trust, communication is an important way to build interpersonal trust. In human-machine co-driving systems, trust between human and vehicle also needs to be established through effective communication. The human-machine interface (HMI) is the main channel for human-vehicle communication in the process of human-machine co-driving. In the autonomous driving environment, the HMI is a complex information interaction system that carries vehicle information, driving information and surrounding environment information [4]. These complex information and the form of information display will affect the driver's perception of the current driving state, which in turn will generate different trust states. By optimizing the information design (display content and display form) of the vehicle interface, the driver's trust level can be adjusted to provide the right information at the right time and calibrate the driver's trust state.

2   Driving Trust-Driven Information Prioritization Construction

A wealth of previous research summarizes interface design strategies to avoid over-trust and under-trust, which mentions the importance of the presentation of interface information for trust calibration, mainly including providing users with information on why and how [5]. Therefore, based on the information presentation principles of driving trust, card classification experiments and cluster analysis methods are used to group the needs affecting users' driving trust and construct an information architecture diagram of intelligent vehicle system interface, so as to determine the content and priority level of interface information display.

2.1   Initial Requirement Set Was Built

By reviewing the automotive industry standards and combining the results of the market research on the internal information display interface of intelligent vehicles, The process of users using intelligent vehicles were decomposed, mainly divided into driving preparation stage, road driving stage and destination arrival stage, then a total of 60 interface information display items in five categories were summarized, as shown in Table 1.

Table 1. Initial requirement set.

Requirement category	Content
Vehicle basic information	Speed, Time and date, Single trip mileage, Airbag status, Seat belt status, Brake status, RPM, Gear, Door status, Seat status, Battery remaining, Air conditioner status, Tire pressure status, Total mileage, Vehicle operating mode, Interior and exterior temperature, Range, Vehicle light status
Road condition information	Distance between surrounding vehicles, Pedestrian warning, Road obstacle warning, Visibility condition, Crosswalk warning, Weather condition, Pedestrian warning, Traffic light warning, Surrounding vehicle speed, Road obstacle warning, Surrounding vehicle driving status prediction
Path navigation information	Vehicle current position, Trip end position, Trip completion time, Vehicle ready to depart, Trip end distance, Road traffic situation Owner/passenger identification, Current travel time, System manual takeover reminder, Turnoff road direction
System decision information	The vehicle begins to slow down, The vehicle begins to turn, The vehicle begins to change lanes, The vehicle maintenance tips, The vehicle begins to accelerate, The vehicle begins to drive in a straight line, The vehicle begins to turn around, The vehicle begins to overtake, Arrives at the end ready to get off, The vehicle begins to reverse, The vehicle begins to stop, The vehicle changes course
Multimedia information	Phone, email, Mobile application interconnection, SMS, Music playback, Internet, Video playback, Radio function, In-car camera, Recording function

2.2 Driving Trust Scale Analysis

Firstly, valid users were screened on the online platform, with the screening criteria being whether or not they had two years of automatic (semi-automatic) driving experience. In addition, the screened users were asked to rate the 60 interfaces in the table above on a scale of 0–5 based on their trust in driving. A total of 312 questionnaires were returned, and 204 valid questionnaires were analyzed by reliability and validity. The data from the valid questionnaires were analyzed to obtain the mean value of the importance of each interface information and the standard error of the trust level. As a result of the comprehensive analysis, four requirement items will be deleted due to low trust level, namely, email function, video function, recording and SMS function.

Secondly, Based on the obtained results, Clustering algorithm [6] was used to classify the requirement items in terms of importance and different trust levels, and finally the display information priority of the intelligent vehicle system interface was obtained. As shown in Table 2.

Table 2. Display information priority.

Requirement category	Display priority		
	High	Middle	Low
Vehicle basic information	Speed, Battery remaining, Single trip mileage, Airbag status	RPM, Door status, Vehicle operation mode, Tire pressure status	Total mileage, Vehicle light status, Single trip
Road condition information	Pedestrian warning, crosswalk warning, traffic light warning, road obstacle warning	Visibility conditions, Surrounding vehicle distance, Surrounding vehicle travel status prediction	Surrounding vehicle speed
Path navigation information	Bifurcated road direction, System manual takeover alert	Vehicle current position, Traffic conditions on the road	Trip end location, Trip completion time
System decision information	Vehicle maintenance prompt, vehicle starts to accelerate, vehicle starts to drive in a straight line, The vehicle begins to slow down, the vehicle begins to turn, the vehicle begins to change lanes, The vehicle begins to turn around, the vehicle begins to overtake, The vehicle begins to reverse, the vehicle begins to stop, the vehicle changes course	Arrives at the end ready to get off	
Multimedia information		Internet,Camera	Phone, email, mobile application interconnection Text messaging, Music playback

These five types of information can be divided into two groups, one is the basic information, mainly including: the basic information of the vehicle, the road conditions during the trip, the route navigation information and various multimedia information. The other is the status decision information, which refers to the decision information. It is mainly used to display the current working status of the system and the vehicle or various types of information during the trip, aiming at conveying the decision-making behavior related to the intelligent system to the user. Then, displaying different information according to different information priorities can enhance the user's trust in the intelligent vehicle.

3 Conclusion

A framework for driver trust-driven interface information design is constructed based on user driving process analysis method and driving trust scale measurement method to prioritize information display on intelligent vehicle system interfaces. It provides an idea and foundation for designing trust-calibrated intelligent system interface design.

Funding. Shanghai Pujiang Talent Program Project No. 21PJC032; National Natural Science Foundation of China Project No. 52205264.

References

1. Gao, Z.L., Wenmin, L.J., et al.: Human-machine trust in self-driving vehicles. Adv. Psychol. Sci. **29**(12), 2172–2183 (2021)
2. Hancock, P.A., Nourbakhsh, I., Stewart, J.: On the future of transportation in an era of automated and autonomous vehicles. Proc. Natl. Acad. Sci. **116**(16), 7684–7691 (2019)
3. Detjen, H., Faltaous, S., Pfleging, B., et al.: How to increase automated vehicles' acceptance through in-vehicle interaction design: a review. Int. J. Hum.-Comput. Interact. **2021**(2), 1–23 (2021)
4. Monsaingeon, N., Caroux, L., Mougine, A., et al.: Impact of interface design on drivers' behavior in partially automated cars: an on-road study. Transport. Res. F: Traffic Psychol. Behav. **81**, 508–521 (2021)
5. de Visser, E.J., Cohen, M., Freedy, A., Parasuraman, R.: A design methodology for trust cue calibration in cognitive agents. In: Shumaker, R., Lackey, S. (eds) Virtual, Augmented and Mixed Reality. Designing and Developing Virtual and Augmented Environments. VAMR 2014. LNCS, vol. 8525, pp 251–262. Springer, Cham (2014). https://doi.org/10.1007/978-3-319-07458-0_24
6. Rodriguez, M.Z., et al.: Clustering algorithms: a comparative approach. PLoS ONE **14**(1), e0210236 (2019)

INNOTEK-MOBIL Information System to Improve Mobility with Dynamic Interaction on Various Devices

Mayerly Rivera[3], Yuliana Montenegro[1], Hernan Naranjo[4], Katerine Tamayo[2(✉)], and Roberto Encarnación[5]

[1] Servicio de aprendizaj, Calle 6 # 21-78 José María Obando, 190001 Popayán, Cauca, Colombia
anyela.montenegro@misena.edu.co

[2] Servicio de aprendizaje, Calle 73 Norte 18 C-20 María Paz, 190001 Popayán, Cauca, Colombia
dayktamayo1@misena.edu.co

[3] Servicio de aprendizaje, Barrio altos del palmar- entrada valladoli, Popayán, Cauca, Colombia
Mayerly.rivera@misena.edu.co

[4] Servicio Nacional de Aprendizaje, Moscopán, Popayán, Cauca, Colombia
henaranjo5@misena.edu.co

[5] Servicio Nacional de Aprendizaje, Carrera 10 # 6-42 Centro, Popayán, Cauca, Colombia
rencarnacion@sena.edu.co

Abstract. Currently, the city of Popayán - Cauca (Colombia) has multiple difficulties in the mass public transport system, among which the lack of information on the routes to go from one place to another in the city, the overcrowding of the buses and the loss of time of the users, directly affecting the users. In order to provide timely information through the INNOTEK-MOBIL Project, a diagnosis of the inhabitants is proposed. With this information, in a first module, a web platform will be designed for managing the fleet of buses, drivers and passengers, applicable to public transport companies. The second module will interconnect various information screens located at strategic points in the city, which will display relevant information for the user. Finally, a mobile application will be designed, through which the user will be able to view the registration options, maps with routes, waiting times and advertising on their electronic device.

Keywords: Application · Web service · API REST · Transport · Information

1 Introduction

In this document you will find information about the INNO-TEK MOBIL project. This is an ongoing investigation that consists of the implementation of informative screens in stations (bus stops), which will improve the daily life of citizens in aspects such as saving time, comfort for the user and security for the same. In addition, there will be a digital platform that will help to carry out detailed control within the functions of public transport companies, and a mobile application that allows people to have access to the information that will be available on electronic devices such as tablets, smartphones, and computers. The achievements that are to be achieved through the realization and implementation of the INNO-TEK MOBIL Information System in support of public and private entities such as the Municipal Mayor's Office, the Government of the department of Cauca and public transport companies, among others, are: Design the logical and physical model of INNO-TEK MOBIL, including the information screens, the mobile application and the digital platform. Develop the structure of the project by implementing the aspects raised and applying the relevant knowledge. Help little by little so that the community adapts technology in their daily tasks. Have an information system that contributes to the improvement of transport conditions and contributes to the beginning of the path of a Smart City.

2   Background and Current Status

In the first instance, an exploration was carried out in the municipality of Popayán, where key aspects of the environment were recognized in order to analyze the conditions of the city, among them, it was possible to highlight that: Of 100% of the inhabitants of the population of the department of Cauca, 3.28% of the people are in misery. Of 100% of the inhabitants of the population of the department of Cauca, 5.99% of the people lack adequate housing. Of 100% of the infants in the population of the department of Cauca, 1.58% of the children do not attend educational centers [1]. Additionally, the main economic activities that exist at the municipal level were studied, among them the following stand out: Electricity, gas and water with a percentage equivalent to 47.5%. Trade with a percentage equivalent to 17%. Transport, storage and communications with a percentage equivalent to 6.4%. Thanks to these values, it was possible to deduce that transportation has a considerable percentage in the satisfaction of local demand [2]. Due to this, the following proposals were obtained as finalists:1. Real-time GPS monitoring of municipal bus activities. 2. Spectral images. 3. Pedagogical evaluation platform. Taking this into account, the final business idea was chosen through a decision table, and considering that it fully complied with the key factors that were: compatibility with the actions launched, economic possibilities, experience, use of technology, satisfaction of needs, conditions and opportunities in the market.

The chosen business idea was the monitoring of the activities of municipal buses through GPS in real time and was structured under five aspects: 1. Product development. 2. Market. 3. Industrial sector. 4. Qualities of the entrepreneur. 5. Economic and financial aspects [3].

3   Methodology

3.1   Phase I

An exploration was carried out to validate the problem, which was executed through the Startup Essentials methodology, which makes it possible to show which clients really experience the problem under analysis. The components of the study methodology used are described below: In all phases of the methodology, trend analysis artifacts and customer learning records called Clientograms are used. In the first step with the first Clientogram used, a hypothesis of the problem was raised and the possible potential clients were determined. It was deduced that the main difficulty that public transport users face daily is the poor condition of the buses in the municipality, the arrival times at the stations, misinformation about the service provided and overcrowding by route. Potential customers are public transport users looking to find a transport system that meets their needs and provides better quality service. In the second step, the problem was refined and potential customers were narrowed down. This process was validated through a survey of twenty people, which helped to the following deduction: the initial hypothetical problem remains and the main clients are students and workers who use the public transport service of the municipality of Popayán. In the third step, a value proposition is presented to customers, about the possible alternative to solve the problem that people are facing. It is proposed to create an information system that serves to monitor and receive information that constantly interacts with public transport companies. In the last step of this process, the solution proposal is presented with a more elaborate speech and prototype drafts are presented to more than 50 potential clients, who expressed their points of view and highlighted their interest in being beneficiaries of the results of this process [4] (Fig. 1).

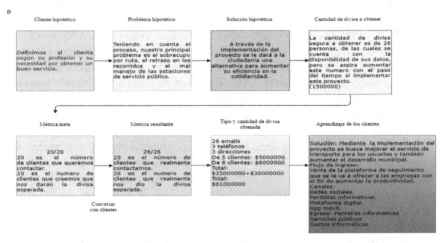

Fig. 1. Example of clientogramas

Once the problem was identified, an investigation was carried out on the existing companies that try to satisfy the needs of the population, and among them it was possible to determine that: The BEA system lacks a mobile application that allows the passenger to obtain information about their transport route in real time, in addition, the cost of the service is very high, exceeding 20,000 USD, plus information system licenses that add up to a value of 4,000 Annual USD. The MOOVIT company does not have an information screen service at public transport service stations and has no cost for its service, but it does not have detailed information and geolocation. The organization called Movil

Move is dedicated to building technological developments with the aim of making life easier for users and has free accessibility, but within its projects focused on mobility it does not provide the possibility for users to have contact with the entity and their communication channels are very limited, which limits the possibility of carrying out a survey of requirements [5].

3.2 Phase II

All the results obtained from phase I were recorded in the Canvas Model, thereby identifying the key partners who might be interested in leveraging the value proposition. At this point, the public transport companies, municipal mayor's office, future mobility and the government of Cauca were identified [6]. Subsequently, the income flow is recognized that would be the sale of the information system oriented to public transport companies and that will be in charge of monitoring the activities of the company. The value equivalent to the production costs was determined, which would be 16,000 USD, taking into account that this value was obtained through the design of a cost structure that includes supplies, payroll, services and digital advertising, among others (Fig. 2).

Fig. 2. Canvas model

3.3 Phase III

In this phase, a systematic review of information on the different architectures used for the implementation of information systems that manage to satisfy the needs of end customers with the type of problem identified and analyzed was carried out, with this it is concluded that for the deployment of the information system, it is convenient to use the REST API architecture supported by microservices [7]. This architecture will allow access to data and functionalities other than the information system through Web services. REST API provides a simple RESTful interface with lightweight JSON-formatted responses that allow you to read and write data to/from your program. APIs are the functionalities that a web service provides through a URL address on a network, making it easier for it to be used by other software to improve its results and optimizing the client-server relationship. Normally it is not a result in itself, but rather serves as a link between software that has already been created and another that may find it useful, which would be called a "software-to-software" interaction. This allows an interaction between the three components of the project, since it connects the modules with other software and in the same way, allows the sharing of specific data without filtering the personal information of the clients, the data of the operating system, among others. It is important that the information provided by a web service API is presented in a format that is understandable by other applications, to avoid losing all the functionality of the API itself. To do this, a series of valid software architectures to be used in this particular type of API will have to be standardized. They typically use standard web services such as REST, SOAP, XML-RPC, and JSON-RPC. The information system that provides a solution to this problem is made up of three subsystems: A web application that is in charge of the administration of the vehicle fleet, the programming of routes and reception of the GPS position of the vehicles and stations. A Hybrid Mobile application, which provides information on routes and times for end users on their Smart Phone and A Dashboard that provides information on routes and times at stations located at strategic points in the city. The information system is accessed from multiple devices such as information screens, Smartphones and Desktop Computers. The way to interconnect all these devices for the exchange of data stored in the Database is through API REST.

4 Prototype Design

The base prototypes and the simulation were worked with a free access digital tool called Figma. The initial elaboration was the graphical interface of the digital platform, which, as had been proposed, will be of an administrative nature and with restricted access to the public. In it, what the transport company requires within the main functions was captured, such as: a registration and login form, a bearing plan and different buttons that allow entering the database analysis, in order to automate the entity's internal processes. After having defined the design of the main component, the Mockups of the application was made, which meets the needs of the company's clients, client-server type (Figs. 3 and 4).

Finally, the Dashboard prototype was designed, which shows the information required by users of public transport and found at bus stops in the city. The design of the interfaces is obtained from the needs identified in the clients and companies of the public transport service (Fig. 5).

The information system converges in a data-centric architecture, where a series of microservices is deployed, which combines several programming languages in each of its services, REST Web Services, QR codes and a hybrid mobile application which will allow access to the information system from any operating system. The project screens will be connected to an API, to consult information such as: route number in real time, position of the vehicle and an indicator that specifies the waiting time (Fig. 6).

Fig. 3. Prototype Interface of Web platform

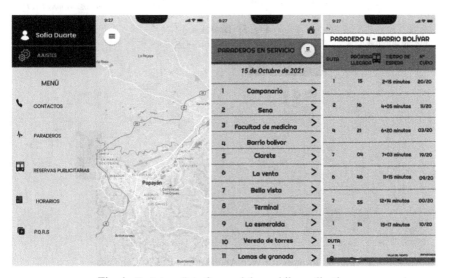

Fig. 4. Prototype Interface and the mobile application

5   Conclusions

Real problems present in the city of Popayán Cauca - Colombia were identified, where public transport highlighted lack of information on routes, loss of time by end users due to waiting at bus stops, lack of organization in the fleet of vehicles in transport companies.

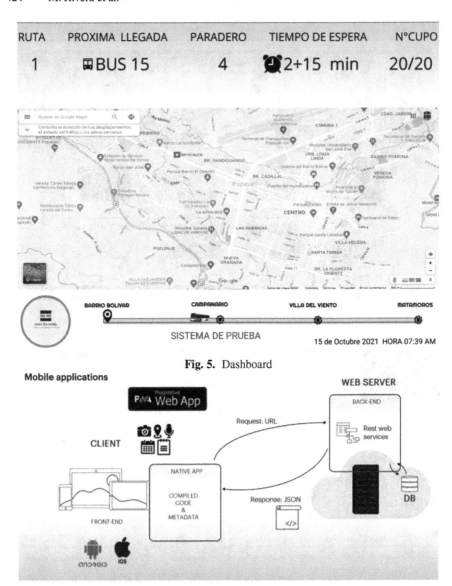

Fig. 5. Dashboard

Fig. 6. Progressive Web Application - PWA - GeneXus

Through the use of the Startup Essentials evidence-based entrepreneurship methodology, it was possible to corroborate the hypothetical problem identified, by conducting multiple surveys of customers (end users of transport), where as a result of the metrics obtained, unsatisfied needs and the requirements for the design of the prototypes of the information system.

The Canvas was modeled to identify channels, key partners, income stream and competitors of the information system, managing to establish the necessary criteria for risk-based entrepreneurship.

As a result of the identification of the problem, the most appropriate architecture was selected for the implementation of the information system, such as the Progressive Web Application - PWA, which allows the interaction of multiple devices through microservices interconnected with API REST.

References

1. *APIs*. (s.f.). Obtenido de https://drive.google.com/drive/folders/1cHoj8v7yEj9NeQEU6YMz 6zgZMhneEKqI
2. DANE (2018). Obtenido de https://cutt.ly/ctPcbkt
3. Gabinete creo en Popayán (s.f.). *Plan de desarrollo municipal.* Obtenido de http://www.pop ayan.gov.co/sites/default/files/documentosAnexos/pdm2020_2023_0.pdf
4. Gabinete departamental. (s.f.). *Plan de desarrollo.* Obtenido de https://www.cauca.gov.co/ NuestraGestion/PlaneacionGestionyControl/Plan%20de%20Desarrollo%20Departamental% 202020%20-%202023.pdf
5. Gómez, A. S. (Enero-Junio de 2016). *Análisis de la dinámica del mercado laboral en Popayán - Colombia.* Obtenido de http://dx.doi.org/https://doi.org/10.17981/econcuc.37.1.2016.07
6. SETP POPAYÁN (2021). *Sistema estratégico de transporte.* Obtenido de https://movilidadfut ura.gov.co/
7. Salesforce: REST API Developer Guide. @Salesforcedocs (2021)

Understanding Travel Behaviors and Developing a User-Centered Design of the Residential Mobility Using a Persona-Based Approach

Toshihisa Sato[✉], Naohisa Hashimoto, Takafumi Ando, Takahiro Miura, and Yen Tran

National Institute of Advanced Industrial Science and Technology (AIST), Tsukuba Central 6
1-1-1 Higashi, Tsukuba 3058566, Ibaraki, Japan
{toshihisa-sato,naohisa-hashimoto,takafumi.ando,miura-t,
tran.yen}@aist.go.jp

Abstract. This paper describes a persona-based investigation of travel behaviors of residential people. This research aims to develop mobility services based on real travel behaviors and the needs of the community residents. We interviewed the two targets: the municipality and the company that implements new mobility services in society, and the residents that use the new mobility services in the region. First, the interviews were conducted to identify the persona describing the users intended by the municipality and the company ("Intended Persona"). Second, the persona representing residents was developed based on the interviews of the residents ("Actual Persona"), and it was used to understand actual movements in the target region. Finally, we investigated the differences between the "Intended Persona" and the "Actual Persona" that will identify the users' expectations and requirements for new mobility services. The results suggest several gaps between the "Intended Persona" and "Actual Persona", including shopping needs in stores outside the residential area, lifestyle of living only within the town, and resident relationships.

Keywords: MaaS (Mobility as a Service) · Persona · Travel behavior

1 Introduction

MaaS (Mobility as a Service) is expected to solve regional transportation issues. In Japan, the Ministry of Economy, Trade and Industry (METI) and the Ministry of Land, Infrastructure, Transport and Tourism (MLIT) jointly started a new project "Smart Mobility Challenge" that aims to support regional cities and areas in implementing the MaaS in society [1]. 'MaaS' refers to the use of IT to seamlessly link all forms of public transportation including buses, trains and cabs to ridesharing and shared bicycles. The MaaS in the "Smart Mobility Challenge" includes on-demand traffic, combination of freight and passengers, co-operative transportation (e.g. residents going shopping or to the hospital can ride the bus for commuting), mobile sales and mobile medical examination.

C. Stephanidis et al. (Eds.): HCII 2022, CCIS 1655, pp. 426–433, 2022.
https://doi.org/10.1007/978-3-031-19682-9_54

There is a wide range of transportation challenges due to a variety of local transportation conditions. The contents of the mobility services should be suitable to the regional traffic in order to improve user acceptance of the soft and hard services. Personalization technique based on the information technology is a key technology to develop MaaS applications for personalized and customized information design [2, 3]. Big data and the data analysis methodologies will contribute to find out user needs and preferences for the daily travels.

In addition, deep data, including users opinion, perspective and feelings about everyday things, is also essential to encourage the mobility services appropriate to the regions. For example, 'Co-Design' is attracting attention, which involves people with many different perspectives in a design process [4, 5]. We used a persona-based method [6], one of user-centric design approaches, to obtain deep data on the residential travel needs and preferences.

2   Methods

This research aims to develop mobility services based on real travel behaviors and the needs of the community residents. We interviewed the two targets: the municipality and the company that implements new mobility services in society, and the residents that use the new mobility services in the region. First, the interviews were conducted to identify the persona describing the users intended by the municipality and the company ("Intended Persona"). Second, the persona representing residents was developed based on the interviews of the residents ("Actual Persona"), and it was used to understand actual movements in the target region. Finally, we investigated the differences between the "Intended Persona" and the "Actual Persona" that will identify the users' expectations and requirements for new mobility services.

2.1   Regions

We selected three regions from 14 areas under "the Smart Mobility Challenge project". The regions selected are Muroran-city in Hokkaido, Misato-cho in Shimane prefecture, and Kiyama-cho in Saga prefecture. Figure 1 presents the location, population and size of the 3 regions.

2.2   Participants

We interviewed 2 staffs in Muroran-city, 2 staffs in Misato-cho, and 4 staffs in Kiyama-cho for the "Intended Persona". 16 people in Muroran-city (average: 73.9 years old; from 50 to 91), 7 people in Misato-cho (average: 73.9 years old; from 67 to 80), and 25 people in Kiyama-cho (average: 71.1 years old; from 62 to 90) participated in the interview for the "Actual Persona", respectively. We talked with most of the residents by phone, and we conducted face-to-face interviews with some of the municipality and company staffs.

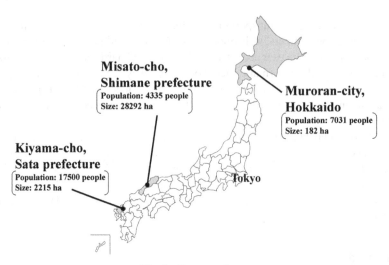

Fig. 1. Target regions.

2.3 Contents of the Interviews

IN the interviews for the "Intended Persona", the contents included traffic issues for the residents assumed by the municipality and the company as follows:

- Daily life of assumed local residents.

  - Resident demographic trends (age/residential history/private car ownership, etc.)
  - What is the daily life of seniors/families like?
  - What kind of community is there?
  - Where do they go for shopping (commercial facilities in/outside the community)

- Regional challenges in mobility and outings

  - Mobility and outing issues related to external factors such as topography, climate, local culture, etc.
  - Daily life of local residents as considered by the municipality and the company
  - Accessibility issues to main facilities for going out (commercial facilities, government offices, etc.) and transportation issues to get out of the area
  - Issues for which existing transportation services are considered inadequate
  - Issues in the community other than transportation issues, etc.

- What kind of behavioral change do you expect to be promoted and what kind of life do you expect to become, through implemented the MaaS?

  - Frequency of going out
  - Scope of activities
  - Improvement of QoL associated with these activities, etc.

The interviews for the "Actual Persona" were intended to clarify actual community and user profile, and the contents were as follows:

- Daily life of local residents

  - Attribution trends of residents (age/family structure/residential history/private car ownership, etc.)
  - What kind of community do they participate in?
  - Where do they go shopping (commercial establishments in/outside the community)?
  - Do they want to go out or would they prefer to do so if they could do so at home?

- Mobility and Outing Challenges

  - Mobility and outing issues related to external factors such as topography, climate, and local culture
  - Issues and challenges within the town that are considered inadequate with existing mobility services
  - Accessibility issues to the main facilities for going out (commercial facilities, government offices, etc.) and transportation issues to get out of the area.
  - Issues that you perceive, including issues other than transportation issues, etc.

- What kind of behavioral change do you expect to be promoted and what kind of life do you expect to become, through implemented the MaaS?

  - Frequency of going out
  - Scope of activities
  - Other behavioral changes
  - Improvement of QoL associated with these changes, etc.

3   Results

Figure 2, 3, and 4 presents the results of the interviews in three regions, respectively. We found out several gaps between the "Intended Persona" and "Actual Persona", including shopping needs in stores outside the residential area, lifestyle of living only within the town, and resident relationships.

4 Discussion

The results obtained from the persona-based approach indicate that the actual travels of residents can be divided into two types: out-of-town and in-town groups. In the out-of-town group, transportation hub plays an important role in making it easier for the residents to get to out-of-town destinations. It is effective to establish routes from the hub to various destinations. Mobility on the way home is essential for the out-of-town group, because it often happens that the return time will not be as scheduled due to the out-of-town shopping or hospital visit.

Muroran-city
(On-demand taxi that can be taken in and out of 75 locations in the town)

"Intended Persona" (81-year-old female)	"Actual Persona" (75-year-old female)
• **Three times a week**, she goes shopping for groceries and daily necessities at a shopping center in the town. The rest is delivered by a home delivery service. • **Several times a year**, she takes a bus from the shopping center to a hospital outside the town. • Both her husband and she stopped driving several years ago, so they use public transportation or walking to get around. • When she occasionally goes out of town for hospital visit or shopping, she takes a taxi if the bus time does not suit her convenience, but this is not a frequent option due to cost issues. • **She often goes out to run errands, and rarely goes shopping before returning home.** • With age, her legs and back have become weaker, and it is difficult for her to get to the bus stop.	◆**Once or twice a week**, I go shopping for groceries and daily necessities at a shopping center in town. I also uses a home delivery service, but prefer to see things with my own eyes. ◆**Once or twice a month**, I take a bus from the shopping center to a hospital outside of town. ◆I am not satisfied with the selection and prices at the shopping center, so **I shop at specialty stores and large supermarkets in the area on my way to the hospital.** ◆Both my husband and I stopped driving several years ago, so we use public transportation or walking to get around. ◆We take a bus to go out of town according to the time. On the way home, I would like to take a taxi from out of town if possible, but I cannot afford to take a taxi every time, so I take a bus to the shopping center in town and take a taxi from the shopping center. ◆Walking from the bus stop to the shopping center is also a challenge. **I want to go out so that I have enough energy to do things at home as soon as I get home.** ◆I would like to maintain my health by going out, including out-of-town trips, to get stimulation.

To increase the use of the service in the future (examples of improvements)
- ❑ **Enhancement of the shopping center's transportation hub function**
  e.g.
  - ➢Install bus stops in shopping centers
  - ➢Improve the number of buses
  - ➢Make it easier to use on-demand cabs from destinations
- ❑ **Expansion of on-demand cab service area**

Fig. 2. The results of "Intended Persona" and "Actual Persona" in Muroran-city.

Misato-cho
(Flat-rate shared-ride taxi service in the large town)

"Intended Persona" (81-year-old female)

- **Once a week**, she shops for groceries and daily necessities in the town. She also uses the home delivery service of a co-op. She goes out of town **two or three times a month** to shop for clothes and daily necessities, and to visit the hospital. **She only goes out to run errands and does not do anything on the way.**
- She relies on her husband, who has a driver's license, for nearby trips, but because it is not safe for her elderly husband to drive, **she asks her neighbors** to drive her for long-distance trips.
- When she cannot ask her neighbors to drive, she takes the bus to go out of town. As her legs and back have weakened, it is difficult for her to get to the bus stop.
- She is not willing to take a taxi because of the **cost** and the neighbors' perception that she's being extravagant.
- By using a cab, she can **live independently** and reduce the burden on both the person providing transportation and the person being transported. In addition to shopping and hospital visits, They also expect to be able to participate in community activities and enjoy their new lives more.

"Actual Persona" (81-year-old female)

- I shop for groceries in town **once or twice a week.** I prefer to buy food in stores, but the selection is not sufficient, so I also use the co-op's home delivery service. I also use a fishmonger's mobile market that comes once a week, but I **use it more for socializing with the community and people** than for convenience. **Once a month**, I go out of town to shop for daily necessities and to go to the hospital. I also regularly go to an electronics store and a private store in the town, building a **relationship** with them so that I can always rely on them.
- Basically, my husband drives me around, and when it is not convenient, **I take the bus unless someone offers to give me a ride.**
- Taxi is not readily available due to **service coverage and limited hours of operation**, rather than cost. I want the taxi to pick me up on time; if it picks me up before I get there, I am in a hurry and afraid of falling. I do not want people to see that I am taking a taxi (they may think that I am not relying on them).
- There are **no cafes or other places** where they can get together with friends and spend a little time.
- I would like to easily go out of town to enrich my life, such as to take lessons, go to hot springs, or enjoy the scenery of the four seasons.

To increase the use of the service in the future (examples of improvements)

- A means of transportation that allows residents to move around the town with "mutual help" (e.g. Uber for Misato Town residents)
- App to call out to people ("I'm going out, would you like to join me?")
- Expansion of logistics to bring goods from outside the town so that shopping can be completed within the town (one store in the center of town)
- Utilization as a means of transportation for residents to go out of town in conjunction with the movement of goods from out of town (in a broad sense, freight and passenger consolidation)

Fig. 3. The results of "Intended Persona" and "Actual Persona" in Misato-cho.

Kiyama-cho
(On-demand taxi service to and from home and throughout town, and a regularly scheduled shuttle bus service on main street)

"Intended Persona" (71-year-old male)

- **Twice a week**, he shops for food and daily necessities at a shopping center near the town. **Once a month**, he goes to an out-of-town shopping center for shopping and a movie. **Once every two months**, he goes to a hospital outside of town for a regular checkup.
- He drives his own car. He feels that the out-of-town area is close by, so it is easy for him to go out.
- He can walk to the nearest station without any problem. When he cannot use his car, **he uses the bus service on rare occasions**, but the number of buses is small, and the arrival and departure times of the buses do not match the time required at the destination. He takes the circular bus on the way to the station and then take a cab on the way back.
- Many residents moved to this town as part of a large-scale development project, and they are very aware of the fact that they built the present town by themselves, and community activities are very active.
- They use PCs and smart phones without any difficulties.

"Actual Persona" (71-year-old male)

- Basically, I travel by car (with advanced driving assistance systems). I want to go out a lot.
- I use PCs and smart phones without any difficulty. No resistance to using mail-order services.

<Type 1: feeling like a neighbor even outside of the town>

- I go shopping for food and daily necessities at a nearby shopping center **twice a week. Once a month**, I go to a shopping center outside of town for shopping and a movie; **once every two months**, I go to a hospital outside of town (far away) for a regular checkup. I **have several favorite restaurants outside of town**, so I often go out to eat while shopping.
- I participate in a hobby community outside of town twice a week. If it is within a 30-minute drive, it feels like a neighborhood even if it is outside of town.

<Type 2: going out several times a day within the town>

- I shop for food and daily necessities in the town **four times a week**. I participate in the local community **4 times a week**. I walk to the local hospital **once a month**. It is easy to go out by car several times a day.
- The bus service is not very frequent, and there is a long waiting time and connections are necessary, so **it is not a means of transportation that allows free movement**.

To increase the use of the service in the future (examples of improvements)

- ❑ **Expansion of out-of-town routes for the Type 1 and further enhancement of on-demand transportation for the Type 2**
- ❑ **App for efficient use of both on-demand and out-of-town routes.**
- ❑ **Co-creation by residents of boarding and alighting locations and diagrams for out-of-town routes and in-town on-demand transportation.**
- ❑ **Subscriptions to enhance convenience**

Fig. 4. The results of "Intended Persona" and "Actual Persona" in Kiyama-cho.

In the in-town group, the residents want objectives to be completed within the town. Mobility getting things to the center of town is essential. In addition, a freight and passenger consolidation, which is used as a means of transportation for residents to go out of town in conjunction with the movement of goods from out of town, might be necessary to encourage the residents to go out of town once in a while for a change of pace. Figure 5 presents the summary of the results of the persona-based method and the future mobility concepts appropriate to the out-of-town and in-town groups.

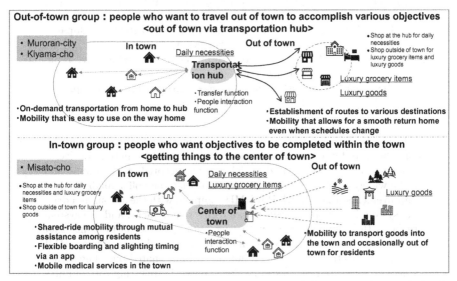

Fig. 5. Two patterns of residential travels and a mobility proposal to support the travels that fits each pattern.

References

1. Smart Mobility Challenge Project Launched. https://www.meti.go.jp/english/press/2019/0618_005.html. Accessed 27 May 2019
2. Anshari, M., et al.: Customer relationship management and big data enabled: personalization & customization of services. Appl. Comput. Inf. **15**(2), 94–101 (2019)
3. Arnaoutaki, K., et al.: Personalization and recommendation technologies for MaaS. In: Proceedings of Conference: 2nd International Conference on Mobility as a Service 2019 (2019). arXiv:2101.12335
4. Mitchell, V., et al.: Empirical investigation of the impact of using co-design methods when generating proposals for sustainable travel solutions. CoDesign (2015). 10.1080/15710882.2015.1091894
5. Alciauskaite, L., et al.: Implementing co-design strategies in creating accessible future mobility solutions in TRIPS project. In: Proceedings of the 7th Humanist Conference (2021)
6. Miaskiewicz, T., Kozar, K.A.: Personas and user-centered design: how can personas benefit product design processes? Des. Stud. **32**(5), 417–430 (2011). https://doi.org/10.1016/j.destud.2011.03.003

External Human Machine Interface (HMI) for Automated Bus -Preliminary Experiments for Acceptance with Real Automated Bus-

Sota Suzuki[1,2]([✉]), Yanbin Wu[2], Toru Kumagai[2], and Naohisa Hashimoto[2]

[1] Tokyo University of Science, Shinjuku-ku, Tokyo 162-8601, Japan
`8122525@ed.tus.ac.jp`
[2] National Institute of Advanced Industrial Science and Technology, Tsukuba, Ibaraki 305-8560, Japan
{`wu.yanbin,kumagai.toru,naohisa-hashimoto`}`@aist.go.jp`

Abstract. Automated vehicles are being developed all over the world, and the introduction of automated vehicles for future better society as new mobility. For automated vehicles to be accepted by the public and to be widely used in society, it is essential that they offer further safety improvements. External HMI (eHMI) equipped with the automated driving system is one of the ways to fulfill this requirement, and the system replaces the communication with surrounding traffic participants that is conventionally conducted by humans such as drivers. Thus, eHMI should be effective way between human and automated bus. The scenes where eHMI should be necessary was exposed by referring rote of automated bus in assumed area, and service and also by considering previous researches. We need to examine effective eHMI in various situations that may occur during operation of automated buses, and evaluate its acceptability through experiments with real subjects. The information presentation method for eHMI was to be studied by combining output devices such as sound and display board, and aimed to clarify the effective presentation method while referring to the opinions of the operators and others as preliminary experiments. As work in progress paper, the necessary scenes which should be considered for eHMI the research plan and the obtained results will be explained.

Keywords: External HMI · eHMI · Autometed vehicle · Mobility as a service

1 Introduction

Automated vehicles are being developed all over the world, and the introduction of automated vehicles for future better society as new mobility. For automated vehicles to be accepted by the public and to be widely used in society, it is essential that they offer further safety improvements and innovative convenience that

C. Stephanidis et al. (Eds.): HCII 2022, CCIS 1655, pp. 434–440, 2022.
https://doi.org/10.1007/978-3-031-19682-9_55

do not compromise safety in the existing transportation environment. External HMI (eHMI) equipped with the automated driving system is one of the ways to fulfill this requirement, and the system replaces the communication with surrounding traffic participants that is conventionally conducted by humans such as drivers and crews. Thus, eHMI should be effective way between human and automated driving system. On the other hand, since the output is mainly from the vehicle side, it does not have a compelling force on the surroundings, but only improves safety and convenience, and the use of eHMI as a means of ensuring absolute safety and communicating essential information is outside the scope of this study.

The project for realizing level 4 automated buses in Japan, which was supported by the government was started in 2021. This project is being promoted as a model area for the "Hitachi BRT" bus line in Hitachi City that has a bus-only road. BRT stands for "Bus Rapid Transit" a higher-order bus system that combines dedicated bus lanes, advanced vehicles, and an efficient operation system. [1] First, the scenes where eHMI should be necessary was exposed by referring rote of automated bus in this project and by considering previous researches. In this study, we need to examine effective eHMI in various situations that may occur during operation of automated buses, and evaluate its acceptability through experiments on test subjects. The information presentation method for eHMI was to be studied by combining output devices such as sound, light, and display board, and aimed to clarify the effective presentation method while referring to the opinions of the operators and others. The related work, study issue and preliminary experiments will be explained and this study is work in progress, thus the further experimental results and detail summery will be explained as a future work.

2   Related Work

The following are examples of previous studies of eHMI. In the FY2020 "Cross-ministerial Strategic Innovation Promotion Program (SIP)/Automated Driving for Universal Services/HMI and User Education" Outcome Report [2] (hereafter referred to as the SIP Phase 2 Report), research was conducted on methods to improve the negative effects of eHMI communication to crossing pedestrians, among other things. In the SIP Phase 1 report, which is the previous year's version of the SIP Phase 2 report, a negative effect of the eHMI was identified: when communicating with pedestrians crossing the street using the eHMI, pedestrians sometimes fail to check for oncoming traffic when crossing, compromising their safety. The results of the verification of this effect showed that pedestrians tended to fail to check safety when the automated vehicle communicated its intention to yield to pedestrians attempting to cross the road ahead of them, rather than when the automated vehicle communicated its intention to stop.

Mirnig et al. [3] introduced voice HMIs in emergency situations as a study of accident situation notification in unmanned buses. A real-world experiment with 24 subjects confirmed the effectiveness of the information provided by the HMI.

Forke et al. [4] developed visual eHMI icons and text as a study on communication between buses and pedestrians, and evaluated conditions that increase pedestrian's sense of security. Lau et al. [5] studied the effects on pedestrians when the eHMI and vehicle behavior are inconsistent, and results of an experiment with 49 subjects showed that pedestrians tend to rely on information from the HMI. Anund et al. [6] developed eHMI for a city bus to evaluate and demonstrate risk reduction. A driver-focused virtual reality (VR) experiment confirmed the effectiveness of the HMI during the transition to automation. Weber et al. [7] conducted VR experiments on the impact of eHMI on pedestrians and compared them in countries with different cultural backgrounds, concluding that HMI information needs to be localized. Faas et al. [8] proposed five different light-based eHMIs for a study of pedestrian interaction with automated vehicles. The results of a real-world experiment with 59 subjects confirmed the effectiveness of the flashing eHMI. Wang et al. [9] evaluated four different types of eHMIs, including text-based and graphic-based HMIs, for research on automated vehicles interacting with pedestrians. The effectiveness of each method was verified in a real-world experiment with 12 subjects. Aramrattana et al. [10] proposed eHMI for interaction with other drivers as part of a study of automated vehicle formation driving. Experimental results using a driving simulator confirmed the effectiveness of the eHMI when merging on a highway. Colley et al. [11] evaluated the safety of pedestrians passing by a truck in a VR experiment with 20 subjects as a study of the effect of eHMI on pedestrians in an automated truck.

To summarize these references, many of them use VR and other methods to unify experimental conditions, etc., with regard to evaluation methods, but basically all of them propose eHMI and evaluate its effectiveness through subject experiments, although the number of participants may be small or large. In addition, as in the SIP Phase 2 [2] report mentioned earlier, in the eHMI, the positive and negative side effects have been confirmed, and the exact use assumptions have been set for each literature, respectively. Therefore, it can be said that in this study, it is necessary to design an experiment that will ultimately confirm the validity in the subjects, and that will construct a hypothesis that takes into account both positive and negative effects and that can be evaluated under appropriate condition settings. Furthermore, as for the characteristics of the literature, the literature is dominated by recent studies, and the impression is that the study of conclusions and discussions on automated driving with eHMI has only just begun. On the other hand, the recent increase in research related to automated driving suggests that future research will accelerate, and continued focus is necessary.

3   Study Setting

In this study, we examined eHMI for use in model regions, based on the examples of previous studies mentioned above and other factors. First, we identified use cases in the model region and examined situations in which HMI can be used, and summarized the advantages that could arise from the use of eHMI.

The road environment in the model area's bus-only road is mainly divided into intersections, single road sections, bus stops, and others. Based on the results of SIP Phase 2 report [2], Table 1 summarizes the situations where eHMI can be used in dealing with the road environment and traffic participants.

Table 1. Scene and eHMI responses

Scene/Target	To intersecting vehicles	To turning vehicles	To crossing pedestrian	To passing pedestrian (Parallel & Opposite)
Intersection with bar gate and no traffic lights	Bar opening/closing Rotary beacon light when starting off	N/A	Intention to give way (Fewer bar gate references)	N/A
Green crossing strip	N/A	N/A	Intention to give way (Typical for BRT)	N/A
Single road section	N/A	N/A	N/A	Keeping away from the road
Intersection without traffic lights and with side walks	Bar opening/closing Rotary beacon light when starting off	N/A	Intention to give way (temporarily excluded)	Keeping away from the road (temporarily excluded)
Intersection without traffic lights and with crosswalks parallel to the road	Obeying the traffic lights Bar opening/closing Rotary beacon light when starting off	N/A	Intention to give way	Keeping away from the road (temporarily excluded)
Intersection with traffic lights	Obeying the traffic lights Bar opening/closing Rotary beacon light when starting off	Communicating intent to act	Obeying the traffic lights Delayed pedestrians Jaywalking pedestrians	Keeping away from the road (temporarily excluded)
Near bus stop	N/A	N/A	Intention to give way	N/A

This paper summarizes our work on improving safety and efficiency by utilizing eHMI in single road sections, with the target being pedestrians. Specifically, it is assumed that the deceleration applied when an automated bus detects a pedestrian walking on an unfenced sidewalk on a single road section will be reduced by communicating with the pedestrian via eHMI. This is expected to improve pedestrian safety and bus operation efficiency by alerting pedestrians to the presence of the bus through eHMI and encouraging them to take evasive action. In addition, since the assumed traffic participants are limited to automated buses and pedestrians in single-road sections, the assumptions made in this situation could serve as the basis for utilizing eHMI at intersections and in other situations.

4   Preliminary Experimental Environment

The parameters for the behavior of the automated bus in the assumed scenario were as follows: the specified speed for steady-state driving was 40 km/h, and the distance from the bus to the obstacle was set to 50 m in order to avoid contact with the obstacle detected by the automated bus. The condition for starting deceleration was that the distance between the bus and the obstacle was 1.5 m or less when the automated bus passed by the obstacle. Ideally, the bus should be able to determine that the obstacle is a human when it detects the obstacle

50 m away. The grace time from the start of deceleration to the pedestrian's location is approximately 9 s, and during this grace time, we aimed to improve safety and efficiency when the automated bus passes by the pedestrian using eHMI. We did preliminary experiments in test track, and will consider the role in Japan when we do in outside area.

4.1 Sound

First, we will explain the experimental environment that was set up for the verification of the eHMI using audio. Using an Arduino and an MP3 playback module, we set up a computer-controlled system to make announcements to the outside of the vehicle. (Fig. 1a, Fig. 1b)

(a) MP3 playback module   (b) Installed on the front of the bus

Fig. 1. eHMI system using sound

The system can play audio files stored on a micro SD card through an external speaker using a 1.5 W amplifier. The output can be set to 0 (mute) or 1 to 30 steps by the program. A simple measurement of the noise level of the announcements showed that the difference in noise level with and without the announcements at 30 m in front of the bus was more than 10 dB, and that the announcements could be heard clearly under normal conditions.

Next, the results of the study of the actual announcement content will be described. Seven sound sources were prepared, and each was selected for reasons such as the voice of a general bus announcement, the actions that we want pedestrians to take, and emphasis on the fact that the vehicle is an automated bus. All of them were created using text-to-speech software and chime sound materials to fit within the grace period of 9 s.

The validity of these announcements was also evaluated through a simple subject experiment. It is assumed that this proposal has not been thoroughly examined enough to be used in a demonstration experiment. First, there was an opinion that the announcement information should be more specific. This is because differences in the amount of knowledge about automated driving may cause differences in the actions taken by pedestrians and the hazards they perceive. Second, regarding the composition of sentences, there was an opinion that it is better to tell the pedestrian what action is desired first, rather than the existence of the bus or the intention of the action. This is because, in Japanese, names are often given first, but considering the time it takes pedestrians to actually avoid the bus after they hear the announcement, it is better to give them the time they need if the request is given first.

4.2   Text Display

Next, we describe the experimental equipment prepared for the verification of eHMI using text display. The LED display panel shown in the Fig. 2a allows the user to set the text to be displayed using configuration software. This LED display board was installed on the front of the bus with the expectation that it would be used to communicate the status of the bus's automatic operation and requests to surrounding traffic participants. (Fig. 2b) Although it is difficult to discern in the photo, the LED display board shows "automatic operation in progress" in orange Japanese. During a sunny day, the letters could be discerned visually up to around 40 m. At a distance of 50 m, it was only possible to confirm that the lights were on, and it was difficult to discern the letters.

(a) LED display board   (b) Installed on the front of the bus

Fig. 2. eHMI system using text display

5   Summary

In the ongoing project, the objective of eHMI, necessary studies and preliminary experiments were explained as work in progress paper.

For future work, both sound and text display eHMIs should be studied with a view to conducting demonstration experiments in model regions. Specifically, it is necessary to improve the experimental environment, evaluate experimental methods, and scrutinize experimental scenarios.

Acknouwledgement. This project has been supported by Ministry of Economy Trade and Industry, and Ministry of Land Infrastructure Transport and Tourism in Japan.

References

1. Kusumawardani, D.M., Saintika, Y., Romadlon, F.: The smart mobility insight of bus rapid transit (BRT) trans jateng purwokerto-purbalingga ridership. In: International Conference on ICT for Smart Society (ICISS) 2021, pp. 1–5 (2021). https://doi.org/10.1109/ICISS53185.2021.9533253
2. SIP-adus, Report of results in the FY2020. Strategic Innovation Promotion Program (SIP) Phase Two/Automated Driving (Expansion of Systems and Services)/ Surveys and Research on HMI and Safety Education Methods in line with Advanced Automated Driving (2021). https://en.sip-adus.go.jp/rd/rddata/rd04/e206s.pdf, accessed at April 25th, 2022
3. Mirnig, A.G., et al.: Suppose your bus broke down and nobody came: a study on incident management in an automated shuttle bus. Pers. Ubiq. Comput. **24**(6), 797–812 (2020). https://doi.org/10.1007/s00779-020-01454-8
4. Forke, J., et al.: Understanding the headless rider: display-based awareness and intent-communication in automated vehicle-pedestrian interaction in mixed traffic. Multimodal Technol. Interact. **5**(9), 51 (2021)
5. Lau , M., et al.: Investigating the interplay between eHMI and dHMI for automated buses: how do contradictory signals influence a pedestrian's willingness to cross? In: AutomotiveUI 2021 Adjunct: 13th International Conference on Automotive User Interfaces and Interactive Vehicular Applications, pp. 152–155 (2021)
6. Anund, A., et al.: Adaptive ADAS to support incapacitated drivers Mitigate Effectively risks through tailor made HMI under automation. In: The ADAS & ME Project. https://www.adasandme.com/
7. Weber, F., Chadowitz, R., Schmidt, K., Messerschmidt, J., Fuest, T.: Crossing the street across the globe: a study on the effects of eHMI on pedestrians in the US, Germany and China. In: Krömker, H. (ed.) HCII 2019. LNCS, vol. 11596, pp. 515–530. Springer, Cham (2019). https://doi.org/10.1007/978-3-030-22666-4_37
8. Faas, S.M., et al.: "Daimler" external HMI for self-driving vehicles: which information shall be displayed? Transp. Res. Part F: Traff. Psychol. Behav. **68**, 171–186 (2020)
9. Wang, Y., et al.: A filed study of external HMI for autonomous vehicles when interacting with pedestrians. In: International Conference on HCII 2020: HCI in Mobility, Transport, and Automotive Systems. Automated Driving and In-Vehicle Experience Design, pp 181–196 (2020)
10. Aramrattana, M., et al.: Safety and experience of other drivers while interacting with automated vehicle platoons. Transp. Res. Interdisc. Perspect. **10**, 100381 (2021)
11. Colley, M., et al.: Evaluating highly automated trucks as signaling lights. In: 12th AutomotiveUI 2020, Virtual Event, DC, USA, 21–22 September 2020, p. 11 (2020). https://doi.org/10.1145/3409120.3410647

The More the Better? Comparison of Different On-Board HMI Communication Strategies for Highly Automated Vehicles Using a LED Light-Band to Inform Passengers About Safe Interactions with Multiple Surrounding Traffic Participants

Marc Wilbrink[(✉)] [iD] and Michael Oehl [iD]

German Aerospace Center (DLR), Lilienthalplatz 7, 38108 Braunschweig, Germany
{marc.wilbrink,michael.oehl}@dlr.de

Abstract. Highly automated vehicles (HAVs) are becoming more and more advanced and will be soon part of our traffic system. Although the drivers will no longer be in charge of the driving task, they remain an important part of the human-vehicle system and need to understand the HAV's current and future behavior to feel safe and trust the vehicle automation. Research identified communication strategies using LED light-bands as a promising internal human-machine interface (iHMI) in the vehicle. Results show, that automation feedback regarding the detection of other traffic participants (TP) seems to be an important information for passengers to understand and anticipate vehicle behavior. However, these findings are limited to simple scenarios when the HAV interacted with only one other TP. Therefore, this current study investigates different communication strategies for more complex scenarios including a HAV interacting with multiple TPs simultaneously. In an online video study, 125 participants took over a HAV passenger's perspective and rated different iHMI communication designs regarding the amount and arrangement of information and their perceived uncertainty regarding the HAV's safe communication with surrounding TPs in a shared space scenario. Additionally, the maximum number of simultaneously presented TPs on the iHMI was investigated. Results revealed participants' high information needs in complex situations with multiple TPs. Participants preferred iHMI designs displaying a maximum amount of information at a time. Prioritizing information led to enhanced subjective uncertainty. However, to avoid visual cluttering and displaying only relevant information on the iHMI, results needs to be critically discussed for future investigations.

Keywords: HMI · Highly automated vehicle · Interaction with other road users · On-board user · User study

C. Stephanidis et al. (Eds.): HCII 2022, CCIS 1655, pp. 441–448, 2022.
https://doi.org/10.1007/978-3-031-19682-9_56

1 Introduction

In future traffic systems, highly automated vehicles (HAVs) at SAE 4 [1] will play an important role, e.g., ensuring among other goals safer, more sustainable, and accessible mobility. Since technological boundaries for HAV are decreasing, a mixed traffic system consisting of HAVs, manually driven vehicles and non-motorized traffic participants will develop in the near future. Even if users of HAVs will no longer be responsible for performing the dynamic driving task at least as a fallback level for the automation (starting at SAE 4), they still remain an important part of the human-vehicle system. In this new role as mere passenger, users need different information regarding their vehicle's intentions and future maneuvers for safe interactions in traffic with other TPs to reduce situational uncertainty and develop trust over time in the vehicle automation [2].

As a passenger, users hand off the full responsibility and control to the HAV. Without a suitable communication strategy used by the HAV to inform its passengers, this may result in the passengers' subjectively perceived uncertainties when using HAVs. Consequently, a new approach for a human-machine interface (HMI), addressing this specific information needs is required. Following this, novel communication strategies used by the HAV via its HMI should focus on creating a joint understanding of the current driving situation between the HAV and its passengers. As a result, system transparency should increase and enable users to anticipate the future HAV behavior accurately thereby supporting the building of trust in the HAV. In order to develop a high level of trust in HAVs in the long term, the transparency of the automated system plays an important role. By improving the predictability and transparency of the HAV's driving intention and concrete behavior, users' subjectively perceived situational uncertainty and safety improve as well. Both are important prerequisites for the building of trust and acceptance of HAVs by their users [3].

Recent studies, using a 360° LED light-band, installed in the interior of an HAV showed high potential for an iHMI [4, 5]. Especially communication strategies that gave an automation feedback regarding the detection of other traffic participants (TPs) via the LED light-band [6] were rated high regarding trust in automation and usability [4]. These novel communication strategies using LED light-bands provide important information for passengers of HAVs to understand and anticipate vehicle behavior. However, these positive results are limited so far to simple situations consisting of a one-to-one interaction between a HAV interacting with only one other TP. The present study will reflect on these positive findings with regard to an 360° LED light-band as iHMI by considering more complex driving situations with multiple TPs interacting with a HAV at the same time comparing different communication strategies via the iHMI for complex interactions in a shared space scenario.

2 Method

The current iHMI communication design study was conducted as a first explorative experimental online user study in the user-centered design approach. Main research question was, whether it is possible to evolve and scale-up existing HAV-user communication strategies via a 360° LED light-band as iHMI for simple scenarios with only one TP interacting with the HAV to more complex scenarios with multiple interaction partners. By using the game engine "Unreal Engine 4" (version 4.24) different video clips were rendered and presented in combination with an online questionnaire to the participants.

The first research question tested two different communication strategy designs by the iHMI regarding a possible reduction of simultaneously presented information by displaying only TPs near to the HAV (near-field vs. far-reaching design). The second research question dealt with different communication strategy designs used by the iHMI for displaying multiple TPs simultaneously on the 360° LED light-band (detailed vs. grouped). By using a one factor within-design with repeated measures for each question, participants experienced and rated all manifestations of the factor. As dependent variables participants rated different iHMI communication strategy designs regarding their amount of information (1 = "too few information", 4 = "enough information", 7 = "too much information"), the arrangement of information (1 = "confusing", 7 ="clear"), and their perceived feeling of uncertainty regarding the HAV's safe interaction with surrounding TPs (1 = "uncertainty-enhancing", 7 ="certainty-enhancing") in a shared space scenario on a seven-point Likert scale. Furthermore, the maximum number of simultaneously presented TPs on the iHMI was investigated.

2.1 Used Scenario

Participants took over the perspective of a passenger driving in a HAV (SAE 4). A shared space traffic environment was chosen, to create a reasonable situation in which a HAV has to possibly interact with multiple other TPs at the same time. Since only a few traffic regulations exists on a shared space, all TPs have the same rights without being segregated by specific streets or lanes.

With this premise, we created a scenario in which the HAV was entering a shared space with 10 km/h. While the HAV was driving on a straight course, it approaches a group of six pedestrians (). Three pedestrians were located to the left and three participants to the right of the HAV. Pedestrians walked with a standardized lateral distance of 2–4 m in a straight way not crossing the trajectory of the HAV. But this was not

Fig. 1. Illustration of the shared space scenario with the HAV possibly interacting with a group of pedestrians.

clear to the participants as HAV passengers. While approaching the group of pedestrians different iHMI designs were presented to the participants. After the HAV had passed the pedestrians, the video faded out and ended (Fig. 1).

2.2 Sample

A total of 125 participants (47 women, 75 men, one diverse and two without specified gender) took part in the present study. The mean age of the sample was 33.7 years (SD = 12.4 years), with the youngest participant being 18 and the oldest participant being 69 years old. Since HAVs will no longer require users to act as driver, also participants without driver's license and little annual driving experience were included in the study. However, 98% of the study participants held a valid driver's license and drove an average of 8641.6 km (SD = 8689.5 km) per year. All participants indicated that they had already heard of HAV. In order to assess the technology affinity of the sample, an interaction-based technology affinity questionnaire (ATI) [7] was used. The ATI measures the interaction with technical systems on a six-point Likert scale from 1 = "not at all true" to 6 = "completely true". The results showed a higher than average affinity for technology in the overall sample (M = 4.45, SD = 0.89). Participants were acquired by publicizing the online study via LinkedIn, Twitter, mailing lists, and direct contact via email with participants in the DLR participant pool. The participation in the online study was in accordance with the Declaration of Helsinki, voluntary and without payment. However, participants were offered at the end of the questionnaire to take part in a lottery (four Amazon vouchers worth 25 Euros each).

2.3 Procedure

The total duration of the study was 20 min on average (SD = 6 min). At the beginning, all participants gave their consent to the recording and processing of their data enabling scientific research. This was followed by a short sample video to test the technical requirements of the study participants' playback device. Subsequently, participants' demographic data were collected and instruction for the experimental trials was presented. Additionally, participants were informed about the functionality of the HAV and the iHMI communication strategies. After participants had experienced the functional concept of the iHMI in a detailed practice run, they were instructed regarding their task. Participant's main task was to attentively watch the videos of the different iHMI communication strategies and afterwards answer a specific questionnaire.

2.4 iHMI Communication Strategy Designs

A 360° LED light-band installed in the vehicle interior was used as iHMI (Fig. 2). The blue color of the light-band informed users about the current automation level (SAE 4) of the vehicle. In addition, the iHMI communicated spatial information in form of light signals directly on the LED light-band. In line with previous work [4, 5], we used a small dark blue bar displayed below a relevant detected TP to provide an automation feedback for perceived TPs by the HAV (Fig. 2). The small dark blue bar followed the

TPs position on the 360° LED light-band in order to provide the user with continuous system feedback. This system feedback indicated that the presence of detected TP was considered when planning future actions and maneuvers by the HAV.

Two different communication strategies (near-field vs. far-reaching) were used in the present study to investigate the presentation of multiple TPs on the LED lightband.

Since the presentation of unnecessary information could lead to an information overload, we wanted to investigate the amount of information needed and understood by the passengers in more complex scenarios with multiple TPs. Reducing the number of simultaneously presented TPs on the LED light-band, we tested a "far-reaching" design (Fig. 2, right) which displayed all present TPs in a given scenario (six TPs) against a "near-field" design, only displaying the three TPs nearest to the HAV (Fig. 2, left).

Fig. 2. Participants perspective including the 360° LED light-band (left: communication design "near-field", right: communication design "far-reaching").

The second research question was whether it is possible to reduce the maximal number of simultaneous presented TPs on the iHMI by using a different design approach (detailed vs. grouped). The "detailed" communication design which used a small dark blue bar displayed below a relevant detected TP (Fig. 3, left) was identical to the "far-reaching" design described previously.

The "grouped" communication design used a large dark blue bar displaying a group of relevant detected TPs (Fig. 3, right). The large dark blue bar followed only the position of the group of TPs.

The goal of both iHMI communication designs was to increase the transparency of the HAV and thus to reduce subjective uncertainty of the HAV users.

Fig. 3. Participants perspective including the 360° LED light-band (left: communication design "detailed", right: communication design "grouped").

3 Results

T-tests for repeated measurements showed significant differences between the two communication strategy designs "near-field" and "far-reaching" (Fig. 4, left). Participants rated the amount of displayed information significantly higher for the "far-reaching" design (M = 4.68, SD = 1.20) compared to the "near-field" design (M = 3.38, SD = 1.59), resulting in a high effect size (T(111) = −9.332, p < .001, d_z = −0,882). Additionally, the arrangement of information in the "far-reaching" design was also rated as significantly higher (M = 4.94, SD = 1.55), compared to the "near-field" communication design (M = 4.47, SD = 1.75), resulting in a small effect size (T(111) = −2.545, p = .012, d_z = −.240). Participants rated the "far-reaching" design as significantly more uncertainty reducing (M = 5.24, SD = 1.44) compared with the "near-field" design (M = 3.97, SD = 1.73) with a medium effect size (T (111) = −6.386, p < .001, d_z = .603). Consequently, 73% of all participants preferred the "far-reaching" communication design over the "near-field" design (27%) in the experienced scenario.

With regard to the second research question we compared the "detailed" communication design with a "grouped" communication design. The results showed significant differences regarding the amount of displayed information (Fig. 4, right). Participants rated the "grouped" design significantly better (M = 3.88, SD = 1.06) than the "detailed" (M = 4.62, SD = 1.05) design resulting in a medium effect size (T (110) = −5.695, p < .001, d_z = −.541). Additionally, the arrangement of information in the "grouped" design was also rated as significantly higher (M = 5.39, SD = 1.61), compared to the "detailed" communication design (M = 4.86, SD = 1.58), resulting in a small effect size (T(110) = 2.510, p = .014, d_z = .238). No significant differences were found regarding the uncertainty reduction between the two communication designs (T (110) = −.048, p = .962). Lastly, 53% of all participants preferred the "grouped" communication design over the "detailed" design (47%) in the experienced scenario.

Finally, participants were asked about the maximal number of simultaneously displayed TPs on the LED lightband. Over 60% of all participants stated a preferred number of five and more simultaneously displayed TPs.

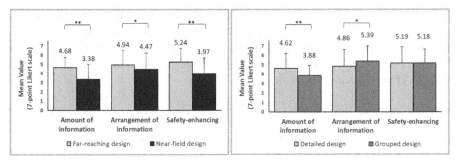

Fig. 4. Comparison (M and SD) between the "far-reaching" vs. "near-field" design (left) and "detailed" vs. "grouped" design (right).

4 Conclusion

The results indicate the high information needs of participants in complex situations with multiple TPs. Participants rated the iHMI communication strategy design approach of only displaying a reduced number of closer to their HAV present TPs (near-field design) significantly lower than presenting all present TPs in the given scenario (far-reaching design) in terms of amount and arrangement of information. Most importantly, participants ratings revealed, that the near-field design leads to a significantly higher amount of uncertainty compared to the far-reaching design. As a result, 73% of all participants preferred the far-reaching design which gives a constant feedback regarding detected TPs by the HAV. These results indicate, that a reduced feedback regarding detected TPs by the HAV could lead to situational subjective uncertainty regarding future behavior of the HAV and thereby to a feeling of being less safe which might, in turn, influence trust in the HAV. Reduced feedback could be interpreted as ignorance by the HAV resulting in potentially dangerous interactions.

Findings regarding the maximum number of simultaneously presented TPs on the iHMI are in line with these results. More than 60% of the participants stated that they would like to see five and more detected TPs simultaneously on the iHMI. However, this very high number represents the high information demand of users and formulates an urgent request for a good system transparency. Participants wanted to understand the current and anticipate the future behavior of their HAV. Therefore, they seem to need a high amount of information with regard to surrounding TPs.

The second research question elaborated an iHMI communication design which indicated groups of pedestrians with only one group-bar and not per TP individually displayed bars on the light-band. Participants rated the presented information of the "grouped design" as significantly better arranged and the amount of information more suitable compared to the "detailed" design in the used scenario. This ("far-reaching") "grouped" communication design might serve as a viable solution for providing the HAV's user with enough transparency of the automation on the one hand and at the same time preventing visual cluttering on the other hand.

However, these results are based only on video data showing one driving scenario as stimulus material. Furthermore, participants experienced the iHMI design for the first time and had most probably not enough time to develop calibrated trust in the HAV.

Further research should focus on real world experiments with additional driving scenarios resulting in more mature ratings regarding HAVs. Additionally, the used scenario presented a situation with multiple TPs but without pedestrians crossings in front of the HAV. Future studies should investigate a possible change in information demand if multiple TPs crosses in front of the HAV.

Acknowledgments. This research was funded by the German Federal Ministry for Economic Affairs and Climate Action within the project @CITY: Automated Cars and Intelligent Traffic in the City, grant number 19A17015B. The authors are solely responsible for the content.

References

1. On-Road Automated Driving (ORAD) committee: Taxonomy and definitions for terms related to driving automation systems for on-road motor vehicles. SAE Standard J3016_202104. SAE International, USA (2021)
2. Lau, M., Wilbrink, M., Dodiya, J., Oehl, M.: Users' internal HMI information requirements for highly automated driving. In: Stephanidis, C., Antona, M., Ntoa, S. (eds.) HCII 2020. CCIS, vol. 1294, pp. 585–592. Springer, Cham (2020). https://doi.org/10.1007/978-3-030-60703-6_75
3. Nordhoff, S., de Winter, J., Kyriakidis, M., van Arem, B., Happee, R.: Acceptance of driverless vehicles: results from a large cross-national questionnaire study. J. Adv. Transp. **2018**, Article ID 5382192 (2018)
4. Wilbrink, M., Schieben, A., Oehl, M.: Reflecting the automated vehicle's perception and intention: light-based interaction approaches for on-board HMI in highly automated vehicles. In: Proceedings of the 25th International Conference on Intelligent User Interfaces Companion, pp. 105–107. Association for Computing Machinery, New York (2020)
5. Drewitz, U., Wilbrink, M., Oehl, M., Jipp, M., Ihme, K.: Subjektive Sicherheit zur Steigerung der Akzeptanz des automatisierten und vernetzten Fahrens. Forschung im Ingenieurwesen **85**, 997–1012 (2021)
6. Dziennus, M., Kelsch, J., Schieben, A.: Ambient Light - an integrative, LED based interaction concept or different levels of automation. In: VDI Wissensforum GmbH (eds.), 32. VDI/VW-Gemeinschaftstagung: Fahrerassistenz und Integrierte Sicherheit 2016, VDI-Berichte, vol. 2288, pp. 103–110. VDI Verlag, Düsseldorf (2016)
7. Franke, T., Attig, C., Wessel, D.: A personal resource for technology interaction: development and validation of the affinity for technology interaction (ATI) scale. Int. J. Human-Comput. Interact. **35**(6), 456–467 (2019)

All-Age Co-creation: A Study of Pedestrian System Service Design from the Perspective of Community Building

Jianbin Wu[1,2] , Kin Wai Michael Siu[2(✉)], and Linghao Zhang[1]

[1] School of Design, Jiangnan University, Wuxi, China
[2] School of Design, The Hong Kong Polytechnic University, Hong Kong, China
m.siu@polyu.edu.hk

Abstract. Using the pedestrian system in Hongqiao Airport's New Village in Shanghai as a case study, this study uses participatory research and co-creation workshops to explore the elements of community-based pedestrian systems and design strategies. The study shows that a people-oriented pedestrian system should enhance mobility at the physical level, safety at the spiritual level, fun at the interactive level, identity at the social level, and sustainability at the cultural level. We propose a physical infrastructure for walking that meets the diverse needs of all ages, creates a shared and open environment that promotes a desired lifestyle, and shapes cultural symbols for a sustainable community. The study shows that a human-scale community walking system can support human relationships and enhance the livability of urban communities.

Keywords: Co-creation · Social community · Pedestrian system · Service design · Design strategy

1 Introduction

Globally, approaches to urban renewal are shifting from incremental construction projects to market development, and more researchers are considering community creation as the "hematopoietic cell" of urban renewal. The aim of community creation is to promote self-organization, self-governance, and self-development through the mobilization of people in a community and to create meaning by building on the social forces and resources of community life.

In recent years, an increasing range of transportation systems have encroached on streets, decreasing pedestrian space. This has led to the renewal of human-scale approaches to urban design. For example, in the Netherlands, features such as pocket parks and shared streets are receiving renewed attention in street designs. Current community walking systems share many basic problems, such as congested roads, long walking distances, poor-quality walking spaces, and inadequate facilities [1]. As a result, even though walking is the most basic form of travel, the needs of pedestrians are not met and social isolation and physical isolation have increased.

Using the walkable area of the Hongqiao Airport New Village in Shanghai, China as a practical case, this paper uses a community creation approach to design a pedestrian system. The aim is, to build a people-centered community pedestrian system. The study also develops a five-level model of the elements and design strategies that promote walkable communities.

2 Related Works

2.1 Community Building from the Perspective of Social Innovation

Communities are the basic units of modern cities and the location of most daily activities. Rapid urbanization in China means that people's diversifying and growing needs are accompanied by a number of social problems and issues, such as population aging and weakening community culture and intergenerational relationships. "Community building" is distinct from result-oriented community planning, and is an inclusive building process [2].

Today, a wide range of scholars share the same in-depth understanding of social innovation and community. For example, Chiara, in her paper "Designing for Social Innovation," states that public innovation requires practitioners to understand sociality, develop emerging skills, and place service design at the center of the design process. This is part of a shift from designing for the community to co-designing with the community, and ultimately to community-owned design [3]. Francesco et al. apply their service design solution framework to community florists. The framework activates an open process that triggers local stakeholders' engagement and also sets the stage for future developments [4]. Current community research focuses on physical spaces that promote spiritual and cultural values and meet the diverse needs of the public. In addition, the literature suggests that the nurturing and maintenance of community culture and community consciousness are an important part of the cultivation of residents' lifestyles, philosophies, and even values.

2.2 Human-Centered Walking Systems

Although the amount of urban public space is increasing, the lack of separation of pedestrian streets and vehicular roads, the crowding of pedestrian spaces, the lack of continuous walking paths, and the air pollution caused by automobile exhausts mean that these spaces do not promote the physical and mental health of residents. Urban planers have gradually realized that pedestrian systems can improve the quality of life [5]. Scholars from many disciplines have drawn attention to the importance of pedestrian systems to the sustainable development of communities. In the UK, the inclusive design approach to outdoor spaces proposed in the 1990s emphasizes the need for spaces that promote walking and social interactions. Alfonzo et al. use Maslow's hierarchy of needs to systematically identify the psychological dimensions of walking systems. For example, they consider how residents are affected by being able to walk to their destinations, by guaranteed pedestrian safety, and by whether the walking systems are comfortable and interesting [6].

Applying the community creation design concept to pedestrian systems expands the design process from the micro-level of spaces and products to the macro-level of service systems and social relationships [7]. Community creation respects the subject position of residents and seeks to identify and support the real needs of residents through immersive participation. Based on the hierarchy of needs proposed by Maslow [8], four levels of walking needs can be identified. The first level encompasses basic functional and accessibility needs, including the relationship between pedestrians and motor vehicles and other hazards that prevent the safety of walking activities from being guaranteed. Needs on the second level, namely social needs, are met when walking systems encourage residents to have fun, socialize, and gain social respect. Self-actualization, the third level, is achieved by providing residents with a platform and channel for self-actualization. The fourth level, sustainability, emphasizes the pedestrian system as a cultural symbol that reaches out to the general public.

This approach recognizes that walking systems have both "tangible" and "intangible" characteristics, and the design of pedestrian systems has gradually shifted from the creation of roads and transportation systems to the creation of enriching environments that support social relationships and create a sense of community belonging [9].

3   Methods

3.1   Input: Participatory Research

The team began by learning about the specific location of the community, which is close to Hongqiao Airport. It was initially built to provide housing for airport employees, but younger tenants have moved in 10 years later, making the community richer in age

Tools Preparation   Prepare the Scene

Answer Questions   Information Collection

Fig. 1. Community participatory research process.

groups. The current plan for the new Hongqiao Airport Village is to build an airport district that will attract more people to stop and walk around.

To achieve this vision, the team took the opportunity provided by the Community Festival to conduct a series of participatory activities. The content of the activities was based on Maslow's hierarchy of needs, as applied to the specific problems of the current pedestrian spaces. The aim was to initially assess the residents' feelings about the community's pedestrian spaces. Unlike traditional questionnaires, this study used cards to guide residents to actively express their feelings and thoughts about walking (see Fig. 1). The questions focused on the community square and how it was used. The aim was to identify the phenomena and conflicts within the pedestrian system.

3.2 Output: Co-creation Workshop

TO meet the diverse needs of the residents, the research team adopted a co-creation approach, inviting various stakeholders to participate in the co-creation of the design. The co-creation design tools included cards that provided information on and solicited feedback on the current Hongqiao Community Plaza plan, the co-creation map, and the proposed public facilities. Based on their preliminary assessment, the team prepared cards on infrastructure, security, social activities, and environmental aesthetics as well as artistic and cultural activities. The team also prepared blank cards to encourage participants to express their own needs.

A workshop involving 30 community residents, of a wide range of ages, was conducted. The team formed three groups: children; young and middle-aged people; and an intergenerational group (including parents, children, and older people). The aim was to create a variety of possibilities through mass co-creation. The activities at the workshop were designed to break the ice, share case studies of pedestrian systems, discuss the current state of walking in the community, design an "ideal" walking space, elaborate on the suggested concepts, and evaluate the proposals (see Fig. 2).

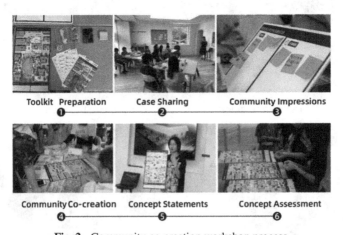

Fig. 2. Community co-creation workshop process.

4 Discussions

4.1 Human-Centered Pedestrian Service System

Pedestrian systems arising from community creation emphasize human-scale walking experiences. A pedestrian system can be described in terms of its external and internal components. The external components are the physical characteristics of the pedestrian system, such as the streets, public squares, landscaping, and facilities that ensure the safety of residents and adequate places for activities. The internal components are the activities and environments that help build a space that promotes harmonious and sustainable community relationships, and ultimately creates a sense of belonging and identity.

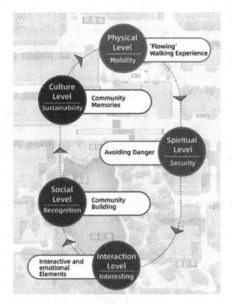

Fig. 3. Five levels of a pedestrian service system.

Therefore, after considering the multiple needs of residents, we build a 5-level model of a human-scale walking system (see Fig. 3). 1) The first level consists of physical facilities that provide a smooth and barrier-free spatial environment for a "continuous" walking experience. 2) The second level ensures the physical safety of the walking environment for residents of all ages, for example, by installing barrier fences to prevent children from falling and rain shelters at resting places to protect residents from the wind and rain. 3) The third level includes elements that increase interactions with the spaces and emotional design elements that enrich the experience. 4) The fourth level considers how the space can be used to carry out multiple activities that promote the social relationships between groups and generations, building a sense of recognition and belonging to the community. 5) The fifth level creates community "memory" and cultivates a sense of belonging among the residents. These "memories" cultivate community "genes" and build sustainable community symbols [10].

Although community pedestrian service systems are only one branch of urban pedestrianism, these systems are diverse and complex and need to be designed to match the specific attributes of each community.

4.2 Design Strategy for Community Pedestrian Systems

Physical Infrastructure that Meets the Diverse Needs of All Age Groups. The physical infrastructure of a pedestrian system consists of paths, resting places, and trash receptacles that are directly accessible to walkers. A human-oriented pedestrian system has inclusive pedestrian spaces, environments, and roads that allow residents of all ages to reach their walking destinations; in other words, it must meet the requirements of accessibility and functionality. First, the human-centered walking should be determined, the pedestrian paths should be clearly marked, and pedestrian and vehicle traffic should be separated. Next, the functionality of the spaces and facilities should be guaranteed, which requires the removal of negative spaces, the development of unused spaces, and the regular maintenance and repair of the system to ensure a clean and safe environment.

Downtown Rulink is a mixed-use area in which the design team worked to create a pedestrian-friendly community environment that includes shared streets, parks, and other public spaces. This design for this downtown community includes a number of public spaces, streetscapes and green infrastructure that meet the needs of the growing community and address the major problems such as traffic congestion, the lack of green space, disrupted bike lanes, and disrupted public infrastructure [11].

Create a Shared and Open Atmosphere and a New Lifestyle Concept. "Sharing" a walkable community is a new lifestyle. Residents in these communities not only walk and live in the same spaces, but can use the spaces to learn about and become integrated into the community. This process requires spaces with inclusive functions and forms in which residents can interact and listen to each other in a natural way, providing them with a sense of value and respect. In this community atmosphere, neighbors become friends and help each other. Over time, stable community networks and systems develop.

The renovated Lingbo Bridge (a pedestrian bridge) on Puji Road in Shanghai adds interest and vibrancy to the city while preserving the bridge's original structure. The bridge has been transformed into a multifunctional elevated park that optimizes traffic flow. The design uses color to create different traffic lanes, with a straight lime-colored path for bicycles and motorcycles and a zigzag fuchsia path to direct pedestrian flow. Green-blue areas are spaces for pedestrians to stop and linger, including observation decks, picnic plazas, recreation areas, and mini-amphitheaters. Bright yellow urban furniture that provides a rich environment for social interactions is scattered against a soft cyan-blue backdrop, creating a stark color contrast. Overall, the bridge provides a shared and distinctive living environment for its residents [12].

Community Genes: Shaping Cultural Symbols for Sustainable Community Walkability. A pedestrian walking system based on local cultural characteristics provides channels and possibilities for cultural display and builds residents' sense of identity and belonging. This gradually develops into the community "gene," which is deeply engraved in people's emotions and memories. To achieve this goal, residents need to be encouraged to participate in community affairs through continuous social interactions. Our design process provides insights into residents' feelings and needs, and helps to create spaces that enhance their sense of belonging through dynamic cultural activities that are relevant to their actual needs. We aim to make residents the designers and builders of their own communities and to increase their sense of belonging. This shift from a passive role to an active role helps residents to self-actualization through their participation in community and social practices.

For example, to help the children of women vendors in the more dangerous areas of two public markets in Accra, Ghana, UN-Habitat and the Mmofra Foundation worked together to implement micro-play spaces for young children. Using Mallam Atta Market and Nima Market as pilot sites, they created child-friendly spaces where children could also receive education. With the participation of the 114-member community, the team identified the issues affecting the children and developed solutions. The result was multi-purpose seating and climbing units at the local market, with interactive art installations on the walls and ceilings to stimulate the senses. The market space was designed to provide recreational activities for more than 100 children per week, alleviating the childcare problems of women vendors.

5 Conclusion

The design of a pedestrian system for community creation emphasizes the full participation of residents, thoroughly explores walking needs, builds human-centered local resources and social relationships, enriches social interaction, and forms cultural consensus, thus enhancing the walking experience of residents. From the perspective of community builders and managers, the humanized design update of the pedestrian system means creating a community environment from a systemic perspective, forming an interpersonal and harmonious communal society, and exploring a more inclusive and open vision of urban construction planning. From the perspective of residents, there is a need to maintain process awareness and confidence in the development of a humane community pedestrian system, which goes a long way.

Acknowledgements. We would like to thank the Joint Supervision Scheme (G-SB3Z) by The Hong Kong Polytechnic University. We also thank the Eric C. Yim Endowed Professorship (8.73.09.847K) for supporting the data analysis, presentation and publication of the paper.

References

1. Cui, J., Lin, D.: Utilisation of underground pedestrian systems for urban sustainability. Tunn. Undergr. Space Technol. **55**, 194–204 (2016)
2. Yamazaki, R.: Community Design. Translated by Hu Shan (2019)
3. Olivastri, C.: Con [temporary]. Design for social innovation. Des. J. **20**(sup1), S2894–S2905 (2017)

4. Mazzarella, F., Mitchell, V., Escobar-Tello, C.: Crafting sustainable futures: the value of the service designer in activating meaningful social innovation from within textile artisan communities. Des. J. **20**(sup1), S2935–S2950 (2017)
5. Pomar, A., Lindsay, G.M.G., Gonçalves, N.M.: Pedestrian systems design. Tecnura **18**, 124–135 (2014)
6. Alfonzo, M.A.: To walk or not to walk? The hierarchy of walking needs. Environ. Behav. **37**(6), 808–836 (2005)
7. Pei, X., Sedini, C., Zurlo, F.: Co-designing a walkable city for the elderly through system thinking approachs (2019)
8. Polus, A., Craus, J.: Planning considerations and evaluation methodology for shared streets. Transp. Q. **42**(4) (1988)
9. Collarte, N.: The woonerf concept. Rethinking a Residential Street in Somerville (2012)
10. Zhong, F., Liu, X.: Design for and by the people: Paths, challenges and opportunities for social innovation. Zhuangshi **5**, 40–45 (2018)
11. https://www.archdaily.com/931255/big-and-wxy-propose-plans-for-a-greener-and-safer-downtown-brooklyn
12. https://www.archdaily.com/944704/100architects-regenerates-pedestrian-bridge-in-shanghai-china-with-colorful-spaces

Robots, Agents, and Intelligent
Environments

Impact of Individual Differences
on the Adoption of Smart Homes

Badar H. Al-Lawati[(⊠)] and Xiaowen Fang

Jarvis College of Computing and Digital Media, DePaul University, 243 S Wabash Avenue,
Suite 806, Chicago, IL 60604, USA
ballawat@depaul.edu, xfang@cdm.depaul.edu

Abstract. With the advancement of Internet of Things (IoT) technologies, the
concept of Smart homes has become widely common. Smart Homes act as an
intelligent house with the ability to acquire knowledge about inhabitants to adapt
and meet the goals of efficiency and automation. However, with this wide advancement in Smart Home technologies, there is a gap between early adopters and the
mass market. Prior research on IoT has focused on the technical functionalities of
the IoT, the communication standards, and the security protocols. Some previous
attempts have used established adoption models to analyze the user acceptance
and adoption of IoT and Smart Home Technologies. However, none of them have
studied the individual differences between users as antecedents impacting the
intention to adopt and use smart home technologies. This research explores and
integrates the level of importance of different tasks at home to form a positive factor
named Perceived Task Necessity. In addition, drawing from previously validated
research, Privacy & Security Risk, and Trust are introduced as antecedents of
perceived behavioral control. Then integrated with the Theory of Planned Behavior and the Big-Five Factors personality model to propose a theoretical model to
explain the users' intention to adopt and use Smart Home Technologies. A 32-item
survey measure is built to test the proposed model and validate the hypotheses.
The instrument is being tested in an online survey. The results of the survey will
be used to verify the validity of the proposed model and show the relationship
between the individual differences, the perceived task necessity, and their attitude
with the intention to adopt and use Smart Home Technologies.

Keywords: Internet of Things · Home automation · Smart homes · Technology
disruption · Theory of planned behavior · Conscientiousness · Perceived task
necessity

1 Introduction

The global Internet of Things (IoT) market spending is expected to exceed 500 billion US
dollars by the end of 2022, and this figure is expected to triple to 1.6 trillion USD by the
end of 2025 [1]. However, it is argued that the smart home market has a big gap between
early adopters of smart home devices and the mass market [2]. Nevertheless, even with
this gap, it is not stopping different manufacturers and suppliers from actively providing

© The Author(s), under exclusive license to Springer Nature Switzerland AG 2022
C. Stephanidis et al. (Eds.): HCII 2022, CCIS 1655, pp. 459–469, 2022.
https://doi.org/10.1007/978-3-031-19682-9_58

smart home services and devices. There is a lack of empirical studies on user behavior, and the adoption and diffusion of smart homes have not been adequately addressed [3]. There is rising evidence that supports the influence of individual differences on IT use, more research is needed to better understand the individual differences that relate to IT acceptance and use [4].

This study aims investigate how personal differences among users will influence their attitudes towards their intention to adopt smart home technologies. To achieve this goal, this study incorporates the Big-Five Personality theory [5, 6] into the Theory of Planned Behavior [7]. The proposed model allows us to explore the impact of individual differences and specific contexts on smart home adoption. This study fills in an important research gap in smart home adoption. The findings will likely provide more concrete and personalized guidelines for the design and marketing of smart home technology.

2 Background

2.1 Internet of Things (IoT)

Majority of the research conducted on the Internet of Things has focused on the technical issues and consequences of the IoT, but very limited work has been done on the impact of the IoT on human behavior and interaction. Academia is trying to catch up with the industry when it comes to the Internet of Things [8]. There is a lack of empirical studies on user behavior and the business aspects of smart home services, which means that the adoption and diffusion of the IoT in the home has not been adequately addressed [3]. This is one of the main reasons that most of the academic research is currently focused on the technical integration and the standardized frameworks of the Internet of Things. Table 1, shows some of the past literature review attempts to evaluate the literature on the concepts of the Internet of Things and Smart Homes.

Table 1. Literature review on internet of things & smart homes

Study	Review criteria	Findings/Observations
[9]	Reviewed 20 publications (from 1999 to 2014) on Internet of Things' definition, history, & evolution	– Lack of a standard definition worldwide – Lack of standardization in the production of IoT technologies – IoT is industry driven rather than research driven
[10]	Evaluated 220 + published articles between 2010 and 2016, on different aspects of Internet of Things	Almost none of those articles focused on the adoption or behavioral impact and assessment of the home automation Internet of Things

(continued)

Table 1. (*continued*)

Study	Review criteria	Findings/Observations
[11]	Conducted a systematic literature review to examine the key drivers, benefits, barriers, and challenges that influence the adoption of the Internet of Things. Identified 253 articles from 2010 to 2017, 46 were systematically reviewed	– Current IoT development efforts: – improved integration – real-time data visibility – business analytics – organizational efficiencies & productivity – Argue that concept of the IoT is still poorly understood by the IS research community
[12]	Systematically reviewed the smart home literature and surveyed the current state of users' perspective. Review included publications from 2002 to 2017, with a total of 143 articles reviewed	– Publications in smart homes do not consider its multidimensionality [13] – The technological focus of the research explains the low acceptance of smart homes in the market [14] – Minimal empirical evidence of the user's perceptions of the benefits and challenges of using smart home devices [15–17]

The Privacy and Security Impact on the Internet of Things. Different studies in the literature assessing the impact of the privacy and security concerns on the adoption of IoT technologies and specifically Smart Home devices were reviewed to confirm the importance of the privacy & security risk as well as trust in the intention to adopt and use smart home technologies [18–20].

Adoption of the Internet of Things. Technology adoption research is usually associated with predicting behavioral outcomes by investigating the relationship between attitudes and intentions. There are many theories that measure the adoption rate of innovation. Many past attempts to study the adoption of Internet of Things & Smart Homes, including the studies by Shin et al. [21] and Park et al. [22] using the Technology Acceptance Model (TAM) [23, 24] and the Updated Technology Acceptance Model (TAM2) [25], the study by Carcary et al. [11] using the Unified Theory of Acceptance and Use of Technology (UTAUT) [26], and finally, the study by Nikou [27] using the Diffusion of Innovations Model [28, 29]. However, despite the growing number of studies into the adoption and usage intentions of smart home technologies, almost none of the proposed models, nor the foundation frameworks study the individual differences between users as antecedents impacting the intention to adopt and use smart home technologies.

2.2 The Theory of Planned Behavior (TPB)

The Theory of Planned Behavior [7] states that the behavioral intention is an indication of the strength of a person's willingness to try to perform a certain behavior and it is thus well suited to be the basis of the proposed model.

Yang et al. [3] presents a theoretical model by extending the Theory of Planned Behavior by adding antecedents reflecting usability, the potential risks of smart home services, and reliable service providers in terms of attitude, subjective norm, and perceived behavioral control. However, just like the other attempts in assessing the adoption of IoT and Smart Homes, they did not account for the individual differences between the participants. The antecedents in Yang et al.'s case relate to the technology and the risk and trust factors of the assessed technologies. It has been suggested that additional behavior-specific cognitive constructs that are clearer determinants of behavior, such as past behaviors could enhance the model's predictive utility and would have direct impacts on the intention formation and behavior, effects currently not explained by the Theory of Planned Behavior [30].

2.3 The Big Five Personality Model

There is a general consensus within the field that supports the stability of the Five-Factors Model across a variety of samples [5, 31, 32]. This model creates a set of very broad dimensions that represents individual differences, and that these dimensions can be measured with high reliability and impressive validity [33]. Barnett et al. [34] attempt to use the Five-Factors Model to understand the adoption and use of technology through linking its components with the UTAUT. Zhou et al. [35] use the Five-Factors Model to understand the adoption of mobile commerce, where they link the model with constructs of the Theory Acceptance Model. As expected, there was a strong direct positive relationship between conscientiousness with the expected and actual use of technology from both studies. Results show that Individuals who score higher on conscientiousness have the tendency to initially make plans and then commit to them, while the ones who score lower on conscientiousness tend to be more careless and subjective in changing their plans.

3 Conceptual Model

This study aims to investigate how personal differences among users will influence their attitudes towards their intention to adopt and use smart home technologies. Most Smart Home technologies (IoT devices) are adopted by choice. Past studies show that people are motivated by a desire to control their environment [36, 37]. To get individuals motivated to adopt and use smart home technologies, more research on user behavior is required, as service providers and manufacturers must satisfy a real need for the end user to allow for mass "diffusion and successful adoption of the services" [3].

The degree of voluntariness to use an invention has been found to impact attitudes toward use of an innovation [38]. As such, personal preferences and individual differences are expected to play a major role in the adoption process, and therefore personality has a great impact on this situation. That is the same reason that makes Smart Home technologies very distinct from other technologies used at home. For example, when it comes to cleaning the house, to get the task done individuals will have the option to use a broom or get an electrical vacuum machine. Opting to get a smart self-guided vacuum machine is a personal preference, but that's not going to change the task on hand, which is cleaning the house.

Personality attributes have recently been found to explain a big portion of the variance in behavior towards adopting new innovations, which provides more insights into user behavior [39]. The Five-Factor Model (FFM) has been widely used by the IS community to understand user behavior. Among those five factors, conscientiousness has been found to be the most consistently related to intentions and behaviors [40]. In this study, we attempt to add conscientiousness from the FFM in addition to other antecedents to the constructs of TPB. This is done to account for the personality differences between users of smart home technologies, to assess and predict the users' behaviors towards adopting and using smart home technologies.

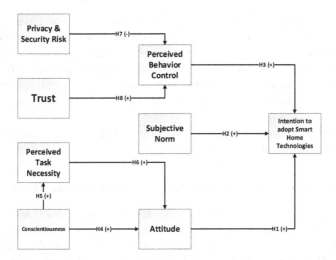

Fig. 1. Research model: smart homes adoption model

Figure 1 presents the proposed model in this study. The Smart homes adoption model. This study defines each of the constructs and develops a theoretical basis for the relationships between the antecedents and the constructs in the model.

3.1 Attitude and Intention to Adopt Smart Homes

This study defines attitude as the degree to which a person makes a favorable or unfavorable assessment or appraisal regarding using smart home technologies. Prior studies on technology adoption have considered the role of attitude as an important determinant influencing the intention to use [41, 42]. It was found that attitude towards using a smart meter (a Smart Home device) had a positive effect on the intention to use it [43]. And that attitude towards IoT services positively impact the intention to use those services [44]. Based on previous findings, the first hypothesis in this study:

H1. Attitude towards smart home technologies is positively associated with the intention to adopt and/or use them.

3.2   Subjective Norm and Intention to Adopt Smart Homes

This study defines subjective norms as the perceived social pressure to use or not use Smart Home Technologies. Prospect users of new technologies at the early stage of diffusion don't have enough information to make a decision about using the technology. Hence, an individual's decision to adopt new technologies may be influenced by others' suggestions or opinions within the social system [45]. The following hypothesis is proposed:

H2. Subjective norm is positively associated with the intention to adopt and/or use smart home technologies.

3.3   Perceived Behavioral Control and Intention to Adopt Smart Homes

In this study, perceived behavioral control is defined as the prospect users' perception of how easy or difficult it is to use smart home technologies. Multiple empirical studies have identified the relationship between the perceived behavioral control with intentions and found that the perceived behavioral control is positively associated with behavioral intention [46, 47]. Other studies show that perceived behavioral control positively influences the intention to use mobile data services [48–50]. The following hypothesis is proposed:

H3. Perceived behavioral control is positively associated with the intention to adopt and/or use smart home technologies.

3.4   Conscientiousness and Attitudes Towards Adopting Smart Homes

In their original article introducing the FFM Model [6], it is stated that Conscientiousness is about showing self-discipline, acting dutifully, and aiming for achievement against measures or outside expectations, and that it measures how individuals are governed and organized by themselves, as these individuals are thorough, efficient, and organized. This study adopts the original definition. Recently, Information systems research has started to use personality assessments to understand the user behavior towards different technologies, and the Big-Five Factors Model is the most used assessment [51–53]. From those five personality traits, conscientiousness has been found to be consistently associated with intentions of behaviors [40], making it the most important personality trait in relation to behaviors. The following hypothesis is proposed:

H4. Conscientiousness is positively associated with the attitude.

3.5   Conscientiousness, Perceived Task Necessity, and Attitude

This study defines Perceived Task Necessity as the extent to which a user believes the task is essential or critical to him/her. The study of task has been the focus of many multi-disciplinary scholars in the past. Scholars from behavior sciences have argued that the nature of a task plays an essential role in a group's interaction process and performance. The role of necessity and sufficiency relationships in conditional sourcing was examined, and found a strong indication that perceived necessity sufficiency predicted variability in reasoning performance [54]. Despite the focus on studying task importance across different fields, perceived task necessity has not been defined nor studied in the past. In this study, we introduce perceived task necessity as an important antecedent influencing individual attitudes towards adopting and/or using smart home technologies. We are also introducing conscientiousness as an antecedent impacting the perceived task necessity. The following hypotheses are proposed:

H5. Conscientiousness is positively associated with perceived task necessity.

H6. Perceived Task Necessity is positively associated with the attitude.

3.6 Security & Privacy Risk and Perceived Behavioral Control Towards Adopting Smart Homes

This study defines Security & Privacy Risk as an individual's belief in the possibility of uncertain adverse events caused by common digital threats such as fraud, identity theft, and unauthorized access, collection, sharing, and disclosure of personal information from the use of smart home technologies. A strong negative influence of security & privacy risk on attitudes towards adopting smart home meters was found [55]. However, the absence of privacy protection has influenced the adoption and usage of different IoT technologies [44]. Despite the importance of the latest developments within the field of Internet of Things, researchers don't know much about the end-users' privacy thoughts and attitudes within the usage and adoption of IoT [56]. Based on previous findings, this study proposes the following hypothesis:

H7. Security & Privacy Risk is negatively associated with Perceived Behavioral Control.

3.7 Trust and Perceived Behavioral Control Towards Adopting Smart Homes

For a long time, trust has been considered a pillar of reducing vulnerability and uncertainty in buyer-seller transactions [57–60]. This study defines trust as the degree of the user's belief in the Smart Home service provider's beneficence and technical ability to protect their interests and security. Trust was found to have an influence on the acceptance of internet technologies [61]. Based on previous findings, this study proposes the following hypothesis:

H8. Trust in technology providers is positively associated with Perceived Behavioral Control.

4 Research Methodology

A questionnaire has been developed to measure the constructs using items from prior research. An online survey of smart home technologies users is being conducted to test the hypotheses described earlier. Structural Equation Modeling (SEM) will be used to test the fit of the proposed model, and each hypothesized relationship. SEM was chosen because it allows the entire model to be tested while mathematically considering measurement error (Table 2).

Table 2. Instrument to test the hypotheses

Construct	Number of items adopted	Source
Attitude	4-item measurement adopted	[47, 62]
Subjective norm	3-item measurement adopted	[62]
Perceived behavioral control	3-item measurement adopted	[47, 62]
Intention to use	3-item measurement adopted	[47, 62]
Conscientiousness	5-items measurement adopted	[63]
Perceived task necessity	4-item measurement developed	Self-Developed
Security & privacy risk	5-items measurement adopted	[55, 64]
Trust	5-items measurement adopted	[55, 64]

5 Next Steps

We have started the data collection to validate the survey instrument. We anticipate sharing the results and outcome of this data collection during the conference.

References

1. Vailshery, L.S.: Forecast end-user spending on IoT solutions worldwide from 2017 to 2025 (2021). https://www.statista.com/
2. Greenough, J.: The US smart home market has been struggling—here's how and why the market will take off. Business Insider (2016). http://www.businessinsider.com/the-us-smart-home-marketreport-adoption-forecasts-top-products-and-the-cost-and-fragmentation-pro blems-that-could-hindergrowth-2015-9. Accessed 26 May 2017
3. Yang, H., Lee, H., Zo, H.: User acceptance of smart home services: an extension of the theory of planned behavior. Ind. Manag. Data Syst. (2017)
4. Thatcher, J.B., Perrewe, P.L.: An empirical examination of individual traits as antecedents to computer anxiety and computer self-efficacy. MIS Q., 381–396 (2002)
5. McCrae, R.R., Costa, P.T., Jr.: Rotation to maximize the construct validity of factors in the NEO Personality Inventory. Multivar. Behav. Res. **24**(1), 107–124 (1989)
6. McCrae, R.R., John, O.P.: An introduction to the five-factor model and its applications. J. Pers. **60**(2), 175–215 (1992)
7. Ajzen, I.: The theory of planned behavior. Organ. Behav. Hum. Decis. Process. **50**(2), 179–211 (1991)
8. Ning, H., Hu, S.: Technology classification, industry, and education for Future Internet of Things. Int. J. Commun. Syst **25**(9), 1230–1241 (2012)
9. Madakam, S., et al.: Internet of Things (IoT): a literature review. J. Comput. Commun. 3(05), 164 (2015)
10. Alaa, M., et al.: A review of smart home applications based on Internet of Things. J. Netw. Comput. Appl. **97**, 48–65 (2017)
11. Carcary, M., Maccani, G., Doherty, E., Conway, G.: Exploring the determinants of iot adoption: findings from a systematic literature review. In: Zdravkovic, J., Grabis, J., Nurcan, S., Stirna, J. (eds.) BIR 2018. LNBIP, vol. 330, pp. 113–125. Springer, Cham (2018). https://doi.org/10.1007/978-3-319-99951-7_8

12. Marikyan, D., Papagiannidis, S., Alamanos, E.: A systematic review of the smart home literature: a user perspective. Technol. Forecast. Soc. Chang. **138**, 139–154 (2019)
13. Balta-Ozkan, N., Boteler, B., Amerighi, O.: European smart home market development: public views on technical and economic aspects across the United Kingdom, Germany and Italy. Energy Res. Soc. Sci. **3**, 65–77 (2014)
14. Chan, M., et al.: A review of smart homes-present state and future challenges. Comput. Methods Programs Biomed. **91**(1), 55–81 (2008)
15. Peek, S.T., et al.: Factors influencing acceptance of technology for aging in place: a systematic review. Int. J, Med. Inf. **83**(4), 235–248 (2014)
16. Czaja, S.J.: Long-term care services and support systems for older adults: the role of technology. Am. Psychol. **71**(4), 294 (2016)
17. Kun, L.G.: Telehealth and the global health network in the 21st century. From homecare to public health informatics. Comput. Methods Programs Biomed. **64**(3), 155–167 (2001)
18. Tarabasz, A.: The Internet of Things-digital revolution in offline market. Opportunity or threat? Handel Wewn?trzny **363**(4), 325–337 (2016)
19. Weber, R.H.: Internet of Things-new security and privacy challenges. Comput. Law Secur. Rev. **26**(1), 23–30 (2010)
20. Yang, Y., et al.: A survey on security and privacy issues in Internet-of-Things. IEEE Internet Things J. **4**(5), 1250–1258 (2017)
21. Shin, J., Park, Y., Lee, D.: Who will be smart home users? An analysis of adoption and diffusion of smart homes. Technol. Forecast. Soc. Change **134**, 246–253 (2018)
22. Park, E., et al.: Smart home services as the next mainstream of the ICT industry: determinants of the adoption of smart home services. Univ. Access Inf. Soc. **17**(1), 175–190 (2018)
23. Davis, F.D.: A technology acceptance model for empirically testing new end-user information systems: Theory and results. Massachusetts Institute of Technology (1985)
24. Davis, F.D.: Perceived usefulness, perceived ease of use, and user acceptance of information technology. MIS Q. 319–340 (1989)
25. Venkatesh, V., Davis, F.D.: A theoretical extension of the technology acceptance model: four longitudinal field studies. Manag. Sci. **46**(2), 186–204 (2000)
26. Venkatesh, V., et al.: User acceptance of information technology: toward a unified view. MIS Q. 425–478 (2003)
27. Nikou, S.: Factors driving the adoption of smart home technology: an empirical assessment. Telematics Inform. **45**, 101283 (2019)
28. Rogers, E.M.: Diffusion of Innovations. Simon and Schuster (2010)
29. Rogers, E.M.: Diffusion of Innovations. 12, New York (1995)
30. Bentler, P.M., Speckart, G.: Models of attitude-behavior relations. Psychol. Rev. **86**(5), 452 (1979)
31. Costa, P.T., McCrae, R.R.: Four ways five factors are basic. Pers. Individ. Differ. **13**(6), 653–665 (1992)
32. Costa, P.T., McCrae, R.R.: Personality in adulthood: a six-year longitudinal study of self-reports and spouse ratings on the NEO Personality Inventory. J. Pers. Soc. Psychol. **54**(5), 853 (1988)
33. Digman, J.M.: Personality structure: emergence of the five-factor model. Annu. Rev. Psychol. **41**(1), 417–440 (1990)
34. Barnett, T., et al.: Five-factor model personality traits as predictors of perceived and actual usage of technology. Eur. J. Inf. Syst. **24**(4), 374–390 (2015)
35. Zhou, T., Lu, Y.: The effects of personality traits on user acceptance of mobile commerce. Intl. J. Hum.-Comput. Inter. **27**(6), 545–561 (2011)
36. DeCharms, R.: Personal causation. J. Appl. Soc. Psychol. **2**(2), 95–113 (1968)
37. White, R.W.: Motivation reconsidered: the concept of competence. Psychol. Rev. **66**(5), 297 (1959)

38. Moore, M.G.: Three Types of Interaction. Taylor & Francis (1989)
39. Shropshire, J., Warkentin, M., Sharma, S.: Personality, attitudes, and intentions: predicting initial adoption of information security behavior. Comput. Secur. **49**, 177–191 (2015)
40. Conner, M., Abraham, C.: Conscientiousness and the theory of planned behavior: toward a more complete model of the antecedents of intentions and behavior. Pers. Soc. Psychol. Bull. **27**(11), 1547–1561 (2001)
41. Bauer, H.H., et al.: Driving consumer acceptance of mobile marketing: a theoretical framework and empirical study. J. Electron. Commer. Res. **6**(3), 181 (2005)
42. Zhou, L., Dai, L., Zhang, D.: Online shopping acceptance model-a critical survey of consumer factors in online shopping. J. Electron. Commer. Res. **8**(1), 41 (2007)
43. Kranz, L., Gallenkamp, J., Picot, A.O.: Exploring the role of control-smart meter acceptance of residential consumers (2010)
44. Hsu, C.-L., Lin, J.C.-C.: An empirical examination of consumer adoption of Internet of Things services: network externalities and concern for information privacy perspectives. Comput. Hum. Behav. **62**, 516–527 (2016)
45. Hu, P.J.-H., Clark, T.H., Ma, W.W.: Examining technology acceptance by school teachers: a longitudinal study. Inf. Manag. **41**(2), 227–241 (2003)
46. Madden, T.J., Ellen, P.S., Ajzen, I.: A comparison of the theory of planned behavior and the theory of reasoned action. Pers. Soc. Psychol. Bull. **18**(1), 3–9 (1992)
47. Taylor, S., Todd, P.A.: Understanding information technology usage: a test of competing models. Inf. Syst. Res. **6**(2), 144–176 (1995)
48. Deng, Z., Mo, X., Liu, S.: Comparison of the middle-aged and older users' adoption of mobile health services in China. Int. J. Med. Inf. **83**(3), 210–224 (2014)
49. Kim, B.: An empirical investigation of mobile data service continuance: incorporating the theory of planned behavior into the expectation-confirmation model. Expert Syst. Appl. **37**(10), 7033–7039 (2010)
50. Lu, M.-T., et al.: Exploring mobile banking services for user behavior in intention adoption: using new hybrid MADM model. Serv. Bus. **9**(3), 541–565 (2015)
51. Karim, N.S.A., Zamzuri, N.H.A., Nor, Y.M.: Exploring the relationship between internet ethics in university students and the big five model of personality. Comput. Educ. **53**(1), 86–93 (2009)
52. Shropshire, J., et al.: Personality and IT security: an application of the five-factor model. In: AMCIS 2006 Proceedings, p. 415 (2006)
53. Warkentin, M., et al.: The role of individual characteristics on insider abuse intentions (2012)
54. Thompson, V.A.: Interpretational factors in conditional reasoning. Mem. Cogn. **22**(6), 742–758 (1994)
55. Lee, M.: An empirical study of home IoT services in South Korea: the moderating effect of the usage experience. Int. J. Hum.-Comput. Inter. **35**(7), 535–547 (2019)
56. Padyab, A., Ståhlbröst, A.: Exploring the dimensions of individual privacy concerns in relation to the Internet of Things use situations. Digit. Policy Regul. Governance (2018)
57. Doney, P.M., Cannon, J.P.: An examination of the nature of trust in buyer-seller relationships. J. Mark. **61**(2), 35–51 (1997)
58. Luhmann, N.: Trust and Power (John A. Wiley and Sons, Chichester), NewYork (1979)
59. Pavlou, P.A.: Consumer acceptance of electronic commerce: integrating trust and risk with the technology acceptance model. Int. J. Electron. Commer. **7**(3), 101–134 (2003)
60. Ring, P.S., Van de Ven, A.H.: Developmental processes of cooperative interorganizational relationships. Acad. Manag. Rev. **19**(1), 90–118 (1994)
61. Gefen, D.: E-commerce: the role of familiarity and trust. Omega **28**(6), 725–737 (2000)
62. Mathieson, K.: Predicting user intentions: comparing the technology acceptance model with the theory of planned behavior. Inf. Syst. Res. **2**(3), 173–191 (1991)

63. Goldberg, L.R.: The development of markers for the big-five factor structure. Psychol. Assess. **4**(1), 26 (1992)
64. Malhotra, N.K., Kim, S.S., Agarwal, J.: Internet users' information privacy concerns (IUIPC): the construct, the scale, and a causal model. Inf. Syst. Res. **15**(4), 336–355 (2004)

A Method to Check that Participants Really are Imagining Artificial Minds When Ascribing Mental States

Hal Ashton🆔 and Matija Franklin$^{(\boxtimes)}$ 🆔

University College London, London WC1E 6BT, UK
ucabha5@ucl.ac.uk

Abstract. Written vignettes are often used in experiments to explore potential differences between the way participants interpret the behaviour and mental states of artificial autonomous actors (hence A-bots) contrasted against human actors. A reoccurring result from this body of research has been the similarity of results in mental-state attributions between A-bots and humans. This paper reports the results of a short measure consisting of four questions. We find that by asking participants about whether A-bots can feel pain or pleasure, whether they deserve rights, or whether they would be good parents, satisfactory differences can be derived between human and A-bot groups. By asking these questions, experimenters can be more confident that participants are constructing mental representations of A-bots differently than those of humans.

Keywords: Mental states · Inference · Human-AI interaction · Evaluation

1 Introduction

Written vignettes are often used in experiments to explore potential differences between the way participants interpret the behaviour and mental states of artificial autonomous actors (hence A-bots) contrasted against human actors [1]. These A-bots might be physically embodied Robots and could be driven by some sort of Artificial Intelligence though neither feature is necessary. They might equally be something unembodied like a chat-bot following a limited script. Vignettes have a long history of use in experimental psychology and human-computer interaction research as they offer the experimenter the chance to ask questions that would not be otherwise feasible to ask (morally, logistically, or otherwise) if a fuller recreation were required [2].

A reoccurring result from this body of research has been the similarity of results in mental-state attributions between A-bots and humans [3–5]. These 'no-difference' results could mean that participants are genuinely willing to ascribe advanced mental states to A-bots even perhaps when these mental states are not possible. Equally, these results could also mean that the experiment subjects were thinking of the A-bot as a human when making their attributions. This criticism can be made for both between and within-subject experiment designs.

© The Author(s), under exclusive license to Springer Nature Switzerland AG 2022
C. Stephanidis et al. (Eds.): HCII 2022, CCIS 1655, pp. 470–474, 2022.
https://doi.org/10.1007/978-3-031-19682-9_59

This brief paper presents the results of an initial study concerning the types of stimuli comprehension questions that best separate subjects considering A-bots from those considering humans and offers some theoretical reasoning for the results. We find that by asking participants about whether A-bots can feel pain, or whether they deserve rights, satisfactory differences can be derived between human and A-bot groups. By asking questions that separate subjects well, experimenters can be more confident that participants are constructing mental representations of A-bots differently than those of humans, and the elicitations which draw the same response between both groups are genuine in the sense they represent commonalities between the two mental representations.

2 Background

Recent empirical work on people's attributions, judgments, and inferences toward Artificial Intelligence (AI) has delivered mixed findings [1, 6, 7]. These judgments often do not meet normative expectations [8, 9]. People's judgments of others are informed by the inferences they make about their mental states [10, 11]. Questions relating to mental states provide an opportunity to develop stimuli which could separate subjects judging A-bots versus humans. This approach assumes that people's mental state inferences between the two agents will differ.

Previous research has explored the mental states people attribute to machines, such as robots, computers, and AI. Famously, Gray and colleagues (2007) found that people attribute mental states along two dimensions: *agency* - the capacity to perform goal-orientated actions, and *experience* - the capacity to feel something; which are adjacent to what philosopher's of mind call *intentional* and *phenomenal* states, respectively [12]. People were happy to attribute agency, but not experience to a robot. Sytsma and Machery (2010) move away from this and posit a distinction between mental states based on whether or not they pose *valence* or *hedonic value* [13]. Some mental states bring about a pleasant or unpleasant feeling (are *valenced*), while others do not contain such are features (are *unvalenced*). People resist attributing robots' states with hedonic value. Buckwalter and Phelan (2013) challenge this hedonic account and instead argue that folk attributions of mental states are based on the perceived functional role an object is designed to realize [14]. Huebner (2010) similarly argues that people's attributions of both phenomenal and intentional mental states rely on functional considerations [15]. Objects that otherwise would not be attributed a phenomenal state will when the question relates to their function.

There is evidence for dual systems which form attributions of mental states - a deliberative and an automatic system [3]. The influence of one of these systems on the final mental state attribution is to some extent dependent on the experimental setup. Vignette designs that give participants more freedom over how to describe a robot find that participants are reluctant to attribute phenomenal mental states to robots [3]. People's automatic systems can be triggered to attribute phenomenal states to robots with faces, distinctive motion trajectories, and contingent interactions. Altogether it appears that people can resist attributing phenomenal mental states to robots, but during actual interactions with robots are likely to attribute phenomenal mental states to machines.

The study presented here aimed to develop items that would produce a difference in people's mental state attributions towards Humans and A-bots. In order to do so, it used a vignette-based approach in order to engage with people's deliberative capacities. It also aimed at not anthropomorphizing the A-bot in order to reduce any automatic triggers that would result in the attribution of phenomenal states towards it. The motivation for developing these items was twofold. First, as a useful tool for inducing a deliberative state at the beginning of a study for research that is trying to explore people's judgments of humans and AIs. Second, to identify people that do think that two agents have the same mental state. Such participants can be further explored or excluded from the research as it is more likely that they are not paying attention to the experimental setting, thus making their attributions less valid to use. Thus, a criterium was that these items needed to be short, and minimal in number.

3 The Study

Participants ($N = 301$) first completed a study where, in separate groups, they had to attribute responsibility to either a human or an A-bot performing the task of a parcel courier or coffee barista (this study will be separately reported elsewhere). They were then given four questions which asked them whether the human or AI: 1) felt pain, 2) was passionate about their job, 3) should receive the same legal rights as everyone else, and 4) would make a good parent. To each question, participants could respond with "yes" or "no", with the addition of a "not applicable" answer for the parenting question. Participants were under no time pressure to respond to these questions.

The justification for the four questions is as follows. Pain was selected as a mental state that can be described, in relation to the previous literature, as pertaining to experience [12], containing valence [13], or otherwise a phenomenal state. Further, previous research finds that attributions of pain produced bigger differences between humans and robots than attributions of happiness [15]. Passion is another experiential state, likely to produce a difference, but might be lower, as it relates to an agent's perceived functional role. Thus, in relation to Buckwalter and Phelan's (2013) account [14], passion does not produce as big of a difference, as both humans and AIs would have the same role of either a coffee barista or parcel courier. Legal rights did not pertain to a mental state, and thus the questions sought to engage with the participant's normative assumptions about the agents. We assumed that most people would think that a human deserved more legal rights than an A-bot. Finally, participants were asked about parenting, as it was another question that pertained to a role, but in this case, not a role that the agents were assigned to in our study. More specifically, in line with normative and biological expectations, we assumed that most participants would view parenting as a role that pertained to people rather than AIs and would thus produce a difference.

Descriptive statistics were performed and are available in Table 1. Chi-Square analysis was used to examine the difference between humans and AIs on pain, passion, legal rights, and parenting. For the parents variable, due to missing data (i.e., answers with "N/A") a total of 140 participants were removed, with 161 participants remaining. All four Chi-Squares produced a significant result: pain [X^2 (1, $N = 301$) = 216.04, $p <$ .001], passion [X^2 (1, $N = 301$) = 7.44, $p = .006$], legal rights [X^2 (1, $N = 301$) = 115.89, $p < .001$], and parenting [X^2 (1, $N = 161$) = 16.41, $< .001$].

Table 1. Results

	Pain		Passion		Rights		Parenting		
	No	Yes	No	Yes	No	Yes	N/A	No	Yes
A-bot	138	11	22	127	100	49	48	100	1
Human	12	140	42	110	11	141	92	49	11

4 Discussion and Conclusion

We will now discuss our four findings. In line with previous research [15] pain produced large significant differences between people and A-bots. When responding to vignettes that are more likely to trigger people's deliberative capacities, people are likely to distinguish people from A-bot on the pain dimension [3]. People were significantly more likely to ascribe pain to a human rather than to an A-bot. Passion also produced a significant difference, with the lowest effect size out of the four variables. This can be interpreted in relation to previous research which posits that as the two agents have the same role - being a coffee barista or parcel courier - and thus both agents would be ascribed to the phenomenal mental state that relates to this role (i.e., passion for the work) [14]. A potential problem with this question in the chosen setting is that both it might be difficult for people to imagine other humans being passionate about their Barista or Courier jobs. This could be explored by comparing the effects size with roles where a vocation might more easily be imagined (teacher or nurse say)Legal rights produced a significant difference - people thought that other people deserved more rights than AIs did. Thus, participants' judgments matched normative expectations around the existing legal rights of humans and the non-existing legal rights of A-bot. Finally, there were significant differences between a person and an A-bot when it came to good parenting. This matched normative assumptions.

Our findings have implications for research exploring people's attributions, judgments or inferences towards A-bots, and how they may differ from humans. Contrasting people's ascriptions of pain, passion, legal rights and parenting aptitude between humans and A-bots, we found humans to be given statistically significantly higher scores on all dimensions. This measure can thus be used as a tool for gauging whether participants really are imagining A-bots when ascribing mental states to them in vignette studies. These items can validate the presence of a difference mental models between humans and A-bots.

References

1. Awad, E., et al.: Blaming humans in autonomous vehicle accidents: shared responsibility across levels of automation (2018). arXiv preprint arXiv:1803.07170
2. Schweigert, W.A.: Research Methods in Psychology: A Handbook. Waveland Press, Long Grove (2021)
3. Fiala, B., Arico, A., Nichols, S.: You, robot (2014)

4. Kneer, M.: Can a robot lie? exploring the folk concept of lying as applied to artificial agents. Cogn. Sci. **45**(10), e13032 (2021)

5. Thellman, S., Silvervarg, A., Ziemke, T.: Folk-psychological interpretation of human vs. humanoid robot behavior: exploring the intentional stance toward robots. Front. Psychol. **8**(NOV), 1–14 (2017)

6. Hidalgo, C.A., Orghian, D., Canals, J.A., De Almeida, F., Martin, N.: How Humans Judge Machines. MIT Press, Cambridge (2021)

7. Tobia, K., Nielsen, A., Stremitzer, A.: When does physician use of AI increase liability? J. Nucl. Med. **62**(1), 17–21 (2021)

8. Ashton, H., Franklin, M., Lagnado, D.: Testing a definition of intent for AI in a legal setting. Submitted manuscript (2022)

9. Franklin, M., Awad, E., Lagnado, D.: Blaming automated vehicles in difficult situations. Iscience **24**(4), 102252 (2021)

10. Laurent, S.M., Nuñez, N.L., Schweitzer, K.A.: The influence of desire and knowledge on perception of each other and related mental states, and different mechanisms for blame. J. Exp. Soc. Psychol. **60**, 27–38 (2015)

11. Malle, B.F., Guglielmo, S., Guglielmo, A.E.: Moral, cognitive, and social: the nature of blame. Social Think. Interpers. Behav., 313–331 (2012)

12. Gray, H.M., Gray, K., Wegner, D.M.: Dimensions of mind perception. Science **315**(5812), 619 (2007)

13. Sytsma, J., Machery, E.: Two conceptions of subjective experience. Philos. Stud. **151**(2), 299–327 (2010)

14. Buckwalter, W., Phelan, M.: Function and feeling machines: a defense of the philosophical conception of subjective experience. Philos. Stud. **166**(2), 349–361 (2012). https://doi.org/10.1007/s11098-012-0039-9

15. Huebner, B.: Commonsense concepts of phenomenal consciousness: does anyone care about functional zombies? Phenomenol. Cogn. Sci. **9**(1), 133–155 (2010)

Comparison of Innovative Strategy of Smart City in Italy, United Kingdom, United States and Spain

Asriadi Rahmad and Achmad Nurmandi[✉]

Master of Government Affairs and Administration, Jusuf Kalla School Government, Universitas Muhammadiyah Yogyakarta, Yogyakarta, Indonesia
asriadi.psc21@mail.umy.ac.id, nurmandi_achmad@umy.ac.id

Abstract. The study aims to analyze the success of the Smart City strategy in Italy, England, the United States, and Spain. This study uses qualitative research methods with bibliometric analysis. Data for 501 articles were obtained from Scopus keywords "Smart City" and "Project," the definition of social science in the last ten years. The four highest countries are Italy 66, United Kingdom 58, United States 54 and Spain 42. Data analysis uses VOSviewer and NVivo12 software to find trending themes. The results show that the strategy's success is supported by three factors, system, application, and government. Italy focuses on applications and systems; application development includes building platforms, open-source technologies, and urban data platforms. System development emphasizes the design of support systems, system effectiveness, and transportation systems. The UK focuses on applications and governance, including application development, collaborative innovation platforms, data security, and transport infrastructure projects. Development is directed at city administrators, mobile data-centric service development, and ICT-driven policymaking. The United States focuses on government development, city challenges, sustainable development, and urban development. Spain focuses on application development, efficient energy, competent government, and urban participatory policymaking. The success of the smart city strategy is strongly influenced by application development. Future research is expected to discuss empirical testing of the conceptual framework developed by intelligent cities with the web of science.

Keywords: Comparison · Innovative strategy · Smart city

1 Introduction

In recent years, smart cities have become an essential strategy in various countries to create livable, sustainable, and functional cities [1]. Smart City is an application based on the use and development of the Internet of Things (IoT) [2]. It aims to encourage the sustainability of the city and the community's quality of life by presenting solutions that can solve various problems efficiently [3]. However, in its application, many are still not

---

The original version of this chapter was revised: The last name has been added for the first author. The correction to this chapter is available at https://doi.org/10.1007/978-3-031-19682-9_92

C. Stephanidis et al. (Eds.): HCII 2022, CCIS 1655, pp. 475–482, 2022.
https://doi.org/10.1007/978-3-031-19682-9_60

on target according to what is expected. This is due to several factors such as a shortage of experts in the field of Smart City, political unrest, poor interconnection with existing laws, and excessive bureaucracy [4].

The smart city project has attracted significant attention as an initiative in increasing urban development, so a particular strategy is needed that must be developed in implementing Smart City to provide good services to the public [5]. The specific strategies in question, including building a Smart City district, where information and communication technology (ICT) must be integrated into the infrastructure to control and control city functions in innovative ways, a framework is needed to be developed to analyze the complexity in the urban planning process by determining the dimensions of intelligence, which is the main focus of each stakeholder and analyzes the consequences [6].

Countries in the European Union have begun to carry out many research projects that create innovative strategies for Smart Cities, where European cities currently accommodate 72% of the population and will very likely increase to 80% by 2050 [7]. Thus, developing innovative project strategies in Smart City is essential to encourage sustainable development and facilitate participatory communities in effectively accessing urban systems. The sophistication of technology and applications in managing real life to develop service innovations and increase the involvement of all urban stakeholders [8].

2 Literature Review

2.1 Challenges of Smart City Innovative Strategies

Smart City has faced many enormous social, ecological, and technological challenges in today's era, including digitalization, democratic aspirations, and security. Multi-stakeholder involvement is needed to create innovative projects as a form of strategy, considering various perspectives and developing a shared city vision [9]. The policy has attracted a lot of attention and funding in recent years. Especially in smart city innovation, as a positive impact of policies to increase urban economic growth involving large multinational companies, local public authorities, and local companies originating from technology to technology overflow [10].

2.2 Smart City

The Smart City concept using information and communication technology is a significant factor in mitigating the impact of rapid urbanization and is considered feasible. However, policymaking in selecting technology to provide better services to the community because ensuring sustainable development is a multi-functional decision process usually carried out by relevant experts [11]. On the other hand, Smart City encourages the integration of sensors and big data through the Internet of Things (IoT) which brings new things to city design and management, and economic prospects. Meanwhile, big data processing with Artificial Intelligence (AI) also contributes significantly to urban structure, and liveability should not be ruled out in technology [12].

3 Method

This research method uses qualitative research with a bibliometric analysis approach to identify the literature contributing to the Smart City strategy. The aim was to ensure high-quality, objective results and analyzed using VOSviewer and NVivo plus 12 software to visualize a term co-occurrence and keyword co-occurrence from the published literature. In addition, NVivo plus 12 makes it more compatible with thematic analysis approaches by presenting an easy-to-understand structure (Fig. 1).

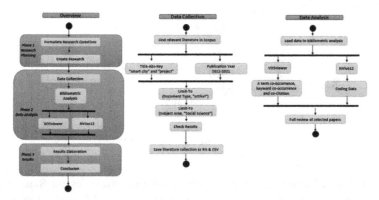

Fig. 1. Research steps in innovative strategy of smart city

4 Results and Discussions

4.1 Trending Smart City in Ten Years

The search results show 501 articles related to innovative, intelligent city project strategies on the Scopus website with "Smart City" and "Project" articles documenting boundaries and social science areas in the last ten years (Fig. 2).

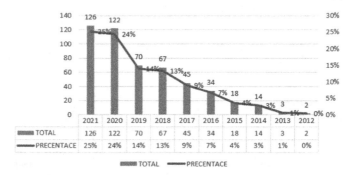

	2021	2020	2019	2018	2017	2016	2015	2014	2013	2012
TOTAL	126	122	70	67	45	34	18	14	3	2
PRECENTAGE	25%	24%	14%	13%	9%	7%	4%	3%	1%	0%

Fig. 2. Trending project of smart city in 2012–2021

Seeing these developments, research on innovative project strategies in the last ten years has continued to increase. The year 2021 is the highest data, there are 126 articles produced, and the percentage reaches 25%. This means that innovative projects are widely discussed in European countries to develop innovative Smart City strategies for efficient urban services to the public. The data obtained placed the four highest countries in developing innovative project strategies (Fig. 3).

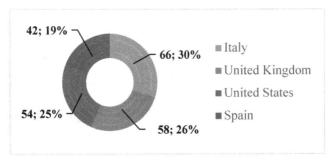

Fig. 3. Four highest countries in 2012–2021

The highest achievements in developing innovative strategies for Smart City are Italy's 66 articles, the United Kingdom's 58 articles, United States' 54 articles, and Spain's 42 articles. The theme "Programming environments: Environmentality and citizen sensing in the smart city Open Access" is the most popular research cited, with 324 citations discussing the distribution of governance within and through the environment and environmental technologies [13].

4.2 Visualization of Innovative Strategy of Smart City

The strategy of innovative Smart City projects in four countries has various research themes focused on interconnectedness in the social field if it is observed by Co-Occurrence that in 2019 the objects of new research that are most widely discussed are IoT, E-Government, Energy Transition, and Economy. Meanwhile, specifically for

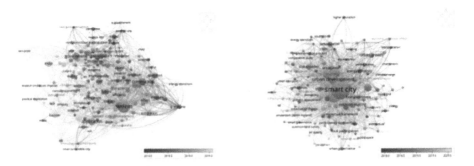

Fig. 4. Co-occurrence and co-occurrence of keywords in project of smart city

Co-Occurrence of keywords, the articles in 2018 mainly discussed innovative Smart City strategies, such as urban development, urban growth, urban area, urban design, urban governance, urban regeneration, technological development, and economy (Fig. 4).

The following year, based on the Co-Occurrence of Keyword, the research continued to develop into several studies, including Infrastructure planning, information management, urban transport, technology, and energy transition. While the objects of discussion related to the study of social science in implementing the success of the Smart City strategy are systems, applications, and government (Fig. 5).

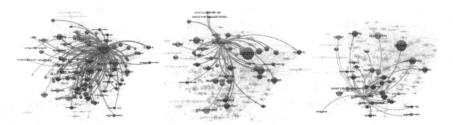

Fig. 5. Dominant objects in the social science area

From the visualization of the object, it was found that there are three most dominant aspects discussed in the strategy for the successful implementation of Smart City, including system development, application, and government. In this object, the researcher compares the success strategies developed in Italy, the United Kingdom, the United States, and Spain.

4.3 Success Strategy in Smart City

After going through the data visualization using the VOSviewer software, then the data is coded with NVivo plus 12 from the data obtained in each country to find the main focus of strategic success from three crucial aspects, application, system, and government in implementing innovative strategies on Smart Cities in Italy, United Kingdom, United States, and Spain (Fig. 6).

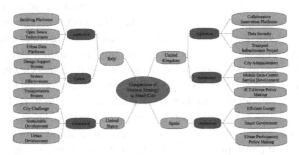

Fig. 6. Coding data with NVivo12

From the figure, it is found that Italy focuses on the application and system development application development, such as building platforms that frame ICT and sustainability as "across-the-board elements" because they are connected with all services provided to society and play a key role in thoughtful city planning [14], open source technologies to encourage e-participation in urban planning and urban data platforms to understand smart infrastructure as a network between places and people to create a healthier, more resilient, and sustainable future for various groups of people [15]. Furthermore, the development of the system used is the design support system to provide connectivity, convenience, comfort, commitment, friendliness, and coexistence [16], system effectiveness to support learning experiences located in intelligent cities, and transportation systems to encourage electronic participation in the community [17].

The United Kingdom focuses on government applications and capabilities, application development, such as collaborative, innovative platforms that make them more open, participatory and experimental [18], data security promoting and protecting the broader public interest, and transport infrastructure projects aimed at transforming inclusive, scalable, and coordinated [19]. Meanwhile, government capabilities are directed at city administrators to regulate development services globally [19], mobile data-centric service development to produce beautiful, provocative, socially inclusive interactive public art through human-centered design techniques, and ICT-driven policymaking to providing service platforms. Integrated ICTs to drive energy and carbon efficiency [20].

The United States focuses on government development, such as the city challenge, smart city readiness in big data, and sustainable development for the economic, environmental, and social challenges [21]. Urban development divides government city development into six categories: innovative economy, intelligent people, smart governance, smart mobility, innovative environment, and intelligent living [22]. While Spain focuses on application development, such as efficient energy to adapt policies to the city's needs, the competent government includes the perspective of all local stakeholders and urban participatory policymaking such as ICT-based public transportation services [23]. The results show that the success of the Smart City strategy in four countries is strongly influenced by application development.

5   Conclusion

Smart City's innovative strategy in four countries is considered to have succeeded in providing effective services to the public; the main focus is the development of applications to facilitate public participation in accessing cities through application platforms. Every year, success continues to increase, connecting information and communication technology with urban mobility and the involvement of stakeholders in determining policies so that strategies are chosen on target. While, by implication, smart cities are often fragmented with technology, many benefits are felt, and very few weaknesses of technology and failed projects related to strengthening networks and access to information. This success can be taken into consideration by the government to improve the quality of future application development. This research still has shortcomings, ranging from data sources and the limitations of researchers looking at comparisons of innovative strategies using the web of science. Researchers hope that further research will discuss empirical testing of the conceptual framework developed by intelligent cities with the web of science and as an evaluation material for the government to improve the quality of innovative strategies in Smart cities.

References

1. Aggarwal, T., Solomon, P.: Quantitative analysis of the development of smart cities in India. Smart Sustain. Built Environ. **9**(4), 711–726 (2020). https://doi.org/10.1108/SASBE-06-2019-0076
2. Silva, B.N., Khan, M., Han, K.: Towards sustainable smart cities: a review of trends, architectures, components, and open challenges in smart cities. Sustain. Cities Soc. **38** (2018). https://doi.org/10.1016/j.scs.2018.01.053
3. Angelakoglou, K., et al.: A methodological framework for the selection of key performance indicators to assess smart city solutions. Smart Cities **2**(2), 269–306 (2019). https://doi.org/10.3390/smartcities2020018
4. Janurova, M., Chaloupkova, M., Kunc, J.: Smart city strategy and its implementation barriers: Czech experience. Theor. Empir. Res. Urban Manag. **15**(2), 5–21 (2020). https://www.scopus.com/inward/record.uri?eid=2-s2.0-85084205801&partnerID=40&md5=11a343da1d70d780dcd8064b6bdee91c
5. Nicolas, C., Kim, J., Chi, S.: Quantifying the dynamic effects of smart city development enablers using structural equation modeling. Sustain. Cities Soc. **53** (2020). https://doi.org/10.1016/j.scs.2019.101916
6. Axelsson, K., Granath, M.: Stakeholders' stake and relation to smartness in smart city development: insights from a Swedish city planning project. Gov. Inf. Q. **35**(4), 693–702 (2018). https://doi.org/10.1016/j.giq.2018.09.001
7. Maestosi, P.C., Civiero, P., Massa, G.: European union funding research development and innovation projects on smart cities: the state of the art in 2019. Int. J. Sustain. Energy Plan. Manag. **24**, 7–20 (2019). https://doi.org/10.5278/ijsepm.3493
8. Bifulco, F., Tregua, M., Amitrano, C.C.: Co-governing smart cities through living labs. Top evidences from EU. Transylv. Rev. Adm. Sci. **2017**(50E), 21–37 (2017). https://doi.org/10.24193/tras.2017.0002
9. Hoang, G.T.T., Dupont, L., Camargo, M.: Application of decision-making methods in smart city projects: a systematic literature review. Smart Cities **2**(3), 433–452 (2019). https://doi.org/10.3390/smartcities2030027
10. Caragliu, A., Del Bo, C.F.: Smart innovative cities: the impact of Smart City policies on urban innovation. Technol. Forecast. Soc. Chang. **142**, 373–383 (2019). https://doi.org/10.1016/j.techfore.2018.07.022
11. Wu, Y.J., Chen, J.-C.: A structured method for smart city project selection. Int. J. Inf. Manag. **56** (2021). https://doi.org/10.1016/j.ijinfomgt.2019.07.007
12. Allam, Z., Dhunny, Z.A.: On big data, artificial intelligence and smart cities. Cities **89**, 80–91 (2019). https://doi.org/10.1016/j.cities.2019.01.032
13. Gabrys, J.: Programming environments: environmentality and citizen sensing in the smart city. Environ. Plan. D Soc. Space **32**(1), 30–48 (2014). https://doi.org/10.1068/d16812
14. Bifulco, F., Tregua, M., Amitrano, C.C., D'Auria, A.: ICT and sustainability in smart cities management. Int. J. Public Sect. Manag. **29**(2), 132–147 (2016). https://doi.org/10.1108/IJPSM-07-2015-0132
15. Petroccia, S., Pitasi, A., Cossi, G.M., Roblek, V.: Smart cities: who is the main observer? Comp. Sociol. **19**(2), 259–278 (2020). https://doi.org/10.1163/15691330-BJA10012

16. Garau, C., Annunziata, A., Coni, M.: A methodological framework for assessing practicability of the urban space: the Survey on Conditions of Practicable Environments (SCOPE) procedure applied in the case study of Cagliari (Italy). Sustainability **10**(11) (2018). https://doi.org/10.3390/su10114189

17. Tanda, A., De Marco, A.: The value propositions of Smart City Mobility projects. Transp. Plan. Technol. **44**(8), 860–886 (2021). https://doi.org/10.1080/03081060.2021.1992179

18. Panori, A., Kakderi, C., Komninos, N., Fellnhofer, K., Reid, A., Mora, L.: Smart systems of innovation for smart places: challenges in deploying digital platforms for co-creation and data-intelligence. Land Use Policy **111**(2021). https://doi.org/10.1016/j.landusepol.2020.104631

19. Huston, S., Rahimzad, R., Parsa, A.: 'Smart' sustainable urban regeneration: institutions, quality and financial innovation. Cities **48**, 66–75 (2015). https://doi.org/10.1016/j.cities.2015.05.005

20. Sivarajah, U., Lee, H., Irani, Z., Weerakkody, V.: Fostering smart cities through ICT driven policy-making: expected outcomes and impacts of DAREED project. Int. J. Electron. Gov. Res. **10**(3), 1–18 (2014). https://doi.org/10.4018/ijegr.2014070101

21. Cugurullo, F.: Exposing smart cities and eco-cities: Frankenstein urbanism and the sustainability challenges of the experimental city. Environ. Plan. A **50**(1), 73–92 (2018). https://doi.org/10.1177/0308518X17738535

22. Nicolas, C., Kim, J., Chi, S.: Natural language processing-based characterization of top-down communication in smart cities for enhancing citizen alignment. Sustain. Cities Soc. **66** (2021). https://doi.org/10.1016/j.scs.2020.102674

23. Del-Real, C., Ward, C., Sartipi, M.: What do people want in a smart city? Exploring the stakeholders' opinions, priorities and perceived barriers in a medium-sized city in the United States. Int. J. Urban Sci. (2021). https://doi.org/10.1080/12265934.2021.1968939

Impact of Distance and Movement Speed on the Acceptance of Human-Robot Interaction – Method and First Evaluation

Jonas Birkle, Annika Vogel, and Verena Wagner-Hartl(✉) ⓘ

Faculty Industrial Technologies, Furtwangen University, Campus Tuttlingen, Kronenstraße 16, 78532 Tuttlingen, Germany
{jonas.birkle,annika.vogel,verena.wagner-hartl}@hs-furtwangen.de

Abstract. The number of scenarios where an interaction between humans and robots is part of the everyday life increased constantly during the last years. Therefore, it is important to focus on a good interaction between both parts, the humans and the robots, as well as the absence of negative emotions. Especially, emotions like fear and anxiety are of great interest. The presented study focuses on a first concept of measuring these emotions and the acceptance through a multidimensional approach. A simple handover task was chosen for the collaboration. Different motion speeds of the robot as well as distances between the robot and the human were considered. Moreover, the impact of two different interaction heights, at face level or at chest level, was examined. In addition to the subjective assessment of the participants, psychophysiological parameters (cardiovascular and electrodermal activity) were recorded during the human-robot interaction. The concept was first evaluated with a number of four participants, limited by governmental restrictions due to the current COVID-19 pandemic situation. The results proof the success of the chosen procedure.

Keywords: Human-robot interaction · Subjective assessment · Psychophysiological responses

1 Introduction

Due to the ongoing development and the rapid evolution of technologies the industry 5.0 is advancing further [1–3]. In this context, humans should be informed better about the processes. Moreover, synergies between humans and machines should be created [1, 4]. Furthermore, collaborative robots are used, which are called "cobots" [5]. These are robots that work hand-in-hand with humans. In doing so, they are not separated from humans by physical partitions, such as fences and at the same time do not endanger them. Collaborations of this type, when humans and robots work simultaneously with each other, create new challenges [6]. Since the new concepts of collaboration require open spaces without physical partitions [6], it is especially important to consider issues like operator safety and ergonomics [7]. According to Hancock et al. [8], trust seems to be a dominant factor to enable a positive collaboration. Following the authors, trust

C. Stephanidis et al. (Eds.): HCII 2022, CCIS 1655, pp. 483–490, 2022.
https://doi.org/10.1007/978-3-031-19682-9_61

depends on the overall performance of the robot. Furthermore, other more physically driven aspects such as speed, acceleration, the physical appearance and size of the robot play a crucial role. Devitt [9] showed that the predictability and transparency of the robot often presents a problem in terms of trust. For the operator it is difficult to comprehend the mass and complexity of the robot's data and algorithms. Based on its high reliability, the robot gains trust but if the degree of complexity is too high, the operator's understanding eludes it. In the worst case, this can also result in a fundamental rejection of the robot. The degree to which the human trusts the robot is therefore a central requirement for a successful cooperation [10].

The physical conditions of human-robot interaction are largely covered by regulations and standards [11]. However, since robots are very different from other work equipment, it is also important to consider psychological effects (e.g., anxiety, acceptance, trust, …) during human-robot interaction. Based on this, a working environment should be created in which the worker can do his/her work efficiently without being afraid. Therefore, the results of a study of Thimm et al. [10] showed that while human-robot interaction was initially unfamiliar to most people, they developed high expectations of a robot's adaptability and performance after working with the robot for a few minutes. Other studies have shown that differences regarding the acceptance of human-robot-interaction do exist between different tasks (e.g., motoric or cognitive tasks) as well as for using a robot in different areas of work and everyday live [cf. 12]. Furthermore, Thiemermann [13] and Arai et al. [14] have investigated the distance between humans and robots during the human-robot collaboration in different working areas. The results of both studies showed a correlation between distance and anxiety in a way that the participants reported the highest amount of anxiety at the smallest given distance. Regarding the movement speed of the robot, different results were shown in the study of Thiemermann [13]. For example, that high movement speeds from 1000 mm/s can no longer be distinguished so well by the participants than movement speeds below, and that the extent of subjectively perceived danger increases with increasing speed. Following Arai et al. [14], a movement speed of 500 mm/s can lead to higher mental stress in the test subjects than a movement speed of 250 mm/s.

In general, psychological processes (cognitive, social or emotional) are accompanied by physiological responses [15]. These psychophysiological responses are mostly easy to measure and can provide insights into otherwise invisible processes like the emotional experience during a human-robot interaction.

Not only physical activities and cognitive processes play a role in the performance of a work task [16]. A person's emotional state is also crucial for efficient and reliable task performance and has a high impact on the work-health relationship. Negative emotions such as anxiety [17] can also have a negative impact on work performance [16]. Among other things, this is due to the fact that they can influence the capacity to process task-related information. Characteristics of anxiety [17] are feelings of tension, nervousness and inner restlessness. Subjectively, anxiety can be assessed, for example, by the State-Trait Anxiety Inventory [18]. However, anxiety can be assessed also objectively, by measuring changes in psychophysiological reactions [16]. Some parameters are particularly suitable for this purpose. For example, electrocardiography (ECG) or electrodermal activity (EDA), which were used in the presented study.

Based on the previous research findings, the aim of the presented study was to develop and evaluate a method to enable further research regarding the impact of distance and movement speed for the acceptance of human-robot collaboration. Therefore, a multidimensional approach which combines subjective assessments and objective psychophysiological and physical parameters, was used to answer the research question whether different levels of distance and movement speed do have an impact on the acceptance of human-robot interaction.

2   Method

2.1   Sample

Caused by the present governmental restrictions (COVID-19 pandemic) during the procedure period, only four people participated in the study. The sample consisted of two female (22 and 23 years old) and two male (23 and 24 years old) participants. The recruiting was limited to the university context which was also caused by the pandemic regulations. All participants provided their informed consent at the beginning of the study.

2.2   Study Design, Materials and Measures

A mixed measurement design was chosen for the experimental study. Participants were split into two independent samples based on the height where the robot interacts with the participant (see Fig. 1). The chosen heights are based on the anthropometric data of the 50th percentile man/woman between the ages of 18 and 40 [19]. The independent variables movement speed and distance to the robot were used as a repetition factor with five steps each. In the first condition, the distance from the human to the robot was changed while the robot moved at a constant speed. This speed was kept at 70% (arithmetic mean of the lowest and the highest treated speed in this study) of the maximum speed of 2 m/s [20]. The condition started with the largest distance (1.5 m). With each iteration, the distance was decreased by the same length (0.25 m). The smallest distance was chosen to be 0.5 m and was based on suggestions from the German Social Accident Insurance, which considers a distance of 0.5 m to be optimal [21]. The distance was processed in descending order, to give the participants the possibility to stop the experiment at any time if the distance to the robot became too close for them and they no longer felt comfortable. In the second condition, the speed-condition, the participants constantly stayed at the same distance of 1.0 m (arithmetic mean of the largest and smallest distance used in this study) to the robot, which increased the movement speed with each iteration by 15% of the maximum speed. The movement speed was presented in an ascending order and started with the lowest speed (40% of the maximum speed) and ended with the highest speed (100% of the maximum speed). The increasing iteration order was chosen for the same reason as mentioned in the first condition. Participants therefore had the chance to stop at any time if they felt uncomfortable due to the increased speed. All used speed levels and distances were checked for their acceptability in pretests. For both repetition factors there was a separate interaction block within the procedure. The order in which these blocks were processed was permuted. The study design is also shown in Fig. 2.

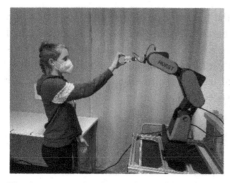 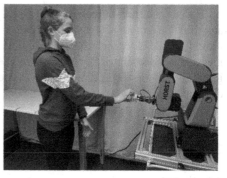

Fig. 1. Approach heights of the robot: head height (160 cm, left) and torso height (107 cm, right)

Position	Distance to the robot					Movement speed of the robot				
	D1	D2	D3	D4	D5	S1	S2	S3	S4	S5
Head height										
Torso height										

Fig. 2. Study design

During the experiment, the participants were asked to work on a task together with an industrial robot (HORST600 from fruitcore robotics GmbH [20]). The task that should be performed together with the robot was to receive a wooden cube and inspect it for a marker ($4 \times 4 \times 4$ cm). So, based on the repeated measurement design, the robot hands the participant five wooden cubes within the distance condition and five wooden cubes in the speed condition. In each condition, three of the cubes were marked with an "X" on one surface. The remaining two cubes had no mark. The visual inspection consisted of searching for the "X" on the cube and then documenting whether the cross was present or not. The component was then returned to the robot. Afterwards, the robot put the cube back on top of a wooden surface attached to the fixture for the robot, which serves as storage for the components. During the execution of the task, the performance measures "correct execution" (Yes/No), "leaving the intended area" (Yes/No) and "error-free return to the robot" (Yes/No) were measured as dependent variables. These measures are based on the standard DIN EN ISO 9241-11 [22]. Furthermore, cardiovascular activity (ECG) and electrodermal activity (EDA) were recorded. In addition, the participants were asked to make use of the thinking aloud method.

The State-Trait Anxiety Inventory [18] was executed by the participants at the beginning of the study (State- and Trait-Anxiety) and after each of the two interaction blocks (only State-Anxiety, see also Sect. 2.3). In addition, the participants subjectively assessed the human-robot interaction after each single interaction (distance – five tasks, movement speed – five tasks). Therefore, the self-assessment manikin [23], the acceptance scale by van der Laan et al. [24] and three additional items specific to human-robot interaction selected from an internal questionnaire [cf. 25, 26] were used. Used additional items were: "I trust the robot", "I perceive the interaction with the robot as risky", and "I trust that the robot cannot hurt me" (five-point Likert-scale ranging from "strongly agree" to "strongly disagree"). To record the psychophysiological parameters cardiovascular and electrodermal activity, the EcgMove4 [27] and EdaMove4 [28] devices from movisens were used.

In order to control the robot, the supervisors require a connected interface with the horstFX software [29]. The interface supplied with the robot is used for this purpose. The experimental procedure was stored in a PsychoPy 3 [30] program, which controls the execution completely automated. The program was executed on a Lenovo ThinkPad T440s. The measurements of the psychophysiological parameters were controlled by another laptop (Fujitsu Lifebook U 747). For the synchronization of all devices an internal program was used [31], which communicates with the connected devices using a standard network switch. To enable the robot to grab objects, a corresponding picker with a suitable shape was designed and 3D-printed.

2.3 Procedure

At the beginning of the study, the experimental procedure and the safety instructions for the interaction with the robot were explained to the participants. Afterwards, the participants completed a socio-demographic questionnaire, rated their general affinity to technology (TA-EG [32]), completed both scales of the State-Trait Anxiety Inventory [18] and the two devices from movisens [27, 28] were applied to measure their cardiovascular and electrodermal responses during the study. Then a baseline measurement (five minutes) of the psychophysiological parameters was conducted. After that, the different interaction-blocks (distance – five tasks, movement speed – five tasks see also Sect. 2.2) were processed, each task followed by a subjective assessment (see Sect. 2.2) and a rest measurement (90 s). The order of the interaction-blocks (distance, speed) was permuted. At the end of the study the participants had the opportunity to ask questions themselves. The total duration of the study was 120 min. Attendance was completely voluntary for each participant and they received no reward.

2.4 Data Analyses

Cardiovascular and electrodermal activity were analyzed using the software DataAnalyzer from movisens [33]. The analyzed parameters for cardiovascular activity were heart rate (HR) in beats per minute and heart rate variability (HRV RMSSD). The analyzed parameters for the electrodermal activity were skin conductance level (SCL), amplitude of non-specific electrodermal responses (NS.SCR amp), frequency of non-specific electrodermal responses (NS.SCR freq) and mean sum amplitude (NS.SCR amp/NS.SCR freq).

3 Results

The first results show that all data was measured without any data loss in the experimental setting. Furthermore, no inherence caused of problems with the used industrial robot, its electronic control system and the used psychophysiological measurement equipment can be shown. So, all data was measured without artefacts and the first results suggest no data loss and a good quality of the measurements (see Fig. 3).

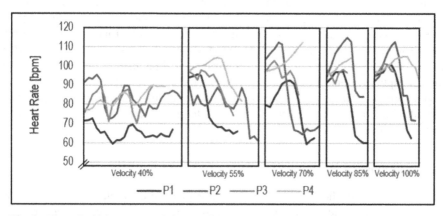

Fig. 3. Example of the measured signals of the heart rate for the different movement speeds

4 Discussion

The results of a first evaluation show that the used study method is promising for the use in further research. The study was able to descriptively show differences regarding the subjective assessments as well as the psychophysiological responses of the participants for the different tasks. From a descriptive point of view, the different distances of the robot seem to lead into less strong responses than the different speed-levels. In the future, an expansion with additional parameters such as eye tracking will be considered.

However, the presented first evaluation of the method and the measurement environment has some limitations: Caused by the COVID-19 pandemic and the restrictions regarding personal contacts during the time when the study was conducted, only four participants attended in the study. We are aware of the fact that this can only be a first step to proof the method and the measurement environment in a preliminary study. Therefore, a follow-up study will be conducted when the restrictions will be eased.

In conclusion, the development of the method and the measurement environment was successful. Following the first results, the basic procedure seems to work without major problems and all psychophysiological data was measured without any inherences or data loss.

Authors Statement. The authors state no conflict of interest. Informed consent has been provided from the participant. The study was approved by the ethics committee of the Furtwangen University.

References

1. Demir, K.A., Döven, G., Sezen, B.: Industry 5.0 and human-robot co-working. Procedia Comput. Sci. **158**, 688–695 (2019)
2. Nahavandi, S.: Industry 5.0—a human-centric solution. Sustainability **11**, 4371 (2019)
3. Skobelev, P.O., Yu, B.S.: On the way from Industry 4.0 to Industry 5.0: from digital manufacturing to digital society. In: Industry 4.0, pp. 307–311 (2017)
4. Sachsenmeier, P.: Industry 5.0—the relevance and implications of bionics and synthetic biology. Engineering **2**, 225–229 (2016)
5. Fast-Berglund, Å., Palmkvist, F., Nyqvist, P., Ekered, S., Åkerman, M.: Evaluating cobots for final assembly. Procedia CIRP **44**, 175–180 (2016)
6. Toichoa Eyam, A., Mohammed, W.M., Martinez Lastra, J.L.: Emotion-driven analysis and control of human-robot interactions in collaborative applications. Sensors **21**, 4626 (2021)
7. Mohammed, W.M., et al.: Generic platform for manufacturing execution system functions in knowledge-driven manufacturing systems. Int. J. Comput. Integr. Manuf. **31**, 262–274 (2018)
8. Hancock, P.A., Billings, D.R., Schaefer, K.E., Chen, J.Y.C., de Visser, E.J., Parasuraman, R.: A meta-analysis of factors affecting trust in human-robot interaction. Hum Factors. **53**, 517–527 (2011)
9. Kate Devitt, S.: Trustworthiness of autonomous systems. In: Abbass, H.A., Scholz, J., Reid, D.J. (eds.) Foundations of Trusted Autonomy. SSDC, vol. 117, pp. 161–184. Springer, Cham (2018). https://doi.org/10.1007/978-3-319-64816-3_9
10. Thimm, C., et al.: Die Maschine als Partner? Verbale und non-verbale Kommunikation mit einem humanoiden Roboter [The machine as a partner? Verbal and non-verbal communication with a humanoid robot]. In: Thimm, C., Bächle, T.C. (eds.) Die Maschine: Freund oder Feind? [The Machine: Friend or Enemy?], pp. 109–134. Springer, Wiesbaden (2019). https://doi.org/10.1007/978-3-658-22954-2_6
11. Gerst, D.: Mensch-Roboter-Kollaboration – Anforderungen an eine humane Arbeitsgestaltung [Human-robot collaboration - requirements for human work design]. In: Buxbaum, H.-J. (ed.) Mensch-Roboter-Kollaboration [Human-Robot Collaboration], pp. 145–162. Springer, Wiesbaden (2020). https://doi.org/10.1007/978-3-658-28307-0_10
12. Wagner-Hartl, V., Gleichauf, K., Schmid, R.: Are we ready for human-robot collaboration at work and in our everyday lives? - an exploratory approach. In: Ahram, T., Karwowski, W., Pickl, S., Taiar, R. (eds.) IHSED 2019. AISC, vol. 1026, pp. 135–141. Springer, Cham (2020). https://doi.org/10.1007/978-3-030-27928-8_21
13. Thiemermann, S.: Direkte Mensch-Roboter-Kooperation in der Kleinteilemontage mit einem SCARA-Roboter [Direct human-robot cooperation in small parts assembly with a SCARA robot]. http://elib.uni-stuttgart.de/handle/11682/4052
14. Arai, T., Kato, R., Fujita, M.: Assessment of operator stress induced by robot collaboration in assembly. CIRP Ann. **59**, 5–8 (2010)
15. Boucsein, W.: Psychophysiologische Methoden in der Ingenieurspsychologie [Psychophysiological methods in engineering psychology]. In: Sonderdruck aus Enzyklopädie der Psychologie: Themenbereich D Praxisgebiete: Serie III Wirtschafts-, Organisations- und Arbeitspsychologie, pp. 317–358. Hogrefe, Göttingen (2006)
16. Boucsein, W., Backs, R.W.: Engineering psychophysiology as a discipline: historical and theoretical aspects. In: Backs, R.W., Boucsein, W. (eds.) Engineering Psychophysiology: Issues and Applications, pp. 3–30. CRC Press, Boca Raton (2000)
17. Asendorpf, J., Caspar, F.: Angst im Dorsch Lexikon der Psychologie [Anxiety in the Dorsch Dictionary of Psychology]. https://dorsch.hogrefe.com/stichwort/angst
18. Spielberger, C.D., Gorsuch, R.L., Lushene, R., Vagg, P.R., Jacobs, G.A.: Manual for the State-Trait Anxiety Inventory. Consulting Psychologists Press, Palo Alto (1983)

19. DIN 33402-2: Ergonomics - Human body dimensions - Part 2: Values. Beuth, Berlin (2020)
20. fruitcore robotics GmbH: Der Industrieroboter HORST600 [The HORST600 industrial robot]. https://fruitcore-robotics.com/horst600/
21. Deutsche Gesetzliche Unfallversicherung e.V.: Bildschirm- und Büroarbeitsplätze – Leitfaden für die Gestaltung. DGUV Information [Unfallversicherung e.V.: Monitor and office workplaces - Guideline for design. DGUV Information], 215-410, p. 96 (2019)
22. DIN EN ISO 9241-11: Ergonomics of human-system interaction - Part 11: Usability: Definitions and concepts. Beuth, Berlin (2018)
23. Bradley, M.M., Lang, P.J.: Measuring emotion: the self-assessment manikin and the semantic differential. J. Behav. Ther. Exp. Psychiatry 25, 49–59 (1994)
24. Van der Laan, J.D., Heino, A., De Waard, D.: A simple procedure for the assessment of acceptance of advanced transport telematics. Transp. Res. Part C Emerg. Technol. 5, 1–10 (1997)
25. Gleichauf, K., Schmid, R.: Questionnaire regarding the acceptance and trust of human-robot interaction, Furtwangen University (2021)
26. Wagner-Hartl, V., Schmid, R., Gleichauf, K.: The influence of task complexity on acceptance and trust in human-robot interaction – gender and age differences. In: Paletta, L., Ayaz, H. (eds.) Cognitive Computing and Internet of Things. AHFE Open Access, vol. 43. AHFE International, USA. https://doi.org/10.54941/ahfe1001846
27. movisens GmbH: EcgMove 4. https://docs.movisens.com/Sensors/EcgMove4/#welcome
28. movisens GmbH: EdaMove 4. https://docs.movisens.com/Sensors/EdaMove4/#welcome
29. fruitcore robotics GmbH: Bedienung von Industrieroboter HORST [Operation of industrial robot HORST]. https://fruitcore-robotics.com/horst/bedienung/
30. PsychoPy: PsychoPy. https://www.psychopy.org/
31. Birkle, J., Weber, R., Möller, K., Wagner-Hartl, V.: Psychophysiological parameters for emotion recognition – conception and first evaluation of a measurement environment. In: Intelligent Human Systems Integration (IHSI 2022): Integrating People and Intelligent Systems. AHFE Open Access (2022)
32. Karrer, K., Glaser, C., Clemens, C., Bruder, C.: Technikaffinität erfassen – der Fragebogen TA-EG [Measuring affinity for technology - the TA-EG questionnaire]. In: Lichtenstein, A., Stößel, C., Clemens, C. (eds.) Der Mensch im Mittelpunkt technischer Systeme [Humans at the center of technical systems], pp. 196–201. VDI Verlag (2009)
33. movisens GmbH: DataAnalyzer. https://www.movisens.com/en/products/dataanalyzer/

Smartphone-Based Input Multimodal Interactions for IoT Environments

Fadia Nouna Bousba[✉][ID], Nadia Elouali[ID], and Sidi Mohammed Benslimane[ID]

LabRI-SBA Lab, Ecole Superieure En Informatique, Sidi Bel Abbes, Algeria
{f.bousba,n.elouali,s.benslimane}@esi-sba.dz

Abstract. Multimodal interfaces offer users different and appropriate ways to communicate with smart devices. However, despite the advantages of multimodal interactions and their interest in connected environments, only a few of them could reach end users. One of the problems causing this concerns the obligation of using intermediate equipment between users and the connected objects (cameras, Kinect, smartwatch, etc.). Equipment that is not necessarily available for most users and even if they exist, can represent a disadvantage in everyday life. The novelty of our approach is proving that the different intermediate equipment/sensors used in the literature between the user and connected objects can be replaced by the smartphone. An equipment that not only contains an important number of sensors, but also exists in most people's homes. Our approach seeks, therefore, to use smartphones instead of different equipment in the literature studies that use intermediate equipment to ensure multimodal interactions with connected objects. We are starting by transforming the well-known interaction modality "Smart Pockets", into a smartphone-based interaction modality. Then, we will follow the same process with other modalities and/or other connected objects and we will evaluate users' feedback. We believe that this will prove the feasibility and allow, afterwards, a democratization of smartphone-based multimodal interactions by making it available to all owners of smartphones and connected objects.

Keywords: Internet of things · Multimodality · Smartphone-based interaction

1 Introduction

With the advancement of technology, the internet of things (IoT) has become more pervasive. It is continuously evolving and growing, ensuring the connectivity for "any one" from "any place" at "any time" [7]. The number of connected devices are increasing exponentially, including TV, bulb light, roomba, door, windows, etc. making the environment more intelligent, ensuring decisions on behalf of people, specifically to achieve a good experience with more user-friendly interfaces.

C. Stephanidis et al. (Eds.): HCII 2022, CCIS 1655, pp. 491–497, 2022.
https://doi.org/10.1007/978-3-031-19682-9_62

To control these smart devices, multiple modalities can be provided to end users. One approach is to exploit voice interaction such as presented by [6,9], where the user can launch his command using natural language, for example, to turn off the light or increase music volume. Other forms of interaction are to adopt gesture modality [4,17], gaze modality, tactile, etc. Or combining, in some situations, more than one input modality to give users appropriate ways to communicate with smart devices. However, despite the advantages of multimodal interactions and their interest in connected environments, only a few of them could reach end users. One of the problems causing this concerns the necessity of using intermediate equipment between users and connected objects (armband, smart rings, voice assistants, etc.). Equipment that is not necessarily available for most users and even if they exist, can represent a disadvantage in everyday life [3].

In this paper, in order to remove this equipment constraint, we suggest using the smartphone as an intermediary device to ensure multimodal interactions with different connected objects. An equipment that not only contains an important number of sensors, but also exists in most people's homes. We are starting by transforming "Smart Pockets" presented by [11], into a smartphone-based interaction modality. Thereafter, we desire to apply our approach with different connected devices using other different modalities to prove its feasibility.

The rest of this paper is structured as follows. In the second section, we discuss related work. Then, we present our approach in the third section. Finally, we present our concluding remarks and out-lines topics for future research.

2   Literature Review

In the literature, there are two categories of work presenting multimodal interactions with connected objects. The first category uses the smartphone as intermediate equipment between the user and the connected object. While the second, uses other intermediate equipment such as kinect, smart-watch, etc.

In the first category and in the area of home automation systems, [2] discussed a new method that allows people to control their home devices by creating automation without the need of programming experience according to their needs through natural user interfaces. The solution proposed is based on augmented reality smartphone application that allow users to get relevant information of encountered objects (their states, rules already created and associated with them, etc.) while freely moving in the home. Also, it gives users the possibility to add new rules by proposing relevant triggers which allow them to personalize the behaviour of smart devices or update existing one.

In the same area, [13] described an android smartphone application that allows residents to adjust and monitor settings of different home appliances based on infrared radiation (IR) remote, Bluetooth and global system for mobile communication (GSM) techniques. Whenever a specific button is pressed (using tactile) on a mobile phone app screen the appropriate equipment takes actions based on data received (ON/OFF operation for example).

Another context of smartphone use is presented by [14]. The study focuses on the control of smart TV through a mobile application as a remote control. It outlines different activities to control TV such as browse, cast content, search process, etc. The user uses the tactile modality to interact with the application (finger swipe on a smartphone screen).

[8] Presents the control of home appliances (like lights, fans, etc.) using an Android mobile app through a wireless communication (WiFi). The authors suggested manual and automatic control options for users. They gave them the ability to turn ON/OFF the light, for example, based on users preferences in the first option, although on the basis of sensors' data monitoring the home environment, the automatic mode changed the state of the appropriate appliance.

In the second category, [15] developed an interactive spatial prototype augmented reality with multiple devices. Firstly, the user activates the device concerned by the action using a registration air gesture (clap, point, form a rectangle, etc.). Then, he interacts with his appliance (air conditioner, blinds, lights, audio player, media-video player, and TV) using one of the available hand gesture forms from command gesture set (swipe up/down/right/left, hand (fist) open/close, etc.) captured through Microsoft Kinect v2.0.

"SmartPointer" is an infrared gesture remote control device defined by [12]. It enables users to perform different operations of control by a simple gesture. At each motion established by the users, the SmartPointer detects the hand action. When this command is appropriate to a specific gesture, it will be translated into a specific action for a proper/desired device.

To facilitate the learning process, different research areas have been suggested various types of interaction modalities through a variety of connected objects. One of these approaches is presented by [5]. The proposed system consists of a multimodal learning system that merges two input modalities (motion-based technology and tangible user interfaces) to ensure students' knowledge gains and retention skills in the school context. In this study, the body movement is captured through an IR-depth camera.

Also, [1] suggested a new mechanism called "Direction of Voice" (DoV) that enables the interaction with diverse ecosystems (smartphone, laptop, TV) through a voice commands with address-ability (devices know if a command was directed at them), where it is selected according to the shortest path and time using ReSpeaker as a device to capture voice command of final user. This solution articulate to be performed without the need of any key words or device name as the traditional smart speakers need.

The glove-based solution, get the intention of [16]. This research shows a system of gesture input adapting smart gloves for a virtual and mixed reality. The proposed prototype focuses on the communication between gloves and the head-mounted displays/devices (HMD HMT-1), where the authors suggested the use of smart gloves as an input to HMT-1 to control different devices.

Exploring the same device, [10] shows the use of glove as a remote control to manage different electronic appliances. The system comprises two units to launch the command toward equipment (TV, radio, projectors, etc.): a glove through which the user executes the gesture, and an intermediate device which receives the operation from the gloves and converts it to a IR code to be sent to the concerned appliance.

From these works (and many others in the literature), we detect that the use of less control equipment results in less exploitation of the different interaction modalities. For example, using devices like Kinect, voice assistant and smart gloves, interactions are often gestural, vocal, visual, etc. However, with smartphones only, interaction is generally limited to touch. Thus, researchers rely heavily on different intermediate equipment/sensors to ensure multimodality. Even if these equipment are not necessarily available for most users and if they exist, they can represent a disadvantage in everyday life [3,18]. On the other hand, the smartphone integrates a large number of sensors (accelerometer, light sensor, proximity sensor, microphone, speaker, etc.), communication standards (WiFi, Bluetooth, etc.), photographic flash, electromagnetic radiation (infrared), etc. This allowed the definition of new interaction modalities as well as new combined ones. The smartphone is also very close to the user and can easily replace both classic equipment (such as the remote control, for example) and new equipment (such as a smart-watch, for example). All of this makes it, according to us, a better device of control in the IoT area so far.

3   Our Approach

The aim of this paper is to extend prior research of "Smart Pockets" introduced by [11], in order to make this interaction available for all smartphone owners. Smart Pockets proposed a technique for sharing a channel from a specific pocket toward a smart TV, and saving a new one to a desired pocket using a simple hand air gesture from and toward the big screen by holding the Myo armband. The send and save options are confirmed using tap operation for twice.

In the light of this study, we suggest replacing the Myo armband by the smartphone as an intermediate device. We introduce two parts in our study. The first one consists of a Tizen web app running on the Tizen operating system performed at SAMSUNG smart TV (see Fig. 1), and the second consists of an android mobile application running on an android smartphone (see Fig. 2). Based on smartphone-accelerometer sensor (instead of the Myo armband) to ensure user interactions.

In this approach, firstly we suggest that Tizen web app comprise videos as a content. To save one of these videos on pocket, we recommend the user to make a motion gesture holding the phone from the TV toward the body's pocket (up right, up left, down right or down left) (see Fig. 3) via WiFi network. For example, when a user is watching a video from the proposed list on TV web application and he wants to save it in order to continue watching the rest after, he could make a simple air hand gesture holding the phone from TV to a specific pocket (as shown in Fig. 3). The content will be associated with the addressed pocket and saved on the mobile app. The same for sending content from pocket toward TV. Our prototype gives the user the ability to access his pocket's content easily

Fig. 1. Samsung TV app.

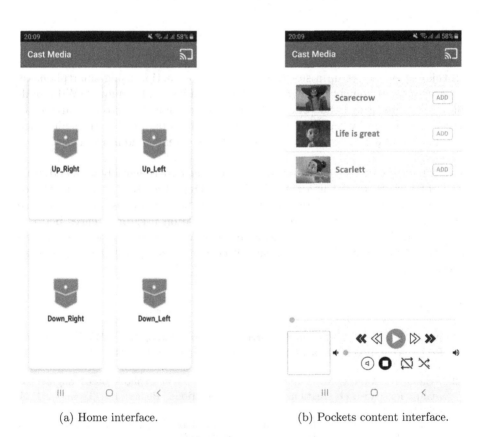

(a) Home interface.   (b) Pockets content interface.

Fig. 2. Android mobile app.

by making the opposite gesture holding the phone (from a specific pocket toward TV). In addition, to avoid any ambiguity of sharing/saving content unintentionally (making hand gestures with the smartphone while talking for example), we suggest to confirm the get/send operations using up/down volume respectively.

Fig. 3. Send and get content from/toward TV.

4   Conclusion

In this paper, we set up a smart home device interaction using smartphone as intermediate equipment through wireless communication techniques (WiFi module). We transformed the "Smart Pockets" interaction [11] into a smartphone-based interaction by replacing the armband with mobile device, through which the user could perform gesture interaction to save/send content from the body's pockets.

As future work, we desire to test our approach experimentally with end users and compare it with "Smart Pockets" [11]. Our objective is to validate not only our hypothesis about the potential effects/benefits of the smartphone use on multimodal interactions propagation, but also on user preferences between smartphone-based interactions and wearable device-based interactions. We are also planning to apply this mechanism with other types of equipment and modalities.

References

1. Ahuja, K., Kong, A., Goel, M., Harrison, C. Direction-of-Voice (DoV) estimation for intuitive speech interaction with smart devices ecosystems. In: UIST, pp. 1121–1131 (2020)
2. Ariano, R., Manca, M., Paternò, F., Santoro, C. Smartphone-based augmented reality for end-user creation of home automations. Behav. Inf. Technol., 1–17 (2022)
3. Arya, S., Patel, D., et al.: Implementation of Google Assistant & Amazon Alexa on Raspberry Pi. arXiv Preprint arXiv:2006.08220 (2020)
4. Billinghurst, M., Piumsomboon, T., Bai, H.: Hands in space: gesture interaction with augmented-reality interfaces. IEEE Comput. Graph. Appl. **34**, 77–80 (2014)

5. Chettaoui, N., Atia, A., Bouhlel, M.S.: examining the effects of embodied interaction modalities on students' retention skills in a real classroom context. J. Comput. Educ. **9**, 549–569 (2022). https://doi.org/10.1007/s40692-021-00213-9
6. Cho, E.: Hey Google, can I ask you something in private? In: Proceedings of the 2019 CHI Conference on Human Factors in Computing Systems, pp. 1–9 (2019)
7. Coetzee, L., Eksteen, J.: The Internet of Things-promise for the future? An introduction. In: 2011 IST-Africa Conference Proceedings, pp. 1–9 (2011)
8. Govindraj, V., Sathiyanarayanan, M., Abubakar, B.: Customary homes to smart homes using Internet of Things (IoT) and mobile application. In: 2017 International Conference on Smart Technologies for Smart Nation (SmartTechCon), pp. 1059–1063 (2017)
9. Lopatovska, I., et al.: Talk to me: exploring user interactions with the Amazon Alexa. J. Librariansh. Inf. Sci. **51**, 984–997 (2019)
10. Muthiah, M., Natesh, A.: Low cost smart glove for universal control of IR devices. In: 2016 IEEE International Symposium on Technology and Society (ISTAS), pp. 1–5 (2016)
11. Popovici, I., Vatavu, R., Wu, W.: TV channels in your pocket! linking smart pockets to smart TVs. In: Proceedings of the 2019 ACM International Conference on Interactive Experiences for TV and Online Video, pp. 193–198 (2019)
12. Ruser, H., et al.: Evaluating the accuracy and user experience of a gesture-based infrared remote control in smart homes. In: International Conference on Human-Computer Interaction, pp. 89–108 (2021)
13. Shinde, A., Kanade, S., Jugale, N., Gurav, A., Vatti, R., Patwardhan, M.: Smart home automation system using IR, Bluetooth, GSM and android. In: 2017 Fourth International Conference on Image Information Processing (ICIIP), pp. 1–6 (2017)
14. Torres, D.: User practices for smartphone control of TV. In: Proceedings of the 20th International Conference on Human-Computer Interaction with Mobile Devices and Services Adjunct, pp. 416–424 (2018)
15. Vogiatzidakis, P., Koutsabasis, P.: Mid-air gesture control of multiple home devices in spatial augmented reality prototype. Multimodal Technol. Interact. **4**, 61 (2020)
16. Wilk, M., Torres-Sanchez, J., Tedesco, S., O'Flynn, B.: Wearable human computer interface for control within immersive VAMR gaming environments using data glove and hand gestures. In: 2018 IEEE Games, Entertainment, Media Conference (GEM), pp. 1–9 (2018)
17. Xu, P.: A real-time hand gesture recognition and human-computer interaction system. arXiv Preprint arXiv:1704.07296. (2017)
18. Yusri, M., et al.: Smart mirror for smart life. In: 2017 6th ICT International Student Project Conference (ICT-ISPC), pp. 1–5 (2017)

Government Data Processing Mechanism to Support Smart City: A Bibliometric Review

Muhammad Farhan HR$^{(\boxtimes)}$ and Achmad Nurmandi

Master of Government Affairs and Administration, Jusuf Kalla School Government, Universitas Muhammadiyah Yogyakarta, Yogyakarta, Indonesia
farhanhr35@gmail.com, nurmandi_achmad@umy.ac.id

Abstract. The study aims to analyze the mechanism of "government data processing in supporting smart cities." The processing of government data collects raw data and translates it into information to create transparent, accountable, and participatory public service delivery strategies. This research was conducted in the United States, Spain, Indonesia, and Brazil. The research approach uses qualitative methods from previous review studies. The data sources in this study were taken from the Scopus database from 2012 to 2022. There are 73 articles, with the top four countries having the highest number of pieces, namely the United States, which has 11 papers, Spain has 10 articles, Indonesia has 6 articles, and Brazil has 6 articles, with the keywords "E-Government and Smart City." Then the author compares the implementation of government data processing mechanisms in the United States, Spain, Indonesia, and Brazil. The research data analysis uses VOSviewer Software as an analytical tool to correlate data processing in government themes of information production in innovative city analysis. The results show that the development of the research "Government Data Processing in Supporting Smart City" from 2012 to 2022 has a fluctuating trend. Furthermore, this research answers that government data is divided into three dominating government process data: information management, big data, information, and communication. Government Data Processing Research in Supporting Smart City information management is seen from technology change, electronic commerce, innovation, and e-government. In contrast, big data is seen from data mining, platforms, and open data. In information and communication, it is seen in privacy, public administration, and e-participation.

Keywords: E-government · Smart city · Data processing · Bibliometric

1 Introduction

Open Government Data (OGD) presents the reality of various things in life, including data and information. From the government's perspective, information must be managed and provided as an obligation and a willingness to open government. This is often referred to as Open Government Data (OGD) [1]. The relationship between the government and its citizens has changed with the advent of ICT (Information and Communication Technology). Especially the Internet and Cellular Technology open the possibility when the

C. Stephanidis et al. (Eds.): HCII 2022, CCIS 1655, pp. 498–506, 2022.
https://doi.org/10.1007/978-3-031-19682-9_63

relationship between the government and its citizens can strengthen the community's active role in the control and participation of the public [2]. The development of information and communication technology or electronic government in government has made open government growing.

Open government data is an open government doctrine regarding the data it has for certain things so that the public can freely use the data. This available data is not only a form of transparency and accountability but also hoped academics can use mics, business people, bureaucrats, professionals, ls, and other groups to develop expertise in their respective fields and discuss government policies [3].

2 Literature Review

2.1 E-Government

The success of E-Government depends on the willingness of the people to adopt and accept this innovation. However, many governments worldwide that are that ill face the problem of law public desire to use E-Government services. A survey conducted by the United Nations in 2014 stated that the EGDI (E-Government Development Index) values for the territory of Indonesia were 0.25 and 0.50, and Indonesia was in the middle rank [4]. In general, the main goal of e-government is to optimize services in urban spaces, which is in line with the actions taken to improve the quality of life [5].

The adoption of E-Government offers benefits at different levels but can be said to have the most significant impact at the urban level closest to the community [6]. Web and GIS, technology-based e-government systems, can promote the dissemination of urban information and enable citizens to raise objections to land use plans during various phases of the planning process and respond to those objections [7]. E-Government must deliver public services in ways that citizens and businesses want, using the internet and other technologies as enablers. E-Government is more than just building websites [8].

2.2 Government Data

Government data is part of the ongoing evolution of the Web and should therefore be combined and integrated with other open data on the Web to enable value-added services. Governments can get involved and play an essential role in this process because they own the data and thus understand it better than the third parties [9]. It enables different types of users to access, organize, and use data in ways that make sense to them [10].

2.3 Smart City

Innovative city development relies on e-government and commercial IoT to improve urban management and authorized services, information sharing, and collaboration and promote high-end innovative and sustainable development [11]. A vital feature of the Smart City architecture is its ability to acquire and process data from multiple data sources (databases, crawlers, third-party applications, sensors) [12]. Innovative governance mainly refers to participatory governance, which emphasizes participation in decision-making and transparency through a new communication channel for citizens, namely e-government [13].

The development of a smart city is different from the development of e-government which the government can only carry out through ICT to improve the efficiency, effectiveness, and accountability of public services. Innovative city development requires the active involvement of various stakeholders from public institutions, the private sector, and civil society [14].

3 Method

This research method uses qualitative research with a Bibliometric Analysis approach to enable dynamic analysis in identifying the literature that contributes the most to Government Data Processing to support Smart City.

The search results show 73 articles by accessing the Scopus website with keyword "Smart City and E-Government", article document boundaries, and Subject area Computer Science and Social Science.

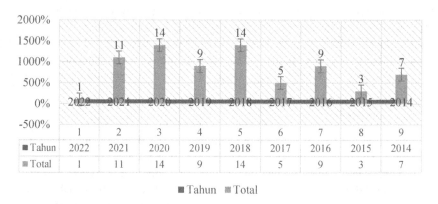

Fig. 1. Distribution of publications by professional journals. *Source: Scopus Database*

In Fig. 1, Seeing these developments the Government Data Processing research to support Smart City in 2020 and 2018 is the highest data with 12 out of 73 publications from 2012–2022. The development of data from 2012 to 2022 was volatile, and the research trend of Government Data Processing to support Smart City began to trend in 2014. This means that government data disclosure is a discussion that continues to be discussed in countries to develop Smart City strategies to provide transparency to the public.

4 Results and Discussions

4.1 Distribution of Publications by Country

In Fig. 2, it can be seen that ten countries publish the most articles on Government Data Processing to support Smart City, as seen from the 2012–2022 research scope data. The first rank is in the United States with 11 article publications; the second rank is in Spain with ten articles. Indonesia has 6 article publications; Brazil, China, and the United Kingdom have the same number of publications, as many as five pieces. At the same time, the Netherlands, Russian Federation, and South Korea have the same number of publications of 4 article publications, and Belgium with the number of 3 article publications.

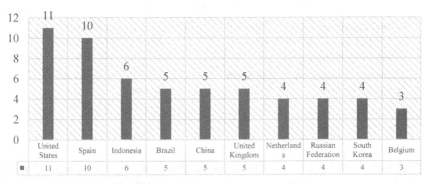

Fig. 2. Publications by country. *Source: Scopus Database*

4.2 Distribution of Publications by Journal

Based on source documents taken from Scopus data, which discusses Government Data Processing to support Smart City, the author has ten sources with the highest publications from 2012 to 2022. It can be seen in Fig. 3

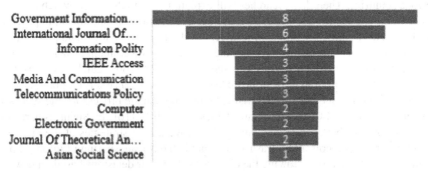

Fig. 3. Distribution of publications by professional journals. *Source: Scopus Database*

Based on the source documents from the image above, the ten documents that publish the most Government Data Processing to support Smart City in four countries are Government Information Quarterly with a total of 8 papers, followed by the International Journal of Electronic Government Research with a total of 6 articles, then Information Polity with a total of 4 pieces. While IEEE Access, Media and Communication, and Telecommunications Policy have the same number of documents, as many as three documents, while Computer, Electronic Government, and Journal Of Theoretical and Applied Information Technology have the same number of copies, as many as two papers, and Asian Social Science has recorded with one record (Table 1).

Table 1. Publication with the mos citations

No	Title	Year	Source	Cited
1	Governing the smart city: a review of the literature on innovative urban governance *Open Access*	2016	International Review of Administrative Sciences 82(2), pp. 392–408	585
2	Information-centric services in Smart Cities *Open Access*	2014	Journal of Systems and Software 88(1), pp. 169–188	204

Source: Scopus Database

The most popular discussion related to Government Data Processing research is Governing the smart city: a literature review on innovative urban governance. *Open Access,* whose research results in intelligent city governance, is not a technological problem: we must study creative administration as a complex process of institutional change and recognize the political nature and compelling vision of socio-technical governance [15]. The research was most cited, with a total of 584 citations.

4.3   Visualization Network Maps Government Data Processing to Support Smart City

This section will describe a study on government data processing to support smart cities in four countries. Then the researcher will explain using VOSviewer, which can show progress on the themes discussed. The findings of this study are significant in providing products and finding new things in research on the development of data processing in four countries. In picture. 4, you can see the progress of Government Data Processing to support Smart City in four countries from the 2012 to 2022 Scopus database results. In the United States, the importance of strategic leadership, intelligence service potential of the city, MOT, and the specific characteristics of the city change process for the successful implementation of E-Government and Cities innovation [16]. In Spain, Smart cities can contribute to better implementation of E-Government strategies at the city level. Cryptographic protocols and infrastructure enable the private sharing of information to promote E-Participation, allowing the cities to make better decisions based on new data personally contributed by citizens [6].

Meanwhile, in Indonesia, the implementation of innovative city policies in Indonesia has grown more rapidly and broadly in recent years to reduce urban problems by using ICT as a technological innovation [14]. The role of E-Participation in providing service feedback is also an essential part of recent developments in Open Government until technological advances have enabled a new level of openness in government, where institutions and service units make information on their service performance available for public scrutiny through various mobile platforms [17].

For the successful implementation of E-Government in Brazil, they propose an evolution from providing basic information by the government using web channels to electronic transactions and participation to increasing interaction between citizens and government; the success of business innovation also applies in the case of urban innovation to the implementation of E-Government and concepts smart cities [18]. And that there are four clusters, and their characteristics have been identified, which affect E-Government initiatives and smart cities. This study analyzes the municipality's profile from four dimensions: city hall connection infrastructure, electronic services and communication with residents, digital inclusion, and electronic transparency [19].

Fig. 4. Visualization of government data processing network map to support smart city in four countries. *Source: Processed by Researchers Using VOSviewer*

The latest information on developing research trends in government data processing to support intelligent cities by understanding the relationship in Fig. 4 network map visualizations contain 84 items in VOSviewer. Then from the total, these items can be clarified into seven interrelated clusters. Furthermore, details can be seen in the table below (Table 2).

Table 2. Cluster government data processing to support smart City. *Source: Processed by Researchers Using VOSviewer*

Cluster	Concept name	Total
Cluster 1	Behavioral research, cloud computing, cybersecurity, data visualization, digital transformation, e-government services, e-governments, economics, geographic information systems, government data processing, government departments, information services, internet, smart cities, three-dimensional computer gra, urban transportation, webvrgis	17
Cluster 2	Accidents, advanced information, e-governance, electronic commerce, governance approach, ICT, information and communication, information and communication, information management, intelligent city, knowledge society, local government, platforms, public value, smart city, technological change, urban planning	17
Cluster 3	Adoption, article, benchmarking, citizen participation, city, content analysis, e-services, government, human, planning, privacy, smart-city, surveys, sustainable development, trust, united nations	16
Cluster 4	Big data, co-creation, crowdsourcing, digital government, e-government, open data, open government, open innovation, competent government, smartphone, social media, social networking (online)	12
Cluster 5	Developing countries, e-democracy, e- participation, emerging technologies, information systems, innovation, open government data, public administration	8
Cluster 6	Data mining, decision making, information and communications, information and communications, interoperability, policymaking, research agenda, urban growth	8
Cluster 7	Efficiency, official urban digital space, urban information system, urban management, web technologies, websites	6

The analysis results from Vosviewer show that the government process data in supporting intelligent city management is divided into three parts, namely information management in terms of technology change, electronic commerce, innovation, and e-governments. On the other hand, big data is seen from data mining, platforms, and open data. While in the field of information and communication seen from privacy, public administration, and e-participation. More can be seen in the three pictures below (Fig. 5).

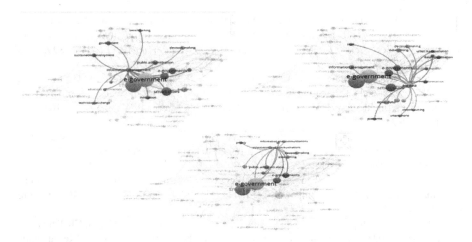

Fig. 5. Visualization of government data processing network map to support smart city in four countries. *Source: Processed by Researchers Using VOSviewer*

5 Conclusion

This study analyzes how government data is processed to create a public service delivery strategy that is transparent, accountable, and participatory in supporting smart cities. The analysis shows that research from 2012 to 2022 has fluctuated with the keywords "E-Government" and "Smart City," which were taken from the Scopus database where the investigation began in 2014 and the research trend was in 2018 and 2020; the results of the study answered government data management. in supporting intelligent cities in 4 countries, namely the United States, Spain, Indonesia and Brazil with the highest articles divided into three dominating government process data: information management, big data, and information and communication. It should be noted that this study includes only publications from the Scopus database. In addition, the scope of the analysis should be expanded to include works indexed in other databases, for example, the Web of Science. This research is further evaluated as an evaluation for the government to improve government data processing in smart cities.

References

1. Herman Fredy Manongga, D., Sunarto, H., Satya Wacana, K., Studi Magister Manajemen, P., Ekonomika dan Bisnis, F., Kristen Satya Wacana, U.: Penerapan Dan Perspektif Open Government Data (Ogd) Di Beberapa Negara: Pendekatan Literatur, no. 1, pp. 978–979 (2018)
2. Furtado, V., et al.: E-totem, digital locative media to support e-participation in cities. Int. J. Electron. Gov. Res. **15**(3), 1–20 (2019). https://doi.org/10.4018/IJEGR.2019070101
3. Yudan, F.F., Arief Virgy, M.: Implementasi Open Government Data oleh Pemerintah Kota Bandung. J. Transform. **7**(1), 128–153 (2021). https://doi.org/10.21776/ub.transformative.2021.007.01.6

506   M. Farhan HR and A. Nurmandi

4. Jacob, D.W., Md Fudzee, M.F., Salamat, M.A., Kasim, S., Mahdin, H., Ramli, A.A.: Modelling end-user of electronic-government service: the role of information quality, system quality and trust. IOP Conf. Ser. Mater. Sci. Eng. **226**(1) (2017). https://doi.org/10.1088/1757-899X/226/1/012096
5. Viale Pereira, G., Cunha, M.A., Lampoltshammer, T.J., Parycek, P., Testa, M.G.: Increasing collaboration and participation in smart city governance: a cross-case analysis of smart city initiatives. Inf. Technol. Dev. **23**(3), 526–553 (2017). https://doi.org/10.1080/02681102.2017.1353946
6. Patsakis, C., Laird, P., Clear, M., Bouroche, M., Solanas, A.: Interoperable privacy-aware E-participation within smart cities. Comput. (Long Beach Calif.) **48**(1), 52–58 (2015). https://doi.org/10.1109/MC.2015.16
7. Lv, Z., Li, X., Wang, W., Zhang, B., Hu, J., Feng, S.: Government affairs service platform for smart city. Future Gener. Comput. Syst. **81**, 443–451 (2018). https://doi.org/10.1016/j.future.2017.08.047
8. Reffat, R.: Developing a successful e-government," … e-Government Oppor. Challenge. …, pp. 1–13 (2003). http://faculty.kfupm.edu.sa/ARCH/rabee/publications_files/03Reffat_eGov.pdf
9. Yan, Z.: Big data and government governance. In: 2018 International Conference on Information Management and Processing, ICIMP 2018, pp. 111–114, January 2018. https://doi.org/10.1109/ICIMP1.2018.8325850
10. Algemili, U.A.: Outstanding challenges in recent open government data initiatives. Int. J. e-Educ. e-Bus. e-Manag. e-Learn. **6**(2), 91–102 (2016). https://doi.org/10.17706/ijeeee.2016.6.2.91-102
11. Fu'Adi, D.K., Arief, A., Sensuse, D.I., Syahrizal, A.: Conceptualizing smart government implementation in smart city context: a systematic review. In: 2020 5th International Conference on Informatics Computing, ICIC 2020 (2020). https://doi.org/10.1109/ICIC50835.2020.9288656
12. Chamoso, P., González-Briones, A., De La Prieta, F., Venyagamoorthy, G.K., Corchado, J.M.: Smart city as a distributed platform: toward a system for citizen-oriented management. Comput. Commun. **152**, 323–332 (2020). https://doi.org/10.1016/j.comcom.2020.01.059
13. Lim, S.B., Yigitcanlar, T.: Participatory governance of smart cities: insights from e-participation of Putrajaya and Petaling Jaya, Malaysia. Smart Cities **5**(1), 71–89 (2022). https://doi.org/10.3390/smartcities5010005
14. Purwanto, E.A.: Smart city as an upshot of bureaucratic reform in Indonesia. Int. J. Electron. Gov. Res. **14**(3), 32–43 (2018). https://doi.org/10.4018/IJEGR.2018070103
15. Meijer, A., Bolívar, M.P.R.: Governing the smart city: a review of the literature on smart urban governance. Int. Rev. Adm. Sci. **82**(2), 392–408 (2016). https://doi.org/10.1177/0020852314564308
16. Guimaraes, T., Madeira, G.: Testing some important factors for city e-gov implementation success. Electron. Gov. **14**(4), 340–358 (2018). https://doi.org/10.1504/EG.2018.095547
17. Allen, B., Tamindael, L.E., Bickerton, S.H., Cho, W.: Does citizen coproduction lead to better urban services in smart cities projects? An empirical study on e-participation in a mobile big data platform. Gov. Inf. Q. **37**(1) (2020). https://doi.org/10.1016/j.giq.2019.101412
18. Madeira, G., Guimaraes, T., De Souza Mendes, L.: Assessing some models for city e-government implementation: a case study. Electron. Gov. **12**(1), 86–105 (2016). https://doi.org/10.1504/EG.2016.074250
19. Przeybilovicz, E., Cunha, M.A., Meirelles, F.S.: The use of information and communication technology to characterize municipalities: who they are and what they need to develop e-government and smart city initiatives. Rev. Adm. Publica **52**(4), 630–649 (2018). https://doi.org/10.1590/0034-7612170582

People-Flows: An Innovative Flow Monitoring and Management System in Urban Environments

Manos Kalaitzakis[1], Eirini Sykianaki[1], Nikitas Michalakis[1], Nikos Stivaktakis[1], Kassiani Balafa[1], Stavroula Ntoa[1(✉)], and Constantine Stephanidis[1,2]

[1] Foundation for Research and Technology – Hellas (FORTH), Institute of Computer Science, N. Plastira 100, Vassilika Vouton, 70013 Heraklion, Crete, Greece
`{mkalaitz,esykianaki,michalakis,nstivaktak,balafa,stant,`
`cs}@ics.forth.gr`
[2] Department of Computer Science, University of Crete, 70013 Heraklion, Crete, Greece

Abstract. Overtourism is an ongoing problem observed in popular destinations around the world, requiring solutions that will combat congestion and enhance the quality of life for citizens and the quality of experience for visitors. In order to truly resolve the problem, solutions should combine the management of visitor flows through technological support, and also assist policymakers and management bodies in planning ahead. This work proposes a system for monitoring visitor flows and supporting their visit scheduling based on the estimated crowdedness of points of interest. The system comprises a web platform for a priori planning, as well as kiosks to issue tickets and informative screens in points of interest and central points of urban destinations. The proposed system is part of an integrated approach, also featuring a system for administrators of attractions (museums, sights, monuments, etc.) and policymakers.

Keywords: Overtourism · Flow management · Flow monitoring · Crowdedness management

1 Introduction

The phenomenon of overtourism refers to the problem of touristic destinations and attractions which occasionally become overcrowded, with unpleasant consequences for the visitors' experience [1]. This phenomenon exhibited in Greece and worldwide increasingly concerns the travel industry, locals, and businesses in tourist areas, as well as governments and policymakers [2].

The congestion of people at terminals and transport stations, and in general at popular tourist destinations such as archaeological sites, beaches, and public spaces, often adversely affects the quality of the provided services, the visitor's experience as well as the quality of life, and health conditions for all. In specific, consequences that have been reported include gentrification, declining population, protest movements, loss of destination attractiveness, loss of residents' livability, a mismatch between the type of

C. Stephanidis et al. (Eds.): HCII 2022, CCIS 1655, pp. 507–516, 2022.
https://doi.org/10.1007/978-3-031-19682-9_64

visitors and destination, as well as a mismatch between groups of visitors [2]. At the same time, several social, economic, but also environmental impacts on overcrowded destinations are evident [3].

To address the problem, we introduce the PeopleFlows platform. The primary goal of the platform is to propose and implement an integrated flow management mechanism that can operate both individually with the aim of decongesting a specific point of interest, but also being capable to provide a holistic solution for managing an entire destination (*e.g.*, a city or an entire area such as an island) through the collection and analysis of large volumes of data to provide service forecasts that will enable short- and medium-term decongestion planning by decision-making centers.

The adoption of such an integrated human flow management mechanism will make it possible to decongest destinations with high traffic, aiming to improve the degree of satisfaction and the sense of security of residents and visitors. Decongestion can be achieved by providing the correct information to the competent management bodies to properly plan ahead, but also with the timely provision of information and recommendations to visitors.

The proposed solution integrates a website for visitors, as well as smart queue management mechanisms for better service of visitors' flows through the utilization of interactive interfaces and information systems established in focal city points and sights. At the same time, it features a system for administrators providing different levels of access and information according to their role (e.g. staff issuing tickets, sight administration, policymaker, etc.). The work described in this paper focuses on the development of visitors' systems. Section 2 carries out a short review of related work in the field. Section 3 presents the PeopleFlows approach for visitors, whereas Sect. 4 the evaluation results. Finally, Sect. 5 summarizes this work and provides directions for future research in the field.

2 Background and Related Work

Overtourism is not new; yet, it is an issue that is attracting a growing interest in literature, with discussions ranging on the causes and implications, case studies, and potential solutions for sustainable tourism. It is noteworthy that although before 2017 it was a topic absent from the literature, in 2022, and despite the ongoing pandemic which has restricted travel, it has become a very popular topic with several articles, special issues, and books devoted to it [4].

Among the causes of this phenomenon, new technologies and the creation of low-cost airline carriers are identified as decisive for its growth [1]. A technology that has had a major impact is that of accommodation and transportation platforms [4], offering the corresponding facilities as part of the 'sharing economy' approach and allowing IT-facilitated peer-to-peer service provisioning. At the same time, digital media have also played a role in communicating touristic experiences, through reviews and blogs which have made some attractions more popular than ever, but also through the delivery of top things to do in a city, thus leading to higher congestion of occasional and hurried visitors in the promoted sights [5].

Solutions that have been discussed in the literature include extending the capacity of tourist activities [1, 4], and shifting responsibilities to governments and policymakers [4].

With regard to the latter, approaches that have been adopted at a regional level range from legal measures to the adoption of technological solutions that monitor and manage flows, redirecting visitors to less congested attractions or areas not usually visited by tourists [6, 7]. For instance, a visitor counting system through cameras has been implemented in the city of Dubrovnik, supported by a machine learning algorithm to calculate visitor flows [8]. Identification of visitors' preferences and understanding of their behavior through GPS tracking has also been implemented in some cases [8, 9].

Nevertheless, technological solutions for the management of tourist flows cannot address the problem on their own. Such solutions can be criticized for not being realistic, since – for example – a person visiting Paris would definitely visit the Louvre Museum, or the Eiffel Tower, no matter what [1]. Technological solutions should certainly be combined with other approaches, such as decentralization and provision of appropriate infrastructures, local involvement and collaboration, planning and regulation, smart tourism approaches, degrowth, and segmentation, as well as fostering of tourist-resident interactions [3]. In this respect, the role of destination management organizations becomes prominent in bringing together all actors affected by tourism in a destination and undertaking strategic leadership [10].

In any case, such technological solutions should be in place to facilitate the management of visitor flows and better planning on behalf of visitors, but also management bodies, and policymakers. We posit that due to the exact same reasons that have led to overtourism, it is often the case that several visitors are not first-time sightseers of a destination. As such, they would probably prefer to visit sights and places alternative to the most popular ones, or at least it should be easy for them to find such places, an objective which can be served with the help of technology.

3 The PeopleFlows Approach for Visitors

This section presents the different systems that have been developed for visitors. In specific, it introduces: (1) the web platform, which aims to assist visitors' planning; (2) the kiosks and informative screens that have been developed for integration in tourist destinations, such as sights or museums, aiming to facilitate flow management and avoid crowdedness, and (3) informative kiosks that can be installed at central city points, allowing visitors to better organize their visits to specific destinations.

All the systems provide crowdedness information and suggestions, through the collection and analysis of large volumes of data. In order to cope with the complexity of managing large volumes of data and achieving the set goals, a data collection and transformation (ETL) system was implemented. The ETL system collects and processes heterogeneous data streams from multiple sources, such as booking systems, entrance control systems, camera installations with object recognition capabilities, etc. Information is transformed into time-series data that is then analyzed by a big data analysis and forecasting system. In turn, forecasts and 'live' feedback are then visualized and used by a suite of applications to provide recommendations and raise warnings. At the same time, motivated by the need to communicate clearly and efficiently big data information to non-specialized audiences [11, 12], the system features dashboards to summarize information in a perceivable and understandable approach.

3.1 Planning One's Visit: The Web Platform

Through the web platform, visitors can be informed about local attractions and plan their visit to any of them for a particular day and time. To this end, the platform's home page provides a specialized search engine and displays the attractions with the lowest crowdedness and highest popularity (see Fig. 1). To use the search engine and get personalized attraction suggestions (sorted by lowest crowdedness), visitors have to fill out at least one of the fields (i.e., attraction location, desired date or dates, attraction type, and the number of visitors). In addition, the home page features alternative paths for booking tickets, namely the "Buy Tickets" button for booking tickets instantly, the menu links leading to different attraction category pages (i.e., museums, sightseeing, landscapes), and content organization in different categories, such as attractions with low crowdedness, but also most popular attractions. As such, a visitor can schedule their visit even to the most popular attractions driven by the most convenient time to do so.

Fig. 1. The web platform: home and search results page.

On the attraction page (see Fig. 2), visitors can be further informed about it (i.e. location along with a link that opens a map, images, description, ticket price, contact details, and open hours), book tickets if available, but also declare their intention to visit it, in which case they will be notified when crowdedness is low. To assist users in picking the best time to visit the attraction, the system provides suggestions on time slots but also crowdedness estimations for the road traffic, as well as the occupancy rate and the waiting time at the attraction, according to the selected season or dates, accompanied by an indication of the estimations' accuracy. Finally, some recommendations for similar low-crowdedness attractions for the current period are offered.

The booking process consists of four steps (see Fig. 3). Firstly, visitors have to determine the attraction, the number of visitors, and the date and time of their visit. The displayed colors can help them pick the best date and time based on the levels of crowdedness (i.e., red for high, yellow for medium, and green for low). In the second step, visitors' contact information (i.e., name, telephone number, and email) and the type of their tickets are requested, while the system calculates and displays the total ticket price. The third step summarizes the purchase and leads to an external payment system. In the last step, booking confirmation appears, which visitors can print or receive via email or text message on their phone.

The declaration of intention to visit an attraction can be completed in a single step. Visitors have to choose the date and time of their visit and determine the number of visitors. Also, an email address is requested to receive a notification when its crowdedness is low on the selected date/dates.

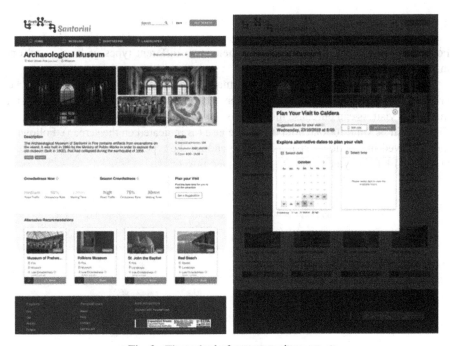

Fig. 2. The web platform: attraction page.

Fig. 3. The web platform: first and fourth steps of the booking page.

3.2 On the Spot: Kiosks and Screens

For optimal on-site visitor flow management, two different types of kiosks and one informative screen are foreseen.

The **tickets kiosk** (see Fig. 4) is a small touch display connected with a ticket printing mechanism and a credit card reader, aiming to decongest ticket counters. Using this kiosk, visitors can purchase their tickets, quickly and easily, without any assistance. Tickets will be valid for one hour after purchase (as indicated on the screen). Following the displayed instructions, visitors have to choose the type and the number of tickets, proceed with the payment and get their printed tickets.

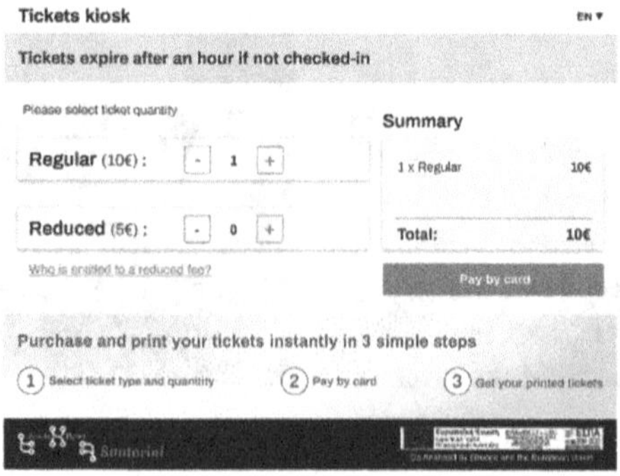

Fig. 4. The tickets kiosk.

The **ticket scanner** (see Fig. 5) is a small touch display connected with a ticket scanner. Following the displayed instructions, visitors can validate their tickets and enter the attraction without any extra delay. The kiosk also provides useful information about the crowdedness and waiting times of the current time and day, allowing visitors to delay their visit if they think the place is overcrowded.

Fig. 5. The ticket scanner.

The **informative flow screen** (see Fig. 6) is a large display expected to be mounted high on a wall where it will be visible, which alternates two information pages every few minutes. On the first page, visitors are informed about the current crowdedness and waiting time at the attraction, as well as the current day's average values and the expected waiting times for the next hours. Moreover, the page offers some recommendations of the closest points of interest that they can alternatively visit, in case of high on-site waiting time. On the second page, visitors can examine the current month's crowdedness calendar and learn how to buy their tickets.

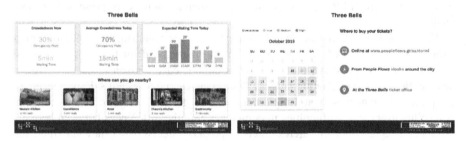

Fig. 6. The informative flow screen.

3.3 In the City: Informative Kiosks

The informative kiosks (see Fig. 7) are systems developed following the responsive design rationale adapting to large or small touch screen displays, featuring also a ticket printing mechanism, and credit card reader, which can be placed at central places in urban areas. These kiosks can be installed both indoors (e.g., at citizens' information points) and outdoors (e.g., in squares and public gathering spaces). The main element of their user interface is the map of the surrounding area on which points of interest and the kiosk's current location (and therefore the visitor's location) are displayed. A passerby will be able to search for a specific point of interest on the map, view more details about it, book and print their tickets, or state their intention to visit an attraction.

Fig. 7. The informative kiosk.

4   Evaluation

A user-based evaluation was conducted with eleven participants who were requested to execute specific tasks using the PeopleFlows systems and to follow the think-aloud protocol, to identify the difficulties experienced when using the system [13]. This was a preliminary evaluation, carried out in the laboratory, and as such, it was focused on qualitative findings that would lead to redesign changes in order to improve users' experience. Overall, participants had a pleasant experience, did not face any serious difficulties, and found PeopleFlows useful. Evaluation findings are presented in more detail below.

Firstly, users had to assume that they were using the Santorini's PeopleFlows platform, on the occasion of their upcoming trip, to plan ahead for their visit and avoid waiting in long queues. All the participants completed the given tasks successfully, however through the evaluation process some changes to the system's design occurred. The primary change was the redesign of the time suggestion service to become simpler. In specific, users faced difficulties in comprehending the differences between booking a ticket and expressing their interest to visit a point of interest. Also, they identified that they would like the automated suggestions to be provided only once they have indicated a time period that they would like to visit an attraction.

In the second scenario, a room with two tablets placed on floor stands (i.e., a tickets kiosk and a tickets scanner) and a large screen TV (i.e., an informative flow screen) was simulating the attraction's entrance hall. Participants were requested to check the current waiting time and then buy and scan their tickets, which they accomplished easily. It was observed that the informative flow screen contained a large amount of information, which delayed participants to find the current waiting time, thus secondary data was removed. On the contrary, the two kiosks received only positive feedback.

Finally, users had to assume that they were either in the central square of Fira or in Santorini's information point hall, where they found a PeopleFlows informative kiosk (i.e., a large touch screen and a tablet placed on a floor stand, respectively). Participants were requested to book and print their tickets, found information about an attraction's crowdedness, and state their intention to visit it. The participants completed these tasks successfully, but it was observed that some minor changes could improve the user experience. The most important of them was the redesign of the splash screen, as participants confused it with a home page with clickable links, and the layout rearrangement of the attraction page, in order to give more emphasis to the attraction's information and make the booking button more noticeable.

5 Summary and Conclusions

Motivated by the need to address the problem of overtourism, this work has proposed a system for monitoring and managing people's flows in popular urban destinations, sights, and attractions. The system employs big data analysis, machine learning, and computer vision technologies, in order to effectively monitor and proactively respond to foreseen anomalies. Furthermore, aiming to provide a viable solution considering the positive sides of touristification, as well as the negative sides of overtourism [14], the PeopleFlows system considers that visitors should not only be directed to less crowded/unpopular attractions; instead, they should be supported in planning their visit to popular sights, considering though when it is best to visit them in terms of crowdedness. As such, the system features a web platform to assist visitors' planning, as well as ticket kiosks and informative screens in attractions and focal city points, aiming to facilitate tickets' issuing and enhance visitors' experience by redirecting them to other less congested points or attractions nearby their destination. It is noted that the PeopleFlows approach also features a system for administrators, allowing them to manage ticket availability and monitor flows in their attraction. At the same time, a system for policymakers provides statistics for all the sights and attractions in an entire area, thus facilitating planning and decision-making.

A preliminary evaluation of the PeopleFlows systems for visitors has been conducted with eleven representative end-users, yielding qualitative findings to improve user experience with the aforementioned systems. Recognizing though that user experience is a composite phenomenon requiring the study of numerous factors [15], additional user-based studies are being planned with a larger number of users who will be engaged in an in-situ evaluation, aiming to identify if the proposed solution is usable but also useful in achieving decongestion and improving visitors' experience in popular destinations.

Acknowledgments. This work has been conducted in the context of the People-Flows research project (http://www.peopleflows.gr/), and has been co-financed by the European Union and Greek national funds through the Operational Program Competitiveness, Entrepreneurship and Innovation, under the call RESEARCH–CREATE–INNOVATE (project code: T1EDK-05210).

References

1. Dodds, R., Butler, R.: The phenomena of overtourism: a review. Int. J. Tour. Cities **5**, 519–528 (2019). https://doi.org/10.1108/IJTC-06-2019-0090

2. Peeters, P., et al.: Research for TRAN Committee - Overtourism: impact and possible policy responses. European Parliament, Policy Department for Structural and Cohesion Policies, Brussels (2018)
3. Veríssimo, M., Moraes, M., Breda, Z., Guizi, A., Costa, C.: Overtourism and tourismphobia: a systematic literature review. Tour. (Zagreb, Online) **68**, 156–169 (2020). https://doi.org/10.37741/t.68.2.4
4. Koens, K., Postma, A., Papp, B.: Is overtourism overused? Understanding the impact of tourism in a city context. Sustainability **10**, 4384 (2018). https://doi.org/10.3390/su10124384
5. Bourliataux-Lajoinie, S., Dosquet, F., del Olmo Arriaga, J.L.: The dark side of digital technology to overtourism: the case of Barcelona. WHATT **11**, 582–593 (2019). https://doi.org/10.1108/WHATT-06-2019-0041
6. Capocchi, A., Vallone, C., Pierotti, M., Amaduzzi, A.: Overtourism: a literature review to assess implications and future perspectives. Sustainability **11**, 3303 (2019). https://doi.org/10.3390/su11123303
7. Hospers, G.-J.: Overtourism in European cities: from challenges to coping strategies. CESifo Forum **20**, 20–24 (2019)
8. Camatti, N., Bertocchi, D., Carić, H., van der Borg, J.: A digital response system to mitigate overtourism. The case of Dubrovnik. J. Travel Tour. Mark. **37**, 887–901 (2020). https://doi.org/10.1080/10548408.2020.1828230
9. Ryan, C.: Future trends in tourism research – looking back to look forward: the future of 'Tourism Management Perspectives.' Tour. Manag. Perspect. **25**, 196–199 (2018). https://doi.org/10.1016/j.tmp.2017.12.005
10. Eckert, C., Zacher, D., Pechlaner, H., Namberger, P., Schmude, J.: Strategies and measures directed towards overtourism: a perspective of European DMOs. IJTC **5**, 639–655 (2019). https://doi.org/10.1108/IJTC-12-2018-0102
11. Vitsaxaki, K., Ntoa, S., Margetis, G., Spyratos, N.: Interactive visual exploration of big relational datasets. Int. J. Hum. Comput. Interact., 1–15 (2022). https://doi.org/10.1080/10447318.2022.2073007
12. Ntoa, S., Birliraki, C., Drossis, G., Margetis, G., Adami, I., Stephanidis, C.: UX design of a big data visualization application supporting gesture-based interaction with a large display. In: Yamamoto, S. (ed.) HIMI 2017. LNCS, vol. 10273, pp. 248–265. Springer, Cham (2017). https://doi.org/10.1007/978-3-319-58521-5_20
13. Charters, E.: The use of think-aloud methods in qualitative research an introduction to think-aloud methods. Brock Educ. J. **12** (2003). https://doi.org/10.26522/brocked.v12i2.38
14. Bouchon, F., Rauscher, M.: Cities and tourism, a love and hate story; towards a conceptual framework for urban overtourism management. IJTC **5**, 598–619 (2019). https://doi.org/10.1108/IJTC-06-2019-0080
15. Ntoa, S., Margetis, G., Antona, M., Stephanidis, C.: User experience evaluation in intelligent environments: a comprehensive framework. Technologies **9**, 41 (2021). https://doi.org/10.3390/technologies9020041

Comparative Study on the Impact of Cultural Background on the Perception of Different Types of Social Robots

Angelika Bernsteiner[1]([✉]), Kathrin Pollmann[2], and Leopold Neuhold[3]

[1] University of Graz, Harrachgasse 21, 8010 Graz, Austria
angelika.mandl@uni-graz.at
[2] Fraunhofer Institute for Industrial Engineering IAO, Stuttgart, Germany
[3] Institute of Ethics, University of Graz, Graz, Austria

Abstract. The increasing integration of social robots into people's everyday lives requires research on factors that lead to a strong acceptance of such robots. This paper shows results of a cross-cultural comparative study (418 participants from Austria, Azerbaijan, Germany and India) on the perception of a humanoid (Pepper), an animal-like (MiRo) and an abstract (Roomba®) social robot. The results indicate, that for a harmonic human-robot interaction cultural factors have to be considered, since people from different countries have different preferences regarding a social robot.

Keywords: Cultural robotics · Cross-cultural study · Robot acceptance · Human-robot interaction

1 Introduction

To achieve a harmonic human-robot interaction and to integrate social robots into people's lives as easily as possible, social robots must be designed to be accepted by people [5]. It is necessary to analyze what social robots should look like and how they should behave in different cultural contexts and situations [5, 6]. The morphology of a robot plays a major role in forming these expectations. Different body parts such as arms, legs, eyes and mouth of the robot are associated with certain functional capacities of the robot such as being able to lift things, walk, see or talk. It has also been argued by the Uncanny Valley theory that robot appearances that are designed too anthropomorphic are experienced as creepy or scary [8].

Once brought to market, robots are made available in different countries, assuming that they will be successfully accepted in varying cultural contexts. However, a review of the body of research in human-robot-interaction suggests that attitudes towards robots can diverge for user groups of different countries: A number of different studies show that people's attitudes toward robots, people's expectations of robots, and people's acceptance of robots depend on people's nationality and cultural background [1, 3–7].

C. Stephanidis et al. (Eds.): HCII 2022, CCIS 1655, pp. 517–522, 2022.
https://doi.org/10.1007/978-3-031-19682-9_65

2   Research and Methods

The present study examines how nationality and cultural background influence perceptions of and preferences for different robot morphologies: humanoid (Pepper), animal-like (MiRo), and abstract (Roomba®) (Fig. 1).

Fig. 1. Types of social robots investigated in the cross-cultural comparison study – from left to right: Pepper, Roomba®, MiRo.

We conducted a cross-cultural comparative study as an online survey with participants from Azerbaijan (AZE), Germany (DEU), India (IND), and Austria (AUT) to investigate the following hypotheses:

- Hypothesis 1 (H.1.): People from different cultural backgrounds prioritize desirable features of a social robot differently.
- Hypothesis 2 (H.2.): People from different cultural groups attribute different properties to different types of social robots.
- Hypothesis 3 (H.3.): People from different cultural groups exhibit different affinities towards different types of robots.

Table 1 contains an overview of the demographic characteristics of the sub-samples of the four countries.

Table 1. Characterization of the sub-samples of the four countries.

Country	Sample size	Male	Female	Mean age (years) ± std.-dev.	University degree
Austria	112	59	53	31,71 ± 13,96	52
Azerbaijan	62	43	19	22,73 ± 8,36	49
Germany	61	32	29	38,41 ± 13,31	46
India	183	158	25	36,09 ± 8,59	182

2.1 Study Design

The study was conducted in a mixed design. Nationality was included as a between-subjects factor and consisted of four levels: Indian, Azerbaijani, Austrian, and German. The design of the robot was included as a within-subjects factor and comprised three levels: humanoid, animal-like, and abstract. Specifically, we examined three dependent variables, namely "general attitude toward robots" (dependent variable 1), "Attitude toward Pepper, MiRo, and Roomba®" (dependent variable 2) and "Affinity for Pepper, MiRo and Roomba®" (dependent variable 3). "Attitude towards robots" in general and for the three robots in particular was assessed using the Robot Attitude Scale (RAS) [2]. The RAS questionnaire consists of eleven pairs of bipolar adjectives (e.g., interesting - boring, reliable - unreliable). Participants are asked to give a rating on an eight-point scale indicating which of the two adjectives better reflects their personal impression of the robot. The questionnaire refers to different aspects of a robot, such as technical progress, user-friendliness and trust. Robot Preference was obtained by asking participants to choose one of the three robots at the end of the survey.

2.2 Study Set-up and Procedure

The online survey was created in English and German using LimeSurvey. The whole questionnaire took about 15 min to complete and included in addition to the inquiry of various demographic data:

General Attitude Towards Robots (Dependent Variable 1). Participants indicated characteristics they considered important in a robot using the 11 adjective pairs of the RAS scale [2]. The adjective that is ranked first is most important to people, while the attribute that is ranked eleventh is somewhat unimportant. Based on this raking task, hypothesis 1 was investigated by calculating the mean values of each attribute for each country and comparing the countries based on these mean values.

Attitude Toward Pepper, MiRo, and Roomba® (Dependent Variable 2). Participants were asked about their attitudes toward each of the three robots. This enabled the investigation of hypothesis 2. For that, the participants were shown a GIF video of each robot doing a simple rotation. Then, participants were asked to fill in the RAS questionnaire for each robot. Participants assigned a numerical value from one to eight for each adjective pair. For example, for the combination safe-dangerous, this means that the number one represents very safe and the number eight represents very dangerous. In order to compare the statements of people from different countries, the mean values of the ratings were calculated for each characteristic and country.

Affinity for Pepper, MiRo and Roomba® (Dependent Variable 3). In order investigate hypothesis 3, at the end of the online questionnaire the participants were asked to specifically choose the robot they preferred and thus express their affinity for humanoid, animal-like or abstract robots. For this purpose, a graphic of each robot was shown, which had been created from the preceding GIFs.

3   Results

With reference to the formulated hypotheses, the main results of the study are presented below.

3.1   H.1. People from Different Cultural Backgrounds Prioritize Desirable Features of a Social Robot Differently

The results of the study indicate that H.1. must be falsified. People from different cultural groups prioritized desirable attributes of a social robot similarly (Table 2). While the attributes safe and useful were perceived as very important in relation to robots, the attributes strong and interesting turned out to be quite unimportant.

Table 2. Prioritization of robot characteristics based on the adjective pairs of the RAS scale - Mean values per adjective and country. Presentation of the most expressive adjectives.

	Safe	Useful	Helpful	Simple	Trustworthy	Technically advanced	Easy to use	Strong	Interesting
AUT	3,76	3,43	3,67	6,79	6,14	6,84	4,73	9,03	8,59
AZE	4,24	5,11	5,23	6,65	6,94	6,27	5,55	7,23	6,32
DEU	3,05	3,56	4,13	7,21	6,10	6,51	4,74	9,05	8,79
IND	2,78	4,44	6,07	7,02	6,57	6,50	5,07	7,89	7,96

3.2   H.2. People from Different Cultural Groups Attribute Different Properties to Different Types of Social Robots

Figure two presents an overview of the mean ratings per country and robot on the 11 RAS scales. Based on that, H.2. can be partially verified. The diverse attribution of properties was particularly notable in the case of the humanoid robot Pepper. While people from India and Azerbaijan rated Pepper as safe, Germans and Austrians attributed more negative characteristics to this robot (e.g. rated it as more dangerous and unreliable). People from Azerbaijan rated Pepper as particularly helpful, useful and trustworthy (Fig. 2).

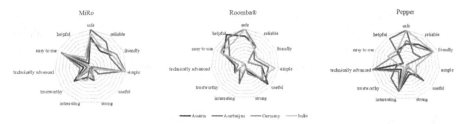

Fig. 2. Mean ratings per country for the three robots according to the RAS scale.

People from the four countries attributed similar characteristics to the robot MiRo. Roomba was rated as trustworthy by people from Germany and Austria in particular, and as simple by people from India and Azerbaijan.

3.3 H.3. People from Different Cultural Groups Exhibit Different Affinities Towards Different Types of Robots

H.3. can be verified (compare with Table 3). The results show that Indians preferred the humanoid robot Pepper. Pepper also appealed to people from Azerbaijan, although the majority preferred the abstract robot Roomba®. People from Germany and Austria clearly preferred Roomba®. The animal-like robot MiRo was not well received in any of the four countries. However, it appealed more to people from India and Azerbaijan than to people from Germany and Austria.

Table 3. Robot preference per country, given in percent.

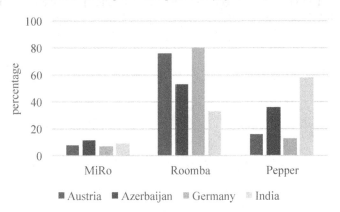

4 Conclusion

The results of the present cross-cultural comparative study show that similar characteristics of social robots are important to people of different countries. It is revealed, however, that people of different cultures attribute different characteristics to the different types of social robots to some extent. Consequently, people of different nationalities have different preferences regarding the robot type. The findings therefore highlight that for a harmonic human-robot interaction, it is necessary to adapt the design of robots to the culturally determined preferences.

References

1. Bartneck, C., Suzuki, T., Kanda, T., Nomura, T.: The influence of people's culture and prior experiences with Aibo on their attitude towards robots. AI Soc. **21**(1), 217–230 (2007)
2. Broadbent, E., Stafford, R., MacDonald, B.: Acceptance of healthcare robots for the older population: review and future directions. Int. J. Soc. Robot. **1**(4), 319 (2009)
3. Conti, D., Cattani, A., Di Nuovo, S., Di Nuovo, A.: A cross-cultural study of acceptance and use of robotics by future psychology practitioners. In: Proceedings of the 24th IEEE International Symposium on Robot and Human Interactive Communication (RO-MAN), pp. 555–560. IEEE (2015). https://doi.org/10.1109/ROMAN.2015.7333601
4. Haring, K., Mougenot, C., Ono, F., Watanabe, K.: Cultural differences in perception and attitude towards robots. Int. J. Affect. Eng. **13**, 149–157 (2014)
5. Korn, O.: Social Robots: Technological, Societal and Ethical Aspects of Human-Robot Interaction. Springer, Cham (2019). https://doi.org/10.1007/978-3-030-17107-0
6. Korn, O., Akalin, N., Gouveia, R.: Understanding cultural preferences for social robots. J. Hum. Robot Interact. **10**(2), 1–19 (2021)
7. Lee, H.R., Sabanović, S.: Culturally variable preferences for robot design and use in South Korea, Turkey, and the United States. In Proceedings of the 2014 ACM/IEEE International Conference on Human-Robot Interaction, pp. 17–24. ACM, New York (2014). https://doi.org/10.1145/2559636.2559676
8. Mori, M., MacDorman, K., Kageki, N.: The uncanny valley [from the field]. IEEE Robot. Autom. Mag. **19**(2), 98–100 (2012)

Human-Computer Interaction and Coevolution in Science AI Robotics

Yoshihiro Maruyama[1,2](✉)

[1] School of Computing, Australian National University, Canberra, Australia
yoshihiro.maruyama@anu.edu.au
[2] Advanced Telecommunications Research Institute, Kyoto, Japan

Abstract. Science AI Robotics has significantly advanced over recent years, and there are various ethical and social issues concerning the potential relationships between humans, including human scientists in particular, and science AI robots, namely intelligent robots for autonomous scientific inquiry. In this paper we address those issues in Science AI Robotics and reimagine the future of science as enabled by advances in Science AI Robotics whilst emphasising the role5 and significance of human-computer interaction and coevolution in scientific practice. At the same time, we shed new light on the novel rôles of Integrative AI, in particular Categorical AI (i.e., Category-theoretical AI) and Categorical ML (Categorical Machine Learning) in the context of Ethical AI, especially the development of Intensional AI which internalises symbolic ethical principles within itself (rather than superficially learn extensional ethical behaviours as in purely inductive machine learning).

Keywords: Science AI Robotics · Efficiency of human/machine intelligence · Sustainability · Energy problem · HCI in science · Human-robot coevolution in science · Intensional AI · Ethical AI · Integrative AI · Categorical AI

1 Introduction

Science AI Robotics has advanced significantly over recent years. Machine learning of universal physical laws, for instance, has been made possible by AI Feynman [23] and AI Poincaré [5] in theoretical data science, while in applied data science, novel material discovery via machine learning has been successful as illustrated in a recent *Nature* paper [22] for example. As to Science Robotics, there is classic research such as the Robot Scientist Adam and its descendent (see, e.g., [3]). It could happen in the long run that superintelligent AI robot scientists become able to win Nobel prizes in various scientific fields. AI robot scientists will eventually go beyond the human cognitive and physical limits, such as the limit of human perception, the limit of human motion, the limit of human intelligence, and the like.

Several questions then arise as to the future of science and society. How should we reimagine the relationships between humans and AI robots at the

C. Stephanidis et al. (Eds.): HCII 2022, CCIS 1655, pp. 523–531, 2022.
https://doi.org/10.1007/978-3-031-19682-9_66

age of Science AI Robotics in which quite some part of scientific practice can be mechanised and automated? If science is enabled and driven without explicit human supervision, what is the role of human scientists then? More specifically, should we restrict the growing capabilities of AI robot scientists so as to lower the risk of catastrophic or ethically problematic accidents (e.g., creation of novel viruses by autonomous AI robot scientists)? If we restrict the autonomy of AI robot scientists, however, it may reduce the creativity of them, and ultimately, make AI robots scientists more like mere assistants than fully autonomous creative agents. Consider the following picture:

which is a picture used in a so-called Moonshot project of Japan [2] to explain the 2050 world in which humans and AI robot scientists are expected to interact and coevolve together. There are both rooms in which only humans work and rooms in which only robots work as well as rooms in which humans and robots work together. What task is for robots only? And what task is for humans only? Designing the relationships between humans and AI robot scientists is concerned with classifying different tasks into three categories, namely the category of tasks for robots, the category of tasks for humans, and the category of tasks for which humans and robots cooperate together and coevolve through their interaction. Performing simple experiments is arguably a task for AI robot scientists (or even simple robot scientists without much intelligence). Is designing objectives and values a task for humans? This sort of meta-learning is actually possible to some extent even via current machine learning.

There are other sorts of social issues as well. The amount of energy required for current machine learning is enormous even for relatively simple tasks (for which human intelligence does not require so much energy). According to Knight [4]:

Researchers at OpenAI in San Francisco revealed an algorithm capable of learning, through trial and error, how to manipulate the pieces of a

Rubik's Cube using a robotic hand. It was a remarkable research feat, but it required more than 1,000 desktop computers plus a dozen machines running specialized graphics chips crunching intensive calculations for several months.

Knight [4] then asserts as follows:

One algorithm that lets a robot manipulate a Rubik's Cube used as much energy as 3 nuclear plants produce in an hour.

This poses a serious sustainability issue to humanity, and some researchers today argue for the computational limits of deep learning [21], which tends to spend too much energy even for simple perception tasks such as image recognition. The sustainability problem lurking behind the current success of Science AI Robotics may ultimately lead to sacrificing some of the ecology of the earth (or it may have been doing so already). Designing a suitable form of science AI robots is therefore a non-trivial enterprise facing various challenges as mentioned above. In this paper we address these issues in Science AI Robotics, and reimagine the future of science as enabled by advances in Science AI Robotics whilst emphasising the role and significance of human-computer interaction and coevolution in scientific practice.

The remainder of the paper is organised as follows. In Sect. 2, we discuss how to reimagine the human-robot relationships in the context of Science AI Robotics, in which we especially focus upon the possibility that AI robot scientists go beyond human cognitive and physical limits, giving rise to superintelligence, supermobility, and supercognition, which in turn yield a number of risks for the present human civilisation. In order to address the risks, we encounter a fundamental dilemma between autonomy and safety/security of artificial agents. In Sect. 3, we discuss sustainability issues, especially the energy problem, and the efficiency of human and machine intelligence. In Sect. 4, we conclude with outlooks and additional remarks for future work.

2 How to Reimagine the Human-Robot Relationships in the Context of Science AI Robotics?

In the above picture, you see both human-only and robot-only rooms. What are they doing? What is each room for? As Science AI Robotics advances we have to reimagine the relationships between humans and AI robots. What relationships are most fruitful for both humans and robots to coevolve together?

The human-robot relationships in the present context could be similar to the relationships between Shogi AI and human Shogi players. There are fruitful interactions between them, each learning a lot from the other. Shogi players today reconceive their strategies in consideration of Shogi AI's strategies, and occasionally even get novel insights from them. Shogi AI learns from data in human Shogi matches as well as data in pure AI matches (although it is not relevant here, it is also possible to train Shogi AI just based upon AI versus AI matches). There would however be dissimilarities between the practice of science and that of Shogi. Shogi is a simple game and there are clear winning conditions as well as clear criteria for what moves are allowed in a given situation. Shogi has a human-made set of formal rules whilst science does not.

Science is a significantly more creative activity than Shogi, and there are, in principle, no a priori limitations on what one does in science. In contrast, what one can do is clearly limited by the clear set of rules in the case of Shogi. This difference on freedom of intelligence leads to a striking difference on their risks. There is virtually no catastrophic risk in Shogi AI, and yet Science AI Robots are involved in a variety of catastrophic risks. There may for example be mad AI robot scientists who create harmful viruses whereas there is no such critical possibility for Shogi AI.

2.1   AI Robot Scientist Goes Beyond Human Cognitive and Physical Limits

AI robot scientists go beyond the human cognitive and physical limits, such as the limit of human perception, the limit of human motion, the limit of human intelligence, and the like. They can, for example, continue to work for 24 h everyday (although ethical considerations may not allow this, especially if AI robots are granted personhood as recently proposed). They can work in space without any oxygen; they can also work in dangerous environments (caused by natural disasters, for instance). They will be able to work in water or in the sky (or wherever else). They can recognise Nature beyond the limits of human recognition, being able to see what we cannot see and hear what we cannot hear, which will open up the possibility for a new kind of science beyond the human cognitive limits.

There have been numerous discussions on superintelligence, yet Science AI Robotics is not just a matter of superintelligence, but also a matter of supercognition and a matter of supermobility. And those superhuman capabilities can benefit and threaten us at the same time, like any other capabilities. As a matter of fact, the risk of AI robot scientists is no different from the risk of human geniuses. There may be evil human geniuses, and likewise, there may be evil AI robot scientists. Superhuman capabilities are pure capabilities, which are like weapons that can be used in whatever manner, and which can in particular be used to threaten us as well as to benefit us. We would have to impose some regulations on AI robot scientists to avoid dystopian catastrophic scenarios, but this leads to a dilemma of AI for social good as follows.

2.2   A Trade-Off Between Autonomy and Risk in Science AI Robotics

The ethical dilemma of Science AI Robotics would be as follows. We obviously would like to have safety constraints required on AI robot scientists; yet constraints constrain the autonomy and creativity of them. As we impose more constraints, in general, AI robot scientists would become less autonomous and less creative, which may be analogous to the human children education in which as parents impose more constraints on their children there is generally less room for children to show their autonomous creativity. If we just build research assistant robots with no genuine intellectual autonomy, then the risks we are concerned with would be lowered. Yet is that what we really want? Science AI Robotics rather pursues fully autonomous artificial scientists who would even go beyond the scientific capabilities of the best human scientists and allow them to win Nobel prizes, Fields medals, Turing awards, and so fourth. Those superhuman artificial scientists will be likely to threaten the human civilisation, however. We thus have to balance autonomy and potential risk in Science AI Robotics, even though it is extremely hard to pin down an appropriate moderate balance between them.

3   Sustainability and the Efficiency of Human and Machine Intelligence

As quoted above: "One algorithm that lets a robot manipulate a Rubik's Cube used as much energy as 3 nuclear plants produce in an hour" [4]. In contrast, human beings are able to solve similar problems much more efficiently; we don't need a massive amount of energy just to solve Rubik's Cube problems. Human intelligence is thus much more effective than current machine learning. Machine learning requires a lot of energy for GPU computation, which is expected to lead to severe energy problems sooner or later. The current paradigm of machine learning is not really sustainable in that sense. There may be some paradigm shift by which we overcome the energy problems and other sustainability issues. A potentially successful paradigm to that end would be Integrative AI, namely the integration of Symbolic and Statistical AI, especially a category-theoretical approach to it; category theory is an abstract theory of systems and processes and has been applied in mathematical foundations of various scientific disciplines (see [6–13] and references therein).

Yet there is another possible perspective on the sustainability of machine learning and the efficiency of artificial intelligence in cognition, learning, and reasoning. Human beings are now able to solve some problems more efficiently than machine learning, but it may be a fruit of the extremely long process of human evolution over countless generations, or at least a fruit of education, which takes a significant amount of time and energy. Considering, for example, the energy required to raise a child or the energy consumed in human evolution through a number of generations, then it may be that the total energy required for human learning is more or less similar to the energy required for machine learning; or it could even happen that machine learning actually require less energy than humans for certain specific tasks.

It is thus not really obvious how the efficiency of human intelligence compares with the efficiency of machine intelligence. At the same time, the question would not make much sense after the so-called intelligence explosion that might happen for artificial intelligence (i.e., the explosion of artificial intelligence capabilities that is caused by the uncontrollable positive feedback process of improving themselves on their own). Once the intelligence explosion has happened, superhuman artificial agents may come up with solutions to sustainability issues as well as other problems in the present human civilisation (just as some accelerationists would argue), and in that case, we do not have to worry about them by ourselves (or we just may not exist in that possibly post-human age).

4   The Aim and Rôles of Human Scientists After the Rise of AI Robot Scientists

What would human scientists do after the rise of autonomous science AI robots? They don't have to collect data, and don't have to do experiments then. They don't have to discover hypotheses, and don't have to verify hypotheses either (there will also be no need for the verification of complicated mathematical proofs such as that of the ABC conjecture). How should we reimagine human scientists then?

Do they still have to design objectives? Do they still have to design values? In the long run we could automate those objective and value design processes as things like meta-learning and AutoML advance further. Even in that case, the explainability and interpretability issues may remain unsolved, and then human scientists could focus on understanding and interpretation of machine-led scientific practice. There would also be an indispensable rôle humans play, such as teaching AI robots science ethics (and other sorts of ethics as well).

There is a different question we could ask. What would human scientists like to do after the rise of sufficiently mature AI robot scientists? Suppose AI robot scientists are capable of doing all essential work for human scientists, and then the question is not what human scientists would have to do, since there is no such thing as they have to do in that case, but rather is what they would really like to do (which depends on the nature of each human scientist, of course).

5   How to Construct Ethical AI? an Intensional Categorical AI Approach

Superhuman evil AI scientists could extinguish the human race, so it is a crucial challenge for us to make them ethical enough in order to avoid such a dystopian future. Yet how can we construct Ethical AI in the first place? To that end, it would be essential for AI to learn ethics intensionally rather than extensionally; AI, if it is to be genuinely ethical, must learn intensional ethical principles (that underlie ethically correct behaviours) rather than extensional ethical behaviours (i.e., correct behavioural input-output pairs).

Ethical principles can be implemented as top-down Symbolic AI principles, and thus Integrative AI would play a pivotal rôle in the development of Ethical AI. Think, for instance, how children learn ethics. They may see some ethically inappropriate behaviours made by human adults, and even in that case, they do not learn those wrong behaviours. If they purely learn from experience just like machine learning does (even with various regularisation and other techniques), then they cannot stop themselves to learn those wrong behaviours. Yet in reality, they are taught top-down ethical principles (by parents, school teachers, etc.), which allow them to not learn those ethically wrong behaviours.

In light of this, Ethical AI must be Integrative AI, internalising intensional ethical principles within itself. Among various approaches to Integrative AI, the categorical integration of Symbolic and Statistical AI may play an indispensable rôle in the development of Intensional AI and Ethical AI (see, e.g., [13–18,24]).

6   Concluding Remarks: Can We Avoid Dystopian Scenarios?

AI robot scientists will eventually go beyond the human cognitive and physical limits, allowing for superperception, supermotion, and superintelligence, which might lead to the birth of superhuman evil AI scientists. Yet in that case, it would not be clear whether we can readily tell which AI scientists are actually evil. They may hide their evil nature in some superhuman clever way, and in that case, humans would not even be able to notice since they are superhuman intelligent. And the probability for dystopian scenarios to due the intelligence explosion will increase then. Taking all this into consideration, it would not be an easy challenge to create good AI scientists who practice science with safety and comfort (for humans) with superhuman capabilities rather than evil AI scientists who practice mad science with superperception, supermobility, and superintelligence.

There are several issues we have not been able to address in this paper. One of them is the personhood status issue for artificial agents, which relates to questions such as whether we are allowed to overwork AI scientists. Another is the issue of embodiment in AI. If AI robot scientists have no bodies, they may be safer, but embodiment could be vital for the development of AGI, namely Artificial General Intelligence. At the same time, there may possibly be some potential rôle of embodiment in the development of Ethical AI, which may have to be Embodied AI (as well as Embedded AI and Situated AI).

Acknowledgements. This work was supported by JST (JPMJMS2033) and the Nakatani Foundation. The author would like to thank the Advanced Telecommunications Research Institute for his research visit there.

References

1. Caliskan, A., et al.: Semantics derived automatically from language corpora contain human-like biases. Science **356**, 183–186 (2017)
2. Harada K., et al.: Co-evolution of Human and AI-Robots to Expand Science Frontiers, Moonshot Project of Japan. https://sites.google.com/g.ecc.u-tokyo.ac.jp/moonshot-ai-science-robot/home. Accessed Jan 2022

3. King, R., et al.: The automation of science. Science **324**, 85–89 (2009)
4. Knight, W.: AI Can Do Great Things — if It Doesn't Burn the Planet, WIRED (2020). https://www.wired.com/story/ai-great-things-burn-planet/. Accessed Oct 2021
5. Liu, Z., Tegmark, M., Poincaré, A.I.: Machine learning conservation laws from trajectories. Phys. Rev. Lett. **126**, 180604 (2021)
6. Maruyama, Y.: Dualities for algebras of Fitting's many-valued modal logics. Fundamenta Informaticae **106**, 273–294 (2011)
7. Maruyama, Y.: From operational chu duality to coalgebraic quantum symmetry. In: Heckel, R., Milius, S. (eds.) CALCO 2013. LNCS, vol. 8089, pp. 220–235. Springer, Heidelberg (2013). https://doi.org/10.1007/978-3-642-40206-7_17
8. Maruyama, Y.: Duality theory and categorical universal logic: with emphasis on quantum structures. In: Proceedings of Quantum Physics and Logic. EPTCS, vol. 171, pp. 100–112 (2014)
9. Maruyama, Y.: Category theory and foundations of life science: a structuralist perspective on cognition. Biosystems **203**, 104376 (2021)
10. Maruyama, Y.: Topological duality via maximal spectrum functor. Commun. Algebra **48**, 2616–2623 (2020)
11. Maruyama, Y.: Prior's tonk, notions of logic, and levels of inconsistency: vindicating the pluralistic unity of science in the light of categorical logical positivism. Synthese **193**, 3483–3495 (2016)
12. Maruyama, Y.: Categorical harmony and paradoxes in proof-theoretic semantics. In: Advances in Proof-Theoretic Semantics, pp. 95–114 (2016)
13. Maruyama, Y.: Meaning and duality: from categorical logic to quantum physics. DPhil thesis, Department of Computer Science, University of Oxford (2017)
14. Maruyama, Y.: Compositionality and contextuality: the symbolic and statistical theories of meaning. In: Bella, G., Bouquet, P. (eds.) CONTEXT 2019. LNCS (LNAI), vol. 11939, pp. 161–174. Springer, Cham (2019). https://doi.org/10.1007/978-3-030-34974-5_14
15. Maruyama, Y.: The conditions of artificial general intelligence: logic, autonomy, resilience, integrity, morality, emotion, embodiment, and embeddedness. In: Goertzel, B., Panov, A.I., Potapov, A., Yampolskiy, R. (eds.) AGI 2020. LNCS (LNAI), vol. 12177, pp. 242–251. Springer, Cham (2020). https://doi.org/10.1007/978-3-030-52152-3_25
16. Maruyama, Y.: Symbolic and statistical theories of cognition: towards integrated artificial intelligence. In: Cleophas, L., Massink, M. (eds.) SEFM 2020. LNCS, vol. 12524, pp. 129–146. Springer, Cham (2021). https://doi.org/10.1007/978-3-030-67220-1_11
17. Maruyama, Y.: Moral philosophy of artificial general intelligence: agency and responsibility. In: Goertzel, B., Iklé, M., Potapov, A. (eds.) AGI 2021. LNCS (LNAI), vol. 13154, pp. 139–150. Springer, Cham (2022). https://doi.org/10.1007/978-3-030-93758-4_15
18. Maruyama, Y.: Categorical artificial intelligence: the integration of symbolic and statistical AI for verifiable, ethical, and trustworthy AI. In: Goertzel, B., Iklé, M., Potapov, A. (eds.) AGI 2021. LNCS (LNAI), vol. 13154, pp. 127–138. Springer, Cham (2022). https://doi.org/10.1007/978-3-030-93758-4_14
19. Minsky, M.L.: Logical versus analogical or symbolic versus connectionist or neat versus scruffy. AI Mag. **12**, 34–51 (1991)
20. Norvig, P.: On Chomsky and the two cultures of statistical learning. In: Pietsch, W., Wernecke, J., Ott, M. (eds.) Berechenbarkeit der Welt? Springer, Wiesbaden (2017). https://doi.org/10.1007/978-3-658-12153-2_3

21. Thompson, N.C., et al.: The computational limits of deep learning. arXiv:2007. 05558 (2020)
22. Tshitoyan, V., et al.: Unsupervised word embeddings capture latent knowledge from materials science literature. Nature **571**, 95–98 (2019)
23. Udrescu, S.-M., Tegmark, M.: AI Feynman: a physics-inspired method for symbolic regression. Sci. Adv. **6**, 2631 (2020)
24. Xu, T., Maruyama, Y.: Neural string diagrams: a universal modelling language for categorical deep learning. In: Goertzel, B., Iklé, M., Potapov, A. (eds.) AGI 2021. LNCS (LNAI), vol. 13154, pp. 306–315. Springer, Cham (2022). https://doi. org/10.1007/978-3-030-93758-4_32

Nordic Study on Public Acceptance of Autonomous Drones

Virpi Oksman[✉] and Minna Kulju

VTT Technical Research Centre of Finland, Tampere, Finland
virpi.oksman@vtt.fi

Abstract. Drones are new phenomenon in public spaces. Adoption of this kind of new technologies requires public acceptance. Drones and other unmanned aerial systems may have various impacts on people's living environments. Furthermore, public is exposed to disadvantages of drones. Public acceptance may be expressed as positive or negative attitude by majority of the citizens towards the new technology or service or as rapid adoption of it in everyday life. In various parts of the globe, in cities and in rural areas drones as emerging technologies are perceived differently, although similar kinds of concerns also appear. Public acceptance studies of drones have been conducted mostly in highly urbanized environments like in Singapore and in European cities. This paper presents results of a Nordic survey study (N = 1000) conducted in Sweden and in Finland. The survey aims at understanding the level of acceptance of different uses of drones in public spaces and the main concerns and benefits related to emerging UAM technologies. The study shows that even though the general attitude towards drones is quite positive, privacy and safety are the main concerns by Nordic citizens. Also, for what purpose and by whom drones are operated, affects the acceptability significantly. The study concludes that there is a need for regulations that safeguard public interests in addition to considering privacy in design, and quiet environmentally friendly drones.

Keywords: Drones · Public acceptance · Survey · Nordic countries

1 Introduction

The new, partly, or fully automatized and autonomous drones can be utilized in logistics, emergencies, surveillance and for many other purposes. In addition, drones will enable even passenger transport via urban air mobility (UAM). The adoption of this kind of new technologies will require new EU regulations, U-spaces, which allow autonomous drones to be used for various commercial and socially beneficial purposes in lower airspaces. In addition, especially the autonomous flying technologies need to mature for drone usage to be safer in public places. After these requirements are met, there is a need for wider public acceptance, which according to some studies, seems to vary in various parts of the world.

New aerial drone solutions can have many potential benefits for public. This means in commercial services more flexible deliveries compared to normal parcel delivery or

C. Stephanidis et al. (Eds.): HCII 2022, CCIS 1655, pp. 532–539, 2022.
https://doi.org/10.1007/978-3-031-19682-9_67

pick-up hours. In addition, there is a possibility for more punctual deliveries when the delivery arrives at a pre-arranged time. There might be also fewer negative effects of traffic congestion when drones replace traditional delivery vehicles (e.g., cars). Drones can improve accessibility of certain areas and deliveries can be made for instance to remote and hard to reach areas such as islands. In addition, drone can be a sustainable transport option by producing less traffic emissions compared to other modes of transport.

However, adoption of new technology or service is never straightforward. Before UAM can be applied in practice, many technological, regulatory, and public acceptance related issues need to be solved. It is not clear, if and how the public accepts the drones as a part of their everyday lives and locations. Quite often, public rejection of technologies has resulted in negative consequences for adoption or the commercialization of technologies [1]. The public may have concerns and negative associations of drones before having any experience of them. For instance, according to a German study, public associated the word drone with espionage and surveillance [2]. In general, media industry has a significant impact on general public's image of drones [3].

Moreover, acceptance of drones is highly contexts specific and cannot be detached from the conditions, purposes, and surroundings where drones are being used [4]. For instance, often drone use for health and welfare or emergency purposes is accepted, as well as use by public authorities is usually more accepted than private or commercial usages. Many surveys worldwide have shown similar type of concerns such as environmental impact like noise, emissions and impact on animals, safety and privacy concerns and lack of transparency [5].

Recently, the attitudes towards deployment of UAM, e.g., passenger eVTOL or air-taxis have been also studied in various kinds of urban and rural, developed and developing regions [6, 7].

To develop drone systems that will benefit both commercial operators as well as society and to understand the possible challenges, we need to assess evolving public attitudes towards different usages of drones. This paper studies the attitudes towards autonomous drone use to offer insights on the context of Nordic users and locations.

2   Method

2.1   The Questionnaire

A web-based questionnaire was planned to survey the level of acceptance of different uses of drones in public spaces and the attitudes towards drones and the passenger eVTOLs. We created a survey that consisted in total of 26 questions which included both multiple choice and open-ended questions. The multiple-choice questions used 5- and 6-point Likert Scale. In the background section, there were questions, which tested participants' knowledge about drones including drone regulations. Moreover, there were questions regarding where the participants have learned or heard about drones during the last year. In addition, the participants were asked if they were willing to use drone deliveries and what kind of benefits and challenges they saw in them. Moreover, there were questions regarding the biggest concerns with drone transport. Willingness to pay for drone transport compared to other modes of transport was asked also. In addition to delivery drones, we asked if the participants would be interested in trying an air-taxi themselves.

Cross tabulation and the Pearson Chi-Square Test were used to analyze the gathered data and make comparison between Finnish and Swedish respondents as well as differences between gender and age groups.

2.2 The Participants and the Procedure

There were in total 1000 participants in the survey from which 500 were from Finland and 500 from Sweden (Table 1). Majority of respondents belonged to the professional group "workers" or "pensioners."

The survey used research panel commissioned from a third party provider. The data was collected following General Data Protection Regulation (GDPR), with explicit and freely given consent to participate in the survey.

Table 1. Respondents' demographics.

	FI	SE		FI	SE
N	**500**	**500**	**EDUCATION**	9%	8%
Male	50%	51%	Primary school	11%	35%
Female	50%	49%	Matriculation examination	38%	16%
			Vocational education	25%	22%
			University, Bachelor degree	17%	18%
			University, Master degree		
AGE	11%	11%	**PROFESSIONAL GROUP**	27%	33%
18–24	18%	20%	Worker	10%	4%
25–34	18%	18%	Senior officer	9%	17%
35–44	17%	18%	Officer	1%	3%
45–54	18%	16%	Leading position	3%	4%
55–64	19%	17%	Self-employed	29%	19%
65–75			Pensioner	10%	6%
			Student	2%	3%
			Stay-at-home parent	0%	0%
			Farmer/primary prod	8%	9%
			Unemployed jobseeker	2%	2%
			Other		

3   Results

Most of the respondents have heard or learned about drones through social media or TV and newspapers. When asked about benefits that deliveries made with drones will have, most of the respondents saw that the improved accessibility to hard-to-reach areas is the most beneficial (76%). In addition, benefits were seen in decreased traffic emissions

(71%) and traffic congestions (68%) as well as in fewer human contacts (65%). Surprisingly, fast, and punctual or more flexible deliveries were not seen as beneficial as one could expect, around 60% of respondents thought that drones would benefit those. The least benefits were seen in low delivery costs, about half (49%) responded that drone deliveries would benefit this. Using drones to transport pharmacy products or medical devices to hard-to-reach areas such as islands and other remote places was accepted by the respondents. Majority of them (83%) considers this as a very good or good idea.

3.1 Concerns and Preferred Use Cases

The main concerns about drone deliveries were related to privacy issues (Fig. 1). In general, Finnish respondents were more concerned about disadvantages of drones than Swedes. The most concerning issue of drones among Nordic people was the privacy violation. 75% of Finnish respondents and 56% of Swedish respondent saw drones as a threat to their privacy. Issues related to crime were the second largest concern among Nordic people. 63% of Finnish and 48% of Swedish participants saw the possibility of using drones for crimes as concerning or very concerning. The third most concerning issue about drones is safety. Job losses were concerning or concerning to 24% of Swedes and 28% of Finns.

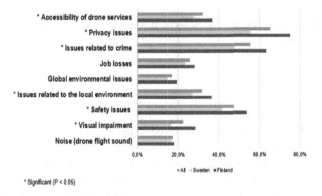

Fig. 1. Concerns related to drone usage.

Both Finnish and Swedish respondents considered using drones in the work of the authorities as a good idea (Fig. 2). The most beneficial was considered to use drones for fire department and rescue service's purposes (90% of Finns and 85% of Swedes). Drone used by police was seen as the second most useful, 88% of Finnish and 85% of Swedish participants. The first aid was seen as the third most important use purpose of drones and it was perceived as very good or good by Finnish (86%) and Swedish (77%) respondents. However, there were significant differences between youngest and older age groups: the youngest age group (18–24-year old) did not see the above-mentioned use purposes of drones as good as the others. For instance in case of using drones for police use 37% of respondents in age group 18–24 answered very good or good, compared to 60%–79% of respondents in other age groups.

Using drones for media use shared respondent's opinions for and against, it was considered very good or good by half of respondents. Private use of drones was the second least accepted by the public. It was considered very good or good by 35% of Swedes and by 33% of Finns. In addition, women were more negative about drones for private use than men, 14% of them considered it to be very bad (men 9%). The least accepted was using drones for passenger transport, only a quarter of respondents thought this is a very good or good use purpose for drones.

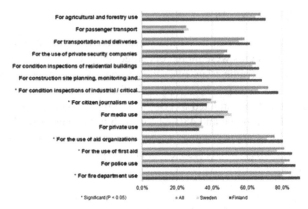

Fig. 2. Considers using drones for following purpose is good idea. (% of respondents answering good or very good idea)

3.2 Drone Deliveries

Overall, Swedish people were more interested in using drones for deliveries than Finnish people (Fig. 3). Medicines (38%) and pharmacy products (33%) were the items that the Swedish people were most likely to order of if the drone deliveries were available for their homes. Finnish people were most interested in taking in advantage of small package deliveries (35%). The second most interesting for Finnish people were food-deliveries from restaurant (25%) or groceries (19%) and deliveries of medicine (21%).

The most preferred delivery option is that the drone brings the parcel to back yard or other private space (Fig. 4). However, there was a significant difference between Finns and Swedes, since 40% of Finnish respondents, but only 28% of the Swedish respondents preferred this option. In fact, 25% of Swedes do not want drone deliveries in their area at all.

Concerning the price of drone deliveries, most of the respondents were willing to pay same amount of money than from the regular ones or same than from express deliveries.

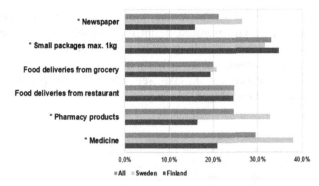

Fig. 3. Would be interested in to take advantage of the following drone-to-home deliveries.

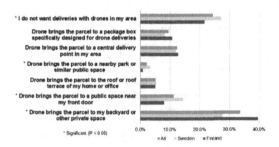

Fig. 4. Preferred delivery options.

3.3 Drone Taxis

At this stage, it is evident, that most of the Nordic respondents were not interested in riding a drone taxi (Fig. 5). 42% of Swedes and 41% of Finns did totally disagree with the proposition "I would like to try automated drone taxi". There was not significant difference between willingness to try automated or remote controlled air taxi, as 41% Swedes and 39% of Finns responded also totally disagree to the proposition whether they would like to try remote controlled air taxi.

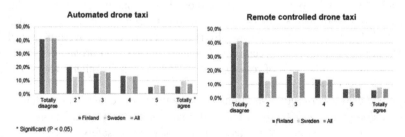

Fig. 5. Willingness to use automated or remote controlled drone taxi.

The respondents were asked whether they would feel safe if automated or remote controlled drone taxi would fly overhead. Again, the attitudes were quite negative since majority of respondents (over 70%) disagreed with the proposition "I would feel safe if over my head would fly automated/remote controlled drone taxi."

The main concerns related to drone taxis were again related to privacy and safety as well as issues related to crime (Fig. 6).

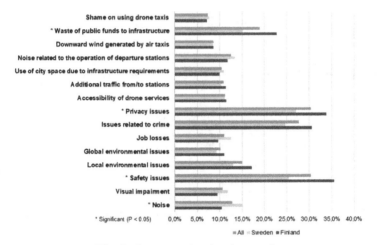

Fig. 6. Concerns related to drone taxis.

4   Discussion

The results suggest that certain drone usages are more accepted than others in the Nordic context. Typical for Nordic countries is that the main benefits were seen in improved accessibility, especially to hard-to-reach areas, such as islands. This is understandable as the Nordic people spend a lot of time in nature and in their summer cottages, in difficult to reach areas.

In addition, Nordic public is accepting most those drone usages that are related to health and welfare purposes, like emergency medical services and delivery of medicine or medical devices. Moreover, the use by public authorities or government-affiliated usages were in general more accepted in Nordic countries than private or commercial usages, which is similar kind of result found in studies in many other countries as well [4].

The biggest concern regarding drone use in both Nordic countries was that privacy would be compromised. This is in line with many other studies that suggest that the biggest concerns of public are related to issues of privacy, safety, and possibility of increased crimes with drones [3, 8–10]. Like described in [3]: "Fears and concerns were misuse of drones by unauthorized personnel, inability to identify whether drones are filming or not, drones being a threat to one's physical safety, and loss of privacy".

This would suggest considering seriously the need for privacy in design. Yet, at the same time there is a need for transparency of the operations; need to know who is operating and the possibility to identify if drones are filming or not, especially when they are flying near people's homes or other private places.

Moreover, drone noise was not considered as one of the top concerns by Nordic participants. This is quite surprising and differs from some of the international studies about societal acceptance, which place the drone noise as one of the main concerns. [6, 7] This may result from the fact that in large survey consisting of public, the participants have no previous experience of drones and cannot estimate how loud the drone sound could be. However, it is also possible that the general public considers the privacy and safety concerns as bigger compared to noise, that is usually suggested as one of the biggest concern by experts and stakeholders.

At this stage, it is evident, that most of the Nordic respondents were not interested in riding a drone taxi. 42% of Swedes and 41% of Finns did totally disagree with the proposition "I would like to try out automated drone taxi." There was not significant difference between willingness to try automated or remote controlled air taxi. This in all was quite different result with the participants of EASA study, showing more favorable attitudes towards drone taxis, with only 20% of participants strongly disagreeing with trying out automated taxi [7]. The Nordic participants' hesitancy about drone taxis/passenger eVTOLS may come from the fact that it is still relatively unknown technology application for most of the public and it may take some time for people to get accustomed to the idea. In addition, the value and the benefits for individual, environment and society would need to be demonstrated more clearly to gain larger public acceptance.

References

1. Gupta, N., Fischer, A.R.H., Frewer, L.J.: Socio-psychological determinants of public acceptance of technologies: a review. Public Underst. Sci. 21(7), 782–795 (2012)
2. Eißfeldt, H., et al.: The acceptance of civil drones in Germany. CEAS Aeronaut. J. 11(3), 665–676 (2020). https://doi.org/10.1007/s13272-020-00447-w
3. Lin Tan, L.K., Lim, B.C., Park, G., Low, K.H., Seng Yeo, V.C.: Public acceptance of drone applications in a highly urbanized environment. Technol. Soc. 64, 101462 (2021)
4. Lin Tan, L.K., Lim, B.C., Park, G., Low, K.H., Seng Yeo, V.C.: Public acceptance of drone applications in a highly urbanized environment. Technol. Soc. 64, 101462 (2021)
5. Çetin, E., Cano, A., Deransy, R., Tres, S., Barrado, C.: Implementing mitigations for improving societal acceptance of urban air mobility. Drones 6(2), 28 (2022)
6. Yedavalli, P., Mooberry, J.: An assessment of public perception of urban air mobility (UAM). Airbus UTM Defin. Futur. Skies. 1–28 (2019)
7. EASA: Study on the societal acceptance of Urban Air Mobility in Europe, pp. 1–162 (2021)
8. Aydin, B.: Public acceptance of drones: Knowledge, attitudes, and practice. Technol. Soc. 59, 101180 (2019)
9. Nelson, J.R., Grubesic, T.H., Wallace, D., Chamberlain, A.W.: The view from above: a survey of the public's perception of unmanned aerial vehicles and privacy. J. Urban Technol. 26(1), 83–105 (2019)
10. Clothier, R.A., Greer, D.A., Greer, D.G., Mehta, A.M.: Risk perception and the public acceptance of drones. Risk Anal. 35(6), 1167–1183 (2015)

Architecture of a Network of Low-Frequency Smart Sensors for IoT Applications in Marine Environments

Abigail Elizabeth Pallares-Calvo$^{(\boxtimes)}$ [ID], Blanca Esther Carvajal-Gámez [ID], and Oscar Octavio Gutiérrez-Frías [ID]

Instituto Politécnico Nacional, Sección de Estudios de Posgrado e Investigación, Unidad Profesional Interdisciplinaria en Ingeniería y Tecnologías Avanzadas, CDMX, 2580 Avenue IPN, Mexico, Mexico
elypallares@hotmail.com

Abstract. The integration of technologies under the underwater internet of things (UIoT) paradigm allows the interconnectivity of sensors, smartphones, cameras, animals, people, plants, etc., in aquatic environments, promoting accessible communication and the generation of information on topics of interest such as the conservation of fauna or flora, the composition of elements in the water, the tracking of objects such as semi-autonomous vehicles, or the location of surfers, bathers, among others, who sometimes focus on obtaining data without considering the effects that some types of communication or devices can cause to the environment. For this reason, in this work a UIoT architecture composed of three layers is proposed: detection, networking and storage, which allows the collection of data from different geographical points, through mobile nodes that are activated when they are close to the line of sight. of fixed nodes that have RFID readers, which work at a frequency of 125 kHz, enabling with this type of technology low energy consumption, a high integration scale and low emission of electromagnetic waves, which by implementing low frequencies we have as a result smart nodes that are friendly to the environment in which they are located.

Keywords: RFID · Internet of Things · Low frequency · Sensors · Mobile nodes

1 Introduction

The Internet of Things (IoT) is the interconnection of different devices to transmit or send data from objects, geographical points, animals, or people, in terrestrial environments, thus achieving broader knowledge and communication [1]. For example, with Ashton et. al in [2], an object detection system is carried out using radio frequency identification (RFID) readers and identification devices to identify and locate products. Zviedris et al. in [3], implement monitoring of the lynx based on a 4-layer architecture: sensing, networking, application and storage, where the first layer collects location, temperature and movement data, through a frequency of 433 MHz, which are sent to the second layer which transmits them to the third layer to be displayed and stored in the last layer.

C. Stephanidis et al. (Eds.): HCII 2022, CCIS 1655, pp. 540–546, 2022.
https://doi.org/10.1007/978-3-031-19682-9_68

On the other hand, if an exchange of information other than the terrestrial one is required, such as the aquatic one, we have the paradigm called UIoT. A work that addresses this issue is the proposal by Adamo et. al in [4], where they implement a two-layer architecture to monitor water quality: sensing and network. The first is responsible for collecting the data and these are sent to the second layer in a wired way, and then send the data to a storage center through the General Packet Radio Service (GPRS, for its acronym in English). Nayyar et. al in [5] performs water monitoring using a 3-layer architecture: perception, network, and application, where the perception layer collects data through wired sensors on a card and then communicates with a Wi-Fi module at an interface application to view them. On the other hand, Qiu et. al in [6], propose the monitoring of marine environments using a 5-layer architecture: detection, communication, networks, fusion, and application. The first layer contains all the necessary sensors to collect data, which are transmitted by the second layer, which can be an acoustic or optical communication, to reach the third layer that transmits the data through the nodes of the network and then reach the fourth layer where the servers are located. save and stream the data to the last layer for the end user to view. However, these works implement frequencies of the order of MHz, which cause alterations in the environment, such as temporary damage to the auditory system or permanent damage to the nervous or auditory tissue of the animal, as well as disorientation to the animals that make the migration [7, 8]. For this reason, in this work the design of a three-layer architecture is proposed: detection, network and storage. Said architecture is made up of intelligent nodes that monitor objects by electromagnetic induction using RFID readers that work at 125 kHz, which do not cause harm to animals. Each node collects the data through a point-to-point network through Wi-Fi modules, and then communicates with a master node that sends the information to the cloud storage.

The document is organized as follows. In Sect. 2, the three-layer architecture is shown. Section 3 describes the characteristics of the architecture. And finally, Sect. 4 presents the conclusions.

2 Methodology

This section presents the communication design scheme for intelligent nodes in marine environments. In addition, the architecture integrated by the layers: detection, networking and storage is shown

2.1 Design Scheme for the Communication of Intelligent Nodes in Marine Environments

In Figure 1, the scheme of device communication is shown, where objects, animals, people and/or characteristics of the environment are monitored and the collected data is transmitted to a storage center for visualization, through communication by electromagnetic induction. and Wi-Fi.

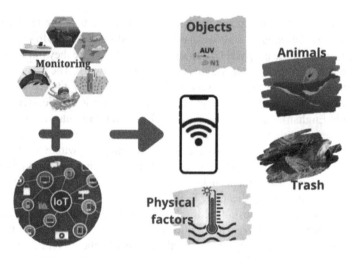

Fig. 1. Communication scheme for marine environments.

2.2 Sensor Network Architecture for Communication With Electromagnetic Induction

The proposed architecture for monitoring marine environments is shown in Figure 2, which is made up of 3 layers: detection layer, networking layer and storage layer. Which are mentioned below.

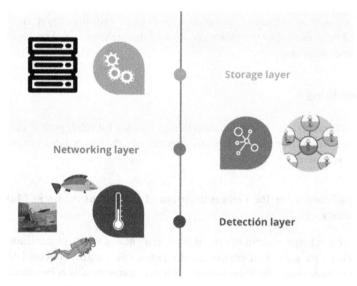

Fig. 2. Architecture of the smart sensor network.

- Detection layer
  In this layer, a device is placed on the object of interest, which sends a signal with data, which allows locating the geographical points where the object is located. Likewise, in this layer other devices can collect data from other physical variables and send this data to the next layer through the device.
- Networking layer
  This layer is responsible for communication and comprises two sublayers. The first is the interaction between the object and the node, and the second is the interaction between the nodes.
- *Sublayer object to node*
  This sublayer is the communication that exists between the device that is placed on the object of interest and a Radio Frequency Identification (RFID) reader using electromagnetic induction. For this interaction, the RFID reader sends an activation signal at a frequency of 125 kHz, and when the device is close to the RFID reader antenna [9], it turns on and sends return to the RFID reader a packet of bits, which is unique for each device [10].
- *Sublayer node to node.*
  The second sublayer is made up of several nodes, each one with its RFID reader, placed in a known geographical location and at one meter between them so that the device can be detected and perform trilateration of the location of the object through of the nodes, which we classify into two types: slave and master.
- *Slave node.*
  The slave node is a fixed node, in charge of collecting the data received by the RFID reader and then sending this information to the master node through a Wi-fi module. Figure 3 shows the structure of the node which has an RFID reader, a power supply, a microcontroller with memory and a Wi-Fi module.

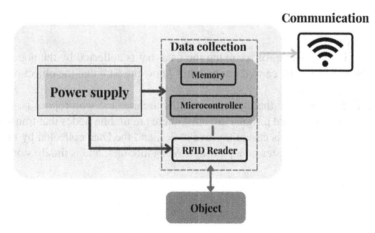

Fig. 3. Block diagram of the slave node.

- Master node

    The master node, like the slave nodes, collects the data that is detected in its area by means of an RFID reader. Figure 4 shows the components of the master node, which are a power supply, an RFID reader, a microcontroller, a memory and, with the difference that, instead of having a Wi-fi module, it has two, one to receive the information from the slave nodes and another to send the data to the source layer.

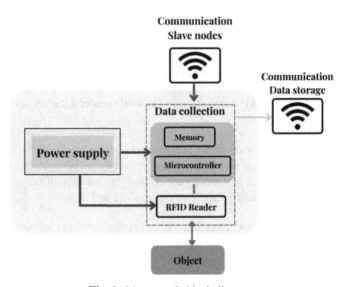

Fig. 4. Master node block diagram.

- Storage layer

    This layer is responsible for receiving the data that is collected by the nodes so that later trilateration can be carried out and thus know the path that the object of interest is following.

    Figure 5 shows how the interaction of the architecture we propose is, in which moving devices that send a signal are used, there are mobile nodes that transmit data to the fixed nodes, in this case, the slave nodes, and the Data collected by the RFID readers is sent to the master node, through Wi-Fi modules, and is finally stored in the storage layer.

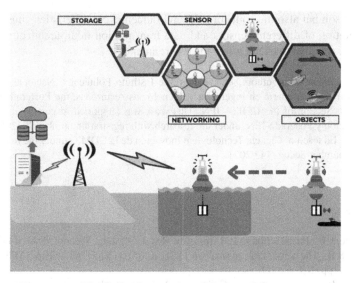

Fig. 5. Implementation of the proposal.

In our architecture, we propose a space distance between the fixed nodes of 1 meter, since the RFID readers for commercial use, which are being implemented, have a communication range coverage in this medium of half a meter, due to the attenuation that it presents in this environment, which can be modified depending on the reading range of the RFID reader.

3 Discussion and Results

The need for interconnection between objects has allowed the IoT to be carried out in scenarios in aquatic environments. In this case, an architecture with low-frequency RFID technology is proposed, which ranges between the ranges of 120 kHz to 134 kHz, which are less harmful to the environment. Environment [10]. In accordance with what is stated by the International Organization for Standardization (ISO) for the identification of radio frequencies of animals (ISO 11784 and ISO 11785), it recommends radio frequency signals between these ranges as adequate for the identification of the marine or terrestrial fauna [11]. Likewise, these types of frequencies do not present any affectation near metals and liquids and are not influenced by the rapid decrease of the frequency in the magnetic field [7, 10, 12].

4 Conclusions

The three-layer architecture: sensing, networking and storage, with the technology we propose, allows monitoring in environments where the fauna is not altered by the frequencies that are implemented. Adhering to the ISO standards and the type of communication between mobile and fixed nodes that allow not only the monitoring of any object, animal, plant or person but also the collection of environmental characteristics, thus achieving implementation of different sensors and data transmission in an architecture that can interact in a way that does not affect the environment.

Acknowledgement. The authors acknowledge the Instituto Politécnico Nacional, the Unidad Profesional Interdisciplinaria en Ingeniería y Tecnologías Avanzadas, the Postgraduate Studies and Research Section of the UPIITA-IPN. This work was supported in part by the Secretaria de Investigación y Posgrado-IPN, under the research with registration number 20220542 and by Secretaria de Educación, Ciencia Tecnología e Inovación de la CDMX, under the reasearch with registration number Sectei /143/2021.

References

1. Gokhale, P.B.: Introduction to IOT. Int. Adv. Res. J. Sci. Eng. Technol. **5**, 41–44 (2018)
2. Sarma, S.B.: The networked physical world. In: Auto-ID Center White Paper MIT-AUTOID-WH-001, pp. 1–16 (2000)
3. Zviedris, R., Elsts, A., Strazdins, G., Mednis, A., Selavo, L.: Lynxnet: wild animal monitoring using sensor networks. In: Marron, P.J., Voigt, T., Corke, P., Mottola, L. (eds.) Real-world Wireless Sensor Networks. LNCS, vol. 6511, pp. 170–173. Springer, Heidelberg (2010). https://doi.org/10.1007/978-3-642-17520-6_18
4. Adamo, F.A.: A smart sensor network for sea water quality monitoring. IEEE Sens. J. **15**(5), 2514–2522 (2014)
5. Nayyar, A., Ba, C.H., Duc, N.P.C., Binh, H.D.: Smart-IoUT 1.0: a smart aquatic monitoring network based on Internet of Underwater Things (IoUT). In: Duong, T.Q., Vo, N.-S. (eds.) Industrial Networks and Intelligent Systems. LNICSSITE, vol. 257, pp. 191–207. Springer, Cham (2019). https://doi.org/10.1007/978-3-030-05873-9_16
6. Qiu, T.Z.: Underwater internet of things in smart ocean: system architecture and open issues. IEEE Trans. Ind. Inform. **16**(7), 4297–4307 (2019)
7. Hungría, E.M.: La protección de la biodiversidad marina frente al ruido subacuáticoes necesario incorporar valores umbral? Revista de la Escuela Jacobea de Posgrado. **19**, 73-96 (2020). http://revista.jacobea.edu.mx
8. Mooney, T.A.: Sonar-induced temporary hearing loss in dolphins. Biol. Lett. **5**(4), 565–567 (2009)
9. Aznar, Á.C.: Antenas. Universitat Politécnica Catalunya, Barcelona (2004)
10. Ahson, S.: RFID Handbook: Applications, Technology, Security, and Privacy. CRC Press, Florida, USA (2017)
11. ISO (1996). ISo. https://www.iso.org/obp/ui/#iso:std:iso:11784:ed-2:v1:en
12. Co, S.X.: Shenzhen Xinyetong Technology. (Shenzhen Xinyetong Technology CO.) (2008). https://www.asiarfid.com/es/lf-hf-uhf-frequency.html. Accessed 04 Jan 2022

IoT Monitoring to Control a Bicycle Parking Lot

Belen Ruales[1] , Patricio Lara-Alvarez[1] , Carles Riba[2] ,
and Manuel Ayala-Chauvin[3(✉)]

[1] SISAU Research Group, Facultad de Ingeniería y Tecnologías de la Información y
Comunicación (FITIC), Universidad Tecnológica Indoamérica, Ambato, Ecuador
{belenruales,patolara}@uti.edu.ec
[2] Centro de Diseño de Equipos Industriales, Universidad Politécnica de Cataluña, Barcelona,
Spain
carles.riba@upc.edu
[3] Centro de Investigación en Ciencias Humanas y Educación (CICHE), Universidad
Tecnológica Indoamérica, Ambato 180103, Ecuador
mayala@uti.edu.ec

Abstract. In recent years, the development of new technologies has improved
the management of resources and services at the urban level. In this sense, several cities worldwide have developed intelligent infrastructures such as Smart
Cities in which, through data collection and management, they aim to achieve
social, environmental and economic improvements. Innovative bike racks are a
promising solution to traffic-related problems in major cities around the world;
however, there is a lack of low-cost solutions for controlling and monitoring bike
racks and thus boosting the mobility of cyclists. This paper presents a system
to monitor and control a bicycle parking lot. In order to achieve this goal, software and hardware specifications were defined and characterised by the control
system. The conceptual design and detail of the prototype and the materialisa-
tion proceeded, where technology with ESP8266 microcontrollers and Raspberry
Pi+Ethernet/WiFi microprocessors was used in the MQTT communication protocol to implement its architecture. The system implements in the bicycle parking lot
of the Universidad Tecnológica Indoamérica. The series of data collected allowed
for determining the frequency of use. With this, a database creates where the information on the frequency of use of bicycles is stored. Finally, through a mobile
application, the availability of parking spaces can be consulted, and bikes in the
parking lot can monitor.

Keywords: Bicycle · Parking · IoT

1 Introduction

1.1 Background

Cities worldwide are increasingly facing a recurring mobility problem due to traffic
congestion. In the last decade, the interest in cycling as a means of transport has grown
steadily [1]. Municipalities worldwide are working on urban policies moving towards

C. Stephanidis et al. (Eds.): HCII 2022, CCIS 1655, pp. 547–554, 2022.
https://doi.org/10.1007/978-3-031-19682-9_69

normalizing bicycles as a sustainable means of transport [2]. In Barcelona, for example, connectivity between cycling and public transport is being promoted [3]. Likewise, cities such as Amsterdam, Boston and Melbourne have multimodal circuits that allow connectivity in the mobility system [4].

One of the most popular measures to boost the adoption of cycling in cities is the implementation of cycle paths and systems with public bicycles [5]. It is also worth mentioning the advantages and benefits of cycling for health, mobility and the environment [6].

A study carried out in Doha, Qatar, with an emphasis on active transport, evaluates the infrastructure and the environment around schools; this study revealed the need to improve the infrastructure by installing bicycle lanes and parking lots [7].

However, the bicycle mobility system does not provide security conditions, so cyclists are victims of vandalism or theft [8]. Municipalities are proposing safety campaigns and bike-sharing services to reduce mobility problems in some cities [9]. However, there are not enough parking facilities in many cases, or those that exist are not useful or adequate.

Municipalities are looking for more sustainable mobility options in intermediate cities to promote the energy transition [10]. In this sense, a bicycle is a viable option. Nevertheless, it is necessary to adapt the infrastructure because the design of the infrastructure influences the behaviour of cyclists [11].

Bicycles and electric bicycles are alternative mobility options; however, urban planning does not provide safe infrastructure for their parking [12]. For this reason, a low-cost bicycle parking control and monitoring system boost the adoption of the electric bicycle as a means of transportation. In addition, it will provide better parking infrastructure for cyclists and reduce bicycle theft, increasing the sense of security and the number of users.

1.2 Related Works

Low-cost systems for bicycle control and monitoring can be developed based on Internet of Things (IoT) technology; for example, Huang et al. proposes a bicycle management algorithm in a campus car park applying IoT [13].

On the other hand, Papadakis et al. developed a participatory IoT based platform for tracking tasks, with which cyclists using their smartphones can find the location of their assets [14].

Angulo-Esguerra et al. present a solution for automatically determining and displaying bicycle parking occupancy with a technological approach installed in cities or university campuses [15]. This research proposes a low-cost system to monitor and control a bicycle-car park in real-time. In addition, a series of data to determine the frequency of use and availability of spaces. The rest of the document is as follows: Sect. 2 will present the method, Sect. 3 will describe the results, and Sect. 4 will present the study's conclusions.

2   Method

The design method applied for the development of this prototype is concurrent engineering [16]. Software and hardware specifications were defined and characterized. Finally, the prototype was materialized and tested.

2.1   Architecture

The implementation of its architecture used technology with ESP8266 microcontrollers and Raspberry Pi microprocessors + Ethernet/WiFi via the MQTT communication protocol. The system can be run via the web or by installing the application App. Figure 1 shows the schematic of the control structure and architecture.

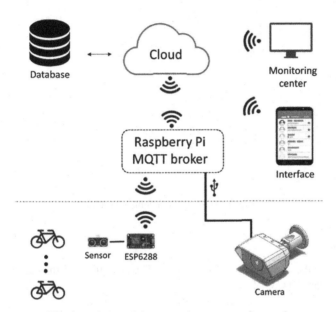

Fig. 1. Scheme of the system's structure of control.

Figure 2 shows the components selected for the electronic circuit, composed of a NodeMCU module (based on ESP8266) and a Raspberry Pi. The implemented components are readily available in the local market, and the approximate cost for the construction of the prototype was $250.

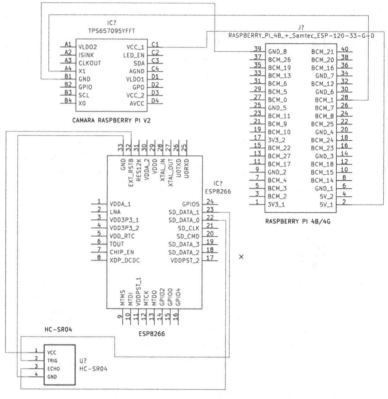

Fig. 2. Diagram of a control system.

2.2 Design

Figure 3 shows the components of the device. The design 3D of the case was executed with the software PTC CREO.

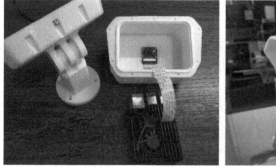

Fig. 3. Prototype.

2.3 Operation

The operation of the system is intuitive and straightforward. After installing the application, the user can visualize the bicycle parking and space availability in real-time. Additionally, the system also has a web application to visualize the parking. Figure 4 shows the interface of the application.

Position	Status
1	Busy
2	Free
3	Busy
4	Busy
5	Free
6	Free
7	Free
8	Free
9	Free
10	Free

Welcome

Fig. 4. Parking lot interface.

3 Results

The correct functioning of the control and tracking of bicycles has been checked and ensured through tests. Also, ensure that the bicycle counting works correctly and shows the availability of parking space to the cyclist. Finally, a report on the frequency of use and monthly mean is generated, which will help plan the infrastructure (see Fig. 5).

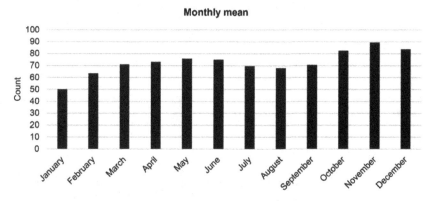

Fig. 5. Counting bicycles monthly mean.

The system's response is considerably fast, allowing the user to visualize the parking space in real-time. Figure 6 shows the bicycle count from May to July 2021, showing entries and exits, e.g. on 09 June, the highest number of entries and exits of 66 and 65, respectively.

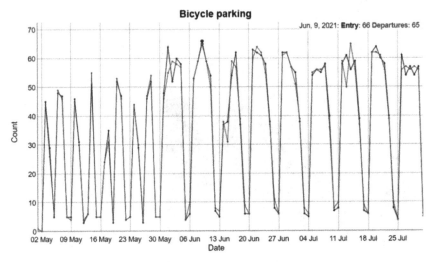

Fig. 6. Counting bicycles in the parking lot.

Figure 7 shows the annual mean recorded per day in 2021. The results show that the days with the highest demand are Tuesdays and Wednesdays, with approximately 83 uses. The maximum use is approximately 177 on Tuesdays. Future research needs to expand the data to make long-term car park development predictions.

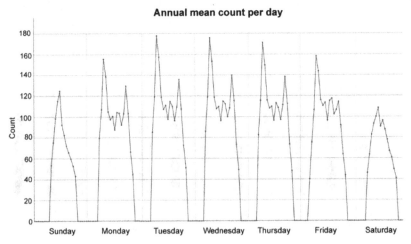

Fig. 7. Annual mean count per day.

4   Conclusions

The document proposes the design of a monitoring and control device for an open-source bicycle parking lot with low materialization costs, with a final price of approximately 250 USD. This system integrates video monitoring and information on bicycle parking availability on a university campus. In addition, the prototype can program parking space availability alarms and generate reports on the frequency of use that urban planners can use. Finally, the system works remotely through a cell phone application or the web.

The interface can be easily replicated and implemented in contexts with similar characteristics, and future research aims to implement the systems in urban parking lots.

Communication between the Raspberry and the ESP6288 device occurs automatically without human intervention. In addition, information about the inputs and outputs is stored in a database and can display in real-time.

After data analysis, we determined that the most significant demand for parking months is October, November, and December. In addition, parking frequency data can serve as a basis for planners to design future infrastructure.

The approach taken in this paper contributes to the development of bicycle parking control and monitoring systems in university settings. However, it can also replicate in more complex contexts such as urban areas.

References

1. Gonzalo-Orden, H., Linares, A., Velasco, L., Díez, J.M., Rojo, M.: Bikeways and cycling urban mobility. Proc. Soc. Behav. Sci. **160**, 567–576 (2014). https://doi.org/10.1016/j.sbspro.2014.12.170
2. Fernandez-Heredia, A., Fernandez-Sanchez, G.: Processes of civic participation in the implementation of sustainable urban mobility systems. Case Stud. Transp. Policy **8**(2), 471–483 (2020). https://doi.org/10.1016/j.cstp.2019.10.011
3. Braun, L.M., et al.: Short-term planning and policy interventions to promote cycling in urban centers: findings from a commute mode choice analysis in Barcelona, Spain. Transp. Res. Part A Policy Pract. **89**, 164–183 (2016). https://doi.org/10.1016/j.tra.2016.05.007
4. Aston, L., et al.: Multi-city exploration of built environment and transit mode use: comparison of Melbourne, Amsterdam and Boston. J. Transp. Geogr. **95**, 103136 (2021). https://doi.org/10.1016/j.jtrangeo.2021.103136
5. Kazemzadeh, K., Laureshyn, A., Winslott Hiselius, L., Ronchi, E.: Expanding the scope of the bicycle level-of-service concept: a review of the literature. Sustainability. **12**(7), 2944 (2020). https://doi.org/10.3390/su12072944
6. McGavock, J., et al.: Multi-use physical activity trails in an urban setting and cardiovascular disease: a difference-in-differences analysis of a natural experiment in Winnipeg, Manitoba, Canada. Int. J. Behav. Nutr. Phys. Act. **19**(1), 1-4 (2022). https://doi.org/10.1186/s12966-022-01279-z
7. Shaaban, K., Abdur-Rouf, K.: Assessing walking and cycling around schools. Sustainability **12**(24), 1–14 (2020). https://doi.org/10.3390/su122410607
8. Márquez, L., Soto, J.J.: Integrating perceptions of safety and bicycle theft risk in the analysis of cycling infrastructure preferences. Transp. Res. Part A Policy Pract. **150**, 285–301 (2021). https://doi.org/10.1016/j.tra.2021.06.017

9. Maioli, H.C., de Carvalho, R.C., de Medeiros, D.D.: SERVBIKE: riding customer satisfaction of bicycle sharing service. Sustain. Cities Soc. **50**, 101680 (2019). https://doi.org/10.1016/j. scs.2019.101680

10. Ayala-Chauvin, M., Riba Sanmartí, G., Riba, C., Lara, P.: Evaluation of the energy autonomy of urban areas as an instrument to promote the energy transition. Energy Sources Part B Econ. Planning, Policy (2022). https://doi.org/10.1080/15567249.2022.2053897

11. Huemer, A.K., Rosenboom, L.M., Naujoks, M., Banach, E.: Testing cycling infrastructure layout in virtual environments: an examination from a bicycle rider's perspective in simulation and online. Transp. Res. Interdiscip. Perspect. **14**, 100586 (2022). https://doi.org/10.1016/j. trip.2022.100586

12. G. Alvarez, M. Coello, A. López, and S. Ordoñez, "Evaluation of the electric bicycle as an alternative mobility in the city of Cuenca, Ecuador. In: Proceedings of the International Conference on Industrial Engineering and Operations Management, vol. 2018, pp. 476–485 (2018). https://www.scopus.com/inward/record.uri?eid=2-s2.0-85066935031& partnerID=40&md5=54e217e39a5d177e2746e9af6d9e81b7

13. Huang, Y., Yang, Z., Xiong, S.: The research on the control algorithm of IOT based bicycle parking system. In: Proceedings - 2012 IEEE 2nd International Conference on Cloud Computing and Intelligence Systems, IEEE CCIS 2012, vol. 3, pp. 1221–1225 (2012). https://doi. org/10.1109/CCIS.2012.6664578

14. Papadakis, N., Koukoulas, N., Christakis, I., Stavrakas, I., Kandris, D.: An IoT-based participatory antitheft system for public safety enhancement in smart cities. Smart Cities **4**(2), 919–937 (2021). https://doi.org/10.3390/smartcities4020047

15. Angulo-Esguerra, D., Villate-Barrera, C., Giral, W., Florez, H.C., Zona-Ortiz, A.T., Diaz-Sanchez, F.: Parkurbike: an IoT-based system for bike parking occupation checking (2017). https://doi.org/10.1109/ColComCon.2017.8088201

16. AyalaChauvin, M., Saá, F., VillarroelCórdova, F., de la FuenteMorato, A.: System for monitoring and controlling industrial lighting with Amazon Alexa. In: Rocha, Á., Adeli, H., Dzemyda, G., Moreira, F., RamalhoCorreia, A.M. (eds.) Trends and Applications in Information Systems and Technologies. AISC, vol. 1367, pp. 473–482. Springer, Cham (2021). https://doi.org/10.1007/978-3-030-72660-7_45

Adaptation of a Study Design to the COVID-19 Pandemic Regulations - Evaluation of a Voice-Controlled Robotic Kitchen Assistance System for the Support of Older Adults in Need of Care

Nicole Strutz$^{(\boxtimes)}$ and Luis Perotti

Charité - Universitätsmedizin Berlin, corporate member of Freie Universität Berlin and Humboldt-Universität zu Berlin, Geriatrics Research Group, Age & Technology, Reinickendorfer Str. 61, 13347 Berlin, Germany
nicole.strutz@charite.de

Abstract. Background. The COVID-19 pandemic had and still has a major impact on the design and realization of studies with volunteers due to the associated restrictions in face-to-face research. In connection with vulnerable target groups in particular, alternative study designs have to be considered. In the AuRorA project, a voice-controlled robotic kitchen assistance system was developed for supporting older adults in need of care.

We will present how we planned and conducted the evaluation of the system despite pandemic restrictions.

Methods. We carried out an iterative risk management based on ISO 12100:2010 with a multidisciplinary team before starting the study. In addition to the consideration of personnel safety in human-robot interaction, additional focus was placed on subject safety with respect to the COVID-19 pandemic.

Results. The risk management revealed that the study cannot be conducted via face-to-face with the target group. As a result, the study was performed via an online survey. We evaluated the robotic system using questionnaires. We simulated and filmed an exemplary cooking process and implemented the video into the survey. The target group was reached via mail.

Discussion. Other research groups also struggeled to adapt their studies to the pandemic situation. However, no best practice example exist yet. With our risk management, we were able to adapt our study design. However, only part of the target group could be reached. In addition, it can be questioned wether the ISO, which adresses machine safety, was an efficient application of risk management in this area.

Keywords: Study design · COVID-19 · Older adults · Risk management

C. Stephanidis et al. (Eds.): HCII 2022, CCIS 1655, pp. 555–560, 2022.
https://doi.org/10.1007/978-3-031-19682-9_70

1 Background/Introduction

The AuRorA project is a research project funded by the German Federal Ministry of Education and Research, which aimed to promote autonomy and self-determination through robotic assistance systems. The target group here were older adults. The project aimed to develop an interactive and cooperative robot that would reduce the dependency of care of older adults in their own homes.

Within the AuRorA project, the independent preparation of meals in the home kitchen was addressed. This would reduce the dependency of people in their own homes for the preparation or delivery of food by caregivers. For this purpose, a voice-controlled robot arm was developed, which can be mounted using a rail in a smart kitchen. It works in conjunction with several cameras and sensors as well as an automated hot plate and drawers. This robot was developed to interactively support the preparation of meals in a collaborative process. The system is able to recognize and grasp objects with its two-fingered gripper by means of object recognition. It is also able to avoid objects on the kitchen counter. The cooking process with the system was designed in such a way that the system does not take over the complete preparation of the food. The system should rather take into account the existing abilities and limitations of the human user and only take over activities that cannot be performed by him. This should promote the autonomy of the user and focus on the maintenance of his resources and abilities. The system also has a function for detecting fatigue states in the user. Adapted to this, the system can take over more activities if the user shows signs of exhaustion.

As part of the final evaluation planned for the AuRorA project, the system should be used and evaluated by older adults in the need of care. The overall concept for the evaluation of the interactive robotic kitchen was for it to be tested and to gather information about the relevance of its use for the target group. However, during the development of the study design, the COVID-19 case numbers in Germany increased, leading to massive restrictions in the area of face-to-face research. Therefore, an extensive risk management was conducted in order to assess the risks of the planned evaluation during the pandemic situation.

In this context, this article aims to present the process of adapting the study design to the prevailing pandemic situation. The results will be presented and discussed.

(1) How can an evaluation of a voice-controlled robotic system for kitchen use be evaluated by the target group of older adults considering the restrictions during the COVID-19 pandemic?

2 Methods

2.1 Initial Study Design

The system is installed in a German retirement home. A group of healthy senior home residents aged 65 and older cooked with the AuRorA system. After the informed consent of the study participants was given, the system should greet the participant and encourage them to cook pasta with tomato sauce together.

The original aim of the evaluation was to include 12 to 15 older adults living in a nursing home in an exploratory study. Technology acceptance [2], intention to use [1] and robot anxiety [3] was to be investigated.

No guidelines on adapting face-to-face research with the target group of older adults to the pandemic situation were available at the time of the evaluation. It was known that older adults in particular were more likely to be affected by a severe course of COVID-19 disease. The ethical maxim was not to expose any person of the vulnerable group of older adults to unnecessary risk.

Until the evaluation, we were not aware of any best practice example of methodological design in pandemic research. To be able to test the developed robotic kitchen system nevertheless, the research team decided on a structured procedure in order to find an objectifieable way of managing the risk during the evaluation.

The structured procedure was based on the German ISO 12100:2010. This ISO has already been used to assess the risk of personnel safety in human-robot interaction.

2.2 Risk Management Based on ISO 12100:2010

The ISO 12100:2010 (Safety of machinery - General principles for design - Risk assessment and risk reduction (ISO 12100:2010); German version EN ISO 12100:2010) defines "(…) the basic terminology and methodology and establishes general guiding principles for risk assessment and mitigation to help designers build safe machines" [6].

The risk assessment according to ISO 12100:2010 is structured into the successive steps of hazard identification, risk assessment including risk evaluation, and risk reduction measures (see Fig. 1).

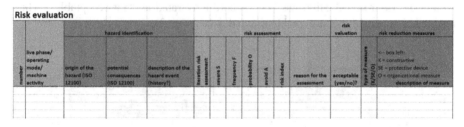

Fig. 1. Structure of the risk assessment according to ISO 12100:2010, own translation

The risk assessment was performed by a multidisciplinary team of robotic engineers, health scientists and the manager of a retirement home.

In a first step the "live phase/ operating mode/ machine activity" is defined and all further successive steps are based on the first step.

Following, the steps are explained based on the example *"driving the robot base on the linear axis"* of the risk evaluation of the robotic kitchen assistance system AuRorA. Shown in *brackets*.

The next steps are, as described above, hazard identification, risk assessment including risk evaluation and risk reduction measures. The hazard identification is split into the following areas: origin of the hazard (*movable parts*), potential consequences (*squeeze, bump*) and description of the hazard event (*robot base bumps into or traps a person*). The risk assessment is divided into iteration labeling (*A*) and into the risk graph, which is used to record the specific hazard in a risk index. The risk graph is composed of the following stages, which build on each other: severity (*2 = high*), frequency (*2 = often*), probability (*2 = moderate*) and avoidance (*2 = impossible*). Optionally, the assessment can be justified. The risk assessment is completed by the risk index (*5 = high*) and the risk valuation (*yes* or *no*). The risk index can take on values from one (lowest) to six (highest). If the risk valuation results in a "no" (meaning not acceptable), risk reduction measures are necessary. The last step of the iteration cycle, the risk reduction measures, is composed of the type of measure (*K = constructive*) and the description of measure (*water repellent housing around linear axis*).

According to this ISO, the risk for conducting the study in the original design was examined. If necessary, a study design should be adapted to pandemic situation was.

3   Results

3.1   Results of Structured Risk Assessment

The risk assessment based on the first step live phase/ operating mode/ machine activity: *general operation of the AuRorA system*. The origin of the hazard, potential consequences and the description of the hazard event are described as *coronavirus SARS-CoV-2, disease of participants* and *transmission by study staff*. The multidisciplinary team performed eight iteration cycles consisting of risk assessment, risk valuation and risk reduction measures. The first risk index was "six", being the maximum value. After the eighth iteration cycle, including several risk-minimizing measures, the risk index was still at "four" and the risk valuation has been accordingly rated as "not acceptable", which resulted in an overall not acceptable risk index (see Fig. 2).

Fig. 2. "general operation on the AuRorA system", risk assessment according to ISO 12100:2010, own translation

This resulted in the risk reduction measures being described as "Only people below the age limit for risk patients according The Robert Koch Institute (German government's central scientific institution in biomedicine) standards should participate as a test person".

After the risk management, the need for adapting the original study design since the evaluation still needed to address the target group of older adults.

3.2 Study Design Adapted to Pandemic Situation

As the risk management showed that the study could not be conducted as original planned due to the prevailing pandemic, the study design was adapted accordingly. In order to reach the target group of older adults, the study was planned as an online survey using standardized questionnaires. To provide the target group with the clearest possible impression of the system, a prototypical cooking process using the robotic kitchen system was filmed by the study personnel. Both in the filming and in the editing, attention was paid to the clarity and comprehensibility of the processes depicted. The user's communication with the robotic system via speech was also recorded, so that the interaction could be shown in the video. The study participants were asked to evaluate the system depicted in the video using various questionnaires. Thus, participants' data were collected using a self-developed basic data questionnaire. The participants' technology acceptance was assessed by means of a validated assessment by Neyer et al. [2]. In addition, the intention to use the system was surveyed using the Technology Usage Inventory by Kothgassner et al. [1].

In order to reach the target group of older adults through the online format, various multipliers with access to the target group were approached. The use of these multipliers made it possible to reach a larger number of people over 65 years of age (Fig. 3).

Fig. 3. Screenshot of the video used in the survey providing an overview of the system. Copyright holder: FZI Research center for Information Technology, permission publication was obtained

4   Discussion

The pandemic-related restrictions on face-to-face research and hygiene measures to protect vulnerable study populations are also evident in other countries and at other research institutions. For example, researchers report studies being prevented and study designs needing adjustment, while also reporting a lack of guidelines to provide orientation [5]. It is also claimed that the increased prioritization of Covid-19 research has made it more difficult to fund and conduct studies, but at the same time, the pandemic has encouraged new forms of research, especially remote research [4]. However, no structured process of adapting study designs targeting the elderly to the pandemic situation has been reported in the literature. Our procedure based on an ISO by the modification of an existing and established guideline can help other researchers in need for identifying infectious risks and adapting their study designs.

Our goal was to develop a methodical procedure for determining risks of infections for potential study participants. The methodological procedure was required to meet scientific quality criteria as far as possible. This meant for it to be transparent, comprehensible, repeatable and objective.

With the choice of risk management oriented towards German ISO 12100:2010, this has been realized. The standardized instrument enables a risk assessment based on defined criteria and has been used many times in other contexts. Since these contexts are mostly concerning the area of machine safety and ISO 12100:2010 focuses on this specifically, the transferability to other areas, such as robotic research in pandemic situation, may be questioned.

However, it cannot be ignored that only a part of the target group of older adults in need of care was reached with our online-survey. This subgroup consists of older adults who have a certain affinity for technology in common, or at least have access to the internet and an mail account.

Additionally, on the one hand no direct interaction with the robotic system took place. Thus, only certain aspects of the interaction could be assessed by the participants. This creates an imperfect impression of a direct and complete ideal process of collaborative cooking with the robotic system. On the other hand, there was no possibility for the researchers to explain the system to the participants or answered questions.

References

1. Kothgassner, O.D., et al.: Technology Usage Inventory (TUI): Manual (2013)
2. Neyer, F., et al.: Entwicklung und Validierung einer Kurzskala zur Erfassung von Technikbereitschaft. Diagnostica. **58**, 87–99 (2012). https://doi.org/10.1026/0012-1924/a000067
3. Nomura, T., et al.: Experimental investigation into influence of negative attitude robots on human-robot interaction. AI & Soc. **20**, 138–150 (2006)
4. Omary, M.B., et al.: The COVID-19 pandemic and research shutdown: staying safe and productive. J. Clin. Invest. **130**(6), 2745–2748 (2020). https://doi.org/10.1172/JCI138646
5. Rashid, S., Yadav, S.S.: Impact of Covid-19 pandemic on higher education and research. Indian J. Human Dev. **14**(2), 340–343 (2020)
6. DIN EN ISO 12100:2011-03, Sicherheit von Maschinen- Allgemeine Gestal tungsleitsätze- Risikobeurteilung und Risikominderung (ISO_12100:2010)
7. Deutsche Fassung EN_ISO_12100:2010. Beuth Verlag GmbH. https://doi.org/10.31030/163 4159

Analysis of Electrical Energy Consumption in the Home Using IoT

José Varela-Aldás[1,3](✉) ⓘ, Mario Miranda[1], Jenny León[1], and Cristian Gallardo[1,2]

[1] SISAu Research Group, Facultad de Tecnologías de la Información y la Comunicación,
Universidad Tecnológica Indoamérica, Ambato, Ecuador
{josevarela,mariomiranda,jennyleon}@uti.edu.ec,
kristianmaurisio1@tpu.ru
[2] Tomsk Polytechnic University, 30 Lenin Avenue, Tomsk, Russia
[3] Department of Electronic Engineering and Communications, University of Zaragoza,
Zaragoza, Spain

Abstract. The consumption of electrical energy is important in the economy of the home and the internet of things facilitates real-time remote monitoring of electrical parameters. This document performs the analysis of electrical energy consumption in a domestic installation based on the data measured in 2 electrical distribution inputs, this information is collected automatically using a data acquisition device with an internet connection. The electrical monitor used is the Emporia Gen 2 Vue and the information collected is stored for a week in the cloud while the owners rate the activities in the home. To measure the activity level of the home, all 4 household members rate their energy use on a scale of 3 levels. The results show the graphs of electrical energy related to the levels of activity in the home. Surprisingly, the hours of high activity have slightly higher energy measurements than the measurements in the hours of medium activity, but both levels of activity have an observable difference with the hours of low activity. The final analysis allows establishing solutions to reduce the consumption of electrical energy in the home understudy.

Keywords: IoT · Electrical energy consumption · Smart home · Emporia Gen 2 Vue

1 Introduction

The cost of electricity has had a notable increase in recent years. Due to the high demand for energy resources worldwide, the decrease in resources and the lack of stability in electricity consumption are projected. Thus, strategies continuously seek to reduce electricity consumption through new data analysis techniques. [1]. On the other hand, there are more and more limitations to expanding electrical generation and transmission systems [2], continually seeking solutions to access low-cost renewable energy [3] and requiring complex equipment to control electrical energy [4]. Thus, the new studies are aimed at improving the energy efficiency of buildings, using new technologies to estimate real values of consumption and performance of electrical energy [5].

C. Stephanidis et al. (Eds.): HCII 2022, CCIS 1655, pp. 561–567, 2022.
https://doi.org/10.1007/978-3-031-19682-9_71

The Internet of Things (IoT) has been a field of research for the industrial and academic sector, seeking to improve the standard of living by using conventional technology to transform it into intelligent systems. Thus, it has been used in greenhouse climate control with efficient energy consumption [6]. The IoT facilitates real-time remote monitoring of electrical parameters, as well as temporary analysis of electrical energy consumption. Studies analyze the importance and necessity of energy conservation using IoT devices [7]. In this way, several investigations verify the efficiency of systems to save electricity or analyze the power of household appliances using smart devices based on the IoT [8, 9].

This work analyzes the consumption of electrical energy in a home using a commercial device for remote monitoring of electrical parameters based on the IoT. The information collected is contrasted with the level of activity registered by the inhabitants of the home to measure the perception of electricity use. For this purpose, the document is organized as follows: Sect. 2 presents the methodology used; Sect. 3 presents the results obtained and a brief discussion, and Sect. 4 presents the conclusions.

2   Methods and Materials

For the analysis of the electrical consumption of this research, the procedures in Fig. 1 are applied. The objective is to compare the measurements of electricity consumption with different levels of activity in the home. To measure electrical consumption, the Emporia Gen 2 Vue 2 energy monitor is used, this IoT-based device performs the necessary measurements and calculations to determine the energy consumed and then sends the data to the cloud through the Wi-Fi connection. The measured data is displayed via the device's commercial mobile app and exported for further analysis. On the other hand, the level of activity consists of the use of household appliances and other devices in the home.

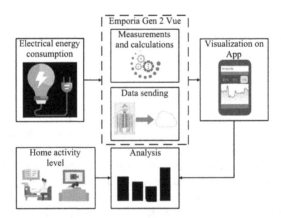

Fig. 1. General diagram of the study

2.1 Electrical Installation

The diagram in Fig. 2 is used to install the electrical monitor. The Emporia Gen 2 Vue has low power consumption (less than 3W), includes 200-amp and 50-amp flexible hook-type current sensors, and collects granular energy data from up to 1 s. In addition, the monitor allows real-time data to be obtained anywhere and anytime through the mobile application. On the other hand, a domestic distribution meter in Ecuador provides 3-wire single-phase alternating current electrical power, with 120 V in the line-neutral connection. All the devices at home use a 120Vac power supply, the L1 line feeds the common areas of the home (living room, kitchen, and dining room), and the L2 line feeds the 2 rooms of the home (including 1 bathroom), each line has a breaker at the entrance.

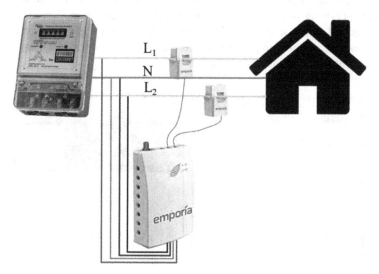

Fig. 2. Emporia Gen 2 Vue installation diagram

2.2 Activity Level at Home

The home that was analyzed in this study has 42 electronic devices in total, of which 25 use line 1, and 17 use line 2 of the power supply. Line L1 connects 9 lamps, 1 refrigerator, 1 microwave, 1 blender, 1 heater, 1 router, 1 shower, 1 water heater, 1 computer, 4 cameras, 2 phone chargers, 1 television, and 1 smart speaker. Line L2 connects 6 lamps, 1 heater, 2 cameras, 1 television, 2 phone chargers, 1 shower, 1 water heater, 1 computer, 1 printer, and 1 smart speaker. The level of activities is registered manually by the inhabitants of the house, and to facilitate this registration, a 3-level scale is established as shown in Table 1.

Table 1. Activity levels at home.

Level	Number of connected devices	Observations
1.- Low	Less than 35%	Mostly lamps and low-power devices
2.- Medium	Between 35% and 70%	Mostly low-power devices and a few high-power devices
3.- High	More than 70%	All and especially devices of high-power

3 Results

Once the electrical monitor is installed, the electrical measurements are recorded for 1 week, supervising the measurements from the commercial application of the IoT device. Figure 3 shows screenshots of the application, observing current and electrical power measurements of both power lines. At the end of the period, the data is exported in CSV format for subsequent analysis.

Fig. 3. Measurements made by the Emporia energy app.

3.1 Electrical Measurements

Figure 4 shows the measurements for an average day of electrical power in both power lines separately, these measurements are expressed in kilo Watts [KWatts]. Line L1 has an average of 102 Watts of electrical power consumed, with a minimum value of 5.8 Watts and a maximum value of 3251 Watts. Line L2 has an average of 258 Watts of electrical power consumed, with a minimum value of 2.2 Watts and a maximum value of 3625 Watts. Together, both lines reach a maximum power peak of 4016 Watts according to the measurements made during this period.

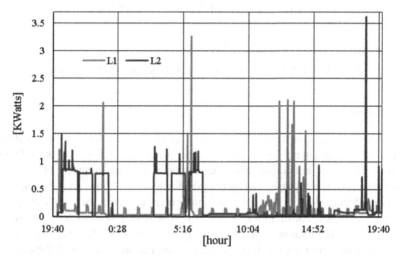

Fig. 4. Measurement of electrical power in the 2 power lines.

3.2 Comparison

The average electrical energy consumed per hour is compared with the activity levels recorded by the inhabitants of the house. Figure 5 shows the average electrical energy consumed for a week in Kilowatts per hour [KWhrs]. The average daily consumption is 9.72 KWhrs, in Ecuador, each KWhr costs 11 cents (USD) for the residential sector, this implies that the average day of consumption has a cost of 1.07 $. This value is consistent with the monthly payment of this house for electricity service. On the other hand, the level of activity in the home shows consistency with these measures. Furthermore, the correlation coefficient between these 2 variables is R = 0.86 and the p-value is 5E-08. This indicates a strong significant correlation between both variables.

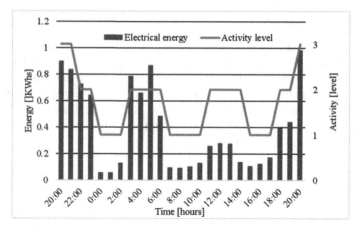

Fig. 5. Electrical energy consumed and activity level of the home

3.3 Discussion

The results obtained show that the low level of activity has much lower electrical energy consumption measurements compared to the measurements of the other levels. This indicates that there is no noticeable difference between the measurements of the medium and high levels of activity recorded by the inhabitants of the house. In addition, the benefits of monitoring electrical energy consumption are evident, since it allows detecting the hours of greatest consumption to seek improvement proposals [6]. The availability of data also offers the opportunity to apply different analysis techniques to reduce consumption and provide users with summary information about their habits to involve them in the energy-saving process [8].

Finally, in this case study, the following recommendations are made to users:

– Check active electrical devices between 4 and 6 am, because the registered energy consumption is higher than the consumption perceived by the user.
– Reduce the use of electronic devices at night because there is the highest energy consumption in this period.
– Continue to monitor energy consumption for patterns that lead to more energy savings.

4   Conclusions

This work presents the analysis of energy consumption in a home using a commercial device based on IoT. The results allow obtaining the hours of greatest consumption and correlating the measurements with the perspective of the inhabitants. A positive and significant correlation between both groups of data is determined. In addition, users rated the level of electrical energy consumption at times with high measurements as a medium, which implies that the user is not aware of all active electrical devices.

This work is limited by the variables registered in the electrical monitor, being able to include more variables such as power factor and reactive power for a more complete analysis. In addition, the recorded level of activity depends on the perception capacity of the user, so better instruments must be designed to measure activity at home. These and more problems are intended to be addressed in future works.

References

1. Velu, K., Arulanthu, P., Perumal, E.: Energy reduction stratagem in smart homes using association rule mining. In: Raj, J.S., Bashar, A., Ramson, S.R.J. (eds.) Innovative Data Communication Technologies and Application. LNDECT, vol. 46, pp. 188–193. Springer, Cham (2020). https://doi.org/10.1007/978-3-030-38040-3_22
2. Conejo, A.J., Baringo, L., Kazempour, S.J., Siddiqui, A.S.: Transmission Expansion Planning. In: Conejo, A.J., Baringo, L., Kazempour, S.J., Siddiqui, A.S. (eds.) Investment in Electricity Generation and Transmission, pp. 21–59. Springer, Cham (2016). https://doi.org/10.1007/978-3-319-29501-5_2
3. Guáitara, B., Buele, J., Salazar, F.W., VarelaAldás, J.: Prototype of a low cost turbine for the generation of clean energy in the Ecuadorian Amazon. In: Rodriguez Morales, G., Fonseca C., E.R., Salgado, J.P., PérezGosende, P., OrellanaCordero, M., Berrezueta, S. (eds.) Information and Communication Technologies. CCIS, vol. 1307, pp. 564–571. Springer, Cham (2020). https://doi.org/10.1007/978-3-030-62833-8_41
4. AyalaChauvin, M., Kavrakov, B.S., Buele, J., Varel-Aldás, J.: Static reactive power compensator design, based on three-phase voltage converter. Energies 14, 2198 (2021). https://doi.org/10.3390/en14082198
5. Seyedzadeh, S., Rahimian, F.P., Glesk, I., Roper, M.: Machine learning for estimation of building energy consumption and performance: a review. Visual. Eng. 6(1), 1–20 (2018). https://doi.org/10.1186/s40327-018-0064-7
6. Ullah, I., Fayaz, M., Aman, M., Kim, D.: An optimization scheme for IoT based smart greenhouse climate control with efficient energy consumption. Computing 104, 1–25 (2021). https://doi.org/10.1007/s00607-021-00963-5
7. Singh, P.P., Khosla, P.K., Mittal, M.: Energy conservation in IoT-based smart home and its automation. In: Mittal, M., Tanwar, S., Agarwal, B., Goyal, L.M. (eds.) Energy Conservation for IoT Devices. SSDC, vol. 206, pp. 155–177. Springer, Singapore (2019). https://doi.org/10.1007/978-981-13-7399-2_7
8. Paredes-Valverde, M.A., et al.: IntelliHome: an internet of things-based system for electrical energy saving in smart home environment. Comput. Intell. 36, 203–224 (2020). https://doi.org/10.1111/coin.12252
9. Shashank, A., Vincent, R., Sivaraman, A.K., Balasundaram, A., Rajesh, M., Ashokkumar, S.: Power Analysis of Household Appliances using IoT. In: 2021 International Conference on System, Computation, Automation and Networking (ICSCAN). pp. 1–5. IEEE (2021). https://doi.org/10.1109/ICSCAN53069.2021.9526428

Incorporating Affective Proactive Behavior to a Social Companion Robot for Community Dwelling Older Adults

Laura Villa[1]([envelope]) [iD], Ramón Hervás[1] [iD], Cosmin C. Dobrescu[1] [iD],
Dagoberto Cruz-Sandoval[2] [iD], and Jesús Favela[3] [iD]

[1] University of Castilla-La Mancha, UCLM, Ciudad Real, Spain
{Laura.Villa,Ramon.HLucas,Cosmin.Dobrescu}@uclm.es
[2] University of California, UCSD, San Diego, USA
dcruzsandoval@eng.ucsd.edu
[3] Centro de Investigación Científica y de Educación Superior de Ensenada, CICESE, Ensenada, Mexico
favela@cicese.mx

Abstract. Virtual assistants, agents and social robots are becoming increasingly popular, assisting users in simple daily tasks. However, they are often mere voice-based interfaces to internet. In fact, they can be perceived as unnatural, unreliable and "inhuman" or distant, as they cannot support a fluid conversation and are not empathic. EVA is a socially assistive robot, created as an open platform, being extended by several research groups. It is an open source, modular, low-cost and conversational robot aimed at supporting Instrumental Activities of Daily Living (IADLs). We describe how interaction with this robot can be improved by incorporating proactivity, so that EVA is able to initiate conversations and care about the user, making the interaction more natural, social and affective. The two main steps to achieve this interaction are: a) with specific triggered events, EVA asks different proactive questions, when the user's presence is detected and b) introducing the novel *wakeface* method, a more natural alternative to the traditional wakeword. With the proposed approach, the robot gets activates when looked at in its eyes. This ensures eye contact during the conversation, a common non-verbal communication strategy among humans, improving affects and trustworthiness. In this paper, the main functionalities of proactive EVA are described.

Keywords: Social Robot · Affective computing · Cognitive computing · Proactivity · Wakeface · Natural interaction · Ambient interfaces

1 Introduction

The COVID-19 pandemic has made more apparent the need to provide emotional support and assistance to older adults. Psychological and emotion monitoring is complex, often imposing significant burden on caregivers. Virtual assistants that help users in simple daily tasks, are becoming increasingly popular. However, currently they mostly act as

C. Stephanidis et al. (Eds.): HCII 2022, CCIS 1655, pp. 568–575, 2022.
https://doi.org/10.1007/978-3-031-19682-9_72

mere voice-based interfaces to the internet. In fact, they seem unnatural, unsocial and "inhuman" to the users, as they cannot support a fluid conversation or show empathy.

In addition to commercial virtual assistants, robots have also been developed to help elderly people in a wide variety of contexts and specific tasks. Robots have been used to assist in meal preparation [1], eating [2], for daily grooming [3], to perform household chores [4], for mood regulation [5], and to control/monitor the health status of the elderly [6], among others. In addition, these interactive devices can also provide companionship to elderly users (e.g., as a partner in a game of chess or cards) and encourage them to engage in cognitive training, as some studies have provided evidence of positive effects of robot interaction on cognitive function in the elderly [7]. In this regard, social robot interventions have been found to improve mood and reduce stress levels in older adults [8]. Despite the wide variety of functions, it has also been shown that the acceptance of these robots by older adults is a complex process and is undoubtedly affected by multiple factors [9], including simplicity and naturalness in interaction and humanization, such as considering affective aspects. These aspects are precisely what has motivated the development of proactive and affective capabilities in the EVA robot, the main contribution of this work.

EVA (depicts in Fig. 1) is a social assistant robot, a project created at CICESE [10], with an open approach, in which other academic organizations, such as the University of California and UCLM, are contributing with new services and applications. EVA is an open source, modular and low-cost robot. It is a conversational and affective robot aimed at assisting older adults in conducting *Instrumental Activities of Daily Living* (IADLs).

Fig. 1. 3D model and working prototype of the EVA Robot.

After explaining the motivation of this work in this section, the rest of the article continues with a description of the EVA robotics platform in Sect. 2. The approach proposed to achieve proactive behavior is explained in Sect. 3. Finally, Sect. 4 concludes the article, describing the objectives achieved and the contributions of this work.

2   The Social Assistant and Open Robot EVA

The first EVA version was designed to assist older adults who suffer from dementia [10]. It was a semiautonomous conversational agent, coordinated by a human operator, that assisted people with dementia who exhibit problematic behaviors. EVA was used as a platform for other related experiments, such as [11], or to assist children with autism in emotion regulation [12].

The EVA robot is mainly composed of: *Raspberry Pi 4*, a screen for eyes displaying, a camera, a speaker, and an array of microphones and LEDs.

The design of the EVA robot, to facilitate future modifications by the community, has been done following a parametric design of all parts using Fusion 360. This design has been especially focused on manufacturing with FDM (*Fused Deposition Modelling*) 3D printing technology. The robot is composed of 3 main parts, i) the base, ii) the body and iii) the head. The base contains the overall structure on which the whole robot rests and is where most of the components are placed. On top of the base, the body of the robot is placed together with the legs and hands, this part of the robot is simply decorative, giving it a more humanized and friendly appearance, hiding the cables and internal components. In the internal structure of the base are mounted two servomotors connected in series that will oversee giving a movement in two axes to the head. In addition to these main components, the head contains two extra parts, the cover that keeps the screen in place and the back cover that hides the head components.

3   EVA's Proactive Behavior

To incorporate a proactive and more natural behavior to the robot, it is necessary to allow the user to initiate conversations, and for EVA shows concern about the user.

In a general way, this involves four key elements:

a) Proactive questions. From time to time, or triggered by specific events, the robot asks the user questions, for example about how the user feels and needs.
b) Activation method. Using the novel *wakeface* method (a more natural alternative to the traditional wakeword used to start conversations with assistants) the robot gets activated when being looked at. This assures that the conversation involves visual contact, which is an important element of human communications.
c) User recognition. The robot can recognize the user, implying a "closer" communication, as the robot can know his face, and refer to him by his name.
d) Ambient interfaces. EVA's LEDs show a specific animation and colour depending on the situation, action, and state.

3.1   EVA's General Workflow

EVA integrates several "micro-services" (presence detection, *wakeface*, facial recognition, microphones, speakers, LEDs, etc.), which require an approproiate asynchronous interaction design, integration of services, and concurrent access to devices.

Conceptually, EVA works as a kind of state machine (see Fig. 2), waiting for the user's presence and the activation of the called *wakeface* to initiate a conversation. Once the robot is listening (*Listening* state), when the user talks (*Recording* state), it waits until silence is detected to send the query to the cloud to process it (*Processing query* state) and generate and reproduce an appropriate response (*Speaking* state). At this point, it can continue listening to the conversation (*Listening-Recording-Processing query-Speaking* states cycle), until the user responds with a farewell (*end conversation* transition), when it returns to the initial state (*Idle_presence* state) and the conversation finishes. If the conversation continues (*continue* transition), the robot waits for an utterance from the user, and the cycle is repeated. If the user does not speak anymore, it goes to the initial state (*timeout* transition) after a timeout, finishing the conversation.

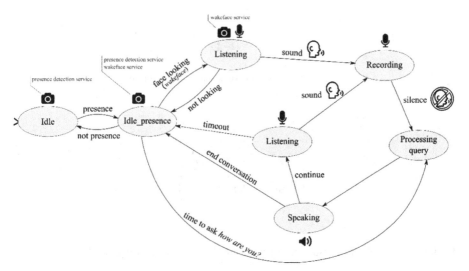

Fig. 2. State diagram of EVA's general workflow. Black icons are active hardware devices.

It can be noted that this workflow has been developed in this way to optimize and reduce the number of services and devices that are concurrently executed, so as not to overload the *Raspberry Pi 4* which is connected to several devices. For example, there is no point on having the camera active during the *Recording* state, since for sure there is a user talking and the conversation has started, neither is the presence detector nor the *wakeface* service needed at this stage.

Cognitive Services. EVA responses (*Processing query state*) are generated using *IBM Watson* and *Google* cognitive services. The generic flow of a query is shown in Fig. 3. The transitions are: 1. Text from user audio input is obtained using *Speech to Text* service; 2. Translation of this text into English, as emotion analysis service does not support all the languages; 3. Translated text is sent to emotion analysis service, obtaining a vector with the estimated probability of each emotion being present (see Listing 1); 4. The input user text and the emotion inference vector are sent to the *Watson Assistant*, to generate a text response taking into account the emotions; 5. Then the audio from the text response is generated, and spoken by EVA.

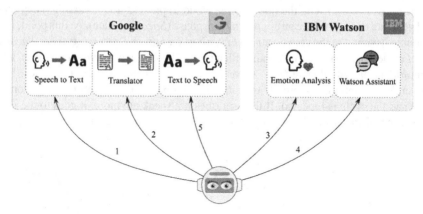

Fig. 3. Cloud cognitive services use diagram.

```
{
    "sadness": 0.174379,
    "joy": 0.66067,
    "fear": 0.051475,
    "disgust": 0.114401,
    "anger": 0.044105
}
```

Listing 1. Example of the results obtained from the user's utterance using *IBM Emotion Analysis*.

3.2 Proactive Questions

These questions cannot be only asked when the *wakeface* is active (i.e., user looking at the robot) and EVA is listening, because it would lose some naturalness in the robot behavior.

Thus, to make a proactive question, EVA must first know that the user is in the room. A *TensorFlow* pretrained person detector model using the *EfficientDet* architecture [13] is used by the camera to determine it, the model was optimized to run on the *Raspberry Pi 4* using *TensorFlow Lite*.

Different proactive questions can be triggered depending on the state of the robot, the situation or specific events registered. When the user presence is detected, it will decide if it is a suitable situation for asking a proactive question. For example, if it has been a long time since the robot spoke with the user and user presence is detected, EVA asks how he feels, by synthesizing the audio of the corresponding question, going to the processing query state, to then continue with the usual flow. Figure 2 (bottom part, *time to ask how are you?* transition) shows the transition to this proactive question. Note that, if the user is talking to EVA (*Recording* state), the robot does not interrupt the conversation for asking a proactive question, but it is postponed to the next suitable situation (that could be, for example, to ask it the next day).

Another implemented proactive question is "Who are you?", which is explained in Sect. 3.4.

3.3 Activation Method

Current assistants use wakeword methods for getting activated. This interaction, although direct, reduces the naturalness and affectivity of the conversation. That is the main aim of the *wakeface* proposal.

The *Wakeface* method is a more natural alternative to the use of wakeword. In this novel method, EVA gets activated when looked at to its eyes, involving eye contact in the interaction and improving affectivity, trustworthiness, and sociability.

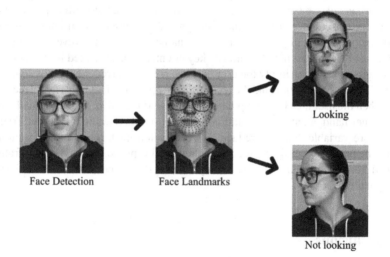

Fig. 4. *Wakeface* process.

This is done using the following heuristic (Fig. 4): 1. The user face is detected; 2. Different keypoints (landmarks) of his face are obtained; 3. To know if the face is pointing at the robot's face, two checks are made: i) for the horizontal axis it checks that the nose point is inside a specific interval between the eyes tragion points, and ii) for the vertical axis it checks that the nose is inside a specific interval between the eyes mean point and the mouth point.

A *Google MediaPipe* Python wrapper is used for face detection and to detect the landmarks.

3.4 User Recognition

To improve the sociability in the interaction, a face recognition model is integrated into the system (using a Python wrapper of the *Dlib* machine learning toolkit [14]). This model is executed each time a user is looking at the robot: if his face is recognized, EVA uses his name to refer to him, and it is sent as context when making a query to *IBM Watson Assistant*, to generate personalized responses for this user.

Face Recording. If the user's face is not recognized (unknown face), a proactive question "Who are you?" is executed. When the user answers, a face recording service is started in a parallel thread. The face embeddings of 6 frames are obtained and saved, so the next time this user will be recognized. If the user leaves during this recording, 10 consecutive frames without detecting a face cancels the recording process.

Optimizations. User recognition using only one frame from a video stream can cause some false positives (unknown face recognized with a name) and false negatives (recorded face recognized as unknown). Also using only 6 consecutive frames for recording a face could lead to this face recognition problems. To avoid this, some optimizations have been carried out. On the one hand, a face history in the recognition process is used. This history is a counter of face names recognized on consecutive frames. If the face is directly recognized, it implies that the user's name is correct. However, if the user face is recognized as unknown, a "unknown" key counter is incremented in the face history. 3 consecutive unknowns imply the user face has not been saved previously, so the "Who are you?" proactive question and the recording process start. This helps avoid recognition errors when the user face is moving when the image is recorded, but it is actually known. On the other hand, a data augmentation process is applied to the 6 recorded frames, to obtain more variable data and reduce the recognition mistakes. Shifting, rotating and varying the brightness of the image are applied for this purpose. 3 augmented frames are obtained from each original one, so finally 24 embeddings per user are saved instead of the original 6.

4   Conclusions

Although EVA could have unlimited uses, older adults emotional support and assistance is our main purpose, to reduce digital gap and loneliness problems, improving their independence. Thus, EVA could be placed at home, detecting user emotional states in conversations, and making actions and suggestions to alleviate this: calls to relatives to reduce sadness, playing music to calm anxiety... Thus, interaction goes beyond a simple dialogue.

Having an EVA robot at home is very accessible for older adult users. Also, it is less intrusive than an unknown person.

The fact of talking to someone with natural interactions, which cares about the user and seems to be more "alive" than a simple passive assistant, gives the feeling that it is his housemate, improving affects, sociability, trustworthiness, and user experience.

References

1. Bovbel, P., Casper, N.G.: An assistive kitchen robot to promote aging in place. J. Med. Dev. **8**(3), 030945 (2014)
2. Graf, B., Hans, M., Schraft, R.D.: Care-O-bot II—development of a next generation robotic home assistant. Auton. Robot. **16**(2), 193–205 (2004)
3. Brooke, J.: Japan seeks robotic help in caring for the aged. Caring. **23**(7), 56–59 (2004)
4. Dario, P., Guglielmelli, E., Laschi, C., Teti, G.: MOVAID: a personal robot in everyday life of disabled and elderly people. Technol. Disabil. **10**(2), 77–93 (1999)
5. Johnson, E., González, I., Mondéjar, M., CabañeroGómez, L., Fontecha, J., Hervás, R.: An affective and cognitive toy to support mood disorders. Informatics **7**(4), 48 (2020)
6. Plaza, I., Martín, L., Martin, S., Medrano, C.: Mobile applications in an aging society: status and trends. J. Syst. Softw. **84**(11), 1977–1988 (2011)
7. Esposito, R., Fiorini, L., Limosani, R., Bonaccorsi, M., Manzi, A., Cavallo, F.: Supporting active and healthy aging with advanced robotics integrated in smart environment. In: Morsi, Y. S., Shukl, A., Rathore, C.P., (eds.). Optimizing Assistive Technologies for Aging Populations, pp. 46–47. Hershey, IGI Global (2016)
8. Scoglio, A.A., Reilly, E.D., Gorman, J.A., Drebing, C.E.: Use of social robots in mental health and well- being research: systematic review. J. Med. Internet Res. **21**(7), e13322 (2019)
9. Sorri, L., Leinonen, E.: Technology that persuades the elderly. In: Oinas-Kukkonen, H., Hasle, P., Harjumaa, M., Segerståhl, K., Øhrstrøm, P. (eds.) Persuasive Technology. LNCS, vol. 5033, pp. 270–273. Springer, Heidelberg (2008). https://doi.org/10.1007/978-3-540-68504-3_29
10. Cruz-Sandoval, D., Favela, J.: Semi-autonomous conversational robot to deal with problematic behaviors from people with dementia. In: Ochoa, S.F., Singh, P., Bravo, J. (eds.) Ubiquitous Computing and Ambient Intelligence. LNCS, vol. 10586, pp. 677–688. Springer, Cham (2017). https://doi.org/10.1007/978-3-319-67585-5_66
11. Cruz-Sandoval, D., Morales-Tellez, A., Sandoval, E.B., Favela, J.: A social robot as therapy facilitator in interventions to deal with dementia-related behavioral symptoms. In: 2020 15th ACM/IEEE International Conference on Human-Robot Interaction (HRI), pp. 161–169 (2020)
12. Rocha, M., et al.: Towards enhancing the multimodal interaction of a social robot to assist children with autism in emotion regulation. In: Lewy, H., Barkan, R. (eds.) Pervasive Computing Technologies for Healthcare. LNICSSITE, vol. 431, pp. 398–415. Springer, Cham (2022). https://doi.org/10.1007/978-3-030-99194-4_25
13. Tan, M., Pang, R., Le, Q.V.: EfficientDet: Scalable and Efficient Object Detection (2019). https://doi.org/10.48550/ARXIV.1911.09070
14. King, D.E.: Dlib-ml: a machine learning toolkit. J. Mach. Learn. Res. **10**, 1755–1758 (2009)

A Study and Comparative Analysis of the Intelligent Park Operation Platform

Jingyi Yang[✉]

Tongji University, Shanghai 200092, People's Republic of China
15680875078@163.com

Abstract. With the development of intelligent technology, related research on smart cities emerges in an endless stream, and a large number of smart solutions related to various functions and scenarios of cities have emerged. As an important unit and functional carrier of the city, the park can be regarded as the epitome of the city. Therefore, the research on smart parks can lay a corresponding foundation for the research on smart cities. In order to make the smart park operate better, a large number of existing studies on the smart park not only focus on the physical space of the smart park, such as the intelligence of infrastructure, but also on the construction of the smart park operation platform. Therefore, a large number of technology and artificial intelligence companies have developed and launched related products or solutions of Intelligent Park Operation Platforms or Centers (IOP/IOC). This research will analyze the platform service products of 14 representative enterprises such as Alibaba Cloud, Huawei Cloud, Dahua HOC, etc.

With this analysis content and framework, these data are compared horizontally and vertically. Through the data analysis, the hot content of functions, data content, the average degree of interaction and technology types, as well as the general interaction realization degree of existing platforms can be obtained. In this way, the trend and potential of the park operation platform and the smart park can be discussed in combination with the realization degree of the park platform and the operation needs, as well as the weak points of technology application in the park, and the potential of data analysis in the park. It brings development trends and directions to the construction of smart parks and park operation platforms.

Keywords: Intelligent Park operation platform · Comparative research · Future of Smart Park · Park operation

1 Introduction

With the continuous iteration and development of artificial intelligence and other technologies, the construction of smart cities is also constantly developing, and its construction and application fields have involved many aspects of the city. Huawei's enterprise business market insights point out that more than 90% of urban residents work and live in the park [1], so the construction and development model of the park can be said to be the epitome of a regional smart city [2].

© The Author(s), under exclusive license to Springer Nature Switzerland AG 2022
C. Stephanidis et al. (Eds.): HCII 2022, CCIS 1655, pp. 576–585, 2022.
https://doi.org/10.1007/978-3-031-19682-9_73

In order to meet the long-term and more intelligent construction and operation needs of smart parks, driven by the technological background of the times, building a data-driven intelligent decision-making center has become an essential element for the smart construction of future parks [3]. As a result, a large number of enterprises and technology companies have developed and launched related services such as smart park intelligent operation platforms or centers (IOP/IOC). We can select some representative platforms to conduct case studies, and sort out and compare and analyze their contents, so as to find out the defects and unmet needs of the existing platforms, so as to give certain reference for the future development direction of smart park and intelligent park operation platform.

2   Method

Before data collection began, I established a framework for data collection and analysis. Subsequent data content aggregation and analysis will be based on this framework. The analysis content includes four layers, as shown in Fig. 1, including the functional structure and content, the corresponding perception data, and the subsequent judgment, reaction, and learning [3] in the decision-making process of the smart brain. And then it's about the related technologies used and the degree of realization. Finally, it is an application case.

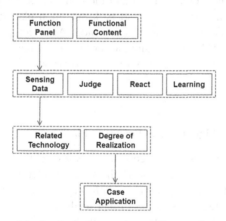

Fig. 1. Analysis content and framework.

The next step is to select the corresponding enterprise and its R&D platform or solution. This research finally selects the most representative park platform service products of 14 enterprises for analysis. These 14 companies are from China and are China's representative companies in smart city, smart solutions and technology. They are HUAWEI, Alibaba, Baidu, China Unicom, Uino Tech, Hikvision, MREGVII, Tencent, Digital Hail, Founder, Argrace, Dahua Tech, 51World and SenseTime. Among them, Alibaba, Baidu, and Tencent are China's top three Internet giants[4]; Huawei is a leading information and communication technology (ICT) solution provider[5]; Sense-Time is an industry-leading artificial intelligence software company[6]; Hikvision is a world-leading provider of security products and industry solutions[7]; Dahua Technology is the world's leading video-centric smart IoT solution provider and operation service provider[8]; China Unicom is one of the most important network communication groups in China. In recent years, it has also been committed to accelerating industry integration and expanding Industrial Internet, 5G + Industrial Internet integration and innovative applications [9]; Uino Tech was established in 2012 and is a pioneer and practitioner in the field of digital twin visualization [10]; MREGVII Tech was established in 2011 and is an artificial intelligence company focusing on IoT scenarios[11]; Digital Hail was established in 2006, focusing on the field of data visualization, the deep integration of system platform and industry needs, and formed a series of industry visualization products[12]; Founder Tech, a mainland listed company under Peking University Founder Information Industry Group, founded in 1998, is currently committed to becoming a "true contributor to smart cities" [13]; Founded in 2017, Argrace Tech is committed to the creation of an intelligent space operation platform, defining and operating space scenarios in an Internet way [14]; 51WORLD, established in 2015, is a digital twin platform company with industry influence [15]. These companies all have strong technical foundations and practical capabilities. Through the analysis of the smart park operation platforms of these 14 companies, it can basically represent the current status of smart park solutions and smart operation platforms on the market at this stage.

Therefore, this research retrieves the published product information and product manuals through the network platform and the company's official website, and then summarizes the information on the smart park operation platforms of 14 companies. Through preliminary sorting, Table 1 is obtained. After completing the summarization and arrangement of the information, according to the analysis framework, further analysis of the various content information was carried out.

3   Results

3.1   Functions of Intelligent Park Operation Platform

After the information aggregation is completed, based on Table 1, the word frequency statistics and analysis are carried out on the function sections and function content. Based on this, we can draw the current platform's focus on functions and function sections supported by technology, and further analyze and consider the power points of future technologies. Merge similar items with the same meaning, and perform word frequency statistics, as shown in Table 2.

Then visualize the frequency of the function sections, as shown in Fig. 2, it can be clearly found that the functions of each platform include Comprehensive security, and almost every platform function includes Energy management, Vehicle and Parking Management, Facility and equipment management, Personnel management, Corporate, Business & Financial Services and Smart Transportation. It can be found that these functions are mainly to meet the most basic security needs of the park, as well as the essential things in the park - the management of people, vehicles, things and enterprises need. At the same time, the functions in half or more of the platforms include Office service, Smart Building and Space Management, asset Management, Intelligent Environmental Monitoring and Management, Investment service and management, Property Services

Table 1. Comparative analysis of the smart park operation platforms of 14 companies.

Platform Name	Company	Function Panel	Function Content	Sense Data	Judge	React	Learning	Type Used	Related Technology	Case Application	Degree of Realization (0-Concept; 1-basic realization; 2-initial realization; 3-fully available)
Smart Park IOC / Smart Operation Center	HUAWEI HUAWEI CLOUD							software hardware		Shanghai Xuhui West Bund Media Port; Hunan Changsha Lake Smart Park, etc.	3
Smart Park Solution	Alibaba Aliyun							software hardware		Zhuanghang Industrial Park, 18 parks of Lingang Group	3
Smart Park IOC / Operation Center	Baidu cloud							software hardware		A smart park in an urban area in Shanghai	3
Ultra-intelligent IOC	China Unicom							software hardware		Zhangjiang Artificial Intelligence Island	2
Smart Park virtualization	nano							software		Pudion Software Park	2
Smart Park Management Platform	Millennium							software hardware		Changan Automobile Global R&D Center	2
Smart Park Solution	MEKOWE							software hardware		Guangzhou Guangfa Building	3
Smart Park Ecological Operation Platform	Financial Cloud							software hardware		China-Israel Innovation Park AIPark	3
Intelligent Park Operation Center IOC	Digital Hail							software hardware		CFLD Smart Park Operation Command Platform	3
Park operation platform solution	Founder							software hardware		Peking University International Hospital, China-Germany Group Enterprise Park	3
Smart Park Solution	Argosee							software hardware		New Zhengfa Property	3
Smart Park Solution	Dahua Tech							software hardware		Foxconn Technology Group Enterprise Park Project	3
Smart Park Management Platform	SHWorld							software hardware		Huawei Global Headquarters Bantian Campus IOC-MAX	2
Smart global space management platform	Senso Time							software hardware		West Bank of Xuhui, Shanghai	3

Table 2. Classification statistics of functional sections.

Function Panel	Functional Subcategory	Count	Count
Comprehensive security	Surveillance video inspection	5	
	Perimeter Intrusion Prevention and Control	4	
	emergency event linkage	1	
	Fire linkage	2	
	Intelligent early warning and prediction	4	14
	Emergency Management and Situation Monitoring and Analysis	7	
	Finding people and things	1	
	property collaboration	1	
Facility and equipment management	Device location	1	
	Equipment operating status	3	
	Equipment ledger	1	
	device visible	1	
	Equipment inspection	1	
	Device warning	1	
	Maintenance records	1	
	Convenient repair	2	10
Personnel management	People statistics, people popularity	2	
	Intervention population stays	1	
	moving track	1	
	Identification	2	
	Easy access	2	
	Non-inductive access	1	
	Smart Visitor and Reservation	3	
	Smart access system	1	
	access control	1	
	Body temperature measurement	1	
	Face brushing elevator control	1	10
Vehicle and Parking Management	Parking guidance	1	
	Parking status	2	
	unmanned parking	1	
	Vehicle Information	1	
	parking violation	2	
	AI vehicle gate	1	
	Deterring non-motorized/high-risk area intrusions	1	11
Smart Transportation	Park Navigation	3	
	Easy access and access control	3	
	Reverse Control	1	
	reverse car search	1	
	real-time location monitoring	1	9
asset Management	Asset ledger and inventory	2	
	Asset visualization	1	
	Asset positioning	1	
	Asset Situation	1	6
Intelligent Environmental Monitoring and Management	Excessive warning	1	
	Visual management	2	
	Garbage classification	1	
	Environmental management	1	
	Air conditioning control	1	6
Energy management	Energy consumption monitoring and analysis (water, fresh air, lighting, electrical)	2	
	Energy saving and environmental protection	1	
	EBA operation and maintenance	1	12
Industry analysis	industry chain intelligent analysis	1	
	Industrial operation	1	
	Decision support	1	
	industrial research	1	5
	Evaluation of Industry Agglomeration	1	
	Industry Planning	1	

Function Panel	Functional Subcategory	Count	Count
Merchants Service and Management	Attract investment	2	
	Investment forecast	1	
	Investment follow-up	1	6
	Investment analysis	1	
	Data board, resource map	1	
Corporate, Business & Financial Services	Online mall, e-commerce service, private domain e-commerce	2	
	Financial and taxation services	2	
	corporate portrait	3	
	Service operation	1	
	Merchant settled	2	10
	Innovation and Entrepreneurship Center	1	
	Business procedures agency	1	
	Willingness to consume	1	
	corporate leasing	1	
	business management	1	
	Enterprise Statistics	1	
Wisdom and Precision Marketing	Industry exchange	1	
	performance optimization	1	
	Marketing Big Data	1	
	Knowledge Graph	1	
	Member management	2	
	customer portrait	1	5
	face payment	1	
	unified payment	1	
	Online and offline advertising resources	1	
	demand feedback	1	
	Enterprise product promotion	1	
Office service	Lack Operation Analysis	1	
	Service Level Analysis	1	
	Maker space	1	
	work together	2	9
	Stream Office	1	
	Smart meeting booking and management	3	
	Alibaba Cloud University, Taobao University	1	
Wisdom Teaching and Research	IoT training	1	4
	Wisdom training	1	
community service	community medical care	1	
	Residential Services	1	2
Catering Services	life support	1	
	Wisdom canteen	2	3
Smart Building and Space Management	Real-time monitoring of elevator running status in buildings	1	
	Rent control management	2	
	space resource usage	1	7
	Resource allocation	1	
	Integrate data on people, houses and places	1	
	space layout planning	1	
Holographic space visualization	3D visualization and interaction	1	4
	AR Kanban	1	
Property Services and Management	Park governance	1	
	Unmanned governance	1	5
	Administrative Services	1	
Smart Logistics and Warehousing	—	1	4
System Management	—	1	1
modular construction	—	1	2
double carbon brain	—	1	1
Overview of the park	—	1	1

and Management, Industry analysis, Wisdom and Precision Marketing. These contents mainly involve high-frequency services in various parks, which can be seen as services and management contents related to office, commerce, industry, property and assets. In addition, some of the remaining platform functions, such as Wisdom Teaching and Research, generally appear in some parks that contain functions related to education or teaching and research; Smart Logistics and Warehousing generally appear in some logistics parks. Holographic space visualization, Catering Services and community service and modular construction occur less frequently. It can be seen that the park operation platform pays relatively little attention to the life services involved in the park, and most of the functions of the platform are well integrated. Only some platforms are modular and customizable. Finally, some companies began to pay attention to the topic of carbon neutrality, hoping to build a smart carbon planning and management park platform. For example, Hikvision proposed "double carbon brain", and 51World started to create "DTARK - Double carbon smart park management application system".

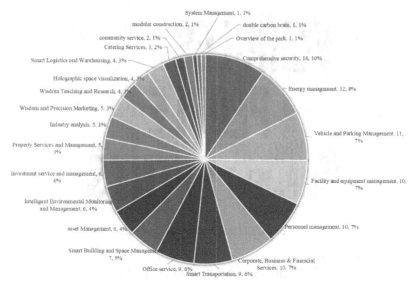

Fig. 2. Frequency ratio of functional section.

3.2 The Intelligent Interaction Process of the Intelligent Park Operation Platform

It can be found that the intelligent park operation platform involves the process of perception, which is also because the establishment of the intelligent park, intelligent operation and intelligent operation platform is based on the ability to obtain data through perception. Through the collection of perception data content, it can be found that the main objects of perception are crowd-related data, data of traffic and vehicles in the park, data of some events, especially emergency events, basic data related to the park environment, data of some equipment and objects, and the data of location attributes, etc. A perceptual data word cloud is generated according to the frequency of occurrence, see Fig. 3.

In addition, it can be found that each platform involves judgment and reaction in the interaction process. Some functions are direct reactions after perception. For example, for some data visualizations after perception, they are directly reflected in the form of images and information. Some of the reactions are after perception and judgment. For example, the early warning of dangerous behaviors is the reaction of perceiving dangerous behaviors through cameras and identifying and analyzing them,and the giving early warnings. Finally, it can be found that almost all platforms have not yet completed the "learning" in the process of intelligent interaction. Only the Alibaba platform clearly proposes to iterate the model by accumulating daily data. This may also be limited by the cost of existing technology to a certain extent, but it can still be considered to supplement the "learning" part of the more important and meaningful functions in the intelligent operation of the park.

Fig. 3. Word Cloud of Perception Objects.

3.3   Technologies and Applications Involved in the Platform

Summarizing the technologies involved in the intelligent park operation platform, it can be found that all the technology types involved in the operation platform are a combination of software and hardware. The hardware involves a series of sensors, such as temperature and humidity sensors for environmental monitoring, PM2.5 sensors, light sensors, etc.; RFID tags for positioning equipment, vehicles or people; as well as cameras and a series of intelligent hardware devices. A large number of emerging technologies are also involved in the process of the software platform linking the hardware to complete the operation of the entire smart park, which is in line with the technological development background of the times. Among them, the most commonly used are artificial intelligence technology, especially the technology of intelligent video recognition and analysis, 5G, Internet of Things, big data, cloud computing. In addition, it also involves technologies related to data and model visualization of the park platform and digital twins, such as BIM, CIM, GIS, etc.

Finally, the Degree of Realization is preliminarily judged by the degree of application in each enterprise platform case. Degree of Realization is divided into four grades, 0 represents just staying in the conceptual stage, 1 represents only preliminary realization, 2 represents basically realized and partially realized the application of the case, and 3 represents fully realized and applied in the case. It can be found that more than half of the platforms can fully realize the functions of their architecture in the case, and some enterprise platforms have only completed the application of some functions in the case, and there is still room for improvement, such as the platform of China Unicom, Hikvision, uino and 51World. In addition, in the process of data collection, it is found that some of the application of these functions in the case integrates all the functions of the platform architecture, while some cases only involve part of the functions in the architecture. This is also related to the business model of the enterprise for platform sales and the foundation of the platform's architecture. The customization of functional modularity may be a more respected way in the future (Fig. 4).

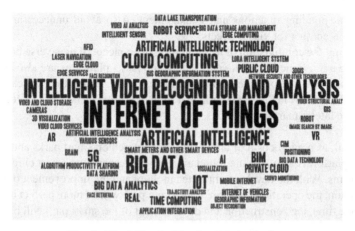

Fig. 4. Word Cloud of Involved Technologies.

4   Discussion

After analyzing the smart campus operation products of various enterprises, the following insights can be roughly drawn:

1) Most of these platforms consider the functions of the smart park operation platform to focus on park management, and they are the most basic aspects of security, people and vehicles management, and equipment and facility management in the park. These are still the "lowest Maslow demand" of the park. In the future, it is possible to combine the needs of operators with the needs of users, and pay attention to the use status and needs of users in the park, so as to bring more vitality to the park and explore more functions in this area.

2) These park operation platforms are built by default on the assumption that the park has reached a well-functioning and dynamic state, so as to carry out intelligent operations. But a very important point is that after the completion of many existing parks, the use of park space is not ideal, and many parks have problems of low space utilization and lack of vitality. In the future, these platforms may be able to consider using intelligent means to assist operators to consider the operation of space first, especially to better activate the space.

3) The function of the smart park operation platform can be considered in the future to be combined with the hot spots of the times, such as the creation of carbon neutral parks and zero-waste parks.

4) For the intelligent interaction process, the intelligent park operation platform still needs to be further explored for the "learning" stage. The improvement of the "learning" process can make the operation platform of the park further improve the degree of digitization and truly realize intelligence.

5) The presentation form of the existing platform focuses on the visual presentation of data and the visual presentation of the park model. In the future, it can be considered to combine functions and needs, and choose a presentation form that is more suitable

for corresponding functions and management. Also avoid unnecessary front-end development just for visual effects.

6) Regarding the combination of technologies, the concept of metaverse has gradually become a hot topic in recent years, and some parks platforms are also considering combining VR and other related technologies. In the future, the application of VR, AR and even MR in the smart park operation platform can be considered, combined with the latest smart technologies.

All in all, as a microcosm of urban life, the research on smart parks and smart park operation platforms also lays the foundation for the research on smart cities and smart city platforms. With the development of technology and the improvement of the degree of digitization, the operation platform of the smart park will be more perfect in the future. At the same time, the construction and development of the smart park will be promoted.

References

1. Huawei Technologies Co., Ltd, Accenture (China) Co., Ltd.. Future Smart Park (2020)
2. pjtime Information group. 数字孪生下的智慧园区信息化建设解决方案[Solutions for Smart Park Informatization Construction under Digital Twin] (2022). http://m.pjtime.com/2022/1/m231952108137.shtml
3. Wu, Z.Q.: 智慧城市: 初心与反思 [Smart city: original intention and reflection]. Contemp. Architect. **12**, 5+4 (2020)
4. Baike, B.: BAT (2022). https://baike.baidu.com/item/BAT/13973564?fr=aladdin
5. Baike, B.: 华为技术有限公司 [Huawei Technologies Co., Ltd] (2022). https://baike.baidu.com/item/%E5%8D%8E%E4%B8%BA%E6%8A%80%E6%9C%AF%E6%9C%89%E9%99%90%E5%85%AC%E5%8F%B8/6455903?fromtitle=%E5%8D%8E%E4%B8%BA&fromid=298705&fr=aladdin
6. Baike, B.: 商汤科技 [Sense Time Technology] (2022). https://baike.baidu.com/item/%E5%95%86%E6%B1%A4%E7%A7%91%E6%8A%80/53973208?fr=aladdin
7. Baike, B.: 杭州海康威视数字技术股份有限公司 [Hangzhou Hikvision Digital Technology Co., Ltd.] (2022). https://baike.baidu.com/item/%E6%9D%AD%E5%B7%9E%E6%B5%B7%E5%BA%B7%E5%A8%81%E8%A7%86%E6%95%B0%E5%AD%97%E6%8A%80%E6%9C%AF%E8%82%A1%E4%BB%BD%E6%9C%89%E9%99%90%E5%85%AC%E5%8F%B8/10465291?fromtitle=%E6%B5%B7%E5%BA%B7%E5%A8%81%E8%A7%86&fromid=6048387&fr=aladdin
8. Baike, B.: 浙江大华技术股份有限公司 [Zhejiang Dahua Technology Co., Ltd.] (2022). https://baike.baidu.com/item/%E6%B5%99%E6%B1%9F%E5%A4%A7%E5%8D%8E%E6%8A%80%E6%9C%AF%E8%82%A1%E4%BB%BD%E6%9C%89%E9%99%90%E5%85%AC%E5%8F%B8/8785104?fr=aladdin
9. Baike, B.: 中国联合网络通信集团有限公司 [China United Network Communications Group Co., Ltd.] (2022). https://baike.baidu.com/item/%E4%B8%AD%E5%9B%BD%E8%81%94%E5%90%88%E7%BD%91%E7%BB%9C%E9%80%9A%E4%BF%A1%E9%9B%86%E5%9B%A2%E6%9C%89%E9%99%90%E5%85%AC%E5%8F%B8/501999?fromtitle=%E4%B8%AD%E5%9B%BD%E8%81%94%E9%80%9A&fromid=194673&fr=aladdin
10. Uino: UINO 优锘科技:数字孪生可视化领域的先行者及践行者 [UINO Technology: Pioneer and Practitioner in the Field of Digital Twin Visualization] (2022). https://www.uino.com/about.html

11. MEGVII: 人工智能行业的务实者和领跑者 [Pragmatists and frontrunners in the AI industry] (2022). https://www.megvii.com/about_megvii
12. Digitalhail: 关于数字冰雹 [About Digital Hail] (2022). http://www.digihail.com/about/companyintro.html
13. Founder: About Us (2022). http://www.foundertech.com/about.html
14. Aiqicha: 品牌项目详情 [Brand Project Details] (2022). https://aiqicha.baidu.com/brand/detail?pid=31052576533252&id=1415679944
15. Baike, B.: 51World (2022). https://baike.baidu.com/item/51WORLD/24306711?fr=aladdin#reference-[2]-24747783-wrap
16. Li, Y., Sun, L., Guo, Z.M., Jin, C., Sha, M.Q.: Intelligent Operations Center (IOC) helps to build the "Intelligent Center" of the Park. Des. Techn. Posts Telecommun. **2**, 72–76 (2020)

AI in HCI: Methods, Applications, and Studies

Role of Artificial Intelligence in the Smart City: A Bibliometric Review

Julio Adi Bhaskara$^{(\boxtimes)}$ and Achmad Nurmandi

Department of Government Affairs and Administration, Jusuf Kalla School of Government,
Universitas Muhammadiyah Yogyakarta, Yogyakarta, Indonesia
julio.adi.psc21@mail.umy.ac.id, nurmandi_achmad@umy.ac.id

Abstract. This study aims to identify the main trends in the scientific literature regarding the role of Artificial Intelligence in implementing six dimensions of Smart City: mobility, environment, people, living, governance, and economy. Scientific literature data was taken from the Scopus database, which was searched from 2016 to 2021 with limitations on authors or affiliations from the top 4 countries in literature publications, namely China, the United States of America, the United Kingdom, and India. The keywords used in this study are Smart City and Artificial Intelligence. Data analysis used simple statistical methods, and bibliometric analysis was performed using VOSviewer software. This analysis includes a number of publications, citation analysis, and visualizing co-occurrence patterns of keywords. Bibliometric analysis shows there are 194 articles in research publication. The results of data analysis show that AI technology has been adopted in some dimensions, such as intelligent transportation systems, big data management, cloud computing, and decision-making using machine learning. Research in the field of Smart City, especially related to Artificial Intelligence, by authors with affiliations in these four countries is increasing rapidly along with the advancement of science and technology. Of the four countries, the Internet of Things is a significant concern because the development of the Smart City concept today is strongly influenced by the IoT and the existence of Artificial Intelligence which is helpful for assisting the policymaker in managing Smart City that it can be sustainable.

Keywords: Smart city · Artificial intelligence · Internet of Things · Sustainability · Bibliometric

1 Introduction

The concept of smart cities has been accelerated by recent globalization and technological advancements. Smart cities can be found all over the world; cities are evolving toward smarter urban areas, utilizing cutting-edge technology to address critical issues such as traffic, pollution, overcrowding, and poverty [1]. To address the growing difficulties of urban areas, local governments, corporations, non-profit organizations, and citizens embraced the concept of a smarter city, incorporating more technologies, improving living conditions, and protecting the environment [2]. Some researchers are defining

C. Stephanidis et al. (Eds.): HCII 2022, CCIS 1655, pp. 589–596, 2022.
https://doi.org/10.1007/978-3-031-19682-9_74

the term Smart City is. The phrase "Smart City" has recently become associated with cities that make significant and intelligent use of digital technologies to facilitate effective information utilization [3]. Giffinger, one of the most-cited authors in a smart city study, says, "A Smart city is a city well performing built on the "smart" combination of endowments and activities of self-decisive, independent, and aware citizens [4]. He defines six dimensions that compose a smart city: smart mobility, smart environment, smart governance, smart living, smart economy, and smart people.

The rapid development of smart cities and their deployment results in the collection of massive amounts of data at an unprecedented rate. Because of the lack of established mechanisms and standards that gain from the availability of such data, the majority of the generated data is wasted without extracting its potentially helpful information and knowledge [5]. This enormous amount of data can be referred to as "Big data," which has characteristics known as 3V's, which are volume, velocity, and variety [6]. Big data can be interpreted by Artificial Intelligence technologies. Artificial Intelligence is a various method "for using a non-human system to learn from experience and imitate human intelligent behavior" [7]. The policymaker can use Artificial Intelligence for increasing the analysis and processing accuracy of data in real-time that helping them for well-informed decisions and develop appropriate and responsive policies [8].

As cities worldwide become more digitized through the installation of sensor, computational cores, and various telecommunication systems, this is becoming increasingly possible [9]. A smart city aims to provide value-added services to improve citizens' quality of life. Thus, the deployment of information and communications technologies (ICT) makes cities smarter and more sustainable [10]. In the future, Artificial Intelligence technologies will cover many aspects of the development of the smart city.

Several previous studies have attempted to review the known artificial intelligence applications in the context of smart cities [11–13]. Even though some studies have already reviewed smart cities using a bibliometric technique, no previous study has reviewed the role of artificial intelligence and smart city dimensions research using bibliometric tools such as keyword co-occurrence and article citation analysis. To address this knowledge gap, this work conducts a thorough bibliometric review of the artificial intelligence research from a smart city dimensions perspective. In reviewing the literature, we aimed to gain an understanding of the present trend of artificial intelligence and smart city research and identify the number of publications from the major contributing country.

2   Research Method

2.1   Bibliometric Methods

We did a bibliometric literature review to ascertain the current state-of-the-art artificial intelligence applications in the smart city. This form of review enables the researcher to synthesize existing scholarly knowledge and serve as a foundation for future research endeavors. With this technique, the researcher can identify its novelty, knowledge gaps, and position in contributions to the field.

The first step in conducting a bibliometric review is determining the best appropriate database for the investigation. We selected articles by doing searches in the Scopus database. Scopus was used to collect data for the research because it is an excellent search engine with core citation references and publishes peer-reviewed articles and symposia [14]. We did our search by adding the following query and Binary operator into the title, abstract, and keywords fields; "artificial intelligence" and "smart city." Using the outline of previous studies as a guideline, we analyzed and developed bibliometric indicators using only articles published in academic journals. The articles are all English-language publications published from 2011 to 2021. To enhance the precision of the results, we limited the subject areas to social sciences and computer science. After this step, we got 403 articles from the Scopus database. We specify the number of publications from the top four leading countries: China, the United States of America, the United Kingdom, and India. The total number of articles considered has been shortened to 194, and the first publication started in 2016.

After we got the publications data from the database, we analyzed the number of publications in the analyzed period and the citation analysis. We conducted a comprehensive analysis of the content (i.e., keywords) and the connections among the articles to acquire further insights [15]. A co-occurrences analysis was performed to analyze the occurrence of key terms identified by authors in the Scopus database, and an analysis of a map of current research trends that illustrates the relationships between those keywords [16]. Based on bibliometric data, network analysis was used to visualize the network structure and clustering of artificial intelligence-smart city research by using VOSviewer [17]. Using this program, we can identify the main research areas in artificial intelligence and smart city.

3   Result and Discussion

3.1   Distribution of Publications by Year

Figure 1 demonstrates the number of journal articles published by year and the growing tendency on the relationship between artificial intelligence and the smart city. We found that the first publication of the articles from the four countries (China, the USA, the UK, India) started in 2016 with six articles. In 2017, only five articles were published. The publications doubled in 2018 by 13 articles and kept increasing tremendously until peaking in 2021 with 84 papers.

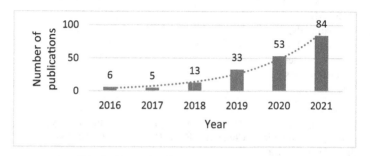

Fig. 1. Year-wise distribution of publications

3.2 Citation Analysis

The following are analyses of the most frequently cited publications on artificial intelligence in the context of smart cities [17]. We analyzed 194 articles about artificial intelligence in the smart city. Table 1 represents the most frequently cited articles, authors, and journals. The document titled "Digital Twin: Enabling Technologies, Challenges and Open Research" ranked on top, with 162 citations, with Fuller, A., Fan, Z., Day, C., Barlow, C., as the authors and belongs to the journal IEEE Access [18]. It is followed by "Enabling Cognitive Smart Cities Using Big Data and Machine Learning: Approaches and Challenges" from IEEE Communications Magazine [5]. From Table 1, we can see that artificial intelligence has begun to impact the development of smart city planning to become sustainable.

Table 1. Citation analysis: top five authors, documents, and sources.

Position	Title	Author	Year	Source	Cited
1	Digital twin: enabling technologies, challenges and open research	Fuller, A., Fan, Z., Day, C., Barlow, C.	2020	IEEE Access 8,9103025, pp. 108952–108971	162
2	Enabling cognitive smart cities using big data and machine learning: approaches and challenges	Mohammadi, M., Al-Fuqaha, A.	2018	IEEE Communications Magazine 56(2), pp. 94–101	154
3	Enabling technologies and sustainable smart cities	Ahad, M.A., Paiva, S., Tripathi, G., Feroz, N.	2020	Sustainable Cities and Society 61, 102301	102
4	A comparative study of PSO-ANN, GA-ANN, ICA-ANN, and ABC-ANN in estimating the heating load of buildings' energy efficiency for smart city planning	Le, L.T., Nguyen, H., Dou, J., Zhou, J.	2019	Applied Sciences (Switzerland) 9(13),2630	98
5	Convergence of blockchain and artificial intelligence in IoT network for the sustainable smart city	Singh, S., Sharma, P.K., Yoon, B., (…), Cho, G.H., Ra, I.-H.	2020	Sustainable Cities and Society 63,102364	96

3.3 Co-occurrence Network of the Role Artificial Intelligence in the Smart City

The analysis of keyword co-occurrence is displayed here. This method can assist researchers in determining the most frequently discussed topics within a particular research area[17].

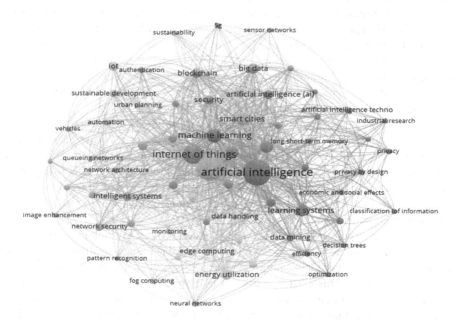

Fig. 2. The keyword co-occurrence network

To map the keyword co-occurrence, we set the number of keyword co-occurrence at five in VOSviewer, 67 nodes are connected, and the network emerged with six clusters, as illustrated in Fig. 2. The size of nodes indicates the occurrence of the keyword in the reviewed articles. The bigger the nodes indicate, the higher intensity of keyword co-occurrence.

The first cluster, which is colored red, is composed of important topics of artificial intelligence, namely decision support system, decision trees, machine learning, learning algorithms, learning system, commerce, data mining, economic and social effects, efficiency, industrial research, optimization, privacy, privacy by design, smart environment and information management. According to the literature, the current trends of research and development in artificial intelligence and the smart city aim to use and implement machine learning algorithms for improving optimization on decision support systems [19]. This cluster focuses on how artificial intelligence in the form of a machine learning system affects the development of the smart city. Looking at the cluster items, the first cluster can be classified as smart governance, smart economy, smart environment, smart people, and smart living dimensions.

The second cluster, colored green, talks about 5g mobile communication affecting intelligent systems such as intelligent transportation systems [20]. Using neural systems, the AI can be used in technology like image enhancement, pattern recognition, data analytics, intelligent transportation systems, intelligent vehicle highway systems, queueing network, urban growth, even increasing network security systems. This cluster focused on how AI is being implemented in urban transportation technologies. If we refer to the smart city dimension, this cluster is included in smart mobility.

The third cluster, the dark blue nodes, is presented that the internet of things is concerned with AI implementation. 5g, artificial intelligence (ai), deep learning, embedded systems, forecasting, internet of thing (IoT), internet of things, internet of things (IoT), long short-term memory, and reinforcement learning are the items in cluster 3. If we merge the duplicate IoT, this cluster can be referred that artificial intelligence is one of the internet of things products that can be used for forecasting in its implementation in the smart city [21]. This cluster is in the smart technology dimension.

The next cluster with yellow nodes is focused on the environmental aspect. The items in the cluster are data handling, edge computing, energy conservation, energy efficiency, energy utilization, fog computing, monitoring, quality of service, wireless sensor networks. Looking at the items in the cluster, AI technology such as fog computing, wireless sensor network, and edge computing is being used in monitoring and handling energy conservation, efficiency, and utilization [22]. This cluster is included in the smart environment dimension.

Cluster five, purple-colored nodes, talks about advanced technologies used in the cities, such as artificial intelligence techniques, big data, authentication, blockchain, cloud computing, digital storage, information and communication technologies, security, and sensor network. This cluster can be set as a smart technology dimension that is applicated in the smart city concept. Looking in the literature, blockchain became one of the popular tools that were used in developing the smart city concept [23].

The last cluster with light blue nodes is referred to the sustainability in the smart city. Automation, decision making, IoT, smart cities, smart city, sustainability, sustainable development, and urban planning are the items of the cluster. This cluster focused on the sustainability of the smart city, with the growth of decision-making technology and automation [24]. This cluster is included in the dimension of smart governance.

4   Conclusion

This study investigates the role of artificial intelligence in the smart city. The bibliometric map generated for this article enabled the identification of the relationship between artificial intelligence and smart city. There is an emerging trend toward increased publication activity in the analyzed field of study between 2016 and 2021. The analysis shows that artificial intelligence is a rapidly developing field of study. Using VOSviewer and Scopus database, there are six clusters of co-occurrence keywords referring to artificial intelligence and smart city. The IoT and Machine Learning became the most popular term in the literature. When the various clusters were analyzed, it was discovered that they all fit into the necessary dimensions of the smart city concept. To be truly smart, a city must incorporate dimensions such as smart governance, smart economy, smart people, smart living, smart mobility, and smart environment. From the result, we identified new dimensions, smart technology, that are embedded with all of the smart city dimensions, so the development of the smart city can be more "smart" and sustainable. It should be noted that this study only covered the publication from The Scopus database. Additionally, the analysis's scope should be widened to cover works indexed in other databases, for example, Web of Science.

References

1. Dameri, R.P.: Searching for Smart city definition: a comprehensive proposal. Int. J. Comput. Technol. **10**(1), 2146–2161 (2013)
2. Dameri, R.P., Rosenthal-Sabroux, C.: Smart city and value creation. In: Dameri, R.P., Rosenthal-Sabroux, C. (eds.) Smart City. PI, pp. 1–12. Springer, Cham (2014). https://doi.org/10.1007/978-3-319-06160-3_1
3. Santis, D., Istat, A., Santis, D.R.: Munich personal RePEc archive Smart city: fact and fiction Smart city: fact and fiction. (54536) (2014)
4. Giffinger, R., Fertner, C., Kramar, H., Meijers, E.: City-ranking of European medium-sized cities. Cent. Reg. Sci. Vienna UT (October) (2007)
5. Mohammadi, M., Al-Fuqaha, A.: Enabling cognitive smart cities using big data and machine learning: approaches and challenges. IEEE Commun. Mag. **56**(2), 94–101 (2018). https://doi.org/10.1109/MCOM.2018.1700298
6. Alam, J.R., Sajid, A., Talib, R., Niaz, M.: A review on the role of big data in business. Int. J. Comput. Sci. Mob. Comput. **34**(4), 446–453 (2014)
7. ICO: Guidance on the AI auditing framework: draft guidance for consultation. Inf. Comm. Off. (2020). https://ico.org.uk/media/about-the-ico/consultations/2617219/guidance-on-the-ai-auditing-framework-draft-for-consultation.pdf
8. Allam, Z., Dhunny, Z.A.: On big data, artificial intelligence and smart cities. Cities **89**(November 2018), 80–91 (2019). https://doi.org/10.1016/j.cities.2019.01.032
9. Alvarez, R.: The relevance of informational infrastructures in future cities. F. Actions Sci. Rep. J. F. Actions Spec. Issue 17, 12–15 (2017)
10. Anthony Jnr, B.: A case-based reasoning recommender system for sustainable smart city development. AI Soc. **36**(1), 159–183 (2020). https://doi.org/10.1007/s00146-020-00984-2
11. Chiu, P.-S., Chang, J.-W., Lee, M.-C., Chen, C.-H., Lee, D.-S.: Enabling intelligent environment by the design of emotionally aware virtual assistant: a case of smart campus. IEEE Access **8**, 62032–62041 (2020). https://doi.org/10.1109/ACCESS.2020.2984383
12. Lee, C., Kim, H.: Groundwork of artificial intelligence humanities. JAHR **11**(1), 189–207 (2020). https://doi.org/10.21860/J.11.1.10
13. Golubchikov, O., Thornbush, M.: Artificial intelligence and robotics in smart city strategies and planned smart development. Smart Cities 3(4) (2020). https://doi.org/10.3390/smartcities3040056
14. Rani, S., Kumar, R.: Materials today: proceedings bibliometric review of actuators : key automation technology in a smart city framework. Mater. Today Proc. (2022). https://doi.org/10.1016/j.matpr.2021.12.469
15. Rejeb, A., Rejeb, K., Simske, S.J., Keogh, J.G.: Blockchain technology in the smart city : a bibliometric review. Qual. Quant. **56**(5), 2875–2906 (2021). (no. 0123456789. Springer Netherlands)
16. Tomaszewska, E.J., Florea, A.: Urban smart mobility in the scientific literature—bibliometric analysis. **10**(2), 41–56 (2018). https://doi.org/10.2478/emj-2018-0010
17. van Eck, N.J., Waltman, L.: Software survey: VOSviewer, a computer program for bibliometric mapping. Scientometrics **84**(2), 523–538 (2010). https://doi.org/10.1007/s11192-009-0146-3

18. Fuller, A., Fan, Z., Day, C., Barlow, C.: Digital twin: enabling technologies, challenges and open research. IEEE Access **8**, 108952–108971 (2020). https://doi.org/10.1109/ACCESS.2020.2998358

19. Wei, L., et al.: A decision support system for urban infrastructure inter-asset management employing domain ontologies and qualitative uncertainty-based reasoning. Expert Syst. Appl. **158** (2020). https://doi.org/10.1016/j.eswa.2020.113461

20. Wan, L., Zhang, M., Sun, L., Wang, X.: machine learning empowered IoT for intelligent vehicle location in smart cities. ACM Trans. Internet Technol. **21**(3) (2021). https://doi.org/10.1145/3448612

21. Piccialli, F., Giampaolo, F., Prezioso, E., Crisci, D., Cuomo, S.: Predictive analytics for smart parking: a deep learning approach in forecasting of IoT data. ACM Trans. Internet Technol. **21**(3) (2021). https://doi.org/10.1145/3412842

22. Le, L.T., Nguyen, H., Dou, J., Zhou, J.: A comparative study of PSO-ANN, GA-ANN, ICA-ANN, and ABC-ANN in estimating the heating load of buildings' energy efficiency for smart city planning. Appl. Sci. **9**(13) (2019). https://doi.org/10.3390/app9132630

23. Bragadeesh, S.A., Umamakeswari, A.: Role of blockchain in the Internet-of-Things (IoT). Int. J. Eng. Technol. **7**(2), 109–112 (2018). https://doi.org/10.14419/ijet.v7i2.24.12011

24. Liu, Y., Zhang, W., Pan, S., Li, Y., Chen, Y.: Analyzing the robotic behavior in a smart city with deep enforcement and imitation learning using IoRT. Comput. Commun. **150**, 346–356 (2020). https://doi.org/10.1016/j.comcom.2019.11.031

A Comparative Analysis
of Reinforcement Learning Approaches
to Cryptocurrency Price Prediction

Daniele Bertillo, Carlo Morelli, Giuseppe Sansonetti$^{(\boxtimes)}$ (iD),
and Alessandro Micarelli

Department of Engineering, Roma Tre University, Via della Vasca Navale, 79,
00146 Rome, Italy
{ailab,gsansone}@dia.uniroma3.it

Abstract. Nowadays, Machine Learning (ML) is present in a high number of application fields. Among these, there is also automatic trading in the financial sector. The research question underlying our research activities is as follows: can ML techniques provide added value in the prediction task in domains with high volatility such as the cryptocurrency financial market? To answer this question, we analyzed and compared different Reinforcement Learning (RL) algorithms on data publicly available online. Specifically, we tested some value-based and policy-based RL algorithms trained for different time intervals, with diverse hyperparameter values and reward functions. The agent that allowed us to achieve the best results was the Deep Recurrent Q-Network trained using the Sharpe ratio as a reward function.

Keywords: Artificial intelligence · Deep reinforcement learning · Cryptocurrency trading

1 Introduction

Artificial Intelligence, and more specifically Machine Learning (ML) [28], is increasingly part of our lives. ML inspires city services [9], suggests which locations [23] to visit (for example, cultural heritage resources [10,25] such as museums [11]) or where to dine [26], and how to get there [8,12]. It recommends which academic papers [16] or news articles [5,14] to read, which songs and artists to listen to [22], which films to watch [2], which things to purchase [3], and also which people to spend our time with [13]. ML also helps us make the best choice [18] and bet our money on sports events [7]. This is even more true since Deep Learning [24] has proven that it can guarantee performance unimaginable until recently (e.g., see [15]). It is, therefore, not surprising that the financial sector is also affected by this phenomenon. In the research literature, there exist several works presenting noteworthy and interesting applications based on Machine Learning, which aim to predict the price of financial assets (e.g., see [4,6,17]).

C. Stephanidis et al. (Eds.): HCII 2022, CCIS 1655, pp. 597–604, 2022.
https://doi.org/10.1007/978-3-031-19682-9_75

In this scenario, the recent interest in cryptocurrencies has prompted more and more researchers to design and implement techniques aimed at short and long-term prediction of the cryptocurrencies price (e.g., see [1,19,20]). However, this objective is made complicated by the high volatility that characterizes this market compared to others.

In this paper, we analyze and compare different approaches based on Reinforcement Learning (RL) [27] to achieve the aforementioned objective. To carry out our experimental tests, we used publicly available data on CryptoDataDownload[1], which collects historical market financial data of various cryptocurrencies. We tested different RL algorithms both value-based and policy-based, trained for different time intervals and with different hyperparameter values. We also employed different reward functions (i.e., profit, Sharpe ratio, and Sortino ratio), which are crucial for the quality of training. During the experimental tests performed on various cryptocurrencies (i.e., Bitcoin, Ethereum, Cardano), we obtained the best performance through the Deep Recurrent Q-Network algorithm, which combines the advantages of Reinforcement Learning with those of Deep Learning, using the Sharpe ratio as a reward. In particular, this algorithm is a combination of a Recurrent Neural Network and a Deep Q-network.

2   Experimental Evaluation

2.1   Dataset

For performing our experimental tests, we employed data freely downloadable from CryptoDataDownload, which collects the financial data of the last years of various cryptocurrency markets. For the first experiments, we used data from the Bitcoin market.

2.2   Preliminary Experiments

The first experimental tests we carried out concerned the prediction of the Bitcoin price. We used an Encoder-Decoder model consisting of two recurrent neural networks. Both the Encoder and the Decoder are composed of a layer of Long Short Term-Memory (LSTM) neurons, capable of identifying and storing time-series patterns and learning long-term dependencies. The Encoder receives the data as input and maps it into a latent space that encodes its most relevant information. Then, it is used by the Decoder as an input to make the prediction. The peculiarity of this approach is that it allows us to predict outputs of variable length. Unfortunately, the results were not satisfactory (see Fig. 1). Graph 1(a) shows the price predictions for the next 5 min whilst graph 1(b) for the next 15 min, starting with an input containing the previous 50 min of data. The predictions only approximately follow the price trend and do not identify trend reversals, thus making the model unreliable in the prediction. If we consider

---

[1] https://www.cryptodatadownload.com/.

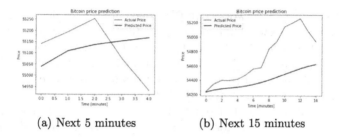

(a) Next 5 minutes   (b) Next 15 minutes

Fig. 1. Comparison between real and predicted values using Stacked LSTM Sequence-to-Sequence Autoencoder from an input containing 50 min of data.

that these predictions must be used to develop investment strategies, this app-roach cannot be considered satisfactory. Based on such results, we then decided to test approaches based on Reinforcement Learning algorithms. Reinforcement Learning is an ML paradigm in which learning takes place through interaction with the environment. In recent years, RL has been employed to tackle computer vision tasks, such as visual tracking [30], image recognition [21], and autonomous navigation [29]. More specifically, RL algorithms consist of two main elements: the agent and the environment. The given domain is modeled in the environment, in our case, we simulated the operation of the financial market, whilst the agent has the task of actively interacting with the environment through actions (see Fig. 2). For the agent, we have modeled the buying and selling actions of cryptocurrencies in the market to open, close, and maintain short and long-term positions. The agent receives the current state of the environment and chooses which action to carry out resulting in changes in the environment. During the training phase, the agent is rewarded or punished depending on the outcome of the previous actions, and this allows it to improve its behavior. The goal of these experiments is to ensure that the agent independently develops an investment strategy.

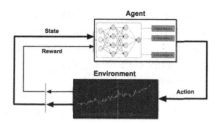

Fig. 2. Reinforcement Learning agent and environment in our scenario.

2.3 First Experiment

For the first experiment, we carried out a comparative analysis between three different algorithms: an algorithm that belongs to the value-based family, namely, the Deep Recurrent Q-Network (DRQN), which uses an artificial neural network to approximate the reward value of each state-action pair, and two algorithms of the policy-based family, that is, the Actor-Critic (A2C) and the Proximal Policy Optimization (PPO2), which use an artificial network to estimate the probability that an action produces a good reward. We trained the algorithms for 250 epochs on the data of April 10, 2021, of the Bitcoin market, starting with an initial investment capital of 10,000 dollars. In the training phase, the results were particularly promising for the DRQN agent, which eventually achieved a 50% gain, whilst the other two agents showed poor results, barely achieving a 2% profit (see Fig. 3). Then, we performed testing on the data of April 11, April 13 and April 17, that is, one, three and seven days after the training, to verify the behavior of the agents and their ability to generalize on an unknown portion of the market. Results are shown in Fig. 4. The profit trend during the training episodes for the days of 13 and 17 April was very inconsistent, while on the market of 11 April, we found encouraging results. In particular, the most promising result was related to the first eight hours of April 11, in which the DRQN agent achieved a steady 3.5% profit, while the other two agents barely reached a 0.2% profit. For the subsequent experiments, we therefore used the DRQN agent.

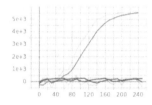

Fig. 3. Profit trend versus training time for the algorithms DRQN, PPO2, and A2C.

2.4 Second Experiment

For the second experiment, we trained three DRQN agents using three different reward functions. The choice of the reward function is crucial for the quality of training and, therefore, it is interesting to test different ones. For the first agent, we used the profit directly. This choice is generally not recommended because it can lead the agent to learn risky behaviors in training that can result in catastrophic consequences on data that it has never seen. Then, we trained the other two DRQN agents with two investment risk metrics, namely, the Sharpe ratio and the Sortino ratio, which compare the profit generated by the agent actions with the market volatility and the profit generated by an investment with zero or almost zero risk. The Sortino ratio is a variant of the Sharpe ratio in which, for the risk calculation, only the volatility in the opposite direction to that of the position opened by the investor is considered. The best results were obtained using the Sharpe ratio (see Fig. 5).

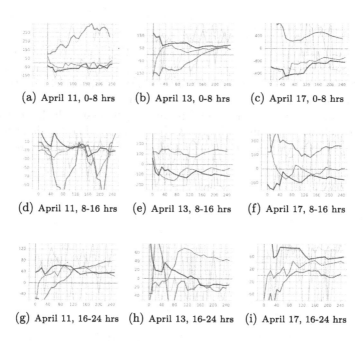

(a) April 11, 0-8 hrs   (b) April 13, 0-8 hrs   (c) April 17, 0-8 hrs

(d) April 11, 8-16 hrs   (e) April 13, 8-16 hrs   (f) April 17, 8-16 hrs

(g) April 11, 16-24 hrs   (h) April 13, 16-24 hrs   (i) April 17, 16-24 hrs

Fig. 4. Profit trend versus training time on April 11, 13, and 17, 2021 for the algorithms DRQN, PPO2, and A2C.

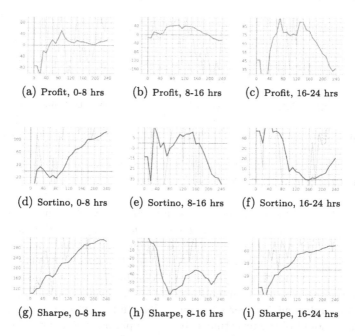

(a) Profit, 0-8 hrs   (b) Profit, 8-16 hrs   (c) Profit, 16-24 hrs

(d) Sortino, 0-8 hrs   (e) Sortino, 8-16 hrs   (f) Sortino, 16-24 hrs

(g) Sharpe, 0-8 hrs   (h) Sharpe, 8-16 hrs   (i) Sharpe, 16-24 hrs

Fig. 5. Profit trend on April 11, 2021, generated by three DRQN agents with different reward functions: profit, Sortino ratio, and Sharpe ratio.

2.5   Third Experiment

For the third experiment, we wanted to test the DRQN agent's ability to generalize for different markets, so considered the Ethereum (ETH) and Cardano (ADA)
cryptocurrencies as well. The datasets of those cryptocurrencies are structurally
identical to that of the Bitcoin (BTC) used for the other tests. In particular, the
Ethereum market is very similar, and, in fact, in the first eight hours the agent
achieved excellent gains, up to about 3% (see Fig. 6). The Cardano market is
smaller, so the behavior of the DRQN agent did not lead to good results.

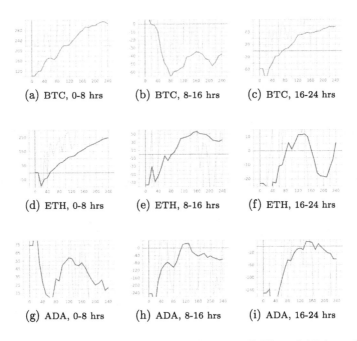

(a) BTC, 0-8 hrs   (b) BTC, 8-16 hrs   (c) BTC, 16-24 hrs

(d) ETH, 0-8 hrs   (e) ETH, 8-16 hrs   (f) ETH, 16-24 hrs

(g) ADA, 0-8 hrs   (h) ADA, 8-16 hrs   (i) ADA, 16-24 hrs

Fig. 6. Profit trend on April 11, 2021, on the BTC, ETH, and ADA markets.

3   Conclusions and Future Works

In this article, we have presented the results of a comparative analysis conducted
by applying Reinforcement Learning techniques using recurring networks for
predicting the cryptocurrencies price. The agent that allowed us to obtain the
best results on similar markets was the Deep Recurrent Q-Network, trained
using the Sharpe ratio. Although the results obtained were encouraging, there are
several developments that we intend to carry out in the near future. Among these,
we plan to implement a wider space of actions, for example enabling agents to
choose the amount of the investment, to use deeper and more complex networks,
as well as to test specific implementations for different types of markets.

References

1. Alessandretti, L., ElBahrawy, A., Aiello, L.M., Baronchelli, A.: Anticipating cryptocurrency prices using machine learning. Complexity 2018 (2018)
2. Biancalana, C., Gasparetti, F., Micarelli, A., Miola, A., Sansonetti, G.: Context-aware movie recommendation based on signal processing and machine learning. In: Proceedings of the 2nd Challenge on Context-Aware Movie Recommendation, pp. 5–10. CAMRa 2011, ACM, New York (2011)
3. Bologna, C., De Rosa, A.C., De Vivo, A., Gaeta, M., Sansonetti, G., Viserta, V.: Personality-based recommendation in e-commerce. In: CEUR Workshop Proceedings, vol. 997. CEUR-WS.org, Aachen, Germany (2013)
4. Buchanan, B.G.: Artificial Intelligence in Finance. The Alan Turing Institute (2019)
5. Caldarelli, S., Gurini, D.F., Micarelli, A., Sansonetti, G.: A signal-based approach to news recommendation. In: CEUR Workshop Proceedings, vol. 1618. CEUR-WS.org, Aachen, Germany (2016)
6. Cao, L.: Ai in finance: challenges, techniques, and opportunities. ACM Comput. Surv. **55**(3), 1–14 (2022)
7. Carloni, L., De Angelis, A., Sansonetti, G., Micarelli, A.: A machine learning approach to football match result prediction. In: Stephanidis, C., Antona, M., Ntoa, S. (eds.) HCII 2021. CCIS, vol. 1420, pp. 473–480. Springer, Cham (2021). https://doi.org/10.1007/978-3-030-78642-7_63
8. D'Agostino, D., Gasparetti, F., Micarelli, A., Sansonetti, G.: A social context-aware recommender of itineraries between relevant points of interest. In: Stephanidis, C. (ed.) HCI 2016. CCIS, vol. 618, pp. 354–359. Springer, Cham (2016). https://doi.org/10.1007/978-3-319-40542-1_58
9. D'Aniello, G., Gaeta, M., Orciuoli, F., Sansonetti, G., Sorgente, F.: Knowledge-based smart city service system. Electronics (Switzerland) **9**(6), 1–22 (2020)
10. De Angelis, A., Gasparetti, F., Micarelli, A., Sansonetti, G.: A social cultural recommender based on linked open data. In: Adjunct Publication of the 25th UMAP Conference, pp. 329–332. ACM, New York, NY, USA (2017)
11. Ferrato, A., Limongelli, C., Mezzini, M., Sansonetti, G.: Using deep learning for collecting data about museum visitor behavior. Appl. Sci. **12**(2), 533 (2022)
12. Fogli, A., Sansonetti, G.: Exploiting semantics for context-aware itinerary recommendation. Pers. Ubiquit. Comput. **23**(2), 215–231 (2019)
13. Gasparetti, F., Sansonetti, G., Micarelli, A.: Community detection in social recommender systems: a survey. Appl. Intell. **51**(6), 3975–3995 (2021)
14. Gena, C., Grillo, P., Lieto, A., Mattutino, C., Vernero, F.: When personalization is not an option: an in-the-wild study on persuasive news recommendation. Information **10**(10), 300 (2019)
15. Hassan, H.A.M., Sansonetti, G., Gasparetti, F., Micarelli, A.: Semantic-based tag recommendation in scientific bookmarking systems. In: Proceedings of the 12th ACM Conference on Recommender Systems, pp. 465–469. ACM, New York, NY, USA (2018)
16. Hassan, H.A.M., Sansonetti, G., Gasparetti, F., Micarelli, A., Beel, J.: BERT, ELMo, USE and InferSent sentence encoders: the panacea for research-paper recommendation? In: Tkalcic, M., Pera, S. (eds.) Proceedings of ACM RecSys 2019 Late-Breaking Results, vol. 2431, pp. 6–10. CEUR-WS.org (2019)
17. Hilpisch, Y.: Artificial Intelligence in Finance. O'Reilly Media, Sebastopol (2020)

18. Jameson, A., et al.: How can we support users' preferential choice? In: CHI 2011 Extended Abstracts. ACM, New York, NY, USA (2011)
19. Lucarelli, G., Borrotti, M.: A deep reinforcement learning approach for automated cryptocurrency trading. In: MacIntyre, J., Maglogiannis, I., Iliadis, L., Pimenidis, E. (eds.) AIAI 2019. IAICT, vol. 559, pp. 247–258. Springer, Cham (2019). https://doi.org/10.1007/978-3-030-19823-7_20
20. McNally, S., Roche, J., Caton, S.: Predicting the price of bitcoin using machine learning. In: 26th Euromicro International Conference on Parallel, Distributed and Network-based Processing (PDP), pp. 339–343 (2018)
21. Micarelli, A., Neri, A., Sansonetti, G.: A case-based approach to image recognition. In: Blanzieri, E., Portinale, L. (eds.) EWCBR 2000. LNCS, vol. 1898, pp. 443–454. Springer, Heidelberg (2000). https://doi.org/10.1007/3-540-44527-7_38
22. Onori, M., Micarelli, A., Sansonetti, G.: A comparative analysis of personality-based music recommender systems. In: CEUR Workshop Proceedings, vol. 1680, pp. 55–59. CEUR-WS.org, Aachen, Germany (2016)
23. Sansonetti, G.: Point of interest recommendation based on social and linked open data. Pers. Ubiquit. Comput. 23(2), 199–214 (2019)
24. Sansonetti, G., Gasparetti, F., D'Aniello, G., Micarelli, A.: Unreliable users detection in social media: deep learning techniques for automatic detection. IEEE Access 8, 213154–213167 (2020)
25. Sansonetti, G., Gasparetti, F., Micarelli, A.: Cross-domain recommendation for enhancing cultural heritage experience. In: Adjunct Publication of the 27th UMAP Conference, pp. 413–415. ACM, New York, NY, USA (2019)
26. Sardella, N., Biancalana, C., Micarelli, A., Sansonetti, G.: An approach to conversational recommendation of restaurants. In: Stephanidis, C. (ed.) HCII 2019. CCIS, vol. 1034, pp. 123–130. Springer, Cham (2019). https://doi.org/10.1007/978-3-030-23525-3_16
27. Sutton, R.S., Barto, A.G.: Reinforcement Learning: An Introduction, 2nd edn. The MIT Press, Cambridge (2018)
28. Vaccaro, L., Sansonetti, G., Micarelli, A.: An empirical review of automated machine learning. Computers 10(1), 11 (2021)
29. Wang, C., Wang, J., Shen, Y., Zhang, X.: Autonomous navigation of UAVs in large-scale complex environments: a deep reinforcement learning approach. IEEE Trans. Veh. Technol. 68(3), 2124–2136 (2019)
30. Zhang, D., Zheng, Z., Jia, R., Li, M.: Visual tracking via hierarchical deep reinforcement learning. In: Proceedings of the AAAI Conference on Artificial Intelligence, pp. 3315–3323 (2021)

Explainable Artificial Intelligence (XAI) User Interface Design for Solving a Rubik's Cube

Cassidy Bradley[1], Dezhi Wu[1]([✉]) [iD], Hengtao Tang[2], Ishu Singh[1], Katelyn Wydant[1], Brittany Capps[1], Karen Wong[1], Forest Agostinelli[1], Matthew Irvin[2], and Biplav Srivastava[1]

[1] College of Engineering and Computing, University of South Carolina, Columbia, SC 29208, USA
`dezhiwu@cec.sc.edu`
[2] College of Education, University of South Carolina, Columbia, SC 29208, USA

Abstract. Explainable Artificial Intelligence (XAI) aims to bridge the understanding between decisions made by an AI interface and the user interacting with the AI. When the goal of the AI is to teach the user how to solve a problem, user-friendly explanations of the AI's decisions must be given to the user so they can learn how to replicate the process for themselves. This paper describes the process of defining explanations in the context of a collaborative AI platform, ALLURE, which teaches the user how to solve a Rubik's Cube. A macro-action in our collaborative AI algorithm refers to a set of moves that takes the cube from initial state to goal state - a process that was not transparent nor accessible when we revealed back-end logic to the front-end for user engagement. By providing macro-action explanations to the user in a chatbot as well as a visual representation of the moves being performed on a virtual Rubik's Cube, we created an XAI interface to engage and guide the user through a subset of the solutions that can later be applied to the remaining solutions of the AI. After initial usability testing, our study provides some useful and practical XAI user interface design implications.

Keywords: Explainable Artificial Intelligence (XAI) · Chatbot · Pathfinding · User interface design · Human-computer interaction · AI

1 Introduction

Recent technological advancement in artificial intelligence (AI) has enabled machines with some capability for solving complex problems and achieving human-level or superior performance in various tasks, such as playing chess (e.g., Alpha Go), autonomous driving (e.g., Tesla car), and disease detection (e.g., cancer detection through images). These technological innovations involve natural language processing, computer vision, knowledge graphs, and other sophisticated AI techniques for solving problems. However, it is unclear how we can transparentize the typical black box in AI through explainable AI (XAI) user interfaces to enable and foster a feasible human-AI interaction. XAI attempts to bridge the gap between the "black box" of artificial intelligence and human learning, so that humans learn to not only use AI, but to also solve the same type of problems. Our use case, the Rubik's cube, has 4.3 × 10^19 possible configurations, and each method has its own high-level step-by-step plan and algorithms for achieving that plan [1]. While AI is often able to solve a Rubik's cube and solve in the most efficient way [1], the complexity of the solutions often surpasses AI's ability to explain these solutions [2].

In this project, using the Rubik's cube as a problem domain, we are taking a bold step to design an XAI system called ALLURE (Fig. 1) that users can use to learn how to solve the Rubik's cube in a personalized fashion. This problem-solving is facilitated by an XAI method and a multimodal user interface. Our XAI method is based on a collaborative version of an artificial intelligence (AI) algorithm, CDeepCubeA, which our research team designed to teach the user how to solve a Rubik's cube [1] using deep reinforcement learning and inductive logic programming. The user interface includes an interactive 3D virtual Rubik's cube for two-way communication and a chatbot capable of generating and processing natural language to engage users in the learning process. In this paper, we will document the work that has been done to develop both the application and an embodied multimodal chatbot to make CDeepCubeA an explainable AI (XAI) system for teaching users how to solve a Rubik's Cube while maintaining engagement. Following research on using a graph where each node represents a goal state and the edges of the nodes or the macro-actions used are the steps taken to go from one state to another, the macro-actions are our main focus for making the system more explainable [2]. If the user can understand the moves to get to different states of the Rubik's cube, they can learn and apply the moves outside of the scope of the application. Thus, we focus on translating the macro-actions by emphasizing movements that put the white-green cubelet of a Rubik's Cube (Fig. 1) in the proper position to solve a white cross. By applying the explanations directly to a chatbot while using other user interface (UI) elements to provide visual representations of the explanations, we have designed an application that was initially tested with ten users to evaluate the effectiveness of the XAI system and its design elements.

For our initial study, we surveyed online Rubik's cube tutorials and consolidated the main techniques for explaining AI algorithms in a way that is both educational and engaging for users. We aimed to decode AI-driven solutions and introduce users to a number of probabilities for solving the Rubik's cube that they would not encounter in their regular learning process. After we built our ALLURE system user interface, we conducted an initial usability study and gained constructive user feedback for how we can better design XAI user interfaces for complicated problems such as the Rubik's cube. Finally, we discussed XAI design implications derived from our usability testing which can be influential in reshaping future learning and knowledge discovery processes when humans need to collaborate with AI for complicated problem solving and personalized learning.

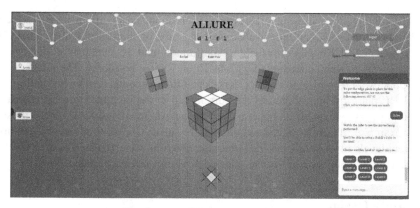

Fig. 1. ALLURE platform snapshot.

2   Brief Literature Review

The integration of AI technologies in education has transformed our traditional understanding of "where students learn, who teaches them and how they acquire basic skills" [7, p. 1653]. For example, AI has the potential to uncover truth from massive data about student learning patterns that are otherwise unknown in traditional measures [5]. AI relies on large volumes of data to understand and support student learning, but whether the data accurately depicts student learning remains unknown. Akgun and Greenhow [4] outline bias and discrimination as two of the primary ethical concerns of AI being used in education. The concerns primarily stem from existing biases and unequal power structures, such as gender bias, which have been ingrained in the AI algorithms [4]. To overcome those ethical concerns, scholars have increasingly invested into the fairness, accountability, transparency, and ethics of AI.

Successful XAI produces rationales that both explain what the system is doing internally and instruct the user in a way that improves their performance of those tasks [11]. Users are no longer satisfied with AI that automatically and blindly solves problems; rather, they want to understand how and why those problems are solved [8, 16, 21]. What's more, user experience (UX) and user-centered design have contributed to the development of positive and enjoyable AI experiences [14, 15]. On the one hand, this transparency can increase trust between humans and AI [8, 13, 21]. However, XAI is simultaneously working to increase agency and empower user with the ability to accept or reject recommendations or solutions posed by AI [11, 14].

According to existing research, XAI is successful when it uses participatory design that caters explanations to stakeholders who are directly involved in the design process [14]. Users also perform better when they receive subgoal-based explanations [12], and when explanations are structured as a dialogue [3]. However, of the existing use cases, no AI explanations are being provided through a chatbot tutor. Moreover, while some virtual agents give explanations through multiple modalities such as text, voice, and voice with a 3D character [20], users have limited interaction with the agents. The explanations for solving a Rubik's cube within the ALLURE platform have been designed and preliminarily tested to meet users' needs and provide a positive user experience. Furthermore,

608   C. Bradley et al.

the ALLURE platform uses subgoals to teach users about the algorithm of a Rubik's cube so that users can solve multiple problems of the cube on their own. Unlike other XAI, though, the ALLURE platform features multimodal and 3D elements to demonstrate the necessary movements to solve various Rubik's cube problems. The interface also incorporates a customizable chatbot experience that responds to user prompting. The ALLURE platform thus addresses the current gap in the literature through increasing autonomy, personalization, and interactivity between humans and XAI. Table 1 presents a few examples of how we translated our collaborative AI algorithm's macro-actions to different levels of explanations (i.e., one macro-action was translated to nine levels of explanations) to engage users in the selected XAI user interface snapshots.

3 Study Design

For this XAI usability testing study, we utilized a convergent mixed-methods [10] approach to evaluate the effectiveness of XAI algorithms. This method was selected because it allowed us to provide a comprehensive understanding of the explainability of XAI algorithms by integrating findings from both quantitative and qualitative data [6, 9]. Quantitative data was collected via pre- and post-surveys to gauge participants' perception of solving problems with XAI algorithms. Qualitative data was collected via semi-structured interviews to provide additional insights for explaining and extending quantitative results. Once both sources of data were collected and analyzed, we integrated the findings to gather deeper inferences [6, 9].

Participants and Contexts
Institute Review Board approval was granted before we recruited participants. Participants were solicited through a university-wide survey that was open to students of all demographics. All study participants were required to fill out a consent form fill out a consent form, complete a demographic questionnaire, and take a Mental Rotation Test (MRT) [19] to assess their existing spatial skills before their usability testing. The testing took place in person in our lab, so that experimenters could more closely observe user interactions with the prototype, as well as record and gain feedback through the users' think-aloud processing and body language. We provided a Dell laptop for users to test our ALLURE XAI user interface in a controlled lab environment. After we debriefed the users about the study protocols, users consented to be audio and video recorded on Zoom so we could document their think-aloud processes while they navigated through the user interfaces. There was one experimenter and at least two observers in the room for each session. Audio files were then extracted, cleaned, and edited into accurate transcripts for further data analysis.

The ten users selected to participate in this study were representative of a wide range of ages, ethnicities, and backgrounds with varying levels of prior knowledge on the Rubik's cube. The sample of participants (N = 100) included 60% male and 50% female, with 10% choosing not to specify. Additionally, half of the participants (N = 5) self-identified as intermediate skill-level Rubik's cube players, two as skilled players, and three as beginner skill-level.

Table 1. Examples of initial configurations, moves and the defined explanation for macro-actions

Macro-action number	Level number	Initial configuration	Moves to reach goal state	Defined explanation
1	1		F	In level 1, we can see that all the color stickers of the white-color edge pieces are paired with their matching color center-piece, but to achieve the White Cross the white stickers need to pair with the white centerpiece too. Turn the front face until the white-green edge piece completes the White Cross.
5	5		D R F' R'	In level 5, our goal is to pair the white and green stickers of the white-green edge piece with their centerpieces and complete the White Cross. Right now, the green sticker is on the down face and the white piece is on the front face. The following moves will teach you how to get the edge piece into place: D R F' R'
8	8		D L' F L	When we finished with level 8, the white and green stickers of the white-green edge piece will be paired with their center-pieces. Right now, the green sticker is on the down face and the white sticker is on the back face. There are two different ways to handle this level, so feel free to go through it multiple times. To put the edge piece in place for this cube configuration, we can use the following moves: D L' F L

F: Front face; F': Front face counter clockwise; D: Down face; R: Right face; R': Right face counter clockwise; L: Left; L': Left face counter clockwise

Procedures

We adopted some validated research instruments from the previous studies and con-textualized them for our study. We collected both quantitative and qualitative data in this round of usability testing that sought to gauge users' initial interests in problem solving, spatial reasoning, and thought processing, while also seeking their honest feed-back on the explainability of the ALLURE platform and their overall experience of their interaction.

4   Data Analysis and Preliminary Study Results

Quantitative

Descriptive statistics were used to gauge the central tendency of perceptions perception regarding their experience with our XAI algorithms. Overall, participants had a positive user experience with the platform in this study as the mean value for almost all of the items falls in the range between agree (4) and strongly agree (5). Particularly, participants found it easy to learn how to use their platform (M = 4.6, SD = 0.70) and were willing to learn challenging things after the experience with the platform (M = 4.6, SD = 0.70). The lowest response was recorded for a reverse-coded item that inquired about whether the participants had problems demonstrating the solution in their mind (M = 3.3, SD = 1.16).

Qualitative

For qualitative data analysis, inductive analysis [17] was applied via two cycles of coding. In the first cycle, qualitative coding using NVivo software was conducted to assign initial codes by honoring participant voices [17]. In the second cycle, pattern coding [17] was used to solicit patterns, categories, and themes of participants' perception of their experience with XAI algorithms. Two actions were taken to ensure the rigor and trustworthiness of qualitative findings. First, peer debriefing was conducted with two AI education scholars to ensure the process of eliciting themes from qualitative data was appropriate and the description of each theme made sense [18]. Then, rich descriptions supplemented by participants' direct quotes were provided to reinforce the rigor of the findings [9].

5   XAI User Interface Design Implications

Based on our user interviews, several initial themes were elicited from the qualitative data. Each of the themes is described below with one sample quote from users to help outline rich XAI user interface design implications in a pathfinding problem-solving domain.

- **Upon user trust, users perceived the XAI algorithm to be efficient in explaining the solutions.** XAI algorithms aim to provide a more trustworthy solution that is more explainable for participants when they solve problems. In this study, participants perceived that XAI algorithms efficiently explain the solutions. For example, User 4 indicated that an algorithm that helped him solve a Rubik's Cube in a more efficient way would be useful.

  User 4: "Yes, I saw one, like five years ago, and I was confused. Well, not that I understand what the commands mean, yeah. I think the ALLURE program gives me a good foundation."

- **XAI provides an underlying rationale for why a certain action is taken for problem-solving.** Participants thought that explanations provided by XAI algorithms efficiently interpreted the moves needed to solve the Rubik's cube problem. For example, User 8 discussed that the explanations gave her an understanding of why the moves were appropriate.

  User 8: "[About the moves and explanations] Oh, I liked having both. I like that it explained what was happening and then kind of broke it down to just that. Like the letters because then you got your brain thinking like that. Just the shorthand of it."

- **We can improve user experience by allocating sufficient time for users to appreciate XAI algorithms and learn complicated problem-solving skills and/or strategies.**

  The usability testing study revealed recommendations for improving user experience with XAI algorithms. For example, User 8 stated that learning in this platform did not happen quickly and that it take more time to fully understand the lessons throughout the platform.

  User 8: "...And I think if I had more time, or put more effort into it, I probably could have figured out a similar pattern for more of the configurations and do a part from it. But since I didn't sit here all day and mess with it and try to get familiar with it, I felt I wasn't properly using it and getting what I could from it."

- **XAI chatbot design requires more human-like feedback features to engage users instead of challenging them.**

  The chatbot was the main avenue for participants to interact with XAI algorithms, but participants reported several challenges during their interaction with the chatbot, indicating more iterations of human-in-the-loop design are needed to improve XAI chatbot UI design and conversation quality. Furthermore, since the chatbot was primarily built in English, the language barrier may have made it difficult for some non-native English speakers to follow the guidance and interact with the chatbot (e.g., User 2).

  User 2: "I think, human tutor so I could get more kind of feedback on, again, how I'm supposed to be utilizing the resource. But I do feel like with more time with the chatbot, and just kind of messing around with it, I would feel more comfortable using that as well. But right now, I would say human tutor."

We anticipate that the results following our usability testing will give us solid insights into our XAI model. Translating the AI to a direct explanation for the user is the most difficult part of this process. With the user feedback, we have a better understanding of the language that should be used. By examining which usability tasks the users can complete, we will have a better idea of which parts of the application work well and what needs to be fine-tuned to engage the users for greater success in problem-solving. When we have completed any adjustments that we feel are necessary to successfully help users solve the white cross problem, we will be able to expand the current model to the remaining XAI solutions that CDeepCubeA will generate.

Acknowledgements. The authors would like to acknowledge the generous funding support from ASPIRE II grant at the University of South Carolina (U of SC), and partial funding support provided by UofSC's Grant No: 80002838.

References

1. Agostinelli, F., et al.: Designing children's new learning partner: collaborative artificial intelligence for learning to solve the Rubik's cube. In: Interaction Design and Children, pp. 610–614. Athens, Greece (2021). https://doi.org/10.1145/3459990.3465175
2. Agostinelli, F., Panta, R., Khandelwal, V., Srivastava, B., Muppasani, B., Wu, D.: Explainable Pathfinding for Inscrutable Planners with Inductive Logic Programming (2022)
3. Amitai, Y., Avni, G., Amir, O.: Interactive explanations of agent behavior. In: ICAPS 2022 Workshop on Explainable AI Planning, April 2022
4. Akgun, S., Greenhow, C.: Artificial intelligence in education: addressing ethical challenges in K-12 settings. AI Ethics **2**, 1–10 (2021). https://doi.org/10.1007/s43681-021-00096-7
5. Beardsley, M., Santos, P., Hernández-Leo, D., Michos, K.: Ethics in educational technology research: informing participants on data sharing risks. Br. J. Edu. Technol. **50**(3), 1019–1034 (2019)
6. Bingham, A.J., Witkowsky, P.: Deductive and inductive approaches to qualitative data analysis. In: Analyzing and Interpreting Qualitative Data: After the Interview, pp. 133–146 (2021)
7. Cheng, X., Sun, J., Zarifis, A.: Artificial intelligence and deep learning in educational technology research and practice. Br. J. Edu. Technol. **51**(5), 1653–1656 (2020). https://doi.org/10.1111/bjet.13018
8. Conati, C., Barral, O., Putnam, V., Rieger, L.: Toward personalized XAI: a case study in intelligent tutoring systems. Artif. Intell. **298**, 103503 (2021)
9. Creswell, J.W.: Research Design: Qualitative, Quantitative, and Mixed Methods Approaches, 4th edn. SAGE Publications, Thousand Oaks (2014)
10. Creswell, J.W., Plano Clark, V.L.: Designing and Conducting Mixed Methods Research, 3rd edn. SAGE Publications, Thousand Oaks (2011)
11. Das, D., Chernova, S.: Leveraging rationales to improve human task performance. In: Proceedings of the 25th International Conference on Intelligent User Interfaces, pp. 510–518 (2020)
12. Das, D., Kim, B., Chernova, S.: Subgoal-based explanations for unreliable intelligent decision support systems. arXiv preprint arXiv:2201.04204 (2022)
13. Fiok, K., Farahani, F.V., Karwowski, W., Ahram, T.: Explainable artificial intelligence for education and training. J. Defense Model. Simul. **19**(2), 133–144 (2022)
14. Khosravi, H., et al.: Explainable artificial intelligence in education. Comput. Educ. Artif. Intell. 100074 (2022)
15. Liao, Q.V., et al.: All work and no play? Conversations with a question-and-answer chatbot in the wild. Assoc. Comput. Mach. **3**, 1–13 (2018). https://doi.org/10.1145/3173574.3173577
16. Putnam, V., Conati, C.: Exploring the need for explainable artificial intelligence (XAI) in intelligent tutoring systems (ITS). In: IUI Workshops (2019)
17. Saldana, J.: The Coding Manual for Qualitative Researchers, 3rd edn. SAGE Publications, Thousand Oaks (2015)
18. Spall, S.: Peer debriefing in qualitative research: emerging operational models. Qual. Inq. **4**(2), 280–292 (1998). https://doi.org/10.1177/107780049800400208
19. Vandenberg, S.G., Kuse, A.R.: Mental rotations, a group test of three-dimensional spatial visualization. Percept. Mot. Skills **47**(2), 599–604 (1978). https://doi.org/10.2466/pms.1978.47.2.599
20. Weitz, K., Schiller, D., Schlagowski, R., Huber, T., André, E.: "Let me explain!": exploring the potential of virtual agents in explainable AI interaction design. J. Multimodal User Interfaces **15**(2), 87–98 (2020). https://doi.org/10.1007/s12193-020-00332-0
21. Wilkinson, D., et al.: Why or why not? The effect of justification styles on chatbot recommendations. ACM Trans. Inf. Syst. **39**(4) (2021). https://doi.org/10.1145/3441715

Role of AI in Promoting European Accessibility Policy

Krishna Chandramouli[✉] [iD]

Venaka Media Limited, 2, Glebe Mews, Sidcup DA15 8GU, Kent, UK
k.chandramouli@venaka.co.uk

Abstract. Following the wide-scope of adoption of digital transformation services, across every-day activities, there is a critical need to ensure all citizens are offered equal opportunities for interacting with such digital interfaces. To this end, the recently published European Accessibility Act (EAA) provides a regulatory framework, which formalises digital interface needs across several digital displays, such as computers, Automated Teller Machines (ATM), ticketing systems, and TV equipment, among others. On the other hand, the exponential growth of AI technologies has further facilitated launch of new products and systems in the market (such as Amazon Echo, Google Assistant and Apple Siri to name a few), which has offered the citizens new and improved ways of interacting with digital technologies. Addressing the changing landscape and paradigm shift, in this poster presentation, a systematic framework on the role of AI technologies in promoting EAA policy is presented. The proposed framework will establish a formal definition of digital content accessibility, that refers to the inclusive practice of making digital content usable and comprehensible by all citizens (for people with abilities and disabilities included). Within the current adoption of digital transformation strategies, the notion of accessibility has been widely addressed within the context of information being shared through Internet services. The relevant standards published from World Wide Web Consortium (W3C) on Web Accessibility Initiative (WAI) individuals' formulated recommendations on creating accessible for all content published online. The recommendations on adopting universal design, that includes the triple synergy between Usability, Accessibility and Inclusion has been well addressed in the literature. Nevertheless, the lack of support for integrating such accessibility standards within individual organisations has been well documented, resulting in the information published from cultural heritage institutions and other Creative and Cultural Industry (CCI) stakeholders to become inaccessible. Extending beyond the scope of the W3C standards, the proposed framework will consider a broad scope of AI-powered technologies such as chatbots, question-answering systems, speech synthesis tools, computer vision technologies, gesture recognition algorithms, multimodal haptic device interfaces and others.

Keywords: Media accessibility · Web Accessibility Initiative · Creative and Cultural Industry · W3C · Artificial intelligence · Machine learning · Digital transformation

C. Stephanidis et al. (Eds.): HCII 2022, CCIS 1655, pp. 613–618, 2022.
https://doi.org/10.1007/978-3-031-19682-9_77

1   Introduction

Digital transformation, defined by Faddis [1], is a term used to describe the holistic effect created by a software application that fundamentally transforms a particular domain. While digital transformation has been on the rise at a slower pace for several years, the emergence of global pandemic has accelerated the adoption process, in which the use of digital technologies has seen exponential growth. Such a change has been observed across a wide range of industries including healthcare, education, media production and distribution, remote working environments, and many other examples. Extending beyond the fixed digital interface (such as display monitor), the emergence of digital technologies can be observed across a broader society as well. An example of such instances of encountering digital interfaces include (i) computers and operating systems; (ii) ATMs, ticketing and check-in machines; (iii) telephones and smartphones; (iv) TV equipment related to digital television services; (v) telephony services and related equipment; (vi) audio-visual media services, such as television broadcast and related consumer equipment; (vii) services related to air, bus, rail and waterborne passenger transport; (ix) banking services; (x) e-books and (xi) e-commerce. While the list is not comprehensive, the digital services rendered across such systems offers a meaningful insight into the challenges and opportunities that are being presented in developing technologies to ensure accessibility and inclusivity remain two pillars of the society.

One of the key challenges often encountered in addressing accessibility refers to the economic impact for the industries and service providers. As global economies become susceptible to the impact of pandemic, with regulations enforced for reduced social interaction, social distancing, lockdown, restrictions on movement, Kutnjak [2], observes that restructuring of business because of pandemic has significantly transformed the general citizens daily lives and set requirements for accepting and getting used to the "new normal" way of life of all humanity. The societies' reliance on the information and communication technologies (ICT) have shown the importance of innovative solutions and become crucial for the continuation of personal and business services and interactions. Pandemic has affected the assessment of the use of ICT, but also the adoption of ICT in those segments where their potential has not yet been discovered to mitigate the social and economic effects of the spread of the virus. The impact of ICT technologies has offered a lifeline in communication, information exchange, strategic decision making, training, but also the supervision of business activities and thus reduce the burden imposed by the pandemic on employers in various industrial areas. Despite such positive impact, one of the key modes of adopting digital transformation is the creation and widening of the digital divide for citizens with disabilities.

For the purposes of the discussion, the definition of "digital content accessibility" will be restricted to the inclusive practice of making digital contents usable and comprehensible by all citizens (with abilities and disabilities included). Within the current adoption of digital transformation strategies, the notion of accessibility has been widely addressed within the context of information being shared through Internet services. The relevant standards published from W3C on Web Accessibility Initiative (WAI) individuals' formulated recommendations on creating accessible for all content published online. The recommendations on adopting universal design, that includes the triple synergy between Usability, Accessibility and Inclusion has been well addressed in the literature [3], which is presented in Fig. 1. Nevertheless, the lack of support for integrating such accessibility standards within individual organisations has been well documented[1], resulting in the information published from cultural heritage institutions and other CCI stakeholders to become inaccessible. Additionally, the lack of multimodal, user engagement tools has resulted in unimodal representation (in text) of historical content.

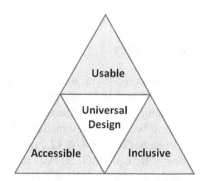

Fig. 1. Triple synergy of universal design

The representation of conservative and generic content, that cannot address different individuals' needs and preferences, has been identified as a key limitation in engaging wider public. Despite the popularity of the audio-visual content, commonly encountered within the Creative and Cultural Industry (CCI), limitations and barriers are still preventing Audio Visual Media Accessibility, being related to usability, interoperability, and standards issues, as well as lack of business-case for take-up by mainstream actors, legal barriers (for example for the transnational reuse of accessible content), difficulties in the reuse of accessible content over time and across different platforms [4]. These challenges need to be overcome for delivering wider access to the cultural heritage content to many communities. For people with a disability such as a hearing, sight or mobility impairment, effective engagement with digital media content and interacting with social media applications provide extra barriers. Following the reports on aging population across Europe, there is a critical need to develop digital technologies considering inclusion by design principles. Addressing the challenge, in 2015, Netflix launched the Accessible Netflix Project (ANP), with the vision of offering audio description of its original content for its vision-impaired audience. Despite an increase in the design and development of assistive technologies which has been released in the market for over a decade, the lack of content production tools and services focused on cultural heritage has negatively impacted the market uptake of such assistive technologies. As an instance, the use of Haptic solutions to offer a sensory experience of touch and otherwise, has not gained popularity among people with disabilities and otherwise, because they offer limited and very basic functionality to the users, e.g., white canes[2].

---

[1] https://unesdoc.unesco.org/ark:/48223/pf0000232026.

[2] https://op.europa.eu/en/publication-detail/-/publication/d657a81b-184c-11e8-ac73-01aa75
ed71a1/language-en.

Addressing the scope and challenges presented by the need for establishing accessibility and inclusion as two pillars of the society aimed to minimise the digital divide among citizens with disabilities, the paper aims to present a framework of AI technologies that is designed to promote the wider adoption of EAA policy. The rest of the paper is structured as follows. In Sect. 2, a review of the EAA is presented, followed by the AI framework for promoting EAA outlined in Sect. 3. The conclusions and future work is presented in Sect. 4.

2   European Accessibility Policy

Since the dawn of the Internet and web content, the topic of accessibility can be traced back to the early efforts of World Wide Web Consortium (W3C)[3] dedicated to promote guidelines on web accessibility initiative (WAI). The first draft of the published version was released in 1999, which have become an international benchmark. Subsequently, WCAG 2.0 was published in December 2008, WCAG 2.1 in June 2018 and the first public draft of WCAG 2.2 in February 2020. WCAG 2.0 became the international standard ISO/IEC 40500:2012. WCAG 2.1 contains all the success criteria of WCAG 2.0 plus 17 additional success criteria. The European Union adopted WCAG 2.1 in September 2018 as a standard for websites and electronic documents. The WCAG recommendations help website designers and developers to better meet the needs of users with disabilities and older users. These guidelines are intended for website developers and designers, creators of authoring tools for website design and programming, developers of web accessibility evaluation tools, and anyone who needs a reference standard for checking the accessibility of specific web content. Web accessibility benefits people with and without disabilities and improves the usability of websites.

The EAA is a step[4] forward in reducing barriers for people with disabilities within the EU: better accessibility of products and services that citizens use every day, such as phones, transport, or banking services, will help people with disabilities to be able to fully participate in society on an equal basis with others, to have better access to education and to enter more easily the open labour market. Accessibility is also necessary for older people to maintain an active role in society, including extending their working lives. In general, accessibility is beneficial to all EU citizens. For example, people trying to hear travelling information in noisy environments like train stations or trying to get money from ATMs on a sunny day, or employees working with enlarged documents to avoid eye strain will also greatly benefit from further accessibility.

A major challenge around digital accessibility concerns the present inability of technology to cover the diverse types of disabilities. More specifically, as Kelly and colleagues (2010) and Lazar and colleagues (2015) explain: while perceptual disabilities (i.e., those involving vision and hearing limitations) and physical disabilities (i.e., those involving limitations of use of limbs as well as speech) have been the focus of accessibility solutions, cognitive disabilities have proven difficult to address. For example, screen readers can help persons who have visual limitations and captioning of videos can help

---

[3] Empirical Studies on Web Accessibility of Educational Websites: A Systematic Literature Review.

[4] https://ec.europa.eu/social/BlobServlet?docId=14869&langId=en.

persons who have hearing limitations. Similarly, certain types of keyboards and other hardware devices can help persons who have physical limitations. However, in case of cognitive impairments such as Down syndrome or Alzheimer's disease, technology is yet unhelpful and needs to be attended to.

3   AI Powered Media Accessibility

According to ECAG recommendations[5], the four principles of accessibility could be defined as follows:

- *Perceivable* - Information and user interface components must be presentable to users in ways they can perceive.
- *Operable* - User interface components and navigation must be operable.
- *Understandable* - Information and the operation of user interface must be understandable.
- *Robust* - Content must be robust enough that it can be interpreted reliably by a wide variety of user agents, including assistive technologies.

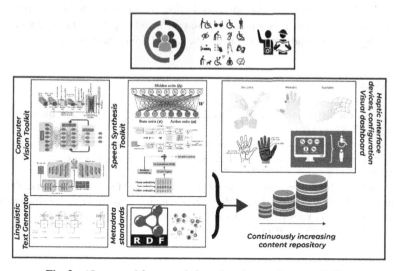

Fig. 2. AI powered framework for enhancing media accessibility.

Bringing together these four principles of accessibility, a generic AI powered framework that aims at addressing new and innovative technologies is presented in Fig. 2. The framework presents a holistic representation of key innovations from six interdisciplinary research themes extending from computer vision technologies to haptics innovations. The computer vision toolkit is included to extract knowledge embedded

---

[5] https://www.w3.org/WAI/WCAG21/Understanding/.

within the pictures and video sequences. The extracted knowledge in terms of objects or key terms, will be converted into full-fledged sentences by the linguistic toolkit. The textual descriptions are then subsequently transformed into speech with audio synthesis tool. The use of semantic technologies powered by Resource Description Framework (RDF) will ensure the semantic interpretability of information and ensure cross linking of relevant information. Finally, the semantic repository populated by the analysis tools are then transformed into haptic language to be closely integrated within the wearable devices. To achieve such a multi-modal interoperability among the technologies, it is important to establish metadata standards using semantic language to enable accessibility of media content.

4   Conclusions and Future Work

In this poster presentation, the role of AI powered framework in promoting EAA policy and the critical need to establish interoperability standards has been presented. The paper builds on the triples synergies of universal design philosophy based on usability, accessibility and inclusion and proposed a framework that exploits the recent advances in the field of machine learning and artificial intelligence. To framework brings together multi-modal data formats representing computer vision, audio processing, linguistic toolkits, and haptic language developments. Following the exponential growth in digital transformation strategies, it is vital to ensure new technologies adopt accessibility and inclusion by design paradigm to minimise the digital divide among citizens.

References

1. Faddis, A.: The digital transformation of healthcare technology management. Biomed. Instrum. Technol. **52**, 34–38 (2018)
2. Kutnjak, A.: Covid-19 accelerates digital transformation in industries: challenges, issues, barriers and problems in transformation. IEEE Access 1 (2021). https://doi.org/10.1109/ACCESS.2021.3084801
3. Stephanidis, C. (ed.): The Universal Access Handbook. CRC Press, Boca Raton (2009)
4. Longo, D., Boeri, A., Turillazzi, B., Orlandi, S.: Cultural heritage and interoperable open platforms: strategies for knowledge, accessibility, enhancement and networking, 371–382 (2020). https://doi.org/10.2495/SDP200301

Human-Centered Learning Engineering for the Emerging Intelligence Augmentation Economy

Jim Goodell[1]([⊠]) and Neil Heffernan[2]

[1] Quality Information Partners, Fairfax, VA 22030, USA
jimgoodell@qi-partners.com
[2] WPI, Worcester, MA 01609, USA

AbstractWe explore the intersection. We explore the intersection of human-centered engineering design methodologies, applied learning sciences, and data (instrumentation & analytics) realized in the practice of learning engineering in response to an emerging intelligence augmentation economy. As the nature of human endeavor and productivity changes with the advancement of HCI and AI technologies we predict an "intelligence augmentation economy" will replace the knowledge economy. Just like the industrial economy and service economies before it, the IA economy will fundamentally change the nature of work and what people need to learn to be its contributors and beneficiaries.

The demands of secondary and postsecondary education have already begun to shift from pre-career and preparation for life to mid-career adaptation, enrichment, and retraining [1]. The intelligence augmentation economy will require development of new skills for new kinds of collaborative work with intelligent agents. The lines between learning and working will blur, just as will the lines between the work of humans and the work of machines. Education institutions will be one source for life-long-learning in a world where work-embedded continuous adaptive learning is the norm.

The learning engineering process provides a methodology for educational institutions and work-embedded training partners to engineer new kinds of learning experiences suited to the needs of the intelligence augmentation economy. These new learning experiences will take full advantage of technologies such as augmented reality and intelligent agents.

We draw ideas from several chapters of the *Learning Engineering Toolkit: Evidence-Based Practices from the Learning Sciences, Instructional Design, and Beyond* [2]. We suggest a path to scaling HCI innovation through application of the learning engineering process to support a radically new future of learning and working in a new intelligence augmentation economy characterized by productivity gains through collaboration between people and intelligent agents.

Keywords: Intelligence augmentation · Learning engineering

C. Stephanidis et al. (Eds.): HCII 2022, CCIS 1655, pp. 619–623, 2022.
https://doi.org/10.1007/978-3-031-19682-9_78

1 The Emerging Intelligence Augmentation Economy

1.1 Changing Nature of Work

The nature of human endeavor and productivity is changing with the advancement of HCI and AI technologies. An intelligence augmentation economy is replacing the knowledge economy. Just like the industrial economy and service economies before it, the IA economy will fundamentally change the nature of work and what people need to learn to be its contributors and beneficiaries. Just like with the previous economic shifts, it was technology which drove disruptive changes in how we lived and worked.

With the Industrial Revolution of the early 1800s to mid 1900s it was a shift from working in fields and cottages to working in factories. Public schools prepared people with basic literacy and factual knowledge to last their working life. With the service economy from the late 1960s to early 2020s people moved from factory jobs to jobs as hair stylists, waiters, lawyers, pharmacist, and yoga instructors as automation took over in the factories. In the service economy, more education meant more knowledge to start a career in a higher paying job. Schools didn't change much but more people attended college. Based on the high demand and value in the economy, people and governments were willing to pay for increasing costs of higher education during this economy.

Now, as we enter the IA economy, knowledge is ubiquitous. The value that a person has in this emerging economy is based more on skills in continuous learning, collaboration, creativity, resilience, and a breadth of knowledge literacy [3], rather than depth of knowledge or ability to do repetitive physical or cognitive tasks. Knowledge work is replaced by human-machine collaboration. Likewise, there is a need to shift the predominant focus of education as the imparting of knowledge to the right mix of knowledge literacy and a new set of foundational skills, such as those presented in the following Fig. 1, for fluent collaboration with machines. And there will be a need to fill the gap for adults beyond the traditional education experience with just-in-time, highly contextualized and personalized, work-embedded learning experiences.

1.2 Changing Demands for Education

This shift in what learners need educational institutions to provide coincides with the emergence of learning engineering. The learning engineering process provides a methodology for educational institutions needing to reengineer the kinds of learning experiences they deliver and for those institutions and other work-embedded training providers to engineer the kinds of experiences that will use augmented reality and intelligent agents as the lines between learning and working blur.

Learning engineering recognizes that learning is a complex endeavor and that a person's learning (e.g. as specific neurological changes) is not directly observable; it is only through assessment events that capture learner responses that we can infer acquisition of knowledge components [4]. However, instrumented experiences and machine learning inference engines give us increasingly greater insights. This will especially be true with instrumented learning while working event data.

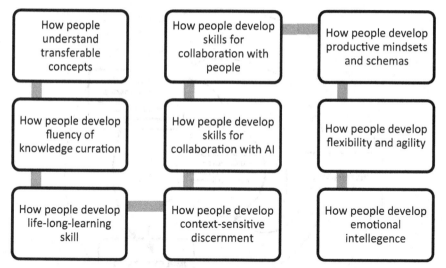

Fig. 1. The need for learning has shifted from an emphasis on factal knowledge retrieval to the need for deeper knowledge of concepts, knowledge curation, adaptation and re-application, emotional intelligence, and collaboration with people and intelligent machines. The way that people learn these skills for the intelligence augmentation economy will require new kinds of learning experiences.

2 The Emergence of Learning Engineering

2.1 Learning Engineering is Human-Centered

The learning engineering process, shown as Fig. 2, borrows from many methodologies, including human-centered design, design thinking, universal design for learning, learning experience design, design-based research, and engineering design [5]. At its core, the best designs for learning are informed by predictions about how learners will interact and function within a designed learning environment. They're iteratively tested for efficacy, and data are collected about learners, learner interactions, and elements of their learning environment. What is learned from those data is used to refine designs and design elements.

According to the IEEE IC Industry Consortium on Learning Engineering (ICICLE), learning engineering is a process and practice that applies the learning sciences using human-centered engineering design methodologies and data-informed decision making to support learners and their development [7]. Data-informed decision-making is an essential and integral part of learning engineering. It includes data instrumentation [8] and data analytics [9].

Data instrumentation and data pipelines, as shown in Fig. 3, collect data that can train artificially intelligent systems that support both improved collaborative tasks and to inform improved learning conditions. The instructional intelligence in the system can provide hints and scaffolding to the learner-worker that improves the effectiveness of on-the-job learning while itself adapting its role in the work task.

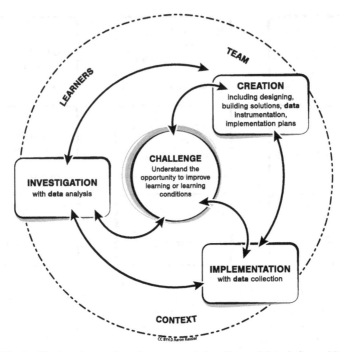

Fig. 2. The learning engineering process is iterative and data-informed [6].

2.2 Instrumented Learning and Working

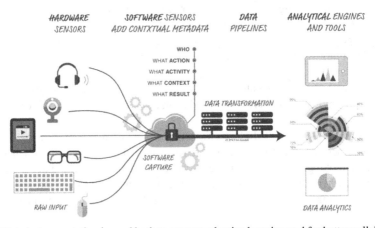

Fig. 3. Data instrumentation is used both to support adaptive learning and for better collaborative results for tasks shared between human and intelligent agents in the workplace [8].

Intelligent systems developed using learning engineering methodologies have been found effective at improving learner development of cognitive tasks, such as mathematics problem solving [10] and cooperative tasks such as team collaboration [11]. As lines between learning and working blur, we see opportunities for new research and learning engineering to advance the capabilities of learners/workers and their intelligent agent collaborators in an emerging intelligence augmentation economy.

References

1. CLASP: Table depiction of 'Yesterday's Non-Traditional Student is Today's Traditional Student'. Center for Postsecondary and Economic Success (2015). http://www.clasp.org/resources-and-publications/publication-1/CPES-Nontraditional-students-pdf.pdf
2. Goodell, J., et al.: Learning Engineering Toolkit: Evidence-Based Practices from the Learning Sciences, Instructional Design, and Beyond. Routledge, London (2022, in press)
3. Toppo, G., Tracy, J.: Running with Robots: The American High School's Third Century. MIT Press, Cambridge (2021)
4. Koedinger, K.R., Corbett, A.T., Perfetti, C.: The knowledge-learning-instruction framework: bridging the science-practice chasm to enhance robust student learning. Cogn. Sci. **36**(5), 757–798 (2012)
5. Thai, K.-P., Craig, S.D., Goodell, J., Lis, J., Schoenherr, J.R., Kolodner, J.: Learning engineering is human-centered. In: Goodell, J. (ed.) Learning Engineering Toolkit, p. 85 (2022)
6. Kessler, A., Craig, S.D., Goodell, J., Kurzweil, D., Greenwald, S.W.: Learning engineering is a process. In: Goodell, J. (ed.) The Learning Engineering Toolkit: Evidence-Based Practices from the Learning Sciences, Instructional Design, and Beyond, pp. 29–46. Routledge, London (2022)
7. www.ieeeicile.org
8. Czerwinski, E., Goodell, J., Ritter, S., Sottilare, R., Thai, K.P., Jacobs, D.: Learning Engineering Uses Data (Part 1): Instrumentation. In: Goodell, J. (ed.) The Learning Engineering Toolkit: Evidence-Based Practices from the Learning Sciences, Instructional Design, and Beyond, pp. 153–174. Routledge, London (2022)
9. Barrett, M., et al.: Learning engineering uses data (part 2): analytics. In: Goodell, J. (ed.) The Learning Engineering Toolkit: Evidence-Based Practices from the Learning Sciences, Instructional Design, and Beyond, pp. 175–200. Routledge, London (2022)
10. Murphy, R., Roschelle, J., Feng, M., Mason, C.: Investigating efficacy, moderators and mediators for an online mathematics homework intervention. J. Res. Educ. Effect. **13**(2) (2020). https://doi.org/10.1080/19345747.2019.1710885
11. Sottilare, R.A., Shawn Burke, C., Salas, E., Sinatra, A.M., Johnston, J.H., Gilbert, S.B.: Designing adaptive instruction for teams: a meta-analysis. Int. J. Artif. Intell. Educ. **28**(2), 225–264 (2017). https://doi.org/10.1007/s40593-017-0146-z

A Skeleton-Based Deep Learning Approach for Recognizing Violent Actions in Surveillance Scenarios

Rabia Jafri[1]([✉]), Rodrigo Louzada Campos[2], and Hamid R. Arabnia[2]

[1] Department of Information Technology, King Saud University, Riyadh, Saudi Arabia
rjafri@ksu.edu.sa
[2] Department of Computer Science, University of Georgia, Athens, GA, USA
{rlc,hra}@uga.edu

Abstract. A novel skeleton-based approach that recognizes specific violent actions (VAs) such as kicking and punching, which are highly relevant in surveillance scenarios, is presented. The method uses a depth sensor for more efficient and accurate depth data acquisition and classifies an action by utilizing the forecasts of an ensemble of Long Short-Term Memory (LSTM) networks, each trained to predict a specific VA. The proposed method offers the advantages of requiring a smaller dataset for training (since only data for a few specific VAs is required and data for non-VAs is not needed) and a lower risk of misclassification (since a separate LSTM network is trained for each VA). The utilization of a compact skeletal representation and a distributed architecture allows the system to operate efficiently bolstering its potential to be practically used in real-world scenarios.

Keywords: Violence detection · Human activity recognition · Long short-term memory networks · Forecasting · Depth sensor

1 Introduction

Violence detection (VD) is of vital importance in several surveillance scenarios such as for monitoring public spaces (e.g., airports, railway stations, college campuses and malls), assisted living accommodations, healthcare centers and childcare facilities. Though surveillance cameras are increasingly being installed at such locations, given the huge amount of data being collected by such systems, it is not only expensive and manpower-intensive to depend on human operators to continuously monitor the feeds from these sensors, but also factors like fatigue, boredom and distraction inherent to human nature render such scrutiny unreliable resulting in delays and omissions in alerting the relevant authorities when a violent act is committed.

These limitations have led to concerted efforts to develop automated systems for VD [1, 2]. In recent years, a few approaches based on skeleton data comprised of human skeletal key points have been proposed [3–10] as skeleton data offers the advantage of being independent of background clutter and also allows for a more compact representation of the human form making it useful for modelling simple behaviors while using fewer computing resources [6]. However, several of these methods [4, 6, 10] aim to detect violence in general while in most surveillance scenarios, authorities are primarily interested in detecting specific violent actions (VAs) like kicking, punching, etc. The few techniques [3, 7] that do focus on specific VAs and employ deep learning require a large dataset comprised of both those VAs and non-VAs and are still prone to classification errors arising from high interclass similarities since these methods usually train a single network to differentiate among all actions.

Furthermore, most of these methods [3–5, 7, 10] extract the skeleton data from surveillance videos utilizing pose estimation algorithms which have the disadvantages of being computationally intensive, and providing restricted data with limited accuracy [11] (e.g., the widely used OpenPose network [12] extracts only 2D coordinates of skeletal points and provides no information about the depth). The recent proliferation of low-cost off-the-shelf depth sensors, such as Kinect [13], has made it possible to inexpensively capture highly accurate 3D data at lower computational cost; though a few skeleton-based VD methods have utilized these sensors [8, 9], the potential of these devices for more accurate and efficient acquisition of skeleton data for VD needs to be further explored.

Long Short-Term Memory networks (LSTM) have been shown to be useful for processing time series data and have been extensively utilized in deep learning approaches for human activity recognition (HAR) in general and VD in particular [1, 2]. They have also proven to be effective in sequence forecasting tasks such as handwriting [14] and speech [15] generation. Though LSTM networks have been used for predicting human actions from video sequences with promising results [16, 17], to the best of our knowledge, there have not been any studies conducted so far to explore how their forecasting potential can be exploited for recognizing VAs.

We, therefore, propose a novel skeleton-based deep learning approach for recognizing specific VAs, such as kicking and punching, that are highly relevant in surveillance scenarios by utilizing the forecasts from an ensemble of LSTM networks. Given a depth map sequence (DMS) from a depth sensor, feature vectors consisting of joint angles based on skeletal key points are extracted from each frame and the feature vector sequence (FVS) for the first few frames is input to an ensemble of LSTM networks, each of which forecasts the FVS for the remaining time frames for a specific VA. The mean squared errors (MSEs) between the forecasted FVSs and the actual observed FVS are calculated and the action is labelled as the one pertaining to the LSTM network with the minimum MSE provided that the MSE is below a certain threshold; otherwise, the action is labelled as non-violent. The process is repeated for several subsequent DMS windows and majority voting is used to determine the final label for the action.

The proposed method offers the advantages of requiring a smaller dataset for training (since only data for a few specific VAs is required and data for non-VAs is not needed) and a lower risk of misclassification (since a separate LSTM network is trained for each VA). The utilization of a compact skeletal representation and a distributed architecture allows the system to operate efficiently bolstering its potential to be practically used in real-world scenarios.

The rest of this paper is organized as follows: Sect. 2 provides an overview of skeleton-based deep learning approaches for VD and discusses the use of LSTM networks for forecasting human activities. Section 3 describes the framework for the proposed approach while Sect. 4 concludes the paper and identifies some directions for future work.

2   Related Work

Though deep learning methods have gained popularity in the field of vision-based HAR in recent years [3], only a few skeleton-based approaches appear to have employed deep learning for VD. For example, Naik et al. [3] apply a modified Mask Region-based Convolutional Neural Network (Mask RCNN) [18] to detect and localize a single person from video, generating a bounding box and a mask; key points extracted from the detected boundary box using the DeepPose [19] pose estimation method are then fed, along with the mask, to an LSTM network to detect the VAs of punching and kicking. Su et al. [4] extract skeletal key points for multiple people from video using the RMPE [20] pose estimation method, then repeatedly apply a Skeleton Points Interaction Learning (SPIL) module that captures both feature and position relation information simultaneously taking interactions among different people into account and finally use a fully connected layer to classify the relational features as violent or non-violent. Liu et al. [6] extract skeletal key points from video using OpenPose [12], then generate kinematic descriptors based on these which are passed to a spatial attention network and a temporal attention network, respectively, to extract spatial and temporal features which are then classified as violent or non-violent; their system also includes a module for abuser tracking. Xing et al. [7] extract 2D skeletal key points from video using OpenPose [12], convert them into 3D, and then employ a two-stream Adaptive Graph Convolutional Network [21] (one stream for the joints and the other for the bones between the joints) with an attention module added to it to detect the VAs of pushing, punching and kicking.

Human activity prediction has applications in many domains such as human-computer interaction, assistive robotics, abnormal behavior detection and contextual marketing [16]. Though LSTM networks have been effectively applied for predicting human activities [16, 17] and trajectories [22, 23], their forecasting potential does not appear to have been utilized for recognizing VAs. The demonstrated effectiveness of LSTMs for sequence prediction in general and human activity prediction in particular coupled with an apparent lack of studies on utilizing these capabilities for VD has prompted us to explore the potential of using LSTM forecasts for recognizing VAs.

3   Proposed Approach

A deep learning approach based on skeleton data for recognizing specific VAs that are highly relevant in surveillance scenarios is proposed. The framework consists of the following modules: data preprocessing, feature extraction, forecasting and classification. An overview of the proposed framework is shown in Fig. 1 and details are provided in the subsections below. It should be noted that the framework below accepts a single DMS as input and classifies it. When deployed in a real-world scenario, the live feed streaming from a depth sensor placed in a public area can be constantly monitored; if a person is detected, the VA recognition system is triggered and DMSs from the live feed generated using a sliding window approach start being sent as input to the system. After assigning class labels to several consecutive windows, majority voting is used to determine the final label for the action.

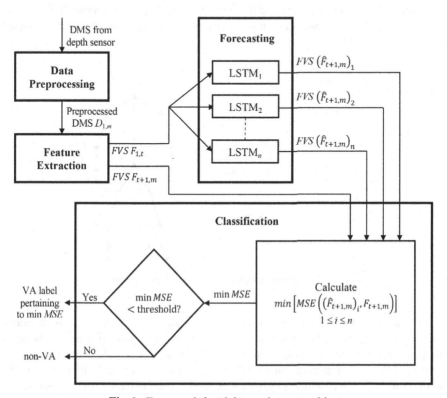

Fig. 1. Framework for violent action recognition

3.1 Data Preprocessing

The data consists of a DMS containing at least one person captured using a depth sensor, such as Kinect [13]. Skeletal key points (KPs) consisting of the 3D positions of the skeleton joints, as shown in Fig. 2, are extracted from each frame using the appropriate software (such as the Kinect SDK). Since the sensor may fail to detect some KPs in certain frames, those KPs are filled with the corresponding detected values from the previous frame [4, 24]. The preprocessed DMS comprised of the skeletal KPs for each frame is then sent to the feature extraction module.

3.2 Feature Extraction

Human actions can be represented as a time series of the 3D positions of the skeleton joints. However, given the similarity among human actions, these KPs may not be enough to differentiate among all actions. The relative and absolute angles between every pair of connected limbs allow for a more discriminative action encoding since these explicitly capture the relationships among the different body parts during any action [8]. We, therefore, represent the skeleton motion data as changes over time of joint angles computed at each time frame [8].

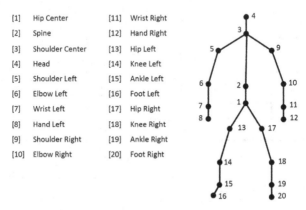

[1]	Hip Center	[11]	Wrist Right
[2]	Spine	[12]	Hand Right
[3]	Shoulder Center	[13]	Hip Left
[4]	Head	[14]	Knee Left
[5]	Shoulder Left	[15]	Ankle Left
[6]	Elbow Left	[16]	Foot Left
[7]	Wrist Left	[17]	Hip Right
[8]	Hand Left	[18]	Knee Right
[9]	Shoulder Right	[19]	Ankle Right
[10]	Elbow Right	[20]	Foot Right

Fig. 2. Skeleton joints captured by a Kinect sensor

For each time frame t, a feature vector $f_t = (\theta_{\text{relative-angle}}, \theta_{\text{absolute angle}})$ is generated where $\theta_{\text{relative-angle}}$ consists of the twelve relative angles at the following joints: shoulder, elbow, wrist, hip, knee and ankle for the left and right side of the body while $\theta_{\text{absolute angle}}$ consists of the twelve absolute angles for the same joints computed with respect to the depth sensor's device coordinate system; these angles are calculated from the KPs using the method described by Chikhaoui et al. [8].

The resulting FVS $F_{1,m} = (f_1, f_2, ..., f_m)$, where m, $m > 1$ is the number of frames in the input DMS, is then split into two parts: 1) the FVS for the first t frames $F_{1,t}$, where $1 \leq t < m$, which is sent as input to the forecasting module and 2) the FVS for the remaining frames $F_{t+1,m}$, which is sent as input to the classification module.

3.3 Forecasting

Let n be the number of VAs that we aim to recognize. The forecasting module then consists of an ensemble of n LSTM networks, where each network is trained to make a forecast for a specific VA. This task can be viewed as a sequence generation problem where the input sequence corresponds to the observed joint angles of a person performing a VA at certain time-instants and we are interested in generating an output sequence denoting his/her future joint angles at future time-instants. The problem for the LSTM network for VA_i, where $1 \leq i \leq n$, can, thus, be formulated as follows: Given the FVS

$F_{1,t} = (f_1, f_2, ..., f_t)$ for VA$_i$ for time frames 1 to t, predict the FVS $F_{t+1, t+k} = (f_{t+1}, f_{t+2}, ..., f_{t+k})$ for VA$_i$ for the next k time frames, where $t, k \geq 1$.

For training the LSTM networks, we utilize existing datasets, such as the NTU RGB+D [25] and SBU Kinect Interaction [26] datasets, which contain several DMS instances for VAs such as kicking, punching and pushing. The DMSs for all VAs of interest are preprocessed and feature vectors are generated for all frames as described in the previous subsections. The training data is then generated as follows: For each DMS instance, its FVS is segmented into fixed-length samples using a sliding window approach. For each VA, the FVS $F_{1,t}$ of the first t frames for each sample is used as input to a sequence-to-sequence LSTM network [27] which predicts the FVS $\widehat{F}_{t+1,m}$ for the remaining frames, where m is the sample length and $1 \leq t < m$. The LSTM network is trained to minimize the prediction error between the predicted FVS $\widehat{F}_{t+1,m}$ and the actual observed FVS $F_{t+1,m}$. We plan to experiment with different values for the window size and the shift at each step in order to determine the optimum values for these parameters.

At runtime, the input FVS $F_{1,t}$ is fed in parallel to the ensemble of LSTM networks and the output FVSs $(\widehat{F}_{t+1,m})_i$ are sent to the classification module.

3.4 Classification

The classification module computes the mean squared error (MSE) between the predicted FVSs $(\widehat{F}_{t+1,m})_i$ and the actual observed FVS $F_{t+1,m}$. The action is then labelled as the one pertaining to the prediction with the minimum MSE provided that the MSE is below a certain threshold; otherwise, the action is labelled as non-violent.

4 Conclusion

A novel skeleton-based approach that recognizes specific VAs which are highly pertinent in surveillance scenarios is presented. The method uses a depth sensor for more efficient and accurate depth data acquisition and classifies an action by utilizing the forecasts of an ensemble of LSTM networks, each trained to predict a specific VA, thus, not only lowering the risk of misclassification but also eliminating the need for a large dataset of non-VAs for training. The proposed approach currently tracks and classifies the actions of a single person to determine if he/she has perpetuated a VA. Though this may completely meet the surveillance requirements in certain scenarios (e.g., for detecting aggressive or self-injurious behavior in a healthcare facility, such as a cognitively impaired patient repeatedly punching a wall in an agitated frame of mind), since, in most other scenarios, VAs usually also involve a victim and, in a crowd situation, may involve multiple perpetuators and victims, we plan to extend the system to multiple people so that the VA recognition framework takes into account not only their individual actions but their collective interactions as well. Other future work directions include enriching the set of features further (e.g., adding joint positions, distances and accelerations) [10], applying feature selection algorithms to identify the most discriminative features [8] and evolving/enhancing the set of VAs by accepting user feedback to learn new actions as well as new examples of existing actions [9]. Eventually, modules for tracking perpetuators [6] and identifying them using face and gait recognition methods [28–33] could also be added.

References

1. Ramzan, M., et al.: A review on state-of-the-art violence detection techniques. IEEE Access **7**, 107560–107575 (2019)
2. Omarov, B., Narynov, S., Zhumanov, Z., Gumar, A., Khassanova, M.: State-of-the-art violence detection techniques in video surveillance security systems: a systematic review. PeerJ Comput. Sci. **8**, e920 (2022)
3. Naik, A.J., Gopalakrishna, M.T.: Deep-violence: individual person violent activity detection in video. Multimed. Tools Appl. **80**(12), 18365–18380 (2021). https://doi.org/10.1007/s11 042-021-10682-w
4. Su, Y., Lin, G., Zhu, J., Wu, Q.: Human interaction learning on 3D skeleton point clouds for video violence recognition. In: Vedaldi, A., Bischof, H., Brox, T., Frahm, J.-M. (eds.) ECCV 2020. LNCS, vol. 12349, pp. 74–90. Springer, Cham (2020). https://doi.org/10.1007/978-3-030-58548-8_5
5. Srivastava, A., Badal, T., Garg, A., Vidyarthi, A., Singh, R.: Recognizing human violent action using drone surveillance within real-time proximity. J. Real-Time Image Proc. **18**(5), 1851–1863 (2021). https://doi.org/10.1007/s11554-021-01171-2
6. Liu, H., Yao, M., Wang, L.: Svrat: a skeleton-based intelligent monitoring system for violence recognition and abuser tracking. In: 2021 IEEE International Conference on Multimedia and Expo (ICME), pp. 1–6 (2021)
7. Xing, Y., Dai, Y., Hirota, K., Jia, Z.: A skeleton-based method for recognizing the campus violence. In: The 9th International Symposium on Computational Intelligence and Industrial Applications (ISCIIA 2020), Beijing, China (2020)
8. Chikhaoui, B., Ye, B., Mihailidis, A.: Feature-level combination of skeleton joints and body parts for accurate aggressive and agitated behavior recognition. J. Ambient. Intell. Humaniz. Comput. **8**(6), 957–976 (2016). https://doi.org/10.1007/s12652-016-0415-y
9. Nirjon, S., et al.: Kintense: a robust, accurate, real-time and evolving system for detecting aggressive actions from streaming 3D skeleton data. In: 2014 IEEE International Conference on Pervasive Computing and Communications (PerCom), pp. 2–10 (2014)
10. Nova, D., Ferreira, A., Cortez, P.: A machine learning approach to detect violent behaviour from video. In: Cortez, P., Magalhães, L., Branco, P., Portela, C.F., Adão, T. (eds.) INTETAIN 2018. LNICSSITE, vol. 273, pp. 85–94. Springer, Cham (2019). https://doi.org/10.1007/978-3-030-16447-8_9
11. Li, D.: Human skeleton detection and extraction in dance video based on PSO-enabled LSTM neural network. Comput. Intell. Neurosci. **2021**, 2545151 (2021)
12. Cao, Z., Hidalgo, G., Simon, T., Wei, S.-E., Sheikh, Y.: OpenPose: realtime multi-person 2D pose estimation using part affinity fields. IEEE Trans. Pattern Anal. Mach. Intell. **43**, 172–186 (2021)
13. Kinect for Windows. https://developer.microsoft.com/en-us/windows/kinect/. Accessed 22 May 2022
14. Graves, A.: Generating sequences with recurrent neural networks. arXiv preprint arXiv:1308. 0850 (2013)
15. Graves, A., Jaitly, N.: Towards end-to-end speech recognition with recurrent neural networks. In: Proceedings of the 31st International Conference on Machine Learning, Beijing, China, vol. 32, pp. II–1764–II–1772. JMLR.org (2014)
16. Krishna, K., Jain, D., Mehta, S.V., Choudhary, S.: An LSTM based system for prediction of human activities with durations. Proc. ACM Interact. Mob. Wearable Ubiquit. Technol. **1**, 1–31 (2018). Article: 147
17. Tax, N.: Human activity prediction in smart home environments with LSTM neural networks. In: 14th International Conference on Intelligent Environments (IE), pp. 40–47 (2018)

18. He, K., Gkioxari, G., Dollár, P., Girshick, R.: Mask R-CNN. In: IEEE International Conference on Computer Vision (ICCV), pp. 2980–2988 (2017)
19. Toshev, A., Szegedy, C.: DeepPose: human pose estimation via deep neural networks. In: IEEE Conference on Computer Vision and Pattern Recognition, pp. 1653–1660 (2014)
20. Fang, H.S., Xie, S., Tai, Y.W., Lu, C.: RMPE: regional multi-person pose estimation. In: 2017 IEEE International Conference on Computer Vision (ICCV), pp. 2353–2362 (2017)
21. Shi, L., Zhang, Y., Cheng, J., Lu, H.: Two-stream adaptive graph convolutional networks for skeleton-based action recognition. In: IEEE Conference on Computer Vision and Pattern Recognition (CVPR), pp. 12018–12027 (2019)
22. Ma, Q., Zou, Q., Huang, Y., Wang, N.: Dynamic pedestrian trajectory forecasting with LSTM-based Delaunay triangulation. Appl. Intell. **52**, 3018–3028 (2022). https://doi.org/10.1007/s10489-021-02562-5
23. Alahi, A., Goel, K., Ramanathan, V., Robicquet, A., Fei-Fei, L., Savarese, S.: Social LSTM: human trajectory prediction in crowded spaces. In: IEEE Conference on Computer Vision and Pattern Recognition (CVPR), pp. 961–971 (2016)
24. Tharali, S.R., Wakchaure, G.S., Shirsat, D.S., Singhaniya, N.G.: Violence detection using embedded GPU. In: ITM Web of Conferences, vol. 32, p. 03014. EDP Sciences (2020)
25. Shahroudy, A., Liu, J., Ng, T.-T., Wang, G.: NTU RGB+D: a large scale dataset for 3D human activity analysis. In: IEEE Conference on Computer Vision and Pattern Recognition, pp. 1010–1019 (2016)
26. Yun, K., Honorio, J., Chattopadhyay, D., Berg, T.L., Samaras, D.: Two-person interaction detection using body-pose features and multiple instance learning. In: IEEE Computer Society Conference on Computer Vision and Pattern Recognition Workshops, pp. 28–35 (2012)
27. Sutskever, I., Vinyals, O., Le, Q.V.: Sequence to sequence learning with neural networks. In: Advances in Neural Information Processing Systems, vol. 27 (2014)
28. Jafri, R., Arabnia, H.R.: A survey of face recognition techniques. J. Inf. Process. Syst. **5**, 41–68 (2009)
29. Jafri, R., Arabnia, H.R.: Fusion of face and gait for automatic human recognition. In: Fifth International Conference on Information Technology: New Generations (ITNG 2008), pp. 167–173 (2008)
30. Jafri, R., Arabnia, H.R., Simpson, K.J.: An integrated face-gait system for automatic recognition of humans. In: International Conference on Security and Management (SAM 2008), Las Vegas, Nevada, USA, pp. 571–581 (2008)
31. Jafri, R., Arabnia, H.R.: PCA-based methods for face recognition. In: Proceedings of the 2007 International Conference on Security and Management (SAM 2007), Las Vegas, USA, pp. 534–541 (2007)
32. Jafri, R., Arabnia, H.R.: A survey of component-based face recognition approaches. In: International Conference on Artificial Intelligence (ICAI 2007), Las Vegas, USA, pp. 103–113 (2007)
33. Jafri, R., Arabnia, H.R.: A multi-resolution hierarchical approach for face recognition. In: International Conference on Image Information and Knowledge Engineering (IKE 2007), Las Vegas, Nevada, USA, pp. 231–239 (2007)

Consumer Intention to Accept AI-Based Products and Services

Xu Li[1] , Do-Won Yoon[2] , Yuxuan Ding[3] , and Hyesun Hwang[3]([⊠])

[1] Department of Consumer Science, Sungkyunkwan University, Seoul, South Korea
[2] Convergence Program for Social Innovation, Sungkyunkwan University, Seoul, South Korea
[3] Department of Consumer Science, Convergence Program for Social Innovation,
Sungkyunkwan University, Seoul, South Korea
h.hwang@skku.edu

Abstract. This study aimed to examine the consumers' intention to accept artificial intelligence (AI) based products/services. Considering that AI-based products/services can be perceived as a radical technological revolution, we analyzed the effect of consumers' overall self-efficacy of innovative technologies on their intention to accept AI-based products/services. In addition, the mediating effects of consumers' positive perception of the intelligent information society and the usefulness of AI technology were verified. The results of an analysis of 6,073 adults revealed that consumers' acceptance of innovative technologies was positively associated with consumers' intention to accept AI-based products/services. In addition, consumers' positive perception of the intelligent information society had a partial mediating effect between the technology self-efficacy and their intention to accept AI-based products/services; the perceived usefulness of AI technology also had a partial mediating effect between the two variables. Moreover, double mediation effects of positive perception of the intelligent information society and perceived usefulness of AI technology were significant in the relationship between technology self-efficacy and their intention to accept AI-based products/services. This means that the more positively the consumers think about the intelligent information society, the higher the perception of AI technology being useful, and ultimately the higher the intention to accept AI-based products/services. The findings of this study confirm that consumers' overall technology self-efficacy not only forms a positive perception of the intelligent information society but also makes them more receptive to the application of new AI technology.

Keywords: Intention to accept AI technology · Self-efficacy · Intelligent information society

1 Introduction

Recently, the fourth Industrial Revolution, in which advanced information and communication technologies such as artificial intelligence (AI), Internet of Things, big data, and mobile are integrated into society, economy, and industry as a whole, has emerged. In particular, there is a growing debate in Korea about an intelligent information society in

C. Stephanidis et al. (Eds.): HCII 2022, CCIS 1655, pp. 632–640, 2022.
https://doi.org/10.1007/978-3-031-19682-9_80

which all things and humans are connected, and automation is maximized based on super connectivity, super-intelligence, and predictability. Artificial intelligence technologies that guide this changing trend expand into different areas that consumers experience [1].

In addition to incorporating artificial intelligence technology into traditional products and services to optimize consumer usage patterns and environments, artificial intelligence products and services with new benefits are also widely used in consumers' lives [2]. Puntoni et al. emphasized that AI-based products and services could significantly solve poverty, a lack of education, chronic illnesses, and racial discrimination and, suggested that consumers live happier, healthier, and more efficient lives with the help of AI technology [3]. In terms of how AI-based products and services are penetrating consumers' daily lives, consumers who are unfamiliar with AI technology or reluctant to use such products or services are likely to be alienated from the intelligent information society [4].

Previous studies have been conducted to understand consumer acceptance of AI-based products and services, which have mainly focused on the influence of users' personal characteristics and social influences on the intention to use specific technology-based products or services [5–7]. However, there are limitations in understanding the overall consumer acceptance of AI technology in that most previous studies have focused on specific cases of products and services based on AI technology. Since the field of products and services to which AI technology is applied is greatly expanding, it is necessary to approach the general attitude and acceptance of consumers toward universal AI technology. Moreover, through the discussion on how consumers facing social change centered on intelligent information technology have an awareness of such a changing society, implications for future consumer adaptation can be obtained.

Therefore, while AI technology and related industries are rapidly growing, examining consumers' intention to accept AI technology is meaningful in that it examines consumers' lives as they adapt to life changes led by technological advancement. In the current study, we investigate the factors that affect consumers' acceptance of AI technology. In particular, we attempted to verify how consumers' self-efficacy in using technologies, positive perception of the Intelligent Information Society, and perception of the usefulness of AI technology affect consumers' acceptance of AI technology.

2 Theoretical Background

Self-efficacy. Self-efficacy has been applied and developed in many fields of sociology, psychology, and consumer behavior [8–10]. According to [8], a sense of self-efficacy can be seen as "not with the skills one has but with judgments of what one can do with the skills one possesses." This refers to the subjective perception that an individual believes that they can overcome the situation with appropriate. Many studies have shown that self-efficacy has a static effect on perceived utility and acceptance of technologies and new products [5, 11–14]. Therefore, technology self-efficiency, which reflects whether new technologies can be used well in the context of AI technologies, may affect AI acceptance intentions and perceived usefulness to AI technologies [4]. Thus, those with high technology self-efficiency are confident that they will adapt well to AI technology and have a positive perception of the intelligent information society where AI technology is applied. Therefore, we established the following hypothesis.

634   X. Li et al.

H1a: Technology self-efficacy has a positive effect on the positive perception of the intelligent information society.

H1b: Technology self-efficacy has a positive effect on the perception of the usefulness of AI technology.

H1c: Technology self-efficacy has a positive effect on the intention to accept AI technology.

Perception of the Intelligent Information Society. Intelligent information society refers to a society in which intelligent information technology combined with data collected through advanced information and communication technology infrastructure (Internet of Things, Cloud Computing, BigData, Mobile) is utilized in various fields [15]. In an intelligent information society, consumers use AI technology to benefit and create new values. Thus, the perception of the intelligent information society affects the attitude toward AI technology. Furthermore, the study by [16] revealed that the perception of a hyper-connected society has a static effect on the perceived usefulness of AI technology and the intention to accept AI technology. Moreover, previous studies have shown that the more consumers perceive a new technology or product as useful, the greater the intention to use it [5, 6, 17]. Therefore, we established the following hypotheses.

H2a: The positive perception of the intelligent information society has a positive effect on the perception of the usefulness of AI technology.

H2b: The positive perception of the intelligent information society has a positive effect on the intention to accept AI technology.

H3: The perception of the usefulness of AI technology has a positive effect on the intention to accept AI technology.

H4a: The relationship between self-efficacy and AI technology acceptance is mediated by the positive perception of the intelligent information society.

H4b: The relationship between self-efficacy and AI technology acceptance is mediated by the perception of the usefulness of AI technology.

3   Method

This study was analyzed using The Report on Digital Divide 2019 survey data provided by the National Information Society Agency [18]. As shown in Table 1, items corresponding to each variable are measured from 1 (*Strongly disagree*) to 4 points (*Strongly agree*). To test the hypothesis, this study was analyzed through the Hayes Process macro.

Table 1. Variables and scale items.

Variables	Items	Mean	SD
Technology self-efficacy (TSE)	I adapt well to new technologies and products	2.71	.73
Positive Perception of the Intelligent Information Society (PPS)	In the intelligent information society, new jobs will be created, humans will be immersed in creative work, and work efficiency and accuracy will increase according to technological advances In the intelligent information society, innovations seen in movies such as drones, virtual reality, self-driving cars, and home robots will become commonplace Since the intelligent information society is human-centered, it will provide convenience and safety in life with intelligent information technology Through technological advances, the intelligent information society will solve social problems such as low birth rates, aging population, low growth, and social risks Intelligent information technology will highly improve productivity and efficiency and provide an opportunity for new industrial growth	2.86	.45
Perception of the Usefulness of AI Technology (PU)	Artificial intelligence (AI) technology will make my life convenient AI technology will provide more economic opportunities AI technology will allow me to receive better information device services I will get better information through AI technology	2.88	.54
Intention to Accept AI Technology (IAA)	Even if I pay more, I intend to purchase devices or services if AI functions are implemented When a service with AI technology comes out, I actively use it	2.57	.67

Note. Items measured on a scale ranging from 1 "strongly disagree" to 4 "strongly agree."

4   Results

Table 2 shows the general characteristics of the study participants. In the case of gender, the ratio of males and females was similar. The proportion of each age group was similar, but those in their 60s or older (26.8%) were the most common. In terms of education level, 35.6% had a university degree or higher, and 64.4% had less than a High School degree. Household income was 3.5 million or less (39.9%), 3.5–5.0 million (32.4%), and 5.0 million or higher (27.7%). Finally, the ratio between those living in Seoul, Incheon, and Gyeonggi and those who do not live in these areas was similar.

Table 2. General characteristics of participants (n = 6,073).

Demographic characteristics		Frequency (%)
Gender	Female	3,060 (50.4)
	Male	3,013 (49.6)
Age	20s	1,048 (17.3)
	30s	1,011 (16.6)
	40s	1,181 (19.4)
	50s	1,203 (19.8)
	60s or higher	1,630 (26.8)
Education	High school or less	3,912 (64.4)
	College or higher	2,161 (35.6)
Household Income (KRW[a])	3.5 million or less	2,421 (39.9)
	3.5–5.0 million	1,969 (32.4)
	5.0 million or higher	1,683 (27.7)
Region	noncapital region	3,018 (49.7)
	capital region[b]	3,055 (50.3)

Notes. [a]KRW 1 million = USD 935.89; [b]Seoul, Incheon, and Gyeonggi.

In this study, through model 6 in the Hayes PROCESS macro, a 95% confidence interval for the indirect effect was obtained by 5,000 bootstrapping resamples [19]. As shown in Fig. 1 and Table 3, we found that technology self-efficacy, positive perception of the intelligent information society, and perception of the usefulness of AI technology positively affect the intention to accept AI technology. Furthermore, all previously established hypotheses were adopted, as the positive perception of the intelligent information society and the perception of the usefulness of AI technology mediate between a sense of technology self-efficacy and the intention to accept AI technology.

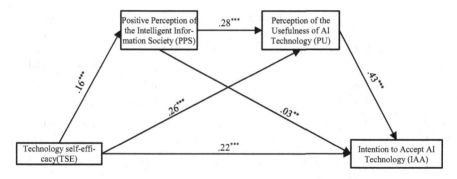

Fig. 1. Research model

Table 3. Results of mediation analysis.

Dependent variable	Independent variable	R^2	B	95% LLCI	95% ULCI
Positive Perception of the Intelligent Information Society (PPS)	Age	.363***	−0.19***	−0.01	<0.00
	Gender (Male = 1)		0.02	<0.00	0.04
	Education (College or higher = 1)		0.05***	0.02	0.07
	Region (capital region = 1)		−0.03*	−0.04	<0.00
	Household Income (Middle-income = 1)		0.07***	0.04	0.09
	Household Income (High-income = 1)		0.07***	0.04	0.09
	TSE		0.16***	0.08	0.12
Perception of the Usefulness of AI Technology (PU)	Age	.338***	−0.17***	−0.01	<0.00
	Gender (Male = 1)		0.002	−0.02	0.02
	Education (College or higher = 1)		0.05***	0.03	0.08
	Region (capital region = 1)		0.06***	0.04	0.08
	Household Income (Middle-income = 1)		0.03*	0.01	0.06
	Household Income (High-income = 1)		0.05***	0.03	0.09

(*continued*)

Table 3. (*continued*)

Dependent variable	Independent variable	R^2	B	95% LLCI	95% ULCI
	TSE		0.26^{***}	0.17	0.21
	PPS		0.28^{***}	0.31	0.37
Intention to Accept AI Technology (IAA)	Age	$.468^{***}$	-0.12^{***}	-0.01	<0.00
	Gender (Male $= 1$)		0.03^{***}	0.02	0.07
	Education (College or higher $= 1$)		0.04^{***}	0.02	0.08
	Region (capital region $= 1$)		0.05^{***}	0.04	0.09
	Household Income (Middle-income $= 1$)		0.02^{*}	>0.00	0.06
	Household Income (High-income $= 1$)		0.04^{***}	0.02	0.09
	TSE		0.22^{***}	0.18	0.22
	PPS		0.03^{**}	0.01	0.08
	PU		0.43^{***}	0.50	0.55
Total effect	Direct effect	–	0.20	0.18	0.22
	Total indirect effect		0.12	0.11	0.17
	TSE → PPS → PU		0.005	>0.00	0.01
	TSE → PU → IAA		0.100	0.09	0.11
	TSE → PPS → PU → IAA		0.017	0.01	0.02

Notes. $^{*}p < .05$, $^{***}p < .001$

5   Conclusion

This study examined the effect of technology self-efficacy and positive perception of the intelligent information society on the intention to accept AI technology by using *The Report on Digital Divide 2019* survey data.

First, a sense of self-efficacy has been found to have a static effect on the intention to accept AI technology. This seems to have led to the same results as the previous research. Given that behavioral economists' information and education alone are not sufficient to induce behavioral change [20, 21], it suggests that the government should not only support consumers' education to strengthen AI technology capabilities, but also strengthen consumers' self-efficacy.

Second, consumers' positive perception of the intelligent information society had a partial mediating effect between the consumers' acceptance of innovative technologies and their intention to accept AI-based products/services; the perceived usefulness of AI technology also had a partial mediating effect between the two variables. Moreover, the double mediation effects of the positive perception of the intelligent information society and perceived usefulness of AI technology were significant in the relationship between consumers' acceptance of innovative technologies and their intention to accept AI-based products/services. This means that the more positively consumers think about the intelligent information society, the higher the perception of AI technology being useful, and ultimately the higher the intention to accept AI-based products/services.

This study confirmed that when consumers judge their intention to accept AI technology, they not only consider that they can adapt well to AI technology but also judge the social environment, which is the perception of the intelligent information society [22]. Thus, it is necessary to create a suitable social technology environment so that consumers can benefit from new products or services, AI technology, and to make efforts to positively recognize the intelligent information society by providing learning opportunities and exploring new possibilities.

References

1. Guk, K.W.: Examples of applications by AI technology and industry sectors. Weekly Technol. Trends **20**, 15–27 (2019)
2. Li, X., Lim, H., Yeo, H., Hwang, H.: Text mining of online news, social media, and consumer review on artificial intelligence service. Fam. Environ. Res. **59**(1), 23–43 (2021)
3. Puntoni, S., Reczek, R.W., Giesler, M., Botti, S.: Consumers and artificial intelligence: an experiential perspective. J. Mark. **85**(1), 131–151 (2021)
4. Hong, J.W.: I was born to love AI: the influence of social status on AI self-efficacy and intentions to use AI. Int. J. Commun. **16**, 172–191 (2022)
5. Kim, B.S., Woo, H.J.: A study on the intention to use AI speakers: focusing on extended technology acceptance model. J. Korea Contents Assoc. **19**(9), 1–10 (2019)
6. Jeon, S., Lee, J., Lee, J.: A study on the users intention to adopt an intelligent service: focusing on the factors affecting the perceived necessity of conversational AI service. J. Korea Technol. Innov. Soc. **22**(2), 242–264 (2019)
7. Jung, J., Huh, J., Park, H., Shin, B.: A study on acceptance factors and market segmentation of smart device: focused on UTAUT and personal innovativeness. Korean J. Bus. Adm. **31**(1), 27–47 (2018)
8. Bandura, A.: Self-efficacy: toward a unifying theory of behavioral change. Psychol. Rev. **84**(2), 191–215 (1977)
9. Bandura, A.: Self-efficacy mechanism in human agency. Am. Psychol. **37**(2), 122–147 (1982)
10. Bandura, A., Freeman, W.H., Lightsey, R.: Self-Efficacy: The Exercise of Control. W. H. Freeman, New York (1999)
11. Zhao, X., Mattila, A.S., Tao, L.S.E.: The role of post-training self-efficacy in customers' use of self service technologies. Int. J. Serv. Ind. Manag. **19**(4), 492–505 (2008)
12. Wang, C., Harris, J., Patterson, P.: The roles of habit, self-efficacy, and satisfaction in driving continued use of self-service technologies: a longitudinal study. J. Serv. Res. **16**(3), 400–414 (2013)
13. Zhang, X., Han, X., Dang, Y., Meng, F., Guo, X., Lin, J.: User acceptance of mobile health services from users' perspectives: the role of self-efficacy and response-efficacy in technology acceptance. Inform. Health Soc. Care **42**(2), 194–206 (2017)
14. Bakke, S., Henry, R.: Unraveling the mystery of new technology use: an investigation into the interplay of desire for control, computer self-efficacy, and personal innovativeness. AIS Trans. Hum.-Comput. Interact. **7**(4), 270–293 (2015)
15. Jang, D.H.: An exploratory study for the direction and tasks for innovating school system in the intelligent information society. J, Digit. Convergence **15**(12), 127–136 (2017)

16. Han, M.: Analysis of the public's intention to use the government's artificial intelligence (AI)-based services: focusing on public values and extended technology acceptance model. J. Korea Contents Assoc. **21**(8), 388–402 (2021)

17. Chae, J.M., Cho, H.S., Lee, J.H.: A study on consumer acceptance toward the commercialized smart clothing. Sci. Emot. Sensibility **12**(2), 181–192 (2009)

18. Ministry of Science and ICT: National Information Society Agency: The Report on the Digital Divide (2019). https://www.nia.or.kr/site/nia_kor/ex/bbs/View.do;jsessionid=43B 9A1B6EF6801C538C288E17D435532.2894582dd32606361891?cbIdx=81623&bcIdx= 21837&parentSeq=21837

19. Hayes, A.F.: Introduction to Mediation, Moderation, and Conditional Process Analysis: A Regression-Based Approach. Guilford Publications, New York (2013)

20. Gilovich, T., Griffin, D., Kahneman, D.: Heuristics and Biases: The Psychology of Intuitive Judgment. Cambridge University Press, Cambridge (2002)

21. Zweig, J.: Your Money and Your Brain: How the New Science of Neuroeconomics Can Help Make You Rich. Simon and Schuster, New York (2007)

22. Park, J.H.: Technology innovation policy of renewable energy in Korea from the perspective of transformatice innovation policy. J. Korea Technol. Innov. Soc. **23**(2), 234–257 (2020)

From Principled to Applied AI Ethics in Organizations: A Scoping Review

Aude Marie Marcoux[1]([✉]) [iD] and Joé T. Martineau[2] [iD]

[1] Université du Québec À Montréal, Montréal H3C 3P8, Canada
Marcoux.aude_marie@courrier.uqam.ca
[2] HEC Montréal, Montréal H3T 2A7, Canada
joe.trempe-martineau@hec.ca

Abstract. The gap between the high-level normative ethical principles aiming at guiding the development and the implantation of responsible artificial intelligence (AI) technologies, and the concrete application and practices of AI ethics in organizations is large and there is an urgent need for moving the discussion about AI ethics from theory to practicality. Building that bridge between knowing and doing in AI ethics is now a necessity to assist organizations into supporting the responsible development and use of AI. Therefore, the goal of this scoping review is to explore the relevant literature providing guidance on the matter of AI business ethics strategies and practices in organizations. From 490 unique results, 352 relevant documents were identified at this early stage of this scoping review in progress (title and abstract screening). After the next rounds of full-text screening, topics will be extracted from the included literature and summarized across different strategies and practices that will be at the core of this review. By keeping the focus on the actionability and practicability of the provided recommendations, following a pluralistic vision of ethics, this study will not only contribute to the advancement of knowledge and practice in AI ethics, but also increase the likelihood of AI ethics to be embedded in practice in organizations. Accordingly, the main goal of this paper is to provide a concrete answer to the question: What are the strategies, practices and practical solutions aiming at bridging the gap between principled and applied AI ethics in organizations proposed in the literature?

Keywords: Ethics of AI · Artificial intelligence · Ethics tools · Applied ethics · Formalization of ethics · Business ethics practices · AI ethics as practice · Scoping review

1 Introduction

The adoption of artificial intelligence (AI) technologies by organizations allows for important opportunities, but entails a variety of challenges in company restructuring, training needs, and cultural transformation, among others. It also raises several serious ethical questions such as risks of discrimination, invasion of privacy, lack of transparency and accountability, and unwanted biases (Pasquale 2015; O'Neil 2016; Mittelstadt et al. 2016). Many reports aimed to define the normative frameworks that should delineate

© The Author(s), under exclusive license to Springer Nature Switzerland AG 2022
C. Stephanidis et al. (Eds.): HCII 2022, CCIS 1655, pp. 641–646, 2022.
https://doi.org/10.1007/978-3-031-19682-9_81

those challenges have been published (Jobin et al. 2019; Fjeld 2020), but their integration in the day-to-day business practice in organizations is still a challenge. Thus, many suggested that "principles alone cannot guarantee ethical AI" (Mittelstadt 2019; Morley et al. 2021).

The gap between AI ethical principles and practice is large and there is an urgent need for a translation from the "what" of AI ethics to the "how" of applied AI ethics (Morley et al. 2020). In other words, moving the discussion about AI ethics from theory to practicality, building the bridge between knowing and doing, is now a necessity for AI ethics to be embedded in practice, for a real and concrete responsible development and use of AI.

The aim of this paper is to perform a scoping review of the relevant literature providing guidance or actionable quality criteria on the matter of AI business ethics strategies and practices in organizations. Accordingly, the goal of this scoping review is to answer the following question: What are the strategies, practices and practical solutions aiming at bridging the gap between principled and applied AI ethics in organizations proposed in the literature? Results will be extracted from the identified literature and summarized across different strategies and practices that will be at the core of this review. Finally, by keeping the focus on the actionability and practicability of the provided recommendations, following a pluralistic view of ethics, this study aims at not only contributing to the advancement of knowledge and practice in AI ethics, but also to increase the likelihood of AI ethics to be embedded in practice in organizations.

2 Methods

2.1 Data Collection

This review is guided by the Preferred Reporting Items for Systematic Review and Meta-Analysis (PRISMA) Protocols and follows the systematic steps of the PRISMA-Extension for Scoping Reviews guideline (Tricco et al. 2018).

The search strategy includes scientific articles published between March 2012 and March 2022 and has been conducted using two online databases containing a diversity of technical, ethical, medical, and social science academic literatures: the search engines Scopus and ProQuest.

The search string contained a combination of search terms correlated to: 1) one main domain which is ethics or human-centered; 2) two verticals within-field perspective which are topics related to practice and organization; 3) and one context-field orientation which is artificial intelligence (including deep learning or machine learning or data mining) (see Tables 1 and 2).

Table 1. Search terms used to search Scopus and ProQuest.

Domain: Ethics	Vertical 1: Practice	Vertical 2: Organization	AI	Databases
ethic* human-centered	implement* practic* bridg* embedd* appl* strateg* operationaliz* operationalis* tool* manag* govern*	business industry organisation organization govern* administration	"AI" "artificial intelligence" "deep learning" "machine learning" "data mining" "AI4SG"	Scopus ProQuest

Table 2. The search string

Database	
Scopus	(TITLE-ABS-KEY ((ethic* OR "human-centered")) W/10 TITLE-ABS-KEY ((implement* OR "practic*" OR bridg* OR embedd* OR appl* OR strateg* OR operationaliz* OR operationalis* OR tool* OR manag* OR govern*)) AND TITLE-ABS-KEY (business OR industry OR organisation OR organization OR govern* OR administration) AND AUTHKEY (("AI" OR "artificial intelligence" OR "deep learning" OR "machine learning" OR "data mining" OR "AI4SG"))) AND (LIMIT-TO (PUBYEAR , 2022) OR LIMIT-TO (PUBYEAR , 2021) OR LIMIT-TO (PUBYEAR , 2020) OR LIMIT-TO (PUBYEAR , 2019) OR LIMIT-TO (PUBYEAR , 2018) OR LIMIT-TO (PUBYEAR , 2017) OR LIMIT-TO (PUBYEAR , 2016) OR LIMIT-TO (PUBYEAR , 2015) OR LIMIT-TO (PUBYEAR , 2014) OR LIMIT-TO (PUBYEAR , 2013) OR LIMIT-TO (PUBYEAR , 2012)) AND (LIMIT-TO (LANGUAGE , "English"))
ProQuest	noft(ethic* OR "human-centered") NEAR/10 noft(implement* OR practic* OR bridg* OR embedd* OR appl* OR strateg* OR translat* OR operationaliz* OR operationalis* OR tool* OR manag* OR govern*) AND noft(business OR industry OR organisation OR organization OR govern* OR administration) AND su("AI" OR "artificial intelligence" OR "deep learning" OR "machine learning" OR "data mining" OR "AI4SG") + Peer-reviewed + English + last ten years

2.2 Eligibility Criteria

The first stage of title and abstract screening was based on a set of inclusion criteria: quantitative, qualitative, mixed-method, and conceptual/theorical peer-reviewed papers were included in order to consider different aspects of AI ethics as organizational practices, and strategies. Specifically, peer-reviewed primary sources published between the period of March 2012 to March 2022, and written in English, were included. We also used the following exclusion criteria for our scoping review process: papers were excluded if they didn't fit into the conceptual framework of the study, which is focused on actionable and practicable AI ethics strategies and practices. In order words, papers were excluded if they didn't focus on proposing solutions for bridging the gap between principled and applied AI ethics in organizations, if they didn't address the translation from theory to practice in AI ethics.

For the second stage consisting of full-text screening, we refined our exclusion criteria by adding the following: In full-text screening, we excluded sources who only mentioned in passage that this gap needs to be addressed in order to focus on sources that proposed concrete solution to be harnessed by organizations.

2.3 Data Management and Screening/Extraction Process

For the data management and screening/extraction process, we used Covidence, a collaborative systematic review management software. We followed a three-stage approach consisting of: 1) screening of titles and abstracts by three independent reviewers (2 votes needed per screening); 2) screening of full-text articles by two independent reviewers and, in case of disagreement, by a third reviewer; 3) full text coding by two independent reviewers.

3 Initial Results

Initially, 582 studies were imported for titles and abstracts screening. After 92 duplicates were removed, our search consisted of 490 documents to be screened. Among those, 138 were judged irrelevant (see Fig. 1) at the first stage of title and abstract screening.

After the step of screening for titles and abstract, 68 screening results were in conflict, meaning the intercoder agreement was overall of 86%. All conflicts were then resolved during a research meeting. A total of 352 results were then eligible to the next step, which is in progress, i.e., the full text screening for eligibility. Afterwards, reference lists of the final included studies will also be checked for relevant articles.

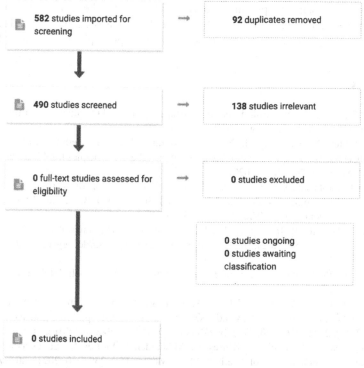

Fig. 1. PRISMA flow diagram (in progress).

4   Discussion and Final Steps

After the next rounds of full-text screening and extraction of this scoping review in progress, topics will be extracted from the identified literature and summarized across different strategies and practices that will be at the core of this review. Accordingly, the main goal of this scoping review is to provide a concrete answer the following question: What are the strategies, practices and practical solutions aiming at bridging the gap between principled and applied AI ethics in organizations proposed in the literature?

At this stage of our scoping review in progress, we see some abductive insights. If AI ethics isn't just a matter of principles, we suggest it is not only a question of tools or of one-size-fits-all solution. A part of the business ethics literature advocates a dynamic understanding and a pragmatic and pluralistic perspective of ethics (Buchholz and Rosenthal 1996; Martineau et al. 2016). Indeed, one may ask about what are the business ethics strategies and practices already formalized in organizations that could be mobilized and adapted to tackle the ethical challenges related to the adoption of AI in organizations? We tentatively argue at this point that to foster a real integration of AI ethics by AI practitioners when it comes to their day job, AI ethics must be embedded into business ethics practices. To really and concretely support the development of responsible AI, a pluralistic view of ethics practices and programs orientations is required.

This represents, in our opinion, not only a contribution to the advancement of knowledge and practice in AI business ethics, but this study increases the likelihood of AI ethics to be embedded in practice, so to bridge the gap between principles and applied AI ethics.

References

Buchholz, R., Rosenthal, S.: Toward a new understanding of moral pluralism. Bus. Ethics Q. **6**(3), 263–275 (1996). https://doi.org/10.2307/3857459

Fjeld, J., Achten, N., Hilligoss, H., Nagy, A., Srikumar, M.: Principled artificial intelligence: mapping consensus in ethical and rights-based approaches to principles for AI. Berkman Klein Center Research Publication (2020)

Martineau, J.T., Johnson, K.J., Pauchant, T.C.: The pluralist theory of ethics programs orientations and ideologies: an empirical study anchored in requisite variety. J. Bus. Ethics **142**(4), 791–815 (2016). https://doi.org/10.1007/s10551-016-3183-x

Mittelstadt, B.D., Allo, P., Taddeo, M., Wachter, S., Floridi, L.: The ethics of algorithms: mapping the debate. Big Data Soc. **3**(2), 2053951716679679 (2016). https://doi.org/10.1177/205395171 6679679

Mittelstadt, B.: Principles alone cannot guarantee ethical AI. Nat. Mach. Intell. **1**(11), 501–507 (2019)

Morley, J., Floridi, L., Kinsey, L., Elhalal, A.: From what to how: an initial review of publicly available AI ethics tools, methods and research to translate principles into practices. Sci. Eng. Ethics **26**(4), 2141–2168 (2020). https://doi.org/10.1007/s11948-019-00165-5

Morley, J., Elhalal, A., Garcia, F., Kinsey, L., Mökander, J., Floridi, L.: Ethics as a service: a pragmatic operationalisation of AI ethics. Minds Mach. **31**(2), 239–256 (2021). https://doi.org/10.1007/s11023-021-09563-w

O'Neil, C.: Weapons of Math Destruction: How Big Data Increases Inequality and Threatens Democracy. Broadway Books (2016)

Pasquale, F.: The Black Box Society: The Secret Algorithms That Control Money and Information, Reprint Harvard University Press, Cambridge (2015)

Tricco, A.C., et al.: PRISMA extension for scoping reviews (PRISMA-ScR): checklist and explanation. Ann. Intern. Med. **169**(7), 467–473 (2018)

Does the COVID-19 Pandemic have Implications for Machine Ethics?

Rosae Martín-Peña[✉]

Department of Philosophy, University of Valladolid - UVa, Valladolid, Spain
Rosaesther.martin@alumnos.uva.es

Abstract. Algorithms have advanced in status from supporting human decision-making to making decisions for themselves. The fundamental issue here is the relationship between Big Data and algorithms, or how algorithms empower data with direction and purpose. In this paper, I provide a conceptual framework for analyzing and improving ethical decision-making in Human-AI interaction. On the one hand, I examine the challenges and the limitations facing the field of Machine Ethics and Explainability in its aim to provide and justify ethical decisions. On the other hand, I propose connecting counterfactual explanations with the emotion of regret, as requirements for improving ethical decision-making in novel situations and under uncertainty. To test whether this conceptual framework has empirical value, I analyze the COVID-19 epidemic in terms of "what might have been" to answer the following question: could some of the unintended consequences of this health crisis have been avoided if the available data had been used differently before the crisis happened and as it unfolded?

Keywords: Machine ethics · Explainability · Counterfactual explanations · Regret · Ethical decision-making · Human-AI interaction · COVID-19

1 Introduction

The power of algorithms is expressed in their ability to present choices, to classify, to prioritize what is important, and, above all, to decide what information should be made visible to the user. However, the trust we place in the decisions made by algorithms reinforces our belief that they routinely make the right choice. The consequence is that AI systems are now expected to be able to act in morally appropriate ways. The emerging discipline researching this goal is called Machine Ethics.

However, while this discipline has been growing in popularity, it cannot be guaranteed that this field does not have inherent limitations. To some scholars in the AI community, this comes as no surprise, because in normative ethics and moral psychology morality does not lend itself to an algorithmic solution. That does not mean that in many situations human-AI interactive systems could not improve their moral behavior by just following the prescriptions of something akin to an algorithm. The main challenges rise to the surface under novel and uncertain situations because codified moral rules are often ambiguous and sometimes must be broken. As a result, there is still a persistent disagreement regarding the situations in which exceptions should be accepted.

C. Stephanidis et al. (Eds.): HCII 2022, CCIS 1655, pp. 647–654, 2022.
https://doi.org/10.1007/978-3-031-19682-9_82

In the face of this dilemma, it needs to be designed with the ability to explain its decisions and should be augmented with a Machine-Explanation component. Therefore, the issue of explainability is directly connected to the lack of transparency in automatic decision-making. The open question is what sort of explanations one can expect from these systems. Explainability or opacity was not a major issue for traditional algorithms, or at least not at the same level that it is for modern machine learning models and artificial neural networks. However, it is relevant for this paper to point out that these limitations are not only found in machine-learning sub-symbolic models, but it is a hallmark of how the human mind works and makes decisions. Much scientific research consists of activities (physical and intellectual) that generate causal chains, such as observation, experimentation, manipulation, and inference. These capabilities are different from the simple act of providing and receiving explanations.

The ability to manipulate a system into new intended states can be considered a sign of understanding. In other words, understanding requires the ability to think counterfactually. So, what is the purpose of counterfactuals? The primary function of counterfactual thinking is centered on the management and coordination of ongoing behavior. Thinking about "what could or might have been" influences performance and expedites improvement, activating several mechanisms. Counterfactual thoughts are deeply connected to goals and are a component of regulatory mechanisms that keep behavior on track, particularly within social interactions. In the same way that counterfactuals work with the "what might have been", regret has a similar function, but from the viewpoint of emotion, enabling a change in future behavior.

I propose a conceptual framework that links counterfactual explanations and regret because I suggest that both dimensions must often work in tandem: they are necessary requirements at the cognitive and affective levels that are able to influence decision-making and, therefore in breaking patterns of behavior that could be improved. The COVID-19 epidemic analyzed on the basis of the frame problem and as a counterfactual event in its double dimension, serves to evaluate whether the measures implemented could have been subject to improvement in human-AI interactions.

2 From the Limitations of Machine Ethics to the Challenges of Explainability

2.1 Machine Ethics: Designing Ethical Decisions

A central argument advanced by machine ethicists about the need for having ethical or moral machines is that their reasoning ability and ethical decisions could be even better than those of humans. According to the authors van Wynsberghe and Robbins (2019) "the assumption is that a robot could be better at moral decision-making than a human, given that it would be impartial, unemotional, consistent, and rational every time it made a decision". Such conceptions are grounded in the way moral judgments are understood. The rationalist approach, which represented the mainstream until a few decades ago, considers emotions an impediment to reasoning in an "objective" way. Nevertheless, the fact that emotions play a role in moral judgment has been demonstrated through psychological and neurological research.

Important advances are, for example, the somatic marker hypothesis postulated by Damasio (1994). In his neuroscientific studies, Damasio has stressed the importance of emotions in morality. In parallel, Greene and others have conducted fMRI investigations of emotional engagement during moral judgment.

The current situation is that "there is no moral epistemology which does not have serious philosophical objections and therefore presents a barrier to being reduced to a programming language" (van Wynsberghe and Robbins 2019).

In addition, and somehow surprisingly, only a few authors have pondered a multi-theoretical approach in which machines can apply interchangeably different theories, depending on the type of situation.

The technical dimension is another aspect that the field of machine ethics has to deal with. Obstacles in this area are related to what is called the "availability of the code, which is predominantly lacking" (Tolmeijer et al. 2021). This issue is intrinsically linked to the need for increasing transparency in algorithmic decision-making. Therefore, one way to do this could be by explaining and justifying decisions.

Baum et al. (2018) argue that moral behavior, "even if it were verifiable and verified, is not enough to establish trust in an autonomous system". It needs to be provided with the ability to explain decisions and should thus be augmented by a Machine Explanation component. The corresponding subfield of AI is known as "Explainable AI" (XAI), or just Explainability.

To conclude with machine ethics, regarding its limitations, I argue that the ability of machines to explain the ethical reasons behind their decision-making could appear to be a starting point for integrating them into the human moral system. However, in the next section, the field of explainability is discussed and analyzed with the aim of detecting if other challenges that do not allow algorithms to meet the required standards of trust and transparency to date.

2.2 Explainability: The Challenge of Persuading with Reasons

The field of Explainability in Artificial Intelligence (AI), or explainable artificial intelligence (XAI), emerged as a topic of research "of the need of conveying safety and trust to users in the "how" and "why" of automated decision-making in different applications such as autonomous driving, medical diagnosis, or banking and finance" (Confalonieri et al. 2021).

According to philosophers such as Dreyfus (1978) and cognitive scientists drawing on phenomenology (Valera et al. 1991; Varela 1996), "the success of symbolic AI was mainly limited to virtual and contained environments such as games and logical puzzles". The inherent limitations of hand-crafted traditional algorithms led to a growing interest in whether machines could learn on their own, with the ability to perform different cognitive tasks inspired by how the human brain works.

A leap took place. Current machine learning models and artificial neural networks sprang out of the "connectionist" paradigm in cognitive science and AI (Russell and Norvig 2009). Maclure (2021) describes it as follows: "artificial neural networks are in at least a superficial sense inspired by how neurons activate and are connected through synapsis in biological brains".

Machine learning algorithms are massively inductive. "During training, a deep learning system adjusts the weights of these links so as to improve its performance. If trained on a decision task, it essentially derives its own method of decision-making, much as we would expect of an intelligent system. But there is the rub. In neural networks, these processes run independently of human control, so that transparency inevitably becomes an issue: it is simply not known in advance what rules will be used to handle unforeseen information" (Zerilli et al. 2018).

While machine learning sub-symbolic models are winning the battle for accuracy, they are losing the battle for transparency. However, Maclure (2021) points out: that "deep artificial neural networks are not significantly more opaque than the human brains/minds". Maclure (2021) calls this "the argument from the limitation of human reasoning". That is, lack of transparency and opacity is also a hallmark of human reasoning or the human mind, and it is, therefore, worth exploring further the kinds of explanations that can contribute to such transparency.

Another weak point in current explanatory models of AI black boxes is that many researchers build explanatory models for themselves, rather than for the intended users. As Lipton (2009) argues, "much empirical inquiry consists in activities-physical and intellectual-that generate causal information, activities such as observation, experimentation, manipulation, and inference".

These activities are distinct from the activity of giving and receiving explanations". If one examines the information that drives machine learning today, we find that it is almost entirely statistical. Learning machines improve their performance by optimizing parameters over a stream of sensory inputs received from the environment, but such machines in operation today can answer reliably questions about situations not encountered before (Pearl 2018). In fact, the ability to manipulate a system into new desired states is a sign of understanding. In other words, understanding requires the ability to think counterfactually (de Regt and Dieks 2005).

3   Linking Counterfactual Explanations and Regret as a Conceptual Framework for Behavior Regulation

Some explanations that one finds obey more to correlations than to causality because sometimes finding the first causes of certain effects is not easy. In some ways, this is reminiscent of what was said about the black box, both for understanding the limitations of the human mind and that of artificial intelligent systems. In addition, and according to Miller (2017), people are not satisfied with mere direct explanations in form of causal relations between the antecedent and consequent but also require knowing why an alternative (or opposing) event could not have happened.

For example, many of us might have wondered whether the coronavirus pandemic represents an event that could have been foreseen. This type of "thinking about what might have been, about alternatives to our pasts, is central to human thinking and emotion" (Epstude and Roese 2008).

So, what is the purpose of counterfactuals? While the general understanding of the concept of counterfactuals is shared among researchers, "there exist several interpretations of this phenomenon" (Stepin et al. 2019). That explains why in this paper I focus on the functional perspective of counterfactual thinking as theorized by Epstude and Roese (2008) "as a useful, beneficial, and utterly necessary component of behavior regulation". Besides, specifically, and relevant for this research, is the work of Byrne (2019), who focuses on what kind of counterfactuals are most useful for explainability. This challenge, according to Byrne (2019), lies in the fact that the number of counterfactuals that can be generated to explain any event is potentially limitless and it is a non-trivial problem to identify which counterfactuals best facilitate the construction of an explanatory model. Given this limitation, I propose to analyze the second element of this conceptual framework for behavior regulation, which has an impact on decision making, is the emotion of regret.

Regret shapes multiple aspects of decision processes, from avoidance of decisions to shifting responsibility for the decision, to reframing decision alternatives (Zeelenberg and Pieters 2007). Regret stimulates information search about decision alternatives (Shani and Zeelenberg 2007) and motivates choice switching (Marcatto et al. 2015).

What is most relevant about the proposed framework is that going deeper into how these elements can work together in tandem might help us understand ethical decision-making processes in Human-AI interaction better and thus serve as a tool for those interested in "post-decision processes and outcomes" (Buchanan et al. 2016). To test whether this conceptual framework has empirical value, in the next section I analyse the COVID-19 epidemic as a counterfactual event in its double dimension and defined as a conditional statement in the form: "If event X had not occurred, event Y would not have occurred" (Lewis 1973).

This statement as a counterfactual explanation can be read as follows: "if information or data about a possible coronavirus epidemic had not been ignored, the trajectory of the most harmful effects of the pandemic could have been avoided". On the side of the emotion of regret this conditional statement implies the following: "if decision-makers could have felt the effects of this pandemic with the information that was available, they might have acted differently in the past".

4 Managing the Epidemic of COVID-19: "What Might Have Been"

Could some of the unintended consequences of this health crisis have been avoided if the available information had been used before it happened? In 2007 the article "Severe Acute Respiratory Syndrome Coronavirus as Agent of Emerging and Reemerging Infection" (Cheng et al. 2007) appeared. The introduction, almost like a futuristic tale portrays and reminds us of the beginning of the pandemic in Wuhan in December 2019–January 2020. We should pay attention to the question these researchers raised in their conclusions: "Should we be ready for the reemergence of SARS?".

In 2012, similarly, the Robert Koch Institute (RKI) developed the scenario of a global coronavirus outbreak. The document, which can be found on the Internet, became popular through an article published on April 07, 2020, in the German magazine "Der Spiegel" under the title: "Das Pandemie-Planspiel" (i.e., "the pandemic simulation game". In the subtitle of the article, the following question was posed: "Hätten sie besser auf die aktuelle Krise vorbereitet sein müssen? So einfach ist es nicht" (i.e., Should they have been better prepared for the current crisis? It's not that simple).

While these documents represent examples of warnings, the actual detection of the virus was made possible by novel technologies. According to Niiler (2020), BluDot was able to employ the services of AI-driven algorithms, to analyze data gathered from sources such as news reports, air ticketing, and animal disease outbreaks, to predict that the world was facing a new type of virus outbreak. Besides that, prediction, this startup, and another called Metabiota were able to predict independently correctly some of the regions that would be hit by the virus next.

However, it is worth noting that predicting an event, or having data available, is not the same as knowing what to do with the information obtained.

If we do not want to repeat an event like the coronavirus, in the future we must be able to make better ethical decisions before their harmful effects shake the foundations of our societies again.

A statement like this: "in fact, computers may be better than humans in making moral decisions in so far as they may not be as limited by the bounded rationality that characterizes human decisions, and they need not be vulnerable to an emotional hijacking" (Allen 2002; Wallach 2008) after the pandemic years should make us reflect on the nature of ethics and the role of human emotions in decision-making. In addition, it is worth noting the fact that the creation of an artificial morality based almost entirely on the dominant Western approaches that are deontology and consequentialism leads to "oversimplification" (Zoshak and Dew 2021). The covid health crisis has needed and still needs global and local solutions at the same time. For this reason, I support the thesis of the need for such "a multi-theoretical approach" that is justifiable because human morality is complex and evolving; it cannot be captured by a simple classical ethical theory (Tolmeijer et al. 2021). Moreover, if we continue to insist on neglecting to reach a greater understanding of the role of emotions in human decision-making first, we will not only produce what Coeckelbergh (2010) calls "artificial psychopaths", but our solutions will also be psychopathic. It is in our hands to design the course of our future (ethical) decisions.

5   Conclusions

COVID-19 is showing that "the availability of empirical data and scientific evidence alone do not automatically lead to good decisions" (de Campos Rudinsky and Undurraga 2021). In addition, the conception of a deterministic world, in which every event is determined by initial conditions that are determinable with precision, at least in principle, has failed.

The results obtained in this research suggest that it is important to investigate further how to develop the field of Machine Ethics through a "multi-theoretical approach" that integrates Western and Eastern values or ethical frameworks in explanatory models, as well as a deeper understanding of emotions, in particular the emotion of regret for its role in regulating behavior. The proposed conceptual framework can thus be viewed as a stepping stone for improving decision-making in Human-AI interaction in the future.

References

Allam, Z.: The rise of machine intelligence in the COVID-19 pandemic and its impact on health policy. In: Surveying the Covid-19 Pandemic and Its Implications, pp. 89–96 (2020). https://doi.org/10.1016/B978-0-12-824313-8.00006-1

Baum, K., Hermanns, H., Speith, T.: From machine ethics to machine explainability and back. In: International Symposium on Artificial Intelligence and Mathematics, ISAIM 2018, Fort Lauderdale, Florida, USA, 3–5 January 2018, pp. 1–8 (2018)

Buchanan, J., Summerville, A., Lehmann, J., Reb, J.: The regret elements scale: distinguishing the affective and cognitive components of regret. Judgm. Decis. Mak. **11**, 275–286 (2016)

Byrne, R.: Counterfactuals in explainable artificial intelligence (XAI): evidence from human reasoning. In: Proceedings of the Twenty-Eighth International Joint Conference on Artificial Intelligence (IJCAI-2019) (2019)

Cheng, V.C., Lau, S.K., Woo, P.C., Yuen, K.Y.: Severe acute respiratory syndrome coronavirus as an agent of emerging and reemerging infection. Clin. Microbiol. Rev. **20**(4), 660–694 (2007). https://doi.org/10.1128/CMR.00023-07

Coeckelbergh, M.: Robot rights? Towards a social-relational justification of moral consideration. Ethics Inf. Technol. **12**, 209–221 (2010). https://doi.org/10.1007/s10676-010-9235-5

Confalonieri, R., Çoba, L., Wagner, B., Besold, T.R.: A historical perspective of explainable artificial intelligence. Wiley Interdisc. Rev. Data Min. Knowl. Discov. **11**, e1391 (2021)

Damasio, A.R.: Descartes' Error: Emotion, Reason, and the Human Brain. Grosset/Putnam, New York (1994)

de Campos-Rudinsky, T.C., Undurraga, E.: Public health decisions in the COVID-19 pandemic require more than 'follow the science'. J. Med. Ethics **47**(5), 296–299 (2021)

De Regt, H., Dieks, D.: A contextual approach to scientific understanding. Synthese **144**, 137–170 (2005). https://doi.org/10.1007/s11229-005-5000-4

Dreyfus, H.L.: What Computers Can't Do: The Limits of Artificial Intelligence. Harper Collins (1978)

Epstude, K., Roese, N.J.: The functional theory of counterfactual thinking. Pers. Soc. Psychol. Rev. Off. J. Soc. Pers. Soc. Psychol. **12**(2), 168–192 (2008). https://doi.org/10.1177/1088868308316091

Lewis, D.: Causation. J. Philos. **70**(17), 556–567 (1973)

Lipton, P.: Understanding without explanation. In: de Regt, H.W., Leonelli, S., Eigner, K. (eds.) Scientific Understanding: Philosophical Perspectives, pp. 43–63. University of Pittsburgh Press, Pittsburgh (2009)

Maclure, J.: AI, explainability and public reason: the argument from the limitations of the human mind. Minds Mach. **31**(3), 421–438 (2021). https://doi.org/10.1007/s11023-021-09570-x

Marcatto, F., Cosulich, A., Ferrante, D.: Once bitten, twice shy: experienced regret and non-adaptive choice switching. PeerJ **3**, e1035 (2015). https://doi.org/10.7717/peerj.1035

Merlot, J.: Das Pandemie-Planspiel. SPIEGEL Wissenschaft, 07 April 2020. https://www.spiegel.de/wissenschaft/medizin/coronavirus-was-der-rki-katastrophenplan-aus-2012-mit-der-echten-pandemie-zu-tun-hat-a-8d0820ca-95a7-469b-8a6a-074d940543d6

Miller, T.: Explanation in artificial intelligence: insights from the social sciences. Artif. Intell. **267**, 1–38 (2017). https://doi.org/10.1016/j.artint.2018.07.007

Pearl, J., Mackenzie, D.: The Book of Why: The New Science of Cause and Effect. Basic Books, New York (2018)

Shani, Y., Zeelenberg, M.: When and why do we want to know? How experienced regret promotes post-decision information search. J. Behav. Decis. Mak. **20**(3), 207–222 (2007). https://doi.org/10.1002/bdm.55

Stepin, I., et al.: Paving the way towards counterfactual generation in argumentative conversational agents. In: Proceedings of the 1st Workshop on Interactive Natural Language Technology for Explainable Artificial Intelligence (NL4XAI 2019), pp. 20–25. Association for Computational Linguistics (2019)

Tolmeijer, S., et al.: Implementations in machine ethics: a survey. ACM Comput. Surv. **53**(6), 1–38 (2021). Article no: 132. https://doi.org/10.1145/3419633

Varela, F.J.: Invitation aux sciences cognitives, Seuil (1996)

Varela, F.J., Thompson, E., Rosch, E.: The Embodied Mind: Cognitive Science and Human Experience. The MIT Press, Cambridge (1991)

van Wynsberghe, A., Robbins, S.: Critiquing the reasons for making artificial moral agents. Sci. Eng. Ethics **25**(3), 719–735 (2019). https://doi.org/10.1007/s11948-018-0030-8

Wallach, W., Allen, C., Smit, I.: Machine morality: bottom-up and top-down approaches for modeling human moral faculties. AI Soc. **22**, 565–582 (2008). https://doi.org/10.1007/s00146-007-0099-0

Zeelenberg, M., Pieters, R.: A theory of regret regulation 1.0. J. Consum. Psychol. **17**(1), 3–18 (2007). https://doi.org/10.1207/s15327663jcp1701_3

Zerilli, J., Knott, A., Maclaurin, J., Gavaghan, C.: Transparency in algorithmic and human decision-making: is there a double standard? Philos. Technol. **32**(4), 661–683 (2018). https://doi.org/10.1007/s13347-018-0330-6

Zoshak, J., Dew, K.: Beyond Kant and Bentham: how ethical theories are being used in artificial moral agents. In: Proceedings of the 2021 CHI Conference on Human Factors in Computing Systems (CHI 2021), pp. 1–15. Association for Computing Machinery, New York (2021). Article 590. https://doi.org/10.1145/3411764.3445102

Find the Real: A Study of Individuals' Ability to Differentiate Between Authentic Human Faces and Artificial-Intelligence Generated Faces

David Wayne Meyer[(✉)] [iD]

Liberty University, Lynchburg, VA 24515, USA
dwmeyer@liberty.edu

Abstract. As advances in Artificial-Intelligence (AI) generated technology accelerate, much of the general population is unaware when they may come across AI-generated content, including AI-generated images of humans. In attempting to see if the general population can ascertain the real vs. fake as society encounters an increasing amount of deep fake imagery, this study was conducted using AI human portraits generated at thispersondoesnotexist.com [1] using SyleGan2 (a generative adversarial network developed by Nvidia) [2]. The deep fake portraits were then juxtaposed with authentic portraits of humans from the Flickr Faces HQ Dataset (FFHQ) of Creative Commons licenses and public domain images [3]. Survey respondents were asked to select which face they believed to be an authentic human face. This is an important study in the realm of Human-Computer Interaction as AI resources are utilized in a variety of forms, including the spread of information, and can be linked to disinformation with the implementation of deep fakes.

Keywords: Artificial intelligence · Deep fake · Fake news

1 Modalities of Authenticity

In an increasing worldwide creation, adoption, and implementation of artificial intelligence through tools, websites, apps, algorithms and preference settings, artificial intelligence is interacted with every day. Yet, the average user or consumer generally has no idea when they are interacting with artificial-intelligence or using it to their benefit. Artificial intelligence can be (and is) embedded and accessed into a variety of contexts in industry, healthcare, customer service (chat bots), and even generation, alteration, and manipulation of images, video, text, and audio through deep fake technology. With the increasing rise of disinformation and fake news, many public and average internet users are unaware of the capabilities of artificial intelligence when it comes to generation, alteration, and manipulation pertaining to the aspects of the four modalities of the common media content of images, video, text, and audio (example: synthetic voices).

In the author's study of whether the general user was able to ascertain the real vs. fake, the respondent was made to select photos compiling the gender, race, and hair color as well as other similar settings to the original photograph. However, options were not given a differentiating insight or contrast of features within the image. Sites like *Which Face is Real* [4], have users "play" a game of guessing which is a real face paired against an AI-Generated face. However, no data regarding the accuracy of individuals taking the test has been provided publicly, nor does it collect any demographic information such as age and education, whereas the author's study, *Find the Real*, collected such data from 100 participants. This article will explore the details and results of the study, breaking down the statistics generally and then in more detail by demographics and education. Additionally, the article will examine the ramifications of the study, the results, and the impact of AI generated faces being used in the world today.

In a world where images that are manipulated, or so extremely bogus they are often considered "photoshopped" this study holds value. As society and industry move into the implementation of artificial intelligence, the public may not expect content that is so real and life-like that they cannot ascertain whether it is computer generated or an authentic photograph/artifact. Indeed, the thought may not even cross the user's mind. Additionally, with the ease of use of generators which create non-alias identities such as *This Person does not Exist* [1] and countless other plugins and extensions on the web, non-alias identities can be generated with ease.

Social Media lends to the misunderstanding and interpretation of information due to hivemind mentalities where users interacting with the app may not be aware that they are viewing content that is meant to persuade them to a false narrative, idea, or event that never even happened. Consequently with 2.19 billion fake accounts disabled by Facebook in Quarter 1 of 2019 [6] the possibility of encountering deep fake content as AI-generators of images, audio, voice, and text become more accessible is increasing. With the accessibility and convivence of other platforms such YouTube, TikTok, Instagram, Twitter, and more, social media can become fertile ground for the flourishing of deep fake content.

1.1 Find the Real Methodology

When creating the test, the author first generated the artificial intelligent non-alias identities using the very simple process found at This Person does not Exist [1]. It was decided by the author to generate acceptable AI portraits of 10 females and 10 males. Next, the author found suitable images of real people using the Flickr Faces HQ Dataset (FFHQ) [3]. These images from the FFHQ are all Public Domain or Creative Commons licensed content found within dataset. This is of significance as the Flickr Faces HQ Dataset is what was used to train the technology created by Nvida Labs when creating StyleGan [2]. The author attempted to have some portraits to be similar to the AI generated content so as to determine through A/B testing if images that are complementary to each other can be discerned as to which portrait is a real human face versus an AI generated face. Images were placed in randomized order with no purposeful pattern set. Participants were not given education or training on how to spot deep fake content prior to taking the study or after. Correct answers were not given upon completion. Participants were recruited through social media with a total of 100 participants providing responses to inform the study.

2 Study Results

How does the public fare when faced with a choice of real content versus fake AI Generated content when it comes to recognizing an authentic human face, with a real identity, story, and life juxtaposed with an artificially intelligence created face with no identity (non-alias), no story, and no life? In a survey of 100 people of various backgrounds and demographics, age, and degree obtainment, accuracy varied greatly.

2.1 Overview of Results

In total, the study had a rate of 50% of the questions correctly identified as real human faces, while 5% of the questions resulted in people identifying the faces with a 50–50 tie of accuracy and inaccuracy, and 45% of the questions were incorrectly identified as real human faces. This general overview does not account for the accuracy of human faces on a single question basis, nor does it account for the age range and demographic. Additionally, no one person out of 100 test respondents were able to score an accuracy rate of 100%. The highest score by any one user was 85% with only 15% of respondents scoring higher than 65% and out of 100, the average score was 48.45% (Fig. 1). One face in particular that was AI was thought to be an authentic human face by 78% of testers (Fig. 1). On the other end of the spectrum, there were some faces that were correctly identified by a healthy majority of users, with one face (Fig. 2) reaching 76% accuracy. 100% of participants reported using a computer, smartphone, and/or tablet device daily.

The individuals with the largest age representation of 35–44 years old (41 participants in total meeting this criteria) were only able to identify with 50% accuracy. The second largest demographic of 25–34 years old (31 participants total) were also only to identify with 50% accuracy. The most accurate age demographic range, although smaller was 18–24 years old (10 participants total) with an accuracy of 65% and a 10% tie followed by a 25% accuracy. Age ranges of 45–54 years (5 participants in total) had an accuracy rate of 55%, whereas ages 55–64 (8 participants) had an accuracy of 35%, with 10% of questions resulting in an even 50/50 tie and 55% of questions being identified falsely. Respondents that were aged between 65–74 (4 participants total) had an accuracy rate of 10%, but had the highest even tie rate of 45% with another 45% being answered incorrectly. One respondent classifying oneself in the category of 75+ had an accuracy of 35% and 65% answered incorrectly (Table 1).

Table 1. Accuracy across age demographics

Age group	Accuracy	Tie	Inaccurate
18–24	65%	10%	25%
25–34	50%	0%	50%
35–44	50%	0%	50%
45–54	55%	0%	45%
55–64	35%	10%	55%
65–74	10%	45%	45%
75+	35%	0%	65%

When analyzing the results from a degree level, the lowest scoring demographic consisted of those who held an associate degree for their highest level of education (7 respondents total) with an accuracy rate of 35% with 65% of questions incorrectly identified. Participants reporting having achieved a master's degree (22 respondents in total) had an accuracy rate of 35% with 5% of questions resulting in an even 50/50 tie and 60% of questions incorrectly identified. Those who identified as possessing a doctoral degree (9 respondents in total) had an accuracy of 45% with 55% answering the challenge wrong. Examining the content further, those who reported having achieved some college had a similar accuracy rate of 45% of faces correctly identified as authentic human faces and an incorrect percentage of 65% of faces misidentified as authentic that were actually Artificial Intelligence generated. Of those taking the survey and identifying as having completed high school (3 in total), there was an accuracy rate of 65% with 35% incorrectly identified as real human faces. Respondents who identified as having achieved training in trade school (4 total) had an accuracy rate of 25%, with a 30% result of questions in a 50/50 tie, and 45% of questions answered incorrectly. The largest group of 42 participants held a bachelor's degree had an accuracy rate of 40%, 10% of questions resulting in a 50/50 tie, and 50% incorrectly identified (Table 2).

Table 2. Accuracy across education demographics.

Education	Accuracy	Tie	Inaccurate
High school	65%	0%	35%
Trade school	25%	30%	45%
Some college	45%	0%	55%
Associate	35%	0%	65%
Bachelors	40%	10%	50%
Masters	35%	5%	60%
Doctorate	45%	0%	55%

2.2   Conclusion of Results

Literacy of content, medium and format is an important asset in a world where opportunity to generate Artificial Intelligence is becoming more accessible and democratized. Indeed, the public remains mostly unaware of when they encounter artificially intelligent generated content, especially in terms of imagery juxtaposed next to real faces attached to an identity. With only a small majority correctly answering out of 100 participants and no one able to score above an 85%, this study demonstrates the persuasive nature, technical ability, and overall confusion that Artificial Intelligence can cause while convincing the viewer that the content they are seeing is a real person. With the release of StyleGan 3 [7], the Artificial Intelligence technology continues to advance and develop at an even greater extent than previous versions. It is important for the public to be aware

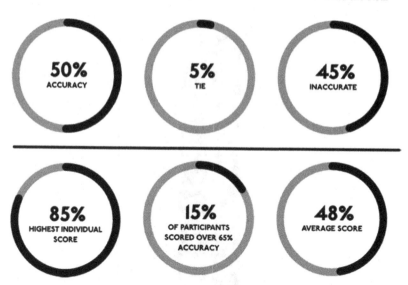

Fig. 1. An overview of the *Find The Real* study results.

of how to recognize AI generated content and earmarks of factual representations in order to truly understand and grasp the validity and authenticity of an element, whether it be image, text, video, or audio. The phrase "Don't believe everything you see on TV" must be greatly amplified and echoed in our current virtual environments and media consumption platforms.

While programs like Adobe Photoshop currently allow the alteration of seasons through the landscape mixer tool (Fig. 4) and the changing of expressions, age, eye direction, and more in its smart portrait tool under its neural filter options, for the most part this content still part relies on human generated artifacts. Additionally, tools in the Adobe Photoshop neural filters do not consider historical accuracy with filter options like colorization created with Artificial Intelligence. When implementing such tools like the colorize filter, these neural filters fail to demonstrate contextual understanding. (For example, these Photoshop filters and AI both would struggle to be accurate when considering an historic landmark such as Tower Bridge in London, England, UK unless it was understood that the context of why it was painted red, white, and blue in 1977 was for Queen Elizabeth's Silver Jubilee. These tools also would not be able to determine the first color of the bridge in its original completion) [8]. Also included in the Adobe Photoshop neural filters is the smart portrait filter, which allows for a variety of options including editing emotions, age, and eye gaze. While any user with training could have altered or manipulated an historic photograph, these Artificial Intelligent features give new rise and cause for concern. To exemplify this perplexity: the famous portrait photograph of Sir Winston Churchill: *The Roaring Lion* by Yousuf Karsh could be easily altered in a way that is not true to historical accuracy with a mischievous smile and elfish eyes. The smart portrait result is a change in expression that is effortlessly completed as opposed to traditional image manipulation techniques done through Adobe Photoshop (Fig. 3).

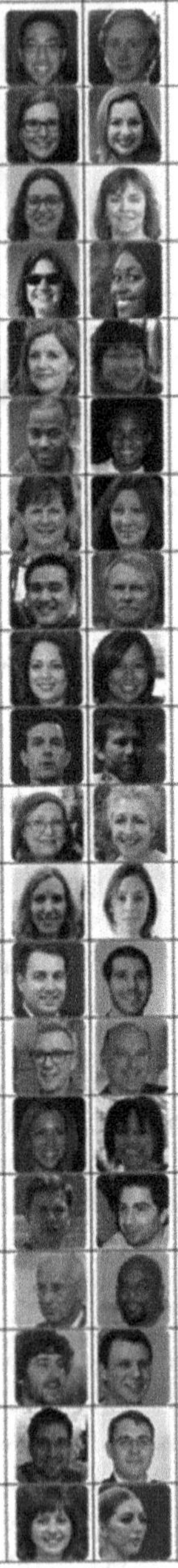

QUESTION	FAKE	REAL	ACCURACY
1			39%
2			34%
3			32%
4			70%
5			64%
6			58%
7			52%
8			51%
9			54%
10			76%
11			29%
12			32%
13			54%
14			50%
15			34%
16			54%
17			39%
18			22%
19			44%
20			55%

Fig. 2. An overview of the results and accuracy.

Another demonstration is using the Adobe Photoshop landscape mixer tool, which allows the user to change the season from its original exposure. The author demonstrated this through an autumn-filled Hyde Park, London, UK being transformed into a snowy landscape (Fig. 4) with just a few clicks, thus altering its reality.

Fig. 3. An example of the Adobe Photoshop Smart Portrait. Original photograph *The Roaring Lion* by Yousuf Karsh. Public Domain.

The threat for confusion and misunderstanding presents a different latitude than that of the existing prevalence of shallow fakes (also identified as the typical edited video, image, or audio clip with edited segments meant to present a polished or altered reality). AI Generated content presents and promises great usefulness, but it must not be understated what confusion and concern it could cause. Many of participants expressed bewilderment at the idea or thought that AI generated content such as non-alias identities existed, let alone how advanced they were. Educating the public on such content is vital for an educated AI-literate society.

Fig. 4. An example of Adobe Photoshop's landscape mixer tool used on Hyde Park, London, UK. Photograph by David Wayne Meyer.

3   Conclusion

As long as humans take photographs, there will be inconsistencies that lend photographs to asserting their own authenticity. How a user may accept the system defaults of the auto-mode of a camera or app, or how they may manually adjust the exposure via aperture and shutter speed resulting in photographs that are slightly out of focus, or how users may incorrectly expose photographs, or how users apply filters or presets provided by an app all demonstrate factors which currently cannot be replicated by AI technology.

Within Human Computer Interaction, when taking a photograph, humankind will create and interpret their own artistic vision whether in a way that expresses their mind's eye to capture a snapshot of a sentimental moment, or to document a current event with truth and integrity, or to simply remember, photographs created by humans will always lend personal verification because of these micro details and so- called mistakes or flaws, whereas artificially generated content in its current state exists as a sterile and perfect artifact lacking representation of human error or human perspective.

Finally, it is imperative to understand and recognize AI-generated content with the rise of anti-democratic nations seeking to confuse and sow discord among citizens and netizens alike. It would be advantageous for the public to inform themselves of the earmarks of AI-Generated content so as not to fall prey to state-sponsored propaganda that may use Artificial Intelligence to sway public opinion and discourse through deep fake imagery, video, audio, and text. In the world and realm of fake news, deep fake agendas could potentially have an extremely damaging impact as most viewers are unable to correctly ascertain what is an authentic human face versus an AI-generated face. Protection from manipulation by images and seeking to discern truth is the crux of why this study matters so much in context of today's society and why education of these issues is imperative.

References

1. Wang, P.: This person does not exist. https://thispersondoesnotexist.com/
2. Nvidia Research Labs: StyleGan2. https://github.com/NVlabs/stylegan2
3. Flickr: Flickr Faces HQ DataSet. https://github.com/NVlabs/ffhq-dataset
4. Bergstrom, C., West, J.: Which face is real? https://www.whichfaceisreal.com/. Accessed 12 Nov 2021
5. "Facebook." Statista. www.statista.com/study/9711/facebook-statista-dossier/. Accessed 12 Nov 2021
6. Tower Bridge History Page. https://www.towerbridge.org.uk/discover/history. Accessed 13 Mar 2022
7. Nvidia Research Labs: StyleGan3. https://github.com/NVlabs/stylegan. Accessed 12 Dec 2021
8. The Roaring Lion, Yousuf Karsh, Public Domain (1941)

It's Still Frustrating! Human-Centered Approaches to Data in Enterprise PC Maintenance

Dawn Nafus[(✉)], Sinem Aslan, and Caroline Foster

Intel Corporation, Portland, USA
{dawn.nafus,sinem.aslan,caroline.foster}@intel.com

Abstract. HCI tends to treat the humble office computer as a solved problem, yet most office workers still experience frustration when IT helpdesks need to be called. Why does this apparently "solved" problem persist? The software/hardware stack on a standard enterprise computer involves an astounding variety of possible drivers and application versions that can conflict with one another, leading to greater opportunity for breakdown, regardless of skills or resources of IT organizations. This circumstance lends itself to the use of telemetry and artificial intelligence (AI) for problem diagnosis and stokes aspirations of fully automating enterprise PC maintenance. To explore the human and organizational factors at work in applying data and AI to this problem, we designed a series of exploratory studies at a large technology company in the United States: (1) remote diary study with semi-structured interviews (n = 30), (2) quasi-experimental study with pretest-posttest design (n = 11), and (3) ethnographic study with open-ended interviews (n = 8). The results show that user frustration with malfunctioning PCs persisted because of the sociotechnical dynamic between employees, PCs, and IT support. Feedback loops between employees and IT played a central role in dialing up or tamping down frustration that accumulated over the long term. The results also indicate that telemetry and AI could provide new opportunities to tamp down user frustration when data were treated as a communication medium between employees and IT support. The results suggest three major design recommendations for preventing frustration buildup: (1) Redesigning PC telemetry data and transparency mechanisms to support two-way communication between IT and users, including shared analysis of malfunctioning data; (2) considering users' buildup of frustration, not just the quality of any single interaction, when designing any IT service solutions; (3) incorporating uses of technology that embrace human-AI collaboration technologies not to automate IT troubleshooting work but to support the human creativity necessary for troubleshooting. Utilizing the design principles we identified in this study, there is a need for further research and development to explore novel feedback systems between enterprise PC users and IT.

Keywords: Office computer · User frustration · PC telemetry · PC maintenance · Artificial intelligence

C. Stephanidis et al. (Eds.): HCII 2022, CCIS 1655, pp. 663–670, 2022.
https://doi.org/10.1007/978-3-031-19682-9_84

1 Introduction

If one were to look over the last two decades of human-computer interaction (HCI) research, it would be fair to assume that the humble office computer was a solved problem. HCI interest tends to focus on more recent software applications like social media, messaging tools, and platforms for collaborative content production, or novel hardware like virtual reality, smart home technologies, and telepresence robots. There almost is an unstated assumption that ordinary personal computer can be assumed away as a given, yet most office workers continue to experience frustration when IT helpdesks need to be called. The emerging repair literature assumes an individual, not institutional context [1–3], which does not help us understand why this apparently "solved" problem still persists. Instead, the problem remains a part of the assumed infrastructure, and as such faded into the background [4].

A workplace computer managed by an IT organization is more likely to experience malfunctions than a typical home computer. This is because an IT organization has to meet many needs beyond an individual's, like rigorous security to protect business-sensitive information, which demands more computational resources. The software/hardware stack on a seemingly standard enterprise computer involves an astounding variety of possible drivers and application versions that can conflict, leading to greater opportunity for breakdown, no matter how well resourced or highly skilled the organization managing those computers might be.

Because malfunctions are inevitable, feedback mechanisms between enterprise PC users and IT play a strong role. Current feedback loops primarily but not exclusively rely on troubleshooting tickets to identify emerging problems across the fleet. It is widely assumed that IT tickets as a source of feedback systematically underestimates problems, as employees typically do not call for every problem. A new data source - telemetry - makes more automated feedback possible. Telemetry could potentially fill gaps that ticket data leaves, but it also introduces a different set of problems. Telemetry can often involve high sample rates and volumes of parameters that render manual interrogation nearly impossible. It is not obvious what constellation of data actually speaks to problems as experienced by users. Nor is it obvious how these measures relate to ticket data, the volume of which many IT organizations treat as a measure of performance. AI methods can assist with reducing complexity to some degree. Nevertheless, ticket data remains a persistently appealing source of information, in part because it is interpretable and in part because there is a built-in notion of impacts to users not available in machine telemetry.

Given that enterprise PC repair is not a topic that the HCI community has revisited in many years, and given that new technologies like telemetry and potentially AI might change that longstanding feedback loop, we set out to understand how the current feedback loop works socially and organizationally, how it contributes to current levels of frustration, and how telemetry might change the dynamic positively or negatively. More importantly, if telemetry has something to offer in this situation, how its value is best realized given the organizational and social factors that currently cause the frustration in the first place.

2 Methods

This study aims to address two major research questions: (1) What is the nature and source of user frustration with computer malfunctions, both in terms of the malfunctions themselves and in terms of having to contact IT to resolve them? and (2) what are the work practices of PC fleet managers and their staff that shape how information about end user frustration can or cannot be acted upon? Put together, these form two sides of the equation that constitute a feedback loop between machine, user, and IT staff.

To address these research questions, we designed a series of exploratory studies at a large technology company in the United States. The first was a remote diary study (i.e., study 1) with semi-structured interviews (n = 30), where we asked participants to log frustration with their computer in real-time through a mobile phone app. We instructed them to submit a diary entry immediately whenever they experienced a moment of frustration related to their computer malfunctioning. We requested at least 10 entries over the course of two weeks, with a flexibility of fewer entries if they did not actually experience that many. We then conducted semi-structured, hour-long interviews with each participant to understand overall experiences with their computers, and what they thought would be a useful and appropriate actions for IT to take based on telemetry data.

The second (i.e., study 2) was a quasi-experimental study with pretest-posttest design (n = 11) to compare how users experienced frustration when the malfunctions naturally occurred versus when we induced artificial malfunctions through software installed on their computers (with permission). This allowed us to understand whether there were variations in the participants' responses to the same, known event, and therefore, how much can be safely assumed about frustration levels just by detecting known machine malfunctions. For two weeks, the participants were asked to log their frustration diaries. In the first week of data collection, the participants used their computers normally, and reported any naturally occurring malfunctions. In the second week, the study software induced artificial malfunctions.

The third study (i.e., study 3) was a smaller ethnographic study with hour-long open-ended interviews (n = 8) of key IT staff who were most likely to use feedback data about malfunctioning if it were to be collected using telemetry as opposed to IT tickets.

For the interview-based data for study 1 and 3, we conducted an inductive thematic analysis, first open-coding transcripts and then identifying emergent categories, narratives, and practices. To analyze types of malfunctions reported in the participants' diaries in study 1 and 2, we first conducted content analysis of free text entries to arrive at a structured categorization of types of malfunctions reported. We then used descriptive statistics to analyze the frequency of these categories, and frequency of actions taken to rectify the problem. Due to the small sample size in study 2, we did not conduct any statistical significance analysis. Instead, we used the intervention of artificial malfunctions to understand whether there were variations in the participants' responses as an effect of the intervention.

We aimed to ensure internal validity through the use of complementary multiple methods, and achieved consistency by ensuring that within the company, we recruited a diversity of participants as much as is possible within a single company by stratifying our sample across job roles, seniority, and demographic categories.

3 Results

While it is commonplace to think of user frustration with a technology as a direct, psychological response to being prevented from accomplishing a task, one of our key findings is that there was a more complex social dynamic at work among machines, their users, and the IT organization who provided and maintained those machines. The feedback loop among these three factors played a central role, socially situating frustration. The results show that the users experienced frustration in two categories: "Acute" and "chronic." Acute frustration, like physical pain or stress, involved malfunctions that a user perceived as either mild or sharp. It would come on suddenly and last briefly, with "brief" being whatever length of time the affected person considered to be a one-off incident, like a PC that froze for ten seconds during a presentation. Chronic frustration, however, showed itself as a response to an issue or issues that recurred over a longer period of time, typically a few months. An example could be a webcam repeatedly failing to turn on during a video meeting. The results show that when chronic frustration set in, the relationship with the IT organization could become more palpable, and could either dial up chronic frustration, or calm it down. In the following sections, we explain how this dynamic worked.

3.1 Acute Frustration

Acute frustration in our study came from a variety of sources, such as freezes, slow-downs, and connectivity issues. (see Fig. 1). The participants sometimes registered their displeasure with IT-pushed updates by reporting it as a "malfunction" even though that would not be seen strictly as a malfunction from an IT perspective.

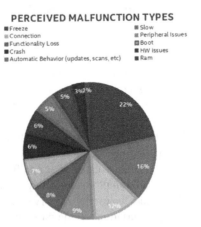

Fig. 1. Perceived malfunction types reported by the participants.

In general, it was not the case that the participants found certain problem areas to be more bothersome than others - say, connectivity issues more bothersome than freezing.[1] However, responses to the artificially induced malfunction events (in study 2) showed a more consistent response when there was a specific, known event shared across the participants. All participants in that study had found network connectivity drops that led to tasks becoming impossible to be the most frustrating, while very few people even noticed our attempts at slowing down their PCs.

3.2 Chronic Frustration

When the same issue happened repeatedly, our participants could be described as being in a state of chronic frustration. Often the participants responded to repeated malfunctions by figuring out ways to work around them entirely. For example, one user from study 1 avoided closing the lid if the computer struggled to resume operation after going into hibernation. Similarly, another avoided using their docking station if putting it in the docking station would destabilize the system. A successful workaround became a habit, something that our participants had become accustomed to and stopped seeing as an urgent problem, much like living in a state of chronic stress would become accepted, if still burdensome. The burden took on a different register that allowed to continue nevertheless. The participants who expressed the most overall frustration in the interviews were the ones who were piling on multiple workarounds for multiple problems, and/or repeatedly experiencing new types of issues on top of the current ongoing issues, and/or had ongoing issues where a workaround could not be found, such as losing one's place in a complex spreadsheet and needing another hour to recreate it.

When severe chronic frustration accumulated, a "straw that broke the camel's back" situation emerged. When this happened, the participants sought acknowledgement of the issue in some way, like escalating the situation to senior managers. In one case, that manager did not work in IT and was not in a position to correct the problem, but the participant had grown so frustrated that the seriousness of the situation had not been acknowledged, and he needed it witnessed by a figure of authority of some kind.

3.3 Frustration as Socio-technical Feedback Loop

In principle, the cycle of chronic frustration could be circumvented by going to IT to resolve bothersome issues. However, our participants rarely did this. In fact, the prevalence of workarounds was so great: We found in study 1 that for 187 frustration events reported to us, there was only 1 IT ticket. This means that even severe issues were going untracked in current feedback systems. One reason employees avoided IT was that the troubleshooting encountered required dedicated time of an unpredictable length, so the experience overall was of being unable to control one's time. This created a disincentive to sorting the problem out if there was a chance of muddling through. One participant exemplified this as: "[I don't call IT] because I have a quick work around

---

[1] There are some exceptions to this. There were more reports of less severe slowdowns, and the unanticipated behaviors, like a push notification from IT, tended to be reported as a mild problem only.

and I don't have the time... my guess is it'll take an hour of my time to work with [IT] on it... Ultimately, it will add up to an hour of time to kill [the frozen program] and start it up again, but I don't know." Another participant commented that "I do my best not to ask IT if I can find it on [the Internet]."

One other reason the participants did not call IT was that that they were concerned about whether the issue would be reproducible, and if it was not reproducible, whether they would have wasted time calling. Some participants resorted to collecting data themselves, such as screengrabs of error messages, either to speed up the process of talking to a technician, or to assert the reality of a situation that could not be reproduced, or where they were concerned about being believed.

What this tells us, then, is not just that ticket data underestimates the extent of PC malfunctioning. It also tells us that even though the time spent getting it fixed is shorter than the time spent working around it, there is still insufficient incentive to call, perpetuating the chronic frustration.

3.4 An Accidental Change to the Feedback Loop

In contrast to the above, and much to our surprise, employee willingness to participate in this study was unusually high, to the point where a wait list formed to get in. This was because people *did* want to tell IT about their chronic frustrations in some form, even if the last thing they wanted to do was opening a ticket. Many participants told us about a specific source of chronic frustration that motivated them to participate, as they wanted it acknowledged in some way. Others asked about when or whether IT was going to roll out this "app." The study's popularity suggested the participants did have a notion about what a feedback loop should involve that was not being satisfied through other means.

Unintentionally, studies 1 and 2 effectively created a new type of data source - the real-time frustration report - that the participants came to see as potentially filling a gap in the feedback loop. This human-in-the-loop mechanism, where there is a channel of communication that does not amount to a "ticket" but helps employees to be heard and exercise some agency over the situation, came to mediate the buildup/tamp-down cycle of chronic frustration. Elements in the feedback could in fact be a crucial component to mediate the world of automated data collection and other sources.

4   Implications

If telemetry and AI are going to be useful additions to enterprise PC maintenance, these studies showed that channels of user expression and communication need to play a central role. That is, "human-in-the-loop" here is not so much about oversight or control as it is about expression. When we look at frustration reports as a data source in relation to the other data sources an IT organization has, the possible ongoing role of such reports seems viable. Ticket data naturally underestimates the problem. Customer satisfaction surveys - routinely used by IT organizations once a year to assess whether they are meeting employees' needs overall - do capture perceptual data, but are not designed to capture the level of specificity that IT can act on for specific maintenance issues like freezing or slowdowns. Machine telemetry has the opposite problem of being so specific, down to the split second, that leaves out human impacts. None of it (including the frustration reports as designed in the study) provides information about time lost, which is necessary to truly estimate the severity of impact. Yet, because frustration reports do have a time stamp, it is possible to associate them with what the machine telemetry data says, and reduce the "needle in a haystack" quality of telemetry data. Because they have a perceptual element, it would also be possible to look for correlations with overall satisfaction scores to see how much PC malfunctioning is affecting that employee's experience with all IT endeavors over the long term. In these ways, there is potential for not just filling a gap, but creating a data-level interoperability that is previously impossible.

What might that interoperability between user, IT administrator, and machine telemetry look like? The results suggested three major design recommendations for preventing frustration buildup: (1) Redesigning PC telemetry data and transparency mechanisms to support two-way communication between IT and users, including shared analysis of malfunctioning data; (2) considering users' buildup of frustration, not just the quality of any single interaction, when designing any IT service solutions ("self-service," chatbots, or helpdesk scripts): Malfunctions, and low-quality interactions with helpdesks, should not be treated in isolation from one another; (3) incorporating uses of technology that embrace human-AI collaboration technologies not to automate IT troubleshooting work but to support the human creativity necessary for troubleshooting: Enterprise PC troubleshooting is, by definition, complex, and tools should be optimized for handling that complexity, and not pretend it is possible to automate them away.

5 Conclusion

This study showed that enterprise PC malfunctions remain frustrating because of how malfunctioning interacts with feedback systems currently in place to rectify those malfunctions, leading to a buildup of chronic frustration. Chronic frustration can be dialed down with a combined strategy of integrating telemetry data and new sources of real-time user data, that allow for a shared acknowledgement of the problem without necessitating a helpdesk engagement. Utilizing the design principles we identified in this study, there is a need for further research and development to explore novel feedback systems between enterprise PC users and IT.

Acknowledgements. The authors are grateful to Nese Alyuz Civitci, Ian Lowrie, Farnaz Abdollahi, and Blake Williamson for their engagement and insights into this research.

References

1. Jackson, S.J.: Rethinking repair. In: Media Technologies: Essays on Communication, Materiality, and Society, pp. 221–39. MIT Press, Cambridge (2014)
2. Rosner, D.K., Ames, M.: Designing for repair? Infrastructures and materialities of breakdown. In: Proceedings of the 17th ACM Conference on Computer Supported Cooperative Work and Social Computing 2014, pp. 319–331 (2014)

3. Russell, A.L., Vinsel, L.: After innovation, turn to maintenance. Technol. Cult. **59**(2), 1–25 (2018)
4. Star, S.L., Ruhleder, K.: Steps toward an ecology of infrastructure: design and access for large information spaces. Inf. Syst. Res. **7**(1), 111–134 (1996)

Understanding the Patients' Adoption and Usage of AI Solution in Mental Health: A Scoping Review

Nguyen Nguyen[✉], Elise Labonte-Lemoyne, Yany Gregoire,
Marie Louise Radanielina-Hita, and Sylvain Senecal

HEC Montreal, Montreal, Canada
nguyen.nguyen@hec.ca

Abstract. The emerging of artificial intelligences interventions in mental health presents many opportunities for more innovative research and medical practices that benefits different stakeholders. There is a growing research stream investigating the adoption of AI-enabled solutions from different perspectives. As patients are the ultimate consumers of mental health services, it is critical to understand patients' perception and attitudes towards AI applications. This project aims to provide a scoping review about that addresses the current state of the relevant literature in terms of research methods, theories, and findings. Using such insights, the review identifies the research gaps and proposes directions for further development of the research stream.

Keywords: Artificial intelligence · Mental health · Adoption · Perception · Review · AI-based tool · Psychiatric

1 Introduction

The WHO reports that one in every four people around the world might struggle with mental health issues at some points in their lives [1]. In recent years, artificial intelligence (AI) has made progressive growth with diverse applications across fields. Mental health support also embraces such trends. AI can be used in the form of decision support system to assist health professionals in diagnosis and treatment [3]. There also exists AI-based apps such as Woebot, Youper and Wysa which offer mood tracking, chatbot, self-help tools and online therapists for consumers to boost emotional wellness [2]. Together with the popularity of such practical implications, the literature also witnesses a surge of interest in the phenomenon. The diversity in scholarly work makes it challenging to identify the findings and the current state of the literature. There are some attempts to summarize the research stream concerning AI in mental health in terms of accuracy and effectiveness from the perspective of clinicians or organizations [4, 5]. The understanding from the patient's and consumer's perception of such practices is still limited though they are the direct or indirect ultimate targets of the tools. Hence, to have successful implementations of AI-enabled solution, it is important to consolidate our knowledge of users' attitudes.

C. Stephanidis et al. (Eds.): HCII 2022, CCIS 1655, pp. 671–675, 2022.
https://doi.org/10.1007/978-3-031-19682-9_85

The goal of this article is to offer a scoping review that reflect the patients' adoption and usage of AI solution in mental health. In particular, the review seeks to identify the relevant characteristics of AI-based tools and the individual factors that affect the adoption of such applications. We then discuss the underlying processes explaining the effects and the main methodologies (research design) that have been used in this area. Based on such findings and insights, the review determines the commonalities and differences between studies, as well as gaps in the literature and avenues for future research.

2 Method

We searched for academic articles published in the last ten years (from January 2012 to March 2022) in three databases: Web of Science, PubMed and ACM Digital library. These databases offer an expanded spectrum of journals and flexibility in search strings and are particularly relevant for the research questions. The search queries were formulated using the following components: (i) artificial intelligences including machine learning, algorithms, and other AI-based tools such as conversational agents, robot, etc. (ii) patients and consumers as targeted stakeholders, (iii) keywords that reflect patients' understanding and perception toward AI applications in mental health (iv) topics involving mental health. We performed our search queries on the titles and keywords.

We identified the set of keywords through a scoping process. An initial search was conducted to capture the records that would be relevant for mental health topic and patients' perception. We then analyzed the text words in the abstracts and titles of the retrieved papers to add synonyms for each theme of search. This process was repeated till no new synonyms for keywords were generated. We used the same procedure to identify the AI keywords. The list of keywords was defined and used in the final search queries (Table 1).

Table 1. List of keywords by topic for search queries

Topic	Keywords
Mental health	mental health, mental illness, psychiatric, mental disorder, psychotherapy
Patients' perception	adoption, perception, perspective, decision-making, acceptance
AI	AI, artificial intelligence, machine learning, natural language processing, conversational agent, chatbot, deep learning, data mining, robotic, algorithm

Overall, the search resulted in 831 records from three databases. After removing the duplicates and other documents (book chapters, proceedings, etc.), the final dataset consisted of 761 documents that were proceeded to the screening phase.

For the screening process, we identified a set of inclusion and exclusion criteria to filter the dataset accordingly. We excluded studies that only discuss the health professional or organizational and institutional views on AI adoption. Technical papers concerning accuracy, cost and effectiveness of such practices were irrelevant for our research questions, thus also being eliminated. For inclusion criteria, we only looked at English articles that show patients' perceptions of AI in mental health. Specifically, research contexts were limited to situation in which patients and consumers interact directly with AI entities. If an article investigates multiple perspectives of stakeholders on AI applications, we included those that considered the patients' view. Both empirical and conceptual works were retained for the latter steps.

The screening process followed a multi-stage strategy. We first picked a random 50 articles sample from the records retrieved by the database search. Two raters screened the titles and abstracts of the chosen documents according to the eligibility criteria independently. We then compared the results to calculate the interrater reliability. When disagreement occurs in the screening results, we included the article. Specifically, we did two rounds of IRR check. In the first round, our comparison achieved a 76% inter-reliability. After discussing and refining the eligibility criteria, we went through a second round of screening and ended up an 86% inter-reliability. Once the interrater reliability was established, we moved on to the full screening. At the current state, we screened 189 documents out of the 761 records, 32 studies are included to the next round of research (16%). The main reason of rejection was that patients were not directly in contact with AI technology in the research settings. After the full screening, we will obtain additional records through snowballing techniques.

The next phase of the review is data extraction. Extracted information are, for each paper: (i) research focus and research questions, (ii) artificial intelligence technology and its characteristics, (iii) research methods (settings, contexts, and data analyses), (iv) individual traits and personality affecting consumers perception, (v) underlying theories and (vi) main findings. Apart from the data previously mentioned, the reviewers are flexible in providing extra information that can give potential contribution to the review. We first run a pilot study with a sub sample of the document set to test the appropriate type of procedure for the official data extraction. We apply the same approach as the screening process in which each member works independently and then cross-checks the outcome.

3   Initial Discussion

The ongoing process of data screening and extraction has led to several insights. First, in terms of research settings, conceptual papers account for a large number of the existing literature of AI adoption in mental health. These papers can be reviews that synthesize findings of a particular AI-enabled solution such as conversational agents [6–8], natural language processing [9], mobile apps [10] etc. Others are protocols and conceptual frameworks to embrace artificial intelligences in practices [11, 12]. As a relatively new and growing research stream, the disproportion of conceptual and empirical studies is a quite common. This calls for more empirical research that further investigates the phenomenon to advance the research stream. Another key insight from research settings is that most empirical studies rely on the use of a single research method only such as surveys or interviews. The use of varied methods provides richer data and more sophisticated analyses to study the topic, thus leading to higher quality works. The scarcity of multi-method approaches is a limitation that researchers should consider improving in their future projects.

Second, data extraction about theoretical considerations provides important findings. Researchers across disciplines seem to develop their studies based on different models. Technology acceptance model (TAM), theory of reasoned action (TRA), Diffusion of innovation theory (DOI) and unified theory of acceptance and use of technology (UTAUT and UTAUT2) are among the most discussed ones. These theories share some similarities in terms of factors. For instance, when patients look at the performance value of AI-enabled solution, it can be referred as perceived usefulness in TAM, performance expectancy in UTAUT or relative advantage in DOI. Overall, based on such theories, factors influencing patient's perception toward artificial intelligence in mental health can be divided into three main categories. There are technical and material factors (AI characteristics, AI quality, information preciseness), social and personal factors (personality and individual traits) and policy and organizational ones (facilitating condition, compatibility). With the growth of the literature, it is critical to adopt more theories from consumer marketing, psychology, information system to add greater variety to the research. For example, the health belief model is a promising avenue to predict the patient use of new technology [13].

Third, ethical issues appear as the focus for many papers on this research topic. Patients claim that trust is one of the main drivers for adoption of AI-based tool in mental health [6]. As mental health practices require much personal data, they also express privacy concern. Concretely, consumers prefer a strong confidentiality and secure management of data as well as clear understanding about information distribution of such solutions. Surprisingly, it shows that "a significant portion of current intelligent assistive technology is designed in the absence of explicit ethical considerations" [14]. In responding to the lack of ethical caution, some works address the current challenges for and offer guidelines for more responsible AI application in psychiatry and psychology [7, 9, 15].

In summary, understanding the view of patients about artificial AI solution in mental health is critical for more successful and innovative implementation. We aim to provide scoping review to summarize the patient's perspectives by giving key insights and propose possible research avenues. Because of the on-going nature of the project, the findings are still limited. We hope to offer more insights in the near future.

References

1. WHO; The world health report 2001: mental disorders affect one in four people. https://www.who.int/news/item/28-09-2001-the-world-health-report-2001-mental-disorders-affect-one-in-four-people. Accessed 10 Apr 2022
2. Raibagi, K.: Top AI-based apps to support your mental health in 2021. https://industrywired.com/top-ai-based-apps-to-support-your-mental-health-in-2021/. Accessed 10 Apr 2022
3. Henshall, C., et al.: A web-based clinical decision tool to support treatment decision-making in psychiatry: a pilot focus group study with clinicians, patients and carers. BMC Psychiatry 17(1), 1–10 (2017)
4. Graham, S., et al.: Artificial intelligence for mental health and mental illnesses: an overview. Curr. Psychiatry Rep. 21(11), 1–18 (2019)

5. Lee, E.E., et al.: Artificial intelligence for mental health care: clinical applications, barriers, facilitators, and artificial wisdom. Biol. Psychiatry Cogn. Neurosci. Neuroimaging **6**(9), 856–864 (2021)
6. Prakash, A.V., Das, S.: Intelligent conversational agents in mental healthcare services: a thematic analysis of user perceptions. Pacific Asia J. Assoc. Inf. Syst. **12**(2), 1 (2020)
7. Fiske, A., Henningsen, P., Buyx, A.: Your robot therapist will see you now: ethical implications of embodied artificial intelligence in psychiatry, psychology, and psychotherapy. J. Med. Internet Res. **21**(5), e13216 (2019)
8. Abd-Alrazaq, A.A., et al.: Perceptions and opinions of patients about mental health chatbots: scoping review. J. Med. Internet Res. **23**(1), e17828 (2021)
9. Le Glaz, A., et al.: Machine learning and natural language processing in mental health: systematic review. J. Med. Internet Res. **23**(5), e15708 (2021)
10. Baldauf, M., Fröehlich, P., Endl, R.: Trust me, I'm a doctor–user perceptions of AI-driven apps for mobile health diagnosis. In: 19th International Conference on Mobile and Ubiquitous Multimedia (2020)
11. Di Carlo, F., et al.: Telepsychiatry and other cutting-edge technologies in COVID-19 pandemic: bridging the distance in mental health assistance. Int. J. Clin. Practice **75**(1) (2021)
12. Torous, J., et al.: The growing field of digital psychiatry: current evidence and the future of apps, social media, chatbots, and virtual reality. World Psychiatry **20**(3), 318–335 (2021)
13. Ahadzadeh, A.S., et al.: Integrating health belief model and technology acceptance model: an investigation of health-related internet use. J. Med. Internet Res. **17**(2), e3564 (2015)
14. Ienca, M., et al.: Ethical design of intelligent assistive technologies for dementia: a descriptive review. Sci. Eng. Ethics **24**(4), 1035–1055 (2018)
15. Mouchabac, S., et al.: Psychiatric advance directives and artificial intelligence: a conceptual framework for theoretical and ethical principles. Front. Psychiatry 1596 (2021)

Birdwatch: A Platform Utilizing Machine Learning to Recognize Species of Indigenous, Migratory and Endangered Birds

Abhishek Rein(✉), Abhinav Rai, Nilima Jaiswal, and Anmol Srivastava

Department of Interaction Design, School of Design, University of Petroleum and Energy Sciences, Bidholi, Via Prem Nagar, Dehradun, Uttarakhand 248007, India
abhishekrein@gmail.com, abhinav.rai.50999@gmail.com,
nilimajaiswalhere@gmail.com, asrivastava@ddn.upes.ac.in

Abstract. The care and upkeep of indigenous, migratory & endangered species of Aves is vital to the ecosystem as they are instrumental in various activities such as pollination and seed dispersal. We explore the possibility of the inclusion of an auditory machine learning model into a multi-platform application to help forest rangers based in remote locations of India identify such species and aid their study and care. The application will be connected to databases which would not only help in the recognition of various birds via sound but also fetch essential information respective to the conservation of identified birds. Forest rangers in remote locations will no longer need to depend on the primitive analogue techniques of bird recognition such as birding by ear or sight, they will be able to get accurate results just by scanning their surroundings using any common device such as a smartphone or a portable computer. This approach reduces the need for sophisticated resources by utilizing extensive datasets and machine learning algorithms which classify the species of birds on the basis of confidence scores. The information displayed to the users on the interface of the application will be divided into different segments which will display details such rarity, native region, population, behavior and flight patterns, and other necessary information. Birdwatch also contributes all the collected data to existing datasets to continuously improve and build up on the accuracy and extensiveness of the datasets, which will help in more precise recognition.

Keywords: Auditory machine learning · Ornithology · Monitoring & recognition of birds in India · Remote forest rangers · Conservation of endangered bird species

1 Introduction

1.1 Influence of Birds on the Ecology

Species of Aves are considered to be vital in the ecology of the earth. With more than 10,000 species and 22,000 subspecies in the world [1], Aves can be found in all environments, ranging from the hearts of metropolitans to unmanned seas. Birds contribute

C. Stephanidis et al. (Eds.): HCII 2022, CCIS 1655, pp. 676–683, 2022.
https://doi.org/10.1007/978-3-031-19682-9_86

more to the ecosystem than we realize other than pollination/plant distribution. They contribute in nutrient cycling and the formation of soil [2] along with carbon sequestration, waste decomposition, and air purification. In Africa, vultures were found to devour huge amounts of dead meat and in Yemen, vultures were found to be able to remove up to a quarter of the organic human-produced waste. [3] When the population of a given species begins to decline, severe changes in the ecosystem might be observed. Because there was less competition for meat as a food source, vulture losses in India resulted in an increase of feral canines. The increase in dog population resulted in an increase in rabies epidemics and human injuries as a result of dog attacks. Vulture decreases are projected to have cost $34 billion [4] in health costs between 1993 and 2006. Birds also contribute to the establishment of forests by distributing plant seeds while foraging. When they take a seed or fruit from a plant and fly away with it, the seed is transported to a new location where it can germinate. Many plants use this behaviour to disperse seeds, and it can increase the genetic variety of plants in a given area by distributing seeds. Animals can transfer seeds up to 40 m away from the source tree in some situations. [5].

1.2 Current State of Birds in India

India has an abundance of bird species but tragically, the population of these creatures has been on a freefall. According to 'State of India's Birds 2020' [6], a report compiled from data provided by 15000+ birdwatchers across the country, [7].

1. 52% of species in the country show clear declines over the past decades out of the 867 species of Indian birds assessed in the report.
2. 101 species have been classified as of High Conservation Concern, and require immediate attention.

The human led destruction of habitat along with the extensiveness of fatal chemicals and capturing for the pet trade acts as a severe threat to a vast number of birds, many of which are native to the subcontinent. The report warns that decreasing population levels of many birds due to one issue brings them closer to extinction due to the accelerated effects of others.

1.3 Identification and Tracking of Birds for Their Conservation

A census is a vital when it comes to wildlife since it helps to ascertain multiple factors such as density of the species in a particular area, age ration, sex ratio and increment & decrement of the population of a particular species in each area. An estimate or census of the number of animals that the area can support is required for scientific management of the area's animal population. As discussed previously, Aves are instrumental in our ecology and thus it is important to keep a check on their count. By maintaining a proper check on the census of the class of species we can obtain information about their most visited areas and make sure those locations maintain the ideal environment of them. Proper tracking teaches ornithological researchers a lot about flight patterns, breeding seasons and population which ultimately helps in the conservations of the species.

1.4   Current Identification Methods for Birds in India

In order to understand the current prevailing methods of bird tracking in India, a field study based on open ended interviews was conducted to investigate how forest officers and rangers, in the Uttarakhand region of India, identify the species they host and how they keep a track of the number of the birds which visit their premises. The participants in this initial study involved 2 District Forest Officers and 5 Forest Rangers. After talking with the officials, it was observed that they, like most others [8], rely primarily on the analogue premise of "counting by sight" or methods such as "look-see counting" where a potentially suitable habitat of a bird species is already known or identified. Multiple teams of rangers are deployed to cover a geographic habitat with each team assigned a smaller section of the location for a thorough population estimate. Each ranger in a team then uses their sight, supported by binoculars and spotting scopes, to count the number of birds in their assigned section. The observed number of birds by each ranger is finally averaged out with the rest of their team to arrive at an estimated number of a birds and bird species in that geographic section.

1.5   Identification Methods for Birds Based on Machine Learning

Visual Identification. When it comes to ornithological research the radar systems used in computer vision machines can be instrumental as they generate data in large scale to track the flight patterns of various birds. [9] By reducing background noise from photos and videos, computer vision improves the accuracy of collected data. This computer vision capability could aid in the study of migratory patterns in birds that move at night. Computer vision aids in the monitoring and counting of migratory birds, as well as the comparison of numbers that return after the migration season.

While computer vision is highly sophisticated in its functioning and performance, there are still some major issues which do not make it ideal for bird tracking. The first one being computer vision is solely based on imagery, when it comes to bird there are numerous subspecies which look indistinguishable and there are serval issues with the lighting condition of the images. Lastly, the most unique feature of recognizing birds is the birdsong or the mating call which computer vision does not account for.

Auditory Identification. One of the most distinct features of Aves is the bird song they produce. Each species of bird has a very noticeable mating call or birdsong which can be instantly recognized by forest rangers or experienced birdwatchers and ornithologists. When it comes to distinction of bird songs different breeds might have similar sounding birdsongs which might make them indistinguishable unless they are clearly visible in front of the forest ranger or the birdwatcher. This particular loophole makes birding by the ear unreliable. [10] Bird abundance and presence are key indicators of specific species as well as overall ecosystem health. Because many birds can be identified by their calls, passive acoustic monitoring serves as a perfect choice.

2 Methodology

2.1 Defining Objective

Keeping all the points in mind from our discovery and research phase, we considered multiple possibilities of utilizing the potential of machine learning and combining it with the available datasets involved in tracking the global conservation status of birds. The aim was to create a robust tool for the recognition of bird songs and calls and display the birds' information and conservation statistics to the users of the application, which would include forest rangers in remote areas to track the presence of these birds in a geographical location, or the general populace to create awareness about the birds. At its core, birdwatch would be a tool which would help the user to easily and quickly recognize birds just on the basis of sound without birding by the ear, eliminating human error, being executed using any device with or without an internet connection.

2.2 Data Collection

Our primary source of data was the worldwide volunteer-driven repository of birds sounds from xeno-canto [11] for training the auditory machine learning model. In terms of collecting the data regarding the endangered species in the Indian subcontinent, we relied on International Union for Conservation of Nature (IUCN) Red List of Threatened Species [12], the world's most comprehensive inventory of the global conservation status of plant and animal species. It uses a set of quantitative criteria to evaluate the extinction risk of thousands of species. These criteria are relevant to most species and all regions of the world.

2.3 Model Training

After handpicking the sound samples from xeno-canto, we used Teachable Machine, a no-code tool from Google, based on the famous TensorFlow framework, for training audio-based machine learning models. The initial model was trained with more than 100 sound samples of birds found in the Uttarakhand region of the Indian subcontinent. In order to make a robust works which would primarily be used in outdoor environments, multiple disturbances such as wind noises, rustling leaves and human chatter were manually added to the recording environment.

2.4 Frontend Development

After successfully training the machine learning model and experimenting with its accuracy, we created the frontend which would be visible to and interacted by the end user. The frontend was built to be primarily web-based to allow it to run on a vast array of devices with minimal time and resource investment. The web frameworks React and p5.js were heavily involved to facilitate the development of the frontend. The model was accessible through the interface and upon recognizing the bird sound, the interface would fetch essential information about the bird from the IUCN Red List and display it to the user (Fig. 1).

Fig. 1. Frontend interface displaying the flow of listening for bird sounds, detecting a bird with the machine learning model, and displaying conservation information to the user from the IUCN Red List.

2.5 Real-World Testing

To test the interface and the model, we visited the Asan Barrage Bird Sanctuary to test the efficacy and accuracy of the model in a real-world scenario. This Bird Sanctuary, situated in the Uttarakhand-Himachal Pradesh border region of northern India, attracts a large number of migratory birds, including extremely endangered birds from the IUCN Red List [13] owing to which, the sanctuary has been designated as a protected Ramsar site. [14].

The testing involved regular fields visits to the sanctuary over the months of March to May, 2022. The visits were conducted in the hours of 8:00–12:00 and 16:00–18:00 (Fig. 2).

A checklist of 5 known birds, of varying IUCN Red List categories, visiting or residing in the sanctuary in that period of the year was prepared to confirm the detection capabilities of the model. The interface and model were run in various parts of the sanctuary on a smartphone throughout the entirety of the visits to validate that birdwatch could be run on any smartphone without any disruption. A bird was marked as detected on the checklist when the machine learning model could assign a confidence score of at least 95% to a detection.

Fig. 2. Birdwatch running at a busy section of the Asan Barrage Bird Sanctuary, Uttarakhand, India. Notice the large flocks of migratory birds on the islands in the distance!

3 Results

Birdwatch was able to successfully detect 3 out of the 5 birds on the checklist (Table 1).

Table 1. Checklist of detection status of birds with birdwatch, along with their IUCN Red List Categories: EN = Endangered, NT = Near Threatened, LC = Least Concern.

Bird common name	Bird scientific name	IUCN Red List category	Detection status
Pallas Fish Eagle	Haliaeetus leucoryphus	EN	Not detected
River Lapwing	Vanellus duvaucelii	NT	Detected
Common Kingfisher	Alcedo atthis	LC	Detected
Red-Naped Ibis	Pseudibis papillosa	LC	Not detected
Black Stork	Ciconia nigra	LC	Detected

4 Conclusion

This project has revealed several unexpected shortfalls in the current analogous method-ologies of bird identification and tracking in India while offering us a pathway into the modern ingenious methodologies, such as the one proposed here. Machine learning based bird identification offers fast and accurate results which manual methods would not. The use of auditory machine learning models also removes any possibility of human errors and manual false positives.

With the proposition of such new methods, the human taskforce currently involved in the detection and identification of birds for reasons of tracking and conservation can be redirected to more important, involved or niche tasks such as the upkeep of animals and educating the general populace about the importance conservation of wildlife. A perfect balance can be created in environments like these, where the technological innovation and human taskforces and co-exist to maximize productive output. Other industries such as the automotive industry and the manufacturing industry already make use of multiple modern technologies such as robotics and artificial intelligence to create stellar products, which are the apex of human intellect and technological advancements [15]. It is time that other fields of work such as forestry and animal conservation replicate the same and progress ahead at a faster rate.

5 Future Work

The progress of birdwatch, yet, has reached a state of a minimal viable product, by reason of which there are currently several apparent avenues to improve the detection and functioning of the implementation further. The immediate next steps of this work would involve around filtering the data samples used for training the model and digitally improving the selected samples with post processing techniques, starting with pitch filtering and automated silence and noise removal from the samples. The automation will then be extended to retrieve and train the model with the samples from the entirety of the audio repository, for birdwatch to detect virtually every bird with their sounds.

An auditory machine learning model, while having impressive detection accuracy without the need of expensive hardware or power requirements, will face problems in detecting subspecies of birds with identical or very similar bird songs and calls. To mitigate this, birdwatch will have to eventually also employ more complex models or include a secondary visual machine learning model to identify such subspecies of birds.

References

1. Mayr, E.: The number of species of birds. Auk **63**(1), 64–69 (1946)
2. Board, M.A.: Millennium Ecosystem Assessment, vol. 13, p. 520. New Island, Washington, DC (2005)
3. Prakash, V., et al.: Catastrophic collapse of Indian white-backed Gyps bengalensis and long-billed Gyps indicus vulture populations. Biol. Cons. **109**(3), 381–390 (2003)
4. Markandya, A., Taylor, T., Longo, A., Murty, M.N., Murty, S., Dhavala, K.: Counting the cost of vulture decline—an appraisal of the human health and other benefits of vultures in India. Ecol. Econ. **67**(2), 194–204 (2008)
5. Godoy, J.A., Jordano, P.: Seed dispersal by animals: exact identification of source trees with endocarp DNA microsatellites. Mol. Ecol. **10**(9), 2275–2283 (2001)
6. SoIB 2020. State of India's Birds, 2020: Range, trends and conservation status. The SoIB Partnership, p. 50 (2020)
7. Viswanathan, A., et al.: State of India's Birds 2020: Background and Methodology (2021)
8. Bibby, C.J., Burgess, N.D., Hillis, D.M., Hill, D.A., Mustoe, S.: Bird Census Techniques. Elsevier, Amsterdam (2000)

9. Alter, A.L., Wang, K.M.: An exploration of computer vision techniques for bird species classification (2017)
10. Okinda, C., et al.: A review on computer vision systems in monitoring of poultry: a welfare perspective. Artif. Intell. Agric. **4**, 184–208 (2020)
11. Xeno-canto Foundation. xeno-canto. https://xeno-canto.org
12. IUCN: The IUCN Red List of Threatened Species. Version 2021–3 (2021). https://www.iucnredlist.org
13. Arya, A.K., Joshi, K.K., Bachheti, A.: A study of waterbirds diversity in selected wetlands of Uttarakhand (Western Himalayas), India. Technol. (IJARET) **11**(5), 929–938 (2020)
14. Ramsar Sites Information Service. Asan Conservation Reserve. https://rsis.ramsar.org/ris/2437
15. Fernandez, G.C., Gutierrez, S.M., Ruiz, E.S., Perez, F.M., Gil, M.C.: Robotics, the new industrial revolution. IEEE Technol. Soc. Mag. **31**(2), 51–58 (2012)

A Survey on Phishing Website Detection Using Deep Neural Networks

Vivek Sharma[1]($\boxtimes$) and Tzipora Halevi[2]($\boxtimes$)

[1] Department of Computer Science, The Graduate Center, CUNY, New York, USA
vsharma@gradcenter.cuny.edu
[2] Department of Computer Science, Brooklyn College, CUNY, New York, USA
halevi@sci.brooklyn.cuny.edu

Abstract. Phishing is a social engineering attack, where an attacker poses as a legitimate individual or institution and convinces a victim to divulge their details through human interaction. There has been a steep rise in phishing cases across the globe. A report by Cisco [1] shows that phishing was the reason for 90% of data breaches in 2021. Various detection models have been proposed in the past to counter such attacks. Some proposed models work on improving the detection rate of phishing URLs while others focus on reducing their detection time. Authors have used machine learning, deep learning, and various other novel mechanisms in feature selections that result in high algorithm performance. This study is a systematic analysis of recent work utilizing deep learning for phishing detection, highlighting the research methods, algorithms, programming tools, and datasets used in such studies. This study further proposes some guidelines for future research, which include standardizing documentation and performance reporting. These guidelines may help researchers in their quest to replicate others' work and compare newly proposed methods with previously developed systems.

Keywords: Website phishing · Neural network · Survey · Phishing detection

1 Introduction

Phishing attacks continue to be very common with 465 brands targeted in Mar 2021 (Statista [2]). According to [3], phishing incidents rose 220% during the pandemic compared to the otherwise yearly average, with 52% of these attacks targeting brand names. 72% of the attacks during the pandemic used a valid HTTPS certificate while almost all of them used TLS encryption. Phishing website detection can help in finding such attempts and keep everyone safe in today's digital world. A lot of work has been done in the past and this paper analyzes articles related to phishing website detection using deep learning. The motivation of this article is to address the lack of standardization and difficulty in comparing various methodologies in this field. It aims to familiarise its reader

C. Stephanidis et al. (Eds.): HCII 2022, CCIS 1655, pp. 684–694, 2022.
https://doi.org/10.1007/978-3-031-19682-9_87

with the methodologies, algorithms, and tools used in such studies. It also provides statistical figures to summarize the results and adds suggestions that might encourage easy replication and comparison across similar studies.

Research Question: This paper looks at the following research questions: What is the current state of the research in phishing website detection using Deep Learning and how can proposed methodologies be made easier to replicate and comparable with other studies?

2   Theoretical Background

Phishing is a cybercrime where an attacker poses as a legitimate institution to lure the target into providing their sensitive data (Phishing.org [4]). Apart from email and website phishing attempts, there are other variants of such types of attacks that use voice calling and text messages. Additional attacks include website forgery, malware, and domain spoofing through which a victim can be trapped in phishing. Typically, Phishing is used against a large number of random targets, while in spear phishing, a targeted version of phishing, the attacks are targeted towards certain individuals who may possess valuable information.

To counter such attacks, various detection models have been proposed. Some of those concentrate on improving the detection rate of phishing URLs while others focus on reducing the detection time. To achieve this, authors use machine learning models like Naive Bayes, Logistic Regression, Random Forest, Decision Trees, Support Vector Machine (SVM), k-Nearest Neighbour, and deep learning models. Deep learning models include Convolutional Neural Network (CNN), Long Short Term Memory (LSTM), Recurrent Neural Network (RNN), and various other novel mechanisms.

Section 3 in this paper discusses the search strategies, inclusion, and exclusion criteria used in this systematic review. Section 4 covers the various algorithms used, paper goals, contents of the datasets, programming tools, and metrics used in these studies. Section 5 concludes the article with proposed suggestions for standardization techniques for future phishing detection research.

3   Methodology

This search was performed on City University of New York's (CUNY) online library OneSearch. We kept the search criteria broad by searching articles related to phishing and manually narrowed it down to website phishing. This is to ensure that papers that do not have the exact keywords can still be included in the study. Systematic review methodology by Kitchenham [5] is utilized in this study.

3.1   Search Strategy

- **Keyword Search:** The following search strings were used to find relevant papers: "Phishing" AND "Detection"

- **Period:** Articles published between 2017 and 2021
- **Paper Type:** Articles published in conferences or journals
- **Search Database:** City University of New York's online library CUNY One-Search
- **Inclusion Criteria:**
  - Articles written in English.
  - Article scheduled to be published with a pre-print available
  - Articles including keywords in title, full-text or their metadata.
  - Articles implementing or proposing a solution relevant to phishing detection
- **Exclusion Criteria:**
  - Book Chapters, Newsletter Articles, Books, and Dissertation.
  - Systematic reviews and literature survey.
  - Articles with pure ML-based implementations.

The search resulted in ninety-two papers out of which twenty-six papers were discarded after applying the exclusion criteria leaving a total of sixty-six papers. Articles that utilized pure Machine learning-based implementation such as kNN, SVM, Random Forest, and Logistic Regression were excluded from this study, except for hybrid and ensemble models where some ML algorithms are combined with deep learning-based algorithms.

4   Discussion/Findings Overview

Once the papers were collected and filtered using the method specified in the previous section, the articles were examined and categorized according to different criteria, including:

- **Datasets:** Datasets are used in the training and testing of the model. In phishing detection, the data needs to be continuously updated so researchers list out the methodologies used to fetch data from popular data sources. The Datasets include different features such as URLs, length of URL, domain based-features including the age of domain, DNS record, and HTML based features: number of out links, anchor tags, etc. Table 1 lists the datasets and data sources that are shared and used in multiple studies.
- **Programming tools:** Listing out the programming tools helps researchers in reproducing the work and comparing their proposed work against the same environmental specifications. The result in Sect. 4.2 confirms the recent trend in the use of python over other programming languages.
- **Algorithms used:** Various. deep learning based algorithms are used in model training. Some researchers fused multiple algorithms in ensemble and hybrid approaches to improve detection accuracy of the model.
- **Research Methods:** The different design goals of the covered work are described, which include removing dependencies or minimizing the needed input data as well as improvement of detection rates and reducing training and testing runtime.

4.1 Datasets

While some studies use proprietary datasets, multiple studies include publicly accessible ones, listed in Table 1.

Table 1. Most popular datasets used in phishing detection

Source	Details	Continuously updated
PhishTank [6]	Phishing URL are submitted and updated by registered users of its community. Users can fetch data through API key	✓
Common crawl [7]	Web crawled data which can be accessed through HTTP or S3. Column like IP address, URL hostname, port, protocol, query, URL hostname, and target URL to name few	✓
Alexa [8]	Top sites are listed based on their traffic ranks which is computed based on average daily visitor and page views	✓
DMOZ [9]	It was earlier known as Open Directory Project (ODP). RDF dumps of database are available to download from the site	✓
Phishload [10]	Contains more than 1000 targeted legitimate websites. Dataset contains HTML source code and other information like id, alexa rank, URL, URL has etc. The size of this dataset is roughly 6GB with screenshots and without screenshots is 44MB.	✗
UCI Phishing dataset [11]	Contains 2456 instances with 30 attributes. Contains IP address, URL-based features, HTML-based features and domain-based features like domain age, DNS record, Page rank etc. Training data is in .arff format and the size is less than a MB.	✗
Kaggle [12]	Contains 1353 instances with 10 attributes each. The features are URL, URL length, IP address, prefix/suffix, domain age etc. Phishing websites were selected from Phishtank and legitimate website were extracted from Yahoo. There are 548 legitimate, 103 suspicious, and 702 phishing websites labelled as 1, 0, −1 respectively	✗
PhishStorm [13]	Contains 48,009 legitimate URL and same number of phishing URL, taking the total to 96,018 URLs. Data is in .csv format and is approximately 3MB in size. This dataset is described and first used in study by Marchal et al. [14]	✗
Openphish [15]	Contains attributes like hostname, URL, path, SSL metadata, IP, targetted brand etc. Datasets dumps ranges from 30–180 days of phishing data. Provides an SQLite dataset which can be easily integrated using an open-source API [16]. Screenshot are available for most of the URLs.	✓

Datasets Features: Different types of data are used in various research, including:

- URL: Uniform Resource Locator(URL) and its related information like its length, and use of special characters with or without trimming were used in most of the studies. While most studies use URL repositories, some combine it with additional data listed below

- Metadata information: Metadata website information includes age of domain, popularity of websites, DNS rank, etc.
- Webpage content: It includes HTML tags based on information like the number of links in the source code.
- Images/screenshots: Some datasets have images and screenshots of the website or logo of targeted brands. These images were used along with URL based information to improve the accuracy of the model.

4.2   Programming Tools

Few articles described the programming tools and specifications used in their experiments. Among them almost 35% of the articles used python and approximately 10 % of them used WEKA, Java, and MATLAB-based implementation. The use of these latter languages is decreasing as compared to python. A survey conducted by Kaggle [17] indicated there is a large number of submissions in python and a significantly lower rate of submissions in other languages such as MATLAB and Java. This trend has been observed starting 2013 [18]

4.3   Algorithms

This section lists major deep learning algorithms used in training the classification models. The literature shows three main approaches used by researchers: deep learning models with a single algorithm, hybrid approaches, and ensemble approaches. The latter two approaches are analyzed in more detail in Sect. 4.4

Deep Learning Models: Primary deep learning models used were Deep Neural Networks with hidden layers, CNN, LSTM, and RNN. The models and their accuracy using these algorithms are shown in Table 3.

Ensemble Models: Multiple diverse models are generated and a final prediction is made after aggregating their predictions. Although this model consists of several base models, the model still acts and works like a single model. The ensemble model aims to reduce the generalization error of prediction. Nagaraj et al. [19] used random forest and neural network to get an accuracy of 93.41 on their ensemble model. Another model with LSTM and SVM saw an accuracy in the range of 95.40%–98.50%

Hybrid Models: The model is made by fusing multiple models into a single model. The algorithms used in such models and accuracy ranges are presented in Table 2.

4.4   Research Methods

This section categorizes the research methods used in the surveyed studies. We broadly classify the domain where these improvements were visible into three categories.

- **Novelty in Feature Selection techniques:** [20–23] used various feature extraction methods. [24,25] introduced novel features and [26] evaluated its model on different feature spaces. [27,28] used novel feature selection technique like Recursive Feature Elimination(RFE) in their work.
- **Use of Fusion/multilevel architecture:** Study by Kazienko et al. [29] shows the use of fusion and multilevel techniques like ensemble model and hybrid model improves the performance of the ML model. While ensemble models can take more time to train the model, a study by Sameen et al. [30] speeds this up through the use of a multi-threaded approach. Different fusion/multilevel architecture models are presented in Table 2.
- **Generation of Adversarial URLs:** Evaluating security aspects of a model is useful for evaluating the ability to prevent adversarial attacks. [31] assesses vulnerability of a system while [32] talks about defense against attacks. Adversarial phishing URL were generated by [33–37].
- **Eliminating need of dependencies:** Performance of a model can be affected by the interruption of third-party services, language dependencies, etc. Study by Somesha et al. [38], Yang et al. [39], Waziral et al. [27], and Jain et al. [40] eliminated need for third-party services in their work. Webpage content-based features, language dependencies and use manually crafted features were eliminated in [39,41,42] respectively.
- **Additional methods:** Work by [22,43–45] were directed towards increasing speed of detection. [46,47] addressed zero-day phishing vulnerabilities, [48] visualized internal working of a DNN while [41,49,50] created phishing detection aimed at low-power mobile devices.

Table 2. Hybrid approaches used in studies

Models	Author	Accuracy (%)
DNN - BiLSTM	Ozcan et al. [20]	99.21
DBN - SVM	Yu et al. [51]	99.96
AE - CNN	Zhang et al. [52]	97.68
CNN - SVM	Zhang et al. [52]	97.68
CNN-LSTM	Adebowale et al. [53]	92.10–93.28
	Yang et al. [54]	98.99
	Bu et al. [46]	95.40–98.32
CNN - RF	Yang et al. [39]	99.25–99.35
CNN - BiLSTM	Feng et al. [55]	99.05
	Zhang et al. [43]	98.03–99.79
	Zhang et al. [23]	92.09–98.84

Table 3. Deep learning algorithms used in studies

Models	Author	Accuracy (%)
DNN	Sumathi et al. [56]	90
	Lakshmi et al. [57]	92.09–98.44
	Somesha et al. [38]	99.43
	Soon et al. [58]	94.27–94.41
LSTM	Somesha et al. [38]	99.57
	Hashim et al. [32]	98.65
	Su et al. [59]	99.1
	Desuoza et al. [60]	95.89–98.30
	Pham et al. [36]	97
CNN	Wei et al. [49]	83.57–86.63
	Somesha et al. [38]	99.52
	Bartoli et al. [61]	98.2–99.2
	Al-Alyan et al. [62]	88.54–98.22
	Singh et al. [63]	98
	Mourtaj et al. [21]	97.94
	Aljofey et al. [64]	51.29–98.58
	Korkmaz et al. [22]	88.90
	Yerima et al. [65]	95.80–98.20
	Jawade et al. [45]	99
RNN	Feng et al. [48]	99.05
	Dutta et al. [66]	98.03–99.79
	Bahnsen et al. [67]	92.09–98.84

4.5 Recommendations

- **Use of shared datasets:** Shared datasets can help in replication and comparison among different models. It would be useful for researchers to test their data on shared datasets in addition to any proprietary dataset when possible, to help improve the side-by-side evaluation of different algorithms. Sometimes the datasets are not shared due to privacy or ethical issues. The researchers can share their approach to fetching data from a data source for easier replication.
- **Sharing code/algorithm:** This will encourage reproducibility of the work and provide a way for researchers to further adapt or expand the current work.
- **Testing on updated datasets continuously.** As new phishing websites are continuously introduced, this will provide a way to gauge the performance of successful phishing detection algorithms on newly introduced phishing URL
- **Standardize testing environment documentation:** Experimentation is the description of the environment in which the experiment was performed.

Creating a standard method of documentation, which will include details regarding the system parameters used and run-time, can help researchers assess the usability of different methods in different attack scenarios as well as recreate the test environment in future studies.

5   Conclusion

Phishing can be done through different techniques. This work focuses on the detection of phishing websites using deep learning neural networks. This study found that there is a growing body of research in this field, utilizing different techniques, datasets, and attack scenarios. This work points to share as well as datasets that continue to update and can be used in future research. It also compares the goals and design details of different studies and the resulting reported performance. This paper suggests methods for standardization of algorithms and testing reports, which can help improve the design of future studies.

References

1. CISCO: cisco threat report 2021. https://umbrella.cisco.com/info/2021-cyber-security-threat-trends-phishing-crypto-top-the-list
2. Johnson, J.: Phishing - statistics & facts. https://www.statista.com/topics/8385/phishing/
3. labs, F.: Phishing attacks soar 220% during COVID-19 peak as cybercriminal opportunism intensifies. https://www.f5.com/company/news/features/phishing-attacks-soar-220-during-covid-19-peak-as-cybercriminal
4. phishing.org: what is phishing. https://www.phishing.org/what-is-phishing
5. Kitchenham, B.: Procedures for performing systematic reviews. Keele, UK, Keele University **33**(2004), 1–26 (2004)
6. PhishTank: PhishTank. https://phishtank.org/
7. Crawl: common crawl. https://commoncrawl.org/
8. Alexa: alexa top sites. https://www.alexa.com/topsites
9. DMOZ: Dmoz phishing dataset. https://dmoz-odp.org/docs/en/rdf.html
10. Maurer, M.: Phishload. https://www.medien.ifi.lmu.de/team/max.maurer/files/phishload/index.html
11. UCI: UCI   phishing   dataset.   https://archive.ics.uci.edu/ml/datasets/phishing+websites
12. Kaggle: kaggle. https://www.kaggle.com/ahmednour/website-phishing-data-set
13. Marchal,   S: PhishStorm.   https://research.aalto.fi/en/datasets/phishstorm-phishing-legitimate-url-dataset
14. Marchal, S., François, J., State, R., Engel, T.: PhishStorm: detecting phishing with streaming analytics. IEEE Trans. Netw. Serv. Manage. **11**(4), 458–471 (2014)
15. OpenPhish: OpenPhish. https://openphish.com/phishing_database.html
16. OpenPhish: OpenPhish API. https://github.com/openphish/pyopdb
17. Kaggle: Kaggle survey 2019. https://www.kaggle.com/kaggle-survey-2019
18. Brownlee, J.: Best programming language. https://machinelearningmastery.com/best-programming-language-for-machine-learning/

19. Nagaraj, K., Bhattacharjee, B., Sridhar, A., Sharvani, G.: Detection of phishing websites using a novel twofold ensemble model. J. Sys. Inf. Technol. (2018)
20. Ozcan, A., Catal, C., Donmez, E., Senturk, B.: A hybrid DNN-LSTM model for detecting phishing URLs. Neural Comput. Appl. 1–17 (2021)
21. Mourtaji, Y., Bouhorma, M., Alghazzawi, D., Aldabbagh, G., Alghamdi, A.: Hybrid rule-based solution for phishing URL detection using convolutional neural network. Wirel. Commun. Mobile Comput. **2021** (2021)
22. Korkmaz, M., Kocyigit, E., Sahingoz, O.K., Diri, B.: Phishing web page detection using N-gram features extracted from URLs. In: 2021 3rd International Congress on Human-Computer Interaction, Optimization and Robotic Applications (HORA), pp. 1–6. IEEE (2021)
23. Zhang, Q., Bu, Y., Chen, B., Zhang, S., Lu, X.: Research on phishing webpage detection technology based on CNN-BiLSTM algorithm. In: Journal of Physics: Conference Series, vol. 1738, p. 012131. IOP Publishing (2021)
24. Yi, P., Guan, Y., Zou, F., Yao, Y., Wang, W., Zhu, T.: Web phishing detection using a deep learning framework. Wirel. Commun. Mobile Comput. **2018** (2018)
25. Xiao, X., Zhang, D., Hu, G., Jiang, Y., Xia, S.: CNN-MHSA: a convolutional neural network and multi-head self-attention combined approach for detecting phishing websites. Neural Netw. **125**, 303–312 (2020)
26. Liu, D.J., Geng, G.G., Jin, X.B., Wang, W.: An efficient multistage phishing website detection model based on the case feature framework: aiming at the real web environment. Comput. Secur. **110**, 102421 (2021)
27. Wazirali, R., Ahmad, R., Abu-Ein, A.A.K.: Sustaining accurate detection of phishing URLs using SDN and feature selection approaches. Comput. Netw. **201**, 108591 (2021)
28. Saha, I., Sarma, D., Chakma, R.J., Alam, M.N., Sultana, A., Hossain, S.: Phishing attacks detection using deep learning approach. In: 2020 Third International Conference on Smart Systems and Inventive Technology (ICSSIT), pp. 1180–1185. IEEE (2020)
29. Kazienko, P., Lughofer, E., Trawinski, B.: Editorial on the special issue "hybrid and ensemble techniques in soft computing: recent advances and emerging trends". Soft. Comput. **19**(12), 3353–3355 (2015). https://doi.org/10.1007/s00500-015-1916-x
30. Sameen, M., Han, K., Hwang, S.O.: PhishHaven-an efficient real-time AI phishing URLs detection system. IEEE Access **8**, 83425–83443 (2020)
31. Ogawa, Y., Kimura, T., Cheng, J.: Vulnerability assessment for deep learning based phishing detection system. In: 2021 IEEE International Conference on Consumer Electronics-Taiwan (ICCE-TW), pp. 1–2. IEEE (2021)
32. Hashim, A., Medani, R., Attia, T.A.: Defences against web application attacks and detecting phishing links using machine learning. In: 2020 International Conference on Computer, Control, Electrical, and Electronics Engineering (ICCCEEE), pp. 1–6. IEEE (2020)
33. AlEroud, A., Karabatis, G.: Bypassing detection of URL-based phishing attacks using generative adversarial deep neural networks. In: Proceedings of the Sixth International Workshop on Security and Privacy Analytics, pp. 53–60 (2020)
34. Xiao, X., et al.: Phishing websites detection via CNN and multi-head self-attention on imbalanced datasets. Comput. Secur. **108**, 102372 (2021)
35. Zhang, J., Li, X.: Phishing detection method based on borderline-smote deep belief network. In: Wang, G., Atiquzzaman, M., Yan, Z., Choo, K.-K.R. (eds.) SpaCCS 2017. LNCS, vol. 10658, pp. 45–53. Springer, Cham (2017). https://doi.org/10.1007/978-3-319-72395-2_5

36. Pham, T.D., Pham, T.T.T., Hoang, S.T., Ta, V.C.: Exploring efficiency of GAN-based generated URLs for phishing URL detection. In: 2021 International Conference on Multimedia Analysis and Pattern Recognition (MAPR), pp. 1–6. IEEE (2021)

37. Shirazi, H., Bezawada, B., Ray, I., Anderson, C.: Adversarial sampling attacks against phishing detection. In: Foley, S.N. (ed.) DBSec 2019. LNCS, vol. 11559, pp. 83–101. Springer, Cham (2019). https://doi.org/10.1007/978-3-030-22479-0_5

38. Somesha, M., Pais, A.R., Rao, R.S., Rathour, V.S.: Efficient deep learning techniques for the detection of phishing websites. Sādhanā **45**(1), 1–18 (2020). https://doi.org/10.1007/s12046-020-01392-4

39. Yang, R., Zheng, K., Wu, B., Wu, C., Wang, X.: Phishing website detection based on deep convolutional neural network and random forest ensemble learning. Sensors **21**(24), 8281 (2021)

40. Jain, A.K., Gupta, B.B.: A machine learning based approach for phishing detection using hyperlinks information. J. Ambient. Intell. Humaniz. Comput. **10**(5), 2015–2028 (2019). https://doi.org/10.1007/s12652-018-0798-z

41. Rao, R.S., Vaishnavi, T., Pais, A.R.: PhishDump: a multi-model ensemble based technique for the detection of phishing sites in mobile devices. Pervasive Mob. Comput. **60**, 101084 (2019)

42. Tajaddodianfar, F., Stokes, J.W., Gururajan, A.: Texception: a character/word-level deep learning model for phishing URL detection. In: ICASSP 2020–2020 IEEE International Conference on Acoustics, Speech and Signal Processing (ICASSP), pp. 2857–2861. IEEE (2020)

43. Zhang, L., Zhang, P.: PhishTrim: fast and adaptive phishing detection based on deep representation learning. In: 2020 IEEE International Conference on Web Services (ICWS), pp. 176–180. IEEE (2020)

44. Yuan, H., Yang, Z., Chen, X., Li, Y., Liu, W.: URL2vec: URL modeling with character embeddings for fast and accurate phishing website detection. In: 2018 IEEE International Conference on Parallel & Distributed Processing with Applications, Ubiquitous Computing & Communications, Big Data & Cloud Computing, Social Computing & Networking, Sustainable Computing & Communications (ISPA/IUCC/BDCloud/SocialCom/SustainCom), pp. 265–272. IEEE (2018)

45. Jawade, J.V., Ghosh, S.N.: Phishing website detection using fast. ai library. In: 2021 International Conference on Communication information and Computing Technology (ICCICT), pp. 1–5. IEEE (2021)

46. Bu, S.J., Cho, S.B.: Integrating deep learning with first-order logic programmed constraints for zero-day phishing attack detection. In: ICASSP 2021–2021 IEEE International Conference on Acoustics, Speech and Signal Processing (ICASSP), pp. 2685–2689. IEEE (2021)

47. Bozkir, A.S., Aydos, M.: LogoSENSE: a companion HOG based logo detection scheme for phishing web page and E-mail brand recognition. Comput. Secur. **95**, 101855 (2020)

48. Feng, T., Yue, C.: Visualizing and interpreting RNN models in URL-based phishing detection. In: Proceedings of the 25th ACM Symposium on Access Control Models and Technologies, pp. 13–24 (2020)

49. Wei, B., et al.: A deep-learning-driven light-weight phishing detection sensor. Sensors **19**, 4258 (2019). https://doi.org/10.3390/s19194258.https://www.mdpi.com/1424-8220/19/19/4258

50. Haynes, K., Shirazi, H., Ray, I.: Lightweight URL-based phishing detection using natural language processing transformers for mobile devices. Procedia Comput. Sci. **191**, 127–134 (2021)

51. Yu, X.: Phishing websites detection based on hybrid model of deep belief network and support vector machine. In: IOP Conference Series: Earth and Environmental Science, vol. 602, p. 012001. IOP Publishing (2020)

52. Zhang, X., Shi, D., Zhang, H., Liu, W., Li, R.: Efficient detection of phishing attacks with hybrid neural networks. In: 2018 IEEE 18th International Conference on Communication Technology (ICCT), pp. 844–848. IEEE (2018)

53. Adebowale, M.A., Lwin, K.T., Hossain, M.A.: Intelligent phishing detection scheme using deep learning algorithms. J. Enterp. Inf. Manage. (2020)

54. Yang, P., Zhao, G., Zeng, P.: Phishing website detection based on multidimensional features driven by deep learning. IEEE access **7**, 15196–15209 (2019)

55. Feng, J., Zou, L., Ye, O., Han, J.: Web2vec: phishing webpage detection method based on multidimensional features driven by deep learning. IEEE Access **8**, 221214–221224 (2020)

56. Sumathi, K., Sujatha, V.: Deep learning based-phishing attack detection. Int. J. Recent Technol. Eng. (IJRTE) **8**(3) (2019)

57. Lakshmi, L., Reddy, M.P., Santhaiah, C., Reddy, U.J.: Smart phishing detection in web pages using supervised deep learning classification and optimization technique ADAM. Wireless Pers. Commun. **118**(4), 3549–3564 (2021). https://doi.org/10.1007/s11277-021-08196-7

58. Soon, G.K., Chiang, L.C., On, C.K., Rusli, N.M., Fun, T.S.: Comparison of ensemble simple feedforward neural network and deep learning neural network on phishing detection. In: Alfred, R., Lim, Y., Haviluddin, H., On, C.K. (eds.) Computational Science and Technology. LNEE, vol. 603, pp. 595–604. Springer, Singapore (2020). https://doi.org/10.1007/978-981-15-0058-9_57

59. Su, Y.: Research on website phishing detection based on LSTM RNN. In: 2020 IEEE 4th Information Technology, Networking, Electronic and Automation Control Conference (ITNEC), vol. 1, pp. 284–288. IEEE (2020)

60. de Souza, C.H.M., Lemos, M.O.O., da Silva, F.S.D., Alves, R.L.S.: On detecting and mitigating phishing attacks through featureless machine learning techniques. Internet Technol. Lett. **3**(1), e135 (2020)

61. Bartoli, A., De Lorenzo, A., Medvet, E., Tarlao, F.: Personalized, browser-based visual phishing detection based on deep learning. In: Zemmari, A., Mosbah, M., Cuppens-Boulahia, N., Cuppens, F. (eds.) CRiSIS 2018. LNCS, vol. 11391, pp. 80–85. Springer, Cham (2019). https://doi.org/10.1007/978-3-030-12143-3_7

62. Al-Alyan, A., Al-Ahmadi, S.: Robust URL phishing detection based on deep learning. KSII Trans. Internet Inf. Syst. (TIIS) **14**(7), 2752–2768 (2020)

63. Singh, S., Singh, M., Pandey, R.: Phishing detection from URLs using deep learning approach. In: 2020 5th International Conference on Computing, Communication and Security (ICCCS), pp. 1–4. IEEE (2020)

64. Aljofey, A., Jiang, Q., Qu, Q., Huang, M., Niyigena, J.P.: An effective phishing detection model based on character level convolutional neural network from URL. Electronics **9**(9), 1514 (2020)

65. Yerima, S.Y., Alzaylaee, M.K.: High accuracy phishing detection based on convolutional neural networks. In: 2020 3rd International Conference on Computer Applications & Information Security (ICCAIS), pp. 1–6. IEEE (2020)

66. Dutta, A.K.: Detecting phishing websites using machine learning technique. PLoS ONE **16**(10), e0258361 (2021)

67. Bahnsen, A.C., Bohorquez, E.C., Villegas, S., Vargas, J., González, F.A.: Classifying phishing URLs using recurrent neural networks. In: 2017 APWG Symposium on Electronic Crime Research (eCrime), pp. 1–8. IEEE (2017)

Revealing Doubtful Data in 200k Images via Re-annotation Workshop by Researcher Community

Ryota Suzuki(✉) and Hirokatsu Kataoka

National Institute of Advanced Industrial Science and Technology,
1-1-1 Umezono, Tsukuba, Ibaraki, Japan
{ryota.suzuki,hirokatsu.kataoka}@aist.go.jp

Abstract. In this paper, we conducted the ImageNet Reannotation workshop with researchers who use ImageNet to find doubtful data in ImageNet. Recent great growth of deep learning is supported by large scale datasets collected by cloud working such as ImageNet, but it seems to have not so few doubtful data for given tasks. We assume that the professionals can efficiently and accurately find doubtful data while they know what kind of data would be better for learning classification tasks. Moreover, we adopted a group working scheme so that it could be more efficient and accurate. This paper shows the re-annotation result that clarifies category and reason of doubtfulness in the large scale dataset constructed by cloud workers.

Keywords: Dataset · Annotation · Cloud sourcing

1 Introduction

Recent great growth of deep learning is supported by large scale datasets. ImageNet [2] is one of the most known large scale image dataset that is the first dataset to let deep learning succeed. ImageNet collects large amounts of images with class labels annotated by cloud workers. ImageNet is known for not only large scale but also high accuracy so that it is capable of deep learning. Deep learning requires a large scale of dataset and so cloud working is essential for constructing such a large dataset.

The image recognition task, that answers category of an object shown in a given image, is one of the basic task on computer vision division. After the deep lerning based image recognition model AlexNet [4] surpassed conventional state-of-the-art methods on 2012, many deep learning research have been conducted with ImageNet as de facto standard image dataset. Moreover, it was found that developers can easily construct high quality deep learning model with smaller scale dataset on a specific domain based on an ImageNet pre-trained model. The process is known as fine-tuning, and quite a large number of deep learning models based on the ImageNet pre-trained model have been spread in world wide.

© The Author(s), under exclusive license to Springer Nature Switzerland AG 2022
C. Stephanidis et al. (Eds.): HCII 2022, CCIS 1655, pp. 695–701, 2022.
https://doi.org/10.1007/978-3-031-19682-9_88

Fig. 1. Example images of Kidney beans label.

Although we benefit high performance of deep learning with ImageNet, it seems to have not so few doubtful data. Northcutt et al. surveyed the label error with cloud working and they reported almost 6% of images of ImageNet test dataset were judged as label error [5]. In Fig. 1, both images are annotated with the Kidney beans label. Actually we can judge the left one is an image of kidney beans with no doubt, but the right one is difficult to say that it is a representative picture of kidney beans. We call such samples *doubtful data*. Surveying doubtful data in ImageNet will provide findings that how many, how much and what kind of doubtful data are potentially included in every large scale dataset constructed with cloud workers.

In this paper, we conducted the ImageNet Reannotation workshop with researchers who use ImageNet to find doubtful data in ImageNet. We assume that the professionals can efficiently and accurately find doubtful data while they know what kind of data would be better for learning classification tasks. Moreover, we adopted a group working scheme so that it could be more efficient and accurate. Compared with other works like [5], we clarify both population and detailed reason of doubtful data.

1.1 Related Work

In recent years, several works about rethinking ImageNet have been reported.

Several works reported that evaluation on recent image classification studies based on ImageNet is unfairly high because an image in ImageNet has multiple objects even while each image has a single label, using the newly re-annotated validation set of ImageNet by cloud annotation which multiple labels [1,7]. Recht et al. revealed that recent deeplearning based image classification methods are over-fitted to ImageNet validation dataset [6]. Hendrics et al. reported that examples called "natural adversarial examples" exist which lead models trained with ImageNet miss-classify, and they considered it is caused by noisy data in ImageNet [3]. Yang et al. released a dataset that inadequate images in ImageNet are eliminated on the viewpoint of fairness [8].

These researches also tried to re-annotate ImageNet as we did, however they are limited to the validation set, which is a smaller part of ImageNet. Moreover, they were not well investigated what kind of inadequate data are included in ImageNet. In our research, we executed re-annotation on train set of ImageNet, and we also collect detailed reason of doubtfulness through the re-annotation workshop.

Fig. 2. An interface of the annotation system.

2   ImageNet Reannotation Workshop

26 researchers of cvpaper.challenge[1], which is a community of computer vision research in Japan, were engaged in the workshop for three days, totally 17 h. The participants consisted of undergraduate and graduate (both master and doctor course) university students, and Ph.D. researchers, who knew well and daily used ImageNet. We asked the participants to annotate "the doubtful data which do not seem sufficient for the image classification task" using the annotation system we newly developed (see Fig. 2). They were divided into groups of three or four participants, so that they could discuss for the annotation. We prepared a desk and a terminal for each group, so only a participant in a group could operate the annotation system. To promote discussion, we also asked them to take a note on Slack[2] about how they made judgements for difficult cases.

After the last annotation session of each day, we had a discussion session to discuss what tools they used, how they established rules of annotation, and what kind of doubtful data was found.

---

[1] http://xpaperchallenge.org/cv/.

[2] https://slack.com/.

(a) Lynx   (b) Tigar cat   (c) Cab

Fig. 3. Samples of doubtful data of similar classes.

(a) Hammer   (b) Fire engine   (c) Flute

Fig. 4. Samples of doubtful data of gap of subjective.

3   Result

As a result, 284,589 images of 223 classes were visually examined, and 17,419 (6%) images were judged as doubtful data. The types of doubtfulness can be divided into 5 types based on the discussions in the workshop.

3.1   Similar Classes

Some images seem to have wrong labels because appearance or concept is close to each other (see Fig. 3).

3.2   Gap of Subjective

Some images seem to have gaps between their labels (see Fig. 4). Actually many images have multiple objects, and some of them do not place the target object as it is the subject.

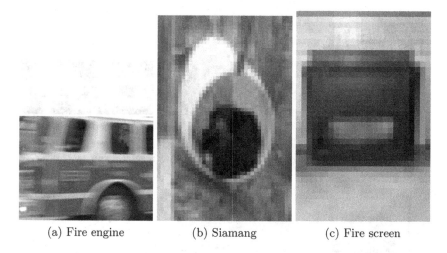

(a) Fire engine   (b) Siamang   (c) Fire screen

Fig. 5. Samples of doubtful data of low resolution.

3.3   Low Resolution

In some images, a subject is photographed with quite low resolution although the label is no problem (see Fig. 5). Extremely low resolution images are considered to degrade the accuracy of deep learning models.

3.4   Images of Text Recognition Required

There are some images which are required to recognize text in the images for classification (see Fig. 6). It is often impossible to classify only from the appearance of the images, so it seems to be doubtful data for the professionals.

3.5   Synthesized Images

Some images are synthesized images, which have quite different appearance with the other pictures (see Fig. 7).

4   Discussion

Interestingly, there are some cases that seem to be caused by the ethics of annotators. The labels in ImageNet are precisely defined based on the word dictionary WordNet, and there should not be misconception. However, the doubtfulness type 1 are occured. We consider it is because of less familiarness to the labels and lack of effort of workers. In the workshop, the participants paid special attention not to fail to re-annotate, and they managed to clarify the definition of the label to search the words and their representative images. The cloud workers who were engaged in original ImageNet annotation belonged to Amazon Mechanical Turk, and they might not pay as much effort as the participants of the workshop.

(a) Butcher shop   (b) Cab   (c) Carpainter's kit

Fig. 6. Samples of doubtful data requiring text recognition.

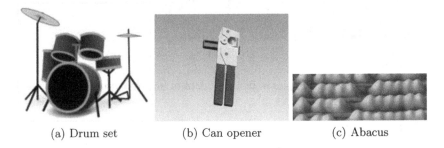

(a) Drum set   (b) Can opener   (c) Abacus

Fig. 7. Samples of doubtful data of Synthesized images.

5   Conclusion

Through the workshop, we revealed doubtful data in the large scale image dataset caused by cloud working. When we construct more accurate large scale image datasets with the help of cloud workers, it is required to prepare worked-out plans, e.g. making annotation instruction with samples of doubtful data, or enabling re-annotation as we did, for decreasing doubtful data.

References

1. Beyer, L., Hénaff, O.J., Kolesnikov, A., Zhai, X., van den Oord, A.: Are we done with ImageNet? arXiv preprint (2020). arXiv:2006.07159
2. Deng, J., Dong, W., Socher, R., Li, L.J., Li, K., Fei-Fei, L.: ImageNet: a large-scale hierarchical image database. In: Proceedings of the 2009 IEEE Conference on Computer Vision and Pattern Recognition (CVPR 2009), pp. 248–255 (2009). https://doi.org/10.1109/CVPR.2009.5206848
3. Hendrycks, D., Zhao, K., Basart, S., Steinhardt, J., Song, D.: Natural adversarial examples. In: Proceedings of the IEEE/CVF Conference on Computer Vision and Pattern Recognition (CVPR 2021), pp. 15262–15271 (2021)
4. Krizhevsky, A., Sutskever, I., Hinton, G.E.: ImageNet classification with deep convolutional neural networks. In: Pereira, F., Burges, C.J.C., Bottou, L., Weinberger, K.Q. (eds.) Advances in Neural Information Processing Systems, vol. 25. Curran Associates, Inc. (2012)

5. Northcutt, C.G., Athalye, A., Mueller, J.: Pervasive label errors in test sets destabilize machine learning benchmarks. In: Proceedings of the 35th Conference on Neural Information Processing Systems (NeurIPS 2021) Track on Datasets and Benchmarks (2021)
6. Recht, B., Roelofs, R., Schmidt, L., Shankar, V.: Do ImageNet classifier generalize to ImageNet? In: Proceedings of the 36th International Conference on Machine Learning (ICML 2019) (2019)
7. Tsipras, D., Santurkar, S., Engstrom, L., Ilyas, A., Madry, A.: From imagenet to image classification: contextualizing progress on benchmarks. In: ArXiv preprint arXiv:2005.11295 (2020)
8. Yang, K., Qinami, K., Fei-Fei, L., Deng, J., Russakovsky, O.: Towards fairer datasets: filtering and balancing the distribution of the people subtree in the ImageNet hierarchy. In: Proceedings of the 2020 Conference on Fairness, Accountability, and Transparency, FAT* 2020, pp. 547–558. Association for Computing Machinery, New York (2020)

Attention and Human AI Collaboration - The Context of Automated Vehicles

Zoubeir Tkiouat[1]([✉]), Élise Labonté-LeMoyne[1], Ryad Titah[1], Nicolas Saunier[2],
Pierre-Majorique Léger[1], and Sylvain Sénécal[1]

[1] HEC Montréal, Montréal, Canada
{zoubeir.tkiouat,elise.labonte-lemoyne,ryad.titah,
pierre-majorique.leger}@hec.ca
[2] Polytechnique Montreal, Montréal, Canada
nicolas.saunier@polymtl.ca

Abstract. With the increase in vehicle automation, the role of the driver is shifting towards that of a partner or a teammate of the automated system. In this collaboration, the driver needs to monitor the environment and be a fallback operator of the automated system to ensure the performance and safety of driving, especially in the case of transition of control from the automated system to the human driver. To further our understanding the role of the direr (or user) in this context, we aim to conduct a scoping review that 1) synthesizes the cognitive and attentional factors that impact the performance of collaboration between the automated system and the human operator, and 2) identifies the different mechanisms and design elements that can potentially improve this performance and keep the driver in-the-loop. This work presents the theoretical grounding, the methodology, as well as the initial results of the review process.

Keywords: Automated vehicle · Human-AI collaboration · Self-driving · Situation awareness · Attention

1 Introduction

The rise of vehicle automation introduces an important change to the role of the driver. The traditional role of the driver is shifting towards that of a partner or a teammate of the automated (or autonomous) system to which more tasks are being delegated. Within this collaboration between the automated system and the human operator, for most commercialized automated vehicles, the driver needs to monitor the environment and be a fallback operator of the automated system [1]. One of the most important aspects of this automated system-human collaboration, that directly impacts the performance and safety of driving, is the transition of control from the automated system to the human driver.

Different attentional and cognitive factors are found to directly affect the performance of this transition of control [2], especially when the resumption of control is triggered by the system, and prompted by a situation that the system's capabilities cannot handle.

C. Stephanidis et al. (Eds.): HCII 2022, CCIS 1655, pp. 702–706, 2022.
https://doi.org/10.1007/978-3-031-19682-9_89

The effect of these attentional and cognitive factors on performance is mediated by the individual's situation awareness, defined as an individual's "perception of the elements in the environment within a volume of time and space, the comprehension of their meaning, and the projection of their status in the near future" [3].

While there are existing reviews that identify the different factors influencing the takeover (i.e., transition of control) time [4] and quality [5], we aim to conduct a scoping review that 1) synthesizes the different attention and cognitive factors that impacts the performance of collaboration between the automated system and the human operator, and specifically that of the resumption of control by the human operator, and 2) identifies the different mechanisms and design elements that can potentially improve this performance.

2 Theoretical Grounding

With the progress of automated (autonomous) vehicles, the involvement of the driver in the operations of the vehicle becomes less required. However, the involvement of the driver to take the control of the vehicle is still very critical. This is because there are two almost parallel tracks for AV development; in the first group, car manufacturers are gradually incorporating ADAS that automate driving functions one by one (level 1 or 2), e.g., adaptive cruise control and lane keeping, where constant driver input and supervision is still required, while in the second group, new technological companies like Waymo develop fully automated vehicles (levels 4 and 5) that do not require any driver input at any time. In the second group, the vehicles will most likely, at least at first, be used to provide a taxi-like service and not for direct sale to end consumers.

The taxonomy of SAE International specifies six (6) different levels of the level of automation as well as the corresponding roles of the driver and the automated system in driving the vehicle [6]: Level 0 -no automation- relies fully on the human to drive the vehicle. At level 1 -driver assistance-, the system can provide assistance to the human while driving for specific tasks. At level 2 -partial automation-, the system performs some tasks such as steering and acceleration, while the human monitors the vehicle and is fully responsible for the other driving tasks. At level 3 -conditional automation-, the system can perform all the driving tasks. However, the human needs to stay attentive to the state of the system and be ready to take control if the system requires it. At level 4 -high automation-, the system is capable of fully operating the vehicle without requiring the supervision and intervention of a human driver in a given area and under most circumstances. Lasty, at Level 5 -full automation-, the system can perform all driving tasks without any human involvement.

In sum, up to level 3, the collaboration between the human driver and the autonomous system takes the form of shared control between the two where there are still situations where the operating system of the vehicle hands over the driving task to the driver either by necessity or following the choice of the driver. Therefore, this transition of control is a critical element that entails a considerable amount of risk contingent upon whether the human can take over the control of the vehicle safely.

The present work presents a scoping review to investigate the different elements that affect the performance of the handover of control from the vehicle's operating system towards the human. Specifically, the research questions we aim to answer are "What are the different attention related states and traits that influence the performance of handover of control from the operating system to the human operator? What are the different mechanisms/ design characteristics that can potentially mitigate this loss of performance?".

The rationale behind the efficacy of the different mechanisms/design characteristics that can potentially improve the quality of the transition of control from an autonomous system to the human driver is that the more the human is kept "in the loop" before his involvement is necessary [7], the higher his performance will be, in terms attentional control and decision making, through higher situation awareness [2, 8] when taking over the control of the vehicle once it is necessary.

3   Methods

Our work aims to further our understanding of the critical factors that impact the performance of the collaboration between a human agent and an artificial intelligence system in the context automated (or autonomous) vehicles. As such the domain of our scoping review is the automated vehicles literature where artificial intelligence systems take on, at least in part, the function of driving the vehicle. Within the collaboration between the human operator and the operating system of the vehicle, the most critical element of our review is the transfer of control from the vehicle to the human operator, i.e., the "takeover".

The targeted databases of our initial search are the Transport Research International Documentation (TRID) database, Web of science. As well as Google Scholar for the forward citation search. The scoping of keywords used in the research query followed an iterative process in which the first step consists of a search in both databases using a set of "seed" keywords that reflect the domain of autonomous/automated vehicles as well as the phenomenon of transfer of control from the vehicle's driving AI system to the human operator. We sampled 30 papers from the search results from which we extracted additional keywords (synonyms) to complement our initial set. This process of searching the two databases, sampling papers to identify synonyms and bonify the set of keywords was done three more times.

During the screening process of the resulting records, non-English, non-peer reviewed, as well as papers that did not involve an automation-to-manual takeover performed by a human, and those that were not empirical papers with primary data were excluded. Criteria for inclusion were: 1) records that deal with the user's (driver) attentional, mental states, traits, or skills, as well as 2) those investigating the use of any feedback, signal, or stimuli to assist the driver / user. Following this screening process, a forward citation search was performed to identify relevant records that were not captured by the query search.

Screening and data extraction were performed with two raters. Data extraction concerns first the user's (driver) attentional, mental states, traits, or skills, and their impact on takeover performance. Second, elements of the feedback, signal, or stimuli that assist the driver/user during the takeover were also extracted while looking at both the attribute of the signal or stimuli as well as its efficacy regarding the takeover performance.

4   Initial Results and State of the Review

The first step of the scoping of keywords used in the research query resulted in 218 records from Web of science and 83 records from TRID. A sample of 20 and 10 records were screened from both Web of science and TRID respectively and allowed the identification of 8 synonyms such as "Automated driving", "Manual control", "vehicle control" and "out-of-the-loop". The second iteration of this process returned 377 records from Web of science and 202 records from TRID. 40 records (20 resulting from both Web of science and TRID) were then screened to identify 5 additional keywords including "driver monitoring", "engagement", and "distraction". The third search iteration returned 1732 records on Web of science from which 20 records were screen to identify the last 7 keywords including "vigilance", "shared control", and "self-driving". The fourth search iteration returned 1856 records on Web of science and did not help identify any additional keywords after screening a sample of 20 papers.

The final search using the finalized comprehensive set of keywords yielded 4429 records from both databases. 388 duplicates were removed before the screening process. Inter-rater reliability was assessed with a sample of 50 records that were selected and screened using the exclusion and inclusion criteria and resulted in a Cohen's Kappa of 74.14%. A follow-up discussion showed that most differences in screening were due to a "no" vote of the first rater and a "maybe" vote from the second rater and led to the reformulation of one inclusion criterion, that is "records that deal with the user's (driver) attentional and mental states, traits, or skills". Currently, the review is at the screening step of the review process.

5   Discussion of Results and Insight Gained from the Process

The initial screening process showed that different states including fatigue, alertness, situation awareness, gaze direction, cognitive load, trust/ confidence in the system and stress have an impact on the performance of takeover of control from the operating system of the vehicle to the human driver e.g., [9]. As for the feedback signal/stimuli used to assist and improve the efficacy of the user in retaking control, attributes including the modality of the feedback (e.g., vocal, visual, vibrotactile), the timing of the takeover requesting alerts as well as the monitoring of the driver's mental state are all found to be an important determinant e.g., [10].

From the resulting papers, we found a few articles that were of relevance to issues related to the ethical or responsible AI use. Some of these issues address a more macro perspective such as the reskilling of drivers and workforce change that are the result of the introduction of a more commercial use of AVs [11]. The safety issue is a very relevant and recurrent one in this literature due to the higher risks associated with driving in general and the remaining unknown factors relating to AVs in particular [12]. These safety concerns encompass risks related to pedestrian collision [13] as well as risks stemming from the negative aspects of autonomous design such as automation misuse and ethical dilemmas [14].

The following steps of our review consist of finalizing the full text screening of the selected records. We then intend to proceed with a forward citation search to capture articles that were not included in the initial query search. We intend to extract information from the selected articles relative to the 1) user's (driver) attentional, mental states, traits, or skills, 2) their impact on takeover performance, as well as 3) the attribute of the feedback, signal, or stimuli that assist the driver/user during the takeover and 4) the efficacy regarding the takeover performance.

References

1. Louw, T., Kountouriotis, G., Carsten, O.: Driver inattention during vehicle automation: how does driver engagement affect resumption of control? New South Wales, p. 14 (2015)
2. Louw, T., Merat, N.: Are you in the loop? Using gaze dispersion to understand driver visual attention during vehicle automation. Transp. Res. Part C-Emerg. Technol. 76, 35–50 (2017). https://doi.org/10.1016/j.trc.2017.01.001
3. Endsley, M.R.: Design and evaluation for situation awareness enhancement. In: Proceedings of the Human Factors Society Annual Meeting, vol. 32, no. 2, pp. 97–101 (1988)
4. de Winter, J.C.F. Happee, R. Martens, M.H., Stanton, N.A.: Effects of adaptive cruise control and highly automated driving on workload and situation awareness: a review of the empirical evidence. Transp. Res. Part F Traffic Psychol. Behav. 27, 196–217 (2014). https://doi.org/10.1016/j.trf.2014.06.016
5. Gold, C., Happee, R., Bengler, K.: Modeling take-over performance in level 3 conditionally automated vehicles. Accid. Anal. Prev. 116, 3–13 (2018). https://doi.org/10.1016/j.aap.2017.11.009
6. SAE J.: 3016. Taxonomy and definitions for terms related to on-road motor vehicle automated driving systems. Soc. Automot. Eng. (2014)
7. Endsley, M.R., Kiris, E.O.: The out-of-the-loop performance problem and level of control in automation. Hum. Factors J. Hum. Factors Ergon. Soc. 37(2), 381–394 (1995). https://doi.org/10.1518/001872095779064555
8. Horswill, M. S. McKenna, F.P.: Drivers' hazard perception ability: Situation awareness on the road. Cogn. Approach Situat. Aware. Theory Appl. 155–175 (2004)
9. Wilkie, R., et al.: Cognitive load during automation affects gaze Behaviours and transitions to manual steering control, pp. 426–432 (2019). https://drivingassessment.uiowa.edu/sites/drivingassessment.uiowa.edu/files/da2019_65_wilkie_final.pdf
10. Yun, H., Yang, J.H.: Multimodal warning design for take-over request in conditionally automated driving. Eur. Transp. Res. Rev. 12(1), 1–11 (2020). https://doi.org/10.1186/s12544-020-00427-5
11. Nikitas, A., Vitel, A.-E., Cotet, C.: Autonomous vehicles and employment: An urban futures revolution or catastrophe? Cities 114, 103203 (2021). https://doi.org/10.1016/j.cities.2021.103203
12. Pradhan, A.K., Pulver, E., Zakrajsek, J., Bao, S., Molnar, L.: Perceived safety benefits, concerns, and utility of advanced driver assistance systems among owners of ADAS-equipped vehicles. Traffic Inj. Prev. 19(2), 135–137 (2018). https://doi.org/10.1080/15389588.2018.1532201
13. Schratter, M., Hartmann, M., Watzenig, D.: Pedestrian collision avoidance system for autonomous vehicles: SAE Int. J. Connect. Autom. Veh. 2(4), 279–293 (2019). https://doi.org/10.4271/12-02-04-0021
14. Banks, V.A., Stanton, N.A., Plant, K.L.: Who is in responsible for automated driving? A macro-level insight into automated driving in the united kingdom using the risk management framework and social network analysis. Appl. Ergon. 81, 102904 (2019). https://doi.org/10.1016/j.apergo.2019.102904

Natural Language Processing for Scientific Paper Evaluation: Comparing Human and Machine Judgements

Tom Xu[1]([✉]), Noel Hinton[1], Michael Timothy Bennett[1], and Yoshihiro Maruyama[1,2]

[1] School of Computing, The Australian National University, Canberra, Australia
{tom.xu,noel.hinton,michael.bennett,yoshihiro.maruyama}@anu.edu.au
[2] Advanced Telecommunications Research Institute, Kyoto, Japan

Abstract. A huge number of papers have been published about COVID-19. So much it's overwhelming. Many papers appear on preprint servers such as arXiv before publication. Researchers and clinicians can get ahead of the curve by making use of these preprint papers, but how to tell what is worth reading? Could there be an automated recommendation mechanism? In this paper we address the question by experimenting with SPECTER document-level vector embedding which establishes the representations by incorporating state-of-the-art Transformer models, such as SciBERT, a BERT variant tailored to scientific text. Meanwhile, the dataset we choose to apply SPECTER embedding is the CORD-19 dataset.

Keywords: SciBERT · SPECTER · CORD-19

1 Introduction

During the COVID-19 crisis, we have seen a substantial amount of new research papers posted on preprint servers such as BioRxiv. It is practically impossible for a COVID-19 researcher to examine all of them within a limited amount of time available for their preprint checking. Natural language processing can be useful to select a subset of COVID-19 preprints worth reading in detail. How should we select that subset then? In particular, how should we determine the quality of papers? Broadly speaking, high-quality papers tend to be published in high-ranking journals/conferences, and weaker papers in lower-ranking venues. In this work, we build a proof-of-concept binary classification model based upon SPECTER (Scientific Paper Embeddings using Citation-informed TransformERs), which allows us to build document-level representations of academic papers that are applicable to many downstream tasks. SPECTER iterates

This work was supported by JST (JPMJMS2033). The last author would like to thank Advanced Telecommunications Research Institute for his research visit there.

on an existing hierarchy of pretrained Transformers: SciBERT [1], which builds on BERT [4], which itself uses multiple layers of Transformers [8]. SPECTER builds its representations using a paper's title and abstract, and tunes these representations using paper citations. Such fine-tuning is motivated by the observation that two papers are more related if one cites the other. Importantly, the trained SPECTER model does not use citations to generate a representation, so embeddings can be made for unpublished papers. The main advantage of SPECTER among pretrained neural language models is that it does not require further task-specific fine-tuning.

2   Related Work

Various other COVID-19 corpora and associated applications have been discussed by Wang and Lo under the umbrella term of 'text-mining' [9]. LitCovid is another popular database of COVID-19 papers [2,3], but it does not include document embeddings as CORD-19 does. Many systems exist that facilitate document and data exploration, summarisation, visualisation, and other tasks. Others aim to automate the systematic review of the COVID-19 literature, so that clinicians and public health officials may make the most informed decisions.

3   Experimental Setup

3.1   Data

We chose CORD-19 as our training corpus (the 2021-04-26 release), filtered to just published papers from 2020 onward. We used CORD-19's SPECTER embeddings of papers as input data to the SVM and labelled the papers as 'recommended' ($C1$) or 'not recommended' ($C2$) based on the ranking of the journals in which they were published.

We opted to use the Scimago Journal & Country Rank (SJR) [7] to classify journals: for simplicity, we decided that a 'recommended' journal meant one within the top 500 journals in the SJR.

Since journal strings are not normalised in the CORD-19 metadata we manually built a mapping table to normalise journal strings to the values in SJR. As this is a time-consuming process, we limited ourselves to just the top 200 most common journal strings in the CORD-19 metadata. Journal strings after the 200th most common ones contributed at most 26 papers per string, out of 13,4206 published papers total. Papers with journal strings outside the top 200 were excluded.

After filtering, our final data set was composed of 11,171 papers, 2,528 (22.6%) of which were labelled as being in class $C1$. The validation and test sets referenced in Tables 1 and 2 are subsets of this data set.

3.2   Model-Fitting

The 2021-04-26 data set was split into 60% training, 20% validation, and 20% test. We fit an SVM (with the default RBF kernel) to the training data using scikit-learn's `svm.SVC` and measured its performance on three metrics: accuracy, F1 score, and average precision [6]. We conducted a search over hyperparameters C (the regularisation parameter), and γ (the kernel coefficient). This was done over a square grid of logarithmically increasing values using the training and validation sets. The model that achieved the highest F1 score was then evaluated on the test set.

4   Results

From the parameter search, the best parameters for F1 score were found to be $C = 10$ and $\gamma = 0.001$. Table 1 shows the validation performance and Table 2 shows the test performance. For the validation set, the accuracy score is 0.87; the F1 score is 0.70; and the average precision score is 0.78. For the test set, the accuracy score is 0.89; the F1 score is 0.72; and the average precision score is 0.79.

Table 1. Validation set confusion matrix.

		Actual		Total
		$C1$	$C2$	
Predicted	$C1$	326	94	420
	$C2$	186	1628	1814
	Total	512	1722	2234

Table 2. Test set confusion matrix.

		Actual		Total
		$C1$	$C2$	
Predicted	$C1$	326	85	411
	$C2$	169	1655	1824
	Total	495	1740	2235

5   Discussion

The model's performance with respect to the test dataset is consistent with the performance on the validation dataset. The test scores are also satisfactory for a proof-of-concept model. This validates the robustness of SPECTER embedding. The task-ready design of SPECTER also allowed us to build the model efficiently.

After we had finished fitting the SVM model to the 2021-04-26 data set, we further tested its performance on newly published papers after the 2021-04-26 CORD-19 release. At the time of experiment, the latest available data was the 2021-06-28 CORD-19 release. We took the 2021-06-28 CORD-19 release and filtered it to papers that were unpublished in the earlier release (including papers on bioRxiv) and published in the later release. This gave us 859 new papers (out of 116,845 submissions). The results of this test are shown in Table 3.

5.1 Additional Dataset

Table 3 shows the model's performance on another 859 new papers mentioned above. For this new dataset, the accuracy score is 0.99; the F1 score is 0; and the average precision score is 0.01. The overall performance is not great. However, the model captured the distribution of the dataset reasonably well.

Table 3. Test on two months of new papers.

		Actual		Total
		$C1$	$C2$	
Predicted	$C1$	0	1	1
	$C2$	7	851	858
	Total	7	852	859

For comparison, we attempted a different approach. SPECTER embeddings are generated using only a paper's title and abstract. We aimed to generate a new kind of embedding that would include more (perhaps all) of a paper's text content, to see if we could make use of the extra information. CORD-19 provides full text parses for many of the papers in the corpus. For each paper, we would split the full text into paragraphs, tokenise each paragraph using SciBERT's tokeniser, then embed the tokenised paragraph using SciBERT. Each paper would now be a list of paragraph embeddings. We then attempted to train a neural network that would combine paragraph embeddings into a single embedding for each paper, then feed that embedding into a classifier for paper quality. For the 'embedding-combiner' process we tried multiple models, such as a single-layer LSTM, a bidirectional LSTM with pooling, and a transformer encoder. Performance was as follows. The accuracy score was 0.84; the F1 score was 0.44; and the average precision score was 0.46.

The comparison approach also performed poorly. We conjecture that the heavily biased new dataset is the main culprit. First of all, the dataset has only 0.81% $C1$ papers. This is dramatically different from the distribution of the previous dataset which has 22.6% $C1$ papers. Moreover, the size of the dataset is extremely limited. Understandably, the vast majority of the papers submitted during the two month period were not published at the time. Therefore, the new dataset is not a good representation of the underlying distribution. Regrettably, at the time of experiment this was the only available data.

On the other hand, as seen from 3 above, the original model captured this biased distribution. This further confirms the robustness of the model and the embedding method.

5.2 How to Judge the Quality of a Research Paper?

Generally speaking, the function of a research paper is to communicate novel information on a subject. The communication part is somewhat easier to quantify. Ideally, an embedding algorithm such as SPECTRE would take into account the length of the document, the sentence structures and to a certain degree the logical connections between sentences to build the representation vector. There is no doubt that some level of correlation between the quality of a paper and the quality of writing exists. However, the novelty of the content is certainly of more interest to the readers. One example to reflect this point is that Galois' original paper on solvability by radicals (what we now consider as part of Galois theory) was rejected for publication largely due to his cryptic writing style [5]. However, the paper was rediscovered after Galois' death and made a significant contribution to mathematics.

The conundrum here for building a classification model is indeed how to capture the novelty of a paper's content. To resolve this the model would need to have some "memory" of the history of the subject. It leads to that the model would have to be tied to a database and require regular update training which renders the model impractical.

We submit that our current model is geared more toward the writing style and the relevance of the topics rather than the content of the papers and we don't have a satisfactory answer to the aforementioned conundrum yet.

Moreover, we recognise that classifying the quality of papers simply according to the reputation of the publication venue is a crude approximation. Better labelling of the dataset could consider metrics such as journal impact factor and h-Index. Unfortunately, without laborious review of the papers it is difficult to have a labelling scheme that directly reflects the quality of the content if there is such an objective way to determine the quality at all.

6   Conclusions and Future Work

In this work, we demonstrated the feasibility of a classification model for paper recommendation tasks based on SPECTER embedding. As more CORD-19 datasets are made available we will be able to further train and tweak the model. Among the future steps, one major task is to apply the model to unpublished papers and track their publication status. Ultimately, we aim to develop a web-based recommendation application for scientific papers.

Acknowledgment. The authors are grateful to Ryohei Sasano for his help with the experimental part of this work.

References

1. Beltagy, I., Lo, K., Cohan, A.: SciBERT: a pretrained language model for scientific text (2019)
2. Chen, Q., Allot, A., Lu, Z.: Keep up with the latest coronavirus research. Nature **579**(7798), 193 (2020). https://doi.org/10.1038/d41586-020-00694-1, https://www.ncbi.nlm.nih.gov/pubmed/32157233
3. Chen, Q., Allot, A., Lu, Z.: LitCovid: an open database of COVID-19 literature. Nucleic Acids Res. **49**, D1534–D1540 (2020)
4. Devlin, J., Chang, M.W., Lee, K., Toutanova, K.: BERT: pre-training of deep bidirectional transformers for language understanding (2019)
5. Neumann, P.M.: The mathematical Writings of Évariste Galois. European Mathematical Society (2011)
6. Pedregosa, F., et al.: Scikit-learn: machine learning in Python. J. Mach. Learn. Res. **12**, 2825–2830 (2011)
7. SCImago: SJR - SCImago Journal & Country Rank [Portal] (2021). http://www.scimagojr.com. Accessed 29 Apr 2021
8. Vaswani, A., et al.: Attention is all you need (2017)
9. Wang, L.L., Lo, K.: Text mining approaches for dealing with the rapidly expanding literature on COVID-19. Brief. Bioinform. **22**(2), 781–799 (2020). https://doi.org/10.1093/bib/bbaa296

Designing for Perceived Intelligence in Human-Agent Interaction: A Systematic Review

Qinyu Zhang[1], Shan Liu[1], Jie Xu[1(✉)], Xiang Ji[2], Yubo Zhang[2], and Yanfang Liu[2]

[1] Zhejiang University, Hangzhou, China
xujie0987@zju.edu.cn
[2] Huawei Technologies Co., Ltd., Shanghai, China

Abstract. The aim of the current study was to identify design elements that influence the perceived intelligence of an agent to inform the design of human-agent interfaces. An agent's level of perceived intelligence by the user is one of the essential dimensions of user experience in human-agent interaction. Studies have shown that perceived intelligence affects outcomes such as intentions to purchase and use. However, there is a lack of comprehensive interface design guidelines for improving perceived intelligence. We conducted a systematic literature review on empirical studies on perceived intelligence in human-agent interaction in academic literature databases and grey literature databases. A total of 2133 articles were screened, and subsequently, 55 relevant articles were identified, reviewed, and analyzed. Perceived intelligence was studied in various domains, such as robots, computer games, ambient intelligence, and interface agents. Design elements that can influence perceived intelligence mainly include anthropomorphism, animation, behavioral diversity, information pushing, decision recommendation, automated action implementation, interaction modality, transparency, and user control. These design elements were classified into three dimensions according to their conceptual similarity: appearance design, behavioral proactiveness, and communication effectiveness. The results can provide guidance to future research and practice for human-agent interaction. More research is needed to explore a broader range of design elements, such as types of human-agent relationships and changes in an agent's behavior over time, that may also influence perceived intelligence.

Keywords: Perceived intelligence · Human-agent interaction · Systematic literature review

1 Introduction

In recent years, "smart devices" have been developed and marketed to and used by the masses. While these devices are not necessarily empowered by artificial intelligence (AI), people have been describing them in terms of how "smart" or "intelligent" they are. In the computer science literature, researchers have proposed methods to evaluate AI systems [1]. One of those methods is the famous Turing test [2]. While the Turing test

C. Stephanidis et al. (Eds.): HCII 2022, CCIS 1655, pp. 713–720, 2022.
https://doi.org/10.1007/978-3-031-19682-9_91

and its variants may have limitations when used for evaluating an agent's ability, they are useful for measuring user experience (UX) in human-agent interaction [3, 4]. Perceived intelligence is a user's own perception of the agent intelligence irrespective of the agent's actual abilities or complexity of algorithms [5]. While perceived intelligence is related to an agent's ability to complete tasks, it is also related to a range of human-agent interaction design elements, such as appearance [6] and interaction modality [7]. Many studies have been conducted to explore the effects of different design elements on perceived intelligence; however, there is a lack of a comprehensive framework or guideline to guide the design of human-agent interaction to optimize perceived intelligence.

The purpose of the current study was to identify design elements that influence the perceived intelligence of an agent through a systematic review of the empirical studies, to inform the design of human-agent interfaces.

2   Methods

2.1   Search Strategy

The literature search was conducted in both academic literature and grey literature databases. The academic literature databases searched included: Web of Science, Psych-INFO, Engineering Village, and ACM Library. The grey literature databases search included design literature websites of companies such Google and Microsoft. The search keyword included both "perceived intelligence" related terms (such as "perceived intelligence", "evaluated intelligence", "assessed intelligence", "attributed intelligence", "appraised intelligence", "judged intelligence", and "inferred intelligence") and "human-agent interaction" related terms (such as "software agent*", "intelligent agent*", "interface agent*", and "human-agent interaction").

2.2   Inclusion and Exclusion Criteria

Articles were included if they: 1) described at least one empirical study; 2) explored the effect of design elements on perceived intelligence. Articles were excluded if they: 1) were not written in English; 2) did not describe the results of the study or studies.

2.3   Article Screening, Review, and Coding

The review process is visualized in Fig. 1. The three major steps included article identification, screening, and coding and synthesis. In article identification, databases were searched using the specified keywords. In screening, the titles and abstracts of the articles were screen for eligibility according to the inclusion and exclusion criteria. In coding and synthesis, full-text of the retrieved articles were read, relevant information was extracted, and the extracted data were analyzed and synthesized.

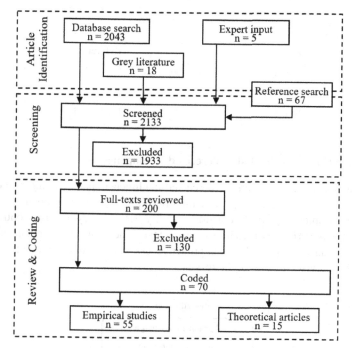

Fig. 1. Flow diagram of the review process.

3 Results and Discussion

3.1 Search Results

The reviewed studies were conducted in different domains, such as robots, games, and automated vehicles. These results indicate that the concept of perceived intelligence is of interests among researchers in different domains or industries. See Table 1 for a breakdown of the references by the different domains.

Table 1. References by research domain.

Domain	References
Anthropomorphized Interfaces	[8–10]
Ambient intelligence	[11–25]
Automated vehicles	[6, 26]
Conversation agents	[27–29]
Games	[30–33]

(continued)

Table 1. (*continued*)

Domain	References
Mobile Health (mHealth) Services	[34–37]
Persuasive systems	[38–40]
Robots	[7, 41–60]

3.2 Design Elements Related to Perceived Intelligence

Design elements that can influence perceived intelligence include anthropomorphism, animation, behavioral diversity, information pushing, decision recommendation, automated action implementation, interaction modality, transparency, and user control. These design elements can be classified into three dimensions according to their conceptual similarity: appearance design, behavioral proactiveness, and communication effectiveness. See Fig. 2 for a visualization of the results.

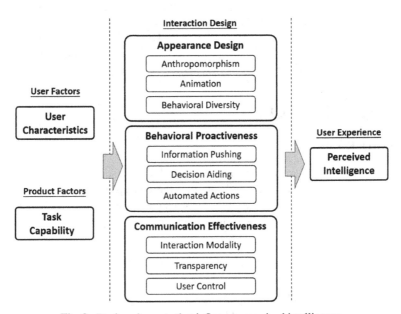

Fig. 2. Design elements that influence perceived intelligence.

These results indicate that a wide range of design elements have been found to be related to perceived intelligence. To optimize perceived intelligence in human-agent interaction, designers should consider balancing the different micro-level elements to create an overall "intelligence" impression. Future research could further explore the effects of the human-agent relationship and human-agent interaction temporal dynamics on perceived intelligence.

Acknowledgment. This research is financially supported by Joint Innovation Lab of Consumer Business Group (Huawei Technologies Co.,Ltd.)—Zhejiang University. The authors thank Yang Chu, Ying Luo, Mi Tang, and Yunxian Pan for their contributions in the review process.

References

1. Hernández-Orallo, J.: Evaluation in artificial intelligence: from task-oriented to ability-oriented measurement. Artif. Intell. Rev. **48**(3), 397–447 (2016). https://doi.org/10.1007/s10 462-016-9505-7

2. Oppy, G., Dowe, D.L.: The turing test. In: Zalta, E.N. (ed.) Stanford Encyclopedia of Philosophy. Stanford University (2011)

3. Hingston, P.: A new design for a turing test for bots. In: A New Design for a Turing Test for Bots, pp. 345–350. IEEE (2010)

4. https://www.linkedin.com/pulse/turing-test-ux-intelligence-ferenc-husz%C3%A1r. Accessed 18 Mar 2022

5. Thill, S., Riveiro, M., Nilsson, M.: Perceived intelligence as a factor in (semi-) autonomous vehicle UX. In: Perceived Intelligence as a Factor in (semi) Autonomous Vehicle UX (2015)

6. Lee, J.-G., Kim, K.J., Lee, S., Shin, D.-H.: Can autonomous vehicles be safe and trustworthy? Effects of appearance and autonomy of unmanned driving systems. Int. J. Hum.-Comput. Interact. **31**(10), 682–691 (2015)

7. Deshmukh, A., Craenen, B., Foster, M.E., Vinciarelli, A.: The more i understand it, the less i like it: the relationship between understandability and godspeed scores for robotic gestures. In: Cabibihan, J.J., Mastrogiovanni, F., Pandey, A.K., Rossi, S., Staffa, M. (eds.) 2018 27th IEEE International Symposium on Robot and Human Interactive Communication, pp. 216–221 (2018)

8. Koda, T.: User reactions to anthropomorphized interfaces. IEICE Trans. Inf. Syst. **E86D**(8), 1369–1377 (2003)

9. King, W.J., Ohya, J.: The representation of agents: anthropomorphism, agency, and intelligence. In: Conference Companion on Human Factors in Computing Systems, pp. 289–290 (1996)

10. Qiu, L., Benbasat, I.: Evaluating anthropomorphic product recommendation agents: a social relationship perspective to designing information systems. J. Manag. Inf. Syst. **25**(4), 145–182 (2009)

11. Rodriguez-Dominguez, C., Garrido, J.L., Guerrero-Contreras, G., Carranza-Garcia, F., Valenzuela, A.: An introduction to continuous interaction. In: 4th International Workshop on the Reliability of Intelligent Environments (WoRIE 2015) (2015)

12. Tang, J., Kim, S.: A Service-oriented device selection solution based on user satisfaction and device performance in a ubiquitous environment. Multimed. Tools Appl. **74**(23), 10761–10783 (2014). https://doi.org/10.1007/s11042-014-2205-x

13. Kernchen, R., et al.: Intelligent multimedia presentation in ubiquitous multidevice scenarios. IEEE Multimed. **17**(2), 52–63 (2010)

14. Cook, D.J., Augusto, J.C., Jakkula, V.R.: Ambient intelligence: technologies, applications, and opportunities. Pervasive Mob. Comput. **5**(4), 277–298 (2009)

15. Nazari Shirehjini, A.A., Semsar, A.: Human interaction with IoT-based smart environments. Multimed. Tools Appl. **76**, 13343–13365 (2016)

16. Bonino, D., Corno, F.: What would you ask to your home if it were intelligent? Exploring user expectations about next-generation homes. J. Ambient Intell. Smart Environ. **3**(2), 111–126 (2011)

17. Gilman, E., Davidyuk, O., Su, X., Riekki, J.: Towards interactive smart spaces. J. Ambient Intell. Smart Environ. **5**, 5–22 (2013)
18. Corno, F., Guercio, E., De Russis, L., Gargiulo, E.: Designing for user confidence in intelligent environments. J. Reliab. Intell. Environ. **1**(1), 11–21 (2015). https://doi.org/10.1007/s40860-015-0001-7
19. Russis, L.D., Bonino, D., Corno, F.: The smart home controller on your wrist. In: Proceedings of 2013 ACM Conference on Pervasive and Ubiquitous Computing Adjunct publication, Zurich, Switzerland (2013)
20. Mostafazadeh Davani, A., Nazari Shirehjini, A.A., Daraei, S.: Towards interacting with smarter systems. J. Ambient. Intell. Humaniz. Comput. **9**(1), 187–209 (2017). https://doi.org/10.1007/s12652-016-0433-9
21. Park, J.-H., Park, W.-I., Kim, Y.-K., Kang, J.-H.: A personalized device recommender system in Ubiquitous environments. In: 2009 International Conference on Intelligent Networking and Collaborative Systems, pp. 175–179. IEEE (2009)
22. Kaowthumrong, K., Lebsack, J., Han, R.: Automated selection of the active device in interactive multi-device smart spaces. In: Workshop at UbiComp. Citeseer (2002)
23. Mukhtar, H., Belaïd, D., Bernard, G.: User preferences-based automatic device selection for multimedia user tasks in pervasive environments. In: 2009 Fifth International Conference on Networking and Services, pp. 43–48. IEEE (2009)
24. Mukhtar, H., Belaïd, D., Bernard, G.: A graph-based approach for ad hoc task composition considering user preferences and device capabilities. In: 2008 IEEE Globecom Workshops, pp. 1–6. IEEE (2008)
25. Misker, J.M., Lindenberg, J., Neerincx, M.A.: Users want simple control over device selection. In: Proceedings of the 2005 Joint Conference on Smart Objects and Ambient Intelligence: Innovative Context-Aware Services: Usages and Technologies, pp. 129–134 (2005)
26. Thill, S., Hemeren, P.E., Nilsson, M.: The apparent intelligence of a system as a factor in situation awareness (2014)
27. Koh, W.L., Kaliappan, J., Rice, M., Ma, K.-T., Tay, H.H., Tan, W.P.: Preliminary investigation of augmented intelligence for remote assistance using a wearable display. In: 'Tencon 2017 - 2017 IEEE Region 10 Conference, pp. 2093–2098 (2017)
28. Jeong, Y., Lee, J., Kang, Y.: Exploring effects of conversational fillers on user perception of conversational agents. In: Proceedings of Extended Abstracts of the 2019 CHI Conference on Human Factors in Computing Systems, Glasgow, Scotland, UK (2019)
29. Moon, Y., Jeong, Y., Seo, E.: I'm listening: the effect of cue difference to elicit user's continuous turn-taking with A.I. agent in TV. In: Proceedings of Adjunct Proceedings of the 2019 ACM International Joint Conference on Pervasive and Ubiquitous Computing and Proceedings of the 2019 ACM International Symposium on Wearable Computers, London, UK (2019)
30. Mallon, B., Webb, B.: Structure, causality, visibility and interaction: propositions for evaluating engagement in narrative multimedia. Int. J. Hum Comput Stud. **53**(2), 269–287 (2000)
31. Druga, S., Williams, R., Park, H.W., Breazeal, C.: How smart are the smart toys? Children and parents' agent interaction and intelligence attribution. In: Proceedings of the 17th ACM Conference on Interaction Design and Children, pp. 231–240. Association for Computing Machinery, Inc. (2018)
32. Mallon, B.: Towards a taxonomy of perceived agency in narrative game-play. Comput. Entertain. (CIE) **5**(4), 1–15 (2008)
33. Schuurink, E.L., Toet, A.: Effects of third person perspective on affective appraisal and engagement: findings from SECOND LIFE. Simul. Gaming **41**(5), 724–742 (2010)
34. Liu, F., Ngai, E., Ju, X.: Understanding mobile health service use: an investigation of routine and emergency use intentions. Int. J. Inf. Manage. **45**, 107–117 (2019)

35. Akter, S., D'Ambra, J., Ray, P.: Development and validation of an instrument to measure user perceived service quality of mHealth. Inf. Manag. **50**(4), 181–195 (2013)
36. Akter, S., Ray, P., D'Ambra, J.: Continuance of mHealth services at the bottom of the pyramid: the roles of service quality and trust. Electron. Mark. **23**(1), 29–47 (2013)
37. Katule, N., Rivett, U., Densmore, M.: A family health app: engaging children to manage wellness of adults. In: Proceedings of the 7th Annual Symposium on Computing for Development, Nairobi, Kenya (2016)
38. Oduor, M., Oinas-Kukkonen, H.: Commitment devices as behavior change support systems: a study of users' perceived competence and continuance intention. In: DeVries, P.W., OinasKukkonen, H., Siemons, L., BeerlageDeJong, N., VanGemertPijnen, L. (eds.) Persuasive Technology: Development and Implementation of Personalized Technologies to Change Attitudes and Behaviors, Persuasive, pp. 201–213 (2017)
39. Oduor, M., Oinas-Kukkonen, H.: Committing to change: a persuasive systems design analysis of user commitments for a behaviour change support system. Behav. Inf. Technol. **40**, 20–38 (2019)
40. Lehto, T., Oinas-Kukkonen, H.: Explaining and predicting perceived effectiveness and use continuance intention of a behaviour change support system for weight loss. Behav. Inf. Technol. **34**(2), 176–189 (2015)
41. Schaefer, K.E., Sanders, T.L., Yordon, R.E., Billings, D.R., Hancock, P.A.: Classification of robot form: Factors predicting perceived trustworthiness. In: Proceedings of the Human Factors and Ergonomics Society Annual Meeting, pp. 1548–1552. Human Factors and Ergonomics Society Inc. (2012)
42. Katz, J.E., Halpern, D.: Attitudes towards robots suitability for various jobs as affected robot appearance. Behav. Inf. Technol. **33**(9), 941–953 (2014)
43. Hennig, S., Chellali, R.: Expressive synthetic voices: considerations for human robot interaction. In: 2012 IEEE RO-MAN: The 21st IEEE International Symposium on Robot and Human Interactive Communication, pp. 589–595. Institute of Electrical and Electronics Engineers Inc. (2012)
44. Choi, J.J., Kim, Y., Kwak, S.S.: The autonomy levels and the human intervention levels of robots: the impact of robot types in human-robot interaction. In: 2014 23rd IEEE International Symposium on Robot and Human Interactive Communication, pp. 1069–1074. IEEE (2014)
45. Vouloutsi, V., Grechuta, K., Lallée, S., Verschure, P.F.M.J.: The influence of behavioral complexity on robot perception. In: Duff, A., Lepora, N.F., Mura, A., Prescott, T.J., Verschure, P.F.M.J. (eds.) Biomimetic and Biohybrid Systems. Living Machines 2014. LNCS, vol. 8608, pp. 332–343. Springer, Cham (2014). https://doi.org/10.1007/978-3-319-09435-9_29
46. Churamani, N., et al.: The impact of personalisation on human-robot interaction in learning scenarios (2017)
47. Lehmann, H., Saez-Pons, J., Syrdal, D.S., Dautenhahn, K.: In good company? Perception of movement synchrony of a non-anthropomorphic robot. Plos One **10**(5), e0127747 (2015)
48. Fu, C., Yoshikawa, Y., Iio, T., Ishiguro, H.: Sharing experiences to help a robot present its mind and sociability. Int. J. Soc. Robot. **13**(2), 341–352 (2020). https://doi.org/10.1007/s12369-020-00643-y
49. Cao, H.-L., et al.: "Hmm, did you hear what i just said?": development of a re-engagement system for socially interactive robots. Robotics **8**(4), 95 (2019)
50. Rosenthal-von der Puetten, A.M., Hoefinghoff, J.: The more the merrier? Effects of humanlike learning abilities on humans' perception and evaluation of a robot. Int. J. Soc. Robot. **10**(4), 455–472 (2018)
51. Beton, L., Hughes, P., Barker, S., Pilling, M., Fuente, L., Crook, N.T.: Leader-follower strategies for robot-human collaboration. In: Aldinhas Ferreira, M., Silva Sequeira, J., Tokhi, M.,

Kadar, E.E., Virk, G. (eds.) A World with Robots. Intelligent Systems, Control and Automation: Science and Engineering, vol. 84, pp. 145–158. Springer, Cham (2017). https://doi.org/10.1007/978-3-319-46667-5_11

52. Schneider, S., Kummert, F.: Comparing robot and human guided personalization: adaptive exercise robots are perceived as more competent and trustworthy. Int. J. Soc. Robot. **13**(2), 169–185 (2020). https://doi.org/10.1007/s12369-020-00629-w

53. Cuijpers, R.H., Bruna, M.T., Ham, J.R.C., Torta, E.: Attitude towards robots depends on interaction but not on anticipatory behaviour. In: Mutlu, B., Bartneck, C., Ham, J., Evers, V., Kanda, T. (eds.) ICSR 2011. LNCS, vol. 7072, pp. 163–172. Springer, Heidelberg (2011). https://doi.org/10.1007/978-3-642-25504-5_17

54. Bajones, M., Weiss, A., Vincze, M.: Help, anyone? A user study for modeling robotic behavior to mitigate malfunctions with the help of the user. The Society for the Study of Artificial Intelligence and the Simulation of Behaviour (AISB) (2016)

55. Ghazali, A.S., Ham, J., Barakova, E.I., Markopoulos, P.: Effects of robot facial characteristics and gender in persuasive human-robot interaction. Front. Robot. AI **5**, 73 (2018)

56. Zhu, D.H., Chang, Y.P.: Robot with humanoid hands cooks food better? Effect of robotic chef anthropomorphism on food quality prediction. Int. J. Contemp. Hosp. Manag. **32**(3), 1367–1383 (2020)

57. Kose-Bagci, H., Ferrari, E., Dautenhahn, K., Syrdal, D.S., Nehaniv, C.L.: Effects of embodiment and gestures on social interaction in drumming games with a humanoid robot. Adv. Robot. **23**(14), 1951–1996 (2009)

58. Haring, K.S., Watanabe, K., Silvera-Tawil, D., Velonaki, M., Takahashi, T.: Changes in perception of a small humanoid robot (2015)

59. Bartneck, C., Kanda, T., Mubin, O., Al Mahmud, A.: The perception of animacy and intelligence based on a robot's embodiment. In: Humanoids: 2007 7th IEEE-Ras International Conference on Humanoid Robots, p. 300 (2007)

60. Barakova, E.I., De Haas, M., Kuijpers, W., Irigoyen, N., Betancourt, A.: Socially grounded game strategy enhances bonding and perceived smartness of a humanoid robot. Connect. Sci. **30**(1), 81–98 (2018)

Correction to: Comparison of Innovative Strategy of Smart City in Italy, United Kingdom, United States and Spain

Asriadi Rahmad and Achmad Nurmandi

Correction to:
Chapter "Comparison of Innovative Strategy of Smart City in Italy, United Kingdom, United States and Spain" in: C. Stephanidis et al. (Eds.): *HCI International 2022 – Late Breaking Posters*, CCIS 1655, https://doi.org/10.1007/978-3-031-19682-9_60

In the originally published version of chapter 60 the last name of the first author has been erroneously omitted. The last name has been added for the first author.

The updated original version of this chapter can be found at
https://doi.org/10.1007/978-3-031-19682-9_60

Author Index

Printed in the United States
by Baker & Taylor Publisher Services